Building the Gort Line

The BEF and its Defences in France 1939-40

Dave Thurlow

Helion & Company Limited

Helion & Company Limited
Unit 8 Amherst Business Centre
Budbrooke Road
Warwick
CV34 5WE
England
Tel. 01926 499 619
Fax 0121 711 4075
Email: info@helion.co.uk
Website: www.helion.co.uk
Twitter: @helionbooks
Visit our blog http://blog.helion.co.uk/

Published by Helion & Company 2019
Designed and typeset by Mary Woolley (www.battlefield-design.co.uk)
Cover designed by Paul Hewitt, Battlefield Design (www.battlefield-design.co.uk)
Printed by Hobbs the Printers, Totton, Hampshire

ISBN 978-1-911628-76-7

British Library Cataloguing-in-Publication Data.
A catalogue record for this book is available from the British Library.

For details of other military history titles published by Helion & Company Limited contact the above address or visit our website: http://www.helion.co.uk.

We always welcome receiving book proposals from prospective authors.

Contents

List of Figures

Abbreviations & Glossary

AA – Anti-Aircraft
ADGB – Air Defence of Great Britain
AASF – Advanced Air Striking Force
AFV – Armoured Fighting Vehicle
AMPC – Auxiliary Military Pioneer Corps
ATM – Army Training Memorandum
BEF – British Expeditionary Force
CRE – Commander Royal Engineers
DCR - Division cuirassée de reserve (French heavy mechanised division)
DLM - Division légère méchanique (French light mechanised division)
DMI – Director of Military Intelligence
DMO - Director of Military Operations
CIGS – Chief of the Imperial General Staff
FDL – Forward Defended Locality
FSP – Field Security Police
FSR – Field Service Regulations
GHQ – General Headquarters
GOC – General Officer Commanding
GQG – Grand Quartier Général (French General Headquarters)
LoC – Lines of Communication
MTP – Military Training Pamphlet
NCO – Non Commissioned Officer
OC – Officer Commanding
PAD – Passive Air Defence
RAF – Royal Air Force
RF – Région Fortifiée
SD Lille – *Secteur Défensive de Lille*
RE – Royal Engineer
WO – War Office

Abatis – An obstacle formed of felled trees laid side by side as far as possible, with their branches towards the enemy. Wire could be interlaced between the boughs, which should be sharpened to points on the enemy side.
Aggregate – Generally this means all particles of sand, broken stone or gravel etc. used in making concrete.

Battle position – A position from which guns carried out their role of supporting the defensive (or offensive) battle.
Blockhouse – a small 'fort' in the form of a single building. Used in this book to refer to the larger French fortifications along the Franco-Belgian border. The British fortifications were generally smaller, and the term 'pillbox' is used to describe these.
Breastwork – A defence work of which the greater portion is above ground level.
Burster – An additional course of concrete blocks etc added to a pillbox to act as a buffer and take the compressive forces of the detonation of a shell, limiting structural damage to the pillbox and casualties to those inside.

Crawl Trench – A shallow trench, 3ft 6in wide, semi-circular in section and 18 inches deep at the centre. It was used as a first stage to connect weapon pits and posts across the front, and facilitating the rapid development of an extensive trench system.
Cut and Cover – a light shelter, constructed by an excavation being made in which the shelter is built and then covered up.
Coir matting – Loosely woven matting of coco-nut fibre.
Concrete – A mixture of Portland or high alumina cement, sand and water.
Curing – Concrete becomes hard due to the chemical reaction by the combination of a cement and water. During this process it is necessary to prevent as far as possible the evaporation of water from the surface of the concrete: this is known as curing.

Dannert Wire –the term retained by the British for oil tempered barbed spring-steel coil concertina wire introduced by Germans during 1914-18 by Herr Dannert.
Defended Locality – An area of ground organised by defence by a definite unit, such as a platoon, company or battalion.

Enfilade fire – Fire which sweeps the position from a flank.

Fascine – A long bundle of brushwood used for revetting.
Frontal fire – Fire the line of which is perpendicular to the front of the target.
Formwork – Moulds made from timber, metal sheets etc into which the concrete mix is poured into and left to set.

Grazing fire – Fire which is parallel or nearly so to the surface of the ground.

Grout – A mixture of cement and water, or cement, sand and water of a consistency about that of cream.

Loophole – The aperture in the wall of an emplacement through which a gun fires. Alternative term is as an embrasure.

Main Position – That portion of a defensive system, in position warfare, in which the commander decides to fight out the battle and break the enemy's attack.

Oreillion – A projection in fortifications to protect firing positions from flanking fire.

Parados – A bank of earth constructed to give protection against reverse fire, and the back burst of high explosive shells.

Parapet – A bank of earth constructed to give protection against frontal fire, and the forward burst of high explosive shells.

Penetration task – Defensive fire in front of reserve localities put down to check further enemy penetration when a break-in occurs.

Pillbox – See blockhouse.

Poste de tir – A small concrete work for either a light machine gun or anti-tank gun constructed by the French in-between the main blockhouses.

Rear Position – A separate defensive system some miles in the rear of the leading defensive system, which can be occupied in the event of the enemy capturing the leading system.

Reinforcing rods – Steel bars placed into mass concrete to relieve tensile, shearing and impact stresses. Engineering manuals of the time suggest mats – formed from a grid of ½ inch to ¾ inch steel bars arranged to form a square of 6 inch to 10 inch sides wired together at crossing points – were required on the inner surface and outer surfaces of walls and roofs. The inner mat helped to resist tensile stress, localise fractures and distribute the shock so preventing large pieces becoming detached and injuring the occupants of pillboxes. The outer mat helped resist penetration of shells and to distribute the stresses due to impact. Stirrups of 1/4 inch to 5/3 inch spaced at intervals not greater than 9-inch helped to bind the inner and outer mats together.

Revetment – A covering or facing placed upon an earth slope to enable it to stand at an inclination greater than its natural inclination.

Roving position – A temporary position from which guns carried out tasks such as counter-preparation fire or opportunity shooting. Troops often had more than one roving position. They were used to prevent giving away the battle positions.

Scrim canvas – Jute canvas which was loosely woven.

Sitzkrieg – The 'sitting war', a play on the word Blitzkrieg (Lightening War), created by British journalists to describe the eight months inactivity following the declaration of war where both sides 'sat idle'. Other terms in use at the time by the British press included the 'Bore War' and the 'Great Bore War'. American journalists used the phrase the 'Phoney War' while the French referred to the *drôle de guerre* (the 'funny' war). Winston Churchill called it the 'Twilight War'.

Shuttering – Same as formwork.

Template – A pattern, guide or model used to indicate the shape any piece of work is to assume when finished.

Traverse – A buttress of earth provided between two adjacent portions of a fire or communication trench for protection against enfilade or oblique fire and to localise the effect of shell bursts. In practice it is usually formed by a continuation of the parapet to the rear so that the trench, instead of running on continuously straight, bends back and goes around the traverse, with the portions of trench between the traverses called 'bays'.

Tourelle – A small turret sunk into the ground in which housed a light machine gun.

XPM – Expanded metal, mainly used for revetting frames and made in sheets of 6ft 6in by 3feet.

Acknowledgements

First, I would like to thank Duncan Rogers, proprietor of Helion & Company, for supporting this project and 'taking a chance' on a first-time author. I should also like to acknowledge the help and advice provided by Kim McSweeney in getting the maps and illustrations to a suitable standard for publication. I owe a great debt to Robert Liddiard, based in the School of History at the University of East Anglia, Norwich, for kindly agreeing to comment on the manuscript. Without his input, I'm sure the book would not be of a standard to warrant publication. However, any mistakes or errors in the text or illustrations are mine and mine alone.

I wish also to acknowledge the professionalism and generosity of the staff at The National Achieves, Kew. I have made many visits to Kew in researching this book, and it could never have reached this stage without their help. Although a substantial part of this book is based on archival research, much use has also been made of secondary sources and I gladly acknowledge my debt to those authors. In particular, there are some principal secondary references which I would like to fully acknowledge in the writing of this book. The authors of diaries, or those who edited them for publication, in particular the Ironside Diaries edited by Colonel R. Macleod, DSO, MC, and Denis Kelly and the Diaries of Lieutenant-General Sir Henry Pownall, edited by Brian Bond, proved invaluable references for the political and military situation of the time and also placing into context the many primary archive documents. In this context, John Kennedy's *Business of War* was also invaluable. It was hard to find published memoirs of those who experienced the 'Sitzkrieg', so R.H. Medley's excellent book, *Five Days to Live*, was a very fortunate find. Julien Dépret's exceptionally detailed and beautifully presented *Le Nord, Frontière militaire Tome 2* provided much of the detail on the French defences constructed in the BEF sector prior to the war, actually vital information as the French blockhouses provided the framework upon which the BEF defences were built up from. I also owe a debt to Geoff Woodard for obtaining a copy of this book for me from France. To my knowledge, there has only been one book completely dedicated to the BEF during the Sitzkrieg and that is Skene Catling's *Vanguard to Victory*: I have made much use of this book. Lieutenant-Colonel Ewan Butler and Major J. Selby Bradford MBE, MC also give a substantial account of life in the BEF during that strange period of the war in their book *Keep the Memory Green*, as does André Maurois in his book *The Battle of France*, and both these books provided much useful information. Finally, but by no means least, David Divine's book *The Nine Days of Dunkirk* gives an excellent account of the Battle of France and Flanders and was a key reference for the chapter on that battle in this book.

Finally, I would like to thank my brother, Tim, for his company (and driving!) on my visits to the Gort Line and my partner Claire for putting up with me when disappearing for hours on end writing and researching this book.

1

Background

Early on the morning of 10 May 1940, Brigadier Smyth VC, MC commanding 127 Infantry Brigade was awakened by the sound of bombs and the hum of large numbers of aircraft. Leaping out of bed, he switched on the radio and heard a voice in French from Radio Paris announcing that the Germans had invaded Belgium and the Netherlands. Then *Général* Gamelin, the French *Commandant-en-chef*, came on the air exhorting all to acquit themselves as men. The long expected German attack had begun and Brigadier Smyth writes:

> The British Expeditionary Force was to leave the defences upon which it had worked so hard all these long and weary months and, at Belgium's call for help, was to advance immediately on Brussels to meet the greatest mechanised army in the world in the open.[1]

On the night of 3 June, the last ships evacuating the British Expeditionary Force (BEF) and parts of the French Army from Dunkirk slipped away – a period of just over three weeks since the BEF had dashed forward into Belgium. Much has been written about these dramatic three weeks, which cumulated in the evacuation of the BEF: 'The Miracle of Dunkirk'. But, the BEF's campaign had begun in September 1939 and, as Brian Bond has stated:

> The experience of the greater part of this inglorious campaign has been eclipsed in the historiography by its dramatic culmination in the evacuation from Dunkirk and the myths associated with that providential escape from even worse disaster.[2]

1 Brigadier Sir John Smyth, VC, MC, MP, *Before the Dawn: Two Historic Retreats Dunkirk 1940. Burma 1942* (London: Cassell & Company Ltd., 1957), p. 37.
2 Brian Bond, 'The British Field Force in France and Belgium, 1939–40' in Paul Addison & Angus Calder (Eds), *Time to Kill: The Solder's Experience of War in the West 1939–1945* (London: Pimlico, 1997), p. 40.

When the BEF landed in France in September 1939, things were very different from the events of 1914. Then, they were welcomed with cries of 'Á Berlin' from the French public while the French Army, confident of its superior will – élan vital – was rushing northwards and eastwards to attack the invading German Army and the BEF went straight into action with them. This time, the French had a purely defensive strategy. Confident of the superiority of the fire power of modern weapons in strong defences against the offensive, they were content to sit behind concrete defences – the Maginot Line – and wait for the Germans to attack. The BEF took its place alongside its French ally in the defences along the Franco-Belgium frontier.

The BEF was also different to that landed in France during 1914. Then, Britain was able to dispatch seven divisions of its regular Army to France. Described as 'contemptible' by the Kaiser because of its small size in comparison to the armies of the other Continental powers, it was, however, with 10 years in the making magnificently trained. In September 1939, Britain could only manage to send four divisions over to France, of which two had not even completed their training.

Many in the BEF believed they would be moving into strong defences. The observations of two officers, Lieutenant-Colonel E Butler and Major J. Selby Bradford, at the time junior officers in the BEF, were typical:

> Some of the Force expected to find a neat defensive position already waiting for them when we reached the frontier. For weeks before the outbreak of war we had read of the famous Maginot Line, that impregnable fortress against which the Germans were to smash themselves, and many of us (for that matter many of the French also) believed that the Line ran clear of the Swiss frontier to the Channel. The men of 1st Corps who credited this fable were soon undeceived. Some defences there were – an artificial anti-tank ditch, covered by a few concrete blockhouses lay in front of them and with it their winter's work. Something more formidable must be built while there was yet time.[3]

The BEF spent the winter labouring on its defences in the area around Lille, the sector allocated to it by the French. By May 1940 the work that had been achieved was remarkable. According to the Official History of the Second World War, the BEF had constructed 'successive positions and switch lines, strengthened by concrete pill-boxes, wire and anti-tank obstacles...and before the offensive opened about forty miles of revetted anti-tank obstacle, covered by over 400 concrete pill-boxes, had been completed.'[4] A further 100 pillboxes had also been started. These defences are often referred to as the 'Gort Line', after the BEF Commander-in-Chief, Lord Gort. The

3 Lieut.-Colonel Ewan Butler & Major J. Selby Bradford, MBE, MC, *Keep the Memory Green: The First of the Many France 1939–40* (London: Hutchinson & Co. Ltd., no date), p. 18.

4 Major L.F. Ellis, *The War in France and Flanders 1939–1940* (London: HMSO, 1953), p. 21.

term seems to have been in use by journalists from December 1939 onwards: during the British Prime Minister's visit to the BEF front line, Skene Catling observed on 16 December:

> The first place Mr. Chamberlain inspected was a secret workshop where men were banging lustily with hammers at planks of wood or sheets of iron. They were all engineers, the men of 'X Force,' whose duty it is to turn out the essential parts of still more pillboxes and other defensive structures for still another chain of discouraging obstacles with which the B.E.F. is making ever more impregnable what may now be called 'the Gort Line' against a German invasion.[5]

However, it would be equably justifiable to refer to the defences as the 'Belisha Line' after the Secretary of State for War, Mr Hore-Belisha. The idea to raise an engineer brigade – 'X' Force – which carried out much of the concreting was his. He was greatly influenced by the Maginot Line and was keen that the British defences should be just as strong for what he alluded to as 'the new conception of fortress warfare.'[6] But whether it is called the Gort Line or Belisha Line the term 'line' is a bit of a misnomer, as in reality the Gort Line was planned as a series of positions sited in depth.

The origins of this book began one November afternoon at The National Archives while researching Suffolk's Second World War anti-invasion defences. I was curious to find out more about the work in France during the winter of 1939–40 that had preceded the frantic construction of Britain's anti-invasion defences following the evacuation from Dunkirk. The more files I looked at, the more I realised that there was a gap in the literature on Second World War fixed defences. Much has been written on the Maginot Line, the Siegfried Line, the Atlantic Wall and the defences that made up Britain's anti-invasion 'Stop Lines' and 'Coastal Crust' but the Gort Line is almost entirely neglected.

Nick Smart, in *British Strategy and Politics during the Phoney war: Before the Balloon Went Up*, has argued that the period of the Sitzkrieg, or the Phoney War as it is also often referred to, is a distinct phase of the war that broke out in Europe on 3 September 1939. However, like Brian Bond, he also points out that it is largely ignored by most historians. The aim of this book is to tell the story of the Sitzkrieg from the point of view of the BEF and, in particular, to describe the construction of the Gort Line. In writing this book, I hope to answerer four broad questions. Firstly, what events led to the Gort Line being built? Secondly, what form did the defences take and what were the ideas behind them – did they reflect a flawed 'Maginot' mentality? The third question is more or less the same as that asked by Skene Catling in his book *Vanguard to Victory*: what exactly did the BEF do in France during the Sitzkrieg? And

5 Skene Catling, *Vanguard to Victory: An Account of the first months of the British Expeditionary Force in France* (London: Methuen & Co. Ltd., 1940), p. 120.
6 Catling, *Vanguard to Victory*, p. 116.

fourthly, how relevant was the Gort Line to what was done in Britain immediately after Dunkirk?

In answering these questions, it should be realised that the decision to build fortifications is always a result of situations and events of the moment, which means they cannot be looked at in isolation. It is equally important to reflect on how these situations and events were perceived at the time, and not with the benefit of hindsight. With this in mind the book starts by looking at the historical context, with a review of how the inter-war years shaped the grand strategy – both the military and political elements – of Britain, France and Germany. In doing so, it can be understood why the BEF dug in along the Franco-Belgian border alongside their French allies. Having set the historical context, the book will describe how the Gort Line was set out with reference to British principles governing the employment of all arms in positional warfare. Chapters will deal with the construction of the Gort Line and its defences: the pillboxes, field works, obstacles and demolitions. A chapter will describe the activities of the BEF – including training – and a glimpse at what life was like for the ordinary soldier while 'holding' the Gort Line. Allied higher strategy, determined by the French as the senior partner, is outlined in a chapter and this gives the context as to why the BEF did not fight on the Gort Line. Instead, French strategy committed it to rush into Belgium alongside the French Army and the Gort Line was in effect relegated to a reserve position. The Sitzkrieg ended violently with the German Blitzkrieg and the events of those three weeks are described, when the Gort Line was actually occupied – albeit briefly – by the BEF and French. Finally, the book will look at how relevant the Gort Line is to understanding Britain's anti-invasion measures immediately after Dunkirk and then the gradual move away from static defence as the situation in the British Army improved.

The experience of May 1940 has led many to regard the BEF as being 'Maginot minded'.[7] However, this book will argue that the defences constructed by the BEF, when seen in the context of 1939, were an entirely sensible precaution and would likely have required hard fighting to overcome them, and that to some extent – by acting as a reserve position – they did achieve the aims behind their construction.

7 'Maginot minded' is a term which encapsulates everything from a reliance on fixed defences to a belief that the next war would be fought along the lines of the last war.

2

Different Paths: British, French and German Grand Strategies and the Road to War

The Great War, the first example of total war on an industrial scale, left the three main players – Britain, France and Germany – exhausted and with millions of soldiers dead. However, the reaction of the three nations to the outcome of that war was totally different. Britain never wanted to be involved in a Continental war again. France was determined that any future wars would not be fought on French soil again. Germany was determined to revoke the terms of the Versailles Treaty, either diplomatically or by force. These different outlooks required differing grand strategies and military doctrines, which ultimately led to the 'sitting' war – Sitzkrieg – that characterised the opening phase of the next war in Europe, which began on 3 September 1939. A nation's grand strategy is the means by which it seeks to obtain security for itself. Military doctrine is the military component of a grand strategy. Grand strategies are not written documents or plans as such. Rather, as Barry Posen notes, they are a conceptualised framework that can be used to explain a nation's means of seeking security. This chapter sets the historiographical background that ultimately resulted in the BEF spending the winter of 1939–40 adding to the defences of the Maginot Extension by examining the consequences of the grand strategies adopted by Britain, France and Germany.

British grand strategy and military doctrine

Following the end of the Great War, Britain had secured most of her war aims and faced few, if any, threats. Germany was beaten and disarmed, the Rhineland occupied, and the League of Nations formed to settle disputes and guarantee peace. But the cost of the Great War in terms of money and human life had been appalling; Britain, along with France and Germany, had effectively fought herself to exhaustion. A staggering £8,000,000,000 had been spent in four years of war and the British Empire had lost 1,000,000 men killed or missing, the majority coming from the United Kingdom. Even in 1919, the Army was still costing the tax payer £412,000,000. The British population was war weary and wanted the Government to 'seek peace and ensure it'. British politicians adopted a political strategy of appeasement and collective security through the League of Nations and a military strategy that was part defensive and part deterrent in order to avoid being drawn into another world conflict and yet safeguard the Empire and British European interests. In a future war, it was assumed a strong navy and air force would defend Britain and keep the sea lanes open, giving Britain and the Empire plenty of time to mobilise their industrial resources and form alliances to fight and win a long war.

It was in this climate that the first post war Coalition Government under Lloyd George introduced the so called 'ten-year rule'. This was adopted in August 1919 for financial purposes, allowing for spending on the military to be cut drastically to reflect the sudden cessation in hostilities. The ten-year rule was an assumption that Britain would not face another war in the next ten years and that no Expeditionary Force would be required and was renewed on a rolling basis. Britain modelled the threat of any future war by assuming France as a hypothetical enemy: not because such a threat was real, but because France at this stage was the largest European power. Such an approach was valid as long as these assumptions remained current. However, despite growing threats from potential adversaries such as Japan and Germany, the financial health of the nation remained the Government's priority. In *The Defence of Britain,* Liddell Hart observed that as each successive government postponed updating Britain's armed forces, the costs of any modernisation became prohibitive, and so the only action politicians could contemplate was further postponement.

In the immediate years after the end of the Great War there was little threat to British home waters and the Mediterranean as France – Britain's hypothetical enemy – was preoccupied with securing her Continental strength and had no ambitions of naval power. It was only in the Pacific, with the growing strength of Japan, that a challenge to British naval power was perceived. Plans were drawn up for a great new naval base in Singapore; in any conflict with Japan, the Navy envisaged sending the greater part of its strength to the Pacific, while maintaining an adequate presence in home waters and leaving the security of the Mediterranean to allies. Although Britain continued to prioritise maintaining its naval power, the politicians refused to fund a truly two-ocean navy and by the early 1930's Britain could not have met any overseas threat without denuding home defence.[1]

Terrifying aspects of the Great War for Britain's civilians were the naval bombardments on coastal towns and the Zeppelin and Gotha air raids. It was, however, the air raid that generated the greatest fear as bombers now gave an enemy the opportunity to attempt a quick 'knock-out' blow against Britain. During the Great War, there were a total of 103 bombing raids against Britain and about 300

1 Continuing adherence to this policy lead to the sending of Force Z to Singapore and the sinking of the HMS *Prince of Wales* and HMS *Repulse* by Japanese aircraft on 10 December 1941.

tons of bombs dropped causing 4,820 casualties, 1,413 which were fatal. A report commissioned by the Imperial Defence Committee in 1921, with France as the hypothetical enemy, concluded that the French air force could drop 1,500 tons of bombs on Britain each month. The scale of attack against London would be about 150 tons of bombs dropped in the first 24 hours, 110 tons in the second 24 hours and 75 tons in each succeeding 24 hours. By 1923 these estimates had been raised to 200 tons in the first 24 hours, 150 tons in the second 24 hours and 100 tons in each subsequent 24 hours. This would result in 5,000 casualties in the first 24 hours, 3,750 in the second 24 hours and 2,500 casualties in each subsequent 24 hours.

Such a scenario ensured that a view of the superiority of an offensive deterrent over defence prevailed in the RAF during the inter-war years, which was supported politically. Although Prime Minister Baldwin's comment given during a Commons debate in 1932 that the 'bomber will always get through' is frequently cited, Daniel Todman notes in *Britain's War* that his comment justifying the bomber deterrent is much less well known:

> The only defence is in offence, which means that you have to kill more women and children more quickly than an enemy if you want to save yourselves.[2]

The RAF adopted a bomber offensive strategy to act as a deterrent against an enemy contemplating a 'knock out' blow against Britain. In 1922 a scheme to provide 14 bomber squadrons and nine fighter squadrons was decided upon (the superior number of bomber squadrons reflecting the RAF's offensive views). This was expanded to 52 squadrons in 1923 with a total of a first-line establishment of 394 bombers and 204 fighters. The scheme was progressed but postponed in 1925 due to the assumptions of the ten-year rule and the international atmosphere of disarmament current at the time.

Out of all the Armed Forces, it was the Army that suffered the most following the adoption of the ten-year rule. For the next decade and beyond, grand strategy was based firstly on the assumption that there would be no major war in the next ten years and secondly that the ultimate danger lay in the Far East. Even if war broke out in Europe, the bomber deterrent would counteract the need to send an Expeditionary Force to France. With uncertainty as to the role of the Army, there was no serious attempt to develop any tactical or strategical doctrine for it. In such a vacuum, Liddell Hart considered that this lead to Britain's military leaders having an instinctive belief that a future war would be a repetition of the past, and involve the dispatch of an Expeditionary Force to France.[3] On the other hand, Britain's politicians were loath to

2 Daniel Todman, *Britain's War: Into Battle 1937-1941* (London: Allen Lane, 2016), pp. 69–70.

3 Although there is some truth in Liddell Hart's remark, it was also undoubtedly made to justify his belief that AA defences should receive priority in the defence budget.

be involved in any future Continental war and saw no reason for maintaining a large army that would be required for such a role. As late as 1933, the Financial Secretary to The War Office, Mr Duff Cooper, stated 'The British Army is not designed for Continental wars. The purpose of the British Army is to maintain order in the British Empire only.'[4] The Army effectively returned to its pre-Great War role of a colonial police force.

By the early 1930's Britain's politicians slowly began to realise the perilous weak state of all the armed services, having been allowed to be run down since 1918. By 1932 the 'ten-year rule' had been abandoned after a grave warning from the Chiefs of Staff and the obvious decline in international relations. Britain began planning to rearm although little more was done than debate the issue. It was now clear that Germany was the main threat and not Japan. Major Pownall – then Military Assistant Secretary to the Committee of Imperial Defence – noted in his diary on 19 May 1933 that Britain was weak everywhere:

> the whole pivot of interest has shifted from the Far East (where Japan has got all she wants because nobody can possibly prevent her, now or in the future) right back to Europe – our old friend Germany with its ultra-nationalistic, sabre-rattling Nazi Government. And so we go on suffering alarms and excursions all round the world and we are weak everywhere, we panic in turn North, South, East and West.[5]

A measure of rearmament was finally decided upon in 1934, including a recommendation to send an Expeditionary Force of one mobile division and four infantry divisions to the Continent to defend Britain's interests if the need arose. However, by the time of the German occupation of the Rhineland in 1936, little had been achieved. Many in the British Government felt that the terms of the Versailles Treaty were too harsh and if they could be relaxed, an agreement with Germany could be reached. Although the French hoped that British progress on modernising its Army could help counteract their shortfall in armour, French intentions were treated with suspicion: Britain refused to support French moves to enforce the Versailles Treaty and French requests for Staff discussions on the conduct of a future war with Germany.[6] There was still no political will for a rapid rearmament; rather rearmament was regarded as an insurance policy if Hitler's stated peace intentions did not hold true.

4 Colonel R. Macleod DSO, MC & Denis Kelly, (eds.), *Time Unguarded: The Ironside Diaries 1937-1940* (New York: David Mckay Company Inc., 1963), p. 21.

5 Brian Bond (ed.), *Chief of Staff: The Diaries of Lieutenant-General Sir Henry Pownall* (London: Leo Cooper, 1972), p.16.

6 The refusal to enter joint staff talks with the French was largely due to the fear that the French may leak the content of these discussions, revealing British military weakness to the Germans.

If war should break out with Germany, many British politicians wanted to fight a war of limited liability; that is commit sea and air power only to aid Continental allies. The war of limited liability was a traditional British policy, in which security was guaranteed by Britain's island status and naval power along with the provision of small expeditionary forces to allied coalitions. The Great War was the exception because Britain raised and committed a large field force to the Continent. Many thought that abandoning the policy of limited liability and the commitment of such a large field force during that war was a colossal mistake. But the war of limited liability now being contemplated by Britain's politicians lacked any sense of collective security in terms of the provision of even a small expeditionary force to an allied cause.

As a result of German air expansion, the 52-squadron scheme was replaced with scheme A (500 bombers and 336 fighters) in 1934, and then Scheme C (840 bombers and 420 fighters). In February 1936, a new scheme was decided upon - scheme F (1,022 bombers and 420 fighters). Despite the emphasis still on bombers for defence by power of retaliation, no thought was given by the Air Staff to the prospect of success against an enemy geared up for defence against air attack! This is even more surprising given that the Air Defence of Great Britain (ADGB) was to become the main priority from 1937 onwards for politicians – at the expense of both an Expeditionary Force and Bomber Command. It was recognised that a sufficient force of fighters and anti-aircraft (AA) guns were required to destroy and drive away German air forces that may attack Britain – and prevent them from annihilating Britain in a few weeks – as well maintaining an offensive strike force.[7]

The German occupation of the Rhineland in March 1936 convinced the British Prime Minister – Mr Baldwin – that the period of drift in the Armed Forces should come to an end. It transpired that there was no plan in place to deal with hostilities with Germany. The production of such plans was supposed to be the responsibility of the Chiefs of Staff, who had the role of advising the Government on strategic matters. However, each of the Chiefs of Staff also had the responsibility of head of their respective service. To ease the pressure on the Chiefs of Staff, a second committee – the Joint Planning Committee – drafted reports for them. But, the members of the Joint Planning Committee also had the responsibility of Director of Plans for the Admiralty, the Air Ministry and the War Office respectively. This duplication of roles meant that little was achieved in terms of national strategic planning for hostilities. Thus, in true British tradition, a further sub-committee was formed in 1936 to ease the burden on the Joint Planning Committee. When Baldwin asked the Chiefs of Staff for a plan on military action should it be necessary, they were forced to admit that none existed. The new sub-committee of the Joint Planning Committee was tasked with drafting a report even before it had met for the first time! The

7 This switch in emphasis, coupled with the development of radar, probably saved Britain during the summer of 1940 as had the Battle of Britain had been lost the outcome of the Second World War may have been very different.

report caused a storm, and the Cabinet could no longer refrain from acting, although according to Major Hollis (later General Sir Leslie Hollis) – the secretary of the new sub-committee – one of the Cabinet's first actions was to commission an underground shelter so they could continue their work under enemy bombing raids, which was to become the famous 'Hole in the Ground'.

During this period of rearmament both the RAF and Navy benefited, although the politicians determined that the RAF's priority was now the ADGB rather than the provision of a bomber deterrent. Nevertheless, the Army continued to be the 'Cinderella of the Services'. Although an expansion of the infantry and Territorial Army was agreed upon by the Government, no timetable was set. Hollis likened this to an ostrich sticking its head in the sand and ignoring the obsolete state of much of the Army's equipment:

> We had no sub-machine guns, no rimless cartridges, no percussion grenades. There were, of course, no dive-bombers in the Air Force and the tanks were fit only for museums ... It was never questioned, however, that the British Army's cavalry lances and swords, their saddles, horse-shoes, picks, shovels, and tent mallets were the equal of any in the world.[8]

Politicians saw the RAF and the Navy as better value for money than the Army and also viewed both as defensive and thus more in keeping with the policy of avoiding antagonising Germany. They were also convinced that the public would not accept sending an Expeditionary Force to the Continent with the probable outcome of another 'Somme' or 'Passchendaele' and the resultant futile sacrifice. General Ironside, then Commander-in-Chief Eastern Command, records the Cabinet's fear of committing an Expeditionary Force to the Continent in his diary on 29 December 1937:

> The Cabinet, in a muddled kind of way, are terrified of making an Expeditionary Force. They reason that if they have such a force, they may be forced to send it to Europe once more. They dread a Continental commitment such as we had, and honoured, in 1914. I don't blame them, for France will scream louder than ever for help in the next crisis. Belgium will shout equally loudly. Once landed, our commitment is limitless... [our ally] only wish to get us committed, and we are then harnessed to the cart driven by them.[9]

The Army was told to concentrate on the provision of AA defence and small-scale expeditionary forces rather than the provision of a substantial Expeditionary Force

8 James Leasor, *The Experiences of General Sir Leslie Hollis KCB, KBE: War at the Top* (London: Michael Joseph, 1959), pp. 55–56.
9 Macleod DSO, MC & Kelly (eds.), *Time Unguarded*, p. 42.

to be sent to the Continent. Many reasons were given by 'false prophets' as to why no large-scale Expeditionary Force was required:

> Thus the Maginot Line was pronounced impregnable; the attack in modern warfare could not possibly prevail over the defence; air forces alone would suffice to stop the advance. Those years were the heyday for cheapjack purveyors of bogus military nostrums.[10]

By 1938 the strength of the Army was planned at only five divisions and no provisions had been made for the reinforcement of this field force. An entry in Ironside's Diary on 21 April neatly sums up the state of the British Army in 1938:

> I have been going into the training of the 4th Division. There is no good concealing the thing from oneself. With no artillery and insufficient men to make up one brigade of infantry I simply haven't the heart to push these people too hard. They cannot imagine Bren guns and armoured carriers. They have never seen them.[11]

Following 'low level' conversations with the French which started in April 1938, the British Government had also reduced the recommended field force that could be sent to the Continent from the one mobile and four divisions in 1936 to just two divisions. This would be accompanied by an Advanced Air Striking Force (AASF) of either 10 or 20 bomber squadrons based at French airfields for use in a 'strategic' offensive against Germany rather than direct support of the Expeditionary Force. It should, however, be noted the dilemma the politicians faced in the uncertain world of 1938. Did they increase the size of the Army in order strengthen France's frontier or did they continue to economise on the Army in order not to weaken the Navy and ADGB, both vital for Britain's security. If a large Expeditionary Force was sent to France, it would require a large naval commitment to guard its sea communications which would prejudice its ability to keep the sea lanes open. A strong ADGB was vital for Home Security; this would be weakened if any Expeditionary Force was sent to the Continent as it would require fighter cover for the Force on land and the Navy guarding the sea communications. The Government fixed British priorities as firstly home defence and keeping the sea lanes open, then secondly the security of the Empire and lastly coming to the aid of an ally. Today, the Prime Minister of the time, Mr Chamberlain, is still widely blamed for the inadequacies in the Army. However, it should be realised that he had to balance the insatiable demands of the three services with economic reality. Chamberlain insisted firstly on expanding British industrial

10 Kennedy, *The Business of War: The War Narrative of Major-General Sir John Kennedy GCMG, KCVO, KBE, MC* (London: Hutchinson & Co. (Publishers) Ltd., 1957), p. 2.
11 Macleod DSO, MC & Kelly (eds.), *Time Unguarded*, p. 56.

capacity. In this he was undoubtedly right: for example, of 11 large companies that had manufactured heavy munitions in 1914, only one was able to do so in 1934, the rest driven to look for new markets because of the lack of demand for weaponry. It is to Chamberlain's credit that in 1939 British aircraft manufacture almost equalled that of Germany and by the end of 1940 was outperforming it. The issue that Chamberlain had to deal with was the neglect over the last 15 years or so that had resulted in these dilemmas.

Although starved of funding and a clear direction of purpose, this did not mean that there had been no attempts to modernise the British Army. General Milne (Chief of the Imperial General Staff (CIGS) between 1926-32) pushed for the need to enlarge and modernise the Army. In armoured warfare, at least initially, Britain led the world. The British Army understood only too well that modern defensive fire power had got the upper hand in the Great War. What was required in the future was a means of providing armour against small arms fire for the infantry. The petrol engine provided the means of carrying this armour. In the closing year of the Great War, Britain was already moving towards deploying self contained armoured forces; specialised wireless and salvage tanks appeared during the war, while both the Mark IX, specifically designed as an infantry or supply carrying tank, and the 'RE' tank, fitted with mine clearing and bridge laying devices, were in development but the war ended before they came into service. In 1926 General Milne authorised the formation of an 'Experimental Force', the forerunner of the Armoured Division. As he explained to an assembly of senior officers:

> [W]e have the means in the petrol engine of altering methods of warfare. Crowds of men on the battlefield are out of place when you have low-flying aeroplanes against them. Think of their communications and supplies. The hostile machine-gun takes away the tactical mobility of the infantryman, and we add to his difficulties by an enormous artillery preparation. Petrol mobility enables you to carry armour and to break through. Against the machine-gun the solution is the Armoured Fighting Vehicle. We shall also have Armoured Divisions.[12]

So, in 1928 the Experimental Mechanised Brigade comprising of tanks and mechanised infantry and artillery was set up. In 1929 it was designated the Armoured Force. These experimental forces represented the first ever modern tactical force powered by the internal combustion engine alone and started the process of investigating roles for the tank other than close support of infantry for which they were originally produced. Yet, many also felt that if the role of the Army was to police the empire, there would be little need for mechanised forces as the likely battlefields would be unsuitable for their use. The Government was reluctant to finance this new experimental force, which

12 Ibid., pp. 19–20.

retarded both the design and tactical development of the tank in Britain. It should also be noted that the Army could not agree upon what type of tanks it required, or what role they should perform, which did not help matters.[13] Fierce criticism of the Army by Liddell Hart and J.F.C. Fuller – perhaps the greatest armoured warfare intellectuals of the 20th Century – also made a substantial part of the Army hostile to their ideas. Although in 1937 Britain did form a 'Mobile Division', which in 1939 became the 1st Armoured Division, Germany had by then a start of some years in intensive tank production.

In one respect though, the British remained ahead of Germany in that mechanisation was also extended to all arms – to the artillery and engineers for instance – with a resultant enormous increase in mobility.[14] In 1937, Mr Hore-Belisha was appointed Secretary of State for War; he was a strong critic of Britain's appeasement policy towards Hitler, but he was also well aware of the financial considerations which would limit the size of any force that could be sent to the Continent should hostilities commence. Highly influenced by Liddell Hart, he thought that a small force, but better trained, better organised, better equipped and more mobile than the armies of the Continental Powers would still have a great morale effect on Britain's allies. This was the driver behind his Army reorganisations of 1937–39. It was considered that the current infantry division – unchanged since the Great War – based on 12 battalions was too cumbersome for the envisaged role of the Army: that of Imperial Defence and only a limited force to be sent to the Continent to assist an allied land force. A more compact organisation to facilitate movement and management in the field was required. It also required flexibility in the type of division – an infantry division based around the light machine gun and a mechanised armoured division based around the tank.

The infantry division was reduced from 12 to nine battalions, but the ratio of fire power and mobility increased. Each rifle battalion was to possess 52 Bren guns,

13 The case of the Valentine tank is a good example of this. On St. Valentine's Day 1938 plans for a new tank were presented to the War Office. For the time, it was relatively heavily armoured and possessed a 2 pdr gun. The proposition and design were rejected, only to be revived again in June 1939.

14 The Royal Army Service Corps led the way in motorisation in the years following the end of the Great War, under an engineer, Colonel Niblett, 'and their activity embraced every aspect of mechanical transport from the drawing-board to the scrap-heap.' (Colonel G. Williams, OBE, *Citizen Soldiers of the Royal Engineers Transportation and Movements and the Royal Army Service Corps 1859 to 1965* (Institute of the Royal Corps of Transport), p. 69). Their work was absorbed into a new Mechanisation Board and the Mechanical Warfare Experimental Establishment, located at Farnborough in 1927. During the Arab-Jewish troubles in Palestine in 1936, the RASC developed invaluable experience in military convoy work, including its own protection, and techniques in troop carrying. This, along with the impetus given to mechanisation following the decision to rearm, led to the RASC consolidating its position of professional 'movers' and road transport now assumed the level of importance that railway transport had in the past.

meaning the machine gun battalion was no longer required (some machine gun battalions were retained, but now formed part of corps troops). New armoured vehicles would be used to get lighter weapons into action at a closer range and each battalion now included a platoon of 10 armoured carriers each mounting a Bren gun. The fire power of the battalion was to be further increased by the addition of one 2 inch mortar for each rifle platoon. This enabled a reduction from four to two of the heavier 3 inch mortar. Each rifle platoon also had a lorry in which all its equipment could be carried, greatly reducing the load of the soldier on foot. In certain circumstances, the lorry could also be used to transport the troops. By 1939 at least twenty per cent of the infantry were conveyed on wheels or tracks while the German infantry was still largely on foot and relying on the horse for the transport of artillery and supplies. The field artillery was reorganised into 'regiments', each consisting of 24 of the new 25 pdr gun-howitzers towed by their own gun-tractor. Mobile anti-tank regiments were formed (which could move at 30 mph on roads), consisting of four batteries each equipped with 12 2 pdr anti-tank guns. Other important changes included a great improvement in the terms of service to encourage enlistment and changes in the Army Council which was largely reconstituted from officers of a younger generation.

On paper at least, Britain had a military doctrine that was characterised by mechanised and combined arms co-operation, as laid down in *Field Service Regulations (FSR) Vol. III 1935*.[15] Training exercises were also very much focused on the attack. In the offensive, breakthrough of the enemy position would be achieved by a combined infantry and tank attack. Victory would be ensured by the use of mobile and armoured formations which would attack enemy reserves in movement in order to prevent their intervention in the battle. The armoured formations would also attack enemy gun positions, headquarters or other vulnerable points in the rear and be used in direct pursuit of the enemy. Air power would be used to locate, delay and disorganise enemy reserves by attacking them during their move forward, either on foot, by road or rail. Other suitable targets for air attack were enemy headquarters and lines of communication. In defence, the counter-move was to be carried out on exactly the same lines as the offensive.

However, the pre-war Army lacked a way of installing a common understanding of the doctrine, relying on individual commanders to interpret it and decide how it should be implemented. It was also hard to organise any real coherent training, with much of the regular Army scattered around the globe on imperial garrison duties. The rapid expansion and rearmament of the Army over a period of just two years

15 The principles of the organisation of the Army, the tactical principles governing the employment of all arms in co-operation and the principles governing the employment of the armed forces in war were laid out in the Army training manual *Field Service Regulations (FSR)*, which was published in three volumes. Volume I dealt with the organisation of the Army, Volume II dealt with the principles governing the employment of all arms in co-operation and Volume III dealt with the principles governing the employment of the armed forces in war and the tactical employment of larger formations.

also meant little chance of a coherent understanding of the combined arms doctrine. When combined arms training did take place, it lacked a sense of reality because of the shortage of equipment. It also required specialised air forces, properly trained and equipped for the support of the Army, but the 'Bomber Barons' of the RAF were obsessed with their belief that they could win the war alone and that co-operation with the Army would be a 'prostitution' of the Air Force. It was not until Ironside became Inspector-General of Overseas Forces that changes began to be made with regards to higher training but the problem with RAF co-operation was to remain well into the Second War.[16] The RAF cannot entirely be blamed for this state of affairs, as up until 1939 no firm decision had been taken to send an Expeditionary Force to the Continent, or any impetus given to the need for such combined arms co-operation.

French grand strategy and military doctrine

The Great War brought devastation to a large part of France and had cost the French 1,300,000 in killed and missing. France was determined that no future conflict would be fought on French soil. This determination – to preserve the integrity of the French frontiers – was to dominate inter-war French political and military thinking. The terms of the Versailles Treaty were designed to compensate the Allies for the damage caused by the Great War and to prevent Germany becoming a threat to peace in Europe again. In particular, the German military was restricted in terms of men and weapons and was also required to demilitarise the Rhineland and allow a 15-year period of occupation by the Allies. However, even after the Versailles Treaty, Germany had greater resources of industry and manpower than France. A resurgence of German industrial and military power was anticipated by France almost immediately after the end of the Great War.

To deal with a resurgent Germany, French political strategy was twofold: firstly, to ensure that the terms of the Versailles Treaty were adhered to by Germany, and, secondly to forge an anti-German alliance. In the west an accord was formed with Belgium. In the east, France formed alliances with Poland, Czechoslovakia, Romania and Yugoslavia. Britain, with her economic power and the resources of the Empire was regarded as a key ally and throughout the inter-war period French diplomacy tried to gain commitments from Britain to resist German aggression on the Continent. However, Britain, as we have already seen, had little interest in Continental alliances until 1936, although in 1935 it did join a short lived anti-German coalition with

16 This was, to say the least, an unfortunate state of affairs. During the last two years of the Great War, the Royal Flying Corps (and later the newly formed Royal Air Force) had success with co-operation with the infantry and attacking German artillery and command and communication centres. Aircraft co-operation with tanks was also a fundamental part of the Allied 1919 Plan (largely derived from Colonel Fuller's ideas), designed to win the war if it continued into 1919. Charles Messenger writes in his book *The Blitzkrieg Story* that the 1919 Plan was the foundation stone of mechanised warfare and Blitzkrieg.

France and Italy – the so called Stresa Front. The intention of such alliances was to threaten Germany with a war on two fronts. All this began to unravel in 1936 when Italy became involved in the Spanish Civil War and Belgium declared neutrality.

Militarily, in 1918 under *Maréchal* Foch – the victorious Allied Commander-in-Chief – the French formulated a series of offensive plans to deal with a resurgent Germany. The occupation of the Rhineland provided a spring board for an offensive to disrupt any German preparations for attack, as Germany's industrial heartland could be quickly occupied – this was Plan P, adopted in June 1921. This plan, the occupation of the Ruhr, was put into effect in March 1923 when Germany failed to make the huge reparations payments. It was revised with Plan A in 1924 which called for the securing of more Rhine crossings and mobilising additional infantry divisions to support the occupying force and expand the bridgehead. However, in 1925, after the occupation of the Ruhr ended, France adopted a more defensive strategy. In any future conflict with Germany, the French forces occupying the Rhineland were to hold their positions only while full mobilisation took place, and not to go on the offensive. As French military planners began to abandon ideas for offensive action against Germany, they instead decided upon the need to fortify the border with defences strong enough to withstand a future invasion while full mobilisation took place. Such a fortification programme, overseen by *Colonel* Séré de Rivières, had been undertaken following the Franco-Prussian War of 1870-71.

The defensive strategy adopted by the French military was in most part due to the combination of the imbalance in manpower between France and Germany and the reduction in conscription. Conscription had been reduced to 18 months in 1923 and in 1928 was reduced again to one year. There was even talk of eight months conscription as a step towards six or four months. The introduction of the one-year conscription service convinced the French High Command that the Army would be incapable of launching early offensives, as it took time to train specialist troops for a modern war of rapid manoeuvre.[17] The decision to introduce one-year conscription was the result of a long battle between the political French left and right. The right wanted the retention of a professional army while the left wanted an army based on short conscripts to ensure it did not become divorced from French society or be used for domestic repression. It was the left that won when a coalition of centre and left-wing parties came to power in 1924. A defensive strategy also required fewer men than an offensive strategy. The French High Command believed that in the event of war

17 Looking back to the start of the Great War, France had an extreme offensive doctrine – *offensive à l'outrance* – that had seen French infantry advance without co-ordinated artillery support to the shouts of '*En avant à la baionette*' during the 1914 Frontier offensives, believing superior will – 'élan vital'– would always succeed. However, by the end of the war, and at great cost, an obvious lesson was that the fire power of modern weapons made offensives very costly in terms of losses in men. The French concluded that an offensive would require both quantitative and qualitative superiority to overcome the defence and would have to be methodically planned and carried out with highly trained troops.

with Germany, it would not have the number of troops required for offensive action until full mobilisation had occurred. However, a fortified border – the Maginot Line – would make the best use of the limited number of conscripts available. Moreover, the strength and firepower of the forts gave the French Army a much higher strength in defence than a straight forward comparison of the numerical strength of its forces with Germany suggested.

The belief in the ability of the concentrated fire power of modern weapons to inflict devastating casualties on an enemy, rather than the ability for rapid manoeuvre made possible by modern weaponry such as tanks, was the key lesson the French took from the Great War. This required close co-ordination of the artillery and infantry under a centralised control, which resulted in the French doctrine of a 'methodical battle'. It did not mean a purely defensive strategy, but the offensive could only take place after the concentrated fire power had sufficiently depleted the enemy's forces. The emphasis on central control – with the intention to produce harmony of command – led to a culture of limited initiative available to subordinate commanders that was to have disastrous consequences for France in May 1940.

Consideration on the ways to protect the frontier with Germany, especially the recovered territory of Alsace and Lorraine, had actually begun soon after the end of the Great War; Lorraine in particular had vital industrial resources which would be necessary for the French economy to be able to wage any future war. In 1920 the French *Conseil Supérieur de la Guerre* was instructed to study ways of defending the frontier and a commission, under *Maréchal* Joffre, was formed and given the task. There was, however, disagreement as to the type of frontier defences required. *Maréchal* Pétain argued for prepared battlefields, similar to the type of defence first constructed by Germany along the Hindenburg Line, consisting of continuous lines of barbed wire and light defences sited in depth that would form a continuous front. Pétain and his supporters argued that the continuous front would deny enemy mechanised forces the ability to turn flanks, forcing them to undertake frontal attacks which the superiority of defensive fire power would smash. Engineering stores would be held in *parc mobile de fortifications* (mobile fortification parks) allowing the construction of these defences at short notice and giving great flexibility and the opportunity to develop them in depth. Mobile reserves would be rushed to any threatened part of the front. On the other hand, *Maréchal* Joffre argued for strongly fortified regions, along the lines of Verdun. Theses would, he argued, allow manoeuvre for offensives and counter-offensives with the flanks secured by the fortified regions.

Joffre and his supporters advocated fortified regions because they had been impressed by the ability of modern concrete used in the Verdun forts to stand up to the heaviest of high explosive shell fire during the Great War. These fortified regions would block off large sections of the frontier, canalising any German invasion and form pivots on which to launch counter-attacks. The later Verdun forts had been constructed using an extra hard concrete – *Bétonné special* (special concrete) – and reinforced with steel bars. The underground galleries of the forts, which provided cover from shell fire, undoubtedly saved many lives. Although French casualties during the fighting for

Verdun were about equal to German casualties, the defence, which was based around the forts, held the German attacks. The basic idea of an integrated fortified defence was considered sound; it just needed adapting and modernising.

Pétain did not agree. He concluded that it was his hastily erected field defences that had stopped the German attack, not the concrete forts. It is interesting to note that the British reached a similar conclusion regarding the fighting at Verdun. Although the great value of shell proof shelters was acknowledged by the British, it did not appear to them that a fort's defensive capacity was any greater than other parts of the defensive line. Mort Homme, on the left bank of the Meuse, was defended by field works only and resisted German attacks for six weeks, exacting a huge toll of German lives before it fell.

No decision was reached, and the commission was dissolved and a new one, the *Commission de Dfense du Territorie,* formed. It embraced both ideas: fortified zones with depth (the depth was ultimately sacrificed when construction actually began, and costs spiralled upwards). The proposed fortified zones were selected to bar invasion routes, just as the fortification programme from 1870 onwards had been designed to do. The idea of fortified zones was strongly supported by Paul Painlevé when he became Minister of War in 1925 but work on the fortifications did not start until 1929 when André Maginot was reinstated as Minister of War. These works are popularly known as the Maginot Line, after André Maginot. However, to secure the northern Franco-Belgian frontier the *Commission* decided to rely on mobility and a rapid advance into Belgian territory with the intention of establishing a line of resistance along selected river barriers – this would complete the continuous front with no flanks. The French considered the difficult low-lying terrain of Belgium a desirable battlefield. It also made this the most likely place to meet the German Army as the Maginot Line defences narrowed the field of possibilities for it, and it placed the vital industrial regions of northeast France out of danger.

In constructing these new forts, an allowance was made for the increased penetrative power of modern shells. The concrete was tested by heavy howitzer fire, and the concrete made thick enough to withstand the impact of three shells at the same point. The new forts would have dispersed defensive positions both above and below ground. Access to fighting positions was to be via underground galleries that could be defended should the enemy breach the fort's defences. Forts also needed to be self-contained (during the fighting at Verdun, Fort Vaux finally fell when the defenders ran out of drinking water). The gaps between the forts were filled with a chain of blockhouses armed with anti-tank guns and machine guns. Each fort could deliver fire to cover its neighbour and the smaller blockhouses.

Construction of the Maginot Line between the North Sea and the Swiss Frontier was in two phases. Construction on the first phase – under the guiding control of the *Commission de Défense des Frontières* (*CORF*) – began in 1929 and ended in 1934 and was concentrated in two fortified regions facing Germany (*Région Fortifiée de Metz* and *Région Fortifiée de Lauter*). This phase is often referred to as the 'Old Fronts' or the 'Maginot Line Proper'. A gap was left between these two regions in the Saar area, which was low lying country on the traditional invasion route into France and not suitable terrain for the construction of deep subterranean fortifications. The French planned to use this area to launch an attack against the Rhineland, with the two *RFs* guarding the flanks of the attack and to rely on a series of ponds and reservoirs to flood the area if attacked.

By the early 1930's a series of events – the British refusal to support the strict enforcement of the Versailles Treaty, the assassination on French soil of the King of Yugoslavia by a Croat terrorist which marked the beginning of the collapse of the French political strategy of an eastern alliance against Germany, the early withdrawal from the Rhineland which made any offensive into Germany or giving mutual support to eastern allies more hazardous and one year conscription – had resulted in France adopting a defensive military doctrine. In the French Government's mind at least, in complete contrast to the 1920's, all thoughts of an offensive had been rejected, as reflected by *Général* Louis Maurin's reply to Reynaud's statement to the Chamber of Deputies on 3 March 1935 that the only means of defeating German aggression was with armoured forces:

> How could it be believed that we are still thinking of the offensive when we have spent billions to establish a fortified barrier? Should we be such fools as to go beyond that barrier, seeking some God knows what kind of military adventure?[18]

One unnamed French general went even further, commenting after a day of manoeuvres in May 1938: 'we shall make defensive war. We will not have the French people slaughtered'.[19] The next war was going to be clearly defensive. France now believed it could not win a future war of attrition with Germany alone. Such a war with Germany would demand the scale of a mobilisation of an allied coalition as seen in the course of the Great War. These factors gave impetus to the first phase of construction of the Maginot Line and also resulted in the acceptance for a second phase to construct smaller forts in-between the larger fortifications. As already noted, these gaps had originally been intended for manoeuvre but by the mid 1930's the Maginot Line would be entirely for static defence. Work on the second phase, known as the 'New Fronts', started in 1934 and lasted until 1939. The New Fronts included the area between the Maginot Line Proper and the North Sea (known as the 'Maginot Extension') as well as the extension of the defences from *RF* Lauter into the Saar gap. The defences were not as substantial as the Old Fronts due to the need to economise – the construction of the Old Fronts had substantially overrun original estimates and coincided with the worst years of the Great Depression – and the technical difficulties of building large forts on low lying ground. Also, the policy

18 Barry R. Posen, *The Sources of Military Doctrine: France, Britain, and Germany Between the World Wars* (Ithaca and London: Cornell University Press, 1984), p. 128.
19 Charles Messenger, *The Blitzkrieg Story* (New York: Charles Scribner's Sons, 1976), p. 131.

on defences had changed completely by then with the desire to modernise the Army – especially in mechanisation – taking precedence, with defences now built to much reduced standards and most lacking organic artillery.

Initially – to the disappointment of *Général* Maurice Gamelin (the *French Commandant-en-chef*) who advocated defensive strongpoints in the rear in case the proposed advance into Belgium went wrong – the New Fronts ignored the Franco-Belgian border as the French claimed they did not want to offend Belgium by constructing substantial defences along the border. Instead, the area between Maubeuge and the coast was to be defended by large scale inundations and the establishment of mobile fortification parks. The Ardennes sector of the Belgian border, largely believed to be impassable to a modern mechanised army, was to be blocked with demolitions such as a programme of tree felling across roads and tracks.[20] In actual fact, the Belgian Defence Minister, Albert Devèze, was concerned at the lack of strong French fortifications along the border with Belgium, as he believed such fortifications would deter Germany from planning an attack on France via Belgium.

The reality was that France indeed expected a German attack would avoid the Maginot Line Proper and be basically a repeat of the Schlieffen Plan, i.e. an advance through Belgium. Pétain was strongly of the opinion that a defensive battle deep in Belgian territory to ensure the closest of co-operation between the French and Belgian armies was in France's best interest and he opposed any fortifications as they could discourage any advance into Belgium. Pétain's supporters also argued that the construction of further fortifications was a financial dream and would be military disastrous to France as all military planning would be reduced to reliance on fortifications. What was not openly admitted of course was that it was not in the French interest to halt a German advance on the border as the key industrial regions of northeast France would be in easy range of German artillery. France expected a request for assistance from the Belgians and planned to advance into Belgium and establish a secure front that would keep the fighting away from the border. But the decision not to fortify the Franco-Belgian border would leave no backstop positions should the Belgian manoeuvre go wrong and was to dominate French military strategy as it left no real alternative to securing a defensive position deep in Belgian territory. Yet the Belgian manoeuvre, with its requirement for mobile operations and the risk of

20 Pétain believed that any forces attempting to pass through the Ardennes could be destroyed in piecemeal as they emerged. However, not all Frenchmen considered the Ardennes impassable. Charles de Gaulle, in his book *The Army of the Future*, thought the Ardennes formed an appreciable but not very deep obstacle which could easily be lost to surprise, error or neglect. In fact, the whole of the northeast French frontier formed a dangerous salient, open to simultaneous blows from Flanders, the Ardennes and Burgundy; if any one of these succeeded, the whole French system of defence would be broken. He considered that if a solid Ardennes and Luxemburg barrier could be raised against Germany, then at least France would be assured of time and space to act against German aggression. Unfortunately, his book was largely neglected at the time.

battles of encounter, did not fit the French military doctrine of the methodical battle and this issue was never adequately addressed.

Nevertheless, by 1933 Edouard Daladier – then Minister of War – had managed to designate Maubeuge and Escaut as fortified sectors and obtain funding for the work. The works along the north and northeast frontier from Maulde to the North Sea were some of the last notified by Daladier in November and December 1936 (Figure 2.1). This was perhaps of no surprise, as from the North Sea to Armentières, the low lying ground – which would be easy to inundate – and the Monts de Flanders provided good natural obstacles while the Rivers Lys and Escaut and the agglomeration of Lille, Roubaix and Tourcoing which extending into Belgium up to Ghent would surely invite co-operation from the Belgian's in the event of hostilities. Notwithstanding this, the fear that the Liége fortifications and other fortifications in Belgian Limburg and the Ardennes would force the Germans to make an even wider turning manoeuvre than in 1914, i.e. through Dutch Limburg and southern Holland was the impetus for the works from Maulde to the North Sea. However, the defences constructed were only intended to be *l'ossature permanente d'un champ de bataille* – i.e. the permanent framework for a battlefield, consisting of pillboxes, anti-tank ditches, field works and barbed wire. These works suffered from a lack of uniformity in concept, as in December 1935 *CORF* was abolished and responsibility was devolved to the military regions. The line from (excluding) Maulde to (including) Armentiéres would become the *Secteur Défensive de Lille* (*SD* Lille), the sector which would be allocated to the BEF in October 1939.[21]

One key assumption made by the French military in planning for a move into Belgium was that the Belgian Army would delay any sudden German attack long enough for French troops to establish defences inside Belgium to form a continuous front. Gamelin, although in favour of the Belgian manoeuvre, always had in the back of his mind that this may not be the case, but at least he now had his strongpoints in the rear in case the manoeuvre failed. It also gave him the freedom to choose to stay on the border if necessary.

21 On 30 November 1936, Général Doumenc proposed a programme costing 35 million francs (MF) to construct 153 blockhouses from Maulde to the North Sea, of which 33 were to constitute a *Ligne d'Arret*, i.e. a rear line. The blockhouses were to be proof against 210mm shells. The *Ligne d'Arret* was to be sited in the rear of Orchies and the interval between Armentières and Bailleul. On 26 July 1937, Daladier announced a final settlement of 30MF, with no more to follow, and for *SD* Lille, between 1937 and 1938, it was proposed that 5MF would be allocated for the line Cysoing – Planard, 3.3MF for the line Planard – Cense de Choques and 3MF for the line Cysoing – Tressin. By the end of 1937, construction work was underway. The year 1938 was one of increasing tension on the Continent, and further money was allocated to strengthening defences along the north and northeast frontier to cover as fully as possible, and in any eventuality, French territory. This included 1MF allocated in May 1939 for the organising of defences in the Bachy area (the so-called Bachy Switch) and the *Ligne d'Arret* south of Orchies in *SD* Lille. See Chapter 3 for details of the defences constructed by the French from Maulde to the North Sea.

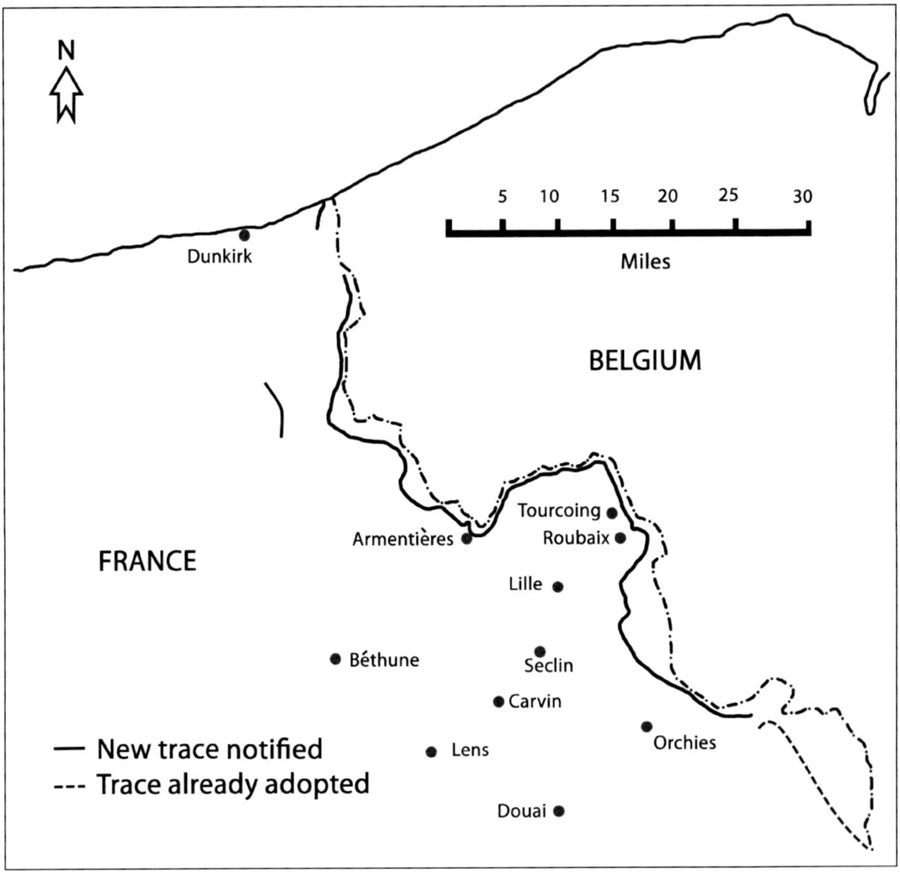

Figure 2.1: Defence works notified by Daladier, November 1936.

So, the role of the French Army was now clear: it was to prevent defeat while France and her allies fully mobilised. The Maginot Line Proper would block invasion routes and protect industries in the northeast required for mobilisation. It would also economise manpower, allowing the French Army to meet the Germans on the flank with an advance into Belgium, which would place the northwest industries out of reach of Germany. A stabilised front would develop, as happened during the Great War, giving France and her Allies time to attain the required superiority over Germany and only then take the offensive.

It would be wrong to conclude that the French military ignored the potential of modern mechanised forces while adopting this defensive doctrine. Gamelin had always advocated spending money on modernising the French Army, and Ironside certainly felt that Gamelin considered that some of the money spent on the Maginot Line would have been better spent on doing just that, although he never admitted it.

However, Gamelin was also a political realist and knew that the French Government and population would never countenance large sums of money being spent on modernising the Army. But they were happy to spend money on securing the French frontier with fortifications, so if money was to be spent on the military, it might as well be spent on fortifications.

It was in the early 1930's that the French seriously began to think about the need for mechanised forces. After the occupation of the Rhineland ended in 1931, French planning for a conflict with Germany and perhaps Italy began to look at the use of mobile forces which could move rapidly to either the border with Germany or Italy depending on where any threat arose. In 1932, the French – inspired by the British exercises on Salisbury Plain between 1927 and 1931 using various experimental mechanised formations – experimented with a mixed cavalry and motorised force. A number of issues arose with this idea and as a result a fully mechanised division was formed in 1933, the *Division légère méchanique* (*DLM*), which was a well balanced combined-arms force.

The French soon realised that the rearmament of Germany would mean they would be faced with anti-tank defence and large tank and motorised formations. Specialist forces were required to deal with these. In a speech given in 1937, Daladier, then Minister of War, announced the need to 'strive for speed and striking power.'[22] New heavy mechanised divisions – *Division cuirassée de reserve* (*DCR*) – were required to supplement the *DLMs*. These *DCRs* would achieve a breakthrough then act as an exploiting force in conjunction with the *DLMs*. There was, however, a crucial difference in French and German thinking about the use of mechanised formations. The French still thought in terms of the methodical battle to achieve a breakthrough, and only then would the mechanised forces restore mobility to the battlefield. The Germans, on the other hand, viewed mechanised forces as the key element to success.[23]

22 Major-General Heinz Guderian, *Achtung – Panzer! The Development of Armoured Forces their Tactics and Operational Potential*, translated by Christopher Duffy, introduction and notes by Paul Harris (London: Brockhampton Press, 1998), p. 146.

23 In 1934, a then obscure French officer – Charles de Gaulle – wrote a short book, *The Army of the Future*. Unfortunately, at the time, his ideas were not taken seriously by the French High Command. When the French did begin to think about the potential of mechanised warfare as outlined by De Gaulle, it was too late to catch up with the lead held by Germany in preparing for this type of warfare. De Gaulle argued that a completely motorised and 'caterpillared' army would make a fortified and continuous front that characterised the Great War a thing of the past. During the Great War, armies moved at a slow pace. Offensives required amassing troops, supplies of all kinds and artillery, which took days to achieve and signalled to the enemy that an offensive was forthcoming. As the attackers advanced, they exposed their own defences. Talk for the attacker was of pivoting, widening breaches and encirclement while the defender spoke of hinging, bracing and strategic withdrawal – all with the purpose of maintaining a continuous front. De Gaulle argued that mechanised armies of the future would avoid this stabilisation of the front. They would carry all the supplies and fire power required to act independently. Such a force attacking at daybreak could be a hundred miles away by night. De Gaulle imagined a professional French Army consisting

But, for the moment, the French were not even thinking in terms of a methodical breakthrough: the French defensive doctrine required these mechanised forces to be used as both a strategic reserve to achieve defence in depth by switching fire power rapidly to any threatened spot and delivering a counter-attack, and a rapid advance into Belgium to establish a defensive front deep inside Belgian territory.

Nonetheless, the French probably had the best tank force in the world by the start of the second European War. They also held frequent tank manoeuvres which convinced even Churchill that the French Army was the finest in the world, but these were in reality no more than practicing crews in the use of tanks rather than rehearsing modern armoured warfare tactics. It was only in the last few years before war broke out that real evolution of thought regarding the use of mechanised forces took place in the French High Command (despite having tank specialists such as *Général* Jean B. Estienne and Charles de Gaulle) and it was only after the fall of Poland in 1939 that the French High Command fully realised the value of independent armoured divisions.

of six divisions, completely motorised and caterpillared, and, partly armoured. Each division would be made up of three complementary brigades: a heavily armoured brigade consisting of a regiment of 500 heavy tanks and a regiment of fast light tanks, a brigade of infantry consisting of two regiments of infantry and an artillery brigade consisting of two regiments, one of heavy short guns, the other of lighter, longer ranged guns. The division would be reinforced by a battalion of engineers to deal with obstacles and a battalion of communication troops. A light division would be attached to these six divisions. This would be of the same make as the other divisions, but equipped with more lightly armoured machines, lighter artillery and more mobile infantry. This division would be responsible for scouting and to prevent surprise. This professional army could act immediately on hostilities, gaining initial success and gaining time for a general mobilisation. In De Gaulle's analysis, the light tanks would lead an attack, making first contact with the enemy and finding favourable routes for the main battle echelon. The battle echelon would consist of medium and heavy tanks, which would attack in independent sections manoeuvring as circumstances dictated. As the tanks produced their effect, the infantry would advance, occupying the ground captured in successive positions protected in depth with machine guns. De Gaulle virtually ignored the role of aircraft in the first edition of his book, and it was only with the experience of bitter hindsight that he realised that technological advances in aircraft design meant they could play a full role in co-operating with the ground forces. Best results would be obtained if great numbers of aircraft could be assembled at short notice to seize temporary control of the skies and to attack the enemy position in depth. The combined effect of the medium and heavy tanks and air support would enable a breakthrough of even fortified positions. Following a successful breakthrough, exploitation that was not available to the armies of the Great War was now possible. Mechanised troops, supported by air power, would rapidly move in the rear of the enemy, striking at his sensitive points and throwing him into confusion. Such operations, being very fluid, would require a change in the working of the higher command. No longer could they be in the rear, working out detailed plans for methodical attacks, but instead they would have to lead from the front, reacting to the rapidly changing situation created by mechanised warfare. The battle would largely be controlled with extensive use of wireless.

It took France ten years after the end of the Great War to decide to rebuild its air force with the creation of the *Armée de l'Air* in the late 1920's. The role of the French Air Force was primarily to support the Army on the battlefield with a secondary role of carrying out operations against the enemy's air force. In this respect, it was similar to the *Luftwaffe*. In 1934 the *Armée de l'Air* became an independent service, and under *Général* Denain, formulated a strategic bomber role to take the air war to the heart of the enemy's industrial power. Although the *Armée de l'Air* was not far off the numerical equal of the *Luftwaffe* by the outbreak of war, these conflicting strategical objectives meant that it developed no real goals or purpose – in effect, it was not much more 'than a pile of aircraft.'[24] The lack of industrial capacity to build modern aircraft in sufficient numbers also resulted in the tendency to maintain nominal strength by preserving obsolete aircraft. The French also dispersed their air force widely, with almost 40 percent deployed uselessly on the Mediterranean fronts.

German grand strategy and military doctrine

In 1900, Germany had been the greatest industrial power in Europe. However, the Great War shattered Germany, with 2,000,000 killed and missing, and now parts of the country were occupied by the Allied armies and the German government, under the terms of the Versailles Treaty, forced to obey the demands of the victorious Allies. German territory had been annexed into old and new European states. With an Army limited to 100,000 men and only light weaponry allowed, and also denied the right to fortify areas of its frontier, Germany was now in a very vulnerable position. Len Deighton, in his book *Blitzkrieg*, shows how these factors caused the political situation inside Germany to disintegrate, with revolutionary communists clashing with the *Freikorps*, a volunteer military force formed of veteran German soldiers dedicated to the defence of the homeland. This violence in the streets resulted in a fall in industrial output and made investors nervous. Over 763,000 Germans were reported to have died of starvation as a consequence of the Allied naval blockade during the war; this blockade was not lifted until long after the Armistice and the German people continued to suffer its effects. Such conditions allowed Adolf Hitler's rise to power, with his promise to restore the German nation.

In this post-war climate, Barry Posen notes that German political and military strategy shared a unified goal – the revision of the Versailles Treaty. While the politicians tried to renegotiate the terms of the treaty with France and Britain, the Army reacted with some subtle and some blatant violations of the treaty. Von Seeckt, who commanded the German Army between 1920 and 1926, viewed France and her

24 Posen, *The Sources of Military Doctrine*, p. 134.

new eastern allies as a grave threat to Germany, and began to prepare for a resumption of war in 1923.[25]

Germany's military doctrine was highly offensive before the Great War and remained so after the end of that war, both during the Weimar Republic and Hitler's Third Reich. It was based on the idea of a short war, with vast encircling movements and annihilation of the enemy forces (*Vernichtungsstrategie*).[26] This strategy of annihilation was attractive to Germany as she did not want to face a war on two fronts. German military leaders planned to use their interior lines of communications to concentrate first against one enemy and defeat them in short war of annihilation, before rapidly shifting forces to the other threatened front.

Von Seeckt was highly influenced by the shock troop tactics developed by *Major* Reddemann and *Hauptmann* Rohr during the Great War. These shock-troop tactics became known as 'Hutier tactics' even though Hutier had nothing to do with their development.[27] Hutier tactics were characterised by surprise, violence, rapidity of execution, manoeuvre and extreme depth of penetration. Von Seeckt concluded that these tactics ultimately failed because of the lack of mobility existing during the Great War; the shock troops advanced so quickly they could not be reinforced or resupplied. Von Seeckt saw the use of infantry transported by lorries as a means to provide the required mobility to allow battles of rapid manoeuvre and annihilation of the enemy to take place. He developed this idea into a theory of *attaque brusquée* – a rapid attack against Germany's enemies before they had time to mobilise. Although Von Seeckt recognised the potential of air power and tanks, his ideas had not reached the stage of what has become known as 'Blitzkrieg'.

German grand strategy under Hitler had much in common with that of the Weimar Republic, although Hitler wanted much more in terms of conquest and at a much faster pace. He aimed to restore German military power, regain lost territory, acquire new German-speaking populations and seize 'living space' in the east for the growth of the new Reich. The scale of Hitler's ambitions, following the publication of *Mien Kampf*, had clearly moved from national politics to vast territorial conquest to fulfil his long-term dream of creating a Germania.

25 Von Seeckt was convinced of a 'fundamental antagonism' between Germany and France. Within three years of the end of the Great War, France had formed alliances with countries surrounding Germany: Belgium, Poland, Czechoslovakia, Romania and Yugoslavia. Moreover, there was Britain and Russia to consider. (Posen, *The Sources of Military Doctrine*, p. 186).

26 During the Great War, Germany did adopt a strategy of attrition (*Ermmattungsstrategie*) under Falkenhayan in 1916 during the Battle of Verdun, before being forced onto the defensive in the West as a result of losses at both Verdun and on the Somme. Germany returned to the offensive in the West in the spring of 1918 with a series of massive assaults making extensive use of 'Hutier' tactics.

27 Hutier's name is associated with the tactics as he was the first to use them successfully against the Russians in 1917.

Hitler pursued an aggressive political strategy backed up with the threat of military action. In March 1935 he announced to the world that Germany would rearm and on 7 March 1936 he reoccupied the Rhineland. The French hesitated – as Britain declared it would not back any move that led to war with Germany – and Hitler had his first victory. This was followed by the forced unification of Austria in February 1938 and the seizure of territory from Czechoslovakia during the Munich Crises. Hitler's approach is referred to as his 'avalanche' theory by German historian Percy Schramm. An aggressive diplomatic policy backed up with a show of military power would overwhelm smaller opponents, and small victories at first would lead to larger victories. General Ironside understood this at the time and noted in his diary on 25 September 1937:

> All the minor nations are now terrified of [Germany]. We shall no doubt be faced with a *fait accompli* one of these days, and the little nation that has been raped will scream in vain.[28]

To achieve these political aims, Hitler needed a large display of military power. If military action was required to fulfil his goals, he needed a speedy victory by a Blitz or lightning war; if military action stagnated this could encourage France, Britain or Russia to become involved. Hitler achieved his display of force by a rapid rearmament programme which emphasised numbers over other military considerations. This was in effect rearmament in 'width' rather than 'depth' with little preparation made to mobilise the economy for the eventuality of total war. The original use of the word Blitzkrieg, or lightening war, referred to this concept. It was a method of achieving a quick victory but avoiding total economic mobilisation for war. Such a policy would have served Germany well if her moves continued to be purely opportunistic, but, in the event of total war it would leave Germany with an eventual irrevocable numerical inferiority in armaments (for example, German fighter and tank production during the first year of the war was less than that in 1944, at a time when the Reich was nearing final collapse). It also resulted in projects that would take time to complete, such as the development of a strategic four-engine long range bomber or the development of jet engines, being postponed.

Hitler achieved speed in military action with what are now familiarly referred to as Blitzkrieg tactics.[29] Heinz Guderian is perhaps the man who was most influential in developing German Blitzkrieg tactics.[30] Guderian believed that tanks alone

28 Macleod DSO, MC & Kelly (eds), *Time Unguarded*, p. 28.

29 The term Blitzkreig was first associated with the new German tactics in a 1939 article on the Polish campaign in the American *Time* magazine.

30 Guderain published his ideas in *Achtung – Panzer*! Guderain elevated tanks, along with aircraft, as the main arms of the services and believed that tanks should be concentrated in specialised divisions – panzer divisions – and accompanied by motorised infantry specially trained in co-operation with the tanks, anti-tank detachments and engineers.

or operating with just infantry could never be decisive; he argued for armoured formations – panzer divisions – which included an all-arms force of tanks, infantry, engineers, artillery, anti-tank guns and anti-aircraft guns in which the tanks played the primary role and the role of the other arms was to enable them to be used to their full effect. The Great War had shown the strength of well-prepared defensive positions. To smash through such positions, Guderian recognised that the whole depth of the enemy position would have to be attacked simultaneously. This required airpower. Unlike the RAF, the *Luftwaffe* had developed with close ties to the Army (being a newly created force, it had no traditional ties and had received a large draft of Army officers) and was prepared and trained for a Continental war where its main role would be reconnaissance, gaining air superiority and co-operating with ground forces. By 1936 Germany was well on the way to developing the art of Blitzkrieg. On a visit to attend German manoeuvres in September 1937, Ironside was impressed with the co-operation of all arms in the German armed forces compared to the British:

> I think that the German Army has developed in a marvellous way. It is madly enthusiastic and very efficient...Everybody watching this effort is terrified, and I am sure nothing will stand up to it when the moment comes...The German Army, Navy, and Air Force are all united and are working for one thing together. They have one direction and as far as I could see no jealousies. They have no

Reconnaissance by light motorised units would send back information to the attacking echelons and identify the mission and offensive deployment of the armoured forces. For a successful breakthrough, Guderian considered that the entire depth of the enemy's position had to be attacked simultaneously. This could be achieved by the use of aircraft to delay the intervention of enemy anti-tank reserves and tanks with attacks on road and rail traffic, command centres and the communication system. These operations could be enhanced with the use of paratroops and air-landing troops. On the ground, tanks were the main weapon of breakthrough, which would be achieved by deploying a large force of tanks in sufficient depth and on a front broad enough to prevent the enemy bringing the central axis of advance under flanking fire, which would prevent the other arms from being able to follow the tanks. Guderain thought that the main armoured forces should attack in four waves. The first wave, after breaking through, would push on to pin down enemy reserves, including tanks, and knock out HQ's and anti-tank guns it came across. However, it was not to get embroiled in the main battle. The second wave would have as its objective the destruction of the enemy artillery and anti-tank defence. The third wave would bring up the infantry through the enemy infantry battle zone. The fourth wave acted as a reserve for the high command. The infantry role was the destruction of the enemy infantry strongpoints left intact during the tank battle. Guderian also realised the importance of the higher command being forward and controlling the battle with the use of wireless. Once through the enemy battle zone, the mobile forces could than rapidly exploit success. Unlike many tank theorists of the time, Guderain also dealt with the unavoidable reality of mechanised warfare: tank versus tank combat. He believed that for success, the use of manoeuvre and reserves would be required in order to concentrate forces so that a greater number of tanks were pitted against a smaller number of the enemy. Other arms should also have as their key objective the contribution to the victory of the tanks.

> watertight compartments. They have thus a great advantage over us, who have made no attempt even to lay down the duties of the various forces. No one will touch the thorny subject.[31]

The defining characteristic of Blitzkrieg was the attack in depth, designed to disrupt enemy command and communications. Blitzkrieg did not remove the need for the traditional German preference for the outflanking and annihilation of enemy forces. However, by causing confusion by disrupting communications, Blitzkrieg destroyed the enemies will to fight and thus reduced the cost of the battle of annihilation.

Not all in the German Army agreed with Guderian's ideas. The Chief of the General Staff, *Generaloberst* Ludwig Beck, dismissed the classic German preference for idea of winning the war in a single campaign of annihilation but instead argued for successive operations based around combined arms tactics grounded within the reality of German industrial and economic means. But Guderian's ideas were attractive to Hitler as they promised speed. After witnessing a demonstration of motorised troops which included the basic elements which were later to comprise the panzer divisions, Hitler is reported to have exclaimed 'That's what I need! That's what I want to have.'[32] Guderian had to fight hard for his panzer divisions, and there is no doubt that Hitler's support was crucial to the adoption of Blitzkrieg. It is ironic that Guderian's thinking was in part influenced by Britain's early experiments with mechanised forces in the late 1920's.

Like France, Germany also constructed defences along its frontier: *Der Westwall* (the West Wall) or the Siegfried Line, which was the name given to it by the Allies. However, Hitler's reason for constructing fortifications was different to that of France. The Siegfried Line was intended to deter any action by France as Hitler extended his Reich eastwards. The fortifications were also different in nature to the French Maginot Line, being based on numerous small reinforced concrete pillboxes and shelters arranged in depth and protected by anti-tank obstacles. In this regard, they closely resembled the defences of the Hindenburg Line constructed by the Germans in 1917, based on the 'Hedgehog' or *Igel* pattern of strongpoints arranged in depth rather than the chain of immensely strong large forts which made up the Maginot Line. To further ensure that the Allies would not dare attack these defences, German propaganda greatly played up the 'impregnability' of the Siegfried Line.

These differing grand strategies of Britain, France and Germany ultimately led to the peculiar state of affairs of the opening months of the next European War – the Sitzkrieg – which ended abruptly with Blitzkrieg.

31 Macleod DSO, MC & Kelly (eds), *Time Unguarded*, p. 30.
32 Guderian, *Achtung – Panzer!*, p. 12.

The Munich settlement and the reluctant British return to collective security

Hitler was an astute politician and achieved his aims by calculating that Britain and France would not act against him. Indeed, Britain and France did not act to stop Hitler seizing Czechoslovakia. Today, it is still widely believed that this was because Germany was thoroughly prepared for war while the Allies were not. But the reality was that there was no political or military will on the part of either France or Britain to act against Germany because of the British determination not to be involved in another Continental war and the French determination not to act alone. If there had been a will to act, France, supported with a British contribution of a naval blockade and air support, could have acted decisively. *Generaloberst* Jodl, giving evidence at the Nuremberg Trials, stated that if France had attacked in support of Czechoslovakia, it 'was out of the question to hold out against a hundred French divisions with only five fighting divisions and seven reserve divisions in the western fortifications which were nothing but a large construction site.'[33] *Generalfeldmarschall* Manstein shared the same opinion, believing that if war had broken out Germany would not have been able to defend either her border with France or Czechoslovakia. Even Hitler, inspecting the Czech fortifications later, acknowledged that the German armies would have run into serious trouble if they had attacked the defence system. Churchill was of a similar opinion and he lamented the lack of any offensive action by the Allies during these aggressions by Hitler. At the time the French Commander-in-Chief, *Général* Gamelin, actually did formulate a counter-offensive against the Siegfried Line between the Rhine and the Moselle, with holding actions on the Upper Rhine and on the Luxemburg sector. However, as already noted, the French were unwilling to act alone and Gamelin was able to use the overstated strength of the Siegfried Line to justify not acting even though he privately thought it would take at least another year before it became a serious obstacle. The plans were shelved following the Munich settlement.

After the Munich settlement, which was regarded as harsh but fair, the British Prime Minister – Mr Chamberlin – was determined to secure a broad peace. But Hitler was preparing plans for the full occupation of Czechoslovakia. Contrary to popular belief, intelligence of Hitler's plans did reach the British and French governments, but such intelligence was of no use if there was no will to act on it. It has been suggested that Chamberlain accepted the occupation of Czechoslovakia as the necessary conclusion to Munich. On 22 March 1939, Hitler occupied Memel – some years later, he is said to have recalled that 'Chamberlain informed me through a third party that he understood very well that this step had to be taken, even though he could not approve of it publicly.'[34]

33 Jon Kimche, *The Unfought Battle* (London: Weidenfeld & Nicolson, 1968), p. 10.
34 Ibid., p. 23.

With the elimination of Czechoslovakia following the Munich settlement, the relative position of military strength between Germany and France was swinging in Germany's favour. The loss of Czechoslovakia meant the loss of 35 well-armed divisions and freed up German divisions that would have had to be held to face them. Germany could now in theory utilise all her divisions against France. In addition, Germany seized the military equipment, including many heavy guns and tanks, as well as the munitions factories of Czechoslovakia; in particular, without the additional Czech tanks it is debatable whether Germany could have launched its Blitzkrieg in May 1940. The elimination of Czechoslovakia also placed Germany one step nearer to the domination of south-eastern Europe, and the natural resources that would allow her to fight a long war.

Immediately following the March crises, Chamberlain received intelligence that Germany was imminently going to attack Poland. In response, he announced an agreement to guarantee Polish security. The Polish guarantee was not, however, a will to swiftly mobilise to help the Poles should they be attacked. Chamberlain still firmly believed Hitler wanted to avoid war, and was convinced that the guarantee would act as a deterrent and a broad peace agreement could still be secured. In this matter, Chamberlain seriously underestimated Hitler's willingness to take risks. The French basically wrote off the Polish guarantee the minute it was signed. The Poles claimed they could mobilise an army of 52 divisions, although they were short on heavy artillery and tanks. At no point did Gamelin take this into account in the balance of power, unlike the Dutch and Belgian forces, which he calculated would be added to the Allied strength if the French and British advanced into Belgium to support these allies in waiting.

Although the intelligence of an immediate attack was false, Hitler had no intention of seeking a peaceful agreement. This was the final step of his plan to settle with the Poles and gain living space for the Reich in the east. By 3 April, the German Army had been told to be ready for 'Case White' – the invasion of Poland – no later than 1 September. At the end of April, Hitler denounced the Anglo-German naval agreement and the German-Polish Non-Aggression Pact.

Another consequence of the events of March 1939 was the realisation by the British Government that the French Army may not be able to secure the Low Countries against German aggression, the loss of which would give Germany airfields and submarine bases from which to attack Britain. France had made it clear that she would not stand alone against Germany and demanded more help from Britain. The British now finally agreed to full Joint Staff talks with the French and reluctantly returned to a policy of collective security and agreed to the deployment of an Expeditionary Force of four divisions, almost the entire Regular home strength, and to reinforce it as soon as possible after the outbreak of war by a further five or six Territorial divisions. Britain intimated that eventually 30 or more divisions could be mobilised. The Government felt able to make these promises to France with the introduction of conscription during the spring.

This then, was the background to the Anglo-French staff talks.

Anglo-French staff talks

During the first talks, which started on 27 March, the French reiterated their aim to defend French territory and remain on the defensive. They would rely on an economic blockade and the industrial capacity of the Allies to obtain quantitative and qualitative superiority over Germany and only then launch an offensive. Both the French and British Staffs realised they would be facing an enemy superior in land and air forces, but not sea forces. A large-scale offensive against France or Britain or both could be expected. The Anglo-French Staffs agreed that such an offensive would have to be first defeated and that Germany would have to be held in static war conditions such as those in the Great War while the Allies built up their economic resources.

The Anglo-French Staffs were also in agreement in the probable action that would be undertaken by Germany. It was expected that Germany would avoid an attack on the Maginot Line, instead attempting to outflank it by attacking through Belgium and Holland. Such a move would also place air landing grounds along the North Sea in German hands, putting German bombers in range of British and French strategic targets. Both Staffs agreed that Holland could not be helped in such a scenario, but it was hoped that with the co-operation of Belgium, an advance could be made to the main line of Belgian resistance along the Meuse-Albert Canal. As a minimum, an advance could be made to the River Scheldt (known as the Escaut to the French). Such an advance would connect the French frontier defences at Maulde to the national Belgium redoubt above Ghent.

Although the French were dismayed at the pace which the British intended to build up the BEF, they were assured of Britain's strength on the sea and in the air; in particular that Britain was on the way to obtaining a bomber strength equal to that of the *Luftwaffe*. But, both the French and British Staffs agreed that the Allies would not initiate air action other than on military targets in the narrowest sense of the word because of the fear of retaliation. The British and French governments were paralysed by the fear of German air attacks – a calculation by the Air Staff estimated that Germany could maintain a daily attack on London with a thousand bombers for 14 days. Germany had deliberately contributed to this fear – the concept of *Risikoflotte* – by continually supplying the Allies with intelligence on their air strength. The Allies agreed to only use bombers against German points of concentration, communications and airfields once France had been attacked. The British Air Staff thought this a poor use of bombers, and, hardly in the spirit of co-operation, told the French 'that they must not expect much result from the assistance of British bombers', and that it was not prepared to see Bomber Command frittered away by operations on such minor targets.[35]

Germany was also guilty of overstating the strength of the Allies, in particular the RAF – or rather its preparedness to strike against Germany – and French armoured

35 Ibid., p. 43.

forces. An assessment of the French Army prepared for Hitler stated that 'the French Army must be rated the same as in the first world war, [sic] as the most formidable of all our potential enemies'.[36] In the summer and autumn of 1939, Hitler was preoccupied with the thought that Germany could be defeated swiftly by a combined air and land attack on the industrial Ruhr. Hitler was not so much worried about Britain and France declaring war on Germany if he attacked Poland – his concern was whether they would do anything about it. Hitler's instinct was that that the French political system was rotten to the core and this would paralyse any action by the French Army and that Britain was pacifist. On these matters, his intuition seemed good: all reports he received suggested inaction by both Britain and France. Typical of these reports was that from Hans Seligo, the press director of the British section of the *Auslandsorgainisation*. Seligo noted that although the British were preparing for war as if it was imminent, Chamberlain and the Cabinet were 'definitely working to prevent the outbreak of war and would prefer a compromise over Danzig and the Corridor acceptable to their people, to any recourse to force.'[37] Key in Seligo's report was the following statement:

> [G]reat gaps in armament remain, especially in the army in the field, but this is not so very important [to the British] because their tactical plans, particularly at the beginning of the war, do not assign any sizeable tasks to the British army in the field.[38]

If Hitler needed any more convincing that Britain would do nothing, it surely came from intelligence supplied from his London embassy by Ambassador Dirksen. Dirksen informed Hitler that in discussions with Sir Horace Wilson, permanent Head of the Civil Service and close advisor to Chamberlain in dealings with Germany, that if Germany was nearing the end of its territorial demands, the British Government would be prepared to enter secret talks with Germany, at first excluding France, to ensure peace and 'one of the greatest political combinations it was possible to imagine.'[39] This was in July 1939 – the British Government still believed Hitler wanted peace. Dirksen's intelligence is revealing because it illustrates why throughout the Sitzkrieg some senior politicians still did not believe Hitler would attack the Allies and the complacency with the slow progress of equipping the BEF. With his territorial ambitions in the east satisfied, perhaps these politicians believed Hitler would accept peace without the need for any further hostilities.

Ironside, when tasked with a mission to find out what Polish intentions were in the event of war was 'profoundly distressed' when, as part of his mission, he read

36 Ibid., p. 57.
37 Ibid., p. 62.
38 Ibid., p. 63.
39 Ibid., p. 81.

the papers and plans prepared by the British and French Staffs. It was clear that the Joint Staffs were quite prepared to let Poland be overrun; in the meantime, this would give the French and British more time to complete their mobilisation. Poland would only be saved in the long run by an Allied victory. Gamelin emphasised that he had no serious intention of attacking the Siegfried Line to come to Poland's aid as this would require long preparations which could not be undertaken in haste. The Anglo-French Joint Staffs, under Gamelin's initiative, was working on what was described as non-provocative warfare. The Joint Staffs discussions also considered the possibility that Germany may attack France first. Here, the benefit of the Polish guarantee was the belief that at least 30 to 35 German divisions would be tied up to guard against any attack in the east.

By the spring of 1939 British politicians had committed to a 32-division strong Expeditionary Force within two years. To meet this commitment, the British Government decided to double the size of the Territorial Force and introduce conscription.[40] Although the British Government had finally woken up to the need to openly confront Hitler and the inevitability of war, it was far too late to raise enough forces to redress the balance of forces between France and Germany. France was promised an initial deployment of two corps, each with two divisions, and that the first armoured division would now be available in eight months. It was also anticipated that the first Territorial divisions could be dispatched in four months' time. It was also decided that 'collaboration with the French Army and Air Force in the land battle' if Germany invaded the Low Countries would be the 'primary commitment of the British Bomber Command during any critical phase of the invasion.'[41]

It seems unbelievable that Hore-Belisha, strongly supported by Churchill, went on to propose a 55 division Army within the same time scale. This was a pure flight of the imagination: in the first place, the BEF's initial four divisions faced chronic equipment and ammunition shortages of all kinds – the Committee of Imperial Defence was informed that hardly a unit of the BEF sent to France was fully equipped. This even extended to uniforms: some men had not even been issued with Battle Dress – or 'Battle rompers' as they were sometimes referred to – but went over to France in

40 The effect of doubling the size of the Territorial Force had a particularly negative effect on unit identity. The Territorial Force had already suffered under the conversion of certain units to AA units and the subsequent 'Partial Deployment' when the AA defences of London were manned in the spring of 1939. Now the Territorial Army had 'to bleed the existing establishments of their trained men' to form second line units and the second line units in their turn 'were decimated to produce third line units, and so it went on until the original identity of the TA was submerged in the flood of conscript manpower' (Williams OBE, *Citizen Soldiers*, p. 93).

41 Basil Collier, *The Defence of the United Kingdom* (London: HMSO), p. 72. This decision was largely taken as an Air Staff analysis had found that Bomber Command lacked the resources for a strategical bombing role.

ill-fitting Reservists clothing.[42] Although supposedly a mechanised army, the BEF also faced transport shortages. Many units had not had the full complement of trucks and civilian vehicles, in various states of repair, had to be requisitioned to fill the gaps.[43] Unfortunately, as Montgomery recalled, many of these quickly broke down due to lack of spares and servicing:

> The transport was inadequate and was completed on mobilisation by vehicles requisitioned from civilian firms. Much of the transport of my division consisted of civilian vans and lorries from the towns of England; they were in bad repair and, when my division moved from the ports up to its concentration area near the French frontier, the countryside of France was strewn with broken down vehicles.[44]

Particularly, there were major shortages in specially fitted vehicles, such as wireless trucks and 30 cwt winch lorries and gun tractors. Some temporary reductions in the B Echelon transport of the Royal Artillery, Signals and Infantry had to be made to keep the frontline units up to strength in motor transport. *FSR Vol. III 1935* makes the point that the 'introduction of new weapons and the increasing mechanization [sic] of armies ... necessitate the most careful considered allocation of the national resources for the purpose of prosecuting the war. The demands for warlike stores of all kinds will in any major war only be met with the mobilization [sic] of industry in accordance with plans prepared in peace.'[45] The 55 division Army would require production plans of 66,000 artillery guns, 192,000,000 rounds of artillery ammunition and 31,000 tanks in the first two years of war! Although Chamberlain had taken steps in the final few years before war broke out to expand industrial capacity, they reflected the government's priorities of aircraft and AA guns. The production figures for a 32 or 55 division Army were plainly unattainable; It would take many months for the British economy to gear up for total war, and the Army would have to compete with both the

42 The 9 Brigade War Diary entry for 15 October 1939 notes that men were still waiting for battle dress; they had had no fresh issue of clothing since the beginning of May pending the issue of battle dress and no unit had any reserve clothing.

43 In 1935 a small nucleus of officers formed the Inspectorate of Supplementary Transport to administer the vehicle impressment scheme. They had representatives in every county of the country and their role was to carry out an inspection of vehicles suitable for military use and maintain records of them. In the event of mobilisation, orders were to be issued to the owners of the vehicles to drive them to designated vehicle collecting centres.

44 Bernard Law, Viscount Montgomery of Alamein, *The Memoirs of Field-Marshal Montgomery*, (London: Collins, 1958), p. 50.

45 *Field Service Regulations Vol.III: Operations – Higher Formations 1935* (London: The War Office, 1935), p. 3.

demands of the RAF and Navy.[46] Chamberlain, at the start of the war, was adamant that the RAF would take priority:

> To my mind the lesson of the Polish campaign is the power of the Air Force, when it has obtained complete mastery in the air, to paralyse the land forces... Accordingly, as it seems to me...absolute priority ought to be given to our plans for rapidly accelerating the strength of the Air Force, and the extent of our effort on land should be determined by our resources *after* we have provided for the Air Force extension.[47]

One of the effects of conscription was to hold up the training of the Regular Army, whose ranks had been thinned by the need for trainers and specialists to train the new conscripts: there were just not enough officers and non-commissioned officers who had had any experience in teaching and training to go around. Another effect was a temporary retarded armament production due to the withdrawal of labour from the factories. General Pownall, then Director of Military Operations and Intelligence, summarised the situation as 'a proper Granny's knitting' but conceded that at least the measures had been introduced in peace time and not on the outbreak of war, and that 'We shall get some of the muddles off our chests before the war begins'.[48]

At this stage, it was understood that France could mobilise 72 divisions in addition to fortress troops (equivalent to 12 to 14 divisions). Of these, 12 would be required to guard the Italian frontier, leaving 72 to 74 to guard the Maginot Line and for operations against Germany. With the addition of the four British divisions, there would be 76 to 78 divisions to meet a German attack. It was considered that Germany would not attack until Poland was disposed of, but once that was done Germany would likely have about 100 divisions for operations against the Allies. Germany would also have the advantage of being able to concentrate a force against the decisive point while the Allies would be forced to disperse their force in the defences along the 500 mile French frontier from Switzerland to the North Sea.

No similar Staff conversations took place with Belgium as she continued to remain neutral. With no effective exchange of information, the planning for the proposed

46 This is amply demonstrated in the officially published statistics relating to the war effort, which shows that it was not until early 1943 that output reached its peak. For instance, 314 tanks were produced from September to December 1939, 1,397 in 1940, 4,844 in 1941 and 8,611 in 1942. The same figures respectively for field, medium and heavy artillery equipment was nil, 968, 3,780 and 3,946. The figures for filled gun ammunition (in millions) were 1.9, 12.8, 29.3 and 59.4. Source: *Statistics Relating to the War Effort of the United Kingdom* (London: HMSO, 1944).

47 Winston Churchill, *The Second World War: Volume I – The Gathering Storm* (London: Cassel & Co. Ltd., 1948), p. 360.

48 Bond (ed.), *Chief of Staff*, pp. 201–202.

advance into Belgium by French and British troops was severely hampered. This then, was the background to the dispatch of the BEF to France.

Dispatch of the BEF to France

Because the French plan of campaign was based upon a defensive attitude until full mobilisation of the Allies had taken place, the plan of operations for the BEF could go little beyond than the safe transport to France and establishing a safe area for concretion and a base. In the last six months of peace much detailed planning was undertaken with regards to the dispatch of the Expeditionary Force.[49] The Army element, plan W4, envisaged the use of the French ports of Cherbourg, Brest, St Nazaire and Nantes; all these ports were on the French western coast and the decision to use them was taken so that the risk of air attack was minimised. Once landed, troops not employed on bases or lines of communication (LoC) were to move at once to an assembly area south of Abbeville and from there go to their allotted stations on the left of the French Armies. In addition a 'Maintenance Project Plan' was prepared to ensure the supply of the Expeditionary Force. The Air Force plan, W.A.4, involved arrangements for the Air Component (intended for reconnaissance and protection of the Expeditionary Force) and the AASF (intended for the strategical bombing of Germany or the support of the Allied armies in any critical stage of an enemy invasion of the Low Countries). With the co-operation of the French, reconnaissance for bases was carried out during the run up to war. The Navy also finalised its plans before the outbreak of war to ensure the safe transportation of the Expeditionary Force.

Meanwhile, France was still promising to come to the aid of her ally Poland with a counter-offensive in the west if Germany attacked in the east. This included a proposal by Gamelin to attack Germany in the west through Belgium, Luxemburg and Holland, which he presented to the French Government on the outbreak of war, but the plan was rejected. Britain also had no intention of exploiting the pre-occupation of the Germans in the east. It did not matter if Poland held out for three weeks or three months, as both France and Britain had already written off the Poles and made independent plans.

On 24 August, Germany secured her eastern border by signing a non-aggression treaty with Russia. Britain, on 25 August, signed an Anglo-Polish Defence Alliance. At dawn on 1 September, Germany attacked Poland without warning. Britain gave Germany an ultimatum to withdraw from Poland, which was timed to expire on 3 September. Germany ignored the ultimatum and at 11:00 a.m. on 3 September

49 During the summer of 1938, a 'Preparations Section' in the War Office was charged with the task of making administrative arrangements for the dispatch of an Expeditionary Force to the Continent. A similar section had been formed in 1914. However, as we shall see, no arrangements were put in hand for an Engineer appreciation of the tasks required once the BEF was in France, which was to result in huge difficulties in the supply of labour for the BEF during the Sitzkrieg.

another European War started.[50] Although Hitler's instinct that neither the British nor French would come to Poland's aid was correct, he was nevertheless taken by surprise by the declaration of war on Germany by both countries following the invasion. In this respect, he seriously underestimated both British and French resolve to halt further German territorial expansion in Europe.

The War Cabinet decided to give command of the Expeditionary Force to Lord Gort. This may well have been a political move to part Gort and the Secretary of State for War, Mr Hore-Belisha, as they were barely on speaking terms. Within his first year of office, Hore-Belisha had made Gort CIGS as part of a move to replace members of the Army Council he considered too old an un-progressive. Hore-Belisha had met Gort whilst skiing in Switzerland and had been impressed by his personality. He was also aware of his war record: Gort had commanded the 4th and 1st Grenadier Guards during the Great War and had been awarded the MC, three DSO's and the VC, which made him well known and popular with the public. Hore-Belisha 'thought Gort was the man. I said to myself, "Here is a man the public and the Army will accept as a soldier – with a V.C., three D.S.O.s and all that." I knew he wouldn't make a good C.I.G.S., and he didn't.'[51] He made the appointment as he felt Gort would 'put the Army on the map'.[52] Gort's appointment as Commander-in-Chief was a complete surprise and was made over the heads of several senior generals; many expected Lieutenant-General Sir John Dill to get the appointment. Unfortunately for Gort, this made him many enemies. As his Chief of Staff, Gort selected Lieutenant-General Pownall.

Ironside, who was bitterly disappointed not to get the command of the BEF, replaced Gort as CIGS.[53] He was told he did not get the command as he was considered unreliable and difficult to get on with. In fact, this was the reason he had also been passed over for the role of CIGS in 1937; instead he was given the post of Governor of Gibraltar, a traditional staging post before retirement. However, this time his appointment as CIGS was widely welcomed as he was in the public eye and had the complete confidence of the Prime Minister and Churchill. Ironside, in all likeliness, would not have been considered for such a position had not Hore-Belisha brought him back from Gibraltar in May 1939, to take up the role of Inspector-General of Overseas

50 Nick Smart, in *British Strategy and Politics during the Phoney war: Before the Balloon Went Up*, makes the point that the Second World War did not start until December 1941 when Japan attacked Pearl Harbour, and Hitler, with Mussolini in tow, declared war on the USA. Until then, the fighting was just a European affair.

51 Kennedy, *The Business of War*, p. 37

52 Ibid., p. 4.

53 The CIGS was not the same role as it had been in the Great War, when then the CIGS had been able to issue orders to the Commanders-in Chief. Commanders-in-Chief were now appointed by either the War Cabinet or the Army Council. The CIGS could issue orders to those Commanders-in-Chief appointed by the Army Council under the authority of that Council, but what about those appointed by the War Cabinet? This matter was to result in much friction between Gort and Ironside.

Forces. Hore-Belisha was impressed by Ironside's personality – 'If Ironside comes into a room, everybody will take notice of him.'[54] He was warned that Ironside would probably try and dominate but thought he could handle such a situation. Ironside knew he had not got the temperament for such a job as the CIGS and wrote as much in his diary. Brigadier Kennedy (then Deputy Director of Military Operations) – who enjoyed his encounters with Ironside, finding them amusing and inspiring confidence – noted that someone had told him 'Hore-Belisha does not know it yet, but he has raised a regular Frankenstein's monster in bringing Ironside back from the dead.'[55] In fact, most in the War Office did not consider that the combination of Ironside and Hore-Belisha could last. They were right, as within a year Hore-Belisha was gone.

On the declaration of war, Chamberlain formed a War Cabinet – to determine British strategic policy – consisting of the top ministers of the government and often attended by the Chiefs of Staff: Admiral Sir Dudley Pound, General Sir Edmund Ironside and Air Marshal Sir Cyril Newall. To ensure co-ordination of the Allied effort, Britain and France set up a Supreme War Council, consisting of the top government ministers and military officers of both countries. However, it did not mean the two countries saw eye to eye on the way the war should be run. Although, at least on the Western Front, uniformity of command was established early on by placing the British Expeditionary Force under the control of the French Commander-in-Chief North-East Theatre of Operations. The terms of the conduct of the operations of the Expeditionary Force issued to Gort observed:

> 1. His Majesty's Government have decided to send a Field Force to France and entrust its command to you.
> 2. The role of force under your command is to co-operate with our Allies in the defeat of the common enemy.
> 3. You will be under the command of the French Commander-in-Chief 'North-East Theatre of Operations'. In the pursuit of the common object, the defeat of the enemy, you will carry out loyally any instructions issued by him. At the same time, if any order given by him appears to you to imperil the British Field Force, it is agreed between the British and French Government that you should be at liberty to appeal to the British Government before executing that order. Whilst it is hoped the need for such an appeal will seldom, if ever, arise, you will not hesitate to avail yourself of your right to make it, if you think fit.[56]

The French Commander-in-Chief North-East Theatre of Operations was *Général* Georges, *Commandant-en-chef (Nord Est)*, subordinate to *Général* Gamelin. Although

54 Kennedy, *The Business of War*, p. 38.
55 Ibid., p. 18.
56 Ellis, *The War in France and Flanders 1939-1940* (London: HSMO, 1953), pp. 11–12.

this decision was taken to ensure uniformity of command from the outset, Brian Bond has remarked on the irony of the situation that after years of military and political establishment opposition to sending an Expeditionary Force to France, both the Government and General Staff readily accepted a more binding and less independent position than in 1914. This situation was of course forced on the British by their refusal to take part in collective security until compelled to do so and hence losing the opportunity to enter the war on their terms.

The RAF component of the Air Force accompanying the Expeditionary Force was to be under Gort's command, but the AASF was to remain under the command of the Air Officer Commanding-in-Chief, Bomber Command, in the United Kingdom. Surprisingly, if the BEF required air support above and beyond the RAF component, Gort had to apply directly to the Air Officer Commanding AASF!

Because of the state of the British Army, Ironside had doubts about the wording in the right of appeal to the British Government. Quite simply, at that moment in time, he did not believe the BEF was ready to go into the line and that Gort would be too loyal to make any appeal:

> Gort ... is a boy – he has a one-track mind – quite rigid. He will play for the side, and that is all. That is not good enough for me. This force is the mother of the British Army. I do not want it to go into the line at first. I have told Gort that he is to *train* his army first when he gets to France.[57]

The BEF had no definite role other than to be part of the French plan to hold a defensive line to guard against a German advance through Belgium. This defensive line, dependant on the duration and extent of Belgian resistance, and the time at which Belgium asked for Allied help, could either be on the Meuse, joining up with the Belgians at Namur; the Escaut, joining up with the Belgians at Ghent; or along the Franco-Belgian border. As nothing could be done on the first two possibilities until an appeal from Belgium for help had been received, this committed the BEF to preparing a strong defensive position along the Franco-Belgian border. Lieutenant-General Dill, who was given command of I Corps, thought that holding a defensive line was all the BEF was capable of. Ominously, he thought that the weakness of the British Army sent to France would expose it to the risk it had run in 1918, when Ludendorff's last big attack had almost succeeded in breaking through to the Channel.

Advanced parties sailed from Portsmouth on 4 September while the first troop convoys sailed on 9 September. On landing, troops moved rapidly to assembly areas at Le Mans and Laval by road and rail. The Expeditionary Force was landed by 27 September without any loss of life; Hitler still hoped to avoid war with the Western Powers during the first three weeks of September, so the consequent action of U-boats was limited by his orders.

57 Kennedy, *The Business of War*, p. 22.

As the invasion of Britain was not anticipated, Home Forces, under the command of General Sir Walter Kirke, had as its main tasks the absorption of the flow of recruits created by conscription and preparing drafts for dispatch to the Expeditionary Force and other British Forces abroad.

3

Defending Secteur Défensive De Lille

The BEF was allocated the defences in front of Lille along the Franco-Belgian border – *SD* Lille. The defences in this area consisted of a complete anti-tank ditch covered by anti-tank gun blockhouses every 1,000 yards or so. A second line in the rear was mostly just a 'project'. This came as a shock to many in the BEF: they were expecting to find something similar to the world-famous Maginot Line. The existing French defences required much additional work to be undertaken if they were to stop an attack with modern mechanised forces. The BEF did have the advantage of being able to study German methods of attack following the Polish campaign. The principles laid out in the pre-war Army manuals were not altered by the lessons from Poland, but it was now clear that they had to be applied to stop a mass tank attack. Defence in depth against tanks became the principal consideration and the defences of the *SD* Lille were largely laid out with this in mind. The layout of anti-tank guns, artillery and obstacles created anti-tank zones while the role of the infantry was to separate the un-armoured enemy infantry from supporting their tanks. As a long-term project, the BEF aimed to develop an integrated defence with the air force and AA guns as a German ground attack would be a combined operation with the *Luftwaffe*.

French defences along the Franco-Belgian border

The British got their first look at the defences along the Franco-Belgian border during early May 1939 as part of the Staff talks with the French. Pownall, who was present on this occasion, recorded his impressions of the defences in his diary:

> West of Montmédy we came to the fieldwork's kind [of defences]. A continuous wire belt (not a very good one, rather low wire about 8 yards broad) and a continuous anti-tank obstacle. The latter here mostly of the ditch type about 12–15 feet across with a 70-deg. face revetted with fascines (to be concreted later). Not a very formidable obstacle if it were not under fire. The defence consists of a large number of concreted posts each holding about twelve men, one 25 mm A.T.

> Gun, one M.G. and one or two light automatics. The orders and fire plans are carefully worked out and the posts capable of withstanding heavy shell fire. But very conspicuous and badly camouflaged – they obviously rely on strength, little effort at concealment. In thick weather or heavy smoke I should say this line is by no means impregnable but it would form a very admirable beginning towards a strong defensive system, which is of course the way the French propose to use it as soon as their field formations come up … Work is still proceeding along most of the line which they have now prolonged as far as Cassel. How much further they will go is doubtful as they may rely on flooding beyond that.[1]

Following this visit, in an acknowledgement of the much weaker field fortifications of the northern extension to the Maginot Line compared to the Maginot Line proper, *Colonel* Petibon (*Chief de Cabinet* to Gamelin) felt the need to make an 'apologia' to Pownall, although Pownall considered it was barely needed.

On the outbreak of war, the state of the defences along the Franco-Belgian border from Dunkirk to Maulde was described to Ironside in a report issued by the *Grand Quartier Général* (*GQG*). The line followed the frontier as nearly as possible while using the obstacles of Les Moëres (an area of inundations), the Ey-Becque stream, the Monts de Flanders, the Lys River and the built-up areas of the suburbs of Tourcoing, Roubaix and Lille. The French system of defence was based on two lines: the principal line (*Ligne Principale*) in front of which the enemy was to be engaged by all the weapons of the defence and the second line in front of which the enemy was finally stopped (*Ligne d'Arret*).The defences were linear except in the area of Cysoing and Maulde where works had been started to form the second line (Figure 3.1). The defences consisted mostly of field fortifications although in places fortifications of a permanent type had been constructed, particularly on Mont Noir and from Cysoing onwards, and were fully developed at Maulde. A continuous anti-tank obstacle was obtained by using water ways and the construction of ditches in places where there was no natural obstacle. The defence works were sited to ensure flanking fire on the anti-tank obstacle.

In detail, the French defences along the border with Belgium were described as follows by the *GQG* report. From Bray-Dunes to Ghyvelde a complete anti-tank obstacle and some anti-tank gun positions had been constructed. The front between Ghyvelde and Hondeschoote was protected by inundations. Little had been done between Hondeschoote and Ostcappel, with only the obstacle completed and some pits dug for turrets and machine guns. The Ey-Becque stream which ran near the border from Ostcappel to Godewaersvelde had been improved to act as an anti-tank obstacle and some pits for turrets had been dug. From Godewaersvelde to Bailleul more had been completed: the organisation of the *Ligne Principale* was almost complete with

1 Brian Bond (ed.), *Chief of Staff: The Diaries of Lieutenant-General Sir Henry Pownall*, (London: Leo Cooper, 1972), p. 205.

both field works and blockhouses constructed. Likewise, the organisation of the *Ligne Principale* was almost complete from Bailleul to the River Lys but no blockhouses had been constructed. The River Lys had been improved as an anti-tank obstacle and some observation posts constructed. From Halluin to Cysoing the *Ligne Principale* was complete and the *Linge d'Arret* had been sited and a few blockhouses constructed along it. From Cysoing to Mouchin the *Ligne Principale* had been fully organised, complete with blockhouses, but the French had decided to site a new *Ligne Principale* in front, the original front line now becoming the *Ligne d'Arret*. Work on this new line (known to the British as the Bachy Switch) had begun but was not complete. From Mouchin to Maulde the *Ligne Principale* was complete and work had started on the *Ligne d'Arret*. The French also had a project under the French Inspector General of Fortifications to construct a powerful defence line along the La Bassée – Douai Canal line, but no works had started on this by the time the BEF moved into the line.

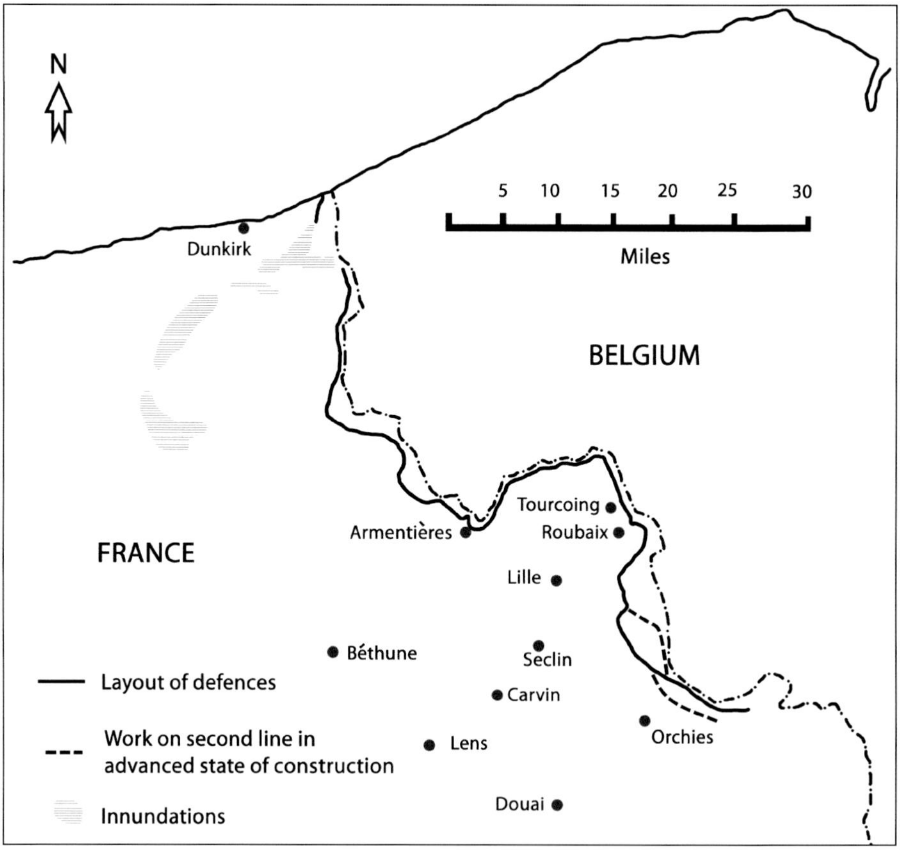

Figure 3.1: Defences along the Franco-Belgian border at the outbreak of war.

An appreciation by MO4 (the Topographical Branch of the DMO), given on 8 September, concluded:

> The French Fortifications along the Franco-Belgian frontier provide the framework of a position which could quickly be made immensely strong by the addition of field works; even in its present condition this line could not probably be breached without lengthy preparation and development of powerful offensive means.[2]

However, Ironside clearly reached a different opinion and on 19 September told the War Cabinet: 'The existing defences on the Franco-Belgian frontier were inadequate and only reached as far as Givet. From Givet onwards to the sea there were only light field defences.'[3]

BEF allocated the *Secteur Défensive de Lille*

Intelligence suggested to Gamelin that Germany was intending to follow up its victory in Poland with an imminent attack on the Low Countries and France. The French were thus keen that the BEF should take over a sector of the frontier defences as quickly as possible. Astonishingly, before hostilities broke out, it had not been decided which sector of the front British troops should be deployed on, although it was strongly presumed that it would be to the south of Lille. On 20 September, Hore-Belisha, Lord Hankey and Major-General Dewing (Director of Military Operations) held discussions with Gamelin and Daladier and reached an agreement that the BEF would be allocated an initial position in front of Lille, which suited the BEF's lines of communications. On 22 September, Gort was handed a telegram from *Général* Georges informing him that the envisaged part of the front to be held by the BEF ran from Maulde to Menin (Figure 3.2). Gort made a reconnaissance of the line during 24 and 25 September and agreed to accept the sector offered to the BEF. The BEF was to take over the *SD* Lille from the French 51st Division (*Général de Brigade* Gillard) within the zone of the French First Army Group (*Général* Billotte) but was to be independent and directly under the command of *Général* Georges. Because of the large front, Georges placed the French 51st Division under Gort's command, which he decided to use on his left flank covering the towns of Roubaix and Tourcoing.

The *SD* Lille defences ran for some 55 miles from (excluding) Maulde on the right, running roughly north to Halluin, thence turning in a south-westerly direction along the River Lys to (including) Armentières and formed a pronounced salient in the Allied line. On the right of *SD* Lille was *SD* Escaut and on the left *SD* Flanders.

2 The National Archives (TNA): WO106/1720, 'APPRECIATION OF THE SITUATION IN THE "MAIN THEATRE"', 8 September 1939.

3 TNA: CAB/65/3/9, 'Confidential Annex to W.M. (39), 19th Conclusions, Minute 3', 19 September 1940.

Included within *SD* Lille were the important roads Tournai – Lille and Tournai – Douai and the industrial areas of Tourcoing, Roubaix and Lille. The left flank of the sector was protected by a natural anti-tank obstacle, the River Lys from Halluin to Armentières. The right flank was secured by the strong French defences at Maulde along with excellent natural anti-tank obstacles formed by the inundated valley of the River Scarpe and the Raismes Forest. Lord Gort, in his first Official Dispatch described the countryside as:

> East of the Tournai–Orchies road the country is flat, much wooded and intersected by small streams. Further to the north lies open and undulating agricultural land which lends itself to artillery observation and to the movement of armoured fighting vehicles. Further north again, the sector is for the most part on the fringe of a highly industrial and mining area.[4]

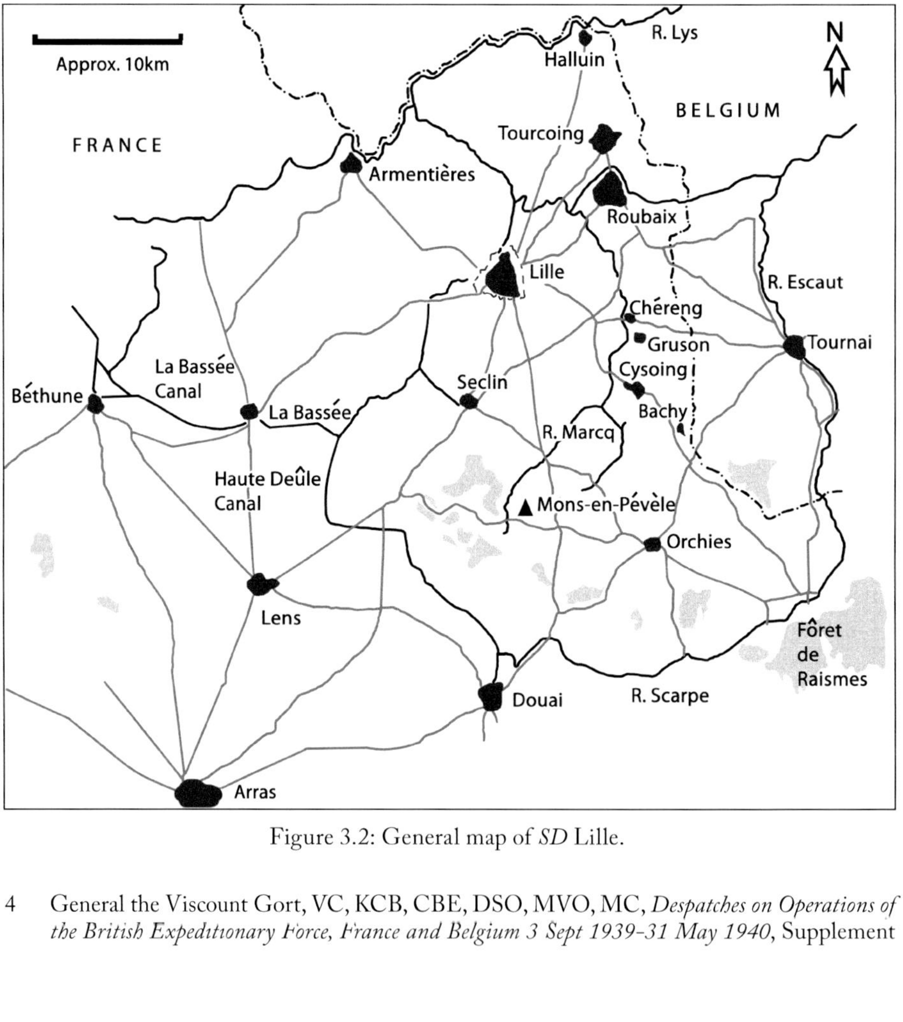

Figure 3.2: General map of *SD* Lille.

4 General the Viscount Gort, VC, KCB, CBE, DSO, MVO, MC, *Despatches on Operations of the British Expeditionary Force, France and Belgium 3 Sept 1939-31 May 1940*, Supplement

Geologically, the *SD* Lille consisted of two very different types of country. It was predominately chalk on a line south of Béthune – La Bassée. A tongue of chalk country ran north-west towards Lille, its northern boundary running through the centre of Lille then east to the Belgian frontier near Baisieux. The southern boundary of the chalk tongue ran from Wannehain on the Belgian frontier west through Avelin to Carvin. In these chalk areas, the chalk is close to the surface, covered by two to six metres of loam. There is very little surface water except in valleys. North of Béthune – La Bassée and north of Lille and around Roubaix – Tourcoing, the sub-soil is mainly stiff clay, but the valleys and hollows were filled with thick deposits of waterlogged alluvium. The area northwards of the Scarpe valley is similar, except that it contains large areas of waterlogged sand and comparatively small areas of thick clay. This geology would determine the amount of digging that could be carried out for defence works.

It had originally been intended that once assembled, the BEF would move to a concentration area and wait in readiness to occupy the line. Georges decided it inadvisable to await the arrival of the whole of the BEF in the concentration area and expressed a wish that I Corps, commanded by Lieutenant-General Sir John Dill, should move into *SD* Lille without delay. Gort agreed to this, even though it would mean I Corps would temporarily hold the entire British frontage. Accordingly, on 26 September, I Corps began the move from the assembly area and was ready to take over its allocated sector on the agreed date of 3 October. It was responsible for the area (excluding) Maulde to (including) Gruson with two divisions in the line. The French 51st Division was responsible for the area Gruson to Halluin with a defensive flank along the River Lys from Halluin to Armentières. It was anticipated that II Corps would move into the line on about 12 October. As planned, from 12 October, II Corps (Lieutenant-General Brooke) was allocated a sector. The sectors in the BEF zone were now as follows (Figure 3.3):

> I Corps: (excluding) Maulde to (including) Cysoing with two divisions in line – 2nd Division (Major-General H.C. Loyd) on the right and 1st Division (Major-General Hon. H.R.L. Alexander) on the left.
> II Corps: (excluding) Cysoing to (excluding) Toufflers with one division in the line – 3rd Division (Major-General B.L. Montgomery).
> 51 French Division: (including) Toufflers to Halluin to Armentieres.

GHQ reserve: one division from II Corps – 4th Division (Major-General D.G. Johnson VC – with its units west of the Haute Deûle Canal; one brigade was detailed to occupy the high ground at Mons-en-Pévèle quickly in the event of an attack. In addition, one machine gun battalion and the 4th Battalion Royal Tank Regiment.

to the London Gazette, 17 October 1941 <http://www.ibiblio.org/hyperwar/UN/UK/londongazette> (accessed 24 August 2017).

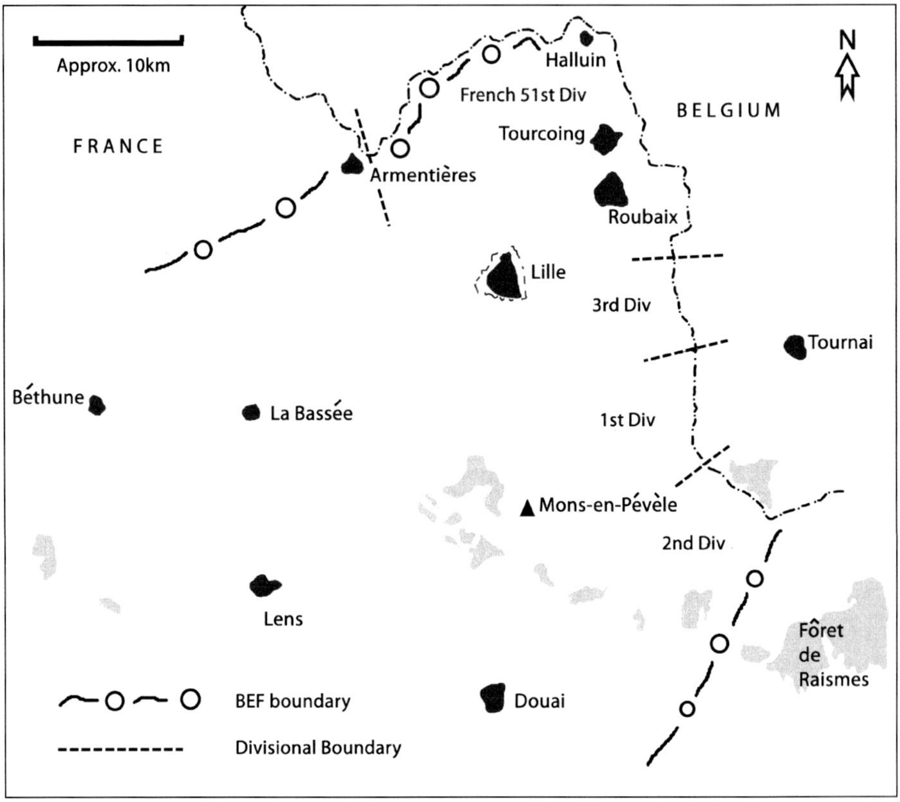

Figure 3.3: BEF Divisional sectors, *SD* Lille, October 1939.

As the British moved into the line at the start of October, there was nothing between them and the sea except for the French 51st Division on their immediate left flank and the French 53rd Division just south of Dunkirk; the French XVI Corps (*Général* Fagalde) which was to move up to the left of the BEF was still some 30 miles to the rear. The British were initially holding the *SD* Lille with four divisions (which included the French 51st) and one division in reserve. The front of each British division was approximately 10,000 yards. The French 51st Division was responsible for a front of approximately six times that of any of the British divisions! On taking over the front, Gort had enquired about the large frontages. Georges had informed him that 10,000 metres (about 11,000 yards) was not considered abnormal and that if a large attack was indicated against the northern section of the line, divisions from the General Reserve would be brought up as necessary to reinforce that front. Gort accepted that divisions would have to hold large fronts, just as the Germans had held long fronts on the Hindenburg Line during the Great War. He noted that the 'Aldershot' conception of a front of 6,000 to 7,000 yards was unrealistic compared to the French and German fronts of 8,000 to 9,000 yards.

The long fronts meant sacrificing depth and both the BEF Corps commanders were unhappy about this. Dill considered that the frontage held by each British division should not exceed 6,000 yards if a serious German attack was to be resisted.[5] The manuals of the time stated a front of about 1,000 yards for a battalion, i.e. 6,000 yards for a division with two brigades forward and one in the rear to add depth. Although French infantry divisions were expected to hold fronts up to 11,000 yards and British infantry divisions had about equal fire power to a French division, the man-power of a French division was about 25 percent greater than a British division which would make a great difference in conditions of night, fog, or if the enemy employed smoke.[6] Other factors requiring a limited divisional front in Dill's opinion were the lack of tanks available to meet and defeat a German tank attack and the lack of AA defence and fighter cover to ensure local air superiority. Brooke also considered the front was too wide and offered no scope for defence in depth if the Germans decided to attack in strength, as he noted in his diary: 'Position would be strong except for the serious shortage of men in the long fronts held. With such a frontage serious resistance becomes impossible. There is no depth to the defence.'[7] At least when winter arrived, the waterlogged ground meant any attack would be confined to the roads and the wider frontages were easier to live with.

GHQ did not express the fears of its corps commanders. The Germans were still 150 miles away and would be unlikely to be able to concentrate enough divisions for a major attack until mid-October, when it would be a gamble to attack so late in the year. Gort, at least on the outside, seemed very upbeat after his initial reconnaissance of the British front, and wrote to Ironside: 'When all the party is collected, we shall be able to put up a good battle. I am quite confident of that.'[8]

Pownall, in his diary, recorded that Gort was especially concerned with Brooke and thought he had a very defeatist frame of mind and showed no signs of confidence of being able to withstand an attack from tanks. Pownall himself regarded the British sector as excellent country in which to defeat tanks:

5 Gamelin considered 10,000 yards was acceptable for a divisional frontage for a sector not likely to be attacked, but even he agreed that if there was evidence that a sector was going to be attacked, such a frontage was too great, and a frontage of about 5,000 yards was more appropriate.

6 Gort did point out that one problem of the Army reorganisations of 1937–39 was that the infantry battalion did not possess the manpower for the type of static warfare the BEF found itself having to prepare for. He went on to successfully argue for an increase in the War Establishment of an infantry battalion by 96 men – an increase of two men per rifle section and two men per platoon HQ. This allowed for extra patrols, observers and the like without reducing the capacity of each section to find its own sentry group.

7 Alex Danchev & Daniel Todman (eds.), *War Diaries 1939 – 1945: Field Marshall Lord Alan Brooke* (Berkeley and Los Angeles: University of California Press, 2001), p. 8.

8 TNA: WO106/1777, Gort to Ironside, 2 October 1939.

> I know of no part of Europe, bar the mountains, so well adapted to dealing with anti-tank defence. We have a continuous A.T. obstacle along our front, another behind us in the La Bassée-Douai canal, we shall construct one behind these two...What more can the heart of man desire? All that apart from the fact that we have a higher proportion of A.T. weapons (even excluding the A.T. rifle) than either German or French divisions. [9]

Georges raised concerns about the front allotted to the French 51st Division and pointed out that it held much more than any of the British divisions. Gort reassured Georges that there was no question of the French 51st Division being asked to withstand attack on this large front and that a British division was in reserve to support it if necessary. It was also considered that the most likely line of attack lay in the fronts held by the British divisions and it was for that reason that the fronts had been allotted. Gort also offered to allocate a machine gun battalion to the French sector along the River Lys, which Georges gladly accepted.

General Headquarters was opened near Arras, with its various branches dispersed in neighbouring villages and in the town itself due to the principal of dispersion against air attacks. Life was reputably spartan for GHQ staff as Gort was determined his staff should not develop a reputation for high-living.[10] Communication was at first difficult until field telephones had been arranged by the signallers – French civil telephone was obviously out of bounds except in emergencies due to security concerns. During the conversations between the British and French Staffs, Gamelin had stressed that one of the mistakes of the last war was the failure to set up adequate military liaison to ensure effective communication between the Allies. To avoid repeating this mistake and to ensure effective communication with the French, a military mission under Major General Sir Richard Howard-Vyse was opened at the HQ of the French Supreme

9 Bond (ed.), *Chief of Staff*, p. 243.

10 Gort's HQ was set up in the small Chateau Habarcq west of Arras. Gort, however, was no luxury loving General and was determined that his Staff should not gain a reputation for high-living. It was reported in the press that 'Tiger' Gort (a nickname only used by the Press and never in France) did not even have a private bath. André Maurois describes his desk as 'no more than a bare plank on a couple of trestles'. Apparently, HQ messes 'sat down dismally to food far inferior to that provided for the troops in the line, prepared under conditions admittedly difficult, by pessimists who had allegedly attended courses at the Army School of Cookery, though, as it seemed, with little benefit to themselves' (Lt. Colonel Butler and Major J. Selby Bradford, MBE, MC, *Keep the Memory Green: The First of Many France 1939 –40* (London: Hutchinson & Co. Ltd., no date), p. 24). The Chateau needed a lot of work – rewiring, a new hot water system, drains disinfected to get rid of mosquitoes, testing the water which was shown to be dilute sewage and connecting to the mains instead – before GHQ could be fully open. One or two Generals apparently got fed up with luke warm baths. Nevertheless, the Chateau was made ready in time for Gort to entertain the King and the Royal Party.

Commander, *Général* Gamelin. A second mission under Brigadier J.G. des R. Swayne was opened for liaison at *Général* Georges' HQ.

A permanent French organisation was responsible for constructing defence works in *SD* Lille, under the command of *Colonel* Bertschi. The French defensive system, as already described, relied upon a series of lines which had extremely little depth and were separated by about 1,000 to 3,000 yards. The French front line consisted of a series of blockhouses varying from a few hundred yards apart in close country to well over 1,000 yards apart in more open country. The blockhouses were joined by a continuous anti-tank obstacle, either a natural ditch that had been deepened or an artificially dug trench, often in a straight line from one blockhouse to the next (Figures 3.4 and 3.5). The blockhouses could bring fire to bear in enfilade along the anti-tank obstacle but could not fire to their immediate front. Between the blockhouses the French had constructed occasional machine gun posts. The defence line was sited to closely follow the frontier and not necessarily the best tactical position; the French did not intend to yield an inch of their country. The need for economy on requisitioning land in peace time had also limited the tactical siting of the line. GHQ summarised the existing defences in the BEF Sector as follows:

i. "A" Along the front MAULDE – HALLUIN there is a front line comprising a fairly continuous anti-tank obstacle with concrete pill boxes 800 to 1200 yds apart. Immediately in rear of the A.Tk obstacle is a belt of wire.
"B" A second A.Tk obstacle with pill boxes has been sited 1500 to 2000 yds in the rear, but very little has yet been completed. (known as the "ligne d'arret" by the French).
There are a few completed pill boxes between these two lines (known as "postes de soutient" by the French).
A certain amount of field defence work has been done by the French troops since mobilization [sic] comprising mostly communication trenches and a few fire positions.

ii. All the pill boxes are designed to hold one French A.tk gun and one light automatic; there are two loopholes, with restricted arcs of fire one to each flank along the A. Tk obstacle; the A. Tk gun can only cover one flank unless moved across to the other loophole. The pill boxes as designed have no arrangements for frontal fire or local protection. The front line is sited with a view to getting the best available field of view and is in consequence somewhat exposed to enemy observation. In the area ROUBAIX – TOURCOING there is in many parts no constructed A. Tk obstacle, and dependence is on the mass of houses for this purpose. There are no defences as yet constructed along the R. LYS from HALLUIN to ARMENTIERES, but the river affords an excellent A. Tk obstacle.

In effect there is a single linear defence line, somewhat exposed: but comprising throughout an effective A. Tk and wire obstacle with pill boxes (8-inch shell proof) for A. Tk guns and L. M. Gs approx every 1000 yds.

iii. The existing front line "A" and projected "ligne d'arrret" "B" will comprise the areas to be held by the forward units and will require immediate development by field defences and later with more permanent works.
A divisional reserve position in rear of "A" and "B" will be constructed when labour becomes available.[11]

Figure 3.4: Aerial photo of a French anti-tank ditch enfiladed by blockhouses at Cobrieux, on the original French *Ligne Principale*. Note the limited amount of field works completed by the French, consisting of communication and fire trenches in the rear of the blockhouses (TNA: WO167/350)

11 TNA: WO167/2, 'Instructions for the occupation of the LILLE Sector of the French Frontier Defences by the B.E.F.', 3 October 1939, GHQ General Operations War Diary.

Although there were no defences along the River Lys from Halluin to Armentières, the French Seventh Army had intended to hold the line Comines – Ypres – Furnes as an outpost position but fall back on the Frontier defences if attacked. The French line of blockhouses, with wire and anti-tank obstacles, recommenced on the outskirts of Armentières and ran northwards.

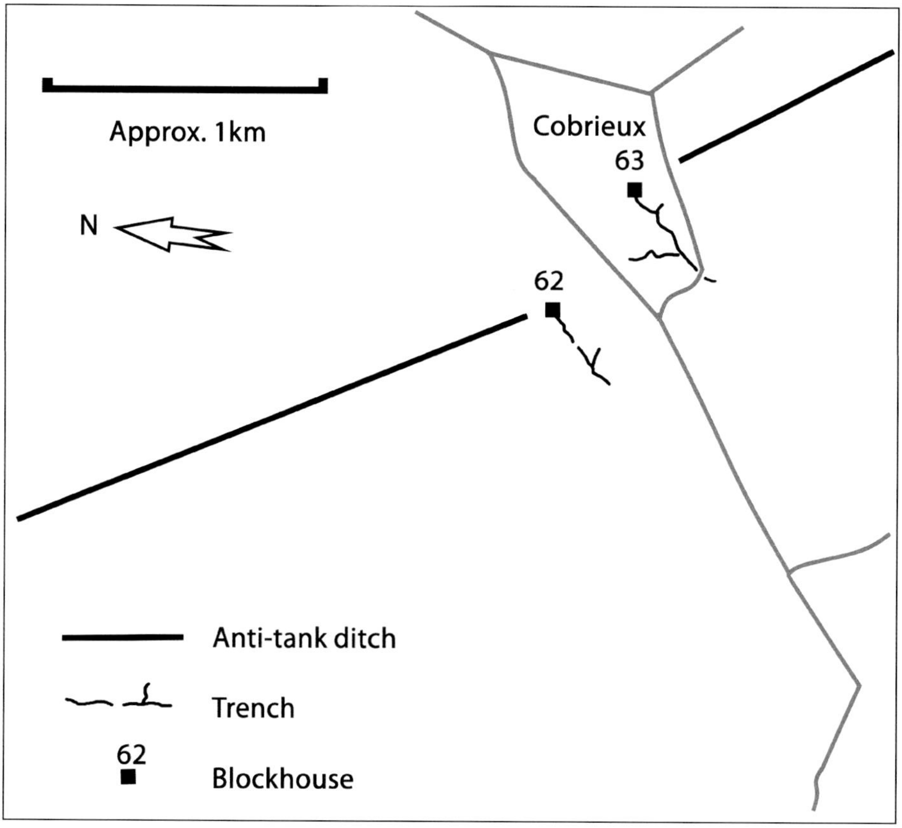

Figure 3.5: Sketch of aerial photograph.

On a visit to France Ironside took the opportunity to visit the front line on 7 October and was shown around by Gort. His observations on the BEF sector of the Lille Defences give a few more details:

> The line follows the frontier fairly accurately and consists of a tank obstacle, which has been dug out by the big machines, built absolutely straight. It is revetted with brushwood in places where it is very watery. The whole country in our sector round Lille is waterlogged in the winter...Everywhere the trench turns to follow a contour or the frontier there is a concrete block-house. They are said

> to be proof even against a direct hit by a very big howitzer...They are built to hold a couple of machine-guns and one or two anti-tank guns. They fire direct down the tank obstacle to the flank and are closed to the front where they are ramped with earth. They have a good prism periscope sticking out of the top which gives an all-round view. The whole place is wired strongly with circles and circles of wire...They are all built with water tanks and sleeping accommodation. It gives one a curious idea of a front line, just long lines of obstacles and barbed wire with great iron rails sticking up in places. Then one began to realize [sic] that in this very flat country artillery observation for accurate shooting upon these fortresses was next to impossible. Also, if the bombardment becomes very heavy the ground will become impossible for machines to move over.[12]

Little, or nothing, was reported about the weakness of the extension to the Maginot Line before war broke out, and, in fact most of the British public assumed it was as strong as the Maginot Line proper. Many soldiers of the BEF were genuinely surprised to find it only consisted of a single anti-tank ditch defended by a line of blockhouses. The expression of disappointment from Second-Lieutenant Peter Vaux, 4th Battalion Royal Tank Regiment was probably typical at the time:

> When we arrived in France, we were told that there was the main Maginot Line and from there to the sea was the Petit Maginot Line... But when we went to the Petit Maginot Line, it didn't exist at all. It was just a few pillboxes at perhaps a mile or two apart...this Petit Maginot Line was nothing more than a line on the map.[13]

The British public were of course reassured of the strength of the defences that the BEF occupied. Skene Catling, Reuters War Correspondent with the BEF, wrote in his dispatch dated 13 October:

> These solid concrete emplacements contain armament for destroying enemy tanks. I visited two of them and was shown the details by N.C.O.s filled with the same pride and sense of fortunate ownership as their commanding officer. These discouraging structures are so placed that they each cover a wide field of fire.
>
> Enemy tanks have not only this deadly fire to contend with. Cunningly contrived tank traps are ready–and more being prepared–from which no floundering vehicle could hope to extricate itself.[14]

12 Colonel R Macleod, DSO, MC & Denis Kelly, (eds.), *Time Unguarded: The Ironside Diaries 1937-1940* (New York: David McKay Company Inc., 1963), p. 123.
13 Joshua Levine, *Forgotten Voices: Dunkirk* (London: Ebury Press, 2011), p. 16.
14 Skene Catling, *Vanguard to Victory: An Account of the first months of the British Expeditionary Force in France* (London: Methuen & Co. Ltd., 1940), p. 3.

British principles for the defence

The War Office manual *FSR Vol.III 1935* makes the point that 'ideas as to strategical planning and conduct can be deduced from the experience of the past: they are often defined and expressed in the form of "principles."'[15] These principles were not laws as such, but simply indicated a course of action that was successful in the past and that to ignore them would involve risk. The main principles in defence as stated in the manual of the time peculiar to the training and tactics of infantry – *Infantry Training 1937* – were:

> Fire – The fire of all weapons must be organised to stop the enemy.
> Surprise – Surprise is as important in defence as in attack. The defence depends largely on concealment to effect surprise.
> Depth – Depth is essential to localise the effects of a successful initial attack.
> Control – The defender should be prepared to act quickly as soon as the attacker has disclosed his intention.
> Information – Reconnaissance is as important in the defence as in attack.
> Determination – All ranks should understand that troops allotted to the defence of a post or locality are responsible for holding it at all costs.

It is worthwhile considering the principle of depth further, as this largely guided the planning and layout of the defences on the ground that the BEF constructed during the autumn and winter of 1939-40. This principle had its origins in the innovations in defence introduced by the Germans during the Great War.

Experience in the Great War demonstrated that an attack with modern weapons could always carry a trench line. The Germans, mainly forced to fight a defensive battle on the Western Front, quickly realised that what was required was not fixed defences in a series of linear lines, but rather a fortified zone. Although a fortified zone did still have its trench lines, a number of strongpoints, which dominated ground of tactical importance, were constructed between the lines of defence. The concept of strongpoints dominating surrounding ground by the fire power of modern weapons was, however, nothing new. The British manual *Infantry Training 1914* noted the importance of such strongpoints, or tactical localities as the manual referred to them, in defence: 'Defensive positions will usually include a number of localities of special tactical importance' which would 'form pivots upon which to hinge the defence of the remainder of the position. The defences of these localities should be arranged so that they may give each other mutual support.'[16]

15 *FSR Vol.III: Operations – Higher Formations 1935* (London: The War Office, 1935), p. 5.
16 *Infantry Training (4-Company Organization) 1914*, (London: General Staff, War Office, 1916 reprint), pp. 153-154.

The manual goes on to say that if these localities were strong enough, and the enemy was forced to expend his strength to overcome them, the defence need not be held in continuous lines. Rather, the intervening ground should be covered by the weapons of these localities by both direct or flanking fire and then utilising the intervening ground for manoeuvre for counter-attacks. What were new in the German ideas were the extreme depth that these localities were arranged and the acceptance that enemy infantry could infiltrate between them. The deeper the enemy fought his way through the defence, the more he would expend his strength and be vulnerable to counter-attack. This was the concept of 'elastic defence'.

By mid-1917, the idea of flexible defence based on a network of strongpoints and weapon positions was clearly established in German defence doctrine. Although *Oberst* von Lossberg and *Major* Max Bauer are credited with the concept, the idea started to evolve from the moment the Western Front became bogged down in a state of siege trench warfare. The defence as conceived by von Lossberg and Max Bauer consisted of three zones. In front was the forward outpost line, one to one and a half miles in depth consisting of a network of pillboxes, strongpoints and machine gun bunkers each defended by a small garrison which could withdraw at will. Behind the outpost line was the main battle zone, again one to one and a half miles in depth, where the enemy was to be stopped. At the front of this zone was a trench system designated the main line of resistance and in the rear another trench system designated the artillery protection line. Finally, behind the main battle zone was a rear battle zone, three miles in depth where the reserve battalions and counter-attack divisions (*Eingreifdivisionen*) were located.

By the end of 1917, the British had followed German ideas and also adopted similar zone defence tactics. The General Staff pamphlet *S.S. 210: The Division in Defence* outlines the policy of defence in depth, laid out in a series of fortified zones.[17] The foundation of the defence was the main battle position. In front of the main battle position and forming part of it was an outpost system organised in depth and behind it in some distance to the rear further positions of defence. The outpost system was designed to act as a buffer, to absorb the first shocks of any attack. The rear positions were to act as a defence system of the last resort and were to be sufficiently behind the main battle zone so as to make it necessary for the enemy to organise a second and distinct operation to assault them.

The defence of each zone consisted of tactical localities, arranged around features that by their nature gave advantage to the defenders, which were to hold at all costs. Tactical localities had to be organised in depth in conjunction with obstacles to confine the enemy or shepherd him to selected avenues of approach covered by the weapons of the defence which would break up the enemy attack. The greater the depth

17 There is an interesting reference in the Chief Engineer's War Diary noting that the WO library was visited to confirm the existence of SS pamphlets of the Great War that might be required for the current campaign.

of defence, the less impact would result on the defence due to an enemy penetration, as he would have to expend energy attempting to widen gaps. For such a system to work, it was essential that it was supported by counter-attacks, to evict the weakened enemy as he fought his way through the main zone and that the main zone resisted gaining time and freedom of manoeuvre for the counter-attack forces. The whole system could be 'compared to a system of springs which contract under pressure, expand at once again when the pressure is removed or overcome, and, if fully compressed, become immovable, but are ready to resume their original form if released.'[18]

S.S. 210 stated that a succession of defensive lines, one behind the other, was not defence in depth. Such a system was rigid and could easily be broken by a succession of blows. If this was not defence in depth, neither was dispersion of the defence garrison into a mosaic of isolated posts. Co-ordination of the plans of all arms and co-operation between the tactical localities was required to make the system work.

This system of defence in depth developed towards the end of the Great War, comprising of a forward and main zone, was codified in the various post-war War Office manuals such as *FSR Vol. II 1935*, which was still in force on the outbreak of war. This manual stated that a defensive position would consist 'of a belt of defended localities arranged with intervals between them, arranged in depth and affording each other mutual support.'[19] The belt of forward localities, when finally settled, became the front edge of the defence, with further defence built up in the rear. The defensive plan was to be made in terms of the co-ordinated fire of all weapons: artillery, machine guns, light machine guns, rifles and if the enemy was equipped with armoured fighting vehicles, anti-tank guns. With regards to tanks in particular, the manual states:

> When the enemy possesses tanks, the question of defence against tanks will always require attention and may be the principal consideration in the plan of defence. Full advantage should be taken of natural obstacles, and mines or artificial obstacles may be used to economize [sic] anti-tank weapons. The plan of anti-tank defence should be co-ordinated by higher commanders in the area for which they are responsible. It may sometimes be necessary to site a proportion of the field guns with the primary object of dealing with enemy tanks.[20]

Behind the main system, rear systems could be constructed or planned, if it was expected the defence would have to withstand a very heavy attack. They should, as already noted in the pamphlet *S.S.210*, be sufficiently distant from the main system to make it necessary for the enemy to organise a second distinct operation in order to attack them.

18 *S.S. 210: The Division in Defence* (London: General Staff, May 1918) p. 7.
19 *FSR Vol. II: Operations – General 1935* (London: The War Office, 1935), p. 137.
20 Ibid, p. 135.

In positional warfare, characterised by static conditions, the principle of depth remained the same. Of note is the statement in *FSR Vol. II 1935* that static conditions could arise from the very outset of war because of the 'tendency of some nations on the continent of Europe to construct elaborate defences along the whole length of a frontier in peace time.'[21] Position warfare is for all practical purposes siege warfare. *FSR Vol. III* makes the point that the length of time for which defence is necessary would determine the depth to which it was organised and *FSR Vol. II* elaborates this point for this extreme type of warfare:

> the defensive system will extend to a depth of several thousands of yards, strengthened by concrete works and shelters, by deep dug-outs, by wide obstacles or inundations.[22]

Lessons from the Polish Campaign

The Polish campaign provided the BEF with evidence of how a German attack would likely unfold. However, a report on the future organisation of the British Army produced in 1935 illustrates that British generals were already well aware that Germany was preparing for a mobile war. The report concluded that in an attack, German air forces would play a major role in close co-operation with mechanised ground forces. Targets for the air forces would be enemy air bases, mobilisation centres, railway nodal points and concentration centres. The air attack was expected 'to paralyse the enemy's movements, concentration and administrative system, and so make possible a break-through by a highly mobile land force.'[23]

The German invasion of Poland largely confirmed the conclusions of this report. The British observed that German tactics used in Poland were based upon the fullest possible use of speed and manoeuvre of tanks in large numbers, combined with air and artillery support, to produce a 'tank infested' area of considerable depth. A heavy air attack and a short but very violent artillery bombardment preceded the attack. The air attack and artillery bombardments concentrated on strongpoints and HQs in the rear with a view to causing disruption and demoralisation. The air attack also had the objective of eliminating the Polish Air Force. Infantry attacks usually avoided frontal attacks against strongly held positions; instead attacks were made on the flanks with a view to envelopment (Polish positions were rarely continuous). Tanks and dive bombers usually supported the infantry attack rather than artillery. Armoured units often penetrated weak points in the defence and subsequently attacked from the rear. In certain cases, armoured units attacked independently from the main zone of attack,

21 Ibid, p. 161.
22 Ibid, p. 162.
23 TNA: WO32/4612, 'The Organization of the Field Force', p. 13, Future Reorganisation of the British Army.

arriving from some distance away to take part in the attack. A feature of the attack was the use of aircraft to bomb and machine gun the movement of reinforcements and to attack rear communications in an attempt to completely isolate the area of the attack. Medium bombers carrying out low level attacks were much more effective than dive bombers in this role.

Once through the enemy position, mechanised units were tasked with destroying communications and liaison and thus paralysing the enemy headquarters. They were called upon to operate as far forward as possible with little regard to flanks, liaison with neighbouring units or the general advance of German forces. The fullest possible use of manoeuvre was made. Obstacles were avoided by rapid manoeuvre and on reaching a defended obstacle such as a town, the tanks swung off until a passable flank was found, when they reverted back to their original course.

Engineers moved with the advance guards with bridging units, allowing the German armour to rapidly cross river obstacles. Engineers also accompanied the infantry, supporting attacks with flame throwers, bridging operations and demolitions.

The British drew two key lessons from the Polish campaign with regards to the use of German armour. Firstly, the success of Blitzkrieg tactics depended upon tanks having liberty of manoeuvre over ground unrestricted by natural or artificial obstacles or subject to any Polish counter-attack. This was only possible, the British concluded, as the Germans were aware there were no Polish armoured forces strong enough to counter-attack and defeat their forward scattered units in detail. The Germans themselves considered such counter-attacks would be of paramount importance.[24] An unfortunate conclusion the British came to was that such circumstances would not be repeated in other theatres of war.

The second conclusion from the Polish campaign was that even if the tanks broke through, such an attack could not be successful if the German infantry was prevented from following up the tank advance. In Poland, British intelligence noted that only one type of pillbox designed for two medium machine guns was used in Polish defence lines. These were arranged in a chess board pattern, approximately one pillbox for every 500 yards of front. There was no depth to the defence to defeat the enemy infantry. The Germans apparently affirmed the view that a position consisting of two or three lines of pillboxes numerous enough to ensure a dense and continuous field of fire was a very powerful obstacle. Ironside clearly held this opinion and in his diary entry for 7 October noted: 'If the position is in sufficient depth there is no fear of attacking infantry ever getting through. The tanks may get through and they may, as they did in Poland, push on till they can go no further, but the infantry cannot.'[25]

24 Von Leeb, who was to lead Army Group North in the invasion of Russia, recognised this as early as 1936 stating that the defence had to use the same weapons and means to defeat a Blitzkrieg style of attack.

25 Macleod, DSO, MC & Kelly (eds.), *Time Unguarded,* p. 124.

British intelligence suggested that the German High Command, following the campaign in Poland, was now convinced that tank attacks on the Western Front should never take place with less than a brigade of tanks (between 400 to 500) at one time. The tactics of a German attack were then expected to consist of at least a tank brigade on a front of about 2,000 yards. Tanks would probably operate in depth (1,000 yards) in three echelons with some tanks in a hull down position supporting other tanks. The first echelon would be tasked with destroying the anti-tank defences and artillery, ignoring infantry positions. The second echelon would attack infantry and machine gun positions. The third echelon, comprising of mostly light tanks accompanied the attacking infantry. The final tank objectives would be in great depth. The whole attack would be supported by artillery and low flying aircraft.

The British concluded that the key to defeating such an attack was co-ordinated anti-tank fire disposed in depth so that each echelon of fire took its toll on the advancing tanks until the attack petered out:

> A strong anti-tank defence, with well supported flanks, is an unsurmountable obstacle for armoured units. The anti-tank gun remains a decisive weapon, if well handled and mobile, and present in sufficient numbers.[26]

Training material of the time made the same point by emphasising the weakness of tanks: they were formidable only in movement but if held up by an obstacle they could be knocked out by artillery fire. It was important that in the early stages of an attack, the enemy be denied the use of tanks and be forced to use infantry through the use of anti-tank obstacles. This was to be achieved by holding a series of mutually supporting anti-tank localities, covered by anti-tank obstacles and anti-tank guns. The primary role of the infantry defence was to prevent enemy infantry securing bridgeheads over the anti-tank obstacle for the use of tanks. Should a bridgehead be secured, then the infantry was to prevent the enemy infantry following behind the tanks, as tanks could accompany little unless followed immediately by their accompanying infantry.

Defence against low flying aircraft was of also given high importance. Passive Air Defence (PAD) such as concealment and deception were important, but it was vital that low flying aircraft should be engaged by fire if this method of close support for the tanks was to be deprived of its efficiency. Against an organised system of air defence, the British concluded that German low level tactics used in Poland would result in casualties on a heavy scale for the Germans.[27] The importance of aerial

26 TNA: WO287/226, 'Western Front', Tactical and Technical Notes on the German Army, Series 7. Over confidence in the anti-tank gun probably arose from experience in the Spanish Civil War, where many observers believed it had gained superiority over the tank. However, this view was mistaken as it ignored the facts that relatively few tanks were used in the Civil War and that the terrain on the whole was not really tank country.

27 Just such a fate awaited the Battles of the AASF sent to bomb bridges in an attempt to stem the German advance in May 1940.

power in defence was also recognised, both in keeping enemy tanks under constant observation and also in taking every opportunity to bomb them with high explosive and possibly incendiary bombs.

To some extent, the layout of the communication and transport network would canalise an enemy infiltration. To protect against this, the use of wire and minefields was considered necessary to deny to the enemy the transport and communication network. As equally important, alternative command centres linked to the front with signal communications were necessary to counter the effect of intensive aerial bombardments. To enable the movement of local reserves forward, the supply of the forward areas or the re-organisation of formations ejected from their original positions, means and equipment were required for opening up an improvised transport and communication network in the shortest possible time. Such equipment included road graders, small stock span bridges and small box girder bridges. Rather optimistically, means of dealing with immobilised armoured formations were also deemed necessary. This was thought largely to be an aircraft role, although ground troops could contribute with mines, booby traps or some form of incendiary mortar or flame throwing apparatus.

The French also drew similar conclusions. At a conference on 6 October, Gamelin stated the chief lesson to be learnt from Poland was the ability of hard-hitting armoured formations combined with close air support to penetrate defences. To meet such an attack, Gamelin also emphasised defence in depth, with the front line held with the minimal number of men needed to resist a German attack. He stated that reserves should be established in depth behind this screen, in two layers deep. The first layer should consist of infantry reserves, while the second was to consist of the mobile reserves, including motorised units, cavalry and *DCR's*. To meet any German armoured breakthrough, he advocated armoured counter-attacks. Gamelin's analysis was sensible, minimising casualties in the front line, using infantry in depth to separate the enemy armour from their infantry before finally counter-attacking the enemy armour. The Allied downfall in May 1940 was largely due to Gamelin's decision to move away from defence in depth and concentrate his best mobile formations in the front line (see chapter 4).

Expected enemy attack against *SD* Lille

In the event of battle being joined near the frontier, the Allies expected the main weight of the German attack north of the Mormal Forest and south of the French coastal inundations. The immediate object of such an attack would be to break through the frontier defences with a view to launching armoured divisions across the open country in the area St Pol – St Quentin – Amiens and securing crossings over the River Somme between Abbeville and Péronne and then threatening the Allied lines of communication. It would be uncertain as to how wide any German turning manoeuvre through Belgium would be. In the first instance, the effort may be made to break through the defences along the Sambre and Escaut with a view to reaching open tank country in the area Le Cateau – St Quentin – Cambrai. If this was held, the drive could develop further north on the Tournai – Douai axis and even by way of Ypres. The crossings over the line of waterways which ran Maulde – Douai – La Bassée – Béthune – St Omer – Graveline would have to be secured before this plan could be affected and it was deemed vital that the Germans be held in front of this line at all costs.

As already alluded to in Lord Gort's dispatch, the countryside in the Lille area is intricate and quite suited to defence. The southern and central part of *SD* Lille, from Maulde to Toufflers is in general a low lying, flat and highly cultivated plain, dotted with woods, water obstacles, and small villages and towns. The countryside from Maulde for a distance of approximately 7,000 yards was low lying and enclosed but the centre was more open and undulating countryside, with good observation over the front from the Bachy ridge. From Toufflers to Neuville, the area was highly industrialised and populated, extending north-east from Lille to Roubaix, with houses running right up to and across the frontier. From Neuville to Halluin the ground was much more open, dominated by Mount d'Halluin. Between Halluin and Armentières the principal feature was the canalised River Lys which followed the frontier, with the only high ground being a ridge running from Halluin to Comines, about 1,000 yards from the canal. The most important access to the canal crossings was impeded by the wooded and built up area between Marchiennes and Seclin and the dominating feature of Mons-en-Pévèle.

The three main approaches to the *SD* Lille were from Tournai – St. Amand, Tournai – Douai and Courtrai – Lille. The Tournai – St. Amand approach was well covered by the French defences at Maulde while the approach from the north from Courtrai was unsuitable for tanks due to the built up urban and industrial areas. As long as the bridges over the Lys were blown, there was no approach from Halluin to Armentières. This just left the approach from Tournai – Douai where a tank attack could be expected. Pownall gives a useful summary of the likely area of attack against the British front in his diary entry of 26 September:

> The right [of the British sector] is not 'attack country' and is strongly supported by Maulde, the floodable area of the Scarpe and, further to the right, a forest and the very strong defensive system at Valenciennes. The only part where it can be attacked in force by tanks is on each side of the road from Tournai – Douai – perhaps a 10,000-yard frontage. Further north comes the edges of the town area extending from Lille north-east into Roubaix. No place for tanks in any numbers but infiltration attack by enemy infantry must be guarded against which will use up a lot of men. From Halluin west along the Lys to Armentières there are no defences, the Lys is a complete A.T. obstacle of course, and the bridges are mined, but the whole of this defensive flank must be watched and reserves handy if wanted.[28]

28 Bond (ed.), *Chief of Staff*, pp. 239–240.

As Pownall noted, the only portion of the front which could be attacked in force with tanks was astride the Tournai – Orchies – Douai road from Mouchin to Bachy, a frontage of around 10,000 yards; it was known German resources were sufficient for a massed tank attack along such a frontage although in Poland the decisive tank attacks were on fronts of around 3,000 yards. The ridge running between Aix and Nomain and the hill feature at Mons-en-Pévèle were vital to the defence of this part of the front. Such an attack might be combined with an advance along the Tournai – Lille road and turning south-west towards Lesquin and Seclin once the forward defences had been penetrated as a gap existed to the north of Bois de Phalempin to the canal at Seclin. Douai was expected to be the first day's objective for the Germans.

Once the enemy had closed-up to the defences, it was expected the attack would open with heavy fire against the loopholes of the blockhouses to try and neutralise them as the leading enemy infantry tried to cross the anti-tank obstacle by all available means. The infantry would likely be accompanied with assault engineers who would blow gaps in wire obstacles and assault the blockhouses with flame throwers. Supporting artillery would attempt to neutralise the defending anti-tank and machine guns, perhaps to the exclusion of other tasks. Once across the obstacle, the ground won would be consolidated to a sufficient depth to allow tanks to cross and form up for the next stage. The next stage, the breakthrough, was expected to be launched at the earliest possible moment by tanks – concentrated and not dispersed along the front – supported by low flying aircraft attacking anti-tank guns, defending troops and British reserves moving forward. As already noted, the tank objectives were expected to be in great depth.

Organisation and layout of *SD* Lille

Gort described the French defences inherited by the BEF as:

> '[A] very good start'. It is no small thing to be handed over a line of strong pill boxes, continuous wire and an anti-tank obstacle. What it needs is depth and we will get on to that at once of course.[29]

As already noted, the lessons from the Polish campaign meant that the defensive system had to be capable of defeating an attack in strength by German forces using large masses of tanks supported by aircraft. In consequence, the defences were to be organised as a series of positions in depth, each protected by a continuous anti-tank obstacle covered by the fire of anti-tank-guns, artillery and small arms. *FSR Vol. II 1935* particularly emphasised the enhanced value of rivers and canals as obstacles because of the development of tanks and transport vehicles, and the technical difficulty of passing a force equipped with these over such an obstacle in the face of opposition.

29 TNA: WO106/1777, Gort to Ironside, 2 October 1939.

The existence of rivers, canals or railway lines with suitable anti-tank properties were fundamental in influencing the siting of the BEF's zones of defence, as it was hoped this would limit the enemy's initial attack to infantry only, which would have to secure a passage for the tanks over the obstacle.

The way the defence was to be organised required careful consideration as it was imperative that the principles and practice of defence were similar between the French and British armies, especially for the purposes of relief. GHQ specified that defence positions were to be organised and developed according to the instructions contained in *Operations. Military Training Pamphlet (MTP) No.23 Part II: Defence.*[30] This coincided very closely with the French principles of defence laid out in *Réglements pours les grands unites.*

The one departure from this pamphlet was the impossibility of a constructing a proper outpost position to cover the main position as the French defences had been built so close to the frontier. With regards to the main position, *MTP No.23 Part II* states that it was to be organized as follows:

A main position will be organized [sic] to provide:

i. The area of forward defended localities protected by a tank obstacle.
ii. The brigade reserve area
iii. The divisional reserve area protected by a tank obstacle.[31]

The defence position for *SD* Lille planned by the BEF can be readily referenced to this pamphlet. The defences were to be developed from the embryonic existing French defences (Figure 3.6). The main position was to consist of a line of forward defended localities (FDL Line, or the French *Ligne Principale de R*ésistance) which formed the front edge of the position and which the defence was to be developed in depth behind it. The reserves of the frontline brigades were sited behind the forward defended localities in the Brigade Reserve Position (the French *Ligne d'Arret*). Behind this were the divisional reserves situated in the Divisional Reserve Position, which was to be made as strong as possible, especially to resist tank attack. Mobile reserves were to be distributed in various parts of the position to check penetration and launch counter-attacks. Behind the main system, when time and labour permitted, a rear position was to be developed. The rear system had to be sufficiently distant from the main system to make it necessary for the enemy to organise a second and distinct operation

30 MTPs formed the bulk of the printed literature setting out the British Army's official doctrine issued during the war. They covered all aspects of the British Army and were the main way that the latest thinking with regards to doctrine laid out in FSRs were communicated. They reflected the fact that the principles laid out in FSRs stayed the same, but that details changed – such as the degree of mobility, fire power etc. Army Training Memorandum's (ATM) were produced more frequently than MTPs and were the method that lessons from recent operations were distilled to the Army.

31 *Operations MTP No. 23 Part II: Defence – 1939* (London: The War Office, 1939), p. 11.

to attack it. It was also to be prepared as a position in depth so it could be organised into a new forward and main position if the forward position was lost. Only in this way could the elasticity of the defence be maintained.

The defences had to be capable of stopping both infantry and tanks supported by artillery. The means of checking these two arms is different. Infantry are chiefly stopped by wire obstacles, small arms fire and anti-personnel minefields while tanks are stopped by anti-tank obstacles, anti-tank guns and anti-tank minefields. As enemy infantry would help the tanks cross obstacles, and the tanks would help the infantry overcome the small arms fire of the defence and wire obstacles, co-ordination of anti-tank and anti-infantry defences was necessary. Artillery was also vital to stopping both arms.

As already noted, each position was to be covered by a continuous anti-tank obstacle. However, the French had made no provision for anti-tank obstacles running from the front to the rear, allowing the supporting defences when constructed to be attacked in enfilade. Therefore, at an early stage, anti-tank obstacles running transversely through the position but not parallel to the front (Switch Lines) had to be constructed to restrict manoeuvre and break up the attack, by causing it to lose direction and cohesion and to canalise and direct the tank attack into areas where it could be dealt with by anti-tank guns, artillery and minefields. It was vital for the defence that 'obstacles are within sight and under direct fire of the defenders'.[32] Anti-tank obstacles had to be under both anti-tank and small arms fire not only to destroy tanks but also prevent the infantry and engineers from attempting to bridge or destroy the obstacle for the tanks.

By the close of October, the general layout on the ground of the defensive position had been decided upon (Figure 3.7). The FDL Line was sited along the line of the French pillboxes and anti-tank ditch of the French *Ligne Principale* which largely followed the Franco-Belgian frontier – as close as 200 yards in places. Starting from the south, it ran from Cense de Choques to Rumegies thence Le Cul de Four – Plannard – north of Mouchin, with the stream L'Elnon forming the anti-tank obstacle. From Mouchin, it ran to Bercu thence along the reverse slope of the Bachy spur to La Posterie. It then followed the line Cobrieux – Péronne-en-Mélantois – Gruson. From Gruson it ran along the River Marcq through Le Marais, Le Heron and Hem when it then turned north-east to follow the Franco-Belgian border, skirting the built up areas of Roubaix and Tourcoing, running through Lys lez Lannoy – La Baillerie – Le Ballun – Halluin. It then turned west to follow the River Lys to Armentières. With the arrival of III Corps in April 1940 (described in more detail in chapter 6), the BEF took over a further section of the French *Ligne Principale*, from Armentières to Bailleul.

The Brigade Reserve Position was initially sited along the original French *Ligne d'Arret* and planned by the French to be 1,000 to 1,500 yards behind the *Ligne Principale*. From the south, the line started south of Rumegies and ran to Haut-Hameau thence

32 *Manual of Field Engineering Vol. I (All Arms) – 1933* (London: The War Office, 1933), p. 40.

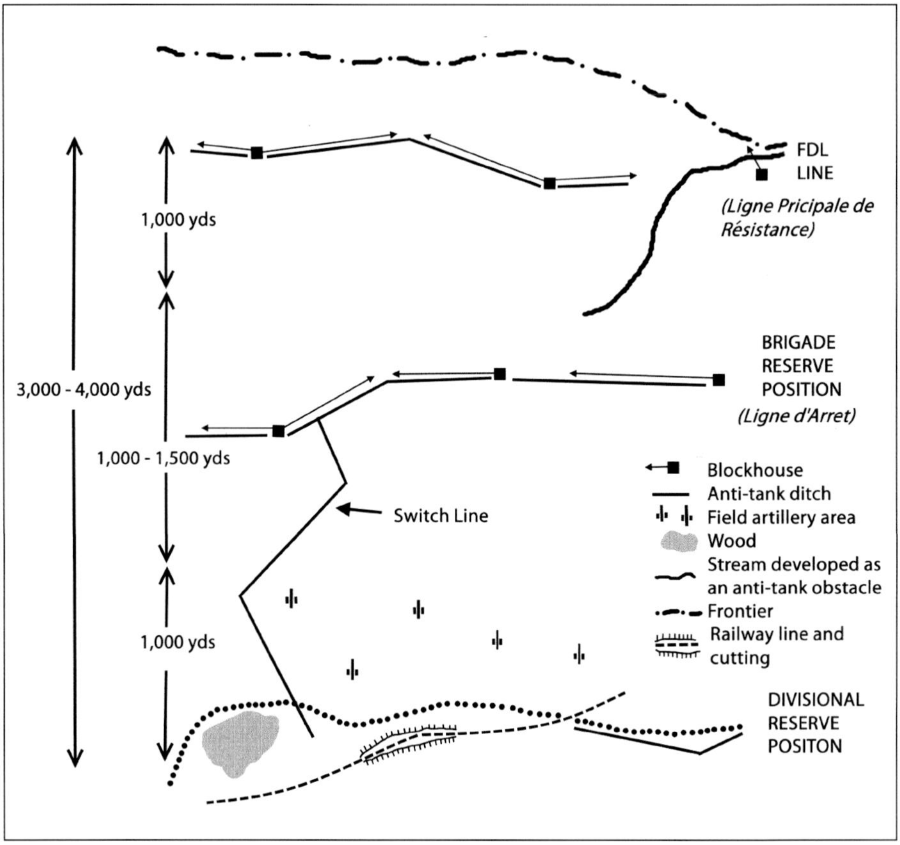

Figure 3.6: Diagram illustrating the layout of the BEF's main position.

south of Lannay to the northern edge of Bois de Bercu thence to Blonde Rue. From Blonde Rue it ran around the northern edge of Genech. The high ground at Genech was the pivot of the position in this area, dominating the plain to the north as far as Bois de Cysoing, the valley to the east and the lower ground to the south. From Genech it picked up the River Marcq from Louvil to Péronne-en-Mélantois, whence it ran to Sainghin, taking in the old fort. From Sainghin, it ran along the line Ascq – Roubaix – Tourcoing – Halluin – Bousbecque.

Starting from the south, the Divisional Reserve Position initially ran in a westerly direction, taking in the dominating high ground of the Aix – Nomain ridge, thence Bois D'Huquin to Templeuve. From Templeuve it then ran north, more or less following the railway line to Lezennes. From Lezennes, it ran around the east of Lille, joining up with the Quesnoy Switch (see below). The line was to be connected with switches to the FDL Line so as to form a defensive pocket on the part of the front along the Tournai – Douai road; the approximate position of the line and switches was Rumegies – Aix – Nomain – Genech – Cobrieux.

As already noted, the French had started work on a new *Ligne Principale* – the Bachy Switch – between Cysoing and Mouchin. The Bachy Switch started from the southern edge of Bercu and followed the line Bachy – Bourghelles – Gruson were it joined up with the original *Ligne Principale.* It took in the high ground of the Bachy spur, a key tactical feature giving good all-round observation, and also cut off the salient in the FDL Line made by the original course of the *Ligne Principale.* The Bachy Switch was initially held as an outpost line while the French completed the blockhouses and anti-tank ditch and as work progressed it was incorporated into the FDL Line. This required further adjustment in the Cysoing – Mouchin sector (see Chapter 5 and Figure 5.4).

A number of other Switch Lines were sited to restrict and canalise any enemy advance or to form the line on which new defensive positions could be organised. The Mons-en-Pévèle Switch and the Lille Switch formed the line on which the Corps Position was to be constructed, to establish a reserve position situated some six to seven miles behind the front. The Mons-en-Pévèle Switch ran west from Marchiennes along the canalised Raches to Montreuil. It than turned north towards Le Boujon, thence to the dominating high ground of Mons-en-Pévèle. From Mons-en-Pévèle it ran around the eastern edge of Bois de Phalempin to Attiches. From Attiches it turned north-west towards Seclin whence it followed the Canal de Seclin to the junction with the Canal de Deûle. It then turned west to Don and the junction with the La Bassée Canal at Bauvin. The Lille Switch was to continue the Corps Reserve Position by joining the Mons-en-Pévèle Switch to Armentières either on the line Wavrin – Armentières or Haubourdin – Armentières; the final route chosen ran from Seclin thence Canal de Seclin to Bac Du Wavrin thence Armentières.

The Quesnoy Switch ran west along the Canal de Roubaix from Croix to Wambrechies. It then turned north, following the Canal de Deûle to Quesnoy thence Deûlémont where the Canal joined the River Lys. This switch considerably shortened the front of the Halluin salient and would make it harder for enemy infantry to infiltrate. The Marcq (or Marque) Switch followed the River Marcq between Tourmignies and Péronne-en-Melentois.

When III Corps moved into the line, the Corps Reserve Position was to run from Bac Du Wavrin – Fromelles – Nouveau Monde thence west along the Canal de la Lys to Merville. It then turned north, following the River La Bourre to La Motte-au-Bois, on the southern outskirts of Hazebrouck. The most likely areas for an enemy attack on III Corps front were the Tourcoing – Halluin gap and either side of Armentières. Further switch lines, to add depth to the defence in these areas, were to be reconnoitred. The Prémesques Switch, facing east and north-east was to run from Hallennes les Haubourdin – Vert Ballot – old fort near Prémesques – Houplines. The Radinghem Switch, facing north-west, was to run from the old fort near Prémesques to Fromelles. Finally, the Lys Switch faced north-west along the line of the River Lys from Armentières to Nouveau Monde. If the BEF had to fight on the frontier defences and as the situation permitted, III Corps intended to advance to the River Lys north of Halluin and to the Comines – Ypres Canal in order to reduce the salient on its front (as noted, the French Seventh Army had planned a similar advance). This new position would include the high ground at Wytschaete and Kemmel.

A rear system, known as the Second Position or Canal Line, was planned some 10 to 15 miles behind the front, utilising the canal lines: Canal de la Sensée – Canal de la Haute Deûle – La Bassée Canal. The L'Allumette Switch ran along the canal from Berclau to L'Allumette to stop attacks from either the south-east or north-west but was not to be organised as part of the Second Position.

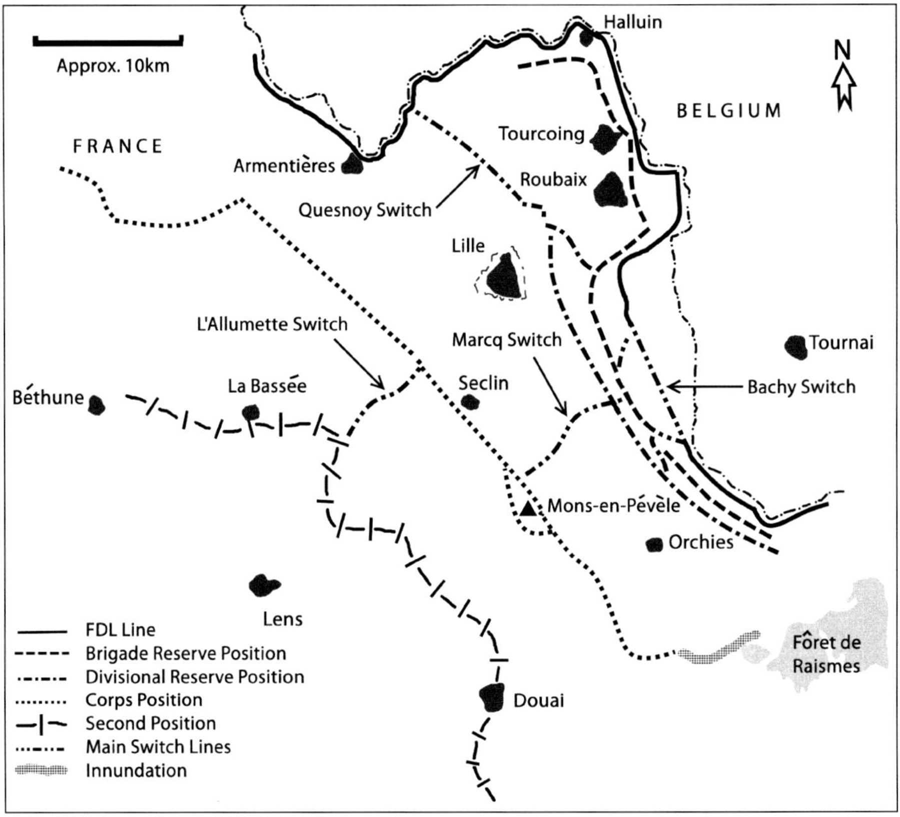

Figure 3.7: BEF defensive positions – *SD* Lille.

Concrete cover

Concrete was the material, apart from steel, that gave the maximum protection with the minimum of bulk. Prior to the Great War, concrete had been used in European fortifications since the 1860's (e.g. the forts around Antwerp in Belgium and Verdun in France) but it was not until that war that it was extensively incorporated into field works in the form of pillboxes. It was the fighting at Ypres during the summer of 1917 that pillboxes really showed their value. The British concluded:

> The concrete "pill-box" system, which held many attacks in 1917, was the most successful manifestation of the system of small posts. These "pill-boxes", besides being a defence against the moving barrage, were also a good defence against the preliminary bombardment. Their construction was strong enough to resist a direct hit by shells up to 6-inch, and their small size and the skill with which they were concealed made them most difficult to hit with larger-sized shells.[33]

Although it may not have been the BEF's initial intention to build a fortified line, at an early stage it was quickly recognised that an 'unexpected opportunity' had arisen in the absence of an enemy to construct concrete defences. A strongly fortified position could to some extent reduce the number of divisions required to hold it. It soon became policy that reinforced concrete pillboxes would be required to afford protection to the key weapons, which formed the backbone of the fire defence throughout the whole depth of the position. Key weapons were guns firing on a pre-determined task, e.g. medium machine guns firing on fixed lines and anti-tank guns enfilading obstacles. In contrast, for weapons of opportunity open emplacements and alternative positions were deemed preferable. Deciding if concrete cover was to be provided depended upon if the weapon could be concealed to obtain surprise, the relative importance of the weapon in the fire plan and if the weapon was located on a site likely to be targeted by the enemy in his preparatory fire plan. If weapons could not be given satisfactory cover or concealment, the policy was to provide shell proof concrete protection. In fact, GHQ issued the following note with regards to pillboxes:

> The frontier positions will be sited and developed primarily with a view to employing semi-permanent and permanent works, and no position can be counted complete unless it has an A Tk obstacle covered by fire, and a due proportion of weapons protected by shell proof concrete shelters. This concrete protection is most important for A Tk guns and the essential machine guns with which a breakthrough can be stopped.[34]

As this took much time and labour, careful consideration had to be given for each site before concrete work was undertaken. Concrete protection was not to be provided for riflemen. Artillery was also not to be afforded concrete protection because of the need for the guns to potentially occupy several alternative positions.

33 *Military Engineering (Vol. II): Defences – 1925* (London: HMSO, 1925), p. 24.
34 TNA: WO167/2, 'Instruction No. 25', 19 December 1939, GHQ General Operations War Diary.

In general terms, the French considered a position could withstand a major attack supported by tanks if it consisted of at least two lines of anti-tank obstacles and essential weapons protected by concrete on a scale of approximately 10 pillboxes per mile of front (six per kilometre) organised in depth and it was to this scale that the BEF planned for. The BEF had 36 kilometres of active front, 10 kilometres of built up area and 20 kilometres of river line. At six pillboxes per kilometre, on the active front the BEF required 216 pillboxes. On the River Lys, a smaller density was acceptable and the BEF worked on a basis of 60 pillboxes to cover the 20 kilometres of front. This gave a minimum total of 276 pillboxes required. The BEF took over 86 French blockhouses on 3 October 1939, meaning a further 190 were needed. This of course took no account of the number of pillboxes required in the rear areas, but it was considered that it should be at least equal to the number required for the main position.

Although the use of concrete pillboxes did not alter the principles of defence outlined in *MTP No.23 Part II*, it did introduce new factors which had to be taken into consideration. Pillboxes took time and skill to construct, and all materials had to be transported to site. It was usually impossible to conceal from the air that a pillbox was being constructed unless it was being built inside an existing building. Under close attack, pillboxes were blind from many directions and the use of smoke could add to this – it was essential that part of garrison should man fire positions outside the pillbox to cover it. Furthermore, it was essential that beforehand the defence zone was divided into brigade sectors and that the disposition of troops in each sector was decided in detail and divided into battalion and company sub-sections. Only then could pillboxes be located in groups so that each group, together with field works, formed a tactical unit i.e. a platoon or company. Such planning was apparently not always carried out due to haste and in order 'to be seen to be doing something'. GHQ had to remind all units not to start concrete works or defence works in general unless they had been planned as a whole.

Concrete pillboxes could be attacked by long range artillery, weapons carried by the advancing enemy infantry and tanks or close-range weapons such as hand grenades. The French also suspected that the Germans planned to use the JU87 dive bomber to attack concrete works. To withstand such attacks, the French policy was to construct principal pillboxes strong enough to withstand two hits in the same place by the largest field gun likely to be employed, i.e. 8 inch shells. For less important pillboxes protection against 5.9 inch shells was to be provided. This standard was adopted by the BEF, with the vast majority of pillboxes constructed to be proof against 5.9 inch shells with a wall and roof 3ft 6in thick. Most tank guns and infantry guns at that time could not penetrate concrete designed to this specification.

Trenches

One of the lessons the British took from the Great War was the defensive power of a trench system:

> The operations leading up to stabilization [sic] of the line on the Western front from the sea to Switzerland and the whole of the trench warfare operations that followed on this afforded ample proof of the high defensive power of an improvised system of trenches and barbed wire held by modern rifles and machine guns. A properly organized [sic] position of this type, if its flanks were secure, was found to be capable of resisting the strongest attacks, even after subjection to heavy bombardment by artillery.[35]

In positional warfare, British military manuals still specified a continuous trench system which should form the framework of the defence. In essence, trenches gave mobility to the defence by linking up defended localities. *FSR Vol. II 1935* lays out further benefits of the trench system, as it facilitated 'reliefs and makes it difficult for the enemy to discover the actual dispositions of the defenders and thus causes him to disperse his fire. Continuous trenches also prevent a feeling of isolation among the troops and thus improve their morale; they also enable additional posts to be established between the main centres of resistance at night or in mist or fog.'[36]

Ironside understood that the large front the BEF had to hold made the digging of a continuous trench system along the lines specified in *FSR Vol. II 1935* impossible:

> Gort and I ... came to the conclusion that the key to the whole question was "ne pas bouger". The troops must be in position, not in a complete trench line. The fronts we have are too big for that. But in islands of defence, each defended by wire...Each covering the country in between the front blockhouses with fire.[37]

However, GHQ initially specified that a continuous trench system was to be developed. It was the weather and saturated ground that put an end to the attempt to dig such a system rather than the impracticality of attempting it.

Fire Power

The defence placed its reliance on fire power:

> The plan of the defence of the main position will be made in terms of fire rather than men and the fire of all weapons – artillery, anti-tank guns, machine guns and rifles – must be properly co-ordinated.[38]

Each part of the defence was to consist of a number of mutually supporting infantry localities prepared for all round defence and protected by tank and infantry obstacles.

35 *Military Engineering (Vol. II): Defences – 1925,* p. 22.
36 *FSR Vol. II: Operations – General 1935,* p.165.
37 Macleod, DSO, MC & Kelly, (eds.), *Time Unguarded,* p. 124.
38 *Operations MTP No. 23 Part II: Defence – 1939,* p. 12.

All infantry localities were expected to hold out to the last, even if enemy tanks and infantry had penetrated round their flanks. They were to continue to engage the enemy infantry with all available fire power and prevent it from supporting the tanks until the situation could be restored by counter-attack.

The French blockhouses on the FDL Line formed the pivot of a forward company locality, from which the platoon areas were built up around, with their section posts located to afford each other and their neighbouring localities mutual support (Figure 3.8). Bren guns firing from the blockhouse would keep the anti-tank ditch under close fire to prevent enemy engineers from bridging the ditch for tanks, while the anti-tank gun engaged the tanks. If the distance between blockhouses was considerable, small intermediate posts were constructed to ensure cover in periods of fog and darkness, consisting of sandbagged or concrete Bren gun posts. A further series of field works were prepared to give depth to the FDL Line.

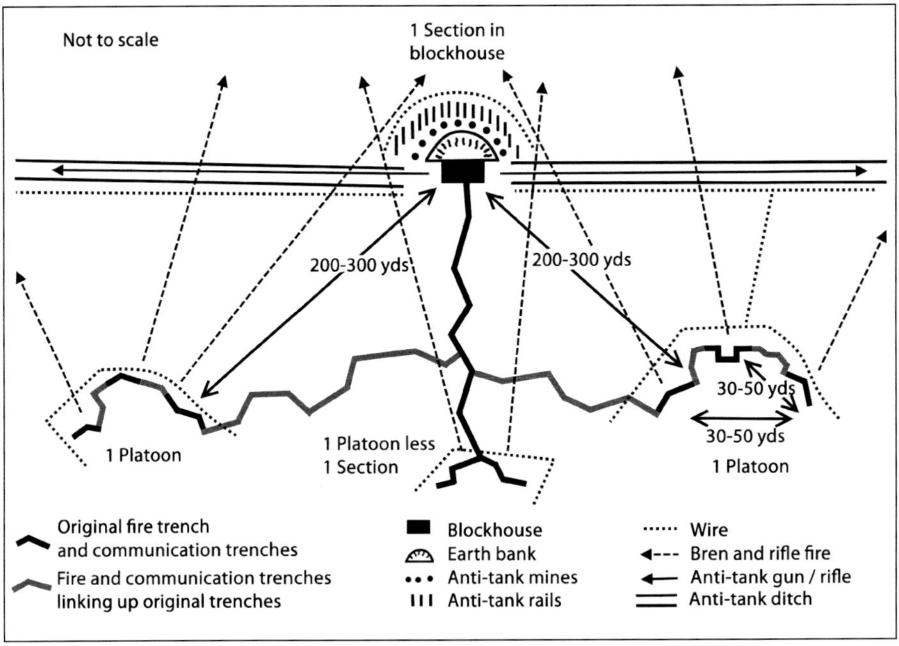

Figure 3.8: Diagram illustrating a forward company locality. The blockhouse forms the pivot of the locality and the two platoon localities to the flanks cover the front of the blockhouse and the locality in the rear prevents interference from the blinded side of the blockhouse.

The Bren light machine gun was the backbone of a section's fire power.[39] Gort considered that one Bren per 60 yards of front was a good yardstick. The Bren gun

39 During the inter-war years, the British had wanted to replace the Lewis and Vickers machine guns with a single general purpose machine gun and in 1935 the War Office adopted a

in each section post was given definite arcs of fire to cover the most likely approaches to be used by the enemy. In many instances, concrete protection was provided for the Bren gun in the form of a hexagonal pillbox. Bren guns were sited in defilade if possible and given arcs of fire such that if one was put out of action, another could cover the same or almost the same ground from another position. In this regard, they could perform short range defensive fire tasks more economically than medium machine guns, which were traditionally used for this purpose. Although allocated such arcs, in principal each section post should be able to bring the whole of its fire power against enemy infantry from whatever direction they approached. For this task the Bren's role was direct fire from its bi-pod from any part of the parapet or any of the loopholes in the standard hexagonal Bren pillbox. In some instances, these interlocking arcs of fire resulted in the need to build barriers between posts to protect them each other's fire. In the forward posts of the FDL Line, fixed lines for night firing or in conditions of fog were generally considered to be of secondary importance because of the requirement of the Bren to able to fire in any direction; if used, they would be co-ordinated with all platoons along a company front and sited to enfilade obstacles that enemy infantry would have to pass for a night attack. An interesting instruction in 11 Brigade's defence scheme for the Halluin area notes that to achieve the aim of building up a network of small arms fire in depth, the defence had to be built up in terms of Bren guns, irrespective of platoon or company. When all the Bren's had been sited, only then was the position to be organised into platoon and company sectors.

The rifle was still the personal protective weapon of the infantry, and riflemen were expected to fight from field works rather than pillboxes.[40] The Infantry was also equipped with both 2 inch and 3 inch mortars. These mortars, if sufficient ammunition

Czech designed weapon, re-designed to take the British .303 inch cartridge, and known as the Bren gun (it was manufactured in its first form at Brno, with British modifications carried out by Enfield, hence the BR of Brno and the EN of Enfield). It was a gas operated, air cooled automatic weapon, fed from a magazine holding 30 rounds. The Bren could fire 120 rounds per minute (i.e. four magazines per minute), but this was for emergencies only. Rather, it was emphasised that full use should be made of the gun's ability to fire single rounds as this saved ammunition and concealed the presence of the gun until a suitable target appeared. In automatic mode, bursts of four to five rounds were recommended to prevent overheating and stress on the mechanism. Instructions were issued in November 1939 to load the magazine with 28 rounds only to prevent stoppages sometimes experienced as a result of certain magazines failing to feed the first round when loaded with 30 rounds. If the magazine had to be kept loaded for any length of time, it was to be loaded with only 20 rounds to prevent the spring becoming weak or even fracturing owing to it being kept fully compressed. Although generally an excellent and reliable weapon, it was never able to adequately perform the role of a general-purpose machine gun, and the Vickers was retained in machine gun battalions under corps control.

40 The BEF was still using the famous Short Magazine Lee Enfield Mk. III, introduced in 1907, with a 10 round magazine and a maximum range of 1,000 yards, although it was rarely effective beyond 600 yards. The best riflemen could attain a rate of fire of 15 aimed shots per minute.

was available, gave the battalion commander a powerful weapon for direct support of a counter-attack, harassing and counter-preparation if sited well forward and supplementing the fire plan of the defence which was not adequately covered by other weapons, when the 3 inch mortar could be laid on fixed lines.

To aid the infantry during darkness, trials were held in April 1940 with Lyon beach lights to test their effectiveness of illuminating the front. In these trials, the lights were mounted in pairs in two forward section posts, about 250 yards apart, so as to give crossed beams in the field of fire from the posts. A mock attack was carried out on the position. The attack was picked up at first with flares and the Lyon light beams were fully on within five seconds of the alarm being given. Although the lights clearly picked up the attack, they could not penetrate a smoke screen laid on with candles. The glare effect on the attackers was considered to be negligible, and indeed would aid attackers by lighting up the ground and also provide an easy target to aim at. It was concluded that they would be of little practical use in the front line, although they may well be of value for emergency work such as bridge repairs as they were easily transportable and easily turned off in an alarm.

Anti-tank defence in the FDL Line was provided by the French 25mm anti-tank gun[41] and the Boys .55 inch anti-tank rifle[42] located within the blockhouses or in

41 The 25mm gun (*canon de 25mm semi-automatique modèle 1934*) was an excellent weapon at the time, with a range of around 1,000 yards. It fired an armour piercing round, with a high muzzle velocity of 3,020 feet per second. The breach was semi-automatic, allowing a high rate of fire to be kept up. It had a traverse of 60°, an elevation of 15° and a depression of 5°. The carriage was of the split trial type. By 11 October, the BEF had received 220 French 25mm anti-tank guns with another 280 promised. On 13 January, the French notified Ironside that 100 of these were to be released to Turkey leaving only 180 to be delivered. The French unofficially notified the British that the 180 guns could only be provided if they accepted 1937 pattern guns. Furthermore, GHQ was still under the impression that it was still to receive the additional 100 guns! The 1937 pattern gun could not be towed behind a vehicle but could be carried on specially fitted trucks. Gamelin promised to deliver 70 by end the end of March; this would mean all the 10 divisions of the first and second contingent would be fully equipped. In return, the French were pressing the British for 10,000 Boys anti-tank rifles and 15 heavy Scammell tractors for recovery of damaged tanks, but delivery was postponed due to operations in Scandinavia. As a long-term policy, it was also intended to equip infantry anti-tank companies with the French 55mm anti-tank guns if made available by the French. Brooke was very impressed with the 25mm anti-tank gun after attending trials of the penetrating power of this gun and the Boys anti-tank rifle; he noted it easily penetrated 2 feet of reinforced concrete. On 25 May the War Office noted the 'most favourable reports of the performance of both the Q.F. 2-pdr and 25 m.m. anti-tank guns and to say that even the 25 m.m., which is a less powerful weapon than the 2-pdr has defeated the heaviest enemy A.F.V's which have yet been encountered' (TNA: WO106/1605, memo from Commander-in-Chief Home Forces to the commands, 25 May 1940).The Germans also tested guns captured after France had been overrun and found it could even penetrate the armour of the Mark IV tanks.

42 The Boys anti-tank rifle weighed 36lb and fired .55 inch calibre bullets held in a magazine containing five rounds. Great faith had been put in the rifle before the war, but few had

prepared field works. The 25mm anti-tank guns were manned by the brigade anti-tank companies. Their task was to keep the anti-tank ditch under close fire and so deny the enemy the use of tanks supporting infantry in neutralising the forward defended localities. Because conditions of mist or smoke could blind anti-tank guns, the guns covering anti-tank ditches were normally not expected to fire over ranges greater than 800 yards. Posts for anti-tank guns were also sited between the FDL Line and the Brigade Reserve Position to add depth to the defence, in what was sometimes referred to as the Battalion Close Support Line. Some of these posts were to be provided with concrete pillboxes, usually along the lines of the French *postes de tir* (see Chapter 8). Although the general policy was to site the 25mm anti-tank guns in the blockhouses, many blockhouses were sited so close to the anti-tank obstacle so as to be considered unsuitable for the fire of anti-tank guns. Furthermore, many unit commanders thought that the enemy would not attempt a serious tank attack against the line in the first instance. It was more probable that an attempt to seize the line with infantry first would be made, and then pass through the armour. Consequently, the anti-tank defence of some blockhouses was to be with the anti-tank rifle only and a proportion of 25mm guns were to be sited in prepared positions in the rear of the FDL Line, designed to deal with any attempt to pass tanks through bridgeheads established over the anti-tank obstacle. The use of 25mm guns in blockhouses was also economised in areas of ground unsuitable for tanks. This was especially the case during the winter months when ground conditions deteriorated, and many guns were removed from blockhouses. It is also worth noting that Montgomery, in his memoirs, mentions a number of 'small one-pounder guns on little hand carts were hurriedly bought from the French and a few were given to each infantry battalion' for use as anti-tank weapons.[43]

any training in its use: 'This weapon, as we firmly but falsely believed, could punch a neat hole in the toughest armour-plate, where after the bullet, its virulence far from exhausted, would hum round inside the enemy tank like an angry hornet, to the great discomfort of its crew. Very few of us, however, had ever fired one of these weapons, since it had, apparently, been impossible to find, in all the United Kingdom, any range on which the men who were to handle the rifle in action might accustom themselves to its use. It was darkly rumoured and widely believed though, that any poor wight who did fire the weapon might expect to have his shoulder broken by the recoil, and this caused the "Boys" to be looked upon with deep, though ill-merited, respect' (Butler & Selby Bradford, MBE, MC, Keep the Memory Green, pp. 15-16). The weapon acquired a bad reputation during the battle of France and Flanders as the above account suggests, as it was only effective at short ranges. The BEF largely used the Boys rifle to supplement anti-tank guns. It was never intended for this purpose: Infantry Section Leading 1938 clearly states the rifle was meant only to provide the infantry with some means of protection against light AFVs. The expectation that the rifle could achieve more was no doubt the reason for its poor reputation. The bullet would penetrate light AFVs from a range of 500 yards and the armour of the Panzer Mk. I and the sides and rear of the hull and turret of the Panzer Mk. II at 250 yards. It would not penetrate the armour of the heavier Panzer Mk. III.

43 Bernard Law, Viscount Montgomery of Alamein, *The Memoirs of Field-Marshal Montgomery*

The Brigade Reserve Position was also to consist of a series of company localities protected by anti-tank obstacles, both natural and artificial ditches. Again, the French blockhouses were to form the basis of company localities with further field works and pillboxes constructed to give depth to the Position. Localities utilised the junction of the anti-tank ditch with woods, small towns and villages, as these could provide a self-contained tank-proof centre of resistance and provided cover for the defences in scrub, orchards, hedges or buildings.[44] These infantry localities, if possible, by their dispositions protected the sites chosen for medium machine guns and anti-tank guns located within the Brigade Reserve Position. The anti-tank guns and machine guns were afforded concrete cover if they could not be otherwise concealed. Further strength to the anti-tank defence was provided by a number of 25-pdr field guns sited for this role behind the Position. The Divisional Reserve Position was to be similarly organised and also provided with a substantial measure of concrete protection.

Although defence in zones of depth was aimed for, the initial three divisions of the BEF had such large fronts to cover, that in reality all that could be manned was a series of localities, or 'islands of defence' laid out in a linear fashion. Only the 4th Division was in reserve to give some depth. Each forward battalion held the FDL Line with three companies forward and one in reserve; the battalion reserve positions for the most being a series of platoon localities prepared in linear defence. The Brigade Reserve Position also consisted of a series of platoon localities, which covered vital ground, but were linear in the nature of their layout, leaving in most cases only one platoon per company to add depth. In some instances, the localities between villages could only be held by skeleton garrisons, consisting of anti-tank gun and machine gun units, with the carrier platoons expected to occupy the positions should the FDL Line be breached. For the Divisional Reserve Position, resources only allowed the provision of a series of field works in the areas of the most likely lines of attack. The problem of holding the Divisional Reserve Position in any strength can be appreciated if we consider the example of the 3rd Division: it had a Divisional Reserve Position of roughly 10,000 yards to hold with one brigade. However, in anticipation of the build up of its forces, the BEF planned positions that were capable of accepting a much larger garrison than was currently available. The 3rd Division, for example, marked out a position appropriate for a corps front. Each of its brigade sectors had to be organised as if it was to be held by two infantry brigades with two machine gun companies and one anti-tank battery. Although in the majority of cases there

(London: Collins, 1958), p. 50. This was presumably the small 37mm gun used by the French in the Great War.

44 *ATM No. 30* made the point that 'The main purpose of a defended village is to produce a self-contained tank-proof centre of resistance.' (*ATM No. 30* (London: The War Office, March 1940), p. 20). Yet experience from the Flanders campaign was to show that villages were liable to be subject to dive bombing attacks and also at risk of being set alight with incendiary bombs. *ATM No. 33* suggested that well concealed positions outside the village locality might be preferable.

was only time to construct defences for existing troops, the 'ghost' positions marked out were to form part of a comprehensive system, capable of rapid expansion and accepting a much larger garrison than that which was available at the time. Even by March 1940, while on a visit to GHQ, the Director of Military Training still got the impression of a linear defence.

The BEF generally reserved the 2 pdr anti-tank guns[45] of the anti-tank regiments to cover the Brigade Reserve Position and the approaches to the Divisional Reserve Position – i.e. out of the area subject to the preliminary bombardment (although a limited number were sited in front of the Brigade Reserve Position). These guns were allocated penetration tasks on the same principle as the 25mm guns located in the FDL Line. The ability to rapidly occupy any position or change position was essential. Anti-tank guns are direct fire weapons, and the principles of deployment of anti-tank guns laid out in *Infantry Training 1937* describes the deployment of the BEF's 2 pdrs:

> The anti-tank guns will be sited to cover the probable avenues of tank approach and localities liable to tank attack. They should be disposed in depth, and concealment will be of importance, as the enemy will attempt to neutralize [sic] them by fire and smoke, if located. Full use should be made of the mobility of anti-tank guns, and alternative positions should be reconnoitred and prepared. It will sometimes be advisable for guns to be kept in mobile reserve under cover ready to move to prepared positions as soon as the direction of the tank attack is disclosed.[46]

This anti-tank gun relied entirely on surprise and concealment and is best sited defiladed from the front so it could engage tanks in enfilade in order to avoid striking the tank in front where the armour is thickest (Figure 3.9). Latest thinking on the handling of anti-tank guns also emphasised reverse slopes so that full use could be made of the flat trajectory of the shell by using grazing fire. The fire unit was a single gun and guns were sited singly rather than closely grouped to ensure that each gun would require attention from the attacker. The anti-tank gun's sole role was to give support to other arms, so its tactical handling was dependant on the tactics of other arms. Therefore, guns had to be sited in relation to anti-tank obstacles, either

45 The 2 pdr anti-tank gun was a semi-automatic weapon firing an armour piercing shell with a flat trajectory up to 2,000 yards, although it was most likely to obtain hits at ranges of under 800 yards. It had a muzzle velocity of 2,598 feet per second, and being semi-automatic, a high rate of fire of 22 rounds per minute could be achieved. It could be fired from its wheels or from its pedestal. As the arc of fire when fired from its wheels was only 23°, it was usual practice to fire it from its pedestal, which gave a 360° arc of fire. The gun had a pronounced flash when fired, which was liable to disclose its position, hence the need to rapidly change position.

46 *Infantry Training 1937: Training & War* (London: HMSO, 1937), p. 170.

with the object of destroying tanks while negotiating the obstacle or destroying those shepherded by obstacles onto a chosen killing area, and hence assisting the commander of the formation, to which the guns were allotted to, in his plan of anti-tank defence. Presumably because some guns hand been badly located in relation to the overall planning of the anti-tank defence, Anti-tank Regimental Commanders were still being reminded at a conference held on 12 March 1940 to locate guns 'where they can best destroy tanks and not merely to defend localities.'[47]

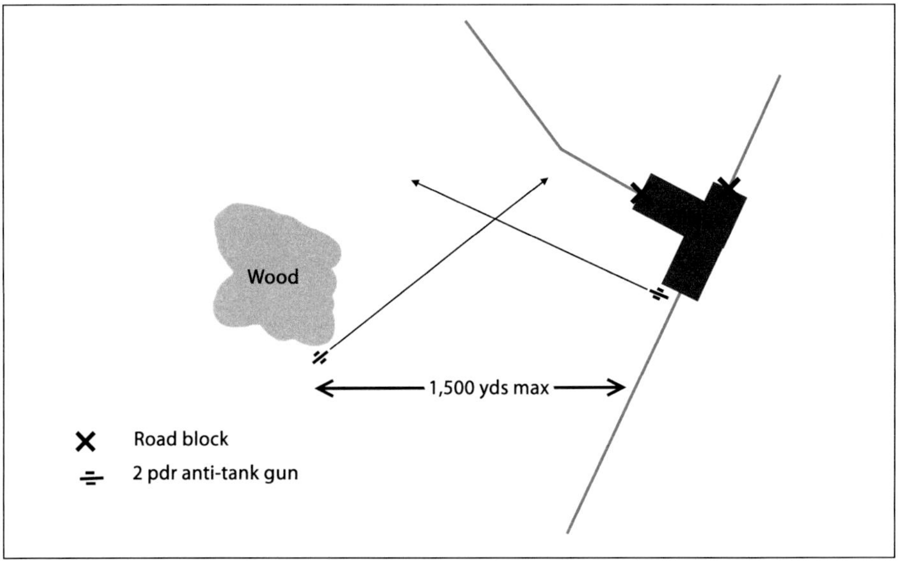

Figure 3.9: Diagram to illustrate the siting of the British 2 pdr anti-tank guns. Anti-tank guns were normally sited so that they are defiladed from the front and fire in enfilade along likely lanes of approach for enemy tanks. In this diagram, the village and woods force the tanks into the cross fire of the anti-tank guns.

Although the BEF was up to strength in the number of anti-tank guns it possessed, the long fronts held by its divisions meant that there were insufficient guns to cover all eventualities and especially there were generally insufficient guns for adequate mobile reserves as suggested in *Infantry Training* and *Army Training Memorandum (ATM) No. 28* made this very point. This was not, however, always a serious issue, because in theory the anti-tank defence was organised on an area basis utilising all available resources. For example, on the northern part of the BEF front which was largely urban, a major tank attack was unlikely. The 11 Brigade defence scheme for

47 TNA: WO167/13, 'Minutes of the Conference of A.Tk. Regimental Commanders held at Regt. H.Q. 20 A.Tk. Regiment on Tuesday 12 Mar 40.' GHQ Major-General Royal Artillery War Diary

the Tourcoing sector stipulated that for such urban areas, anti-tank defence could be obtained using buildings as the obstacle combined with road blocks and only a minimum use of anti-tank guns. The bulk of the Brigade's anti-tank guns could then be deployed in the more open area on its left boundary. In general, though, the shortage of guns resulted in a tendency to spread the anti-tank guns too thin, covering vulnerable areas with only one gun. Given the danger of massed tank attacks and the expected casualties to guns and their crews, it was emphasised that at least two guns should cover the same ground of vulnerable areas. Some of the BEF's commanders hoped that the anti-tank rifle would fill in the gaps between the widely spaced anti-tank guns despite the fact that the rifle was only intended as an infantry weapon to knock out light armoured vehicles.

Pre-war doctrine stated that further depth to the defence was given by medium machine guns which could occupy positions from which long range fire could be employed.[48] The machine gun was 'the most powerful of all infantry weapons in defence, since it is capable of producing a concentrated volume of accurate and sustained fire beyond the effective reach of rifles and light machine guns, and yet presents only a small target in action.'[49] GHQ stipulated that the primary task of the machine gun was to engage with direct fire from concrete emplacements enemy infantry who had penetrated the forward defences. For this task they had to be sited well behind the FDL Line, i.e. immediately behind the Brigade Reserve and Divisional Reserve Positions. Machine guns were also used to provide the nucleus for the defence of rear localities.

Machine guns achieved best results from defiladed positions and the latest thinking emphasised firing at short ranges – indirect fire was seldom required. A small proportion of guns were sited forward for use in defensive fire in front of the FDLs in cases where defensive fire at longer ranges was needed (for instance if shorter range fire using a light machine gun could only be produced from positions unduly exposed). In the first instance, only those guns sited forward could be included in the FDL Line fire plan, but when stream line ammunition became available, the majority of guns could support the FDL Line with map shooting. However, if a gun had a penetration fire task from a defiladed position, it would be difficult to allot that gun a defensive fire task. Guns could, however, be given a harassing fire task from a specially detailed position. Machine guns could also be used as a mobile reserve to check penetration or

48 The medium machine gun in service with the British Army was still the Vickers machine gun used in the Great War, 'the grand old lady of no-mans-land'. It was water-cooled and capable of sustained rapid fire. Its heavy tripod, which weighed 56lb, allowed laying on fixed lines and indirect fire. The maximum effective range of the Vickers was 2,000 yards, and at rapid fire it could fire 250 rounds per minute. Given the great length of the beaten zone in proportion to its width (e.g. 300 yards long by 5 yards wide at 1,000 yards range) fire was most effective when delivered obliquely or in enfilade. The area of ground so swept at close range was practically impassable to infantry.

49 *Infantry Training 1937: Training & War*, p. 4.

support counter-attacks, although the carrier platoon of infantry battalions was better suited to this task.

The BEF's artillery had four main roles in defence: to harass the enemy preparation for an attack, to inflict damage on the attack, to engage enemy artillery and to give depth to the anti-tank defence. The artillery dispositions had to be worked out in advance and the position of every battery and gun fixed. The dispositions in theory should allow the whole, or nearly the whole, of the artillery to concentrate its fire against an attack on any part of the front. Thus, there would be many more battery positions prepared than batteries available, to enable batteries to shift to alternative positions. The need for the artillery to shift to alternative positions meant that the provision of concrete emplacements for artillery would also be very difficult to conceal.

It was obviously advantageous to harass, interrupt and break up enemy preparations for an attack, especially enemy artillery and ammunition echelons during their move forward, with 'counter-preparation' fire. This was to be achieved by siting a proportion of the field artillery in forward roving positions and a high proportion of available ammunition was to be allocated to this role. However, minor targets or 'sniping' at small parties of enemy was to be avoided due to concerns over ammunition supplies.

The general policy was to move artillery back from these roving positions to battle positions when attack was imminent. In order to guard against surprise and attack taking place before guns had been withdrawn from roving positions, 50 percent of the artillery was to occupy battle positions from the start and remain silent so as not to disclose their positions. From the battle positions, the field artillery would switch to 'defensive fire' when the enemy attack began (Figure 3.10). This would be put down on pre-arranged areas and in co-ordination with other weapons, especially machine guns. In general, each defensive fire task could be covered by several batteries firing at the same time. Such fire was to be controlled either by observation or a pre-arranged SOS signal in which gunners could use predicted fire to hit pre-defined target areas.[50]

It would have been difficult for the field artillery to adequately cover the long front the BEF held. I Corps initially held a front of 20,000 yards covered by two hundred and sixty-four 25 pdrs.[51] The burst of a 25 pdr shell covered a maximum frontage of 35 yards, so if all the guns covering I Corps were used side by side they could put

50 In the absence of specific orders, rates of fire to answer an SOS signal were: LMGs – 1 minute rapid, 1 minute normal (repeating according to circumstances); Medium MGs – 2 minutes rapid, 3 minutes normal (repeating according to circumstances); mortars – 5 rounds HE per minute for 3 minutes (if ammunition allowed); artillery – 3 minutes intense then lifting to counter-preparation tasks and fire two bursts of 2 minutes rapid with 2 minutes interval.

51 The 25 pdr field gun was the result of experiments to combine the longer range of field guns with greater power of howitzers. These 25 pdr 'gun-hows' replaced the 18 pdr field gun and the 4.5 inch howitzer in the Field Artillery regiments and the 13 pdr of the Royal Horse Artillery units. It was a 3.45 inch calibre gun firing a 25 pound shell. It used the variable charge ammunition of howitzers to vary range. It had a maximum range of around 13,400 yards and a 'gun-fire' rate of six to eight rounds per minute. It was usually towed, along with its ammunition trailer, by a Morris 4x4 'quad'.

down a barrage on a frontage of 9,240 yards. The position of II Corps was no better. They had one hundred and twenty 25 pdrs to cover 10,000 yards, i.e. a maximum frontage covered of 4,200 yards. In the case of counter-preparation fire, to address the fact that there were insufficient guns to deal with all tasks simultaneously, fire was to be switched from one target to another to concentrate fire in large 'splashes' rather than dispersing fire on a number of targets.

There were still insufficient 25 pdrs to equip the 48th, 50th and 51st Divisions when they crossed over to France (Chapter 6 describes the expansion of the BEF), so their Divisional Artillery was equipped with older 18 pdr guns. This required an exchange of Field Regiments with the 1st to 5th Divisions to ensure a more even distribution of this shorter ranged field gun. The burst of an 18 pdr shell covered a maximum frontage of only 30 yards. The BEF also faced a shortage of equipment and spares for the field artillery. For example, there were heavy deficiencies in clinometers sight and telescopic sight No.22 for the 25/18 pdr – units had indented in the UK for these but had departed before they could be issued – and many guns were temporarily put out of action after road accidents because no spare hub assemblies were carried.

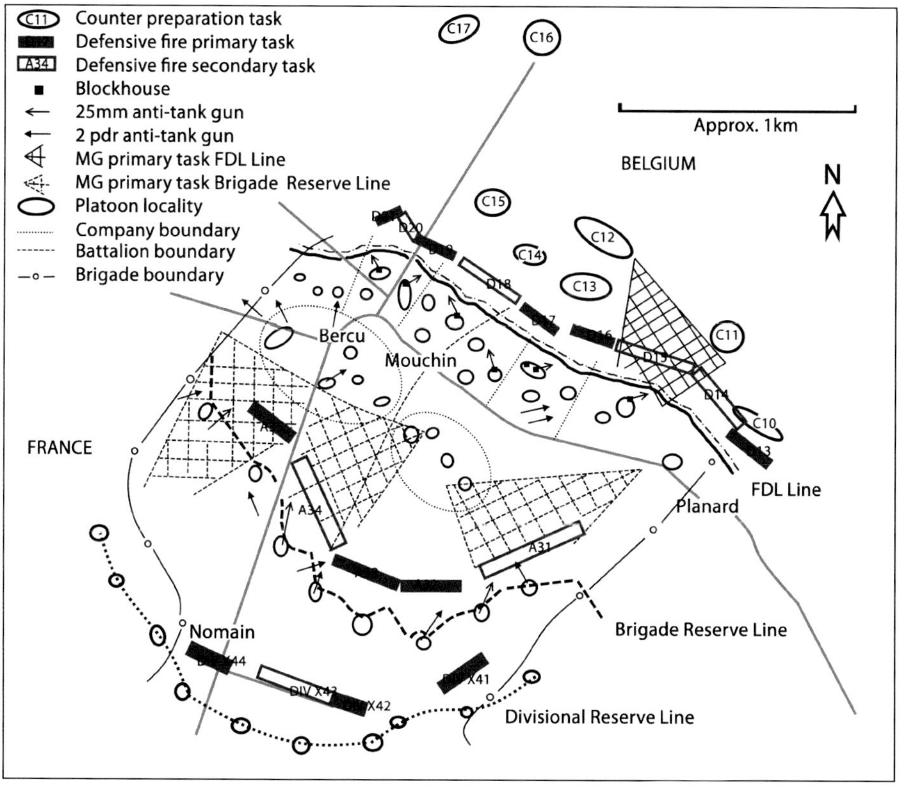

Figure 3.10: Map showing 6 Brigade's artillery fire plan illustrating the various fire tasks. The left-hand battalion was the 1st Battalion Royal Berkshire Regiment, the right-hand battalion was the 1st Battalion Royal Welsh Fusiliers and the 2nd Battalion Durham Light Infantry were in reserve along the Brigade Reserve Line.

With the tank danger in mind, GHQ emphasised the need for the artillery fire plans to be closely co-ordinated with anti-tank guns to form continuous and mutually supporting anti-tank zones. In an anti-tank role, a proportion of the field artillery was sited in depth between the Brigade Reserve and Divisional Positions and was not to take part in artillery tasks other than direct fire at enemy tanks. This was to be extended back behind the Divisional Reserve Line. The latest lessons of anti-tank gun trials with the 25 pdr field gun emphasised that not to site these guns with this in mind was an 'unjustifiable waste of weapon power.'[52] These trials noted that the best position for 25 pdrs were reverse slope positions allowing the advantage of grazing fire; forward slopes were to be avoided. A long field of fire was not necessary: a field of fire of over 800 yards was regarded as dangerous as this would mean opening fire too soon; 500 yards was ample and in many cases 200 yards adequate. The object, as with the 2 pdr anti-tank gun, was to hit with the first round. Now that the field artillery was an integral part of the anti-tank defence, it would not be able to use its mobility to withdraw to positions in the rear to continue the fight if it was in danger of being overrun by a tank attack. It could, however, withdraw if in danger of being overrun by an infantry attack unsupported by tanks.

The heavier guns were under corps control. When an attack began, corps artillery was to fire on counter-preparation and defensive fire tasks until sufficient information became available for counter-battery work. Counter-battery work, i.e. engaging enemy artillery, was necessary to prevent enemy guns from neutralising the fire of the defence. In order to carry out these roles, corps artillery had to be sited in the forward area to achieve the necessary range. There was an even greater shortage of heavier calibre guns to adequately cover the frontage the BEF was tasked to hold (Table 3.1). On the outbreak of war, Churchill raised the question of the heavy artillery he had arranged to be put into storage in 1919. It comprised of thirty-two 12 inch, one hundred and forty-five 9.2 inch, many 8 inch and nearly six-hundred 6 inch guns with large quantities of ammunition. Some parts of the guns had deteriorated during the time they had been in storage and would require renewal and work had actually started on this during the crises of September 1938. Churchill was keen that these guns should be put into the field as quickly as possible so that the BEF did not suffer from a lack of heavy artillery. Only a small number of these guns found their way to France, which, with hindsight, was just as well as they met a vital requirement in Home Defence following the evacuation from Dunkirk.

With the general shortage of medium and heavy artillery, it was inevitable that some of the field artillery would also have to be employed on counter battery work. It was generally not necessary to co-ordinate the medium and heavy guns into the

52 *ATM No. 24* (London: The War Office), p. 11. Although a proportion of 25 pdrs were sited for an anti-tank role, as at 10 May 1940 virtually no 25 pdr armour piercing shot had actually been issued, although experience was to show that tanks could be stopped with HE shell if using direct laying.

anti-tank defence, as they were generally not suited to engaging moving tanks in low density, but their employment in engaging tanks moving in columns through defiles could be profitable. However, if in danger of being overrun by a tank attack, the corps artillery would still have had to stand and fight; although these guns did not have any direct fire anti-tank value, they would have to stay in action to help stem the enemy infantry advance. If in danger of being overrun by a tank attack, the gun crews were to take cover in slit trenches and wait until the tanks had passed by.

Ammunition for all calibres of artillery – as well as the infantry mortars – was in short supply from the start. For instance, in the event of a heavy attack, the expenditure of ammunition for a 25 pdr gun was expected to be about 400 rounds per gun (rpg) and 50 to 100 rpg per day for one day preceding and for two successive days, giving an expenditure of about 600 rpg for an operation. This quantity of ammunition had to be within reach of the mobile echelons. Because of the long LoC, there were shortages in RAOC personnel and labour to handle the large weights involved needed to establish the forward dumps. The expected shipping of ammunition from the UK was also below that needed to build up a sufficient reserve. The situation had not improved much by January, as noted in the War Diary of MGRA for 13 January:

> The main subject during the past week has been the question of ammunition. Production appears to have fallen well behind the promised rate, and serious deficiencies are apparent. The matter was represented to the C-in-C, who has taken drastic action.[53]

The Ministry of Supply had been too optimistic in its estimates of production in the early days of the war, meaning the BEF had less ammunition than it expected by Christmas. Gort had hoped to make up the deficiencies with promised deliveries in January and February, but production of ammunition was severely reduced in these months due to a heavy rate of sickness caused by an influenza epidemic. The situation was made worse by the curtailment of shipments of certain types of ammunition because of the decision to postpone the dispatch of III Corps. In the case of 2 inch mortar HE rounds, the BEF was forced to accept ammunition that produced 10 percent duds rather than wait for the redesign to be completed and have no ammunition. Lord Gort, in his Official Dispatches notes:

> I had on several occasions called the attention of the War Office to the shortage of almost every nature of ammunition of which the stocks in France were not nearly large enough to permit of the rates of expenditure laid down for sustained operations before the War.[54]

53 TNA: WO167/13, GHQ Major-General Royal Artillery War Diary, 13 January 1940.
54 General the Viscount Gort, VC, KCB, CBE, DSO, MVO, MC, *Despatches on Operations of the British Expeditionary Force.*

Table 3.1: The number of guns available to the BEF at 31 March 1940 and the recommended rounds per gun (rpg) per day compared to the approved rounds per gun per day.

Weapon	Total No. Of guns in I and II Corps	Total no. of guns in III Corps	Total no. of guns in I,II and III Corps	Stock with BEF at 31.3.1940	Approved rpg per day	Recommended rpg per day
18 pdr	84	132	216			
HE				243,070	18	7
Shrap.				187,778	15	3
Smoke				31,984	2	1
AP				Nil	1	Nil
4.5" How.	36	60	96			
HE				59,686	22.5	Minimum possible
Smoke				39,580	7.5	
Gas				Nil	N/A	
25 pdr	512	144	656			
HE				1,551,318	30	28
Smoke				206,193	5	2
AP				2,400	1	Nil
60 pdr	16	Nil	16			
HE				28,800	12.5	12.5
Shrap.				26,300	12.5	12.5
4.5/60 pdr H.E.	Nil	32	32	Nil	25	19
6" How.	128	48	176			
H.E.				199,600	30	Minimum possible
Gas				18,000	N/A	
6" gun	8	4	12			
HE				9,996	9	6
Shrap.				2,994	6	6

8" How. HE	12	Nil	12	16,120	24	3.5
9.2" How. HE	12	12	24	28,310	20	8
9.2" gun H.E.	Nil	2	2	890	5	5
12" How. HE	Nil	4	4	Nil	7.5	3
3" Mortar HE Smoke	124	70	194	92,412 53,724	16 10	Minimum Possible
2" Mortar HE Smoke	744	405	1,149	14,062 247,515	1 9	Minimum possible
2 pdr anti-tank gun	240	192	432	440,450	5	5
25mm anti-tank gun	201	81	282	276,000	5	5

The stock of ammunition includes all echelons – i.e. including the reserve held at base depots as well as 1st and 2nd line ammunition. The approved rpg per day was based on the probable rates of fire that may be expected during operations over a considerable period of time, and was based on an extensive study of the previous war, covering both periods of intensive fighting and others of considerably less intensity. It was used to assess the amount of reserve ammunition the BEF required, based on 30 days worth in reserve ammunition depots and 15 days worth in transit. The recommended rpg per day was based on the actual amount of ammunition held by the BEF, including that in reserve. Both the approved and recommended rpg took into account the estimated shipping programme for April 1940 – for example, 1,000 rounds for the 12 inch howitzer were expected in April. The table shows that the most critical shortage of ammunition occurred in the 4.5 inch howitzer, 6 inch howitzer and both the 2 inch and 3 inch mortars. The table also illustrates the shortage of heavier calibre guns.

Demolitions

Demolitions could assist in delaying the forward movement of enemy forces or checking the enemy on the front selected for defence. Uncoordinated demolitions usually only had a local effect. It was of the first importance, therefore, that demolitions be carried out on a definite plan to ensure the creation of an effective obstacle. Such schemes usually consisted of extensive demolitions throughout belts of country. According to military manuals of the time, the first requirement was to develop a primary demolition belt, sufficient to form an effective linear obstacle. Usually a water line was selected for a primary belt. Once the primary belt was completed, its effectiveness could be extended by adding subsidiary belts, or zones of demolitions. However, in the Lille salient there was no water line or other natural obstacles suitable for a primary demolition belt. The only suitable line was that of the Second Position (i.e. the Canal Line). This was adopted as the Primary Belt, with a scheme of demolitions (road cratering and bridge demolitions) in some depth in advance of the Canal Line. This included demolitions a short distance into Belgium – for example the French planned for demolitions along the Courtrai – Bossuyt Canal, which was 10 miles into Belgium from the frontier defences and the BEF inherited this scheme from the French when it moved into the line. Although instructions were issued to destroy military vehicles that had to be abandoned and as a result likely fall into enemy hands, there were initially no instructions to destroy petrol stocks or garages with petrol pumps.[55]

Counter-attack and tank v tank action

Counter-attack was fundamental for defence in depth to work, striking at an enemy weakened as he fought his way through the various zones of the defence. If the enemy succeeded in gaining a foothold, he was to be prevented from widening the gap and ejected by counter attack with local reserves if this was considered to have a chance of success. Such counter-attacks had to be launched during the period of confusion before the enemy infantry established itself, or else the moment had been lost and unnecessary casualties would result. The carriers of a division usually formed the local reserves and as such their Bren guns were not generally included in fire plans.

The BEF could only mount a deliberate counter attack with the mobile reserve under the control of GHQ. However, the GHQ reserve may also have been employed in strengthening the shoulders and foremost limits of any salient made by the enemy breaking into the position. Therefore, the GHQ reserve, which initially consisted of one division and one machine gun battalion from II Corps and the 4th Battalion Royal Tank Regiment, had a number of roles assigned to it depending on the situation

55 Such instructions were issued when the BEF fell back onto the frontier defences in May 1940.

developing after a German attack. It could be required to hold the high ground at Mons-en-Pévèle, along which the reserve division of II Corps was constructing field defences. The reserve may also be expected to counter-attack towards Orchies – Maulde or stop an advance on Seclin from the direction of Ascq. Should the main weight of the attack fall in the north of the *SD* Lille, GHQ reserve had two alternate roles. Either it would be required to extend the II Corps front, allowing the French 51st Division to shorten their front, or it would occupy the Roubaix – Quesnoy Switch along the Canal Croix to support troops in front of that line. Finally, should the situation arise and an adjustment to the front become necessary, GHQ reserve could be required to take up positions along the Canal Line Marchiennes – Douai – Beauvin – La Bassée – Béthune. This line had to be held at all costs as if the Germans crossed it they would be in open country. To ensure that the reserve could fulfil any role allocated to it, arrangements were made to provide the means of establishing alternative routes and switches around defiles that had been subjected to bombing attacks, for example with the use of bridging equipment. If the GHQ reserve could not restore the situation, the BEF would ultimately have had to rely on the French strategic reserve.

The French considered that a tank breakthrough was possible anywhere that the anti-tank defence was not supported by strong natural obstacles, and that the best way to stop it was with tanks. Thus, the French believed tank *v* tank action was a certainty.[56] If enemy tanks succeeded in pushing through, they were to be halted by all available

56 One problem with British tanks – with the exception of the A12 'Matilda' – according to French opinion was that they were not designed to fight in the type of warfare likely to be encountered on the Western front. The French always considered that armour and armament should take precedence over speed. The British never really resolved the balance of these three elements in their pre-war tank design. Furthermore, the principal that tanks should be capable of effectively engaging enemy tanks was not always held in British pre-war thinking. The British, influenced by the theories of Captain Basil Liddell Hart and Major General J.F.C. Fuller, had three types of tank on the outbreak of the War: the heavily armoured but slow A11 and A12 tanks designed for infantry support, three medium Cruiser tanks, A9, A10 and A13 concentrated in Armoured Divisions and the Mk VIB light tank, designed to be cheap and massed produced and used for infantry support in mobile warfare and reconnaissance duties, which sacrificed both armour and armament for mobility. The light tank was, in the French view, not an effective weapon for war on the Western Front, and in this they were proved right. The Cruiser tanks, designed for mobile operations including tank *v.* tank action where there had been little time to organise defences, did eventually arrive in France with the 1st Armoured Division. These were more lightly armoured than the infantry tanks and proved to be vulnerable to dug in German anti-tank guns during the Battle of France. Both Cruiser tanks and the A12 were armed with the 2 pdr gun firing armour piercing rounds only. With the lack of capability to fire HE shells, they could not effectively engage dug-in anti-tank guns. During a conference held on 19 October, General Dill did enquire about using the medium Cruiser tanks as mobile anti-tank guns but was informed they were all being held at home for training. The British eventually came to the conclusion that the light tank had limited value, and in early 1940 closed down production of them in favour of Cruisers.

anti-tank guns, by the action of the field artillery and by minefields and demolitions. Ultimately though, the British recognised that 'the only effective way of dealing with a successful attack of this nature [i.e. an attack with a large number of tanks with the object of achieving a breakthrough] is with our own armoured formations.'[57] Initially, however, GHQ only had the 4th Battalion Royal Tank Regiment under its command for such a role. Although counter-attack was the primary role of the Battalion, which required the Battalion to be kept under Battalion control, *ATM No. 28* did acknowledge that there may be instances in which it could be dispersed in a defensive role in front of the Divisional Reserve Position where it could undertake penetration tasks from positions too exposed for un-armoured troops and use their mobility to move to alternative positions – in effect a mobile pillbox.

Although the British ultimately planned to put proportionately more tanks into the field than either the French or Germans, the reported state of the 1st Armoured Division – which was expected to arrive in May 1940 and have a counter-attack role as well as an exploitation role in conjunction with French armoured formations – in England during November 1939 (Table 3.2) illustrates just how retarded the British actually were in armoured vehicles compared to the Germans.[58] The War Office proposed to send out the next 'I' tank battalion (7th Battalion Royal Tank Regiment) with tracks with only 300 miles left on them. While these 300 miles were being used up it was hoped that reserves of tracks would be built up.[59] In March 1940, the War Office proposed to send out two more Divisional Cavalry Regiments, enabling three brigades of three regiments to be formed. During discussions on this, Gort said that this would be sufficient for the BEF's needs but was forced to admit that for reasons of petrol supply, there was a limit to the number of armoured units that could be maintained in France!

57 TNA: WO106/1777, 'Security of Western Front'.

58 Although the 1st Armoured Division did arrive in France as expected in May 1940, it was never able to join the BEF. As a stopgap, arrangements had been made with the French to purchase 100 Hotchkiss (two men) tanks if the British supplied castings at the rate of two sets for each Hotchkiss available for purchase. The original timetable allowed for the supply of these before the end of April 1940, but the French said they could now only supply 120 by the end of spring 1941. In the end, because of the poor performance of the Hotchkiss, the British decided to enquire if the French would supply Char B's on the same basis of exchange of castings instead.

59 The 7th Royal Tank Regiment did arrive in time to be able to join the BEF, forming the 1st Tank Brigade with the 4th Royal Tank Regiment, and took part in the so-called Arras counter-attack. This action (see Chapter 10) shows what might have been possible if only the Armoured Division could have joined the BEF in time.

Table 3.2: The state of the 1st Armoured Division as at 13 November 1939 compared with the full War Establishment and the proposed modified Establishment it was hoped to achieve by 1 May 1940.

	ACVs.	Scout Cars	Light tanks Mk. VIB	Light tanks Mk. VII	Cruisers Light	Cruisers Heavy	Close support
Full War Establishment	7	93	-	108	159	58	24
Establishment it was hoped to achieve by 1 May 1940	7	93	108	54	163	-	24
Establishment 13 Nov 1939	-	-	201	-	47*	-	-

* Of these, only 27 had gun mountings as at 13 November 1939.

Defence against attack from the air

Any enemy ground attack was expected to be combined with low flying air attacks. PAD measures were to be adopted for the protection of troops and material so as to offer the least possible target to air attack. Camouflage and slit trenches were the main methods of PAD. One of the first tasks all troops had on arrival in the British sector – and specified in all Standing Orders – was digging slit trenches in billeting areas. One recommendation for HQs and bases was the provision of Anderson ARP shelters, although it is unlikely that any were ever shipped over to France. Active defence was achieved with the use of anti-aircraft artillery and small arms fire. It was generally recognised that heavy losses to well entrenched infantry would not be inflicted by air attack. However, it was also recognised that such air attacks were likely to be frequently repeated with a moral effect out of all proportions to casualties inflicted. The only active defence would be by Bren guns mounted for an AA role against low flying aircraft and commanders were to site these guns to ensure a maximum density of fire over their area. Each platoon was responsible for its own air defence scheme and it was anticipated that in the early stages of any attack, they would be more concerned with opposing air attacks rather than ground attacks. Instructions specified that at least one Bren per platoon locality should be capable of being mounted in an AA role. These guns would revert to a ground action once a ground attack was imminent.

AA troops were deployed in the corps areas and on the LoC and were some of the first units of the BEF to disembark. They consisted of the 1st and 2nd AA Brigades, and had a combined resource of 72 heavy guns (twenty-four 3.7 inch and forty-eight 3 inch guns), 84 light guns (40mm Bofors), 192 anti-aircraft Lewis guns and 96 searchlights. Their first task was to protect the base ports of Cherbourg and Nantes during the disembarkation of the first contingent of the BEF and its transit to the assembly area. During the move from the assembly area to the concentration area, 1st AA Brigade undertook the defence of the crossings of the rivers Seine and Somme while the 2nd AA Brigade continued to provide protection for the base ports. The state of the French roads took a toll on the Bofors guns during the move forward with bent axles being reported and a lack of spare tyres meaning delays as punctures were repaired. After the BEF moved into *SD* Lille, the AA resource was divided between the LoC and forward area tasks. The French had asked the BEF to provide the gun defence for Lille, but this request was turned down as the BEF considered it a French responsibility and anyway it did not have sufficient guns to take on the role.

The decision to use the more easterly French ports, in particular Havre, for heavy shipments meant a re-examination of the AA defence. It had been assumed that it would not be possible to provide adequate AA defence for Havre due to the risk of attack from the seaward side. The prospect of the early delivery of Radio Direction Finding (RDF) equipment would largely alleviate this weakness and it was decided to install three heavy batteries and one light battery of AA guns in November to reinforce the French defences. In December, two heavy batteries and one light battery were installed at Boulogne. The first RDF sets (three G/L Mark I sets) were received in January 1940, two allotted to Havre and one to Boulogne. Dunkirk was also given AA protection in the form of one battery of light AA guns and two sections of searchlights, primarily to give some protection against mine-laying aircraft and also to protect the landing of the 1st Cavalry Division during December and January.

In the forward zone, the AA resource was deployed to protect GHQ in the area east of Arras and also for the protection of corps HQs, railheads, the Air Component aerodromes and key French electrical installations. About 75 percent of guns in the forward area were to remain silent so as not to give their position away unless enemy aircraft in formations of three or more were actually engaged on low level machine gunning and bombing attacks. The divisional organisation of light machine guns for AA defence was to be co-ordinated with the light AA guns as far as possible.

The BEF constantly faced shortages in AA equipments. For a start, it was in competition with ADGB for the 40mm Bofors. There simply were not enough guns to go around, so as a temporary substitute 15 mobile Naval Mark VIII 2 pdrs carried in lorries and mounted on baulks were sent out to the BEF along with 30,000 rounds of ammunition, which represented an entire month's worth of production. These guns took two hours to get into action and half an hour to get out of action. The possibility of providing armour piercing rounds for use with the Bofors gun in an anti-tank role was considered by the War Office. However, it was noted that this would interfere with the production of 2 pdr ammunition, and that there would be no spare capacity in production of this ammunition once the Armoured Division proceeded overseas. As it was envisaged that heavy tank attacks would be accompanied by heavy low flying attacks, it was decided not to press for the production of armour piercing rounds for the Bofors. Gort also highlighted the lack of spares for Predictors for the 3 inch anti-aircraft guns and missing height finders and deficiencies in equipment such as Kerrision Predictors and signal lights for the light AA units.

Although by January 1940, the AA resource had increased to 152 heavy guns (seventy-two 3.7 inch and eighty 3 inch guns), one hundred and twelve 40mm Bofors (of which six were on static mounts), thirty-six 2 pdr Mark VIII on static mounts, 136 Lewis guns and 192 searchlights, this was in no way considered sufficient for the adequate defence of the BEF. At a War Office conference on 5 December, Gort's representative had stated the BEF required 384 heavy AA guns and 396 light AA guns. The danger was mitigated to a certain extent by the French fixed defences at the ports of Cherbourg and Havre, and in the industrial areas of Lille, Douai and Bethune.

Because of the doubtful efficiency of searchlights used in conjunction with AA guns, it was the favoured policy of AA Branch GHQ to establish an illuminated fighter zone for the protection of the BEF against night bombing. As resources did not permit all-round protection, the zone was to be established to the north of the BEF barring the enemy's shortest route providing he continued to respect Belgian neutrality. The eastern flank of the zone was to rest on the Belgian frontier while the western flank was to extend to the English Channel in the neighbourhood of Boulogne. One immediate problem with this was that it included French gun zones, which barred the use of fighters. As a long-term project, it was suggested that a continuous illuminated corridor that enemy bombers could not outflank should eventually be established. This would extend from Calais, where it could be considered an extension of the air fighting zone in ADGB, to Switzerland. This required an estimated 1,900 searchlights and some 40 fighter squadrons, which was considered achievable if the French undertook their share of the corridor. This corridor would give good protection to the areas occupied by the Anglo-French armies, but little protection to the rest of France. On the other hand, extensions to the corridor could protect such places as Paris while defence in other areas could be dealt with by AA guns.

Gort decided to reject the proposal to form an illuminated air fighter zone in northern France until there was the possibility of forming the continuous corridor in which both British and French searchlights and fighters would contribute to. Instead, the BEF deployed its searchlights for the defence of the area occupied by the BEF in three roles: in gun zones for the benefit of AA guns in the BEF sector, for dazzle defence of the Air Component aerodromes and for anti-mine laying tasks at Dunkirk, Gris Nez and Boulogne and dazzle defence out to sea in co-operation with light AA guns. In the event of an advance into Belgium, it was the intention to examine the possibility of establishing an illuminated fighter zone to protect the BEF and its new railheads. This was possible as fighters would now be clear of French gun zones.

Perhaps the most unusual AA defence measure proposed was to use smoke generators to produce a thin haze over a wide area to prevent effective air attack against bridges, defiles and HQs. Trails were to take place at Porton to test the feasibility of this idea.

Air support for the BEF was a taxing issue. The question of Allied air co-operation in general and RAF co-operation with the BEF were never adequately settled during the period of the Sitzkrieg. There were several reasons why this was the case. Firstly, the French considered that the defence of their country should be the first priority and were constantly demanding more air support from Britain, especially fighter support. Being separated from the Continent by the Channel, Britain on the other hand, had little fear of being invaded; the only realistic way the enemy could attack Britain was with bombers. Consequently, a large number of fighters were required for ADGB. Secondly, the French believed that the whole bomber effort should be focused on opposing an enemy advance and were totally opposed to any bombing of Germany in fear of retaliation. British policy on the other hand considered that the war should be carried into enemy territory by attacking selected targets in the Ruhr with heavy bombers. Thirdly, it did not help that the Air Ministry and War Office were in sharp disagreement as to using the RAF in direct support of the Army.[60]

The AASF was originally to consist of two Echelons. The First Echelon consisted of ten medium bomber squadrons equipped with Battles while the Second Echelon was to be made up of ten Blenheim squadrons. The Second Echelon was cancelled in favour of the Blenheims operating from bases in Britain. The BEF was also to be accompanied by an Air Component comprising eight Army co-operation squadrons and four squadrons of fighters. The fighters were originally to have been Blenheims but Air Chief Marshal Dowding insisted modern fighters needed speed and climbing power and the decision was taken to send Hurricanes instead. During the first week of the war the ten Battle squadrons of the AASF and the four Hurricane squadrons of the Air Component crossed the Channel unmolested by the enemy.

Both Gamelin and Gort repeatedly called for more fighters and indeed a re-organisation and increase in British air strength was affected during the winter. In total, the RAF forces in France at the start of 1940 consisted of the Air Component with four Blenheim squadrons, four Hurricane squadrons, two Gladiator squadrons and five Lysander squadrons and the AASF of four Hurricane squadrons, two Blenheim squadrons and eight Battle squadrons. The authors of *Keep the Memory Green* noted that an enemy spy may have reported the situation as such:

60 On 27 September 1939, Ironside noted in a memorandum: 'The R.A.F. are devoting their main energies to building enormous bombers for long-distance bombing. Their idea is to destroy German industry and principally oil supplies. They have not trained with the view to close tactical co-operation with the Army. We have put up a paper asking for an Air Arm under our own control, fit to co-operate with us either in offence or defence. The production of such a force of aircraft is essential to our well-being. It should be produced, whatever the method by which it is produced. The question is so urgent that there can be no delay in the starting of production and training' (TNA: WO106/1720, 'NOTE BY C.I.G.S.', 27 September 1939).

> "The Gladiators are obsolete. They were shortly to be replaced; the Battles obsolescent, as slow as tram-cars and based in France only because their range is so short that France is the only place from which they can operate. As for the 'Lizzies' – *ganz ohne Bedeutung, Herr Reichsmarschall* – quite negligible – defenceless, slow, ridiculous."[61]

The commitment of eight Hurricane squadrons was generous though, as at the time there was inadequate modern fighter strength for the ADGB. The British Government's decision not to commit any more fighters above this level proved wise, as even if more were sent to France, it is doubtful if they would have been able to alter the events of May 1940.

With regards to heavy bombers, Bomber Command argued that they were not suitable for attacking small targets such as enemy columns and would be too vulnerable to AA defence in such attacks. They also pointed out the risk to Belgian civilians. Bombing the Ruhr, according to Bomber Command, would have a greater effect on the war in the long run as five of the eight railways that would be required to supply any German advance into Belgium ran through the Ruhr. Gamelin and the senior BEF Commanders were against such a policy and argued it would have no effect on the immediate battle as the German forces would have passed beyond the Ruhr. They also pointed out that the Allied armies would be facing a co-ordinated attack by the German Army and *Luftwaffe*, and the only way to meet this was by similar co-ordination.

In December, the system of command in the RAF was re-organised in France. An Air Officer in Command, Air Marshal A.S. Barratt, now commanded all RAF units in France, under the official title of British Air Forces France (BAFF). Air Marshal Barratt was made responsible for seeing that the BEF had at all times 'full assurance' regarding air support – a much better arrangement than the previous one where Gort had to apply directly to Air Officer Commanding AASF. However, he was also required to operate with regards to the Allied situation on the Western Front as a whole, i.e. he had to satisfy the demands of both Gort and the French High Command.[62] But at least now, a start could be made in training pilots in co-operation with the Army.

61 Butler & Selby Bradford, MBE, MC, *Keep the Memory Green,* p. 38.

62 The chain of communication for this co-operation with the French seems to have been very cumbersome. General Giraud remarked to André Maurois: 'Aircraft! Do you know how many aeroplanes I, the Commander of an Army, have at my disposal? Eight. Just eight. I know of course that there's the Royal Air Force and that it's excellent, but if I want to make a reconnaissance I have to ask General Georges who asks General Gamelin, who asks Marshal Barratt, who asks Vice-Marshall Blount, who has a reconnaissance made for me, but more often than not long after it would have been any real use.' (André Maurois, *The Battle of France,* p. 164).

Thought also had to be given to any advance into Belgium. The Air Component was made semi-mobile, equipped with transport to move ammunition and supplies etc. forward quickly if the advance to the Dyle was ordered. With what little intelligence that could be obtained in the light of Belgian neutrality, locations for airfields in Belgium had to be drawn up and estimates of supplies and materials required for making them useable.

The possibility of the Germans using air landing units was always a worry. Air landing units included both parachutists and air infantry battalions landed by aircraft. It was expected that these forces would be used either as small groups of parachutists tasked with destroying vital points, such as railways stations or bridges, and seizing areas of vantage pending the arrival of reinforcement from the air, or, in large numbers to effect surprise in major operations. In the latter case, both parachutists and air landing infantry would probably be employed in a combined attack, perhaps in the rear of the defences. For such an operation to succeed, air superiority would be required.

British intelligence believed that Germany had 3,000 to 3,600 trained parachutists and between 5,000 to 6,000 men in air landing battalions. The JU 52 was the aeroplane that transported both, which held 12 to 15 men and had a cruising speed of 138 mph with a range of 805 miles. Intelligence had identified a total of seven *Kampf Gruppen* with about 280 JU 52's maintained for special missions and about 700 JU 52's that could be employed as troop carriers.

Thus, theoretically an enemy force of approximately one division without heavy artillery could be landed. To deal with such a force would require the use of fighter aircraft and GHQ reserves. For smaller scale landings, the governing principal placed the responsibility for the defence of vital points or installations in corps or divisional areas on these formations. In particular, the defence of HQs was given a high importance. Neighbouring units were to mutually co-operate to achieve this. Units were expected to detail a piquet to deal with and destroy air enemy troops as soon as they landed. The suggested strength of a piquet for units was one company or its equivalent for an infantry battalion, 50 men for an artillery battery and one section for a field company. Other units were to find a piquet in proportion to their strength.

The normal duties of men selected to form the piquet would not be interrupted except when a landing took place. They were to be armed with rifles and light machine guns. Unit schemes would detail transport for their use. On an air landing being witnessed, these piquets were to take immediate action and call on neighbouring units to co-ordinate. Co-operation and liaison were also to take place with French protective troops stationed at vulnerable points, under the command of *Monsieur le Général Commandant le Group de subdivisions et la subdivisions de Lille Citadelle.* Of course, once altered to the danger, numerous reports were received of parachutists. Every small cloud or puff of an anti-aircraft round exploding could potentially be mistaken for enemy parachutists.

Gas warfare

Gas in its various forms had proved itself an effective weapon during the Great War. There was always the possibility that Germany would use it again to inflict casualties, reduce morale by compelling troops to wear gas masks or render areas of ground impassable. On 30 September, the War Cabinet authorised the despatch of charged chemical weapons to France as a precautionary measure. Initial arrangements were made to send out three thousand 250lb chemical bombs and 300 hundred spray containers to France, but this was delayed firstly due to production delays and secondly because the French would not allow them to be sent through the usual ports used by the BEF. The latter difficulty was eventually resolved by designating Fécamp as a special gas port.

The supply of chemical weapons was made more urgent by intelligence that suggested the Germans were experimenting with a new type of gas called Arsine. The British code word for Arsine was 'ARTHUR', just as gases in the Great War had been referred to as 'DICK', 'CLARK', 'ADAMSITE' etc. It could be deployed in compressed cylinders, shells and aircraft bombs or as a powder known as Calcium Arsenide. It was non-persistent, invisible and had no smell except in very high concentrations when a faint smell of garlic could be detected. The powder was grey-white in colour, and with contact with moisture would give off Arsine gas for up to one hour. High concentrations were fatal; effects were also cumulative, so low concentrations breathed in for long periods or frequently at short intervals were also dangerous.

First symptoms were stated to be blood in the urine. Longer term exposure resulted in headaches, nausea and vomiting. The British respirator gave fair protection against high concentrations – the gas passed through within four minutes, but a large proportion was absorbed by the charcoal in the filter so that the gas did not reach dangerous levels for about two hours. A detector, such as that used for blister gas, was considered an urgent matter, and detector paper Type 'A' was developed for 'ARTHUR'. It was recommended they were to be put in every occupied post, gun emplacement and pillbox, and also at intervals of every 50 yards in trenches.

If gas was used against the BEF, retaliation was to be immediate and chiefly from the air, in the form of gas bombs and spray. Gas spray was considered to generally achieve the best results over a wide area while bombs were effective on a small target, such as demolished bridges in order to delay repairs. Trials in Algeria showed that gas released from high altitude showed up as a white plume from the emission pipes which developed into a curtain which was clearly visible. However, gas from a high altitude at night would have a good chance of the element of surprise, as aircraft would be out of sight and the droplets may not be detected as they fell. But, the problem with high altitude spraying was that it was indiscriminate and demanded extremely accurate meteorological information. Civilians within the area would almost certainly be affected, which was considered politically unacceptable, at least until the enemy had used it extensively first. It was also easy to guard against with gas capes and respirators.

Low altitude spraying was obviously more accurate, but it made attacking aircraft very vulnerable to AA fire. Therefore, the combination of high altitude spraying during the night which could be employed against troops moving up to the front line under the cover of darkness, and at the same time, attacks undertaken with gas bombs on such places as railheads, bridges etc. where a concentration of gas was likely to delay enemy operations was considered the best option.

As at April 1940, the BEF had 261 charged 250lb spray containers, 809 charged 500lb spray containers and 3,330 charged 250lb LC bombs. The 250lb spray containers could only be used by Lysander's, but opinion at the time suggested these would never be spared for spraying, although crews had been trained in it. All aircraft could carry the chemical bombs, and Battle and Lysander squadrons had been trained in their use. The 500lb spray containers could only be used by Battles, although pipes suitable for the Blenheim were being manufactured. A larger 1000lb spray container was also under production, which would have to be carried by Wellingtons.

If chemical warfare was authorised, it was assumed that squadrons would operate at about 48 sorties per squadron per week. This would allow about one week of intensive spraying with available stocks. After that, it was assumed that the element of surprise would be lost anyway, and for sustained operations a smaller commitment would be all that was required after the initial intensive effort.

The Army could also respond in a limited way. By April 1940 there were as yet no gas shells for the 25 pdrs or 5.5 inch howitzers, but there were 28,000 charged mustard gas shells for the 6 inch howitzer. In addition, 1,460 Livens had been issued, equipping four chemical warfare companies, although there were no charged drums yet (4,700 were waiting to be charged at the manufacturing company Randle). Although production of mustard gas was satisfactory, no BBC (a tear gas) was expected until October 1940 and no phosgene until sometime in 1941.

Communications

Effective intercommunication, both from the front to rear and lateral, are essential in military operations. According to *FSR Vol. II 1935*, 'Intercommunication is a factor in which the defence, being stationary, should have an advantage over the attack'.[63] Although the French had provided some separate protected underground military telephone circuits, for instance for *SF* Escuat and *SF* Maubeuge, no provision for such circuits had been made for *SD* Lille. Thus, the BEF had to plan a system of intercommunication from scratch. If time allowed for the establishment of a defensive position, British policy stipulated that cable was to form the backbone of the communication system. The main intercommunication system was based on a permanent grid of rear to front cable arteries connected by laterals. The crossing points of the main arteries and laterals formed signal centres to which the various

63 *FSR Vol. II: Operations – General 1935*, p. 148.

HQs connected to with their own signal personnel. The whole system was to be buried, with priority given to the signal centres. The reason for this, according to the signalling manuals of the time, was that cable had the advantage of security, was quick and accurate, had a great traffic carrying capacity and allowed discussion by telephone which gave a sense of confidence. Although cable was vulnerable to damage by shell fire, the grid system would help ensure that a route was always open. It is interesting to note that one of the findings of a 2nd Division manning exercise was that officers had become 'telephone minded' with the result that telephone lines became badly blocked! The exercise concluded that if telegraph facilities existed, officers should be encouraged to make more use of the 'buzzer'.

Wireless sets were viewed as invaluable in mobile operations, and the sets in use by the Army – the No. 11, No.9 and No.3 – were designed to provide a relatively free use over the ranges required for mobile warfare. However, in defence they were only to be used in emergencies as an alternative means of communication if the line was cut. Wireless silence was to be maintained except in cases of urgency in the face of enemy action. But *ATM No.27* did emphasise the use of divisional cavalry regiments to provide 'battle' patrols in static warfare – in the form of carrier troops working forward – making full use of wireless sets to supply information on the situation of friendly and enemy troops in instances of large-scale assaults. In general terms though, the use of wireless was deemed risky as the enemy could intercept wireless signals, it was subject to interference by atmospheric conditions and the location of wireless sets could be determined by direction finding.[64] Wireless sets of the time were also by no means reliable.

Other means of inter-communication established were visual signalling in forward areas as an alternative to line and wireless communications, a Dispatch Rider Letter Service (DRLS) which ran periodically between HQs on a pre-arranged time table and message dropping stations for use with Lysander's. However, intercommunication between the British and French was almost entirely by civil telephone – supplemented by liaison officers and visits by commanders and their staffs – which was not exactly secure. The French insistence of wireless silence since the start of the war meant that outside the BEF zone, wireless communication hardly existed.

Civil defence

During active operations the BEF would not be in position to provide for the security of the civilians within its zone. The BEF inherited the French scheme to evacuate the

64 It is interesting to note that an R/T test carried out by the 3rd Division on 4 March 1940 from 10:00 a.m. to 11:00 a.m. to practice officers in speech and giving and receiving messages was unsuccessful on the whole, as only one message was passed in the hour, and this was only received by one battalion, interference being too bad for the other two battalions to hear anything.

civil population from Lille, Roubaix and Tourcoing in the event of a German invasion. The scheme was settled and could not be altered in principle. About 400,000 civilians were to be evacuated by rail and the remainder, of which the number was unknown, by road through the zone of the BEF by designated routes to collecting centres. Two Check Lines were established to divert refuges on to the designated routes. The evacuation was expected to last a week. If the evacuation from Lille was followed by refugees from Belgium, GHQ troops were to endeavour to deflect them onto routes laid out for the evacuation from Lille. The French *Gendarmerie* was also to be on duty to guide refugees on reserved routes.

4

Allied Strategy to meet a German Attack

Gort may have been responsible to the King and the British government for the safety of the BEF, but to the French he was no more than the commander of a single army in a group of armies. Pictures widely published in the press at the time, showing Gort and Gamelin standing side by side no doubt gave the impression of an equal relationship. It was not. Gort was not even directly subordinate to Gamelin: between them in the chain of command came Georges. The contribution the BEF made to the Allied cause in terms of manpower and material was small compared to that of the French and all agreed it would be Gamelin who would give the strategic directives which would decide how the Allied armies were to operate. Georges would issue detailed instructions to the BEF within the framework of Gamelin's strategic directives. This was despite the BEF being nominally part of the French First Army Group (*Général* Billotte). Gamelin's strategy to meet a German attack against the West was to result in the BEF not standing and fighting in the defences it laboured on all through the winter of 1939–40, but instead dashing into Belgium alongside the French Army to meet the invading Germans.

Background to Anglo-French relations and discussions

In response to the German attack on Poland on 1 September 1939, the French quickly completed their mobilisation and Gamelin concentrated his forces for a move into No Man's land between the Maginot Line and the Siegfried Line and reduce three salients: the Saar Offensive which opened on 7 September. This offensive was just the preliminary moves to a full-scale offensive once the Allies had fully built up their strength, and Gamelin only committed nine divisions to it. Gamelin intended to do nothing more than 'lean against the Siegfried Line' and test its strength, and to bring up heavy artillery to 'try his experiments upon the line'. Gamelin stated the offensive would fulfil France's commitment to Poland while distracting the Germans as the Allies completed their mobilisation and minimising French casualties at the same time. On launching his attack, Gamelin quickly concluded the situation in Poland was hopeless and he decided against committing further troops and support for the offensive, as Ironside noted on 16 September:

> General Gamelin has now definitely abandoned what little initiative he had seized and is preparing for two things:
>
> i. A local counter-attack [by Germany] against the positions he has taken in between the Maginot and Siegfried Lines. ...This counter-attack may come at any moment.
> ii. [A German] attack on a large scale through Belgium and Holland.[1]

Ironside was also unhappy with the British response, clearly seeing the great opportunity the Allies had missed to act against Germany:

> We have practically been at war a month and nothing has worked out as we thought it would. This wonderful Air Force of ours has not been used at all. A few futile droppings of pamphlets...a few bombings of "military objectives", a few reconnaissances and nothing more. None of the long-distance bombers have been used at all. The political creed is to remain "one behind the Germans" in bombing factories and depots ... Militarily we ought to have gone all out against the German the minute he attacked Poland.[2]

French troops dug in where they had been halted but having no intention of being caught in fieldworks beyond the range of support from the Maginot Line, the French thinned out their lines and by mid-October the Germans had retaken most of their territory seized by the French during the short-lived Saar offensive.

1 Colonel R. Macleod, DSO, MC & Denis Kelly (eds), *Time Unguarded: The Ironside Diaries 1937-1940* (New York: David McKay Company Inc., 1963), p. 108.

2 Ibid., p. 113. Gamelin did actually submit a proposal to bring immediate help to Poland by attacking Germany in the west through Belgium, Luxemburg and Holland. With most of the German Army and air force occupied in the attack on Poland, von Leeb's Army Group C had a force of only 11 trained divisions and 25 incomplete and largely untrained second line divisions to hold the Siegfried Line, still largely a 'construction site'. It has been suggested that the Allies would have enjoyed a temporary superiority of three to one on land and two to one in the air; Germany's industrial heartland would have quickly been occupied and the war over. Attacking Germany through Belgium had always been considered an option by the French, but the Belgian declaration of neutrality in 1936 had the effect of confining the French as they now had no option of attacking Germany other than a direct assault against the Siegfried Line unless they violated Belgian neutrality, and this was rejected by the French government. For their part, British politicians still hoped for a settlement with Hitler. Hitler claimed his invasion of Poland was nothing more than a 'rectification' of the frontier. Britain still hoped that Hitler had no desire for a long war, and that once the German Army had 'rectified' the frontier, Germany would seek peace with Poland, Britain and France.

After the fall of Poland and the rapid shift of German forces westwards a defensive strategy was the only one available to the Allies once other courses had been ruled out such as violating Belgian neutrality to attack Germany or the aerial bombardment of Germany. The French believed the war would be fought in four distinct phases. The first phase would be highly mobile, using largely mechanised forces and aircraft, lasting two to three weeks. If a decisive decision was not reached, the front would stabilise even more rapidly than in 1914. There would then follow a period of static warfare. The final stage would be when one of the armies succeeded in a methodical breakthrough of the other's lines and could exploit its success. With an economic blockade in place and Britain's industrial power, the French believed that the Allies would have the necessary time for a steady build-up of forces to achieve the required superiority over the Germans for the breakthrough, and by the mass employment of mechanised forces a rapid exploitation of success not known during the course of the last war.

The French views on the way the war would unfold certainly suited the British and there was a degree of complacency on the British side. Some in the British military hierarchy believed that Germany had little chance of success in the West unless the Allies were forced to disperse their effort. Most British politicians believed that Germany would not risk an attack against the West and that the determination of the Allies to build up their forces coupled with a British naval blockade would force Germany to the peace table. The French were less confident that Germany would not attack, which is not a surprise as they faced the threat of an invasion against their country.

Although there may have been broad agreement on the way the war would be fought, neither ally fully trusted the other. Those at home may have believed the dispatches from correspondents with the BEF, such as André Maurois and Skene Catling, who spoke of the 'hereditary' friendship between Britain and France. In fact, there was a degree of mistrust between the two allies. This arose first because of the British determination not to weaken the defence of Britain and British sea communications, which conflicted somewhat with the principal concern of the French – the protection of French soil. Secondly, there was an undercurrent of distrust between the two allies dating back to the Great War. British history popularly portrays the British Army having to bail out the French during their mutinies of 1917, then going on to largely win the war by itself in 1918. The French remember shouldering most of the burden during 1914–16, then having to come to the rescue of the British Army during Ludendorff's 1918 spring offensives. It should also be remembered that *Maréchal* Foch had been given the supreme command, placing British and Imperial Forces, along with the Americans, under his control. Furthermore, France, as already stated, was not prepared to carry the main burden of the land fighting again. Many in France also felt that war with Germany had only come about because Britain was spineless in not enforcing the Versailles Treaty, and that Britain could not be fully trusted in any war with Germany.

Although on the surface working relations between the Allies were cordial, that undercurrent of mistrust was always there. Gamelin is said to have believed that the Great War showed 'that one must always keep large French forces alongside the ...British. Whenever these were removed, they had to be rushed back in times of crises.'[3] Because of this belief, Gamelin was unwilling to give key roles to the BEF in any advance into Belgium as he simply did not believe the BEF capable of carrying them out. He is stated to have said:

> It is for us to give them [the British] moral support, to organize [sic] the strategy of the campaign, and to provide the necessary planning and inspiration.[4]

Others in the French Army certainly agreed with Gamelin. In his diary, a French officer, *Commandant* D. Barlone, notes the opinion of another French Officer with the French Mission to the British Army:

> According to the French officers, the British Army is not yet up to the mark. The officers' qualifications are moderate. They say that our Captains know more than British Colonels and that the troops are not sufficiently hardened, although they work much more than ours.[5]

This attitude of the French was noticed by some British officers. General Moulton (at the time a staff officer at GHQ) remembers that the French were patronising towards the British, regarding them as amateur soldiers. In some instances, units on the ground had no contact at all with neighbouring French forces; Captain Barclay remembers that the 2nd Battalion Norfolk Regiment on the right of the British sector, although having good relations with local farmers, had no liaison with the French division on their right.

Although Gort held the French in high regards, other senior British officers had doubts about the efficiency and professionalism of the French Army. Brooke's views on this subject are well known. On landing in France, he wrote about French inefficiency in his diary and wondered if they still had the same spirit and fighting qualities they had shown in the Great War. His doubts increased following a visit to the Maginot Line and witnessing a parade of French troops:

> Seldom have I seen anything more slovenly and badly turned out. Men unshaven, horses ungroomed, clothes and saddlery that did not fit, vehicles dirty,

3 Robert Tombs & Emile Chabal (eds), *Britain and France in Two World Wars: Truth, Myth & Memory* (London: Bloomsbury, 2013), p. 6.
4 Ibid.
5 D. A. Barlone, *A French Officer's Diary: 23 August 1939 – 1 October 1940* (Cambridge: CUP, 1942), pp. 35-36.

> and complete lack of pride in themselves or their units. What shook me most, however, was the look in the men's faces, disgruntled and insubordinate looks, and, although ordered to give "Eyes left," hardly a man bothered to do so.[6]

Ironside also had his doubts. However, he was more reserved with his comments, reflecting instead upon the reality that the BEF relied upon the French Army for its security:

> I tried in my mind to sum up the state of the French Army and its fighting value. I must say that I saw nothing amiss with it on the surface. The Generals are all tried men, if a bit old from our view-point. None of them showed any lack of confidence. None of the liaison officers say that they have seen any lack of morale after the long wait they have had, after the excitement of mobilization [sic]. I say to myself that we shall not know until the first clash comes. In 1914 there were many officers who failed, but old Joffre handled the situation with great firmness. Will the *Blitzkrieg*, when it comes, allow us to rectify things if they are the same? I must say I don't know. But I say to myself that we must have confidence in the French Army. It is the only thing in which we can have confidence. Our own Army is just a little one, and we are dependent upon the French. We have not even the same fine Army we had in 1914. All depends on the French Army and we can do nothing about it, but it is up to us to back it up and not to deny it. The only thing I can say is that the men are not doing the amount of work in digging-in which I should like to have seen.[7]

The British were also well aware of the French sensitivities over the difference between their own manpower and that of Germany. Ironside observed:

> They consider that, at some stage of the war, there will be heavy fighting on the Western Front, and they want us to bear our fair share of the resulting casualties. They are almost certain to continue to pressure on us to send the maximum number of divisions to France, even though such action may not be the best from the strategical point of view. [8]

Another complication arose over the two cardinal rules agreed by both the French and British: that a battle of encounter was to be avoided at all costs and that the enemy would be met in well prepared defensive positions. This certainly held true for the British given the weak state of the British Army, but, as we shall see, it was not so

6 Arthur Bryant, *The Turn of the Tide: Based on the War Diaries of Field Marshal Viscount Alanbrooke* (London: Collins, 1957), p. 71.
7 Macleod, DSO, MC & Kelly (eds), *Time Unguarded*, pp. 203-204.
8 TNA: WO166/1685, 'Our War Strategy'.

straight forward with regards to the French. None of this made for a fully harmonious alliance or approach to planning the strategic direction of the war.

Plan E

The Maginot Line proper ended suddenly: it did not continue along the Franco-Belgian border to the North Sea. In the last war, Count von Schlieffen's plan called for Germany to ignore the fortified border with France and instead swing through Belgium to attack the undefended Franco-Belgian frontier. The French were well aware of the possibility of a similar manoeuvre, and especially the threat to the industrial region centred on Lille. To guard against this possibility, France had five armies along the frontier: the Second Army (*Général* Huntziger) from the end of the Maginot Line roughly to Sedan, the Ninth Army (*Général* Corap) from Sedan to the valley of the Oise, the First Army (*Général* Blanchard) from there to Maulde, the BEF from Maulde to Toufflers, and the Seventh Army (*Général* Giraud) from there to the sea. The coast was further guarded by troops under the command of *Vice-amiral* Abrial – known by British troops as 'Admiral Nord'.

But, as we have already seen, if the Germans tried a repeat of the Schlieffen plan, the French never had any real intention of fighting on the frontier: instead they intended to swing their Armies into Belgium to meet the enemy advance. France had already produced plans for this: Plan C (1930), Plan D (1933), Plan Dbis (1935) and Plan E (1938). Plan D envisaged a defensive line based on the River Dyle while Plan Dbis emphasised rapidity of the Belgian manoeuvre following Germany's declaration of rearmament. Plan E limited the Belgian manoeuvre to forming a defensive position based on the River Escaut. Although the depth of advance into Belgium differed between these plans, they all had the same intention: to form a continuous front and grind down the German Army which would be forced to make frontal attacks. This may well have been possible with Belgian co-operation but was essentially a very risky gamble following Belgium's declaration of neutrality. Still, Gamelin, had no hesitation in pushing forward his forces into Belgium to meet a German invasion from a new defensive line even if the Belgians only called on the Allies the moment they were attacked. He recognised that this risked an encounter battle – and as we saw in Chapter 2 was keen to develop defences along the Franco-Belgian border in case such a manoeuvre failed – but decided the advantages outweighed the risk. It would keep the main fighting off French soil, add the Belgian Army to the Allied strength, and it would provide him with the opportunity to eventually attack the Germans away from the protection of their Siegfried Line.

The British were against any such move into Belgium. With the reluctance of the Belgians to enter direct staff talks, Ironside reported to the Cabinet on 19 September that this put the BEF in a very difficult position. He considered that in the event of a German attack, any Belgian pleas for help would have to be resisted as any move into Belgium would resort in battles of encounter – such as Mons and Le Cateau in the of opening month of the Great War – for which the BEF was unprepared for. Simply put, unless the Belgian attitude altered and concerted plans were made with them in time before the German advance, Ironside considered that the priority should be to build up the defences along the Franco-Belgian border to meet the expected attack. He was very blunt with the War Cabinet in opposing such an advance:

> I gave them a fright this morning. I told them that Gamelin now fears a German attack in the West. I explained to them that the French defences on the left are practically non-existent. Gamelin is the commander of the only army in the field–the British Army has not yet arrived; anyhow it is no good yet. I told them that our Army is not properly equipped, and that the men were thrown together just before they embarked. I gave them my opinion that the B.E.F. is unfit to advance into Belgium or to fight in the open, and that it could only dig in and hang on. I said that, therefore, we most oppose the French plan to put us on the Escaut.[9]

Ironside's statement to the War Cabinet had annoyed rather than frightened them. On 20 September Hore-Belisha, Lord Hankey and Dewing went over to France to discuss the issue with Gamelin and Daladier. Gamelin explained his preference for some form of movement to the Escaut if Belgium was attacked: firstly, it was an excellent anti-tank obstacle in its lower reaches and secondly it gave depth to the frontier defences, a depth that could not be achieved in the rear due to the urban mass of Lille, Roubaix and Tourcoing. He emphasised that the decision would only be taken if time was available to organise defences before being attacked and with note to the conditions in which the Belgian Army withdrew so as to avoid an encounter battle.

Ironside renewed his opposition to the idea, pointing out the danger of being caught out in the open during a forward rush, particularly by low level bombing attacks, and that an improvised defence on the Escaut could only be linear and ineffective. It would mean 'coming out of our good prepared positions and going into others which are quite unprepared' with no dumps, no supplies, no line built, and only 35 miles from the sea with long lines of communication.[10] Georges, on the other hand, was confident that the BEF motor transport echelons would give the BEF a wide radius of action.

To be sure, when the BEF moved into the line at the start of October, it seemed unlikely that there would be a dash into Belgium. At this stage, Gamelin did not anticipate a wide German sweep through parts of Holland and Belgium but expected them to move through the Ardennes and south of the Meuse. The move to the Escaut was just a 'project'. Initial orders issued by the BEF stated that the frontier defences were to be held with outposts established across the Belgian border if the situation

9 John Kennedy, *The Business of War: The War Narrative of Major-General Sir John Kennedy* (London: Hutchinson & Co. (Publishers) Ltd., 1957), p. 24.

10 Macleod, DSO, MC & Kelly (eds), *Time Unguarded*, p. 113.

permitted. The task of the outposts was to gather information and not resist. The French intended to hold their current positions, although the French Seventh Army would carry out delaying actions on the Messines Ridge and Yser Canal and send out reconnoitring cavalry to the Mons – Charleroi line.

As German troops began to move west after their victory in Poland, warnings of an impending attack on the Low Countries began to reach the Allies in mid-October. The probable date for the attack was expected to be between 12 and 15 November. The intelligence was good, as Hitler was indeed planning to attack. Hitler realised that time was not on his side, and that German superiority in arms would soon be offset 'by England, which is constantly growing stronger.'[11] When it became obvious that peace would not be made with the Allies, he planned for an immediate offensive in the West to ensure 'the destruction of the ability of the Western Powers ever again to oppose the development of the German people in Europe.'[12] Preparations went forward for an attack on Belgium and Holland with Hitler informing his Generals that Operation Yellow, the code name for the offensive, was to commence on 12 November.

On 6 October, prompted by Gamelin's fear of a German attack, Ironside visited France. A conference was held at *GQG* to discuss the threat. At this conference both Gamelin and Ironside outlined how they envisaged the German attack would unfold.

Gamelin reiterated that the French would not carry out an offensive as they could not withstand the losses. He hoped that when the German attack came, they would smash themselves on the strong Allied defences. When they were sufficiently weakened, Gamelin would launch a counter-attack. As already noted, the Allied defences were not a continuous line: the Maginot Line was comprised of a series of forts along the Franco-German frontier from Switzerland to Longwy, while along the Belgian border the defences comprised of field works and pillboxes. Gamelin expected the German armour to penetrate the gaps between the Maginot forts, but if all posts held firm, the following German infantry and transport columns could be stopped, isolating the armour from supplies and support. With no supplies of ammunition or fuel, the armour would come to a halt and then be ripe for counter-attack. Gamelin advocated defence in depth. In support of the Allied line were local reserves with a role to support and reinforce the front and to counter-attack. In the rear he had assembled a general reserve of 18 divisions situated around Paris which could utilise the railways to move to any threatened part of the front.

At this point, it is interesting to note that *FSR Vol. III* noted the risk in the type of battle Gamelin planned to fight, and it is almost prophetic in this matter. It stated that planning such a battle promised well, as defence in a prepared position was more economical than attack and the battle was fought on the ground of the defenders choosing and not the enemy's, but it did carry risk: 'The chief difficulty is that the enemy can, unfortunately, seldom be trusted to play the role assigned to him exactly as

11 Bryant, *The Turn of the Tide,* p. 59.
12 Ibid, p.58.

forecasted. He attacks at an unexpected place, at an unexpected time or in unexpected strength' and the defender would 'find himself induced or forced to fight the battle on the enemy's plan rather than on his own.'[13] To fight such a battle successfully and launch the counter-move at the right time would require a great deal of skill, which, for the Allies, was sadly lacking in May 1940.

Gamelin anticipated that at first Germany would launch a pinning attack and push the French back to the Maginot Line. He did not intend to oppose this attack but instead planned to fall back on the Line. He expected the main German attack would come from the north, either a big sweep through Belgium or a shorter move through Luxemburg and the Ardennes then turning south to outflank the Maginot Line. The latter he now thought unlikely as there were good defences behind Luxemburg and he regarded the Ardennes as impassable for tanks (he acknowledged that infantry could still move through and cross the Meuse but considered that such an operation would take a substantial amount of time to organise, allowing French reserves plenty of opportunity to move up and restore the situation). He thought the only place where the decisive battle could be fought was on the Belgian plains. The date of the main German attack through the Low Countries was uncertain, but due to the winter weather he considered the principal threat would have passed by 10 November.

On the other hand, Ironside considered the main attack would come through Luxemburg and the Ardennes, and thence along the Franco-Belgian border, with the Germans using the Meuse to protect their right flank. Despite their differences in opinion as to where the Germans would strike, both Ironside and Gamelin were satisfied with a move into Belgium to the Escaut. If Gamelin was right, the Allies could support Belgium and add their Army to the Allied force as well as holding a shorter line. This would enable more forces to be withdrawn into the general reserve for the eventual counter-attack. If forced back, they could withdraw onto the frontier defences. If Ironside was right, the Allies could hit the Germans in a pincer-like counter-offensive from the north by the move into Belgium and from the south with the general reserve situated around Paris. Liddell Hart had expressed a similar opinion in his book *The Defence of Britain*, but noted that for such a counter-offensive to succeed fully, it was vital that full use of the Meuse was made as an obstacle to the attacker. Ironside had now relaxed his opposition to any move into Belgium as he had become more concerned about allowing Germany to seize territory from which it could then install bombers to attack Britain at short range. Some at GHQ also accepted Gamelin's proposed move into Belgium: Pownall described it as a much better option 'than sitting back on the French frontier and giving up the whole of Belgium'.[14]

Although Ironside no longer opposed a move into Belgium, he was still not entirely happy with the plan. He did not fully trust French intentions. Ironside was well

13 *FSR Vol. III: Operations – Higher Formations 1935* (London: The War Office, 1935), p. 55.
14 Brian Bond (ed.), *Chief of Staff: The Diaries of Lieutenant-General Sir Henry Pownall* (London: Leo Cooper, 1972), p. 253.

aware of the French cynicism towards the British and he felt that if the opportunity arose, the French would push the BEF out to the extreme left in direct touch with the Belgians. At a conference held on 13 October to discuss the projects for the advance of the Allied armies into Belgium, Georges offered the BEF a choice between the most northern sector joining up with the Belgians at Antwerp or to advance more or less directly to its front with its right directed on Brussels.[15] With the former option, Ironside thought the BEF might then be left in a position in which they, along with *les braves Belges*, could be isolated and cut off. Only if there was a French force of at least corps strength between the BEF and the Belgian Army was he confident that the French *GQG* would maintain an interest in the fate of the BEF. Gort strongly agreed with this view and chose the latter option. Ironside was also concerned with comments from Georges, which suggested to him that he may be thinking of grander schemes and moving away from the French determination not to get caught out in the open. At the conference of 13 October, Georges had reiterated that the Belgians were unlikely to ask the Allies into their country until attacked, and hence the Allies should look after their own interests and not be drawn into an unknown and dangerous situation, but that this did not apply to the advance to the Escaut as this was vital for the protection of the Lille industrial area.

Both the BEF corps commanders were also uneasy over the planned move into Belgium. On 17 October, Dill wrote to Gort giving his conclusions of the general situation. Dill recognised that time was the one thing Germany could not afford to give the Allies. Therefore, he considered it unlikely that Germany would be content to just regain lost ground in the Saar sector and resume their 'peace offensive'. Germany could decide to force a result by a decisive attack in the Saar sector by turning the Maginot Line proper by way of Luxemburg. However, this would bring them into contact with a *Secteur Fortifié*, behind which French reserves were then well placed to meet such an attack. He thus thought it unlikely Germany would attempt to reach a decision in the Saar sector.

Dill recognised Britain's sea power as a major threat to Germany. If Germany could gain air and naval bases in the Low Countries her position to launch successful attacks against British naval power would be much increased. Germany may be satisfied to limit any offensive against the West to occupying Holland to secure naval and air bases, but this would not force a quick decision so also seemed an unlikely course of action to him. There then remained the possibility of a strong attack through Belgium aiming at the envelopment of the Allied left flank. If this did not achieve a decisive result, Germany would at least have air and naval bases in Flanders. Such a manoeuvre through Belgium would be a risky operation if resistance was met due to the number of water obstacles. However, as Belgium was neutral and had no clear desire to fight Germany, he considered it prudent to prepare for a sudden German

15 Georges did not want the French 51st Division included in an advance into Belgium; instead he wished it to remain as a reserve in the Roubaix area.

attack, with leading mechanised forces advancing at 50 miles a day. Such an advance could get through these obstacles before the Belgian Army carried out demolitions or organised adequate defence of them.

If the Belgians, supported by the Allied air force, put up a strong defence, Dill believed that a German attack could not gain a quick success. However, given the uncertainty regarding the Belgians, he concluded it 'would be a mistake to abandon the French Frontier Defences, on which much work has been done, for the move forward to the line of the Escaut unless we can be sure of a comparatively undisturbed week in which to organize [sic] its defence.'[16] He made the very valid point that if time was required to organise the present frontier positions to meet a German attack, the same must also be true of Escaut front. Brooke agreed with Dill, noting in his diary 'the danger of leaving our present prepared position for one totally unprepared'.[17] To Brooke, the idea of the BEF meeting the panzers and Luftwaffe on the open Belgian plains before they had become fully equipped and completed their training 'was fantastic and could only have resulted in disaster.'[18] Gort and Pownall were uneasy about the pessimistic views increasingly expressed by the two corps commanders as they feared the pessimism could spill down the ranks. Gort probably shared the views of his corps commanders but only expressed them once to his personnel assistant, the Earl of Munster. He told Munster one evening that he had heard that Germany was planning to attack the West with 10 armoured divisions, and then stated: 'In that case, we haven't an earthly chance.'[19]

So now the BEF had to plan for two scenarios: to stand and fight on the frontier defences or to move forward and fight on the River Escaut. If the decision was taken to sand and fight on the frontier, on receipt of the code word 'BE PREPARED', troops who would garrison the frontier defences were to bring them to a state to meet the attack in two stages. Stage 1 was final preparations and involved completing defence works as fully as possible. Stage 2 was manning the defences. Mobile elements were to move into Belgium to carry out reconnaissance and demolitions. The 12th Lancers would be sent forward for reconnaissance between the River Escaut and River Dendre. Behind the 12th Lancers, forward divisional cavalry regiments (under the command of Brigadier F.E. Hotblack, DSO and Bar, MC and Bar, and known as 'HOTBLACK' Force) would move forward and secure crossings on the River Escaut.[20] Following on, mobile detachments accompanied by demolition parties were to be pushed forward (Force 'J'). The mobile detachments comprised of field

16 TNA: WO167/124, Dill to Gort, 17 October 1939, I Corps General Staff War Diary.
17 Bryant, *The Turn of the Tide,* p. 64.
18 Ibid, p. 65.
19 J.R Colville, *Man of Valour: Field Marshall Lord Gort VC* (London: Collins, 1972), p. 155.
20 Major Hotblack was given command of the newly established Intelligence and Reconnaissance Department of the Heavy Branch of the Machine Gun Corps – later renamed the Tank Corps – during the Battle of the Somme in 1916 and excelled in this role for the remainder of the war. In 1940 he was recalled home and promoted Major-

artillery, anti-tank guns and mobile infantry. Once arrived on the River Escaut, the mobile detachments were to relieve HOTBLACK Force which was then to move forward to the River Dendre to cover the withdrawal of the 12th Lancers and carry out the demolition of bridges over that river. The role of the mobile detachments was to secure the crossings over the Escaut, cover the demolition of bridges over that river and delay the enemy. The French First Army on the BEF right was also to send forward motorised reconnaissance units and if available a light mechanised division to harass and delay the Germans on the line Binche – Mons and the Brussels – Charleroi canal south of Seneffe. On the BEF left, the French XVI Corps was to send forward reconnaissance units to the River Escaut.

If the decision was taken to fight on the River Escaut, the BEF was to push forward reconnaissance units, mobile detachments and HOTBLACK Force as described. The main body of the BEF would move forward to the River Escaut and be prepared to fight on the line Maulde to Rossuyt. Infantry were to march by night while motorised transport moved by day at a density of five vehicles per mile if possible but not exceeding 10 vehicles per mile to minimise the danger of air attack. The French First Army would hold its current position but would send forward the 2nd Light Mechanised Division. The French XVI Corps was to move forward on the BEF left with three divisions to the River Escaut from Rossuyt to the Ghent bridgehead and to connect with Belgian forces there. It was also to send forward reconnaissance units to the River Dendre. At this stage in the crises, the French XVI Corps was still based at St Omer. Both Dill and Brooke feared that German air attacks on communications would mean it may not arrive in time either to reinforce the frontier defences or take part in the move into Belgium. In such a case, the four French and four British divisions on a front of some 60 miles would have little hope of success. Further confusion arose from the fact that the French XVI Corps orders at the time only stipulated weak reconnoitring detachments moving into Belgium, which would have left the British flank in the air if it moved up to the Escaut! Ironside's fears about French intentions appeared to be justified.

It was the weather that saved the Allies, with the meteorological report for 7 November so bad that Operation Yellow was postponed. By mid-November, the apparent tension had considerably eased, and troops were no longer held at notice; HOTBLACK HQ was disbanded on 30 November.

Plan D

By the start of November, the French were taking the question of an invasion of Holland seriously. Gamelin believed Hitler could not remain inactive due to internal politics and would attempt something during the winter; probably a blitzkrieg against

General and given command of the 2nd Armoured Division. His military career came to an untimely end in spring 1940 following a probable stroke.

Holland, with Belgium left intact for the time being. Holland could then be used as a base to attack Belgium, the same method that had been employed in Czechoslovakia and Poland. Gamelin was convinced that if Germany attacked Holland and Belgium, the French and British must go to their aid otherwise both would be defeated in detail, with the loss of 22 Belgian and five Dutch divisions to the Allies. The Belgians had enquired as to what they should do if Germany attacked Holland. Gamelin had replied that he was happy, if the Belgians agreed to join in, to come to the assistance of the Dutch but would need permission to cross Belgian territory. The Dutch plan of defence was based around two systems of inundations, an outer system behind their frontier and an inner system protecting Amsterdam and Rotterdam, known as the 'fortress of Holland'. These defences reached no further south than the Meuse, leaving the mouth of the River Escaut uncovered. If invited by the Belgians to go to the assistance of the Dutch, Gamelin planned to advance at once and occupy it.

On 7 November, Ironside received notice that Gamelin wanted a conference to deal with the action to be taken if Germany attacked Holland only or launched a general attack in the area. He was accompanied to the conference, which was held on 9 November, by both Gort and Air Chief Marshal Newall. Gamelin held a final conference on 16 November, attended by Gort, and *Généráls* Georges Billotte (Commander of the French Army Group No. 1, comprising First Second and Ninth Armies), Blanchard and Corap, when Plan D was finally settled upon.

During these discussions, Gamelin stated that the second situation, i.e. a general attack in the area, was now unlikely until the spring. As the autumn rains closed in, the dykes and streams would soon be full and much of the countryside would become sodden. As the countryside dried up in the spring, Gamelin considered the German options were to launch an attack through Belgium and possibly Holland into northern France or attack down from the north behind the Maginot Line. He had by now completely disregarded an attack through the Ardennes, believing that the countryside with its deep valleys, wooded heights and traversed by the Meuse was unsuitable for armoured warfare.

Although direct staff talks were still not taking place with the Belgians, plans for a deeper advance into Belgium had already been discussed by the Allies but only in terms of a broad outline of possibilities. These plans were based around reinforcing the Belgians on their defences along the Albert Canal and the River Meuse (Figure 4.1 and also see Appendix II for a description of the Belgian defences). It was argued that only with such a deep move into Belgium could the Belgian Army hope to oppose the German invasion, with the support of its French and British allies. Indirect talks between the French and Belgians convinced Gamelin that the Belgian Army could hold out for a considerable period of time on the defences near the German – Belgian frontier. However, *GQG* did rule out supporting the Belgians directly on the Albert Canal and the Meuse as moving so far into Belgium was judged to be a too risky adventure.[21] Instead, the French had suggested to the Belgians that the new Brussels defences that they were working on should be joined up to the River Namur and if this was done, it might be possible for Allied forces to move to this line and reinforce them. Such a move would be a succession of bounds from one anti-tank obstacle to the next. There were three possible lines that could be occupied: the rivers Escaut, Dendre and Dyle.

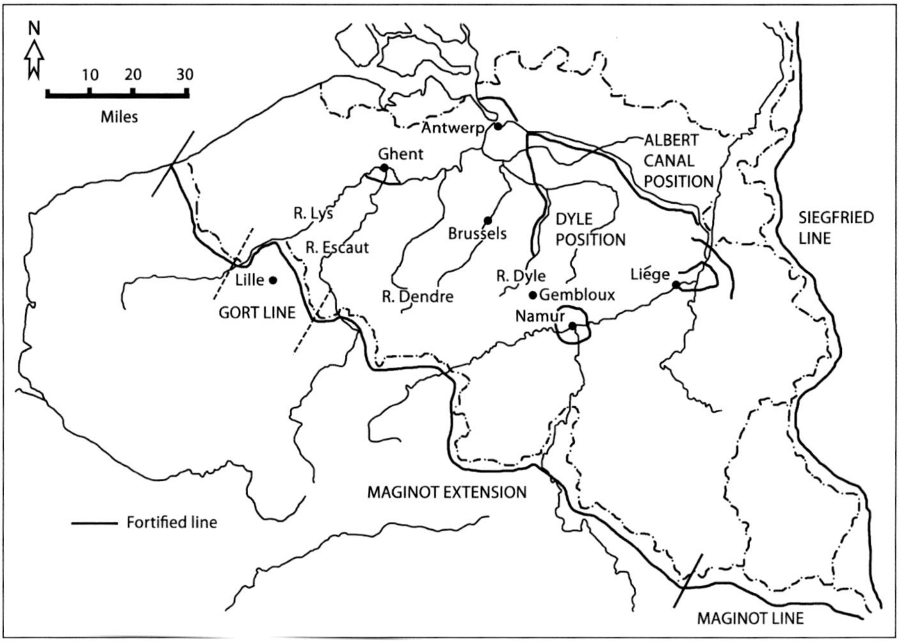

Figure 4.1: Map showing the various Belgian defensive positions, and the Maginot and Siegfried Lines for reference.

21 The War Office considered that supporting the Belgians along the Meuse – Albert Canal was the only chance of success for Plan D because of the weakness of the Dyle Position. In a memo dated 2 February, Dewing (DMO) noted the great strategical advantage of stopping the Germans on the Dyle by the shorter front it would offer but was concerned that the Belgians had far from fully developed the position. Pillboxes had been constructed in its northern area but only along the front line. To the south, even the front line was 'in progress' only. He considered that it would take a week for the Allies to arrive on the position and a further two weeks would be needed to bring it up to strength. In the meantime, the Allies would be relying on the Belgian Army to hold off the Germans. The Belgians neither had the reserves or offensive training to restore the situation if the Germans should break through. He considered that the only way sufficient time could be gained to develop the Dyle position was if the Allies reinforced the Belgians on their front line along Meuse – Albert Canal. Ideally armoured forces would be required to counter-attack German forces that broke through, but as the Allies had insufficient armoured forces for this task, infantry would have to be used to reinforce the Belgians instead. They could at least prevent German infantry from securing crossings over the Canal for tanks. He thought six to eight infantry divisions would be required for this role, and that the Allies would have to accept serious losses in them.

The Escaut had the advantage of a short advance. It was an excellent anti-tank obstacle and covered the mouths of Rhine and Meuse. However, as already noted, it had one serious disadvantage in that there was only a corridor of 30 miles depth between it and the sea for the lines of communication. A German breakthrough on the front would soon reach the sea, threatening all troops in Belgium. Greater depth and more room for manoeuvre were required. The Dendre was ruled out as it was not much of an anti-tank obstacle in the summer. The Dyle was a good anti-tank obstacle, it would be close to the Belgians fighting on the Albert Canal who could fall back on the river if necessary, and it had the fortress of Antwerp on its left flank from which help could be organised for the Dutch or the Dutch could fall back to. It also placed Britain out of range of enemy bombers. However, the move to the Dyle was much further than the Escaut. Although the Allied mobile units where capable of such a dash, they had inherently been trained for a defensive battle; if they could not dig in and establish their artillery on the Dyle before the Germans arrived, the battle would become one of encounter.

Plan D involved four Armies moving into Belgium: the French Ninth to the Meuse south of Namur, the French First to the line Namur – Wavre, holding the so-called Gembloux Gap, the BEF in the centre round Brussels to the Dyle and linking up the Antwerp defences and the French Seventh on the left from Antwerp. The French Seventh Army had an independent role, operating behind and to the left of the Belgians at Antwerp, covering the Allied left flank and acting as an operational reserve. The French Second Army would deploy from Sedan to Longwy and the start of the Maginot Line. The plan was to be undertaken in three methodical advances; lines would only be occupied if they could be reached with certainty before the Germans. The first advance would be to the Escaut, as already planned for. The second move would be an advance with light forces to the Dendre; there was to be no question of fighting on the Dendre, it was to be on the Escaut or Dyle. The third advance to the Dyle would only be undertaken if the main body of the Allied forces could reach it with certainty of not being caught in the open.

Although Gort, Ironside and Newall all accepted Gamelin's plan, the War Office Joint Planning Committee tried to 'shoot it into splinters.'[22] The Committee considered that defensive positions so far advanced could not be prepared in time or that the RAF could be deployed in good time to support ground troops. The spirit of the French was admired but 'their buoyant, ill-founded optimism' was deplored, as no new arguments had been put forward by Gamelin to justify his contention that the Allied armies could reach more advanced lines and establish themselves before being attacked by the Germans.[23] But even as they presented their case, they knew it was doomed, as France, the stronger partner, had the final say. Gamelin, on discovering that his plans had been discussed in such a manor was furious and objected to the

22 Kennedy, *The Business of War*, p. 30.
23 Ibid, p. 31.

criticism of his plan 'by a Committee of junior officers' and 'that it was his plan, it was a very good plan, and that he meant to carry it out.'[24] The Cabinet was reminded by Ironside that, in expressly appointing Gort under the French Command, they could not really intervene as Gort had agreed to the proposal and he had accepted Gort's decision. Following a meeting of the Allied Supreme Council in Paris on 17 November, Chamberlain also placed great importance on holding the Germans as far east as possible. Chamberlain's support for the plan, along with Ironside's statement, closed the matter as far as the British Government was concerned.

Plan D certainly had political and military merits and it is easy to see why Gamelin accepted the risk of an encounter battle. It was certain that if the Allies stayed in the frontier defences, the Belgian Army would collapse quickly once they realised that the Allies would not come to their aid. Plan D would add the Belgian Army to the Allied strength as well as considerable depth to the Allied line. The frontier positions would still be insurance against the failure of the Belgian manoeuvre.[25] The strategic reserves in the north and around Paris would have been well placed to give support to any part of the front. Moreover, it would have been politically disastrous on the world stage if the Allies had abandoned Belgium the way they had Poland. Having recognised the political benefits of Plan D, British planners also recognised the military risk:

> In the best case strategically, the Allies might hold the Germans indefinitely on the line of the DYLE or ALBERT CANAL. In the worst, the Allied left after failing to reach a position in BELGIUM, or after being defeated thereon, might be driven from their defences on the FRANCO-BELGIAN frontier with unpredictable consequences.[26]

A scenario was imagined in which the Germans invaded on say 1 March 1940. A week or so later the Germans had forced the Albert Canal but had been checked by the Allies on the Dyle. A period of three weeks or a month of fighting then could be expected, in which the Germans launched local actions to gain positions of advantage for a breakthrough. The fighting on the Dyle was expected to consume large amounts of ammunition and result in large losses of material. If the Germans achieved the breakthrough, the Allies could not expect to hold the Escaut for long. The Allies would inevitably have to fall back on the defences along the Franco-Belgian border – a withdrawal of some 70 miles under continuous pressure. This withdrawal would also

24 Ibid.
25 The French certainly had confidence that the frontier defences would halt a German attack if the Allies were forced out of Belgium. For example, Major D.A. Barlone writes: 'Our system of defence at the frontier, although imperfect, would shelter us if the Germans drove us back, and there they would break their teeth' (D. A. Barlone, A *French Officer's Diary,* p. 33).
26 TNA: WO106/1664, 'Note on possible course of operations affecting B.E.F. France during 1940, for the purpose of assessing rates of material wastage', December 1939.

result in a large loss of vehicles and equipment. The period of delaying on the Escaut and withdrawal to the frontier defences might be two weeks. Having gained contact with the frontier defences, it was expected the Germans would have to pause for two weeks – although there would still be heavy fighting in local operations – before they were ready to attack in strength. A period of fighting for up to six weeks was then expected as the Germans attempted to break through the frontier positions. If they were unsuccessful, the front would stabilise and trench warfare would ensure. The scenario did not address the question of what would happen if the Germans did successfully break through.

It was not only the British corps commanders who expressed reservations about moving out their prepared defences for an advance into Belgium. Georges was also against both plans. He was particularly unhappy about pushing forward the French Seventh Army up to the mouth of the Escaut as he had planned to keep it behind the Allied left as a strategic reserve. Writing to Gamelin on 30 November, Georges stated:

> In case of an enemy attack in strength on the centre of our line...we could be deprived of the necessary means to strike back. [27]

Gamelin ignored Georges' concerns and even went as far as excluding him from talks with military and civilian leaders to get agreement for the planned move into Belgium.

Plan D: Breda Variant

By the end of November, Gamelin had clearly decided the only options to meet a German invasion of Belgium would be an advance to the Dyle or the Escaut. Which plan was to be adopted would only be decided by the French High Command when the time came, depending on how the Belgian Army was holding up against the German invasion. However, Gamelin was also contemplating a much more ambitious move, which involved incorporating the French Seventh Army in the front line: it was to be pushed into Belgium and beyond, rushing forward to Breda to support the Dutch Army. This would, Gamelin argued, link up with the Dutch Army and form a continuous Allied front stretching from the Ardennes to Breda.

On 10 January 1940, a German light aircraft in bad visibility made a forced landing just inside Belgian territory due to engine problems. On board the aircraft was a German officer carrying instructions to units subordinated to No. 2 Air Fleet about the offensive that the German Army was to carry out across Belgium from the Moselle to the North Sea. Although the officer tried to burn the papers, they were

27 Robert Parker, *"Ou est la Masse de Manoeuvre?": Maurice Gamelin and the Lessons of Blitzkrieg in Poland <spectrum.libary.concordia.ca/977623/1Parker_MA_F2013.pdf> (accessed on 25 August 2017),* p. 36.

retrieved by the Belgians; much was still legible, and the intelligence was passed over to the Allies. By February, Gamelin had decided upon the Breda variant (known to the French as scheme B/H – *Belgique/Hollande*) following this intelligence and secret talks with the Belgians, in which he concluded that they would put up a strong defence along the Albert Canal Line, allowing the Allies enough time to reach the Dyle. Further impetus for this plan came from the Dutch Commander-in-Chief, *Generaal* Winkelman, who gave a discreet warning that his troops could not hold out for long unless Allied support was received quickly. This plan was formerly adopted on 12 March 1940 and Gamelin was given a free hand by both the French and British governments to move into Belgium and Holland depending upon the circumstance, without approaching either government. It was a high-risk scheme as it increased the length of the Allied line and committed the best elements of the strategic reserve without the knowledge of the *Schwerpunkt* – the point at which the weight of the main German attack would fall. It also had no formal agreement with either the Belgians or Dutch.[28] Despite Gamelin being given a free hand by both governments, the French Prime Minister at the time, Paul Reynaud, was opposed to the advance and was on the verge of relieving him just as the German invasion began.

Gamelin has been much criticised for not maintaining a strategic reserve. In holding such a long line, a strong strategic reserve that could deploy to any part of the front that was threatened was fundamental. Recently, Robert Parker has argued that this was no oversight on Gamelin's part. Gamelin's decision to increasingly concentrate his reserves in the front line, and not maintain a defence in depth as he had originally planned, was a direct result of the lessons learned from the Polish campaign. The Polish Army's reserves met the same fate as the frontline troops: movement forward was made impossible due to the activity of the *Luftwaffe* in attacking the reserves in their zones of concentration and devastating the roads and railways. Gamelin was determined to avoid the operational paralysis the *Luftwaffe* imposed in the Polish campaign. He always feared that the *Luftwaffe* would attack Allied reserves moving forward and continually asked the British to provide more fighters to take on the *Luftwaffe*.

Crucially, Gamelin was unwavering in his belief that the main German attack would develop on the northern wing of the Western Front through Holland, central and northern Belgium and northern France.[29] He thus planned to maximise his forces at what he believed would be the critical point and grind the German attack to a halt. Thus, the final disposition of Allied forces was made with this in mind. The most mobile elements of the French Army were allocated to the Seventh and First

28 Unknown to the French and even before operations began *Generaal* Winkelman had decided to pull his southern wing back to defend the southern part of Fortress Holland. Thus, when the Seventh Army rushed forward to Breda in May 1940, it found itself alone.

29 Intelligence did reach Gamelin that the main German invasion route would be through the Ardennes, but Gamelin decided to ignore it, believing it was incomplete, inconclusive and deliberately misleading information provided by the Germans.

French Armies. Along with the mechanised BEF this would ensure the Allied forces could cover the distances needed to fulfil Plan D (Figure 4.2). General Corap's Ninth Army, which only had to carry out a short 'wheel' to the defile of the Meuse facing the supposedly impassable Ardennes, and the Second Army, which occupied the comparatively strong extension of the Maginot Line in the Sedan area, were amongst the weakest in the French order of battle. It was further assumed that these areas could easily be reinforced by the French strategic reserve. His great mistake was not to replenish the strategic reserve with the interval troops held behind the Maginot Line to face any surprises which always come along in war: this was apparently discussed prior to the German invasion but no attempt to carry it out was made until after the invasion had commenced. Although always believing that the main German effort would be directed against Holland and Belgium, Gamelin believed the Germans had enough divisions to attack the Maginot Line at the same, so kept the interval troops in place. This represented a gross misuse of the Maginot Line, as far from economising troops, a great number were stationed behind the line when in all likelihood the main battles would be fought elsewhere.

Gort has been widely criticised for agreeing to Plan D and abandoning the defences on which the BEF had laboured so hard on. However, Gort was quite correct when he stated in his Official Dispatches that it was not his role to comment on the strategic decisions taken, but it was his role to ensure 'that the orders issued by the French for the employment of the British Expeditionary Force were capable of being carried out'.[30] Gort did, however, protest when the idea of advancing as far as the Albert Canal was mooted and this did draw criticism from Reynaud. Gort agreed only to hold the Dyle sector from Louvain to Wavre.

For the BEF, once Plan D had been settled upon, training became a higher priority than constructing defences with the exception of concreting and constructing anti-tank obstacles. The frontier defences were now regarded as a secure jumping-off line or a reserve position in case the BEF had to fall back. To some officers, the time spent labouring on pillboxes seemed a waste of time given that the BEF was to advance into Belgium. For example, Major Donald Wilson-Haffenden, HQ 1st Division, observed:

> We always knew that we were going to try and stop the Germans on the Belgian frontier and it always struck us that it was very stupid, pouring all these tons and tons of cement into pillboxes along the French border, that we were going to leave before the war started.[31]

30 General the Viscount Gort, VC, KCB, CBE, DSO, MVO, MC, *Despatches on Operations of the British Expeditionary Force, France and Belgium 3 Sept 1939 – 31 May 1940*, Supplement to the London Gazette, 17 October 1941 <http://www.ibiblio.org/hyperwar/UN/UK/londongazette> (accessed 24 August 2017).

31 Joshua Levine, *Forgotten Voices: Dunkirk* (London: Ebury Press, 2011), p. 17.

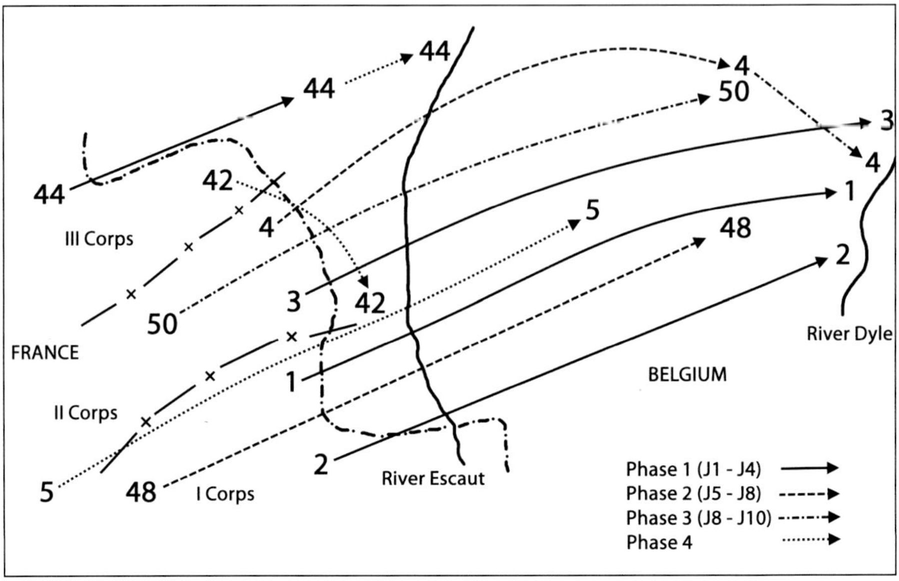

Figure 4.2: Diagram to illustrate the advance the BEF advance into Belgium – Plan D.

Second Lieutenant FitzGerald, 23rd Field Company, was also unimpressed:

> In the first place, having spent eight months fortifying a defensive position, why abandon it at once to occupy a silly little stream like the Dyle, which had no prepared defences at all.[32]

Taking the offensive

Although a defensive strategy was the only one available to the Allies, Ironside still emphasised that the war could not be won merely by trying to avoid losing it:

> Except in the economic field our action is at present confined to countering moves made by the enemy. Our present inferiority in army and air strengths, the long-term nature of our economic weapon, and the time taken to convert our industry to a full war basis, are factors at which at present dictate a defensive strategy.

32 Desmond FitzGerald, *Many Parts: The life and Travels of a Soldier, Engineer and Arbitrator in Africa and Beyond* (London: Radcliffe Press, 2007), p. 91.

> This defensive strategy should not be abandoned likely. A war cannot, however, be merely won by trying not to lose it, and such an outlook is very unlikely to inspire the neutrals, who though their sympathy may be with the Allies, are afraid of Germany and have no wish to share the fate of Poland. In short, to defeat the enemy, we must at some time be prepared to assume the offensive.[33]

However, the Allies never really established a combined staff or organisation to formulate and execute the strategic direction of the war. This state of affairs led to improvised solutions and the Allies certainly did not lack imagination in constructing other fronts against Germany – such as in Finland, the Balkans or the Caucuses – but never gave these secondary fronts anything other than derisory resources which ensured the failure of these projects.

For the French, their whole pre-war political strategy had focused on alliances in the east – threatening Germany with a war on two fronts. Although this strategy lay in ruins, the French government still hoped for a two-front war with a new theatre of operations in the Balkans. The idea was to rally the countries of southern and central Europe against Germany, and, to threaten Germany with a second front. Such an operation received strong support from the French commander in the Middle East, *Général* Maxime Weygand. The British questioned the value of such an adventure, and in this, were backed up by Gamelin, who was reluctant to divert any forces away from the Western Front.

If not looking favourably on action in the Middle East, the British were just as keen to open up other fronts and disperse German effort. Winston Churchill, then First Lord of the Admiralty, suggested mine laying off the Norwegian coast to prevent Swedish shipments of iron ore from Gällivare (during the winter months these were shipped from the Norwegian port of Narvik). The Russian attack on Finland added another dimension: if the Allies were to come to the Finns aid, the only practical route for troops and supplies was from Narvik and thence by rail to Sweden. The iron ore fields at Gällivare could be occupied at the same time. It was calculated that a stoppage of Sweden's iron ore shipments to Germany might well be decisive within a year. Ironside reasoned that the terrain would mean only a small force would be required for such an operation and would not prejudice the security of the Western Front. Churchill wanted to combine this with floating mines down the Rhine – Operation Royal Marine – but the French refused to allow this in fear of retaliatory bombing by Germany. They were willing, however, to support the Scandinavian project, as they saw it as an opportunity to take the war to Germany and reduce the risk of a German invasion of France. Just as important to the French, additional British troops to those on the Saar (see chapter 6) would be involved in active operations.

The Finns were forced to negotiate a peace with Russia before the operation could be launched. The French Prime Minister, Daladier, fell from power as a result of the

33 TNA: WO166/1685, 'Our War Strategy'.

failure to act in time. The Allies, however, still continued planning for a landing at Narvik. But the Germans also had plans for Demark and Norway. The two rival forces clashed in early April, with the Germans coming out on top.[34] Chamberlain was to suffer the same fate as Daladier as a result of the Allied failure, being replaced by Churchill on the fateful 10 May.

These operations, as already stated, were merely attempts to disperse German forces as well as a continuation of the economic war against Germany by denying her Swedish iron ore. At some point, both the French and British realised that the main bulk of the German Army would have to be engaged, quite probably by a direct attack against the Siegfried Line. We have seen that the Allies were not willing to contemplate such an operation until they were assured of both quantitative and qualitative superiority over Germany. Nevertheless, both Allies pressed on with research on how to overcome the defences of the Siegfried Line (see Appendix III). At first, given the mutual suspicion between the Allies, there was little sharing of ideas or technology. However, co-operation between the Allies did markedly improve with French representatives attending demonstrations of British experimental equipment such as the A.20 tank and British representatives attending demonstrations at the French experimental centre at Bourges.

34 During this operation, the Germans lost the majority of their available surface fleet: three cruisers, ten destroyers and eight U boats were sunk, and two battle cruisers, a pocket battleship and two cruisers damaged. Although not recognised at the time, this rendered any German invasion of Britain impossible.

5

Building the Gort Line

If Germany had attacked in the autumn of 1939, there would have been little time to improve the frontier defences. If, on the other hand, the Germans did not attack until the following spring, there would be four or five months in which to work on the defences, and this could include concrete construction. GHQ had to plan to meet both scenarios. To some extent, the situation was further complicated by the various plans to advance into Belgium in the event of a German offensive: was the Gort Line to be a front position, or if the BEF advanced into Belgium, would it become a rear position? This would have a bearing on the nature and priority given to work on the defences. The construction of the Gort Line was dependent upon establishing good LoC which absorbed a large proportion of available labour. Construction of concrete defences and miles of anti-tank ditches also required the raising of an engineering force comprising of Territorial field companies taken from the second to fourth contingents of the BEF, and an excavating company. All this military activity in the British zone needed concealing from enemy eyes. At home, the Secretary of State for War thought that progress on the defences was too slow and this led to the so called 'pillbox affair' which ended with his downfall.

Defence work priorities

The lack of any defined operational role for the BEF led the Chief Engineer I Corps to enquire on 3 October:

> In the absence of any special "Directive" on the subject I assume that the Engineer object will be to improve the defences of the sector to a point in which the Corps will be in a position to stop any major attack by German forces, particularly mechanised forces moving through Belgium.[1]

1 TNA: WO167/129, 'Appreciation by Chief Engineer 1st Corps of the Engineer situation on 1st Corps front on taking over Southern Sector of Lille Defences', 3 October 1939, I

He requested clarification as to whether normal field defences or concrete defences were required, the general plan for the defence of the sector and who was responsible for siting the various lines of defence. To be fair, GHQ did provide some clarification early on, with the issue of a policy for defence works: *Instructions for the Occupation of the LILLE sector of the French Frontier defences by the BEF.* With Gamelin's appreciation that a German attack might be expected any time up to 15 November, troops were fully employed upon making what strongpoints they could and getting themselves undercover close to the FDL Line so they could come into action at once. Works to further develop the FDL Line and the Brigade Reserve Position were to be undertaken with corps resources while the reserve position was to be developed under the Engineer-in-Chief with GHQ resources when these became available. The general priority of work was to be from the front to the rear (Figure 5.1).

Because the French blockhouses could not bring fire to their front, they were open to being rushed or the gaps between them infiltrated by enemy infantry in periods of darkness, fog or under the cover of heavy artillery fire. As a result of this weakness, the immediate priority specified by GHQ was to ensure the local defence of each blockhouse by the provision of infantry posts in the intervals between and behind them and completing the wiring scheme. This required a substantial amount of engineer stores, with shortages from the start. For example, the 2nd Battalion Dorsetshire Regiment, manning the blockhouses in the area Belzanois – Rumegies, indented for 320 coils of barbed wire, 4,000 sandbags, 800 large stakes and 1,600 small stakes. The Battalion managed to complete the wiring of the anti-tank obstacle but on 26 October had to suspend wiring on a second tactical obstacle as all available wire was required for another front.

Next, a series of completely concealed machine gun posts were to be constructed to cover the Brigade Reserve Position; they were to be camouflaged but not occupied until attack was imminent to avoid making tracks. Third priority was the construction of another anti-tank obstacle along the *Ligne d'Arret*, which had already been carefully sited by the French. Work on this was to commence as soon as mechanical trench diggers became available but in the meantime its course was to be marked on the ground with poles and bunting. Forth priority was to begin the construction of trench positions, comprising fire trenches, communication trenches and headquarters. These were to be shallow at first and then gradually elaborated as resources permitted. Fifth priority was to site observation posts in the rear in case of an enemy breakthrough. Lastly, positions to site wire obstacles were to be carefully chosen although not constructed as the wire might be needed for the proposed advance to the Escaut. Instead, wire was to be dumped in locations to allow construction at short notice.

As well as developing the defences, anti-tank guns, anti-tank mines and artillery had to be sited. Positions for the 2 pdr anti-tank guns were to be prepared to cover approaches to the Brigade Reserve Position along with positions for the mobile

Corps Chief Engineer War Diary.

reserve, with forward routes to the positions reconnoitred. Along with some machine gun positions, the anti-tank gun positions were to be prepared at the exact position they were to occupy and, in some cases, would be replaced with a concrete pillbox later. Anti-tank mines were in very short supply and their use was to be limited to blocking gaps in the anti-tank obstacle, such as roads, and to complete the anti-tank defence of the blockhouses. Battle and roving positions, along with alternative and dummy positions, had to be constructed for the artillery. Lines of fire needed to be determined and observation posts sited. Communication was to be by cable laid in open trenches, sited so as to fit in with the main intercommunication system.

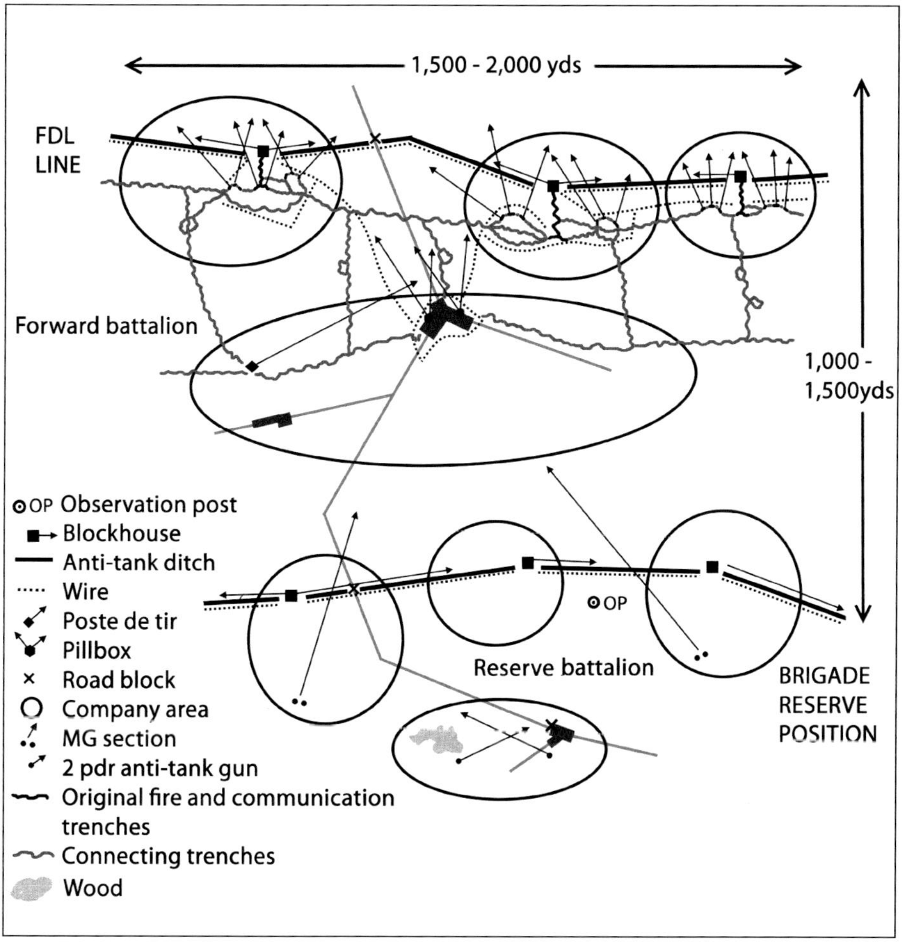

Figure 5.1: Diagram to illustrate the build-up of the defences on part of a brigade sector in the FDL Line and the Brigade Reserve Line as instructed by GHQ in *Instructions for the Occupation of the LILLE sector of the French Frontier defences by the BEF.*

All the defence works outlined above required detailed reconnaissance, survey and liaison before work started to avoid a waste of labour and materials. A consequence of the desire for 'getting a move on' or commencing work to show that men were being employed lead to improvisation, mistakes and a waste of effort, and brigade commanders had to repeatedly warn against it. An acute shortage of maps, along with frequent errors in maps that did exist, also did not help in matters for siting a fully co-ordinated defence. The growth of the defences also required co-ordination and GHQ stipulated that effort must not be dissipated to ensure that incomplete works were not scattered over the area when a lesser number of completed works could be provided at the more important points. The artillery also needed to undertake survey work for positional warfare. Two survey regiments were sent over to France to carry out the necessary surveys required for ranging points, flash spotters and sound ranges of the FDL Line and divisional areas, as well as surveying the target and observation post areas.[2] The 1st Survey Regiment reported that taping out distances in the FDL Line was difficult because of the mud and barbed wire obstacles!

By the end of October, most battalions reported that they were dug in along the FDL Line, either in trenches or breastworks. The field artillery had its guns under cover and had prepared battle positions and fixed routes for the gun tractors from the wagon lines to the gun positions. The medium and heavy artillery was also in position and ready for action, although work was still required to improve the positions. Ammunition for the medium and heavy artillery had been dumped at the gun positions – although, the 5th Heavy Regiment noted in its War Diary that no fuses were included with the ammunition![3]

Such progress was only possible because of the untiring work of the divisional engineers, who struggled with the trivialities of Army life, obtaining materials, supervising the construction of the defences and an ever-increasing demand on 'works services' of all kinds required to sustain the BEF. On 4 October the diarist of CRE 2nd Division's War Diary records the following:

> Now started a period of furious rush. The general idea was to thicken up the defences of the sector. Very few stores could be expected from behind. The

2 The aim of survey in this connexion was to fix the positions of guns and targets on the map to allow 'predicted' fire to be opened with great precision. However, because of the long fronts held by the BEF in *SD* Lille directly observed fire from observation posts would still have been vital. Sound ranging allowed enemy guns to be picked up by 'hot wire' microphones, together with other complicated apparatus, and their position plotted much in the same way that bearings are taken to establish a point on a map. Flash spotting is locating enemy guns by sight from gun-flash and is carried out by a number of observers from as many different posts. When gun-flash was spotted, the observers sent back their bearings and allowed the position of the enemy gun to be plotted.

3 By the end of October, the ammunition had largely been returned to the ammunition points.

> C.R.E. had extensive powers of buying. The Field Park Coy cannot possibly compete with the stores' organization [sic] when the process involves buying, storing, accounting and distribution. Besides this, numerous recces are necessary to find where the stores exist ...
>
> After various re-adjustments of organization [sic] the following has been found the best:
>
> One Field Engineer attached to Field Park Coy as Stores Officer. One Field Engineer employed permanently on projects – most of which could never hope to mature, but when Higher Authority calls, the call must be answered.
>
> A scene in the C.R.Es office is as follows:
>
> An office orderly from the -----shires comes and asks if the R.E. can fix a latrine in the G.O.C's mess. On his heels is a B.Q.M.S. from the Gunners to ask for coconut matting to revet a gunpit. The only place to receive them is the C.R.Es Office which is getting crowded. Next the C.O. of the ---A/Tk Regt R.A. comes in with suggestions for siting minefields. A French Colonel and two liaison officers arrive to protest against the riteway in which the troops are cutting brushwood. Everyone salutes and bows shakes hands and bows again. Then the telephone bell rings and H.Q. I Corps demands an instant reply regarding the number of Mk. I. Primers in the division. Pandemonium reigns from dawn to dusk. The only time for thought is after dinner, and then one's brain is too exhausted to work.[4]

The War Establishment of the divisional engineer units were simply not suitable for the kind of warfare characterised by the Sitzkrieg – a curious mix of peace time and war time duties – where 'no shots would be fired' and a huge fortification programme undertaken. The divisional engineers were in competition with each other and the French Army for what supplies were available and infantry commanders often made unrealistic demands on them. Second-Lieutenant FitzGerald recalls being called to the office of Lieutenant-Colonel Annesley-Cook OC 2nd Battalion Coldstream Guards:

> Ah, FitzGerald, I need 2,000 sheets of corrugated iron to build shelters for my men. Please get them for me, delivered here by midday Friday.

When FitzGerald pointed out that there would probably be only 2,500 sheets for the whole of the BEF in France by Friday, the Colonel replied:

> Well that's great, then. I only need 2,000. See they are here. Good Morning.[5]

4 TNA: WO167/207, 2nd Division Commander Royal Engineers War Diary, 4 October 1939.

5 Desmond FitzGerald, *Many Parts: The life and Travels of a Soldier, Engineer and Arbitrator in Africa and Beyond* (London: Radcliffe Press, 2007), p. 85.

Although by 15 October the CRE 2nd Division was able to report that the 'flow [of stores] comes more smoothly'[6] and that indents from units were beginning to be met, the shortages of materials were to remain a constant headache for the BEF. At first, it was generally accepted that French stores should be used to preserve those of the BEF; and it was up to each division to obtain their own materials locally. CRE 1st Division War Diary describes an engineering officer, Lieutenant Montanaro, sent off on a buying expedition and ordering supplies to the value of 300,000f, which included timber, cement, wire and nails. This policy resulted in rising prices, as noted by CRE 2nd Division:

> The supply of R.E. Materials continues to give anxiety. None comes up from behind and we have to buy what we can. But like this, there is no possible control of prices. Each Div cuts the next one's throat.[7]

Rising prices, the result of the BEF desperately trying to obtain what engineering materials it could, also resulted in complaints from the French! Rising prices were not the only problem; if having successfully purchased materials a shortage of military transport and the requisitioning of most of the civilian lorries by the French military made delivery difficult. By December, GHQ had issued orders that obtaining local supplies was to stop unless in an emergency and only then up to the value of 20,000f per month. Instead, supplies were obtained centrally. However, this did not ease the supply problems with units frequently stating in their War Diaries that only a small portion of materials demanded were ever sent up.

By mid-November, the scare had passed; it was unlikely that an invasion would take place before spring as the wet winter weather closed in. The many small streams and ditches in the area become full of water and the ground in general was unsuitable for armoured attacks. The BEF now had a period of three months to 'aim at attaining a certain degree of completion of defence works by the end of February 1940' in order to meet any German spring offensive.[8] The priority was the completion of the anti-tank ditches in the positions already laid down and the provision of concrete cover for the principal weapons of the defence. However, the engineers were still dealing with the daily trivialities of the Sitzkrieg right up to the move into Belgium, with Lieutenant Clarke's (Engineer Intelligence Officer, 4th Division) diary entry for 9 May having a similar theme to that quoted in CRE 2nd Division's War Diary for 4 October:

6 TNA: WO167/207, 2nd Division Commander Royal Engineers War Diary, 19 November 1939.

7 Ibid.

8 TNA: WO167/2, 'Instructions regarding Defence Works – Lille Sector', November 1939, GHQ General Operations War Diary.

> Telephone active with the usual trivialities; winding the handle is good indoor exercise. 18 Field Park Company have lost the bulldozer again. 30 Field Regiment RA have indented for yet more sandbags; are they to be supplied? A battalion in 10 Brigade has cut up the local dance floor for revetting material and are faced with a bill for £50. The infantry working party for offloading stores has failed to arrive at the goods yard. Corps want our return of outsize boots by tonight's DRLS [Despatch Rider Liaison Service] and 225 Field Company have forgotten that "Nil Returns" are required. A French civilian arrives from the Mairie with a pot of blue paint to say that he has instructions to black out the windows.[9]

Lines of Communication

Logistics are frequently overlooked in military studies despite any army being dependent upon them. Logistics were just as important in the defence as in the attack. The BEF was operating from overseas bases along the French coast, in which its stores and depots, reinforcement camps and base hospitals were grouped. Accommodation of all kinds, workshops, maintenance installations such as laundries, bath houses and bakeries, and training and recreation facilities all had to be provided with the engineers playing the leading executive role. It was estimated that for every man in the BEF about a third of a ton of material of all kinds per month was required. There was also all the materials required for the construction of the defences in the BEF fortified zone and the aerodromes for the AASF and the Air Component to think about. These had to be despatched to RE field parks by road and rail. The logistics of the LoC necessitated an administrative effort for which large numbers of personnel, especially labour, was required and had to be progressed simultaneously with the construction of the defences and aerodromes, with competing demands upon the available labour. Pre-war manuals, such as *Engineer Training – 1937*, stated that engineer services on the LoC would represent fully half the engineer contribution to the entire campaign.

At first, it was intended to form maintenance depots near the ports of Brest and Nantes, but with such long LoC, the need for forward depots soon became apparent. The port of Havre was at first thought unsuitable for a forward base, but these problems were overcome by November and an Advanced Base was set up near this port. In all, the BEF ended up making use of 17 French ports.[10] These ports landed a total of 250,000 men, 45,000 vehicles and a monthly tonnage varying from 60,000 to 100,000

9 Ralph Lionel Clarke, *Three Weeks to La Panne: A Diary of Dunkirk* <http://www.foxearth.org.uk/ThreeWeeksToLaPanne> (accessed 25 August 2017). An interesting observation in the CRE 4th Division War Diary for April was that many billets in the Divisional area were now very comfortable in houses and flats with central heating and hot and cold water laid on. The result was that repairs required skilled tradesmen and the correct stores, not the kind of 'improvisation' in the field usually expected from field companies!

10 Initially two dock groups (organised with four stevedore sections each) were formed to handle the main ports of Brest, Cherbourg, St. Nazaire and Nantes but it soon became

tons of stores of all kinds. A system of field supply depots was established further forward. Some half-dozen railheads were constructed at depots and aerodromes.[11] As the French economy was fully engaged on war industry, great difficulty was found in obtaining suitable buildings for accommodation, depots and workshops and an extensive programme of building and hutting was required.[12] All these activities were under the control of the GOC Lines of Communication Area, Major-General P. de Fonblanque: the BEF eventually occupied about a third of France, stretching from Dunkirk to Brest and from Cherbourg to Marseilles.

The task of organising the arrangements for the reception of the personnel and vehicles of the BEF and their move from the ports to assembly areas, and the subsequent movement and stocking of stores to base and forward depots was the responsibility of Movement Control.[13] With its HQ in Paris, its organisation gradually built up to the deployment of five Movement Control Groups deployed under two District HQs: Q (MC) South covered Marseilles, Nantes, Le Mans, Rennes, Brest, Cherbourg and Caen while Q (MC) North covered Le Havre, Rouen, Dieppe, Boulogne, Calais and Dunkirk. The doctrine of supply to the troops was based upon so-called 'pack trains'. Materials of all kinds were sent forward from base depots in 'pack' trains – loaded as much as possible to reflect the demands received at base depots from units and formations – to railheads.[14] From the railheads they were delivered to units and formations by road in three links of a chain. Third line transport, comprising

apparent that a third docks group was required for the ports of Fécamp, Caen, Rouen, St. Malo, Le Havre and rolling stock and vehicles were switched through Calais and Dunkirk.

11 At first the French railways were able to handle the BEF's rail traffic, but by the end of October it had been decided that the British would have to provide their own rolling stock and train crews and progressively take over the rail transport between the docks and depots. The British provided 100 shunting engines complete with crews for work in the depots and by April 1940 operating companies were also working the main line trains between St. Malo and Rennes.

12 Rather optimistically, it had been hoped that the French would provide billets for the majority of troops along the LoC, and consequently in the planning little provision had been made for hutting. By 15 November, only 1,250 huts had been sent to France.

13 Movement Control was formed in September 1938, although it owed its origins to the managerial function of controlling movement by rail during the South African War. The Directorate of Railway Transport was tasked with movement during the Great War. It was disbanded after the end of the war, only to reappear in the form of Movement Control to apply the doctrine of military movement. In France, apart from 11 regular officers, its personnel were built up from Supplementary Reserve officers and men. Movement Control's first major operational exercise was organising the movement forward into Belgium. It was to play an important part in the 'Overlord' planning – the Allied landings at Normandy in June 1944 – but not all were impressed with this branch responsible for military movement: Admiral Cunningham said 'When we advance, it is all control and no movement. When we retire, it is all movement and no control' (James Leasor, *The Experiences of General Sir Leslie Hollis KCB, KBE: War at the Top* (London: Michael Joseph, 1959), p. 257).

14 Stores were also moved by 'bulk' trains, which contained one or more commodities in bulk, e.g. ammunition, engineer or transport stores, road stone, petrol, etc.

of maintenance companies, RASC and reserve transport units worked between the railhead and refilling points. Second Line transport, made up of divisional and corps RASC, was loaded at the refilling points to convey loads to delivery points, such as field supply depots. From delivery points, supplies were transported to where they were needed by first line transport, which was part of the war organisation of all units.

It had been agreed with the French that the BEF would construct all additional rail track required. At the start of the campaign, one railway survey company, three railway construction companies and one railway construction and operating company were available; these were reinforced early in 1940. In all, 141 miles of track were laid to new rail depots and feeder lines to aerodromes. By the time of the German invasion, immense masses of stores and ammunition had been accumulated in depots all along the LoC. Ten days supply was accumulated between the Seine and the Somme and an additional seven days' supply north of the Somme. This latter provision saved the BEF after the German breakthrough.[15]

The vast amount of materials and equipment required for the construction of the BEF's defences had to be delivered from the field supply depots by road. The roads in *SD* Lille were described as 'indifferent' with the exception of the *Route Nationale* and the *Chemins de Grandes.* The Chief Engineer I Corps noted that in some cases it would be impossible to start concrete construction until approach roads had been constructed. A good road network was also important for the mobility of the Army, especially mobile reserves and artillery. Hence the provision of a system of roads and tracks to all parts of the position was essential and had to be one of the first tasks undertaken and progressively developed. The general layout had to fit in with the existing layout and required traffic control circuits to be established. By-passes around all large towns and villages were marked out and, in certain cases, prepared, and forward tracks avoiding main roads also had to be constructed. Approaches to alternative crossings over the Canal Line also had to be considered and bridging practice carried out at these points.

If the existing roads were not improved, it was feared they would soon break up under the traffic which they would be subjected to. Key traffic routes had to be widened and new surfaces laid. Many roads in the *SD* Lille were pavé which were narrow and readily developed potholes due to the volume of traffic and needed constant repair and maintenance.[16] It was feared that no vehicle over 30 cwt would be able to use the roads when the weather deteriorated. In the 1st Division's area, for example, 70 miles of road needed improvement and it was recognised that to do this it would be

15 Although this reserve undoubtedly saved the BEF, the Germans had cut the BEF's LoC by 21 May but the battle was over before this could materially influence the outcome. Later in the war, the British Army moved away from reliance on the 'pack' train, and often used improvised motorisation of supplies to keep the momentum during offensive operations. The Movement Control organisation of the BEF was never repeated.

16 Pavé is a road surface comprising of uniformly shaped blocks of hard stone laid in courses and bedded on sand or earth.

inevitable that the rate of construction of defensive field works would be slowed down – daily working parties of 300 men were working on roads in the Divisional area during October. The CRE 1st Division noted that 100 tons of road metal was arriving daily at railheads by the end of October, but it was not enough to keep up with the deterioration of roads. By November divisions were handling up to 240 tons of road metal per day. The combination of heavy traffic and rain caused many pavé roads to slide into the roadside ditches; a temporary solution was to replace the mud at the road edge with road metal. Later, it was snow followed by a rapid thaw that caused roads to rapidly deteriorate. It was not so much the snow that caused the problems – although it did lead to a sharp rise in road traffic accidents – but rather the thaw. Water became trapped in the subsoil due to water thawing in the upper layers of soil being unable to escape through the still frozen lower layers. Saturation of the subsoil reduced the load bearing capacity, causing roads to collapse.

Many engineers helped themselves, without permission, to materials from the dumps of the French agency responsible for roads – *Ponts et Chaussées* – which resulted in a number of complaints. To avoid further disputes, a convention was agreed between the BEF and the French civil authorities that in future, work on roads required by the BEF would be undertaken by the agency of the *Ponts et Chaussées*. However, it was found that insufficient French labour could be provided due to reductions as a result of war conditions. It was agreed that the French skilled workmen would continue with pavé road maintenance while the BEF's engineers took responsibility for new road construction, repairs to macadam roads and draining and cleaning all roads. Even this arrangement proved insufficient for the volume of road repairs following the severe winter and subsequent thaw.

To ensure supplies could still be delivered if roads deteriorated to such an extent that they became unusable, pack mules in their hundreds were shipped over straight from the Himalayas along with their own sepoys. The idea was to distribute the Indian contingent into small units within the British forward zone. The first detachments arrived at a railhead in the forward area of the British zone on 5 January.[17] These mules, or 'katchas' as they were known to the soldiers, pulled two-wheeled army transport carts. In his Official Dispatches, Gort records that the mules 'proved their usefulness on many occasions.'[18] The Indian mules were not the only ones sent over to the BEF. A contingent of mule transport units also crossed the sea from Cyprus for service with the BEF. This represented the first occasion on which a force from Cyprus had taken the field alongside British troops. The names of six of these Dominion troops appear on the Dunkirk Memorial.

17 I Corps War Diary notes that the 1st Division constructed an animal transport (mule) company camp during January.

18 General the Viscount Gort, VC, KCB, CBE, DSO, MVO, MC, *Despatches on Operations of the British Expeditionary Force, France and Belgium 3 Sept 1939 – 31 May 1940*, Supplement to the London Gazette, 17 October 1941 <http://www.ibiblio.org/hyperwar/UN/UK/londongazette> (accessed 24 August 2017).

Pillbox requirements

As we have seen, it was intended that the principal weapons of the defence be given concrete protection. Work began immediately in the forward areas; for instance, on 11 October, the 1st Division issued instructions that three pillboxes were to be constructed in each forward brigade area while by 31 October the 2nd Division had completed three pillboxes and had a further 12 under construction. By the middle of November, all divisions had completed their preliminary reconnaissances for siting pillboxes and submitted their requirements to GHQ. The task in hand was enormous. A plan of the 1st Division's concrete requirements shows that 31 anti-tank gun and Bren pillboxes, 16 machine gun section pillboxes and six Bren pillboxes were required (see Chapter 8 for details on BEF pillbox design). Each field company would require 50 tons a day of material for concrete construction. On 18 November, the 3rd Division War Diary noted that fifteen 25mm pillboxes, forty 2 pdr pillboxes and 24 machine gun section pillboxes needed to be completed before the defensive arrangements contemplated could be considered complete. For the Divisional Reserve Position in its sector, 2nd Division stated it required 39 pillboxes which would require 6,150 tons of concrete to complete (Table 5.1), while on the FDL and Brigade Reserve Positions for its 5 Brigade, it was estimated that it would take until the end of June 1940 to complete the required 87 concrete posts.[19]

Table 5.1: Concrete requirements for 2nd Division's Divisional Reserve Position

Pillbox Type	Number	Concrete required per pillbox (tons)	Total concrete requirement (tons)
Hexagonal pillbox for a section	22	127	2,794
Double M.G. pillbox	6	250	1,500
Single M.G. pillbox	4	154	616
2pdr and Bren pillbox	2	240	480
Single 2pdr or 25mm gun pillbox	5	152	760

19 The 11th Field Company, working on the 5 Brigade's Front, limited its work to four types of concrete post: post X, a Bren post for one gun and two men (100 tons), post Y, a section post in a house (180 tons), post Z, a hexagonal section post in the open (280 tons) and post M for a 25mm anti-tank gun (300-500 tons). The Company produced an estimate on 31 October 1939 for 10 X posts, 74 Y posts and three M posts required on the 5 Brigade's front, which could be completed by the end of June 1940.

'X' Force

Following his visit to France in September, Hore-Belisha appointed a team of engineers, both military and civil, to recommend ways to speed up the construction of defences. The result was the decision to mobilise a Royal Engineer brigade of two battalions for pillbox construction. Each battalion consisted of five Territorial field companies and one Territorial field park company, taken from divisions that were to make up the second to forth contingent. This force was known as 'X' Force, under the command of Brigadier Minnis with Colonel French (who was a large building contractor) as his second-in-command. The task of 'X' Force, as outlined by Major-General Collins, Director of Works and Fortifications at the War Office, was to construct a fortified GHQ line of about 40 miles long in the rear of the BEF. This line was to consist of large concrete works on the lines of the Maginot Line. It was noted that the Secretary of State for War 'lays great importance on this work.'[20] This incensed GHQ, which did not think it was the Secretary of State's role to decide upon such matters, and on a preliminary visit to France during 2 to 8 October, Brigadier Minnis and Colonel French found that a fortified line as envisaged by the War Office was apparently not required or intended! If that was not enough, during a conference with the Engineer-in-Chief (Major-General R. P. Pakenham-Walsh) and the officers of 'X' Force, difficulties were envisaged in fitting in their HQ with the existing chain of command. The Engineer-in-Chief, although recognising the value of the extra engineer units, was insistent that any work carried out by 'X' Force should be under his direction, and that the stores it was proposed to send out for their use should be diverted to completing the forward defences if required.

Brigadier Minnis had doubts that the personnel of the field companies would be suitable for reinforced concrete construction. He therefore asked for permission to recruit 100 steel fixers and 100 carpenters, with civil engineering firms circulated for names of suitable men. Although many of the men were already in the Army, permission was refused to transfer them on the grounds that suitable men would exist in the field companies. Brigadier Minnis undertook a survey of occupations in the field companies and the returns revealed that:

> [I]t was learned that the Companies contained Ham Curers, Barman, Organists and Bookbinders and that less than 10 % of the total Force were men whose trades were of any use in reinforced concrete work.[21]

Minnis submitted proposals to raise works battalions containing the right number of skilled and unskilled labour. This proposal was adopted, with the formation of

20 TNA: WO167/43, GHQ Chief Engineer War Diary, 29 September 1939.
21 TNA: WO167/1429, 'Appendix No. 34: Report on "X" Force', HQ 'X' Force War Diary.

the Auxiliary Military Pioneer Corps (AMPC), with enlistment into the AMPC opening in the last week of October.

It was not just the skills of the field companies that taxed 'X' Force. Equipment was in short supply right from the start. Colonel French spent between the 8 to 15 October arranging to purchase plant but it was discovered that the quantities asked for were reduced before the order was placed. For example, 50 concrete mixers were asked for but only 24 ordered; a further 25 had to be subsequently ordered. After the plant was ordered, there was a considerable delay in its arrival in France due to both the slowness in manufacture and delay in transport. The concrete mixers, vital for the work, were ordered before 15 October but the first ones did not arrive in France until 16 November. It was not until December that 'X' Force could report that the balance of the plant ordered from England had finally arrived!

Also vital was transport for the anticipated quantities of road material, ballast, sand and cement that had to be distributed within the BEF zone. Over 100 tipping lorries were requested immediately. The 76 RASC was already being formed for attachment to 'X' Force, and a works operating section of 40 tipping lorries was added to this company. These duly arrived in France on 31 October and were at work at once. Colonel French was promised a further 25 lorries if he could help in recruiting the necessary personnel. This he did, and a list of 50 volunteer drivers willing to enlist were called up within a week of being submitted. The lorries never materialised though, and the drivers remained at stuck at Aldershot, and attempts were even made to draft them to other units. In his report on 'X' Force from 2 October to 5 December, Colonel French wrote that the 'work of "X" Force is strangled through lack of these vehicles.'[22] Eventually, the lorries were supplied and 39 arrived in France on 13 December. Many had tyres worn through to the canvas, some even getting punctures as a result of the drive to the embarkation port! None of the vehicles were supplied with tool kits. As for the men, they had been employed on fatigues while at Aldershot and had received no training in map reading, convoy work, arms drill, PAD or other skills they would require. In fact, in a report on the matter, Major Booth-Scott, OC 76 RASC was scathing:

> Vehicles which have done excessive mileage, as evidenced by badly worn tyres, are useless for the work we carry out, and only entail extra work for evacuation and replacement.
>
> I feel very strongly that the men, who are all <u>Volunteers</u>, have been badly treated, and that it was the responsibility of the authorities at home that these men were at least sufficiently trained, during five weeks at Aldershot, where facilities are not lacking, to take their place immediately in a unit like this one.
>
> As a matter of fact, I have interviewed the men and they have already experienced convoy work in this country, and I am quite prepared to say that

22 Ibid.

> they will carry out their duties efficiently; but it will be done due to the qualities inherent in these men, who have volunteered for Active Service, and not by way of previous training in England.[23]

The total size of the initial force was about 2,500 engineers and 1,300 personnel of the AMPC. HQ of 'X' Force was opened at Douai and the HQs of the two battalions were both at Coutiches. The advance units of 'X' Force began arriving on 24 October to reconnoitre areas for billets, which had to be close to their place of work.

Table 5.2: Location of 'X' Force units

Unit	Division taken from and contingent	Location
HQ – 'X' Force		Douai
HQ 1 Battalion RE		Coutiches
200 Field Coy RE	42nd Div, 2nd contingent	Tempeuve
208 Field Coy RE	44th Div, 2nd contingent	Tempeuve
228 Field Coy RE	49th Div, 2nd contingent	Bonnance
213 Field Coy RE	1st North Midland Corps Troops RE, 2nd contingent	La Broderie
216 Field Coy RE	1st London Corps Troops RE, 3rd contingent	Coutiches
254 Field Park Coy RE	55th Div, 4th contingent	Coutiches
L.A.D. 1 Battalion RE		Coutiches
HQ 2 Battalion RE		Coutiches
242 Field Coy RE	52nd Div, 3rd contingent	La Monilel
245 Field Coy RE	53rd Div, 4th contingent	Coutiches
250 Field Coy RE	54th Div, 3rd contingent	Rue de Rosier
506 Field Coy RE	Taken from Northern Command	Rue de la Quieze
252 Field Coy RE	55th Div, 4th contingent	La Talbot
223 Field Park Coy	1st London Div, 3rd contingent	Coutiches
L.A.D. 2 Battalion RE		Coutiches
Works Motor Transport Coy RASC		La Jonquiere

23 Ibid.

As it was the intention that 'X' Force should start work immediately, large quantities of materials were shipped over with it, although much went to waste. A trainload of 500 tons of cement was received from England early on, but much was wasted due to breakages in bags and deterioration due to the length of time in storage. Two thousand tons of steel bars were ordered before any pillbox designs had been settled. They were therefore cut to random lengths, which required a great deal of time and labour in sorting out and trimming to the required length; it was estimated that this would produce 10 percent wastage. Even when pillbox designs were issued, some were later altered and the steel reinforcement had to be designed afresh, meaning the time that had been spent in cutting the bars to length had been wasted. In order to supply the large construction programme of 'X' Force, gravel pits at Calais were allocated to it but the output was not great and 'X' Force had to send two badly needed tipping lorries to assist in working the pits.

The arrival of 'X' Force caused some confusion as to who was to decide upon the priority for concrete work, as noted in 2nd Division's War Diary:

> 13 November: Concrete priority is giving trouble. What 'X' Force (a collection of T.A. Div Fd Coys into a RE Bde) may or may not do in the way of concrete in 2 Div sector is subject to constant change. As a result, RE planning is rendered very difficult if not impossible.
> 14 November: Still difficulties over concrete priority. We are now told we are not to give priority of construction to Sig comns and Arty O.P.s as we had ordered.
> 18 November: Concreting priority still in the melting pot. We are now told 'X' Force will do 6,000 tons of concreting on the Div Res and 5 Inf Bde Res lines only.[24]

It was finally settled that 'X' Force's first priority would be the Divisional Reserve Position and the switches joining it to the forward positions (Figure 5.2). Second priority was to be the Mons-en-Pévèle Switch, the Lille Switch and the Roubaix – Quesnoy Switch. Third priority was the Marcq Switch and forth priority the Second Position. These priorities reflected GHQ's policy of working on the defences from the front to rear.

Colonel Bertschi, with two concreting companies and five labour companies, was to continue to have responsibility for the work in the French 51st Division area. At first the French concentrated on constructing pillboxes on the front Tourcoing – Halluin – Bousbecque and on completion of these were to start work on a line of pillboxes along the River Lys from Halluin to Armentières. With the planned relief of the French 51st Division by the 4th and 5th Divisions (see Chapter 6), Gort was insistent that the front between Roubaix – Halluin was brought up to strength with the construction

24 TNA: WO167/207, 2nd Division Commander Royal Engineers War Diary, 13 –18 November.

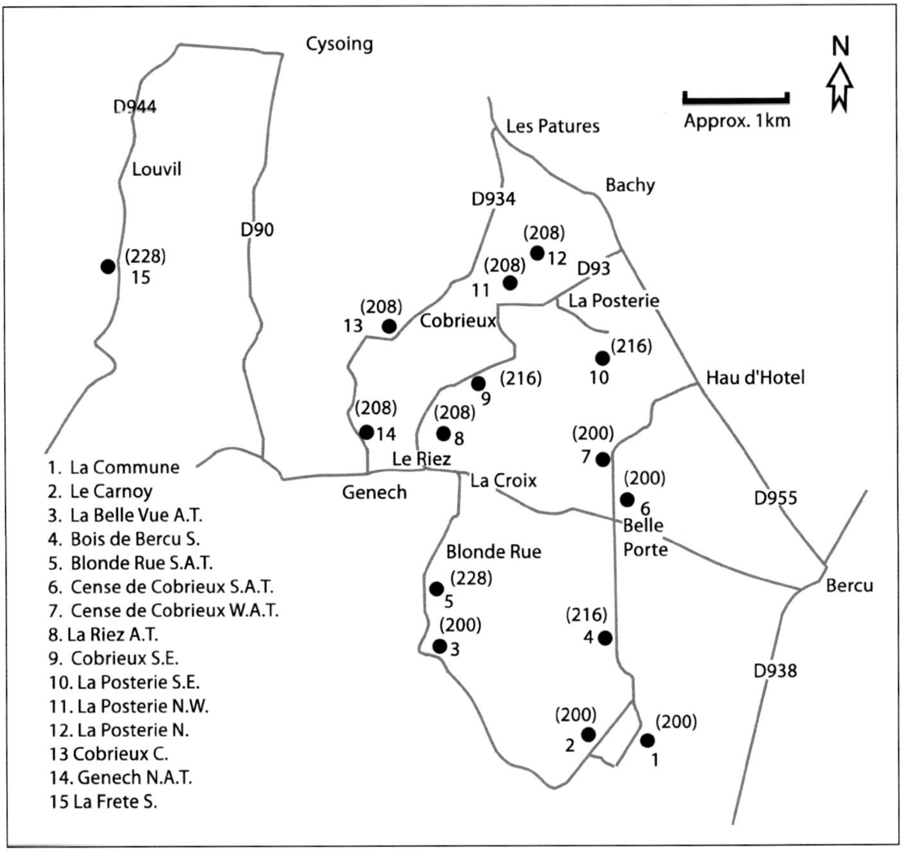

Figure 5.2: 1st Battalion 'X' Force's first programme of anti-tank pillboxes, 1st Division's Divisional Reserve Position. The field company responsible for construction is shown in brackets.

of another 15 pillboxes by the end of February; also required were about 30 pillboxes along the River Lys to be completed around the end of March. It was originally intended that 'X' Force would take on this work and the need for the arrival of 'X' Force's RE battalions was considered urgent; it was suggested that a large building contractor could have been hired from England and the job got on with! It was, however, eventually settled that *Colonel* Bertschi would continue to be responsible for the Lys front and build in accordance with the French scheme and design.

The divisions continued to be responsible for constructing pillboxes in the forward brigade sectors. This was also an ambitious undertaking in some cases. For instance, the 4 Brigade planned a concrete programme to construct 36 concrete posts which represented a total of 81,450cu.ft. of concrete and the weekly delivery of 400 tons of stone, 200 tons of sand, 130 tons of cement and 20 tons of steel to complete it by March 1940. To speed up pillbox construction in the 3rd Division's sector, the 253rd Field Company was instructed to set up a workshop capable of mass production of shuttering and bar cutting and bending. The RE field companies provided the technical expertise with working parties found from the infantry, anti-tank regiments and machine gun battalions. The GOC II Corps, Lieutenant-General Brooke, demanded that the REs must be diluted by infantry who should be trained in concrete work. The OC 1st Division desired something similar with 'Battalion Concreting Parties' and the infantry personnel selected to be given experience in all aspects of constructing reinforced concrete. Orders issued by the 1st Division also specified that REs should only be employed on skilled work; the finishing off of pillboxes, i.e. the heaping up of earth on the defiladed side , camouflaging, turfing etc., should all be completed by other troops.

Work was underway fairly quickly in the forward brigade sectors and by 1 December the 5th Field Company reported it had used its first 1,000 tons of concrete on the forward brigade sector of the 2nd Division. André Maurois observed the progress and noted on 22 November:

> We had visited the position three weeks before. Now it was hardly recognizable [sic]. Naturally it relied still upon the concrete block-house and the anti-tank ditches constructed by the French engineers before the war, but its depth had increased formidably. Well-protected strong points had been drained and the roads re-made. Behind the line of French block-houses, numerous squads were hard at it constructing other cement works. Already long steel hooks marked the outlines of the new casemates, while the cementers nearby mixed the sand and gravel.[25]

Even with 'X' Force's task settled, there was still delay due to constant changes in the siting of pillboxes and the lack of equipment. This meant 'X' Force was not in a position to carry out the task it had been sent out for. Until stores and equipment arrived, it was decided to allot one battalion of 'X' Force to each of the 1st and 2nd Divisions to assist with engineer work such as road repairs. Field company sections were also allocated to various aerodromes to undertake work in preparing landing grounds; work was expected to last for 14 days but the sections were at 48 hours'notice to be withdrawn if required for pillbox work. By early December Brigadier Minnis felt able to state that at last 'X' Force could begin on its task in earnest, as most of the pillboxes had now been sited, and, that as a result, he would be withdrawing 'X' Force labour from divisional tasks. By 31 December, work was underway on 47 pillboxes on I Corps front. Work on II Corps front was only put in hand in the New Year.

The dispatch of new divisions to join the BEF was expected to absorb the field companies of 'X' Force in due course. However, the huge demand from the Army

25 André Maurois, *The Battle of France* (London: John Lane the Bodley Head, 1940), p. 33.

for concrete work on the defences had shown the necessity for a large unit to deal with work of this nature. The field company, designed to meet the operational needs of a fighting division, was a complicated and expensive organisation which had to be capable of taking on work of any nature. Its use in concreting was uneconomical – as we have seen, divisional and corps commanders both insisted that REs must only be used on skilled work, with infantry working parties providing the labour.[26] It was decided to replace 'X' Force with two RE general construction battalions (under Lieutenant-Colonel C.P. Worsfold and Lieutenant-Colonel W.G.R. Nutt), as part of a wider scheme to increase the labour supply, described in further detail later in this chapter. The general construction battalions were intended at first to form part of GHQ (eventually Army) troops and were made up of an HQ, one field park company and four general construction companies. The War Establishment of a general construction company was identical to a field company but made up largely of men with a background in civil engineering concreting (Table 5.3).

General construction companies faced the same problems as the rest of the BEF in equipment shortages. The War Diary of the 655th General Construction Company describes its unit transport comprising of 'Impressed Vehicles in the last stages of usefulness'. Finding sufficient tools was not always easy; for example, CRE 2nd Battalion 'X' Force visited the 109th Field Park Company to draw tools for the general construction companies but none were available! When they did have tools, employing skilled workmen could certainly speed up construction. For instance, the 655th General Construction Company noted that Second-Lieutenant McCall and a picked squad of men completed a Bren pillbox in just under three days, from cutting the first sod to placing the last spade of concrete. Being volunteers from the building trade, most of the men in the general construction companies were only too happy to get down to the work they had joined up for, much preferring it to the usual Army routine of drilling and training. However, Lieutenant R.L. Clarke (Engineer Intelligence Officer with the 4th Division) still thought that the RE field companies could get pillboxes up quicker than the construction companies.

To address the continuing shortage of specialised labour required for the concreting programme, suggestions were put forward to upgrade the tradesman classification of

26 It is justifiably arguable that general labouring was equably a waste of an infantry man's talents as it was an engineer's. The BEF required highly trained infantry specialists to carry out its mechanised doctrine. However, during the inter-war years, the general consensus was that walking behind the guns to be killed was a job which any fool could do – the most technically minded recruits tended to opt for careers in the RAF, RAC or the Artillery. It was not until later in the war, largely thanks to the efforts of General Paget, that it was fully realised just what a specialist role modern infantry undertook, and that the infantryman must have a much wider range of knowledge and skill than he had had before. However, whether or not the BEF commanders understood just how much of a specialist the modern infantryman had to be is a moot point; the reality was that the shortage of man power left little choice but to use infantry as general labourers.

Table 5.3: War Establishment of a General Construction Company for Concrete Work.

	HQ	4 sections each	Total
Tradesmen			
• Carpenters		3	12
• Clerks	3		3
• Concreters		16	64
• Draughtsmen (Architectural)	2		2
• Fitters (Forman bar bender)		1	4
Engine Hands		2	8
Pioneers			
• Bar benders		7	28
• Shuttering hands		8	32
• General	3	16	67
Non Tradesmen			
• Drivers	3	3	15
• Batmen-Drivers	1		1
• Batmen	1	1	5
• Sanitary duties	1		1
• Water duties	1		1
Total Rank & File	**15**	**57**	**243**

concreters and bar benders during April 1940. It was hoped this would induce them to enlist, as at home a concreter foreman or bar bender could earn £5 or £6 per week, which was more than the current Army pay. The current arrangements in the Army also gave them no opportunity of improving their pay by skill in their particular trade.

Following the decision to raise general construction companies, with effect from 10 March it was decided that the units of 'X' Force would come under the command of corps and take all orders direct from corps HQ. HQ 'X' Force was to remain under command of I Corps until all outstanding administrative and works matters had been resolved. HQ 'X' Force was then to be dissolved.

Work on the defences was not to stop if the BEF advanced into Belgium to meet a German attack. The 'X' Force RE field companies (then later the general construction companies following the disbandment of 'X' Force) were to remain and continue their work on concrete pillboxes, as well as other works which it was not possible to carry out until a more active threat had arisen, such as putting buildings into a state of defence. The British were also to hand over all the keys and inventory boards of the French blockhouses to the French. *Colonel* Bertschi was to make arrangements to take over all the blockhouses and prepared demolitions and for work to continue on the defence programme.

135th Excavator Company RE

Although pre-war Army manuals acknowledged that the use of excavating machinery could result in a great economy of labour in preparing defence works, it is perhaps of no surprise that given the pre-war state of the British Army, no provision had been made for mechanical excavators. With the advent of war and the realisation of the advantages presented by excavators in the speed of construction and the replacement of labour, the Army Council reached a decision to form an excavator company – designated 135th Excavator Company RE – in the Royal Engineers. As most excavators and operators in military service in England were fully employed on the large programme of construction of camps and airfields, the Company was an entirely new organisation that had to be built up. The Company was formed under the Director of Works and Fortifications, Major-General Collins and the Assistant Director, Colonel Chippendal. An officer with considerable experience in excavating plant, Major Westrop, DSO, MC, was appointed commander of the Company. The Company was formed at Newark, with a training ground and a selection of machines made available. Men were obtained by circulating leading users of excavating plant for a list of their experienced drivers who had been called up. From this list, units were ordered to send the men to report to the Company at Newark. Further operators were obtained by the War Office and GHQ circulating units and asking for the names of men with experience in excavators with a view to transfer to the Company and by direct enlistment of experienced civilians. The quality of the men transferred from other units as a result of the War Office and GHQ circulation was found to be mixed, with a few experienced operators but also several completely inexperienced ones.

Excavators were chosen to meet the expected requirements in the field and was obtained from the United Kingdom and America. Universal excavators were equipped mainly as dragshovels (also called back-actors) for trench digging with a bucket capacity of ¾ cubic yard down to ¼ cubic yard. Several dragline attachments plus a number of shovel and skimmer attachments were also provided.[27] The Company

27 Universal excavators consisted of a base machine to which a variety of front-end attachments could be fitted. They were usually referred to by the name of their front-end attachments – typically draglines or dragshovels. The dragline was considered the most universal equipment, and consisted of a long steel lattice jib, or boom and a specially designed drag bucket. It was not positive in action but was rapid in operation. It was the most difficult of the equipments to operate and demanded a high degree of skill. The operation is similar to an angler casting a fly – the bucket is thrown or cast by swinging the jib, allowing the bucket to fall forward of a vertical line from the top of the jib. The bucket is then dragged

initially had 26 excavators. A total of 21 tractors were on the Company's strength, equipped with elevating graders, scrapers, angle dozers or bulldozers along with 24 dumpers. The Company also had six cable trench diggers. The Company was set up to be mobile, with eight Scammell 25-ton low loaders which could move all the various plant the Company was equipped with. Six FWD 10-ton diesel lorries were available for transporting the heaviest excavators. It was also intended the Company be self-sufficient and considerable spares were carried for each machine along with workshop plant.

The first detachments of 135th Excavator Company crossed via the train ferry from Harwich to Calais on 2/3 October with a train carrying seven tractors, three scrapers, six excavators and certain trailers and spares. The detachment proceeded to Orchies to start work on the 2nd Division's anti-tank ditches with elevating graders. Their arrival was recorded by CRE 2nd Division:

> Det. 135 Excavator Coy comes under command. There are 20 men and 20 colossal machines, most of which get stuck in the mud.[28]

About half the establishment of machines proceeded by rail ferry on 23 October under the command of Major Westrop. The Company formed part of GHQ troops, with some divisions feeling arrangements would have been more satisfactory if it was under their control. During the start of November, more plant was employed in I Corps and II Corps area: six 10 Rushton-Bucyrus's were employed in II Corps area while four additional draglines and drag shovels commenced work on I Corps Brigade Reserve Position at Belle Porte – Lannoy. The work rate for a pair of machines was on average 50 yards of ant-tank ditch per working day of eight to nine hours. It was believed that there was scope to significantly increase this work rate as operators became more experienced. By the end of November, the Company had 22 excavators, 10 tractors, two cable diggers and 16 dumpers at work and during the last week of the month completed 1,350 yards of anti-tank ditches. As well as anti-tank ditches, the Company was involved in various road works, constructing dump sites and gun pits with skimmers and infantry earthworks with tractors used as bulldozers. It was found

forward towards the machine. The dragshovel, or back-actor, consisted of a stout boom and dipper arm with a bucket mounted on the end of the arm. It was positive in action, with the bucket moving through a fixed arc, the chord remaining constant, but the digging radius is varied by raising or lowering the boom during operation. It was slower than the dragline, but it produced a well-controlled even cut. A skimmer was used to cut material at, or above the level of the base of the machine. It could cut accurately within fine limits, and as its name implies 'skims'. The 10 Ruston Bucyrus was one of the lighter universal excavators of the time and ideal for the BEF due to its relative ease to transport compared to heavier machines.

28 TNA: WO167/207, 2nd Division, Commander Royal Engineers War Diary, 15 October 1939.

that the arrangement of relying on the nearest field company to supervise infantry work parties, which changed daily, was an inefficient way of working and at the end of the month the Company was provided with its own AMPC. In addition to the 135th Excavator Company, some diggers supplied and operated by French contractors were also used to dig anti-tank ditches in the BEF zone, for example in the Bois de Bercu area on the 1st Division's front.

Heavy rain set in during the first week of December, meaning very difficult working conditions for both men and machines. Bulldozers and tractors could not do any effective work. The dragshovels and draglines continued to work but had to be kept on timber mats which slowed down the rate of work. The men of the attached AMPC proved too old to stand the working conditions and infantry working parties had to be resumed. Conditions were to get worse in the New Year as a freeze set in.

Labour shortages

The BEF was working on three major projects: the organisation of the LoC – road and rail construction, bases and depots, and the handling of the vast amounts of munitions and other stores and supplies transported and accumulated in France – the aerodrome construction programme – runway construction and accommodation for personnel and stores – and the construction of the defences in the forward area. Available French civilian labour was almost impossible to hire due to mobilisation. At first, the bulk of the work was undertaken by cavalry and infantry reservists (these were later absorbed into the AMPC). Thus, there was an instant demand for extra RE units that at the time simply did not exist.

An estimate prepared in December for a War Office meeting to discuss labour for the BEF revealed an extra 50,000 men were required, which included trained engineers amounting to 582 officers and 22,000 men. The meeting recorded that there would be 'great difficulty in finding officers, and N.C.Os. just did not exist.'[29] It was the LoC that demanded the lion's share of this labour, even at the expense of constructing defences. The War Office decided that:

> Construction units for L. of C. work were most important and should be provided first, but if possible, some units should be provided at the same time for "X" Force.[30]

29 TNA: WO106/1777, 'R.E. (Works) Organization in the BEF: Record of a meeting held in the War Office on 5th December 1939'.

30 Ibid. Although this may seem surprising at first, the British tendency to emphasise LoC often proved wise. As we have seen, the seven days' supply of ammunition north of the Somme saved the BEF after the German breakthrough.

One method adopted to meet the need for labour was the raising of about 60 new RE units of two types: the general construction company for work on concrete defences (already described above) and aerodromes, largely made up of civil engineering concreters and road construction workers and the artisan works company for general work, with men largely recruited from the building trade. The men that made up both these types of units were hastily thrown into uniform and any men with previous military experience were frequently used to drill the rest in PAD, musketry and squad drill. From these instructors, a nucleus of NCO's was selected and given an acting rank. However, in one company raised, only one member besides the CSM and CQMS had previous military experience, and that was during the South African War of 1899-1902! Training men to some sort of standard was slow, as all were volunteers who had left civil jobs to join up and were not used to a life of hectic drilling. Indeed, skill with weapons was not considered essential, and to get the units dispatched to France as quickly as possible, a level of skill with a rifle to that attained by the AMPC was accepted.

A further memorandum dated 13 March, prepared by the Secretary of State for War, estimated that by June 1940 an additional 60,000 men would be required for labour, rising to 120,000 men by June 1941, the rate of increase after June 1940 taking place at 5,000 a month. By April the supply of labour and engineers was becoming critical due to additional demands. It was estimated that in addition to the total number of formations in the BEF or on existing forecasts an additional 16 general construction companies, 13 road construction companies, three field park companies, nine artisan works companies and one works transport company were required.

The Army Council intensified its efforts to increase the number of voluntary recruits for the AMPC. Recruitment for the AMPC was by the voluntary enlistment of men from the age group 35-50 but this age group also provided the home defence battalions and the overseas defence battalions. Use was also to be made of Grade II enlisted men who had not so far been used. The AMPC was also supplemented with the recruitment of foreigners domiciled in France, mostly refugees, who under French law were liable for ancillary military service. During January 1940, No. 7 Training Company AMPC arrived in France to administer and train batches of foreign labour sent over from Britain and organised into foreign labour companies. A few thousand labourers were also recruited from Cyprus and other Colonies. However, these measures represented only a small pool of additional labour. It was expected that a total labour force of not more than 23,000 would be found from these sources by June 1940, or not more than 30,000 by June 1941.

A temporary measure taken to meet the need for labour was the decision to send portions of three Territorial Army divisions – the 12th (Eastern), 23rd (Northumbrian) and 46th (North Midland and West Riding) Divisions – out to France in April. In ordinary circumstances these divisions, which were neither fully trained nor equipped, would not be sent overseas for some time. These divisions – nicknamed 'digging divisions' – were employed on construction tasks in the rear areas, on aerodromes and acting as working parties for general construction companies. A balanced programme of training was supposed to continue from the point the division had reached on departure from England as time permitted. The men of these divisions were certainly not happy with the labour duties they had to perform or the standard of training they received. One veteran, whose story is told in Mike Rossiter's book *I fought at Dunkirk*, recalls that a fair chunk of the training consisted of route marches, and he thought that the authorities just sent them out on these to keep them occupied. A song about the ex-War Minister was a favourite on these marches:

> We had to join Belisha's army,
> Ten bob a week, nothing to eat, bloody great blisters on
> Your feet,
> *We had to join, we had to join, we had to join Belisha's army!*[31]

The divisions had only just started their pioneer duties at the beginning of May before being thrown into the Blitzkrieg cauldron.

As a longer-term solution, a proposal was put forward to increase labour by allowing the voluntary enlistment in the AMPC of men in the age group 18–20. This was deemed the least politically risky option out of a number of options considered such as the compulsory service of the unemployed in the AMPC or the call up of men for service in the AMPC under the age of 20, which would go against the promise not to send men under the age of 20 to France called up under the National Service (Armed Forces) Act. The voluntary enlistment of the 18 and 19-year- old classes was expected to provide at least 27,000 by the end of August and then 5,000 a month thereafter, as it was anticipated it would satisfy the demand for work for this age group, of which some 40,000 to 50,000 were unemployed.

The expected demand for timber also required a rethink on the number of forestry companies in France. During 1917 it was pointed out that there were 55 British forestry companies in France; in April 1940 there was just one British forestry company of 153 men. Although there was no shortage of round timber in France, the limiting factor was manpower. France had agreed to supply half the timber required for the BEF in 1940, the other half coming from British forestry companies cutting in French forests and by import from outside France. If active hostilities broke out, it was thought that the French may struggle to supply their half due to a lack of manpower in sawmills. To ensure an adequate supply of timber, the Director of Works recommended increasing the number of forestry companies to the scale of one per division.

One obvious conclusion that can be drawn from the labour crisis is that no engineer appreciation had been undertaken prior to dispatching the BEF. In May 1941, Major-General King produced a report on the reorganisation of the Works Services and on the necessity of there being an Engineer-in-Chief at the War Office. He could find

31 Mike Rossiter, *I Fought at Dunkirk: Seven Veterans Remember the German Invasion of France* (London: Bantam Press, 2012), p. 43

no trace of an engineer appreciation having been prepared for any operation. As an example, he cited the requirements of the RAF Component of the BEF, which had been so grossly underestimated it was apparent that they had never been correctly appreciated. His recommendation of an Engineer-in-Chief at the War Office was adopted and in October 1941 he became the first holder of the post.

A 'spot of bother' with the French 51st Division

On 30 September, Ironside wrote to Major-General Howard-Vyse and expressed his concern of the apparent lack of any co-ordination in developing the defences between the French and British. He noted that the 10 field companies of 'X' Force along with mechanical diggers were about to be sent over to France to make the British line along the Franco-Belgian border secure, but that 'it is not much use unless the French continue it either way.'[32] He was concerned that Gamelin was more preoccupied with an expected attack in the north-east, against Holland and Belgium, and was doing very little along the Franco-Belgian border. According to Churchill, Hore-Belisha subsequently raised the question of the gap between the northern end of the Maginot Line proper and the beginning of the British fortified zone with the War Cabinet several times and although representations were made through military channels, the Cabinet and military leaders were shy of openly criticising the French.

As already noted, in the British zone the French were responsible for defence works in their 51st Division area and also for the completion of blockhouses and the anti-tank ditch along the Bachy Switch. GHQ was concerned about the slow progress on the front held by the French 51st Division. According to Pownall, Gillard had been 'squeaking' for weeks about the importance of his sector but had done little about improving it. On a visit to the sector on 24 October, Pownall counted only nine men working on defences compared to hundreds of men in the British sector. Brigadier Kennedy also remarked on the lack of progress on the BEF's flanks:

> [T]he stronger the British defences had become, the greater would the danger have been of the British Army being surrounded and cut off, had we stood on the frontier; the French would undoubtedly have been swept away on our flanks because they had made no proper defences.[33]

The French probably thought why build defences if the French and the BEF where to move into Belgium in the event of a German attack? They were also aware that it was planned to hand over their sector to the BEF. Another factor was that works carried

32 TNA: WO106/1777, Ironside to Sir Richard Howard-Vyse, KCMG, DSO, 30 September 1939.

33 John Kennedy, *The Business of War: The War Narrative of Major-General Sir John Kennedy* (London: Hutchinson & Co. (Publishers) Ltd., 1957), p.150.

out by the French Army were paid out of local taxes. On 27 October, the 11 Brigade was instructed to assist the French 51st Division in the preparation of defences in the Halluin area (Mont d'Halluin – Triez Cailloux – Nouveau Monde). The anti-tank obstacles in this sector included the completed *Ligne Principale,* an intermediate obstacle surrounding Mont d'Halluin, which required a minefield of 1,500 mines on the eastern face of Mont d'Halluin, and the *Ligne d'Arret* under construction with projected blockhouses along the Becque de Neuville (Figures 5.3 and 6.1). The Brigade's tasks were twofold. Firstly, it was to improve the Becque de Neuville as an anti-tank obstacle. Secondly, it was to construct field defences in the forward area of Halluin. The field defences were to fit in with the framework of pillboxes already constructed or sited. If any new pillboxes were required, these were to be constructed under arrangements made by the French.

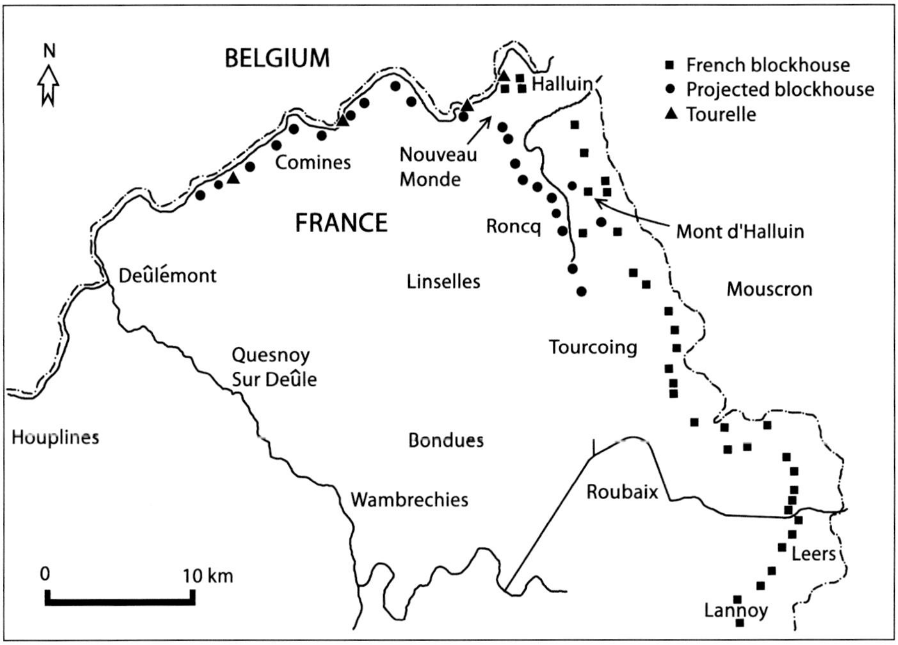

Figure 5.3: Map showing existing blockhouses from Lannoy to Halluin and projected blockhouses along the River Lys from Halluin to Comines and the Becque de Neuville, French 51st Division sector, at the time 11 Brigade were ordered to assist the French with the construction of defences.

The French 51st Division held a wide front, with roughly one and a half companies holding a sector to which the 11 Brigade were allocating a battalion. With the French still occupying the position, some difficulties were experienced in co-ordination, with the Brigade's battalions having to consider the defence of their sectors as a TEWT (Tactical Exercise Without Troops). A compromise was found where the French continued to work on the *Ligne Principale* while the Brigade worked on the *Ligne d'Arret.* On the whole the Brigade's progress was good and the results were noticeable when GHQ staff officers accompanied Georges on a tour of the 51st Division's sector in early November:

> From Armentières to Comines to Bousbecque he met the C.O.'s of the 51st Division who explained the various church spires on the ground, the works that were *envisagés*, the area of fire on their masses of tracing paper. But no sign on the ground, all virgin soil. Then suddenly we came to Mt Halluin, a mass of British soldiers digging like fury. The contrast between words and deeds was almost pitiful! Even Gillard said of the scene 'c'est épatant!'[34]

On 29 November, the Brigade became responsible for the whole of the sector. It should, however, be noted that the lack of progress made by the French on their 51st Division's front was not reflected along their entire front and in places the French actually did much work to improve the defences of the Maginot Line and the Maginot Extension (see for instance, Appendix I).

The pillbox affair

On 17 November the Secretary of State for War, Mr Hore-Belisha, flew over to France to visit the Front. Ironside was also visiting France at the same time in order to address French concerns that Britain was not mobilising fast enough. Hore-Belisha's visit to the Front and the subsequent events lead to what became known as 'The pillbox affair'.

Hore-Belisha became Secretary of State for War in May 1937, probably in an attempt by Chamberlin to raise the prestige of the Army as he had been a popular

34 Bond, Brian (ed.), *Chief of Staff: The Diaries of Lieutenant-General Sir Henry Pownall* (London: Leo Cooper, 1972), p. 251. Other distinguished observers also noted the apparent lack of French activity. Churchill wrote: 'Yet visitors to the French front were often struck by the prevailing atmosphere of calm aloofness, by the seemingly poor quality of the work in hand, by the lack of visible activity of any kind. The emptiness of the roads behind the line was in great contrast to the continual coming and going which extended for miles behind the British sector' (*The Second World War: Volume I – The Gathering Storm* (London: Cassell & Co. Ltd., 1948), p. 442). Churchill was of the opinion that the French Army had deteriorated over the course of the winter and that they would have fought better in the autumn of 1939 than they did in the spring of 1940. André Maurois came to a similar conclusion. He recalled a conversation with Lieutenant de Jumilhac who was his guide on his tour of Corap's Ninth Army in April 1940. De Jumilhac remarked that the 'dust is beginning to settle on us here.' Maurois was also struck by the emptiness of the roads behind the Ninth Army's front: 'I returned from this last tour of the armies with a feeling of uneasiness. The troops in the line seemed good enough, but the disposition was terribly thin. Ten miles behind the line one never saw a soldier. The thought of this emptiness was agonizing [sic]. If ever the enemy were to pierce this thin shell ...' (André Maurois, *The Battle of France* (London: John Lane the Bodley Head, 1940), pp. 171-172).

Minister of Transport. Although he managed to obtain substantial funding for the Army and pushed through some much-needed reforms, he was regarded as a flamboyant, egotistical, impulsive and tactless politician by the military hierarchy. His unorthodox methods of working, especially his association with Captain Liddell Hart, then Military Correspondent of the Times, had resulted in him becoming extremely unpopular with professional soldiers. Gort, Pownall and Ironside all disliked him; Pownall was particularly hostile when writing about him in his diary.

Before they departed from England, Ironside had asked Hore-Belisha whether he wished to visit the troops or defences, so Gort could plan his visit. Hore-Belisha stated he wished to visit the troops and not the defences. On 18 November, Hore-Belisha toured the front of I and II Corps, and saw men working on the defences. The following day was wet, cold and windy. On the way to the western side of the British position, Gort stopped at Vimy Ridge and made Hore-Belisha climb up a very muddy bank and kept him shivering and cold as he explained the battles of the Great War fought in the area. Next, the party stopped at Aubers Ridge where Pownall gave a description of the fighting there. The party met *Général* Gillard in his château where he pointed out the various places in the landscape; Gort opened a window and let in a piercing draft on Hore-Belisha. The party visited Commines and Halluin and climbed another hill to view the landscape. Hore-Belisha was then packed off with bully beef sandwiches supplied by Gort's mess. Years later, Pownall admitted that this rough treatment of Hore-Belisha was quite intentional; no doubt it contributed to Hore-Belisha's subsequent mishandling of the whole affair.

Meeting up with Hore-Belisha in Paris on 19 November, Ironside noted that Hore-Belisha 'had had a wonderful trip. He glibly told me that he now had a grasp of things and had various ideas. He had been disappointed at the way the Sappers had failed to get a pattern of [i.e. a standard design] pillbox and how Gort hadn't used all the extra sappers we had sent him'.[35] Indeed Hore-Belisha was not satisfied and confided to Brigadier Kennedy:

> My impression of the front is that they are working on quite the wrong lines. There ought to be hundreds of pill-boxes, every hundred yards if necessary. Pakenham-Walsh [BEF Engineer-in-Chief] had an enormous file with six designs in it, and no pill-boxes have been built except two, although they have been that position for a month or more. I sent them a good engineer to help them. I found him very crestfallen. He had not been properly used. It is always the same in the British Army. You are always looking for the best design. The best is the enemy of the good. That is why we have got no tanks or anti-tank guns. We must standardize [sic] pill-boxes for mass production. [36]

35 Colonel R. Macleod, DSO, MC & Denis Kelly (eds.), *Time Unguarded: The Ironside Diaries 1937 – 1940* (New York: David McKay Company Inc., 1963), p. 164.
36 Kennedy, *The Business of War*, p. 38.

Pownall also noted Hore-Belisha's impatience in his diary. He recorded that the latter questioned the need for having so many drawings of different types of pillboxes projected, and Pownall clearly felt that he did not understand the need for detailed planning for such a large scale of works. Pownall also writes that Hore-Belisha expected to see 'concrete fortresses' springing up all over the place, but that as usual the soldiers were holding him back from realising his dream of constructing a 'Belisha Line' greater and stronger than the Maginot Line. Pownall clearly illustrates in his diary the great distrust and suspicion, mostly undeserved, he had in the Secretary of State for War.

Hore-Belisha also asked Ironside how pillboxes could be made quickly to which Ironside apparently informed him 'You can't make a Maginot Line with mud'.[37] Remarkably, an engineer that Hore-Belisha quizzed on the matter had suggested just that: a quick way to make pillboxes would be literally to use mud, by freezing it! Pakenham-Walsh was also pressed on why pillboxes could not be constructed more quickly and was urged by Hore-Belisha to 'do all we can to avoid disaster'.[38] Pakenham-Walsh replied that he thought the line was of some strength and that with the intention to fight a long way in front of it, he did not foresee a 'disaster'.

About the same time as Hore-Belisha's visit, the Secretary of State for the Dominions, Anthony Eden, and five representatives of the Empire overseas – Mr. Crerar (Canada), Mr. Casey (Australia), Mr. Fraser (New Zealand), Colonel Reitz (South Africa) and Sir Muhammad Zafrullah Khan (India) – also visited the BEF zone and the Maginot Line. They were all immensely impressed with strength of the French defences along the Maginot Line. Mr. Crerar remarked 'The line is tremendously strong. It would be mighty hard to get through.'[39] Mr. Eden said: 'To visit the Maginot Line is to realize [sic] how much we owe the French Army and the French nation for having constructed it.'[40] They noted the apparent lack of concrete defences in the BEF zone compared to the Maginot Line. These comments reached Hore-Belisha and seemed to confirm his own doubts.

On 24 November Hore-Belisha told a Cabinet meeting after Ironside had left the room that he was not satisfied with the work the BEF was putting into the defences (Hore-Belisha had a particularly difficult relationship with Ironside, as had earlier been predicted, and Pownall suggests that this was the reason why he discussed matters relating to his visit to the front at key meetings when Ironside was absent). He also stated that Gamelin had informed him that the French could construct a pillbox in three days while it took the British three weeks (Gamelin subsequently denied saying this but had stated that it took the French three days to construct a

37 Ibid., p.149.
38 Bond (ed.), *Chief of Staff*, p. 261.
39 Skene Catling, *Vanguard to Victory: An Account of the first months of the British Expeditionary Force in France* (London: Methuen & Co. Ltd., 1940), p. 98.
40 Ibid.

pillbox using French quick-dry cement after the site had been prepared and all the materials were assembled, the whole operation taking 20 days). He also compared favourably what he thought were French defences on the left of the British sector, unaware that they had in fact been built by the BEF. Following the War Office meeting, he summoned an Army Council meeting at which again Ironside was not present, but Pakenham-Walsh was. Hore-Belisha repeated his concerns about the programme for pillbox construction, which he thought was far too slow. It was, he remarked, no use explaining to the House of Commons why pillboxes could not be built more quickly. Pakenham-Walsh was instructed to inform Gort verbally of the War Cabinet's concern at the lack of defence works:

> The Prime Minister, on the report of the representatives of the Dominions, the S of S for Dominions, and myself, has said in the War Cabinet that he is very perturbed at the reported weakness of the British sector of the line. [41]

This message was without a Cabinet mandate, and later Hore-Belisha tried to claim that the message Pakenham-Walsh delivered to Gort was a gross distortion of what he actually said.

When the Prime Minister informed Ironside of the adverse criticisms, Ironside decided to go to France himself to review the state of defences. Arriving in France on 29 November, he naturally found GHQ 'in a devil of a rage' over the message from Hore-Belisha passed on by Pakenham- Walsh. GHQ had good reason for its 'rage'. The War Minister had made no complaint to Gort during his visit to France and appeared completely satisfied with all he saw. Having asked to see the troops and not the defences, he had not been shown the field works. These were well concealed in camouflaged houses, woods and hedges, and many could not have been visible when Hore-Belisha was inspecting the troops, who, in several cases had been formed up near roads to make inspection easier.

On 30 November, Ironside met with both Gort and Brooke. In his diary, Brooke noted that Ironside 'informed me that when Hore-Belisha returned from his trip he informed both the Cabinet and Privy Council that the BEF was doing no work and had left their front unprotected. That we were the laughing stock of the French on either flank and a few similar remarks! The true case is that the French have been doing practically nothing on our flanks'.[42] Brooke was so concerned about the lack of progress on the defences made by the French 51st Division that he had asked Gort to relieve it with his 4th Division so he could secure his flank.

On returning to Britain, Ironside presented a report on the progress of the British defences and stated that he was perfectly satisfied with what had been achieved. He

41 Bond (ed.), *Chief of Staff*, pp. 259–260.

42 Alex Danchev & Daniel Todman (eds.), *War Diaries 1939-1945: Field Marshall Lord Alan Brooke* (Berkely and Los Angeles: University of California Press, 2001), p. 21.

pointed out that the BEF had been working while under short notice of attack and that the first priority had been to dig in to resist an attack. After 15 November, troops were disposed with a view to working on defences rather than meeting a German attack. In his report on the state of the defences, Ironside recorded that I Corps had 51 pillboxes completed (including the French blockhouses taken over on 3 October) and 26 under construction and sites selected for a further 133, while II Corps had 52 completed (also including the French blockhouses) and seven under construction and sites selected for a further 105. Both corps had completed the strengthening of houses, totalling 35. 'X' Force was beginning its work and with standard designs settled should be able to construct 20 to 30 pillboxes a month. Trenches and breastworks in the forward line had been completed to section post stage. Work on wire obstacles had been somewhat limited due to the need to maintain a large reserve for any advance into Belgium; only some 300 tons had been released up to the end of November although a complete wiring scheme had been produced which could be carried out in one to two days. Much work had been completed on digging anti-tank obstacles, with 1,350 yards completed by 18 diggers alone in the last week of November. The layout for a buried cable communication system was well under way, with four mechanical diggers at work which could do half a mile a day each. All battery positions had been prepared and temporary and roving positions reconnoitred and routes to them fixed. Field works for anti-tank gun and machine gun positions had been completed on part of the Corps Reserve Position. Ironside stated that the actual time to complete a pillbox, including getting all materials to site, was around six weeks and that *Colonel* Bertschi 'and other authorities say that it is quite impossible to make a pill box in three days.'[43] He also reminded the Cabinet that the Maginot Line took 10 years to construct.

Just after his return to France, Ironside remarked to Brigadier Kennedy 'Now that I have seen the defences myself, I intend to tell the Cabinet quite straight that Hore-Belisha is wrong. I think he'll have to go. It is time we had a better chap in the War Office.'[44] Apparently, the report Ironside presented came as a surprise to Hore-Belisha. In a conversation he had with Kennedy eighteen months after the affair, he remarked that at a meeting to discuss the slow progress of pillbox construction Ironside had stated 'Jack Gort knows nothing about defences. Let me go and see the front and report.' On his return, Ironside immediately went to see him and observed: 'All France is in an uproar at your criticisms of the defences.' He expected Ironside to 'put them right', but to his astonishment Ironside said 'No – I agree with them'.[45]

It was evident that confidence in the Secretary of State for War had collapsed in the BEF, a situation exploited by Pownall, who did all he could to ensure Belisha's removal. The King, who had become aware of the incident, made a weeklong visit to

43 TNA: WO106/1777, 'Notes of C.I.G.S's Visit to B.E.F. – 29th Nov. – 2nd Dec. 1939'.
44 Kennedy, *The Business of War*, p. 40.
45 Ibid, p. 150.

the Front in December and also saw the discontent in the BEF. He was convinced that Hore-Belisha had to go. Chamberlain also made a brief visit, and in a letter to Gort wrote: 'I was particularly impressed by the great progress made, in so short a time and despite many difficulties, with the construction of defences'.[46] He also became convinced that the friction between Hore-Belish and the senior commanders of the BEF was detrimental to the war effort in France. Eden was apparently equally distressed and emphasised that he and the five Overseas Ministers had been drawing attention to the obvious contrast between the BEF defences and the Maginot Line and had implied no criticism of Gort or his staff. He claimed they were only trying to be helpful in getting extra assistance for concrete defences in the BEF zone.

Hore-Belisha subsequently tried to drop the matter, but even so was still apparently unaware of the deep offence he had caused. This was a key reason why on the next Cabinet reshuffle, Chamberlain offered Hore-Belisha the Board of Trade, which he refused and resigned from the Government (he had been considered for the post of Minister for Information, but being Jewish, this was considered too much of a propaganda opportunity for Goebbels). His resignation – the 'Belisha Scandal' – caused a stir in the press, some papers claiming he had been forced out by the aristocratic generals.

It is certain that the dismissal of Hore-Belisha was more to do with personalities rather than a major tactical disagreement or questions over his competence. Brigadier Kennedy certainly thought that pillboxes were a side issue, with the attack on him being a culmination of a long series of differences. If he had not fallen out with Gort and Ironside on the question of pillboxes, some other issue would have arisen for a test of strength. With the BEF committed fully to Plan D, did it really matter how many pillboxes were being constructed? If he had been a more popular War Minister, the whole matter would probably have blown over. It is likely that what was in reality a minor crisis, in which Hore-Belisha did not follow protocol, was transformed into a 'crisis' in order to finally get rid of him.

Hore-Belisha was probably right in that pillboxes could have been built faster if things were better organised, as a report produced by 'X' Force in March 1940 subsequently demonstrated. In this report, the peculiar problems of pillbox construction were outlined: it required a large amount of material in proportion to the labour, pillbox sites were dispersed over a wide area and specialised equipment was required. Also delays were incurred if the construction of pillboxes were handed over from unit to unit. The report noted that an average pillbox of 150 cubic yards took six weeks to complete, with five to 20 men employed according to the stage reached and 300 tons of material. Certain processes, such as manufacture of shuttering, bending and cutting of steel bars and repairs to plant were best carried out in a central workshop. A centralised dump and transport pool would also speed things up – it was noted that

46 Catling, *Vanguard to Victory*, p. 62.

it took six weeks to establish a workshop and dump, about as long as that required building a pillbox! The report observed:

> In fact, as in all Military Engineering work which takes a considerable time, Blockhouse Construction should be controlled on an area basis and should not be tied rigidly to formations or to formation boundaries.[47]

The report went on to note that if each general construction company was allocated 12 pillboxes to work on simultaneously – one construction section had around 40 men, so should be able to work on three pillboxes simultaneously – this would require 600 tons of material a week per company or 100 tons per working day. To speed things up, it was recommended that no round trip for each load should exceed 12 miles and that labour should be billeted within walking distance of the work. Mechanical loading of trucks would also speed things up and the use of tipper trucks would save time in unloading. The suggested solution was to establish construction HQs, each looking after on average four companies. The HQs would regulate supplies of materials, plant, transport and labour and oversee the manufacturing of shuttering, bar bending and cutting and plant repair. A central location would be chosen for each HQ to hold plant, the transport pool, workshop and dump, which would only move when all work in the area was complete. As a particular construction company may finish its work before the work in that area was complete as a whole, each HQ would have to be capable of coping with between one to six companies. The inference from this report is that pillbox construction could be speeded up by more efficient organisation.

A harsh winter

GHQ noted in its War Diary that December 'has been on the whole quieter than the three preceding' months.[48] This allowed GHQ (Operations Branch) to move to Arras and with more efficient working conditions consolidated instructions could be issued to replace the plethora of instructions issued over the preceding three months. Instructions were also issued to prepare an outline scheme for fitting up a battle headquarters in the caves to the south-east of Arras railway station, to be used by an Advanced GHQ and at a later date by Army HQs (it was planned to divide the BEF into two Armies when the number of divisions in the field, excluding the Armoured Division, rose above 11). These caves had been utilised in 1917 when two divisions had been accommodated in them prior to the Arras offensive. The scheme was never to come to fruition.

47 TNA: WO167/1430, 'H.Q. of Construction Units for Blockhouse Building', 13 March 1940, 1st Battalion "X" Force War Diary.

48 TNA: WO167/2, 'War Diary Summary – December 1939', GHQ General Operations War Diary.

With the advance into Belgium firmly settled, it was now unlikely that the Allies would fight in the northernmost frontier defences. But it was still regarded as essential to be prepared for all eventualities and work was to continue to make the defences in the BEF sector as strong as possible. Work was not necessarily to be connected with the existing frontages of formations and units; if the BEF did have to withdraw from an advance into Belgium, such formations and units would not necessarily end up fighting in their current positions. At the same time, with a German attack highly unlikely until the spring, training took a much higher priority. For example, the 4 Brigade issued instructions that all breastworks under construction were to be completed by 7 December to allow units to devote all time not required for maintenance of existing defences to training. Battalions were to concentrate all available working parties as required irrespective of the company sectors that the work was to be carried out in to achieve this. Work on the defences was now to concentrate on pillboxes and anti-tank ditches only. However, it was only really from February onwards that it was acknowledged that concrete work may have to slow down to allow more time for training.

Resources also allowed work to start on the reconnaissance and siting of permanent defences on the Corps Line along the sector from Marchiennes to Mons-en-Pévèle thence to Seclin. The French, under *Colonel* Bertschi were still responsible for the construction of a line of pillboxes along the River Lys between Halluin and Deûlémont using contractors and French concreting companies. These pillboxes were if possible, to be an anti-tank gun pillbox covering every road approach to the Lys with intermediate single machine gun or Bren pillboxes.

During December the weather turned very cold, heralding the start of what was to be an extremely hard winter, with freezing conditions lasting until mid-February.[49] At first the cold did not disrupt work on the defences. Indeed, after the heavy rain at the start of December, the ground conditions were much more favourable for the excavators of the 135th Excavator Company. On 6 January, the Company's War Diary notes its best weekly progress achieved so far with 2,044 yards of anti-tank ditch completed during the week. As winter tightened its grip, the work rate slowed drastically. It became impossible to use the draglines. The dragshovels could still work, but it resulted in anti-tank ditches not being completed to the full width; it was anticipated that the dragshovels could catch up when the thaw set in. On 19 January, permission was obtained from the Engineer-in-Chief to stop all work due to the excavators being overstrained as a result of the ground conditions, with practically no results to show for the effort. It was not until early February that an attempt was

49 From the end of December, anticyclonic conditions set in over Europe, persisting for much of January resulting in the coldest European winter for at least 45 years. Unfortunately, there is a gap in the Lille weather station temperature data for this period, but the mean temperature for January 1940 at Uccle, 105km east of Lille, was -4.08 °C, a temperature anomaly of -6.89°C compared to the previous decade (1919-29). Source: https://data.giss.nasa.gov/tmp/gistemp/STATIONS/tmp_606064470000_5_0_1/station.txt.

made to restart work with all machines. Working in thaw conditions was not straight forward though. The ground was still too hard to drive in pickets while the ground slush made it difficult to do any effective revetting. A return to frost resulted in only 150 yards being completed during the week ended 10 February.

At the end of February, a review was undertaken on the progress of the defences as a result of the delays caused by the weather. It was estimated that to complete all the proposed anti-tank ditches with the number of mechanical excavators available would require a year. Mechanical excavators had to be employed on a fixed priority (Table 5.4). Where mechanical excavators were not available, ditches could be progressed by working parties; a party of 50 men could excavate a ditch at approximately the same pace as a mechanical excavator. Progress speeded up in March and April, and with the improved conditions the AMPC provided 'good working parties' and showed the value of having a permanent labour on this sort of work. A record weekly yardage of 4,671 yards was completed in April, with the monthly total being nine and a half lineal miles. The 135th Excavator Company was able to report that the FDL and Brigade Reserve lines were complete throughout I and II Corps sectors and the bulk of the Divisional Line also completed. Work was also underway on the sector of the newly arrived III Corps.

Table 5.4: Anti-tank ditch priority, February 1940. This represented three months work for the excavator teams available if full use was made of the hours of daylight.

First Piority	**Length in yards**
II Corps FDL Line	6,350
I Corps Brigade Reserve Line (between 815253-893185)	8,600
Second Priority	
II Corps Divisional Reserve Line (between 768288-740443)	7,000
I Corps Nomain Switch	11,300
Third Priority	
I Coprs Corps Reserve Line (Mons-en-Pévèle)	6,100
	39,350 (say 40,000)

At the start of the freeze, concreting was at a stage which could be left for a few days, with work focused on bar bending and erection of shuttering instead. But with no let up in the freezing conditions, progress soon ground to a halt. Only a limited amount of concreting took place with special frost precautions (see Chapter 8). An attempt was made to resume concreting at the start of February due to a thaw setting in but the return to frost put a stop to work again. It was not until 21 February that concreting could be fully resumed, but the state of the roads due to the thaw caused problems with the delivery of sand and aggregate. Some general construction companies adopted double shifts in March to try and make up for the delays caused by the winter weather. In April, a conference held at the HQ of the 2nd General Construction Battalion in which working hours were discussed decided that a break in the afternoon would only be allowed if tea could be provided and that there was to be no extension to the half hour lunch break. Progress on field works was equally affected as digging was impossible in the frozen ground. Thus, during the height of the freeze, the whole front was effectively snow and ice bound and everything at a standstill.

When the thaw set in at the end of February, training remained a higher priority than the construction of defences, although not road repairs. Instructions issued by I Corps on 28 February, for instance, prioritised tasks in the following order:

1. Maintenance and repairs of roads as a result of the winter weather.
2. Training.
3. Construction of anti-tank ditches.
4. Concrete pillbox construction.
5. Field works.

Although maintenance was supposed to have continued on existing field works after the thaw set in, there were so many calls on the infantry to supply working parties for the engineers to help in road repairs that many trenches and breastworks were still in a bad condition at the end of March. From 16 March the *SD* Lille was upgraded by the French to a Fortified Region – *Sector Fortifié de Lille.*

170th Tunnelling Company

Early on, the decision was taken to mobilise a tunnelling company for work on deep dugouts for key HQs. The 170th Tunnelling Company was mobilised on 19 October and its establishment was based on the Great War establishment for a tunnelling company RE. The personnel of the company consisted of volunteers and men drawn from the service including RE training battalions, AA and search light units, infantry units etc. Most of the men hailed from the mining districts of Northumberland and Durham. Some were from Wales and a few from Scotland. However, because of delays in receiving equipment and effecting transfers, the Company did not get to France until 13 January.

At the beginning of February, the Company was given its tasks. These consisted of battle HQs at Douai and Lens for the HQ of I and II Corps. The work at Lens entailed opening up the old Hulluch tunnel works employed during the Great War, and 'proved very interesting to some of the Old Tunnelling Officers of the unit who had actually assisted to lay down these tunnels some 25 years previously.'[50]

By early March, it was decided to provide underground accommodation for GHQ at Doullens, and it became apparent that expansion of the tunnellers was necessary. The Hulluch tunnellers from were withdrawn along with a section from Douai to carry out the work at Doullens. Work at Hulluch continued under CRE II Corps with personnel from the field companies. On 26 March, approval was given for expansion to a CRE Command consisting of an HQ with four tunnelling companies and a workshop section. Work continued on Douai and Doullens throughout April and additional reconnaissances were carried out for various arms and formations requiring underground accommodation. First Army expected to form in the summer of 1940 (see Chapter 6) required cover at St. Pol and the operations room of the AASF considered proposals for an underground operations room in the old caves in Arras. It was further decided to raise a further three tunnelling groups i.e. 16 tunnelling companies in all. The work at Doullens was almost complete by May 1940, and was the largest work undertaken, excavated 70 ft below the old Citadel and consisting of some 70 chambers with forced ventilation and gas protection.

Other dugout works were also undertaken in the various battle zones. For example, the War Diary of the 3rd Division notes that work was started on a mined dugout for a battalion HQ, but that the work was hampered because of flooding. Specialist mining labour from the 1st Battalion Durham Light Infantry were engaged on 'special works' on the Corps Reserve Position, with I Corps War Diary noting that 15 yards horizontally at a depth were completed during January.

The Bachy Switch

The original *Ligne Pricipale* sited by the French had utilised the River Marcq as part of the continuous anti-tank obstacle. However, this produced a salient in the line between Bachy and Gruson and the French, as already described, had started work on a new FDL Line to cut off this salient, as well as take in high ground. This new section of the FDL Line was known as the Bachy Switch by the British and most of the Switch ran through 1st Division's area (I Corps). It was, however, very exposed and at least one brigadier considered it would be a difficult position to hold. When the BEF took over *SD* Lille, the French continued to be responsible for constructing the blockhouses and the anti-tank ditch along the Bachy Switch although British detachments assisted with the revetting (Table 5.5).

Whilst construction of the Bachy Switch was taking place, it was to be held as an outpost line. Bren and infantry posts were constructed while the anti-tank ditch was wired. Planning to hold the Bachy Switch as a FDL Line on completion, expected to be by 1 February 1940, was progressed simultaneously with the construction of the

50 TNA: WO167/957, 170th Tunnelling Company RE War Diary.

Table 5.5: Report on Bachy Switch on 1st Corps front carried out by Captain K.G. Exham and Captain Smith-Dorrien, 10 October 1939.

Location	Comments
Blockhouse No.1 847235	Blockhouse complete. Troops working on field defences. Anti-tank ditch complete to a point just south of blockhouse No.2
Blockhouse No.2 841248	Blockhouse complete except for covering up the pile of rocks on the front face. The anti-tank ditch starts again beyond this blockhouse after a gap of about 200 yards between it and No.1.
Blockhouse No.3 834265	Blockhouse complete except for piling rocks on forward face, on which a small gang of labour was working on. The anti-tank ditch was complete between No.2 and No.3 except for a gap for a road.
Blockhouse No.4 833268	Blockhouse not complete; a gang at work said it would take a further two weeks to finish. Blockhouse located on an important feature, overlooking the low ground towards Bourchelles. The anti-tank ditch was complete between No.3 and No.4.
Blockhouse No.5 8226	Only half finished. A large gang at work on the blockhouse. The anti-tank obstacle between No.4 and No.5 ceased some 500 yards before reaching No.5. An excavator was at work on this section.
Blockhouse No.6 815296	Blockhouse at foundation level only. Anti-tank obstacle from No.5 ceases at a point near 8226. An excavator was at work on this section.

defences by the French. The Brigade Reserve and Divisional Reserve Positions needed to be modified and additional pillboxes sited in the brigade forward area (Figure 5.4). The original FDL Line remained unchanged as far as and including Bercu. Thence, the new Switch would run on the general line east of Bachy – between Wannehain and Genech – Bourghelles – Gruson. From Gruson, the FDL Line then resumed its original trace. In the south, the Brigade Reserve Position remained unchanged as far as the Bois de Bercu. Thence the new Position would run on the general line Cense de Cobrieux (where it cut the original FDL Line) – La Posterie – west of Bourghelles – east of Cysoing. It then swung round towards Sainghin to pick up the original trace. Very few pillboxes had been projected on this part of the new Position, and those that had were mainly around La Posterie. The Divisional Reserve Position remained unchanged in the south up to Nomain. The new Position then ran east of Genech, joining the original FDL Line southeast of Cobrieux. It then followed the original FDL Line to Péronne-en-Mélantos and then picked up the original trace.

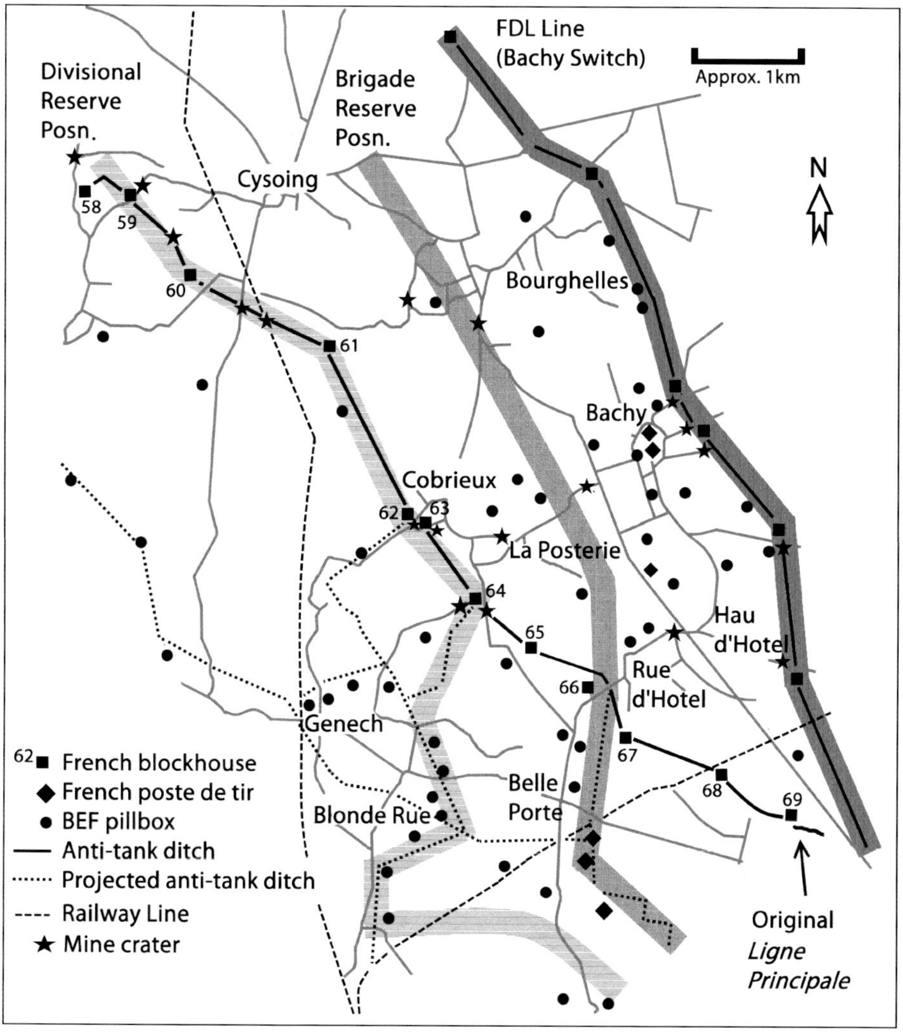

Figure 5.4: Map depicting proposed lines and pillboxes required to incorporate the Bachy Switch into the FDL Line as at 15 November along 1st Division's front.

By the end of November, the engineers had begun work on Bren and anti-tank pillboxes to add the required depth to the line, with an initial programme of four Bren pillboxes, three 2 pdr anti-tank gun pillboxes and one 2 pdr anti-tank gun and Bren pillbox. Additionally, a number of switch anti-tank ditches were to be dug by the 135th Excavator Company to close various gaps.

The Corps Reserve Position and the Second Position

At first, 4th Division – although attached to II Corps – was retained in GHQ Reserve and was tasked with developing the defences of the Corps Reserve Position on the general line Moncheaux to Seclin and the Second Position along the canal line. The 15 Brigade also worked on the Corps Position from Marchiennes to Bois de Flines until it came under the command of 5th Division.

The purpose of the Corps Reserve Position was to hold any enemy tanks that succeed in penetrating the forward defences (and possibly enemy infantry at a later stage) and block the passage to the canals. The Second Position was to be developed to block all crossings over the canals and to prevent the formation of bridgeheads by exploiting forces. At a later date, both Positions were to be organised as systems of defence in depth.

The high ground at Mons-en-Pévèle was the cornerstone of the Corps Reserve Position. The French had also recognised the importance of this position, and when the BEF moved into the line, *Colonel* Bertschi handed over a project for the defence of this feature. In the first instance, and as a high priority, Mons-en-Pévèle was prepared as a defended locality and held by the 2nd Battalion (Machine Gun) Cheshire Regiment and the 21st Anti-tank Regiment. The defended locality was to include the woodland on the line Moncheaux – Thumeries – Bois de Phalempin, which were natural anti-tank obstacles.

The Corps Reserve Position was considered excellent country for defence. Houses and orchards were ribboned along the main roads leading into villages, which provided narrow covered approaches to the villages that could easily be blocked. Either side of villages, the landscape was generally featureless arable land and easy to defilade with anti-tank guns hidden in gardens, orchards, etc. According to 10 Brigade:

> The topography of the position lends itself admirably for the purpose required and it should be possible to prevent any attempt by the enemy to break through either with armoured vehicles alone or in co-operation with motorised infantry supported by only weak artillery.[51]

The general policy was to hold the villages and woods with riflemen guarding anti-tank blocks with Bren guns, anti-tank rifles and anti-tank mines; it was intended that this would force the enemy armour off the roads onto the surrounding countryside where they would come under fire from the anti-tank guns. The siting of defence posts in the villages and woods would also help conceal them from the air. Initially, only 21 anti-tank guns were available to hold the Corps Reserve Position in the 4th

51 TNA: WO167/366, 'Appreciation by Commander, 10th Infantry Brigade', 13 October 1939, 10 Infantry Brigade War Diary.

Division's sector (the remainder of its anti-tank guns were deployed along the Second Position) while the 15 Brigade's sector had a total of 30 guns.

The order of priority for work on the Corps Reserve Position was the construction of the anti-tank gun and anti-tank rifle posts, blocking passage through villages and woods and the construction of section posts in support of the anti-tank gun positions and obstacles. Concealment of the defences was especially important to ensure that surprise was obtained; troops were encouraged to make full use of woods and houses when siting the defences. Although depth was to be aimed for, it was emphasised that this was not to be at the expense of a strong 'crust'. These defences were sited by the units carrying out the work. An anti-tank obstacle was to be constructed, at first to close the gaps between the villages and woods, and later in front of the infantry localities. As this work progressed, it was intended that the anti-tank guns could be thinned out along the line of the FDLs to provide more depth to areas most vulnerable to attack.

Although work on the Corps Reserve Position was temporarily halted when the 4th and 5th Divisions took over the French 51st Division sector during December, the expected arrival of III Corps would place three divisions in GHQ Reserve – 48th Division in I Corps area, 50th Division in II Corps area and 44th Division in III Corps area – which would allow work to proceed on the rear defences, namely the Corps Reserve Position and a Divisional Reserve Line to be sited along the front of the British 51st Division (which started to relieve the French 53rd Division in the area Bailleul – Armentières at the end of January 1940) with a new switch line to connect the Corps Reserve Position at Prémesques to this new Divisional Reserve Line.

Instructions issued to the 48th Division for the Corps Reserve Position in I Corps area specified that first importance was to be given to the defences in front of, and on the flanks of, the Mons-en-Pévèle feature and astride the Orchies – Douai road from the canal at Montreuil to Boujon. Those issued to the 50th Division in II Coprs area stated that first priority was between the Bois D'Avelin and the canal north-west of Seclin and the defences between the old fort at Hallenes-lez-Haubourdin and Prémesques.

GHQ carried out the detailed siting of the anti-tank ditch and pillboxes covering it while the two divisions were to recommend what extra pillboxes were required to add depth to the position. All pillboxes were to be 3ft 6in thick unless 5ft 6in was specified. GHQ instructed that the anti-tank ditch was to run in straight legs of a maximum length of 850 yards covered by pillboxes containing one anti-tank gun and one Bren gun (Figure 5.5). These pillboxes were sited in pairs at angles to the ditch so they could enfilade it without danger to each other. The hastily constructed field defences on the Mons-en-Pévèle position had to be largely re-sited to fit in with the line finally decided upon for the Corps Reserve Position. Priority was attached to the anti-tank ditch, anti-tank gun pillboxes to produce a belt of fire enfilading the ditch and machine gun pillboxes and wire. Work on Bren pillboxes and field works was not to begin until further notice. Only two excavators were available for this work in I Corps area, requiring infantry working parties to be employed on digging the ditch.

The instructions noted that the field works already completed had been prepared for three infantry brigades on an extended front. The new concrete pillboxes were not to fit into the defences for occupation of units of a particular size but were to form the framework from which the defences could eventually be built up. Following a review of the state of defences undertaken in February as a result of the delays caused by the winter weather, GHQ devolved responsibility for the detailed siting of the anti-tank ditch and pillboxes, each corps now responsible for the area within their own boundary.

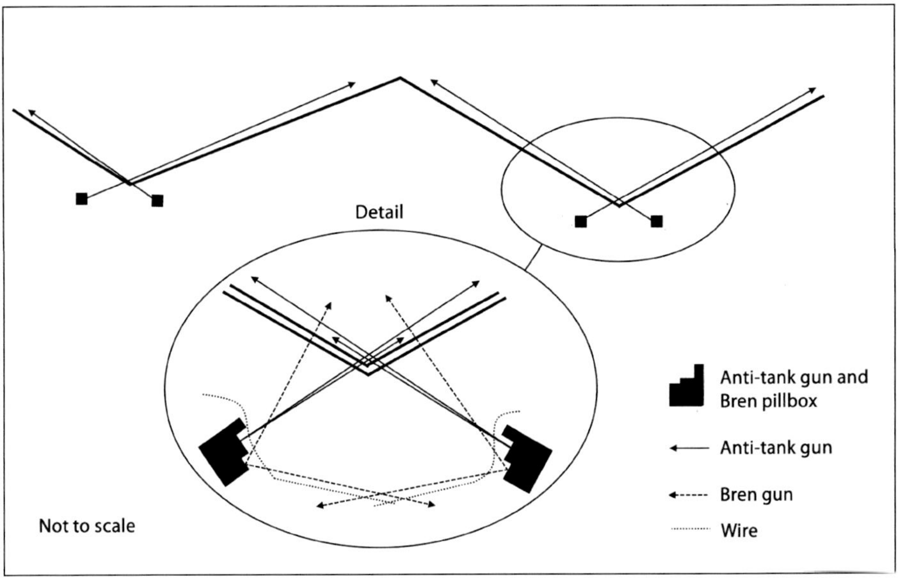

Figure 5.5: GHQ specification for the layout of anti-tank ditches and anti-tank gun pillboxes for the Corps Reserve Position.

Priority work on the Second Position – or Canal Line – was the preparation of defences for all crossings over the canals. This included preparing bridges for demolition, preparing blocks on all bridges, constructing anti-tank gun and anti-tank rifle posts and section posts to cover the gun positions and blocks. In many instances, the anti-tank and Bren guns could be sited in buildings, at first strengthened with propping and sandbags, and later concrete. Until permission was received from the French authorities to carry out the completion of defences in buildings, the weapons were to be given field emplacements. Not all crossings were to be defended by an infantry garrison; larger RE demolition parties than normal were allotted to some crossings to delay the enemy as much as possible. The main roads and crossings over the Second Position would have to deal with traffic and refugees up to the last moment and blocks on crossings over the canals would have to take this into account.

The initial difficulties of holding the Canal Line can be appreciated from the 11 Brigade's War Diary. This Brigade was tasked with holding the Canal Line from Le Pont de Courrieres to Béthune and the L'Allumette Switch, a total distance of 24 miles. There were totals of 20 road bridges, six rail bridges, five-foot bridges and two locks. To defend this front there were only 33 anti-tank guns, which would require most to be sited forward with negligible depth. Although the towns, villages and mines were all excellent anti-tank keeps, there was no obstacle to prevent the enemy's approach to the Canal Line in the Brigade's sector. The countryside was enclosed in some areas in close proximity to the canal, making it difficult to defend by infantry in small dispersed posts. An energetic enemy could approach unseen in daylight and cross the canal unless the defence was alert; during darkness, it was considered impossible to prevent the enemy infantry crossing with 24 miles of front to hold. The 7th Field Company, working on the Brigade's front, made a start on an anti-tank ditch and weapon pits between Seclin and Wavrin to link up with the 10 Brigade and provide an obstacle to bar the approach to the Canal Line.

The 12 Infantry Brigade laid down some basic principles for the defence of the Canal Line against approaches from enemy reconnaissance groups or armoured attacks consisting of light and medium tanks supported by lorry-borne infantry. The first requirement was an anti-tank obstacle to prevent an armoured vehicle up to the size of a medium tank rushing up to a bridge. A combination of three rows of anti-tank mines and three rows of upright rails was suggested as a standard obstacle. In most circumstances the obstacle would be sited on the enemy side of the bridge, and on the road within a few yards of it passing onto the bridge so that it could be kept under effective fire.

As infantry should be sited in tank proof localities, this meant that infantry localities would normally be sited behind the canal. If it was not possible to obtain a clear field of fire from behind the canal, posts comprising a Bren gun and an anti-tank rifle could be sited on the enemy side provided they could be made tank proof, be covered from the main positions and a protected line of withdrawal be provided. Dispositions during the night would likely be different to that during the day. Fixed lines of fire could not be relied upon to prevent enemy infantry from removing blocks. The tank blocks should be surrounded by a wire obstacle and Bren guns brought into a position, not likely to be more than 50 yards from the wire and on the enemy side of the bridge, from which they could effectively fire at night.

In practice, the anti-tank guns were to withhold fire until medium tanks appeared so as not to prematurely disclose their position. If, however, armoured cars and light tanks had got into a position from which their fire was neutralising that of the defence, the anti-tank guns would have to come into operation. Alternative positions for the anti-tank guns had to be provided if possible, so the guns could move during pauses in the fighting and regain the element of surprise.

During November plans were drawn up for a defence scheme along the Second Position. It was envisaged to prepare a position that would be held by two corps. The Position was to be organised as a full defence system with anti-tank obstacles: an FDL

Line (approximately company areas only), a Brigade Reserve Line (approximately company areas only) and a Divisional Reserve Line along with an artillery and machine gun framework and a signal layout.

The defence scheme noted that the area held by the BEF offered the enemy the shortest advance to a tract of relatively open country suited to tank forces. Once the Canal Line was breached there was no continuous anti-tank obstacle to the west and enemy tanks would have access to the area bounded to the west by the sea and to the south by the River Somme. Even a limited penetration of the line would deny the use of the coal fields of Lens and Bruay to the French.

The defence scheme was to be drawn up with the assumption that it would have to defeat a full-scale attack supported by artillery with a tank attack following once crossings over the canals had been made. The right flank of the Second Position was centred on the area Vieux Condé – St. Amand – Marchiennes, an area with good natural anti-tank obstacles. The left flank was less strong, with only a single canal forming an anti-tank obstacle. Thus, it was deduced that an enemy offensive would have its southern flank directed on Douai. The enemy could approach the Position along good road routes, either from Tournai – Douai, Courtrai – Roubaix – Lille – Carvin, Menin – Lille – Haubourdin or Ypres – Armentières – La Bassée or Béthune.

Once the canal bridges had been blown, the canals would form a continuous obstacle to both infantry and tanks, being on average 110 feet wide and 10 feet deep. In places a maze of small woods, water areas and villages or built up industrial areas added depth to the obstacle. In the area between Berclau to Béthune the obstacle was solely the canal itself and would offer the enemy the quickest opportunity of getting across the obstacle into open tank country.

The enemy would have two choices to attack the Canal line. He could either choose to attack the whole area, causing a dispersal of the defence or focus his attack on the weakest area. For the British there was only one option: the line had to be held at all costs. Any enemy attack was expected to be supported by a heavy air attack. The moving of reserves would be problematic, with the Lens area especially expected to form a bottle neck. It was considered vital to have strong sub-sector reserves and a reserve placed well to the west of Lens, provided with motor transport.

Concealing military activity along the Gort Line

The Great War had shown the need for concealment to be both collective and scientific. Collective schemes for the Army were largely forgotten during the inter-war period, until revived by Brigadier Thorne, 1 Guards Brigade, who in the summer of 1936 tested various camouflage schemes in two exercises around Aldershot. He produced a report on the results of the exercises, which was taken up by the War Office the following spring, when it decided to introduce camouflage to the Army on large scale – starting with the disruptive painting of vehicles and testing various type of netting.

However, at the time the BEF sailed for France, it had no camouflage organisation. Brigadier C.G. Woolner (staff officer on the Engineer-in-Chief's staff) visited the

War Office in early September to raise the question of establishing a camouflage organisation and a factory for camouflage material. Indeed, at this stage, the need for camouflage material for rear installations such as camps, dumps, vehicle reception depots etc. was considered more urgent than the equipment's of the fighting troops. Frederick Beddington was appointed to the position of camouflage advisor to the Engineer-in-Chief with the rank of Major. He had developed an interest in the art of concealment during the Great War and at the time was working for the War Office as a civilian assistant advising on camouflage and was apparently the only suitable candidate for the post. He was soon promoted to Lieutenant-Colonel and established what was officially known as the Camouflage Experiential Section. Its function was to produce working specifications and drawings for new devices and materials for concealment.

The static conditions of the Sitz required a high degree of collective concealment, which could only be delivered at the highest level in the BEF, i.e. through the Engineer-in-Chief at GHQ. The opening paragraph *MTP No. 26: Notes on Concealment and Camouflage* stated:

> It should not be assumed that concealment and camouflage are applicable only to field engineering: they are equally important in every form of military activity in the field. [52]

This collective concealment was not instinctive, unlike individual concealment. It required a uniform teaching of theory, and *MTP No. 26* published in 1939 was the standard work on the subject. The following paragraphs deal with the general principals of concealment – the concealment of the individual elements of the defences such as pillboxes and field works are dealt with under chapters that deal specifically with these defences.

It was inevitable that the enemy would try to detect military activity by photographing the territory occupied by the BEF at regular intervals. Scrutiny of successive photographs would show the enemy what was going on unless great skill and care in concealment was undertaken.[53] Although it was recognised that it was

52 *Notes on Concealment and Camouflage – MTP No. 26,* (London: The War Office, October 1939), p. 7.

53 Objects can be identified on aerial photographs by shape and tone. Shape is self-explanatory and the aim of camouflage was to break up regular lines and curves. Tone is due almost entirely to the amount of light which is reflected by the object to the camera. The amount of light reflected depends on several contributing causes, such as the position of the sun when the photograph was taken, the texture of the surface and the strength of the wind. The more light reflected, the whiter the object appears in the photograph. For example, tarred roads appear black while unmade roads and tracks appear light grey. Buildings (and pillboxes), because of their flat surface, generally produce highlights with shadows clear and well defined.

extremely hard to deceive the enemy, and certain objects of military importance could never be hidden whatever efforts were made, certain measures of concealment could be undertaken to hide military activity. *MTP No. 26* details three methods of concealment: natural (adapting to local ground and vegetation conditions), artificial (camouflage) and deception (e.g. dummy works, tracks and defences). In the forward areas liable to bombardment from enemy artillery, absolute concealment from the air camera (as well as the naked eye) was to be aimed for from the start. In the rear areas, which would only be subject to bombing by enemy aircraft, such elaborate precautions were unnecessary: it would suffice to make objects difficult to pick up with the naked eye as for a successful bombing run the man behind the bombsight would need to pick up the target from about five miles range due to the speed of modern aircraft.

For successful concealment from the air, a firm understanding of how the country appeared from the air was essential, and the first step in successful concealment was good siting to fit in with the characteristics of the country along with the clever use of natural materials. This often concealed military activity far better than using artificial material. Furthermore, the supply of artificial material for use by the BEF was often in short supply. The forward areas occupied by the BEF consisted of a patchwork of fields, small woods and villages with a predominance of red tiled roofs and corrugated iron. Walls of buildings were brick or cream painted. The rear areas were similar, but the villages tended to be more frequent. In this way, for example, if new huts, dumps, etc. could be made to fit in with the existing village pattern they would be much less noticeable. The use of natural materials such as hay, grass, branches and foliage were all useful for concealment. These could be effectively supplemented with wire or twine netting (the latter was more portable but less durable). Using such materials, dumps could for instance, be made to resemble sugar beet heaps and haystacks. Care was needed in such methods, and it was suggested that roads bare of these features should be chosen so that the landscape did not become too crowded.

These methods of concealment were also an effective 'anti-eye' medium. The static conditions also allowed the BEF to use painting as a means of concealment, which was chiefly an 'anti-eye' medium and only to a lesser degree 'anti-camera' as from the air texture was more important for concealment. Painting was of two types: scenic, where a picture of the background is painted on the object and disruptive, where contrasting colours are painted to contradict the shape of the object. Three or four masses (green, brown, yellow and grey) were normally sufficient.

According to the War Correspondents André Maurois and Skene Catling the BEF did have some success in concealing itself. André Maurois, for example, subsequently observed:

> In 1939 the British Army has brought the art of camouflage almost to the point of invisibility. Thousands of men, wagons, guns and cars vanish into the countryside, mingle indistinguishably with the haystacks, the woods and the farms, drape themselves with nets, sea-weed and branches and then disperse so ingeniously that finding them becomes a game, which is made more difficult by

> the strictness of orders and 'I don't know' – the soldier's inevitable answer to any question.[54]

There is perhaps some evidence to support André Maurois's claim that that the BEF successfully concealed itself on the ground as one of the reasons given for why the Dominion ministers saw little evidence of the BEF's defences on their visit to the front was because they were cleverly concealed. However, from the air GHQ did have reason to be concerned, with cases of poor track discipline and little effort made to conceal PAD slit trenches.

For all military activity, good track disciple was of paramount importance. In static warfare tracks 'give more information regarding the movement of troops and war material than any other photographic sign.'[55] Lieutenant-Colonel F. Beddington went even further in the GHQ pamphlet *Notes on Camouflage from the BEF*:

> Where one man walks, it is fatally easy for others to follow and in no time the enemy camera will have a distinct record. Such a record has a military significance and will be read and studied by the enemy. THE FIRST MAN THEREFORE TO BE CARELESS OR LAZY IN TAKING A SHORT CUT, WILL BE RESPONSIBLE FOR THE SHELLS OR BOMBS WHICH WILL INEVITABLY FALL ON HIS UNIT.[56]

The layout of tracks had to be part of the planning for any position. Where possible, the cover of hedges and woods could be used. If no cover or natural demarcation existed, tracks should follow the edges of fields and ditches and in general have a rectangular course to match the ground pattern of the country. Use of dummy tracks, leading past a real HQ or position to dummy ones also had to be included in planning. GHQ noted many examples of well concealed defences and HQs betrayed from the air by tracks radiating from them.

With regards to PAD slit trenches, the GHQ pamphlet *Notes on Camouflage from the BEF* noted:

> Nothing is more immediately recognisable from the air than slit trenches defined by uncovered spoil. Cases have occurred of otherwise careful Camouflage being ruined by neglect of these precautions.[57]

54 Maurois, *The Battle of France,* p. 16.
55 *Notes on Concealment and Camouflage – MTP No. 26,* p. 38.
56 TNA: WO167/43, 'Notes on tracks with special reference to static warfare in muddy country', GHQ Chief Engineer War Diary.
57 Ibid.

To conceal PAD trenches, it was recommended that they were sited in the shadow, if possible, under trees and at least 10 yards away from buildings. If this was not possible, they could be sited close to the north face of buildings, although protection from falling masonry had to be provided. In the case of huts, there was no objection to digging them under the huts, so long as adequate exits were provided. In all cases, it was important to cover the spoil with grass sods or brushwood.

Concealment of the BEF's large number of vehicles was primarily by dispersion and using available cover such as trees, edges of wood, orchards, houses and barns. Artificial means – disruptive paint and nets – were used to assist natural cover.

Thought also had to be given to camouflage in snow during the hard winter. As snow melted more quickly on gun pits, pillboxes, dugouts etc., it was recommended that fresh snow should be used to replenish it. Garnished netting would not normally hold snow and would appear as a dark patch from the air. In such cases it was recommended that the net be removed and the ground and guns etc. covered with calico. Contemporary photographs certainly do show guns camouflaged in such a manor, along with troops in 'home made' calico coveralls.

The BEF experienced an acute shortage of camouflage netting, which was used for screening and covering every aspect of the BEF's activities such as aggregate heaps used in pillbox construction, defences, vehicles, aircraft and billets. Until sufficient supplies of netting could be obtained from home, it was decided to open a camouflage factory in France. A disused mill site at Le Houlme was chosen, on the main Rouen – Dieppe road. Plant for the factory was shipped out from England, but French female labour was to be used. The factory was under the command of Captain C. Le Bretton-Simmons (later promoted to Lieutenant-Colonel) and the Chief Supervisor was Company Commander E. Lindsay, CBE, ATS. To ensure the smooth running of the factory, Mrs Lindsay found it necessary to request a male supervisor was appointed as French women would not work under one of their own sex!

Production commenced on 11 December, and in the first instance was limited to garnishing camouflage nets with coloured canvas only. By the end of the Christmas period, the factory was employing a total of 44 women. Production was hampered by a shortage of jute canvas – there would be no supplies from home until supplies were received from India and the French supplier could no longer supply coloured canvas strips after the initial order of 250,000m. The factory also temporarily filled the gap in the shortage of frames for nets until Ordnance were in position to meet the supply.

By March, supply problems had been alleviated to a large extent and the factory was now employing 140 women and was producing 125 nets per week. During April, a long-range forecast for future stores was received and necessitated the investigation of adding more floor space to the factory and increasing the labour force up to 500. There was also a change in policy with regards to netting produced from April onwards. The Chief Engineer's forecast for the next six months envisaged a large increase in the need for camouflage netting, and as twine netting was difficult to obtain both from home and in France, wire netting was to be produced instead. Wire netting was harder to work with than twine netting, and it was considered that a female worker would only be able to garnish 12 sq. yards of wire netting in a day compared to 20 sq. yards of twine netting.

One interesting diversification of the factory's work involved the possible production of dummy tanks, mainly to simulate concentrations of AFVs. During December, Captain Le Brtetton-Simmons received a letter from the War Office informing him that the question of the provision of dummy tanks as a decoy had been raised. Some collapsible models, which could be folded and transported in a truck, had already been made by Sound City Limited, a film production and recording company with set making expertise; the company was to feature prominently in the provision of dummies and decoys at home under the direction of Colonel Turner. The price offered by Sound City for its dummies was prohibitive, and it was considered that the camouflage factory could produce them cheaper.

By March, the factory had received a Sound City dummy tank as a model to work on. The Sound City tank was judged to be sufficient to deceive air photography from 2,000 feet and ground observation from 500 yards. It was however quite heavy and took eight men to assemble and dismantle. No more than three could be transported in a 5-ton lorry. A simplified version manufactured by the camouflage factory was much lighter, requiring just three men to assemble and at least five could be transported in a 5-ton lorry. The factory estimated that with an increased work force of 40, about 50 could be manufactured in a week. The factory's dummy tank received the full approval of GHQ and the Department of Works decided that if the policy of the provision of dummy tanks was approved, the order would be awarded to the factory.

The German breakthrough in May 1940 put an abrupt halt to all the activities of the camouflage factory. Lieutenant-Colonel Beddington supervised the incineration of all the files on concealment compiled during the Sitz by the Engineer-in-Chief's staff in a brewers vat on the road to Dunkirk.

Building the airfields

Perhaps one of the ironies regarding the provision of air support for the BEF was that even if Gamelin and Gort had got their way, and more fighters were sent over to France, it would have been a struggle to find airfields for them. Although from the start, the French did place a number of aerodromes and landing grounds at the disposal of the BEF, many of these were unsuitable for the weight of modern aircraft and required improvement; some had to be abandoned except in the driest of weather. Huts and other infrastructure all had to be provided and at many sites the construction of concrete runways was necessary.

The burden of the construction and maintenance of aerodromes fell upon the already overstretched Royal Engineers:

> The preparation of the surface of aerodromes and the provision of aeroplane hangars is the duty of the air force, but the necessary labour and material will be provided from army sources.[58]

Thus, although the AASF was under the control of the Air Ministry, the Army had administrative responsibility for camp services (water supplies, defence works, electricity supplies), accommodation (for personnel and stores, construction of hangers and base installations), approach roads and runway construction as well as being responsible for the Air Component. The Army was responsible for the transportation of all stores from the ports to the railheads while the RAF was responsible for the transportation forward of the railhead.

To meet this commitment, a Deputy-Director of Works (RAF), Colonel P.W. Clark was appointed to control the works and he was allotted one army troops company, one road construction company and two AMPC's. At the start, it was assumed that French civilian contractors could carry out most of the work, but as described elsewhere in this chapter, this proved not to be the case. One of the reasons for the formation of the additional RE units – general construction companies referred to above – was a direct result of the RAF estimate of future requirements formulated in November. This amounted to a total of 25 aerodromes and 25 satellites, of which five of each were wanted by the Air Component by March 1940 and a further five of each by July 1940, the balance being the requirement of the AASF. As well as labour, what was considered at the time to be a large quantity of machinery such as graders, scoops, excavators, dumpers and concrete mixers had to be assembled.

Runways in particular were a problem due to the lack of permanent pasture in France. The problem was greatest for the Air Component; being allotted to the BEF, its aerodromes were located in Picardy and Flanders, the majority being in Flanders with its notorious mud. The AASF was largely based in the Champagne region, where soils were drier and firmer. At the time, engineers had little knowledge of rapidly laying runways in active service conditions. The grass runways of Flanders could not be relied upon except in the driest of conditions. A temporary surface could be laid at some sites comprising of steel 'grillage' provided by the French.[59] In many cases, it was decided that concrete had to be used until spring allowed for the sowing of grass.[60] The general idea was to have one concrete runway and the rest sowed with grass so that in dry weather a greater area of the aerodrome was operational.

58 *FSR Vol. I: Organization and Administration* (London: The War Office, 1939), p.153

59 Grillage is a framework of steel (or timber) used to spread the load and increase support in areas of soft ground. The British used similar systems of prefabricated steel landing mats later in the war for temporary runways and tracks such as Pierced Steel Plank, Square Mesh Track and Sommerfeld Track.

60 Grass runways were preferable to concrete as they were less obvious, and it was much easier to fill in bomb craters on a grass surface than on a concrete one. Grass seed for the runways came from as far away as New Zealand.

Due to the problems caused by the winter weather, an increase from eight to over 20 concrete runways were required for the Air Component area and three for the AASF area. Because of the problem of transporting large volumes of aggregate required for aerodrome construction, slag from pitheads near Lens was spread and consolidated. Trials were also initiated to devise methods of utilising materials on site. Most of the aerodromes were on sites on which a clay loam overlay chalk. Some method was required to use this loam, either mixed with cement or broken up sufficiently so it could be used as an aggregate. Such methods were used successfully with the Black Cotton soils of Australia. It was first suggested that the loam could be baked in oil or coal powered burners, with the aim of producing a material of a size of between ¾ inch to 3 inch in size that would not break down when wet or scale when frozen and could be used as a matrix with which cement grout could flow to form an adequate concrete. Experiments in Canada had shown that rolling in crushed rock salt on top of clay when the grass had been removed formed an elastic hard surface. Experiments had even been tried with a soya bean crop, which consolidated the surface when the crop was about a foot high.

Nevertheless, and despite these problems, a huge resource had been put into aerodrome construction by the time of the German invasion. In his official dispatches, Gort records the progress up to 15 May:

> Upwards of 10,000 men were employed on this work, and forty-seven aerodromes and satellites (including 19 new aerodromes) were under development or construction. By 15 May eight of the nineteen new aerodromes were capable of use, and at least 50,000 tons of concrete had been laid.[61]

61 General the Viscount Gort VC, KCB, CBE, DSO, MVO, MC, *Despatches on Operations of the British Expeditionary Force.*

6

Taking over more of the line

The British were able to form a fifth regular division by November 1939 and take over the front held by the French 51st Division. Progress in equipping and training the Territorial's at home made it possible to plan for an III Corps and IV Corps to be to be formed in France. III Corps was delayed in taking its place in the line by the Allied landings at Narvik. IV Corps was not expected until June 1940, but the Battle of France and Flanders was over by then. However, there were still concerns that the rapid expansion of the BEF was at the expense of properly equipping it. To help ease the problems caused by equipment shortages, consideration was given to forming purely defensive divisions which would not be as well-equipped as divisions with a mobile role. The expansion of the BEF also caused some confusion of who was to have direct control over it – Gamelin or Georges. By the time the Germans launched their Blitzkrieg, good progress and a degree of depth in the defences had been achieved along the fronts held by I and II Corps, but a great deal of work was still required to be undertaken on III Corps front. As well as taking over more of *SD* Lille, the BEF also sent brigades on a two week rotation to serve in front of the Maginot Line on the Saar front. During these tours, soldiers experienced enemy shelling and raids and also took part in fighting patrols which periodically clashed with enemy patrols.

Expansion of the BEF

Progress in the training and equipment of units at home had it made it possible to dispatch the 15 and 17 Brigades to France during October and November. Also the 13 Brigade was relieved from the LoC by the 25 Brigade. Gort decided to use the 13, 15 and 17 Brigades to form a fifth regular division in France. On 25 November, II Corps received a warning order that the French 51st Division was to be withdrawn and relieved by II Corps on 1 and 2 December. The 4th Division was to take over the right of the French 51st Division front and the 5th Division (Major-General H.E. Franklyn), when fully formed the left part of the front. This meant the BEF was now responsible for holding the entire *SD* Lille front. On the left was II Corps with three divisions in the line and on the right I Corps with two divisions in the line. The 48th Division (Major-General A.F.A.N. Thorne) arrived in January 1940 and was allocated to I Corps although held in GHQ Reserve. A reconnaissance of Doullens was made with a view to moving GHQ there after Army Headquarters had been formed, expected to happen in late June.

Plans were also underway to extend the front held by the BEF with the formation of III Corps. III Corps (Lieutenant-General Sir R. F. Adam), consisting of the 42nd Division (Major-General W.G. Holmes), 44th Division (Major-General E.A. Osborne) and 51st Division (Major-General V.M. Fortune) was expected to arrive in France during February and March. Gort offered to take over a corps front to the north from Armentières to the railway Hazebrouck – Poperinghe. But *GQG* wanted to keep the French Seventh Army in being and offered the BEF a one-division front to the north (Armentières to Bailleul) and a two division front to the south from the BEF's present right at Maulde to Wargnies-le-Grand southeast of Valenciennes. Gort accepted this offer, but then the French Army commanders on each side expressed dissatisfaction. Giraud did not want to give up Bailleul; Pownall thought this was probably because he was hoping to fight a grand battle of mass manoeuvre on the BEF's left and did not like being 'edged in on'.[1] Bailleul was vital for the BEF as the high ground there was necessary for the defence of the line further south. In the south, both Blanchard and Georges were unwilling to hand over part of the French First Army sector as they felt that the role of the First Army in an advance to the Dyle was an important role and should not be given to British troops until they were up to the standard of training required and possessed the necessary transport and equipment to carry out the role.[2] On 29 January, the BEF learned it had got the boundary in the north it wanted, which included Bailleul.

Ironside was concerned about the capability of the BEF taking over more of the front given the ongoing shortages in equipment. During his visit to France to investigate Hore-Belisha's allegations that the BEF was building insufficient pillboxes, Ironside witnessed these shortages of equipment and ammunition himself. He wrote a damming telegram to the Secretary of State:

> The position of the equipment available for ten divisions is in my opinion most depressing, but in view of the insistence of the French and of the necessity for

1 Giraud may not have been as optimistic as Pownall thought. He remarked to André Maurois that it would be difficult to advance and meet the Germans, a move he considered a 'very risky procedure'. He would much rather have entered Belgium at the beginning of hostilities and occupied a solid line despite the protests that would have come from Belgium – a risk worth taking to avoid the worse risk of advancing to meet the Germans.

2 The French First Army, which had been allocated the most mechanised and armoured divisions available to the French Army, was tasked with covering the gap between the Dyle and Meuse, the so-called Gembloux Gap, where it was expected to encounter the German armour.

> taking a greater share in the land defence in France it seems to me essential that we have a force of ten divisions in France by the end of February equipped to the best of our ability. But the Cabinet should realize [sic] that the German Army if it attacks will do so fully equipped with modern weapons. And in view of their well-known tactics the shortage of ant-tank and light anti-aircraft weapons is very serious. Theses must be made up as soon as possible. A minimum of six more anti-tank Regiments (making a total of ten) each comprising twenty-four 2-pr. and twelve 18-pdrs. older pattern with platforms and tracer ammunition should in my opinion be sent out with the new Divisions. As regards light A.A. guns, in view of the German tactics in Poland I regard a scale of forty per cent., including reserves, as most dangerous and the allocation of these guns to B.E.F. should be given first priority. Cannot the R.A.F. be forced to disgorge some Hispano guns in our extremity? They could be put in a simple mounting. The 3.7-inch A.A. guns should be increased by March to fifty per cent. of establishment, i.e. to a hundred and twenty ... ammunition is the lifeblood of all our rifles and automatics and any shortage, which never occurred in the last war, puts an end to all fighting. As regards tanks, no offensive or counter-offensive operation is possible with a shortage of Infantry tanks of sixty per cent. (not counting any reserves) and the Cabinet should realize [sic] this. The medium and heavy artillery ammunition is deplorable, making offensive operations impossible... The Cabinet must clearly understand that divisions armed on such a reduced scale have not the same fighting value even in defence as those which are fully equipped. Moreover, a force not properly found in arms, ammunition and transport cannot take part in offensive action.[3]

The question of taking over more of the line arose again at a conference held on 6 February when the arrival of a British IV Corps, expected in May, was discussed. Georges was still unwilling to hand over part of the French First Army sector and explained that he felt that the expansion of the BEF sector to the north was the only practical solution. But Gamelin did not want the IV Corps to extend to the north as this would interfere with the role of the French Seventh Army. Gort explained he would be happy to take on the role of the French Seventh Army in guarding the sea coast and the south bank of the Escaut and forming a general reserve to the west of Antwerp but not the recently discussed possibility of pushing the Seventh Army forward as far north as Breda to support the Dutch. Gamelin, aware that the British were not keen on the Breda manoeuvre, was then reluctant to agree to the BEF relieving the Seventh Army. Indeed, it is thought that one of the reasons that Gamelin wanted the strong French Seventh Army on the British left was to prevent a British dash back to the Channel. When Lord Gort ordered the retreat to Dunkirk,

3 Colonel R. Macleod, DSO, MC & Denis Kelly (eds), *Time Unguarded: The Ironside Diaries 1937-1940* (New York: David McKay Company Inc., 1963), pp. 399-400.

many in the French Army felt vindicated in their mistrust of the British. The irony of the situation was not lost on Pownall:

> It's an odd inversion. Here are the French NOT wanting to give us line, but rather keeping us cramped. And at the same time the French Government and Gamelin are pushing the W.O. hard to send out as many divisions as possible and as early as possible.[4]

Towards the end of January, the 50th (Motor) Division (Major-General G. le Q. Martel) which was to become the third division of II Corps, 51st Division and III Corps HQ began to arrive in France. II Corps was to be the parent formation of III Corps until it was ready to take over. Then, III Corps was to go into the line on the left of the BEF sector, taking over the 5th Division from II Corps and relieving the French 53rd Division between Armentières and Croix de Poperinghe with the 51st Division. These arrangements were disrupted by the planning for the Allied landings at Narvik, with HQ III Corps and advance parties of the 42nd and 44th Divisions being recalled to England. Gort was also instructed by the Army Council to make available a division for withdraw from the line in France at short notice and prepare to embark it for Scandinavia. In issuing these instructions, Ironside did not consult with Gort as to whether he could carry out his responsibilities if his force was reduced by three divisions. Likewise, Gamelin had not consulted with Georges. Gort selected the 5th Division, stating he would loyally follow the instruction, but under protest as he had been appointed by the War Cabinet and did not recognise the authority of the Army Council. He also made it clear that it would result in difficulties:

> My views have not been invited as to whether the with-holding of two divisions of the 3rd Corps and the projected withdrawal of the 5th Division will affect the ability of the British Expeditionary Force to carry out its allotted roles, but the Army Council will no doubt wish to be made aware of the difficulties, both operational and administrative, which will accrue.[5]

Gort was particularly concerned with the resultant shortage of troops to work on defences, concrete and other, in the reserve and switch lines. He was of the opinion that completion of these lines would be 'deferred for a very long time.'[6] He was also of the opinion that it would severely hamper any planned advance of the BEF. In the case of Plan E, which if the BEF extended its front northwards to Bailleul also

4 Brian Bond (ed.), *Chief of Staff: The Diaries of Lieutenant-General Sir Henry Pownall* (London: Leo Cooper, 1972), p. 278.
5 TNA: WO167/21, Gort to Under Secretary of State, War Office, February 1940, GHQ SD &T Branch War Diary.
6 Ibid.

called for the BEF to take over an equivalent frontage on the River Escaut, he would only have a reserve of a brigade at most, which he found unacceptable and would be forced to ask *GQG* to amend the British commitment. In the case of Plan D, which was originally to be undertaken by five regular divisions, he would be forced to use only four regular divisions supported by three territorial divisions which were 'capable of defensive action but of no form of offence, and that even the movement to the Dyle would impose a severe test unless carried out under peace conditions.'[7] It was not only infantry divisions that were affected. The proposed landings also meant the cancellation of the deployment of the 55th and 58th Light AA Regiments and of the 85th Heavy AA Regiment, leaving the BEF and the AASF short of AA guns. Work on the LoC would also be disrupted by the suspension of the despatch of RE and AMPC units to France.

The proposed diversion of III Corps for the Narvick landings required a reshuffling of divisions, with II Corps temporarily overseeing five divisions, having to fit in the 50th and 51st Divisions into its already overcrowded rear area. The state of confusion lasted into March and was finally resolved by the Scandinavian states refusing to agree to the operation and Finland's surrender to Russia. It was not until the start of April that III Corps arrived to take its place in the line on the Western Front, with the 51st Division relieving the French 53rd Division as originally planned. III Corps now consisted of the 5th, 51st and 44th Divisions while the 50th Division became the third division of II Corps and the 42nd Division moved into GHQ reserve. With the Territorial divisions finally arrived in France, it was decided that each of the Territorial brigades would be strengthened by the inclusion of a regular battalion at the expense of one of the Territorial battalions. This naturally produced a degree of resentment and confusion as battalions were shuffled around.

The Scandinavian affair caused much disquiet in GHQ. In his diary, Pownall writes:

> For five months we have been struggling to make fit for action in the spring a force that last September was dangerously underequipped and untrained ... As spring approached there were signs we were getting some reasonable way to our goal. By the end of this month we would have ten divisions, not nearly fully equipped. God knows, far from fully trained either, but still a force which in defence could make a good showing. If this business goes through...we shall be cut by three divisions, 30 per cent. It is a most disheartening business.[8]

It was not only the loss of troops that caused concern, but also the steady drain on resources and the disruption to training. Ammunition and equipment were not being dispatched to France but were being held in readiness for the Norway expedition

7 Ibid.
8 Bond (ed.), *Chief of Staff*, p. 283.

and six valuable weeks of training were lost. GHQ clearly felt that the whole project was reminiscent of the minor sideshows during the Great War such as Gallipoli, when resources were diverted away from the main theatre of operations. Just as Haig believed that Germany could only be defeated on the Western Front, so did Gort and Pownall believe that the war could only be won or lost on the Western Front.

The German invasion of Denmark and Norway on 9 April caused another minor re-organisation of the BEF. Although the plan to send three divisions was abandoned, the 15 Brigade – part of the 5th Division – was dispatched to England en route to Norway while the remainder of the Division was to be recalled to England to act as a reserve. The advance parties of the 127 Brigade – part of the 42nd Division – had by then once more departed for France; the other two brigades of the Division had already left. All further moves of the Brigade were cancelled on 14 April and on 16 April the Brigade was informed it was intended for Norway and that the advance parties had been ordered back again. Brigadier Smyth remarked that the 'latter must have been getting quite dizzy from all these orders and counter-orders.'[9]

At the same time the DMI announced that an attack on Holland and Belgium was quite likely imminent. Pownall records his frustration: 'There is just no sense in it all, it seems like the War Office is going on like a cage of monkeys, there's no co-ordination and everybody is butting into everybody else's job.'[10] He further remarks that only a year ago, the Government would not accept the need that the Army would be called upon to fight in Europe at all and now it was running two European campaigns! The Allies were completely surprised by the swiftness and decisiveness of the German invasion and events moved so quickly that it was soon became evident that the 127 Brigade would not be required, and it was ordered to France on 20 April. GHQ managed to postpone the removal of the 5th Division; it was to remain in the Amiens area in War Office reserve, relieved in III Corps by the 42nd Division.

The arrival of IV Corps was put back until July due to shortages in equipment. With the Canadian Division preceding them in June, and assuming that the BEF was still on the frontier, two Army HQs were to be formed: First Army (Finlayson) with its HQ in St. Pol and Second Army (Dill) with its HQ in Arras.

4th and 5th Divisions take over the French 51st Division's front

As already noted, II Corps received warning notice that it was to take over the French 51st Division's front on 1 and 2 December. The 4th Division was responsible for the line from the boundary with 3rd Division to Le Purgatoire while the 5th Division held the line from here to Halluin thence along the line of the River Lys to Pont de Nieppe. The lack of progress by the French on this part of the front has already been

9 Brigadier Sir John Smyth, VC, MC, MP, *Before the Dawn: Two Historic Retreats Dunkirk 1940. Burma 1942* (London: Cassel & Co Ltd, 1957), p. 16.

10 Bond (ed.), *Chief of Staff*, p. 304.

mentioned, and the 4th Division War Diarist noted that the 'work taken over was almost entirely "projects"'.[11]

Key to the new sector were Mont d'Halluin and the Triez Cailloux ridge – the sector that the 11 Brigade was working on (see Chapter 5) until relieved by the 17 Brigade (5th Division) on 30 December – which gave excellent views of any enemy approach from the north-east, but if lost, would provide the enemy excellent views over the back areas of the 5th Division. In the north of the sector the River Lys formed the anti-tank obstacle. To the east, there were three anti-tank obstacles: the Frontier obstacle (*Ligne Principale*) an intermediate obstacle enclosing Mont d'Halluin which then continued north on the reverse slope of the Triez Cailloux ridge and a rear obstacle (*Ligne d'Arret*) formed in part by the Becque de Neuville which was to be continued north to Nouveau Monde. The ground around Nouveau Monde faces north, east and southeast and covered the exits from Halluin. The Roncq ridge, about 3,000 yards from the FDL Line, was a natural choice to site the Brigade Reserve Position. One weakness of the whole position was that there were no obstacles behind the River Lys on the north flank except one being constructed on a short stretch between Nouveau Monde and the Du Mont Farm made by cutting into a natural bank, which was to be continued west by 1,000 anti-tank mines. Thus, towns and villages had to be relied upon as obstacles until the new Divisional Reserve Positions could be constructed; this position had to be sited so it could fight facing both north and north-east and even north-west in the event of a breakthrough from the north. Halluin itself posed a particular problem in that the existing defences ran along the border behind the town. The OC 11 Brigade, during his initial reconnaissance of the area in November when the Brigade was sent to help the French 51st Division in preparing defences (see Chapter 5), recognised that to hold the town the border would have to be crossed so as to rest the flanks on the River Lys, which is exactly what was done when the BEF fell back to the Gort Line on 23 May (see Chapter 10).

The OC 11 Brigade also raised some interesting questions with regards to the general policy laid down for the defence of the French blockhouses along the FDL Line during. First, he disagreed with the assumption that the enemy would limit his initial attack to infantry only to secure bridgeheads across the forward anti-tank ditch for his armour. He considered that with the use of fascines or special bridging tanks, combined with heavy shell fire, the ditch could easily be crossed by tanks and he thought it highly likely that tanks would be included in the initial attack.[12] He

11 TNA: WO167/233, 4th Division CRE War Diary, 1–31 December1939.

12 Of interest is the tale by a Belgian officer recounted by Gordon Beckles in *Dunkirk – and After*. According to the officer, a column of tanks arrived at a deep ditch caused by a demolition: 'The leading tank promptly dropped into the ditch...Then the second, third and forth tanks crashed down also; but the fifth tank rocked its way over to the road on the other side by overrunning the other ones. Then the column followed suit. It had cost them four tanks, but the column kept going' (Gordon Beckles, *Dunkirk – and After: The Campaign and Evacuation of Flanders* (London: Hutchinson & Co. Ltd., no date), p. 39).

therefore refuted the assumption that anti-tank defence in the blockhouses could be left to anti-tank rifles and felt that the 25mm anti-tank guns should be retained in the blockhouses.

Secondly, he considered the Bren gun quite unsuitable for the defence of the blockhouses. In his opinion the distance between blockhouses, being up to 1,000 yards, was too great for Bren guns firing from the blockhouse to cover. Even though additional Bren posts could be dug into the banks of the obstacle in the intervening spaces between blockhouses, these would be exposed locations and their fire could not be relied upon. In the event of an infantry attack, he noted that the anti-tank ditch and wire obstacle needed to be covered by a continuous stream of bullets and only the Vickers machine gun or other heavy machine guns could accomplish this. He was undoubtedly right in this matter as the continuous need to change magazines and barrels rendered the Bren unreliable for such a task; the Bren fell short of its intended role as a general-purpose machine gun. It could not deliver the sustained fire of the Vickers, even when mounted on its tripod. Although the Bren was very reliable, accurate, and extremely simple to use, when sustained fire was required by the infantry, such as covering obstacles, the British were at a disadvantage compared to the German infantry armed with the MG34. This versatile light machine gun was belt fed, and when mounted on a tripod it was capable of long sustained bursts of fire, meaning it could fulfil the role of a medium machine gun and successfully pin down the British infantry.

No attempt was to be made to dig an extensive trench system on taking over the front from the French 51st Division. Instead, full use was to be made of the system of fortifications constructed by the French. These were to be supplemented by weapons concealed in small pillboxes and concrete trenches defiladed from the front. Communication trenches were to be limited to main arteries and to exposed pillboxes. As the construction of pillboxes took time, alternative positions made from sandbags and timber were to be built providing they did not prejudice the siting of the concrete pillboxes. To speed up the construction of pillboxes, 5th Division noted it would help if they were sited wherever possible close to a road to facilitate the delivery of materials. Reconnaissance was carried out for cellars which could be used for shelter in conditions of heavy prolonged bombardment. The French, under *Colonel* Bertschi, were still responsible for the completion of the anti-tank obstacle in continuation of the Becque de Neuville and the construction of 10 pillboxes along it and 20 pillboxes between Halluin and Deûlémont. These works were all expected to be completed by 31 March. The 135th Excavator Company began working on the anti-tank ditch in the 4th Division's area along with two French diggers belonging to a civilian contractor.

The British considered that the straight French anti-tank ditch in the Tourcoing and Halluin area was indefensible and a bastion trace ditch was required instead. This was achieved by digging stretches of new ditch in front of the existing French ditch (Figure 6.1). The ditch in this area was completely dominated by the Le Purgatoire ridge, where the enemy could get splendid observation over the rear areas. Consequently, it was decided to site the FDL Line ahead of the obstacle. This would greatly enhance the obstacle as it would now be sited on a reverse slope, it would deny the enemy observation of the defences as far west as Roncq and it would increase the depth of the defences ahead of the built-up area. The defence of the FDLs in this area was to be by section posts – including Bren pillboxes – and anti-tank gun pillboxes, which were to be strongly wired and made tank proof with anti-tank mines. The 11 Brigade had issued orders for a first priority of seven Bren and two anti-tank gun pillboxes forward of the anti-tank obstacle. This work was undertaken by the 7th Field Company with infantry working parties, but there was 'an oath or two' when it was discovered that some of the pillboxes had been sited in Belgium by mistake!

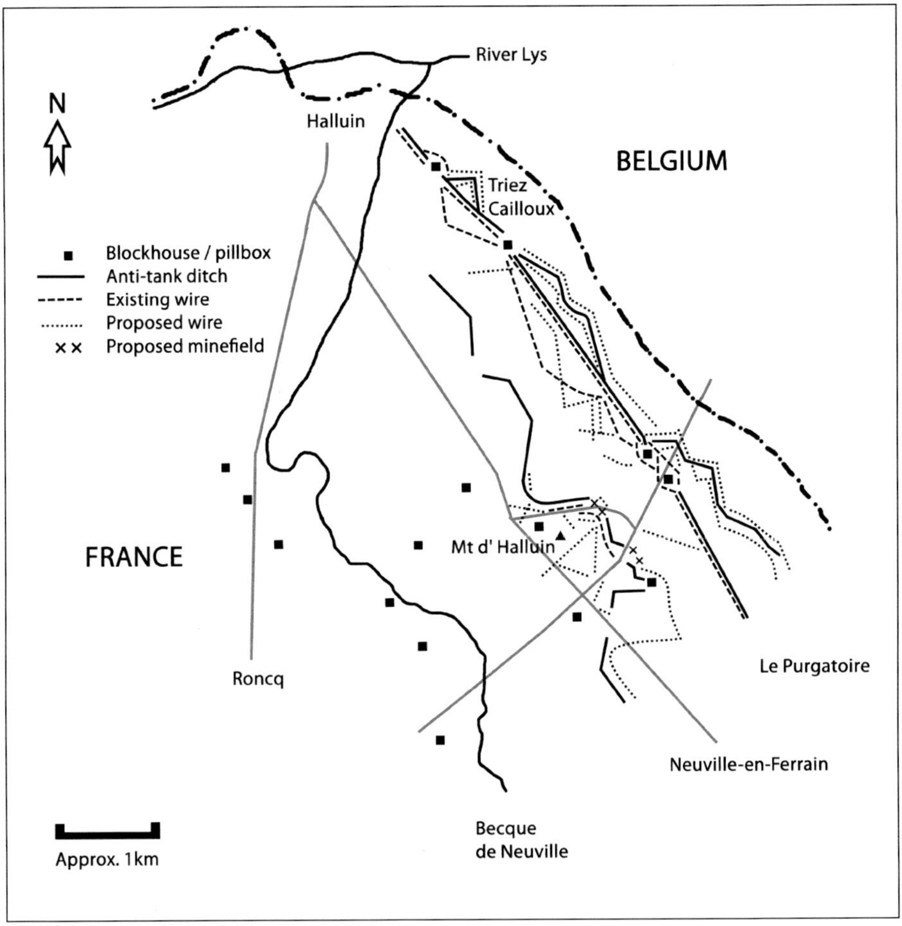

Figure 6.1: Defences on the 5th Division's sector, held by the 17 Brigade. Note the new bastion anti-tank ditch dug in front of the existing French anti-tank ditch.

Virtually nothing had been done by the French along the River Lys in the 5th Division's sector. Not even wire had been put up; a reconnaissance identified that a substantial amount was required for the near side of the River Lys. This part of front was large, meaning in principal the decision was taken to cover the whole river obstacle by fire, with the garrison kept to a minimum and if necessary, sacrificing depth. Reconnaissance by the 5th Division for the preliminary trace of the Divisional Reserve Line and the FDL Line along the River Lys were completed by early January. When work began on constructing breastworks on the 5th Division's front in February, the decision was taken to complete them on a one company front at a time. The reason for this was that if the work had to be suspended or handed over to another formation, it was considered better to have some completed posts rather than a number of partially completed posts, which were likely to fall in if work was not continuous

Work on the reserve positions, especially the Quesnoy Switch, was delayed due to an acute shortage of materials and plant. A first task of 66 pillboxes was required for the Quesnoy Switch and the Divisional Reserve Line (32 on the 4th Division's front and 34 on the 5th Division's front). Work was finally begun on this Switch on the 4th Division's front in February by the 656th General Construction Company (1st General Construction Battalion) and in April two French excavators began to dig the anti-tank ditch. A French pioneer company provided all the labour and revetting materials. The Divisional Reserve Position of the 5th Division was extensive and was in the main to be defended from the occupation of houses, breastworks and utilising First World War German pillboxes. Only a few key section posts were to be constructed on the Divisional Reserve Position, although German First World War pillboxes that had been identified as suitable for use were also to be prepared. Work on the Quesnoy Switch on the 5th Division's front was to be undertaken by the 2nd General Construction Battalion. It was planned to move two general construction companies from I Corps area to undertake the work and relieve the 5th Division's field companies. The 661st General Construction Company were actually tasked with an initial 13 pillboxes (six anti-tank, four double machine gun and three Bren), but instead, along with the 668th General Construction Company, it was decided to use them on the defences between Armentières and Bailleul on the 51st Division's front (see below) which took priority over work on the Quesnoy Switch. Work on this Switch was now postponed until June as there were insufficient materials and plant for work on both positions. The OC 2nd General Construction Battalion also felt he could not simultaneously control work in I Corps area, along the Quesnoy Switch and in the Armentières and Bailleul area.

On 2 May, the 42nd Division relieved the 5th Division (Figure 6.2). It is interesting to note the description of the defences taken over by the 5th Manchester Regiment, one of the 42nd Division battalion's, as it illustrates the progress being made since the BEF took over this part of the front from the French 51st Division. The Battalion moved into the line west of Halluin, including Triez Cailloux and found:

> A/Tk ditch almost completed, two heavy pillboxes complete, numerous RE pillboxes under construction, trenches and concealed light concrete and sandbagged breastworks could accommodate 600 men with concealment and some protection.[13]

51st Division moves into the line

At the end of January 1940, the 51st Division began arrangements to relieve the French 53rd Division in the area Bailleul – Armentières. The front had been organised by the French in such a manner that it was occupied by three regiments; in the first instance the 51st Division planned to hold the position with two brigades up. Later it was intended to develop a defence scheme to hold the position with two divisions, each with two brigades up. In organising the defence, full use was to be made of French constructed and projected defences and fire plans:

> Since the French are past masters in the art siting weapons for defence, all work finished and projected will be taken over and the same policy of defence continued.[14]

The FDL Line consisted of the usual French blockhouses enfilading a continuous anti-tank ditch. The French had started work on defences in the rear, especially around the dominating feature of the Ravelsberg Ridge and the high ground north and north-west of Bailleul. The relief was postponed until 28 March due to the Norway landings. It is of interest to note that on the same day of the relief, the Supreme War Council of France and Britain put on record the will to fight as one, and to live as one when the fighting had ended.

The whole of the sector was overlooked by the high ground Neuve Eglise – Mont Kemmel – Mont Rouge – Mont Noir – Mont des Cats. The British were unsure whether the French wished to leave the present defences to occupy these features if the decision was taken to fight on the frontier line. However, the very strong blockhouses that had been constructed, or projected, suggested that the French would only occupy the high ground as an outpost line.

It was estimated that a programme of 32 new pillboxes would be required in the 51st Division's area, about three months work for two general construction companies. On 17 April the 51st Division began to move to the Saar front, being relieved by the 44th Division on 23 April (Figure 6.2). On the same day, the 2nd General Construction Battalion issued the first task blockhouse programme for the 661st General Construction Company on the 44th Division's front: eight anti-tank

13 TNA: WO167/789, 5th Battalion Manchester Regiment War Diary 29–30 May 1940.

14 TNA: WO167/314, 'Platoon areas', 13 February 1940, 51st Division General Staff War Diary.

pillboxes, four Bren pillboxes, four double machine gun and two unspecified. Neither the 51st nor the 44th Divisions had time to organise the position in depth; the defences in this sector were perhaps the most linear on the BEF front. On the other hand, some of the French blockhouses were larger and stronger than on any other part of the BEF's sector.

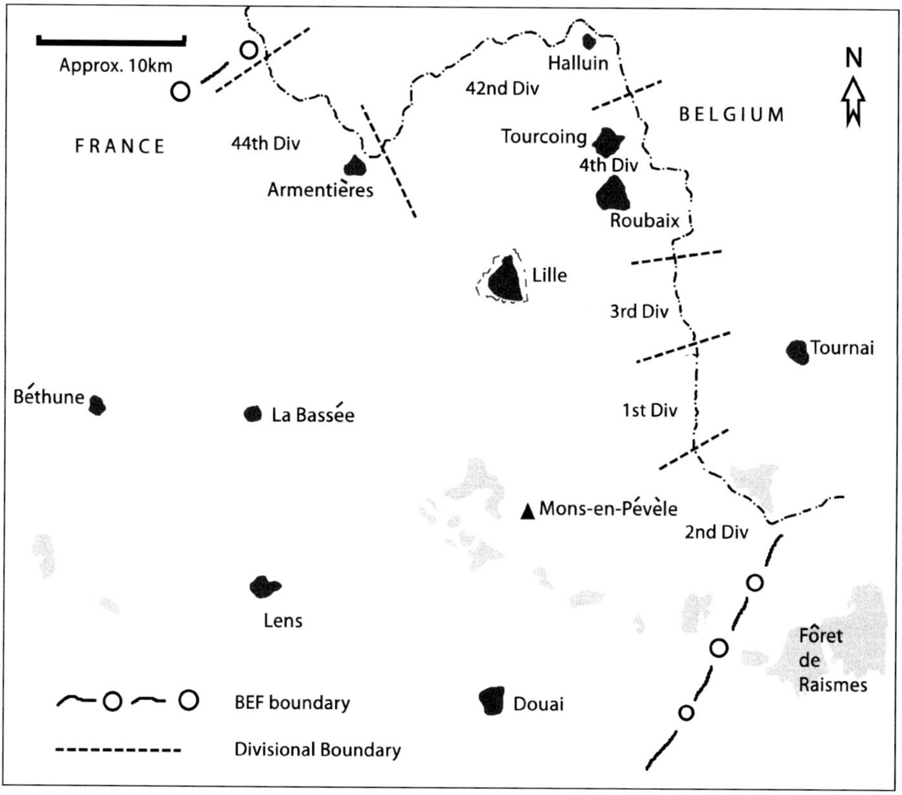

Figure 6.2: BEF Divisional sectors, *SF* Lille, 9 May 1940.

Defensive Divisions

Despite the difficulty of equipping new formations, consideration was being given to the possibility of accelerating the dispatch of the second and subsequent contingents of the BEF to France. If the dispatch of the BEF was to be accelerated, the only way it could be achieved was by a temporary reduction in equipment to certain units:

> French pressure upon us to put on the western front by the Spring the absolute maximum number of divisions of which we are capable, has already begun. Our limitation is presumably equipment. We cannot hold out for a higher standard

> of equipment for the British divisions than for French divisions. We ought to review our equipment in this light and in the light of the effect of inactivity throughout the winter upon our reserves of equipment ...We ought to also to consider whether any modification in the equipment of our divisions would be possible if they were designed primarily for a comparatively static role. The possibility of equipping certain divisions for a static role while others were equipped for a mobile role should not be ignored.[15]

In other words, if a proportion of the BEF was always employed on defensive duties, then a temporary reduction could be accepted in the equipment for these units. To some extent, the War Office considered 'that the divisions of the B.E.F. are equipped on a more lavish scale than is necessary for a purely defensive role.'[16] Such divisions, in the opinion of the War Office, were better suited for operations such as the move into Belgium or for use as a reserve: i.e. they could be replaced with divisions allocated and equipped for a purely defensive role. The question was asked if the French Fortress divisions were a more economical organisation of an ordinary division for defence, but it was pointed out that the Fortress Divisions contained highly trained troops to operate the highly technical equipment of the forts – such units could be compared to the crew of a battleship. These divisions could not be classed as low-grade defensive divisions.

Defensive divisions could have a temporary reduction in motor transport to ensure that corps and divisions assigned a more mobile role could carry all their equipment in one lift. The carrier platoon could be taken from the infantry battalion. Lewis guns were acceptable as a replacement for Bren guns, but each infantry battalion should have a minimum of 36 Bren guns. The biggest drawback of having such a two-tier organisation was that it would prevent the normal system of reliefs. Gort agreed to defensive divisions in principal, but for him the maximum proportion of defensive divisions acceptable was 40 percent and that any reductions could only be acceptable on a temporary basis. Furthermore, only a minimum reduction in anti-tank guns was acceptable to Gort, as defensive units – even those in the rear – may have to deal with an enemy tank breakthrough.[17]

By April, it had been possible to increase the size of the BEF to 10 divisions without too many equipment shortages (although medium and heavy guns and ammunition remained critically short in supply). However, equipping units was only one aspect: Brigadier Smyth noted that his 127 Brigade had only just been issued with its nine 25mm anti-tank guns before advancing into Belgium and that only half the gun teams

15 TNA: WO106/1664, 'Notes on the situation if Germany remains passive' 28 October 1939.
16 TNA: WO166/1685, 'Security of Western Front'.
17 The principal of defensive divisions was adopted in Britain's anti-invasion measures following the fall of France, where lower establishment divisions were assigned a purely static role in the defence of beaches.

had had a chance to fire the guns even once before going into action against German tanks. Despite this increase of the BEF to 10 divisions, French pressure for a faster build up did not diminish.[18]

BEF Command

The expansion of the BEF, along with further planned increases in its size, raised the issue of who should have direct control over it – Gamelin or Georges. The friction between Gamelin and Georges was by January 1940 common knowledge all over France. At the outbreak of war, it was widely assumed that Georges would take full command of the French and British armies, with Gamelin retiring to an advisory position on the French Military Council. However, Gamelin had no intention of yielding his command to Georges. Furthermore, it was widely thought that Gamelin was jealous of the role Georges had, as he was in command of the only front where contact with the enemy was taking place and the decisive front if Germany attacked in the west. This led to a conflict of authority between Gamelin and Georges throughout the eight months of the Sitzkrieg.

In January, Gamelin reorganised *GQG* in an apparent attempt to increase his prestige and cut a bit away from Georges' position. It was also believed that Gamelin wanted direct control over the BEF and not the indirect control he had because of the fact that the BEF was under the command of Georges, his own subordinate. This seemed absurd to the BEF as Gamelin had not the staff at *GQG* to deal with such an arrangement. The official BEF line was that although the BEF was under French command, it was not up to it to decide how Gamelin exercised his command. The BEF could not serve two masters and consequently suggested the status quo, with Gamelin giving the strategical directives affecting the Allies as a whole and within the framework of those directives Georges should issue detailed instructions to the BEF. Ironside met Gamelin to discuss command of the BEF in early March with instructions to maintain the status quo if possible; he was not to agree to any changes as this would be decided by discussions between the British and the French Prime Ministers. Gamelin readily agreed to the status quo until such a time the BEF reached a suitable size to be considered as an independent force.

Relations in the French government were also uneasy after Reynaud replaced Daladier as Prime Minister. Reynaud wanted to replace Gamelin with Georges, but Daladier, who had become the Minister of War, was absolutely opposed to this.

18 General Billotte's comments to André Maurois are probably typical of the French view of the British, in which he said they 'are distressingly slow. Here we are after eight months of war and all they've got is ten divisions! They want to do too well. They're finicky. The Germans appreciate the importance of the time factor. There are times when it's better to have mediocre material on the spot than perfect material after the war' (André Maurois, *The Battle of France* (London: John Lane The Bodley Head, 1940), pp. 157–158).

Reynaud could not get the absolute majority he needed and on 20 April unanimity was obtained and Gamelin remained in post.

If relations in the French camp were difficult, they were no easier in the British camp. The fate of the War Secretary, Hore-Belisha, has already been told elsewhere in this book. Ironside was next in the firing line. Both Gort and Pownall neither liked nor trusted Ironside. Ironside's brusque manner had also not made him particularly popular with the British Government or the War Office. Pownall noted in his diary on 10 April 'C.I.G.S.'s stock is very low, I am told, and it is very probable that he will be 'Limoged' very soon.'[19] In anticipation of the removal of Ironside, Dill was summoned home to take on the role of VCIGS. In reality he was to be CIGS in all but name, as for the moment Ironside could not be removed during the ongoing international crises arising from the Norwegian affair. Lieutenant-General M.G.H. Barker took over I Corps from Dill.

Defences completed by the BEF and French under Colonel Bertschi

The BEF arrived on the *SD* Lille to find that the 'Petit Maginot Line' in most places consisted of only a single anti-tank ditch defended by blockhouses spaced about 1,000 yards apart. The Sitzkrieg gave the BEF time to try and put this right. André Maurois recorded the progress made since the start of the war during a visit on 3 April 1940:

> I had visited that part of the line a long time previously. I remembered the stark simplicity of the countryside: the background a line of naked wood, pale trunks reaching up to a heavy sky. 'That will be where the enemy will come from,' the Colonel had said. And then, as far as the eye could see, the clayey plain, red, rich and damp, almost unwaveringly flat.
>
> Yesterday I went back there, and the change was astounding. This countryside that had been so empty, was now just one immense mason's yard. A little behind the line of casemates a line of pillboxes had arisen, finished and complete. And still further back, in the plain, countless little cement citadels were springing up with an amazing rapidity.[20]

On the ground, some of the troops also noted how the defences had developed. When returning to the Franco-Belgian frontier in April following a stint on the Saar Front and some home leave, Second-Lieutenant R.H. Medley records how the defences had developed since November, and that 'it was now possible to envisage the detailed

19 Bond (ed.), *Chief of Staff*, p. 298.
20 Maurois, *The Battle of France*, pp. 136.

picture more easily. The 'Gort' line of supporting pill boxes sited to support the Anti-Tank ditch defences on the frontier was taking shape.'[21]

I and II Corps had attained some degree of depth of defence by holding vital points in considerable strength. The gaps between localities were wide, but their siting allowed heavy concentration of both small arms and anti-tank fire along all probable approaches. On III Corps front, the defence was more linear, as it had not had the same amount of time as I and II Corps to organise a defensive position. Lord Gort's dispatches record that a total of 400 pillboxes were completed with another 100 under construction, considerable improvement of the field defences made, and 40 miles of anti-tank ditch added to that excavated by the French Army in peace time.[22] But what did this mean in terms of the various positions?

On the fronts of I and II Corps the anti-tank obstacles along the FDL Line and Brigade Reserve Position were practically complete, and the bulk of the Divisional Reserve Line was also near completion. On III Corps front, the front line from the 4th Division's sector to Halluin (42nd Division's sector) was complete. On the 44th Division's front, work had only just started on the FDL Line north of the Armentières – Bailleul road and the Brigade reserve line north of L'Epinette. In total, the Company had excavated about 25 miles of anti-tank ditch since starting work.

The situation with the pillbox construction programme is harder to ascertain. In I Corps area, it would appear that on the fronts of the 1st and 2nd Divisions most pillboxes had been completed between the FDL Line and the Divisional Reserve Line. The situation was less satisfactory on II and III Corps fronts: 'X' Force did not start work on II Corps front until the New Year while III Corps only took over its sector in April. On the 3rd Division's front, records indicate that 91 pillboxes were under construction as at 31 March with work about to start on a further 15, and the 1st General Construction Battalion RE lists another 93 pillbox sites recced in April – presumably none of these had been completed by 10 May (Table 6.1). Most of these pillboxes were on the Divisional Reserve Line and the Bachy Switch. The 4th Division had some 35 pillboxes in hand on 30 April while the 5th Division had 19 pillboxes in hand as at 30 April and the 2nd General Construction Battalion RE also had 55 under construction in its sector (Table 6.1). Work on III Corps Divisional Reserve Positions and the Quesnoy Switch had been fully reconnoitred but largely postponed until June, as the work on the Armentières – Bailleul front was to receive priority. However, reconnoitring of the Armentières – Bailleul front had only just begun by the time the BEF advanced in Belgium.

21 R.H. Medley, *Five Days to Live: France 1939–40* (Abergavenny: Dover & Company, 1992), p. 24.

22 Dépret gives the number of pillboxes constructed by the BEF between September 1939 to May 1940 from French sources as 258 completed and 233 in hand against a *Groupe d'armée no. 1* target fixed at 300. Inventories carried out in 1946 listed approximately 350 BEF pillboxes with an average of $50m^3$ concrete.

Table 6.1: Pillboxes for 3rd, 4th and 5th Divisions either in hand or sites reconnoitred as at 30 April 1940.

Division	Anti-tank pillbox	Bren pillbox	Single MG pillbox	Double MG pillbox
1st RE Battalion – 3rd Div	13	64		16
4th Div Field Coys	17	18		
1st RE Battalion – 4th Div	7			
5th Div Field Coys	5	2	12	
1st RE Battalion – 5th Div	3			
2nd RE Battalion – 5 Div	20	14	4	17

In addition, 2nd RE Battalion settled on the siting of 17 pillboxes in the Bailleul area on 44th Division front on 1 May.

The French, under *Colonel* Bertschi, completed a number of pillboxes in the Halluin sector. But little progress had been made along the line of the River Lys: Dépret and other French researchers list only nine blockhouses completed and 31 'projects'.

Field defences and road blocks had been prepared along most of the Corps Position. However, concrete pillboxes and sections of anti-tank ditch had only been constructed in front of, and on the flanks of, the Mons-en-Pévèle feature and astride the Orchies – Douai road. The Second Position could still be regarded as a 'project'. The only progress had been the construction of some field works and road blocks guarding the crossings over the canal lines.

Saar front

German propaganda made much of the fact that the French were fighting on the Maginot Line while the British apparently did nothing. A typical German broadcast in French was noted by the War Diarist of CRE 2nd Division on 4 December, which claimed that while French soldiers were in the Maginot Line, British soldiers were raping their wives. Germany also dropped propaganda leaflets over France; one particular example showed French troops dying on German barbed wire but when the thin card was held to the light a transparency revealed a contrasting picture of British soldiers in a scene of debauchery. Although the arrival of the BEF was frequently celebrated by the local population in the towns and villages of the British zone, away from *SD* Lille many French never saw any British soldiers and probably hardly believed the BEF existed. A particular worry was that many French troops in the Maginot Line did not even know there was a British army in France. As early as September the possibility of deploying part of the BEF on the Maginot Line had been muted: Ironside noted in his diary on 30 September that 'Daladier [the French Prime Minister] has been talking to the British Ambassador in Paris and telling him the appearance of even one Regiment of British in the Maginot Line would hearten up the French and stop the [German] propaganda that the British are willing to fight to the last Frenchman.'[23]

During November – in order to counter this adverse propaganda and increase co-operation between the Allies, as well as giving British troops much needed experience in day to day activities when in close contact with the enemy – Gort arranged with the French High Command that a British infantry brigade should take its place on the Saar Front under the command of a French division. There they would hold forward positions in front of the Maginot forts. It was intended that brigades would complete short tours of two weeks in rotation on the Saar Front. In this way as many brigades as possible would have a turn in the line, and then whole divisions would take a turn. Before hostilities broke out in May 1940, nine brigades had had the invaluable experience this provided. It also gave a boost to morale, providing a break from the monotony of digging, with most units enjoying their turn on the Saar. Indeed, some units apparently regarded it as sport, which irritated the French. One French officer, who knew England well, described the assembly of a British patrol just about to go out as strongly reminiscent of the meet of a pack of foxhounds on a shooting party! Arrangements were also made to have one brigade in the Alsace front, but the project was dropped.

The Saar sector was within the area of the French Forth Army (*Général* Recuin). The front was inundated in many places, made by damming the Saar south of Sarreguemines. On the outbreak of war, there had been little depth to the Maginot Line. The French had had four months to put things right and had pushed out forward defences in front of the Maginot Line and provided some depth behind it. The forts in the British sector continued to be manned by French Fortress troops, with the British battalions disposed in depth in advance of the fortified line. The enemy front positions were on average 1,500 yards from the British foremost posts. The French position was organised in three zones: the *Ligne de Contact*, the *Ligne de Recueil* and the *Ligne d'Arret*. The forts of the Maginot Line formed the *Ligne d'Arret*. The French were also working on a further line along the River Canner, about three miles behind the fortress line to form the *Ligne d'Arret de L'Armée* which was to constitute the final line on which to stop enemy tanks.

The French did not plan to fight seriously on the *Ligne de Contact*. This was purely an outpost line, intended to prevent enemy patrolling and give warning of any impending major enemy attack. In places the *Ligne de Contact* was supported by a support line – the *Ligne de Soutien*. The purpose of the *Ligne de Soutien* was to facilitate the withdrawal of the *Ligne de Contact* or to act as a second line of defence. The *Ligne de Recueil* had

23 Macleod, DSO, MC & Kelly (eds), *Time Unguarded*, p. 114.

two purposes. Firstly, it was to act as a co-ordinated line for the withdrawal of troops from the *Ligne de Contact*. Secondly, it was to act as a hold-up line, to gain time for reserves to move into the *Ligne d'Arret*. If an enemy attack was correctly appreciated in time and additional formations had arrived at the *Ligne d'Arret*, the French did not intend to fight seriously on the *Ligne de Recueil*. Thus, these two zones, referred to as *Le Couverture*, could allow work to be carried out uninterrupted on developing the *Ligne d'Arret* and also give warning of any serious attack as the enemy would first have to make subsidiary operations to get within striking distance of the *Ligne d'Arret*. For this to work, the distance between the *Ligne de Contact* and *Ligne de Recueil* should be such that both positions could not be overrun in one operation. On the British sector of the Saar, the distance between the two was about three and a half miles (the *Ligne de Contact* was in general seven miles in front of the *Ligne d'Arret* and the *Ligne de Recueil* about four and a half miles in front of the *Ligne d'Arret*).

As noted above, the Maginot forts formed the *Ligne d'Arret*. These were a system of underground forts of varying size, supported in the interval between by troops in field works and blockhouses.[24] The forts were also supported by the field artillery. Immediately in front of the Maginot Line were infantry defences, termed *Brisants*, which were sited to break up any attack in front of the forts. The forts were self-supporting in terms of food and ammunition for a period of many weeks. If overrun, individual forts would act as *points d'appui*, supporting counter-attacks.

The first brigade to visit the Saar front was the 3 Brigade, from 27 November to 18 December. As the Brigade prepared to take its turn in the line, the Brigadier issued the following order:

> I wish every Officer, W.O., N.C.O. and private soldier to realize [sic] that this moment is a historic occasion. The 3rd Infantry Brigade has been chosen to

24 Colonel R Macleod, DSO, MC, gives a good description of the Maginot forts: 'To make each fort the French had scooped out the inside of a hill and made a concrete house of several storeys inside. There was a magazine for ammunition, store rooms, kitchen, dining-room, living-quarters, laundry, and, at the top, the levels from which the weapons were fired, all connected up by lifts and lighted by electricity made on the spot. Periscopes gave all-round fields of vision. At the very top was a disappearing field gun. It was pushed up to fire and brought down to load and lay, without a man exposing himself. The air pressure inside the fort was kept greater than the outside, so no gas could get in, and there were means of expelling the gases from the fort. The fort was ventilated and air-conditioned. Three forts could fire on one area so that if one fort was knocked out two others could still cover the ground. What was remarkable, however, was the small number of weapons in use for the large size of the garrison. Forts, accommodating from five hundred to one thousand men, varied in size according to the size of the hill' (Macleod, DSO, MC & Kelly (eds), *Time Unguarded*, p.202). The larger forts were known as *Gros Ouvrages* and mounted the only real artillery weapons, while the smaller forts were referred to as *Petit Ouvages* and were armed with light infantry type weapons. The forts were not designed for long range artillery duels but rather to actively take part in close combat operations. In between the forts was a chain of smaller pillboxes and blockhouses.

> go into action as the vanguard of the British Army. We shall be in the closest touch with our Allies, who have extended to us the warmest of welcomes. Unless everyone had done his duty since arrival in France, this unique honour would not have been conferred on you. The enemy awaits our arrival with expectancy. The opportunity is yours to maintain and enhance the glorious tradition inscribed on your Colours. Be vigilant, keep cool and fire low. To the last round and the last man and a bit more. Not only the eyes of the Midlands are upon you but those of our Allies and the whole Empire. With justice on our side your proud watchword will be *On ne passé pass* – 'we shall stop them' and *On les aura* – 'We will win.'[25]

The 3 Brigade came under the command of the 42nd French Infantry Division (Hombourg – Budagne sector), holding the centre sector of the front of that Division, after relieving the 80th Regiment, which was then in support of the 3 Brigade (Figure 6.3). Attached to the 3 Brigade was the 26th Field Company, tasked with improving the defences and accommodation for the Brigade's battalions, as well as carrying out work detailed by the *Commandant* of the Divisional Engineers, 42nd French Division.

The French held both the *Ligne de Contact* (a front of approximately 3,500 yards) and *Ligne de Receuil* (a front of approximately 5,000 yards) with just one battalion. The *Ligne de Contact* was covered by only one battery of four 75mm guns. When the British took over, the French agreed to increase the support to one French Regiment of three batteries each with four 75mm guns and one battery of four 155mm guns. The *Ligne de Receuil* was covered by the artillery of the Maginot forts. Tank support was provided by one battalion equipped with Model 35 Renault's billeted at the camp at Veckring.[26] These were only intended for support or counter-attack against local actions; in the event of a major attack the British would stand on the *Ligne de Receuil* in the first instance before falling back on the *Ligne d'Arret*.

The British held the line in similar manor to the French, with one infantry battalion in the *Ligne de Contact*, one infantry battalion in the *Ligne de Receuil* and one infantry battalion in support in the *Ligne d'Arret* area. The *Ligne de Contact* was not heavily entrenched, consisting of a series of section posts, observation posts and machine gun posts. The majority of the Brigade's anti-tank company was placed in the *Ligne de Contact* as the French feared that once the Germans discovered the British were holding this part of the line, they would mount an attack assisted by AFVs to test the British. The machine gun company was also placed in the *Ligne de Contact*, one platoon given forward fire tasks while the other two platoons where given penetration and defensive fire tasks.

25 Lt. Colonel Ewan Butler & Major J. Selby Bradford, *Keep the Memory Green: The First of the Many France 1939–40* (London: Hutchinson & Co. Ltd., no date), pp. 55–56.

26 The Model 35 was a light tank of 11 tons, proof against the German 37mm anti-tank gun and armed with a 37mm semi-automatic gun and machine gun.

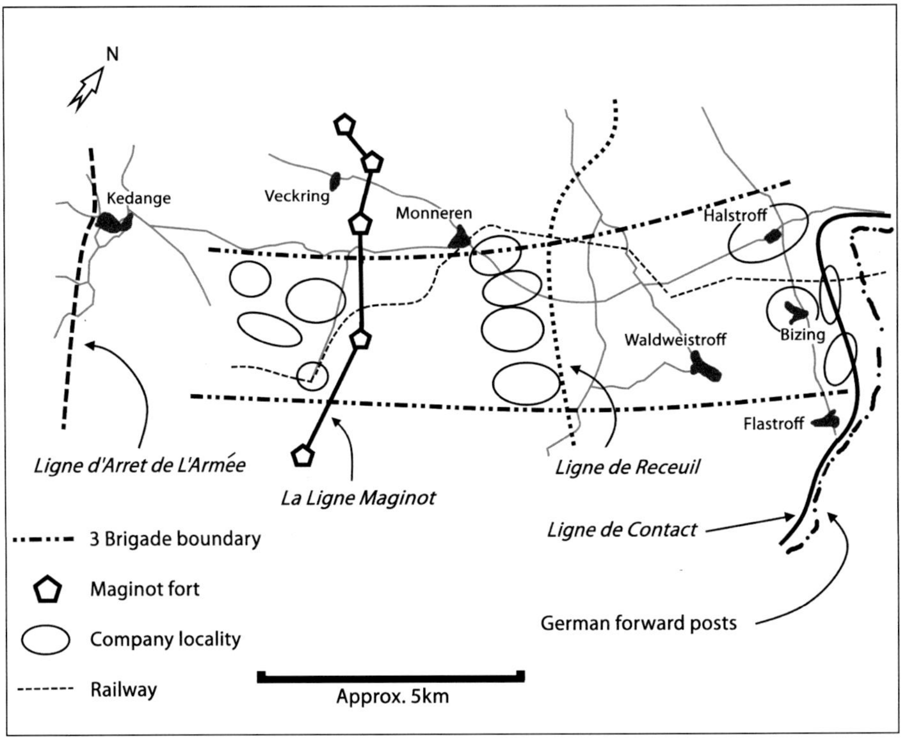

Figure 6.3: Saar Front

The topography of the Saar Front was of a hilly nature, with many streams and patched heavily with forest, and was very suited to defence, giving good observation and good cover for manoeuvre and the artillery. After the flat plains of *SD* Lille, the varied countryside of the Saar Front must have been welcome to the troops. The casemates of the Maginot Line had been built into the hills behind Monneren and were well camouflaged. All the villages, farms and properties between the Maginot Line and the frontier had been evacuated, meaning plenty of available billets for the troops. The scene is described by Second-Lieutenant R.H. Medley during his stint on the Saar Front in February:

> There were no people, there were no animals it was all somewhat eerie. It was sad to see that property had been ransacked, and even the pews in the Church had been ripped out and used as firewood to provide warmth in the bitter winter.[27]

27 Medley, *Five Days to Live*, p. 17.

Medley then goes on to provide a good description of the countryside in the British sector:

> The ground fell away in front of our forward positions quite sharply into a valley along which the Hermsbach stream flowed. In front of 15 platoon on the left the ground rose beyond the Hermsbach stream flowed ... the ground rose beyond the Hermsbach stream forming a spur behind which was another valley with a stream. The two streams joined to our front and flowed through the village of Zedange which lay in noman's land to the right of the company position. The forward German positions were on the slopes of the valley some eighteen hundred yards to our front. The forward German positions on the right overlooked the re-entrant formed by the Hermsbach stream in front of Point 311. It was rolling countryside liberally broken up with woods. The forward positions generally were sited on the forward edges of woods overlooking the Hermsbach stream. There was a lateral road running across the battalion position in dead ground to the rear from Halstroff on the left, through Grindorff Station ('C 'Company Headquarters), to Bizing and Flastroff. Roads ran into no man's land to Waldwisse from Halstroff and from Bizing to Zedange. The railway line ran right through the centre of 'C' Company passing the company headquarters on an embankment and then going into a cutting. All the railway lines in the cutting had been torn up. The cutting fell away near the frontline trenches and the line ran up on to another embankment and bridge over the Hermsbach stream, then ran into another cutting before disappearing from view around a bend towards Waldwisse Station.[28]

Although the French had added some depth to the Maginot Line in the first four months of the Sitzkrieg, as we have seen they had no intention to fight seriously in front of it. This certainly showed in the defence works taken over by the British, which varied from groups of log cabins in forward edges of woodland to revetted and sandbagged field works in open ground. Most of the posts on the front line were on forward slopes, those in open ground being in full view of the enemy. They were also isolated, with no attempt having been made to link them up. The British were keen that the posts be re-sited on the reverse slope, so that in conditions of good visibility the front forward posts could be thinned out and the posts held by observers only. Wire was often badly sited, either too far forward of the posts to keep under effective fire or too close to the post to keep the enemy out of bombing range. Second-Lieutenant Medley was not impressed with the line:

> The positions we took over were disgraceful often no more than two feet deep. Wire was badly sited either in dead ground so it could not be covered by fire,

28 Ibid., pp. 17–18.

> or so close the enemy could throw grenades into our trenches. One sandbag, I remember we found, was filled with biscuits and straw!![29]

Although keen to improve the defences taken over from the French, little could be done because of the freezing conditions. Consequently, when an artillery officer, Captain Twomey (58th Medium Regiment) started his stint on the Saar Front at the beginning of March, little seemed to have changed:

> On our way up to the OP we passed two British posts and had a chat to them. We were struck by the ineffectiveness of their defences; both the lack of digging and protection they have provided themselves and the imbecile way the posts had been sited. A few miles back in the Maginot Line is a perfect example of the ABC of defence laid out in a system of mutually supporting posts with cross fire – no post firing to its immediate front but firing across the fronts of the posts on either flank. Most of our posts are sited so that they see very little and that to the front only and no post can support another. Most of them are sited in woods were shells bursting in the branches do ten times the damage. They seem to be afraid of going and digging themselves in properly on reverse slopes. They are too lazy to dig and get a sense of false security like ostriches in woods. Half the fault lies in the system of each battalion only getting 6 days in the line. They only want to keep quiet for that time and hope they will get away with it for that time and then get relieved, and they are dammed if they are going to do all that digging for another Regiment.[30]

Captain Twomey is perhaps a little unfair, given the impossibility of actually doing any digging in the freezing conditions, although he does highlight a weakness in the system of short tours each unit served on the Saar Front.

A definite policy of 'live and let live' was observed by both sides on the Saar Front, with local 'game laws' adhered to. Villages were strictly preserved from artillery fire and neither side was anxious to deprive the other of winter accommodation. Single vehicles were also not shelled by either side. This allowed single motor transport to approach within a mile of the piquet line at night and commanders' motor cars by day. A report by the12 Infantry Brigade shows how rigidly this was observed. A German working party was observed daily and arrangements were made to engage it with harassing machine gun fire at a range of 3,200 yards. The commander of the local French regiment objected strongly as the reconnoitred machine gun post would mean the projected fire would pass over a village and he feared the church tower might be

29 Ibid., p. 17.

30 Captain L. Twomey, *Notes on attachment to French Arty. Groupement supporting the British SAAR Force* <http://www.wargunner.co.uk/58th/58thtwomey> (accessed on 9 August 2017).

struck. However, in general terms working parties were fair game, and French guns often fired at them if observed from their observation post or reported by British observers as long as they were not working in villages.

The British battalions held the *Ligne de Contact* with all four companies up. Each platoon and company commander was responsible for all that went on in their area, including movement and organising work. As already highlighted, the defences were found wanting on both the *Ligne de Contact* and *Ligne de Receuil* and each battalion did what it could to improve them. Regarding work on the *Ligne d'Arret*, the comments by the Officer Commanding 1 Guards Brigade perhaps illustrate how lax some French officers had become:

> As regards the work on the Ligne d'Arret I was unable to find anyone who knew anything about it or who was interested in it.[31]

Although a 'live and let live' policy was generally in place, active patrolling was strongly encouraged. Each battalion of the brigade serving on the front provided a fighting patrol, nominally of one officer and 16 other ranks which came under the central command of the officer commanding the battalion in the *Ligne de Contact.* The Germans certainly held the initiative in patrolling, as they knew the ground intimately and their use of dogs gave them advantage. Small German patrols of three to four men accompanied by a dog frequently carried out reconnaissance patrols between and round the British posts. Attempts to 'lie-up' and ambush these patrols were fruitless as they were discovered by the dog. The Brigadier of 12 Brigade came up with the idea of obtaining a bitch 'on heat' to decoy enemy dogs, but unfortunately one could not be found. He also considered certain defiles could be made uncomfortable for the German dogs by putting down pepper, but it was obviously impracticable to cover a large front by such means.

The short period that each brigade was in the line also put the British at a disadvantage as it was difficult for patrols to learn the ground thoroughly. The Germans also used large patrols of up to 50 men as a way of training young soldiers. The best way to counter the German patrolling was considered to be by carrying out patrolling right up to the German front line using strong patrols. The French sometimes organised large patrols of up to 80 men so they could undertake what they called a *Coup de Main*, but the British saw no need for this, which was in effect a raiding party strength, instead preferring active and inquisitive patrolling by the smaller fighting patrols. These fighting patrols often split up, one part of the patrol trying to lay up in ambush while a smaller party acted as bait and made as much noise as possible hoping to attract a German patrol. In addition to the battalion fighting patrols, each section

31 TNA: WO167/346, 'Notes on tour of 1 Gds Bde on Saar Front', 1 Guards Brigade War Diary.

post was expected to check it its own wire and dead ground at 'Stand To' and to 'act inquisitively' in conjunction with the battalion organised Fighting patrols.

The fighting patrols were the first British troops to be issued with 'gangster guns' – the Thompson sub-machine gun – for close quarter work.[32] The French advised the British against wearing pullovers and balaclava helmets as the Germans were likely treat any man captured wearing 'civilian' clothes harshly. Standard infantry boots were found to be too clumsy for patrolling; the 51st Division found that 'a water-proof boot, much on the lines of Messrs. Dunlop's shooting boots with rubber soles costing from 10/6d. to 15/- the pair' were ideal for patrolling.[33] Perhaps the most unusual patrol organised by the British was an unarmed 'stalking' patrol carried out by the Reverend Captain J.F. Holt on 7 January along the railway embankment northeast of Grindorff-Ewig. He observed an enemy patrol of six men, which by their behaviour he assumed was not an aggressive patrol. He reported seeing no 'black dogs', although he did hear dogs bark.

The first BEF casualties as a result of active operations were announced on 17 December, when a message was received at British GHQ from French *GQG* stating 'The British now have their wounded and even their dead on French soil once again.'[34] The memo further stated that the casualties 'refer to general patrol activity and not to any particular incident.'[35] It was actually an enemy 'booby trap' that caused the casualties. The first decorations for bravery in the field were also awarded on the Saar Front on 12 January, with the Military Cross for Captain F.P. Barclay and the Military Medal to Lance-Corporal H. Davis, both of the Norfolk Regiment. Both men won their awards for bravery on the same patrol.

The Germans also carried out occasional raids on the British. One raid on the 2nd Battalion Duke of Cornwall's Light Infantry on 4 March was very successful,

32 Although the British had investigated adopting an infantry automatic rifle during the inter-war years, the idea was not taken up, in part because the General Staff felt it would hinder mobility with the need to carry large amounts of ammunition, as they considered troops would just fire off magazines indiscriminately. They preferred the longer range and lethality of a rifle, in the hands of a well trained rifleman. The fear of indiscriminate shooting even led to the re-introduction of the magazine cut-off on the Lee Enfield rifle during the inter-war years. The Germans had used sub-machine guns during the Great War – the Bergmann MP18 issued to special assault troops – and continued to develop them after the war, adopting the MP38 in 1938. Following the success of the MP38, the BEF urgently requested sub-machine guns. Some American M1928 Thompson's happened to be immediately available and 450 of these were shipped over to the Britain. The Treasury rebelled at the cost of £50 per gun and wanted something cheaper. Two other possibilities were a Belgian manufactured sub-machine gun and the Italian Berretta sub-machine gun. The Berretta option fell through on political grounds. Ultimately, Britain developed its own sub-machine gun – the famous Sten gun.

33 TNA: WO167/314, 'Patrolling', 27 April 1940, 51st Division General Staff War Diary.

34 Skene Catling, *Vanguard to Victory: An Account of the first months of the British Expeditionary Force in France* (London: Methuen & Co. Ltd., 1940), *p.* 148.

35 Ibid.

utilising a very effective box barrage to neutralise neighbouring posts; two men were killed and 10 taken prisoner. Captain Twomey, 58th Medium Regiment, gives further details of this raid. The post was shelled by a 6-inch mortar battery and a battery of smaller guns. A German patrol cut the wire under the cover of this concentration and then rushed the post when the fire lifted 100 yards. He considered that the German task was made easier by the very isolated nature of the British posts, and the effectiveness of the shell bursts amongst the overhead tree branches. Making wooden crosses for the casualties was a task that engineers from the 253rd Field Company found themselves having to undertake.

The tour of duty of each brigade was raised to three weeks in March. At the end of March, the decision was taken that the British Army should take over a divisional sector on the Saar Front, with the first (and as it turned out the only) being the 51st Division. One of the Division's battalions, the 1st Battalion Black Watch, had already done a tour in the forward defences, spending Boxing Day in the *Ligne de Contact*. The Division, which arrived on the Saar Front in the third week of April, was allotted the sector Hombourg – Budange. The outpost line ran from Heyden to the Grossenwald wood, then to the village of Remeling to Grindorff-Ewig, to the Hartbuch wood thence through Flastroff towards Neunkirchen, which the Germans held. Many of the French defences taken over were again described as poor, little more than log cabins that were not even bullet proof but within a dense perimeter of barbed wire. The French had also dug many trenches, but more than the Division could possibly occupy. The two pioneer battalions, the 6th Battalion Royal Scots Fusiliers and the 7th Battalion Norfolk Regiment had their work cut out. The surplus trenches were flattened, and the log cabins replaced with more serviceable dug positions. Mules had to be used to carry materials and equipment forward of the Maginot forts.

The 51st Division was very active with patrol enterprises. The following account by Second-Lieutenant A.L. Orr Ewing of the 7th Battalion Argyll & Sutherland Highlanders is very illuminating in explaining what happened when British and German patrols clashed:

> I left our own wire near F 9 in the Grossenwald at 2300 hrs and made my way to the S.E. corner of the Lohwald. I lay-up in the trees on the rt. hand side. About 0130 hrs, I heard someone moving in the wood, and 10 minutes later more movement. I lay quiet for 5 minutes and then decided to investigate. I left 4 men with 2 automatic guns in the trees to cover me, and also to shoot anyone trying to leave the corner of the wood. With the remaining men I moved forward between the stream and the wood. About 40 yds. away from me I saw 3 men running back from the wood towards the stream. I opened fire with my sub-machine gun, and two men dropped. Heavy firing from at least 4 Tommy-guns immediately opened on my flash. My patrol and I all dropped flat and continued to fire and throw grenades. About 8 or 10 men left the wood and opened fire. More men in the wood also fired on us. One man advanced towards us but was severely hit in the stomach. At least two more were hit by grenades,

> as we heard the screaming. The enemy threw stick-grenades, one landing near my batman and me, cutting us both, and temporarily blinding me with blood. Owing to the superior numbers of the enemy, and the fact that our ammunition was low, we withdrew 60 yds. under covering fire from the 4 men we had left in our rear. The enemy then also withdrew, and we heard them talking on the other side of the stream. As it was then our time to return, we made our way back to our own wire.[36]

There can be little doubt that brigade tours to the Saar front were of great value. Firstly, they gave a break from the endless monotonous working parties required for digging and concreting, and secondly, they provided real experience of being in close contact to the enemy. For instance, the 15 Brigade on receiving notice that it was to move to the Saar front put in hand training for the sort of operations it was anticipated would be undertaken. The Brigade's War Diary noted 'The prospect of going to a front where the Brigade would be in contact with the Enemy stimulated all ranks, who entered into the training exercises with zest and enthusiasm.'[37] Although the 'live and let live' policy on the Saar can hardly have represented full on battle experience, it can be compared to the policy of introducing new troops to quite sectors as practised during the Great War. This allowed experience to be gained, including coming under fire: no amount of peace time exercises could prepare a soldier for the momentary confusion as the first enemy shells fell. Mistakes could be made without serious consequences. Many shortcomings in the standards of training were highlighted on these tours to the Saar front; at least there was time to start to put things right before the events of May 1940. In the opinion of Second-Lieutenant Medley, the experience was certainly worthwhile:

> Our experience in the line had brought us face-to-face with enemy across a no-mans-land a mile wide. We had seen shellfire and we had experienced patrolling. It was a gentle introduction. It helped reduce the initial shock when the real battle began.[38]

36 Linklater, Eric, *The Highland Division* (London: HMSO, 1942), p. 16.
37 TNA: WO167/376, 15 Brigade War Diary, 22 January to 17 February 1940.
38 Medley, *Five Days to Live,* p. 21–22.

7

Sitzkrieg: Holding the Line throughout the Long Winter

After moving up to the frontier in October, the BEF immediately began work to dig in and add depth to the French defences, which, for the troops, involved long hours often in atrocious conditions. A German attack was also possible and frequent practice was required in manning the defences. As the autumn passed into winter, and a German attack became unlikely until the following spring, more time could be given to leisure activities for the troops, including home leave which was granted just before Christmas. More time could also be devoted to training, which was sorely needed as all recognised the training deficiency in the BEF. The lack of any military activity on the front – with the exception of the skirmishes along the Saar Front – made the work of journalists reporting on the war difficult and the term 'Phoney War' was coined by American journalists.

Monotonous work

As the BEF moved up to *SD* Lille to take its place in the front line, the first task was to find billets for the troops. These were found wherever possible near the defences on which they would have to work upon. The BEF was spread over industrial areas in the north and rural districts in the south. Billets were easier to find in urban areas, such as cottages, factories and brickworks, and could be made relatively comfortable with clean straw. In rural areas, billets could be quite bleak; the lucky men were billeted with French families in farm houses, but the rest had to make do with lofts, barns, derelict buildings and village halls. In many cases, billets in derelict or empty buildings had no electric light until arrangements were made to put in installations. In one case at least, men shared a cow shed with the cows! Those troops billeted with French families said they were made welcome, but according to Lieutenant R. L. Clarke, the British were generally not popular, as it was said that the British wanted all the houses for themselves.[1] Troops tried to make their billets as comfortable as possible and in

1 The 1st Battalion Grenadier Guards War Diary for 5 February notes that billets taken over

many instances one of the first tasks was to ensure that at least dining areas were under cover. The provision of other infrastructure required for domestic arrangements, such as incinerators, latrines, cookhouses and ablution benches proceeded as rapidly as the supply of timber and corrugated iron permitted. The laying of brick paths and rubble for firmer standing for motor transport also helped.

Work on improving the defences began immediately and working parties were continuous. The fighting troops not only had to prepare their own section posts and connecting trenches, but also provide working parties for road repairs, digging and revetting anti-tank ditches and concreting pillboxes. In at least one case, troops took part in a divisional scheme during the day and then continued digging from 7:00 p.m. to midnight. Instructions were often issued that work would be carried out each day irrespective of the weather, and the War Diary of the 200th Field Company noted that the men worked day and night on the BELLE PORTE pillbox. Men with concrete experience were often tasked with aiding the field companies with pillbox construction. For instance, the 12 Brigade undertook a census of its battalions for men with previous concrete experience – the 2nd Battalion Royal Fusiliers found 27 men and the 1st Battalion South Lancashire Regiment 22 men – who were used to construct one Bren pillbox in their own sector, under their own resource but under the supervision of the 7th Field Company.

Troops must have been surprised to find themselves working as agricultural labourers. Arrangements were made with the French authorities to help with the autumn harvest and the ploughing and sowing for the summer crops, as all the young Frenchmen had gone off to France's eastern frontier.[2] A small BEF film crew actually did some filming, intending to show the film to the French troops in the Maginot Line. The hope was that it may raise their morale by showing that the BEF was doing all it could to ensure their land at home was not being neglected. However, it was feared it may have the opposite effect if they saw Englishmen working on their land while they sat in the Maginot Line, so the film was never shown.

It was a wet autumn and the rain and mud gave rise to conditions only too familiar to those who served on the Western Front during the last war, with fields transformed into lakes. Day after day, men laboured on the defences in thick mud and lashing rain. As happened in the Great War, drills had to be introduced to prevent trench foot. In most cases, troops had no spare uniform so the clothes they had spent the day working in had to be dried before blazing fires – that is if they were lucky enough to have access to one. Eventually most billets and the blockhouses were provided with oil stoves. Only one blanket per man had been issued – according to the 2nd Battalion Dorsetshire Regiment's War Diary, men were not issued with a second blanket until

at Lorry-lès-Metz in the rear of the Maginot Line had been left filthy by former British battalions and that items had also been stolen, so the inhabitants were understandably none too friendly.

2 Film taken at the time even shows Bren gun carriers employed as tractors for ploughs.

the start of November – and for additional warmth, they had to turn to the favourite Army standby: straw. One of the first tasks the divisional field companies undertook was to construct some form of divisional bath houses, and when established they must have been a godsend to the men, although they usually only got one bath a week. Typical of improvised bathhouses was that provided by the engineers for the 2nd Battalion Dorsetshire Regiment. The bathhouse was located in the basement of a brewery in Rumegies and hot water was provided by heating petrol tins on a furnace. The Germans had the used the brewery for the same purpose during the Great War! For some lucky units, laundry contracts were also arranged in Lille. Others had to make do with mobile bath and laundry units.

The rain was followed by an intense cold. The troops wrapped around themselves every kind of garment they could lay their hands on to try and keep warm. One young soldier, Wilfred Leonard Saunders, described how the cold cut right through overcoat, battle dress, scarves, pullovers, and vests, and that soldiers' caps froze onto heads, greatcoats and socks froze solid, hair froze, and bread froze on plates. Conditions were especially bad for despatch riders, as the roads were exceptionally hazardous, and no amount of clothing could keep them warm. Corporal Sykes, 7th Field Company, who volunteered to deliver a message to a pillbox site on one day in January, had to be physically lifted from his motorcycle, stripped and massaged back to life, and revived with 'hot 'grogs'. The I Corps War Diary observed that dispatch rider services were stopped on 17 January due to the conditions and train or local omnibus were used instead. It was almost as bad for the drivers of trucks; they also had the additional worry of frost precautions such as draining the radiators every night. Captain John Horsfall called it the 'Winter of Discontent' and gave the opinion that many troops 'thought they were swindled and were here, in France and in some discomfort, under false pretence. And there were overtones of ignominy.'[3] Large amounts of comforts for the troops such as pullovers, socks, balaclavas, gloves and mitts were sent over from home.

The monotony of the work did not escape the attention of the higher commanders, and given the constraints they were working under and the necessity to improve the defences, they did what they could to provide some relief from digging for the men. The 1st Division, for example, specified that men were to have one and half days per week doing something else than digging. This may have only been route marches or drill but also included bathing, and some time to themselves.

Holding the line

As well as digging the defences, the BEF had to be prepared to hold them against a German attack. Although the enemy was not in front of the FDL Line, a rapid night advance with armour through Belgium was always considered a possibility.

3 John Horsfall, *Say Not the Struggle* ... (Kineton: The Roundwood Press, 1977), p. 12.

Initially, the FDL Line blockhouses were fully garrisoned. Guards were mounted and patrols detailed between the blockhouses. Those not on patrol or sentry duties worked on improving the obstacles and fire positions of each blockhouse, since the blockhouse formed the centre of the platoon post. During the night the garrison slept in the blockhouse – bunks and later hammocks were provided. The 2nd Battalion Royal Warwick's method of holding the line was probably typical. A platoon would be billeted in a farmhouse near the blockhouse. Each section of the platoon would man the blockhouse for 24 hours in turn. After all sections had completed their turn, another platoon would take its place in the farmhouse. As fears of an imminent attack subsided, it was only necessary to mount guards. As a typical example, Standing Orders issued by the 1st Division required a blockhouse guard of not less than one NCO and three men, allowing one sentry to be mounted on the blockhouse by day and night. As well as the blockhouses, a guard was also mounted in the trenches. This must have been particularly unpleasant – just as it was in the Great War – with wet, cold nights and the clinging mud, although at least there was no physical danger. If the need came to hold trenches, the 9 Infantry Brigade got hold of the Trench Standing Orders used by the Guards Division in the Great War.

Following various instructions, the amount of ammunition to be dumped at the FDL blockhouses was settled at 200 rounds per 25mm anti-tank gun, 150 rounds per anti-tank rifle, 5,000 rounds per Bren gun, 100 rounds per rifle and 36 HE grenades. Blockhouses were also to be stocked with seven days hard rations for the full garrison. The water in the blockhouse tanks was unfit to drink unless boiled; a stock of solidified alcohol was to be stored in each blockhouse for this purpose. Range cards were prepared and kept in each blockhouse. Standard range marks were also placed in the field of fire. These would be especially useful if handing over to another unit. The standard markers were a triangle for 400 yards, a circle for 700 yards and a square for 1,000 yards, the colour of the marks varying according to the background.

In the rear, both the LoC and airfields needed troops for local protection. Regular troops could not be spared for such duties, which necessitated the formation of 'Old Soldiers' Garrison Battalions from men deemed too old or unfit for regular service.

By December, when an attack was now very unlikely until the following spring, there was no longer any requirement to garrison or provide a guard day and night for the blockhouses and trenches. For example, the 2nd Division issued instructions that at the discretion of brigade commanders, blockhouses could be locked and left empty during the day, although a guard was still to remain in them at night. Plans were now put in place to man the defences in two stages in the event of an attack. During stage one, wiring and trench digging tasks were to be completed as fully as possible, blockhouses stocked, including the water tanks, knife rests placed in position to close gaps in the wire on the frontier, and artillery, anti-tank guns and machine guns were to complete preparations to move to battle positions, including the dumping of ammunition. Houses which were to be demolished to improve fields of fire would be prepared for demolition and houses that were to be incorporated into the defence were to be taken over and put into a state of defence, including loopholing. Engineers were to prepare bridge and road demolitions, which would be carried out under the orders of the Chief Engineer. Notice boards for refugees were to be prepared and refugee routes policed. Gas decontamination centres were to open. In the rear, troops designated to man the reserve positions would move into place and guards were to be found for the Second Position. Stage two was manning the defences: blockhouses and platoon localities were to be fully manned, artillery, anti-tank guns and machine guns moved into battle positions, unit commands to move to their Battle HQ and patrolling commenced along the frontier and outposts sent out. Anti-tank minefields were to be laid and armed and a wire run around them to prevent friendly troops from becoming casualties, which was to be removed at the last minute. Steel rail road blocks were to be put in place except at designated frontier crossings, which were to be left open for refugees.[4]

Leisure

Until the end of November, there was little time for leisure, Sunday being treated as any other day (church parades, however, were counted as work). While working on the defences along the River Lys, the 15 Brigade did declare Sunday a day off from digging, but it was emphasised this concession was dependent upon the progress of the work on the defences.

Estaminets in the billeting areas were naturally very popular with the troops with some time off, and kept busy. Some estaminets were reserved for officers only and others for Warrant Officers and Sergeants only. Concerts organised by the Entertainments National Service Association (ENSA) were given regularly in Lille and other larger towns by the likes of Gracie Fields, Noel Coward and Leslie Henson. French cinemas also showed British films. B Echelon, 2nd Battalion Dorsetshire Regiment thought that the good cinema in Marchiennes was ample compensation for rather poor billets. It was somewhat irritating for the troops scattered around the small villages where there were no such facilities as there was neither the transport nor tickets for more than a small proportion of men to travel to a cinema or concert in the evening. This made tickets, which were free, very highly prized and of a high barter value.

However, three mobile cinemas did arrive in the British zone on 20 October and later on, ENSA was able to provide small travelling concert parties of 'three or four pretty girls, a comic or two, a trunk of "props" and dresses' which could visit the troops wherever they might be.[5] Mickey Mouse was a popular showing by the mobile cinemas, and it must have brought some relief to the troops, who were 'absolutely starved in the matter of professional entertainment' and had spent the war so far

4 The code words 'Stand To' and 'Action Stations' were adopted to describe these two stages for manning Britain's anti-invasion defences.

5 Lt. Colonel Ewan Butler & Major J. Selby Bradford, *Keep the Memory Green: The First of the Many France 1939–40* (London: Hutchinson & Co. Ltd., no date), p. 23

living in hard conditions 'without the preoccupation of actual operations to break the exacting daily round of digging, building, and wiring in the increasingly severe winter climate, the wet and cold, the deepening water, and the thickening mud.'[6] Travelling around the British zone was not without risk for the entertainers, with Miss Violet Loraine, Miss Binnie Hale and Jack Payne all suffering injuries in car accidents.

As Christmas approached the decision was taken to grant home leave, but it was obviously strictly controlled to ensure only a small part of the battalion strength was away at any one time. Nevertheless, by the end of January ten days leave home had been enjoyed by some 60,000 of all ranks. 'Paris Leave' was never granted but on one occasion during a football match between the French and British during the early spring, a sizeable number of men were allowed to visit the Parc de Princes, the 'Wembley' of France. Men returning from home leave often reported that little interest was shown in the BEF at home because of the lack of active operations. The situation is summed up humorously in one book:

> "But what," civilians would ask the soldier from France, "do you *do* all the time?"
> "Dig," the warrior might reply, laconically. He is tired of this question.
> "Oh, *dig*! I should have thought you could have done that here."[7]

After the New Year, a decision was reached by GHQ to allow various social welfare organisations to set up canteens, recreation rooms and rest rooms in the BEF zone and along the LoC. These were run by organisations such as the Salvation Army, the YMCA, the Church Army, the Church of Scotland and the Catholic Women's League. The Salvation Army also provided canteens for British troops in the Maginot Line. For many senior officers, providing such comforts for their men was long overdue.

Not unsurprisingly, brothels were also a popular pastime. In order to try and reduce the cases of VD, General Montgomery issued an unfortunately worded divisional order. This caused bitter complaints from the Senior Chaplains of both the Church of England and the Roman Catholic Church and almost resulted in him losing his command. One can guess at the activity of some of the men who took the nightly 'Passion Wagon' truck to Douai, which had been organised for the HQ of the 13th Anti-tank Regiment.

In a memorandum prepared for the War Office, it was noted that one of the 'biggest problems through the winter would be the maintenance of enthusiasm and morale' of the troops.[8] Almost certainly it was down to the boredom of the Sitzkrieg that drink and fighting, often both going together, and the occasional charge of 'failing

6 Skene Catling, *Vanguard to Victory: An Account of the first months of the British Expeditionary Force in France* (London: Methuen & Co. Ltd., 1940), pp. 193–194.
7 Butler & Bradford, *Keep the Memory Green*, pp. 54–55.
8 TNA: WO106/1661, 'Notes on the situation if Germany remains passive'.

to comply' or 'striking his superior officer in the execution of his duty' were the most common incidents on soldier's charge sheets.[9] Alan Allport in *Browned Off and Bloody-Minded: The British Soldier Goes to War 1939-1945* explains the obvious temptation of French alcohol to British soldiers, where half a pint of brandy cost two pence or a bottle of Champagne three shillings, while beer at home cost four pence a pint. The 9 Brigade had to issue an order that trucks taking men into Lille for an evening had to return, and not wait for the men. If the men could not catch a train back, then the trucks would have to be sent out later to fetch them; only this way could it be guaranteed that drivers would be sober! The War Diarist of the 101st Army Field Company notes that a party of the Labour Corps sent to collect stores 'took [the] opportunity to get hopelessly drunk. Had to send out Cpl Murphy and two lorries to bring them back handcuffed at 20.00 hours.'[10] Although most pre-war NCO's were aware that drunken men should be kept in custody and away from their superior officers, many NCO's promoted or brought in since the outbreak of war did not realise the importance of this. In many cases, drunken and disorderly soldiers were often allowed to stop in their billets or barracks, often resulting in cases of subsequent insubordination or violence by the drunken man and charges far more serious than that of being drunk. Some punishment was certainly handed out for being drunk: Major D.F. Callander recalled that about six soldiers a day were staked out or suspended above ground, even in the extreme cold. Second-Lieutenant FitzGerald, who was lucky enough to have good billets and access to the attractions of Lille noted that it was probably just as well as the war started when it did:

> It was just as well the phoney war ended when it did, otherwise we might have died of obesity and cirrhosis of the liver. All that high living was not good for us.[11]

Sport was always a popular activity with the troops. Football, rugger and tennis were all played when time and conditions allowed, while indoors, darts was a favourite game. Sometimes troops played against the local inhabitants – the War Diary of the 7th Field Company notes that several games of hockey were played against the Lille Hockey Club in April, with the engineers losing all of the games! The 4 Brigade War Diary notes a football match against the French 43rd Infantry Regiment at St. Amand; the supporters marched to the match through the town, headed by the pipes and drums. The result was a 2-2 draw, no doubt good for Anglo-French relations.

Most, if not all, soldiers kept in touch with loved ones at home with letters or Field Service Postcards. As many as 9,000 bags of mail could be handled on a single day by the BEF Postal Service. To ensure the safety of the BEF, strict rules on what

9 Horsfall, *Say Not the Struggle...*, p. 16.
10 TNA: WO167/925, 101st Army Field Company War Diary, 1 January 1940.
11 Desmond FitzGerald, *Many Parts: The Life and Travels of a Soldier, Engineer and Arbitrator in Africa and Beyond* (London: Radcliffe Press, 2007), p. 90.

could be posted were in place. It was strictly forbidden to post correspondence in the French civil post offices. Picture postcards of places, no matter how well known, were prohibited. Soldiers were also not to write to the press. Subjects that could not be mentioned in letters included details of unit locations, descriptions of billets, particulars of armaments or equipment or criticisms of any kind which might bring the BEF or its allies into disrepute. Officers carried out censorship of their men's letters, although up to three letters could be sent uncensored by unit officers if placed in green envelopes addressed to the Deputy Chief Censor. Field Service Postcards also did not require censoring. According to some of those that had to censor letters, the topics soldiers wrote home about hardly ever varied: 'I am well. The food is good. We are living in mud...' with the rest of the content being family affairs.[12] On average, 3,000 bags of parcels and letters came out to the BEF every day and an estimated 200,000 letters sent home. Letters from the United Kingdom usually took four to six days while a letter sent from France took longer; in most cases though, a soldier could expect a reply to a letter he sent home within 12 days.

The conditions of the Sitzkrieg allowed all in the BEF, including the front-line infantry, to celebrate Christmas. Decorations were put up in barns, school-rooms, farm outhouses and other billets. Pigs, turkeys and other livestock were purchased by various units and fattened up in preparation for Christmas Day. Christmas Day was a complete holiday for all except for a percentage who would have to continue to carry out normal guard duties. Many men were invited to share a Christmas meal with French families. Companies usually provided a free barrel of French beer for the men, as English bottled beer from a NAAFI canteen, at five francs a bottle, was too expensive for most. Many officers also hosted parties for the residents and children of the French villages in which their company was billeted in. The Scottish regiments celebrated Hogmanay in style.

The 'Phoney War'

Publicity and propaganda were now part of modern warfare. Every newspaper, broadcaster and news-real agency demanded their representatives at GHQ. This need to satisfy publicity was jointly managed by the Director of Military Intelligence and his staff at GHQ along with the Department of Public Relations at the War Office. The Newspapers Proprietors Association was responsible for the selection of accredited representatives. In all, the BEF had to look after numerous British journalists, broadcasters, photographers, novelists and writers of every description, various official war artists, nine American journalists and four French journalists – all looking for something, anything, to write about or film. The lack of any active operations in the first months of the war meant lean pickings for these journalists and writers. This undoubtedly led to the lack of interest in the BEF shown at home,

12 André Maurois, *The Battle of France* (London: John Lane the Bodley Head, 1940), p. 71.

which many soldiers experienced while on leave. The Americans coined the phrase 'The Phoney War' while British journalists referred to it as 'The Bore War' or even 'The Great Bore War'. During the British Prime Minister's visit to France, one war correspondent remarked to him that he found the war 'rather hard to write about.' An officer replied: 'Boredom is better than bombs!'[13] One American journalist was even heard to remark, that in the opinion of his employer, the war was not being 'put over at its full entertainment value'.

The Sitzkrieg, however, was not without periods of a heightened state of alert, or in the term frequently used at the time: a 'flap'. The term 'flap' is neatly defined by the CRE 2nd Division War Diarist:

> The word flap has become, if not worthy of inclusion in the Oxford English Dictionary, at any rate at worthy of inclusion in a Glossary of Military Terms. There is no other single word that implies crises, troop movement, orders, counter orders, packing, unpacking, packing again, destroying files, looking for letters destroyed, rescuing them from waste paper basket, and writing more letters at high speed. The word, in fact, implies the whole gamut of military activity when everybody wants to get something done but nobody is quite sure what.[14]

The first 'flap' was the result of intelligence that suggested Germany was preparing to follow up victory in Poland with an attack on the Low Counties and France. This crisis reached its peak early November and the War Diarist of CRE 2nd Division, with characteristic humour, summed up this scare with his diary entries for November:

> There is a general feeling that the Germans, anxious to begin where they left off on 11 November 1918 will begin again now.
> <u>But they haven't</u>
> We now seem to be back to Concrete work. Intelligence reports suggest that the ESCAUT and DENDRE schemes will not be wanted for a bit. So now we sit back and struggle to get Engineer Stores. What a War! One minute we are all "flat out" for Mobile Operations: the next minute we are flat out for Sand and Aggregate.[15]

This 'flap' did not prevent Lord Gort from attending an Armistice Day service at a French military cemetery, although a detachment of French soldiers headed by *Général* Blanchard that was supposed to be present never arrived; it was rumoured they were 'standing to' in view of the latest fears of a German attack.

13 Catling, *Vanguard to Victory*, p. 118.
14 TNA: WO167/207, 2nd Division Commander Royal Engineers War Diary, 25 April 1940.
15 Ibid., 11–17 November 1939.

The outstanding event of January was the acute state of tension that existed between the 12th and 16th of that month as a result of reports that Germany was about to invade Belgium and Holland. From about 9 January there were reports of increased activity on the frontier and on 12 January a German aeroplane made a forced landing in Belgium – the so called 'Mechelen incident' – which contained details of plans to invade the Netherlands and Belgium with a view to destroying the BEF and French forces to its north. Arrangements were made to implement Plan D: mobile troops closed up to the frontier, both corps were placed on four hours' notice and all leave was cancelled. The Belgian Government offered to let in the Allies under certain conditions. Gamelin was ready to order in the French troops but would not do so unless the BEF moved forward with them. It took the War Cabinet two days to authorise this move, but by then it was too late as the Belgians had withdrawn the offer. By 16 January, tensions had eased, and the special precautions relaxed. Many at the time believed the captured plans to be a plant by the Germans in order to induce the allies to move into Belgium and giving them the opportunity to violate Belgium, claiming it was no longer neutral. The 'flap' no doubt did the BEF good, as noted by I Corps War Diary 'since it disturbed the rather too "even tenor of its ways" and made everyone realise that we were at war.'[16]

The 'flap' of 11 to 19 April was generated by the German invasion of Norway and Denmark. It had the usual effect of generating troop movements, thinning the files, cancelling leave and nearly resulted in an 'incident' when a reconnaissance party from the 225th Field Company set foot in Belgium when examining a frontier barrier. It no doubt raised morale, as at last it seemed that the digging and concreting was over and that the enemy could be met away from his fortified Siegfried Line: Captain Barclay (2nd Battalion Norfolk Regiment), for example, recalled that his men were raring to go after the monotonous months of the Sitz. The War Diarist of CRE 4th Division notes another effect of such heightened tension on troops – it encouraged gambling. Unfortunately for the Allies, there was another effect of all these 'flaps', with their preparations for a move into Belgium at short notice: it provided German intelligence with a very good idea of what the Allies intended to do. Although, according to the War Diarist of CRE 2nd Division, if the Germans wanted to know what the Allies intended to do, all they had to do was read the British Press. During the November 'flap' he noted:

> There is a general feeling that we may have to advance into Belgium as the Germans are manning the Dutch Frontier. If they go into Holland we shall go into Belgium or at least we think so – so does the Daily Mail.[17]

16 TNA: WO167/124, 'Summary of the month', January 1940, 1st Corps General Staff War Diary.

17 TNA: WO167/207, 2nd Division Commander Royal Engineers War Diary, 3 November 1939.

It also must be admitted that the code words Plan D or E did not pay much attention to security!

The BEF did suffer some casualties early on, but none were struck down by German gunfire. Most were victims of road accidents. Although these casualties ended up in French hospitals, the RAMC had been busy establishing hospitals in the base areas. Nearer the front there were the casualty clearing stations, and further forward still were the main dressing stations and forward dressing stations. These stations were kept busy with numerous injuries resulting from construction work on the defences. Hundreds of nurses had also arrived in France. At the base hospitals, the establishment provided for 80 nurses for six hospitals which had a total of 1,200 beds and 50 nurses for four hospitals with a total of 600 beds. The establishment for each casualty clearing station was eight nurses. None were allowed nearer the front in the dressing stations, which were staffed entirely by men. Preparations were also made for burials. Within the general area of the British sector were many military cemeteries from the Great War established by the Imperial War Graves Commission. The original plans of these cemeteries – the 'cities of silence' – were examined with a view to finding out if ground existed for new burials. Where ground did exist, new plots were marked out by the Commission and a notice displayed announced:

> This British military cemetery is open for the burial of members of the Allied or enemy forces falling during the present hostilities.[18]

The first causality caused by a British bullet on the Western Front was a French farm worker pushing a barrow at night who was wounded in the arm after a sentry fired at him for failing to respond to a challenge. It turned out the farm worker was stone deaf. However, up in the sky the RAF and the *Luftwaffe* did occasionally clash. Early honours for the RAF and AA guns occurred on 2 November, when two German reconnaissance planes were brought down – one by an RAF fighter and one by the combined shooting of British and French AA guns and pursuing RAF fighters. On 22 November, a Heinkel bomber was brought down by a 22-year-old fighter pilot. However, the RAF did not have its own way all the time, with a total 29 aircraft lost in operations during the seven months before the German Blitzkrieg.

The unreal situation of the Sitzkrieg allowed a succession of 'tourists' – i.e. distinguished visitors – to visit the BEF front line. The troops quickly got fed up with these 'tourists' as it invariably resulted in a loss of leisure time and an uncomfortable few hours trying to keep warm while lined up along a roadside waiting for the VIP. A total of seven Cabinet Ministers visited the front: Mr. Hore-Belisha twice, Sir Kingsley Wood, Winston Churchill, Anthony Eden, Mr. Chamberlain, Sir Samuel Hoare and Lord Hankey – in that order. The King made a weeklong visit from 4 to 10 December, visiting both the BEF and the Maginot Line. In the BEF zone, he was

18 Catling, *Vanguard to Victory*, p. 139.

able to view numerous units lined up along the roadsides to great him. He also visited some gun pits, trenches and blockhouses, and even climbed on top of one blockhouse and viewed the landscape with the aid of maps and plans. According to Captain Townsend, 2nd Battalion Durham Light Infantry, this was blockhouse No. 67 on the main Tournai road, and 'beautiful wooden steps with a hand rail were put up against the blockhouse so that visitors could gaze into Belgium from the top. I often wonder if those steps were still there when the Germans came by.'[19] In the many villages that the King passed through, French school children were given the day off so they could see him. Although there was the ever-present RAF overhead, his visit to the front line certainly resembled a peace time event!

A sense of complacency certainly gripped some British politicians and the press, who were lulled into false security by the 'phoney war'. With the atrocious autumn and winter weather, many guessed – quite correctly – that no major operations could take place until the winter had passed. These same people then reasoned that during this respite, the British and French defences would become stronger, presenting even greater risks to Hitler if he dared to attack. Skene Catling captures the opinion of many:

> At present his [Hitler's] army finds itself pinned on the West by the now fully mobilized [sic], amply supplied, and steadily growing forces of the Allies, who are perfectly content to hold on where they are – with bulldog tenacity.[20]

The idea that it was the Allies who had Hitler 'pinned' down on the Western Front seems ridiculous with hindsight, but it was the opinion of many at the time. On 5 April, Chamberlain uttered his ill-judged statement that Hitler had 'missed the bus' as both Britain and France had made good their deficiencies during the seven months of the Sitzkrieg.[21] Brooke found himself arguing continuously with those who thought the Germans would remain indefinitely passive. In his diary entry for 28 January he records a conversation with the DMO and that he got the impression that the War Office was 'concentrating on ensuring that they are going to win the war in three years' from now', but neglected 'to realise the dangers they run of losing it this year.'[22] On 16 February, he records a conversation with the new Secretary of State for War, The Rt. Hon Oliver Stanley, who expressed the opinion that Germany would

19 Captain Cyril Moseley Townsend, *Diary of 40725 Captain Cyril Moseley Townsend 2 DLI.* <http://www.durhamlightinfantry.webs.com/2dlidyledunkirk1940> (accessed on 10 August 2017)
20 Catling, *Vanguard to Victory* p. 223.
21 Winston Churchill, *The Second World War: Volume I – The Gathering Storm* (London: Cassell & Co. Ltd., 1948), p. 461.
22 Arthur Bryant, *The Turn of the Tide: Based on the War Diaries of Field Marshal Viscount Alanbrooke* (London: Collins, 1957), p. 78.

not attack on the Western Front that year.[23] To Brooke, it seemed that the War Office looked upon the Western Front as one of stalemate.

Along with doubts if Hitler would ever attack, comfort was also taken at home by many in the knowledge that the senior commanders of the BEF had all gone through the Great War. Many felt, if it did come to hostilities, that these commanders having experienced the horrors of the Great War themselves would never waste their men's lives in futile action.[24]

Air activity by the British air force during the Sitzkreig was limited to aerial reconnaissance of the Siegfried Line by No. 70 Squadron Blenheim Strategical Reconnaissance Wing, part of the Air Component, and driving off inquisitive enemy reconnaissance aircraft by fighters of both the Air Component and the AASF. As we have already seen, this led to both some successes and some losses. Bomber Command carried out a number of leaflet drops over German cities throughout the autumn and winter. It was hoped these would convince the Germans of their vulnerability to air attack and disrupt work in factories by having to adopt defence measures. Neither the organisation or equipment of the AA Brigades were seriously tested during the period of the Sitzkrieg, as enemy air activity was almost entirely restricted to reconnaissance at great heights. This meant a daily monotony for the AA gunners, with a gun detachment having to be present at all times, often living a troglodyte lifestyle in a dugout next to the gun pit. However, there was the momentary excitement of the usual morning air raid alert and André Maurois tells the tale of one team of gunners who found that each time after they had loaded the gun, the 'all-clear' was given before they could fire it. He continued: 'It was always the same shell and they were soon on the most intimate terms with it. They called it "Arthur"' Eventually, unable to stand it any longer, they fired the thing.'[25] The battery commander did not know what they fired at, but at least they had got rid of 'Arthur'!

Security

Security was one of the main preoccupations of the BEF Staff, as no attempt had been made to evacuate civilians from the frontier area. When the BEF arrived in the *SD* Lille, over 10,000 Belgians were working on the beet harvest in the British zone and it was estimated over 20,000 crossed the border each day on their normal daily business. The *SD* Lille was densely populated and was full of Belgians, Poles and even Italians working in the mining and cloth industries. The French also employed civilian

23 Montgomery recalled a similar conversation with Chamberlain on 16 December, when after lunch Chamberlain asked him: 'I don't think the Germans have any intention of attacking us. Do you?' (Bernard Law, Viscount Montgomery of Alamein, KG, *The Memoirs of Field-Marshal Montgomery* (London: Collins, 1958), p. 58).

24 The notion of futile sacrifice and a 'lost generation' was how the public increasingly viewed the Great War from the 1920's onwards and is still the dominant view today.

25 Maurois, *The Battle of France,* p. 73.

contractors for work on their defences, with a handful also employed on the British defences. Captain Barclay recounts that conversations with Belgians, who were on one side of the stream L'Elnon and men from his Company on the other, frequently took place! Brooke noted in his diary that there were plenty of opportunities for spying and that Belgium was full of German spies. Traitors such as William Joyce – 'Lord Haw-Haw of Zeeson' – and his fellow betrayer Ferdonnet – the 'Traitor of Stuttgart' – helped to spread German propaganda. The Communists, of which there were many in the industrial and mining areas of Lille, were also trying to cause friction within the Franco-British alliance.

Ironside summed up the situation in his diary on 7 October:

> Gort took me up and showed me the line. A very curious position. Here we are in a foreign country, going in to occupy a line facing a neutral country, in absolute peace. Thousands of people live on one side of the frontier or the other, and cross to their work every day in the fields or the factories. Everything that we do, or build must be reported to the Germans within a few hours. There can be no concealment. Everything will be pinpointed at once...All the inhabitants are living right up to the frontier.[26]

A French officer, *Commandant* D. Barlone, working on defences to the right of the BEF zone, also described the lack of security:

> All our available vehicles are placed at the service of the Engineers, who are building a series of blockhouses along the Belgium frontier. They are sited along an anti-tank ditch which, in its turn, is protected by a net-work of barbed wire and mine-fields right up to the very edge of this anti-tank ditch. Some of these fortifications have been constructed by civilian contractors who employ Italians, Belgians, Czechs. Furthermore, country-folk, inquisitive folk, and spies wander about continuously. No one makes any attempt to preserve any secrecy about our defences... I make frequent visits to view the workings, the progress of which is slow. The most surprising thing is that when the main works are completed, they are neither armed nor guarded. Any one is free to enter, to sabotage anything and everything. When I diffidently make a remark to this effect to Captain Perrier of the General Staff, and Colonel Careme, a friend of his in the Engineers, they answer me confidently, 'What are we to arm them with?'[27]

26 Colonel R. Macleod, DSO, MC & Denis Kelly (eds), *Time Unguarded: The Ironside Diaries 1937-1940* (New York: David McKay Company Inc., 1963), p. 123.

27 D. A. Barlone, *French Officer's Diary: 23 August 1939 – 1 October 1940* (Cambridge: CUP, 1942), pp. 26 27.

Of course, some attempt was made to control civilian traffic across the Franco- Belgian frontier and keeping inquisitive eyes away from the defences. However, the strength of the French border force had been much reduced on mobilisation, requiring it to be supplemented by the BEF. The system in place consisted of primary posts established close to the frontier on main roads, while rail traffic was examined at frontier stations. At nightfall, the frontier was closed to all road traffic. A secondary control of traffic took place at both Lannoy and Chereng, where roads leading from the frontier crossed the anti-tank obstacle. In the sector eventually taken over by the 51st Division, a second line of posts had also been sited along the Nieppe salient. The FDL Line anti-tank ditch and wire formed the link between posts, but in the Nieppe salient the posts had been linked by a barbed wire fence. Control was carried out by the *Gendarmerie*, reinforced by the *Gardes Republicaines* and customs guards (*Douaniers*). The BEF had an officer of the Field Security Police (FSP) based at the HQ of the French Customs in Lille for liaison purposes as well as French speaking FSP stationed at a number of customs posts.

Instructions were issued that small regular patrols, during the day and night, were to be organised under divisional arrangements, and arranged in conjunction with the French *Douaniers*. Purely military patrols were also arranged under the discretion of local commanders. It was hoped that these patrols would provide useful experience of active patrolling, and it was anticipated they should be looked upon as if patrolling in 'no man's land' when in contact with the enemy. Such patrols could be an uncomfortable experience. Richard Dorney, in his book *An Active Service: The Story of a Soldier's Life in the Grenadier Guards, SAS and SBS 1934-1958*, describes one such patrol undertaken by Sid Dowland:

> Sid was sometimes required to accompany his officer on patrols, both in and out of the line, and they often returned soaked to the skin and covered in mud. During one patrol, the two found themselves in a bog and as they tried to find their way around, Sid became stuck fast up to his thighs. The more he tried to free himself, the deeper he sank. He gratefully accepted his officer's outstretched hand when it was offered. Unfortunately, this did little to help his rescue. After a considerable time spent tugging, grunting and heaving, their joint efforts eventually extricated him from the glue-like mud. They now looked more like swamp monsters than an officer's patrol, but they completed the evening's activities none the less.[28]

It was recognised that such patrols would not prevent all unauthorised crossing of the frontier, but it was hoped that they would maintain morale with the local French population and act as a deterrent to clandestine communications and smuggling

28 Richard Dorney, *An Active Service: The Story of a Soldier's Life in the Grenadier Guards, SAS and SBS 1934–1958* (Solihull: Helion Ltd., 2005), p. 55.

cigarettes and luxury goods across the frontier. The French thought that small static patrols at known crossing points were more successful than mobile patrols; one successful technique used was to have dogs on leads barking occasionally at certain crossing points to hopefully divert individuals to other crossing points where a patrol was lying in wait.

Away from the immediate frontier, there was no control over civilian traffic through the defensive zone. Formations were instructed to make sure that such traffic was confined to established roads and paths and that the 'loitering in the vicinity of the defences' was not to be permitted. Suspicious looking individuals or persons refusing to comply with these instructions were to be apprehended and taken to the nearest French control post and handed over to the French authorities.

It was not surprising that there were many 'spy' scares, and several suspicious looking characters were apprehended, although all turned out to be harmless and known to the French authorities. A typical spy scare is that recorded by the 23rd Field Company on 23 October, when orders were issued to keep watch on a farmer who kept pigeons, as a signaller thought he had seen pigeons flying towards the Belgian frontier. Occasionally, the French authorities apparently used the situation to arrest well known trouble makers. Lights were seen from a chalet owned by a woman who was already notorious to the local police authorities as an abortionist. The British were asked to keep a watch on her for a repetition of the lights or any other circumstances which would give the local police an excuse to arrest her.

Training for war

The fact that the BEF was not sufficiently trained for war when it landed in France was obvious to all. Ironside was insistent that Gort should train his Army first before moving into the line. Gort was just as aware as everyone else for the need for training:

> The British Army contains to-day very few regimental officers and other ranks who fought in the last war; much that was common knowledge and accepted practice then, must therefore be learned again.[29]

Of the first four divisions that had landed in France in September 1939, only the two of I Corps were fully trained; the two divisions of II Corps, with half its men reservists, were neither fully trained nor equipped. The Corps Commander, Lieutenant-General Brooke, had drawn attention to mobilising the two divisions for service in France deficient in almost everything required for modern war. Neither had undergone any

29 General the Viscount Gort, VC, KCB, CBE, DSO, MVO, MC, *Despatches on Operations of the British Expeditionary Force, France and Belgium 3 Sept 1939 – 31 May 1940*, Supplement to the London Gazette, 17 October 1941 <http://www.ibiblio.org/hyperwar/UN/UK/londongazette> (accessed 24 August 2017).

collective training at divisional or brigade level. The new 25 pdr guns were only just being issued and the gunners unpractised in their use. Brooke received assurance that his two divisions would remain in western France for a period of training before taking their place in the line. However, on landing in France he was informed that his divisions were to move to the frontier at once. For political reasons – in response to continual French demands for more men – the British Government continued to send out partially trained troops in the hope they could complete their training in France. Ironside thought that the War Cabinet just did not understand that the BEF would have to withstand a German attack in the spring – and it would have to be ready for it with trained and equipped troops. Brooke was also livid at this policy; his diary entry for 26 November reads:

> Went to visit the 4th Gordons (MG) Bn which has recently been added to the Corps. It is totally unfit for war in every respect and will take at least 2 months to render it fit. It would be sheer massacre to commit it to action in its present state in addition to endangering lives of others. I therefore consider that it is a very grave fault by those concerned in sending it out to this country in such a state. Hore-Belisha when he was out here asked me whether it would not be advisable to push units and formations out here to complete their training (mainly with the object of impressing people with the numbers he was dispatching). I told him that I considered that such a procedure was neither fair to the units, the BEF or our allies the French.[30]

If Hitler had been able to attack earlier than he did, the lack of an efficient training organisation and equipment may well have been more disastrous than Dunkirk for the British. Again, according to Brooke:

> On arrival in this country and for the first 2 months the Corps was quite unfit for war, practically in every respect. Even now our anti-tank gunners are untrained and a large proportion of our artillery have never fired either their equipment or type of smoke shell they are armed with. To send untrained troops into modern war is courting disaster such as befell the Poles. I only hope that we may now be left in peace for the next 2 to 3 months to complete the required readiness for war.[31]

The BEF had to prepare and train for a number of roles. It could be required to hold the frontier defences in conditions of static warfare or undertake a rapid move into Belgium to take up new defensive positions. At some point it would be required to undertake offensive action, perhaps requiring an attack against the fortified Siegfried

30 Alex Danchev & Daniel Todman (eds), *War Diaries 1939-1945: Field Marshall Lord Alan Brooke* (Berkeley and Los Angeles: University of California Press, 2001), p. 20.
31 Ibid.

Line.[32] All these scenarios had to be catered for in any training programme. The ten months of breathing space provided by the Sitzkrieg gave time to get things going. This was just as well according to Brooke, as his II Corps sill required 'months of training with the necessary facilities, such as artillery and anti-tank ranges.'[33] With the BEF in the line facing the enemy, even if he was 150 miles away, much needed incentive was given to training. Although this incentive for training was apparent in the BEF, getting the necessary equipment to train with still lacked a sense of urgency within the British Government. Many politicians thought it unlikely Germany would attack in 1940. They hoped the phoney war would persist and that the naval blockade would force Germany to concede without any real hostilities on land.

The BEF was totally unprepared for defence in positional warfare, which it found itself planning for. For a start, British pre-war training always favoured the attack. Also, it seems that the principles of war were not actively studied – perhaps not unsurprising given the Army's main role was to police the Empire and mainly dealing with 'uncivilized' warfare – as Lord Douglas, who in 1939 was the deputy chief of the Air Staff, recalled of his time at the Imperial Defence College:

> we never discussed, in our work as instructors, what might be called the principles or the theory of war; and that we did not waste our time on any high-falutin' pretensions about theory.[34]

Much work was required on the part of senior commanders to get junior officers and men to think in terms of a defensive layout and how to conduct the defence. Gort noted that at first offices and men were 'terrified of lateral fire' and it took them a long time to understand the importance of concealment or reverse slope positions. Battlefield tours were encouraged to enable officers to gain a better grasp of studying the ground and laying out defences. Static defence based around concrete pillboxes also gave Gort cause for concern. On the one hand, he was concerned that men were beginning to think they could not defend unless they were in concrete. On the other hand, it took a certain type of mentality to stand and fight in the confines of a blockhouse or pillbox. Gort was always of the opinion that despite mechanisation, the final result in the end would always depend upon the man. The officer had to learn how to control a concrete post: 'As long as the officer holds out, the show goes [on].'[35]

32 Although an attack against the Siegfried Line was a possibility, in September 1939 this option was certainly deprecated by the DMO as the BEF was not equipped to take part in offensives in first class warfare. Gamelin was of the opinion that the BEF would need to gain experience in defensive warfare before it could take part in offensive warfare.

33 Danchev & Todman, *War Diaries 1939-1945*, p. 12.

34 Jon Kimche, *The Unfought Battle* (London: Weidenfeld & Nicolson, 1968), p. 123.

35 TNA: WO167/21, 'Notes on discussion between C-in-C. and D.M.T. at G.H.Q., 30 Mar 40', GHQ SD & T Branch War Diary.

Standing orders for a blockhouse stated: 'THE BLOCKHOUSE WILL BE DEFENDED BY ITS GARRISON TO THE LAST MAN AND THE LAST ROUND'. Therefore, it was essential that troops knew how to fight from the blockhouses. In order to ensure no confusion or delay during action as a result of the constricted space, it was essential every man knew his role. One or two short periods a day were devoted to 'blockhouse drill' – the OC 2nd Division compared it to the drill in a turret on a battleship. The drill included rapid dismounting of the anti-tank gun and mounting the light machine gun. Fire exercises to practice 'blockhouse drill' and use of the periscope could be carried out if the blockhouse was not near the Belgium frontier; the enemy was represented by men crossing the fields towards the anti-tank ditch and tanks represented by flags.

Exercises in fully manning the defensive positions were frequently carried out. This was certainly difficult during October and November, as in many cases the trenches had not yet been dug deep enough to be manned or were flooded, and few shelters and dug-outs had been constructed. Nevertheless, in the case of flooded trenches, troops were expected to bail them out if at all possible. In one exercise, troops just about managed to stay dry by crouching on fire steps and piles of duckboards. Manning exercises practiced normal trench routine and enemy attacks with the use of 'picture painting' by umpires. Umpires would announce 'heavy shelling' followed by an 'intense bombardment' or that advancing tanks could be heard. A soldier may be told he had become a casualty and had to sit down until the stretcher bearers arrived and took him back to the nearest dressing station. Silent patrols would test the vigilance of certain blockhouses. These exercises where held at brigade, division and corps level and became more elaborate as the BEF settled in. During March, I Corps held a manning exercise to practice various aspects of the defence: holding the Corps sector, mounting a deliberate counter attack, army co-operation with aircraft, supply of ammunition, intelligence work, and artillery in a defensive battle. In some cases, such exercises ended with carriers mounting mock attacks on the position, which provided useful practice for anti-tank weapons to aim at moving targets. The 3rd Division planned to mount an exercise where 200 tracked vehicles attacked the Divisional Reserve Position, but it had to be postponed due to the soft nature of the ground and the certainty that tracks would be left which would be clearly visible from the air. These exercises could sometimes be surreal with units not taking part continuing with daily life: during a I Corps manning exercise in April, the 2nd Battalion Durham Light Infantry felt their efforts to conceal every man was spoiled by RE working parties which did not take part in the exercise and motor transport of II Corps which ignored instructions to use roads in the rear.

That the placing of half-trained troops into trench warfare conditions could result in them losing their sense of mobility was a risk recognised from the start. The need to not neglect mobile warfare, for which a high standard of training had been reached – or at least aimed for – in the regular Army in the pre-war years, was vital if troops were to take advantage of every opportunity in offensive action. This principle was clearly stated in divisional and brigade Operating Instructions and memos, although the continuing shortage of resources made this easier said than done. Furthermore, although it was recognised that the defences being constructed resembled those of the Great War, the need to guard against the assumption that any forthcoming operations would resemble those of that war was also emphasised.

As troops were fully occupied in improving the defences for the first two months, there was little time for other types of training. For many during this early period, training was limited to wet days when work on the defences was not possible. However, with fears of an invasion of Holland and Belgium receding by the middle of November and the arrival of 'X' Force and the AMPC, plans that had been in preparation for training could be put into effect. Ammunition was now allotted for training purposes, ranges improvised or borrowed from the French and training areas organised. Moreover, various GHQ and corps schools were opened, such as a school for the Royal Engineers to learn the most up to date methods of field engineering, a camouflage school and the II Corps Junior Officers School at Bethune. Many officers were also sent home to attend various Army Schools. To overcome the shortage of trained officers in the early stages, many men were given 'Emergency Commissions' from the ranks without the need to graduate through an Officer Cadet Training Unit (OCTU) in the United Kingdom. These tended to be highly experienced men or ex-officers serving in the ranks as reservists. This practice was eventually stopped, with men promoted having to return home and pass through an OCTU. Lectures were another common method of disseminating information. Typical subjects covered included trench warfare, German methods of attack[36], anti-gas and first aid and even the prevention of trench foot. Such lectures were given at company level to all ranks.

In broad terms, military training is split into individual training and collective training. Individual training included PAD, weapon training, and the training of specialists such as snipers and 25mm anti-tank gun teams. Collective training was the practising of an operation by a unit or formation by holding an exercise (alternatively known as a scheme) such as a rapid reconnaissance of a position (by infantry, machine guns and anti-tank guns), fighting patrols, advance of a fully mechanised advanced

36 Training tended to emphasise the German technique of demoralisation of an enemy before the main attack was launched. *ATM* No.32 states: 'All available means are employed to cow opposition and are ruthlessly exploited. Aircraft attack ground forces by H.E. bomb, incendiary bomb, and machine gun, seizing every opportunity to launch such attacks when the ground forces are inadequately protected by anti-aircraft guns or fighter aircraft. Tanks in mass follow up and co-operate with the attacking aircraft…Unlike shell fire, both aircraft and tanks, being visible forms of attack, are apt to give the impression that they are directed against the individual spectator' (ATM No. 32 (London: The War Office, 20 May 1940), p. 6). The weakness of aircraft to AA fire and tanks if held up by an obstacle was emphasised along with leadership, power of endurance and a high level of physical fitness. However, the shortage of spares for armoured fighting vehicles gave little opportunity to expose men to the sight and sound of tanks, with many Dunkirk veterans claiming they never saw a tank during the Sitz. This included Montgomery, who stated in his memoirs that he never saw any tanks during the winter of 1939–40 or during active operations in May 1940.

guard (including embussing[37] and debussing at night), route marches and practice in manning the defences as already described. These were all skills which were to be of great value in May 1940. For collective combined arms training, units could request support from the 4th Battalion Royal Tank Regiment, located in the rear area. Call could also be made upon the cavalry units for training in the movement of a fully mechanised advance guard. However, as we shall see, opportunities for such training were limited by a lack of spares for the AFVs.

Training programmes were largely left to divisional, brigade and battalion commanders, with only broad guidance from corps or GHQ. This was a long-held tradition in the British Army, when in principle every commanding officer of a unit was responsible for the training of his officers and men with as little interference as possible. Unfortunately, this meant that some commanders were more forthright in their approach to training than others. David French, in his book *Raising Churchill's Army*, notes that the 3rd Division held no less than four divisional exercises, each lasting several days, while 2nd Division conducted only two short movement exercises. In order to try and at least ensure a uniform approach to teaching in training, the War Office published a number of training pamphlets and training memorandums, which released GHQ from the need of issuing training pamphlets as had been the case during the Great War. GHQ did issue some pamphlets on specialised subjects of importance to the BEF such as PAD, destruction of vehicles likely to fall into enemy hands and wireless discipline. The War Office also issued a series of pamphlets covering the tactical and technical aspects of the German Army. A magazine published by Messrs. George Newnes Ltd., titled *Battle Training in Words and Picture*, had War Office approval and was recommended reading for all ranks.

Individual weapon training was sorely needed as many men, especially the non-infantry units such as HQ staff and RASC, had little experience in handing the weapons they had been issued with. Such units of the 5th Division, which assembled in France during December, had just such a training deficit. Following a request for the number of men who had never fired their weapons, it transpired that 576 men had never fired their rifle and 114 men had never fired their pistol. Although .303 inch ammunition was available for training, 5th Division was informed by II Corps that no .38 inch revolver ammunition was available for practice purposes! The 51st Division, which moved into the line at the start of January, was reported to have a low musketry standard as they had been hastily put through range practice at Aldershot before having the opportunity of acquiring or training instructors.[38] Its units were also in desperate need for range practice with the anti-tank rifle.

37 The term 'embussing' and 'debussing' is probably a memory of the early days of the Great War when large numbers of London motor-omnibuses carried troops from railheads to their destination along the roads of France and Flanders.

38 Although the Bren was the backbone of the infantry's fire power, the rifle was still an important weapon and Gort emphasised that men had to be able to fire ten aimed rounds per minute, to kill a man at 300 yards.

Individual weapon training could only be practiced on suitable ranges. Ranges for rifle, pistol, anti-tank rifle and light and medium machine guns and grenades were selected at divisional level while ranges for anti-tank guns were made under arrangements of corps. Anti-tank regiments also had their miniature ranges, using air guns and .22 inch rifle attachments. Use was made of existing French ranges where possible otherwise ranges had to be improvised. Improvisation of targets was also required, with pieces of tin suspended from string, tiles obtained from local brick works and cardboard and wood all being used. The 1st Division took over ranges at Dannes from the French. This was an area of sand dunes some two miles in depth and a straight stretch of shoreline. It allowed for firing machine guns at 2,000 to 3,000 yards, anti-tank rifles at 300 yards and light AA guns to practice shooting at hydrogen balloons. The 2nd Division secured the use of some disused sand pits at Flines les Raches to construct three 100 yard ranges and four 30 yard ranges for rifle, anti-tank rifle and light and medium machine gun practice. A mortar range was sited nearby. Despite the BEF's efforts to provide facilities for weapon training, some soldiers still recalled they had little opportunity to actually practice firing their weapons on ranges.

For both the engineers and troops, individual training in the handling of anti-tank mines was problematic at first. One field company War Diary notes that although 12 French anti-tank mines had been issued for training purposes, no British training mines had been issued by the end of October.[39] Training in the use of anti-tank mines could also be dangerous. As part of attending a junior officer's course, Second-Lieutenant Medley witnessed the after effects of a squad of men horrifically injured while carrying out training in the use of the British Mk I anti-tank mine. Only one individual of the squad survived his injuries. Medley was supposed to have been in that squad, but swapped places with a friend at the last moment. This was not a one-off example of tragedy while training with anti-tank mines.

As both corps still had all their divisions in line, collective training was difficult; at best an infantry brigade could be withdrawn to the rear for a short period of training. Even then, there was the need to balance recreational needs of the troops with training during these short periods out of the line, and also daylight hours for training were limited as winter had now arrived. Those planning training had to take into account the need to avoid damaging growing crops – in particular winter wheat, newly sown grass, and beet which was used for the production of industrial alcohol for explosives – and to avoid damaging fences, which all added to limiting the effectiveness of training. In April 1940, for example, the 50th Division noted that collective training was all but impossible due to crops. Another difficulty in planning training was the lack of NCOs who had been through a training cadre due

39 In fact, the vast majority of Army had been unable to gain experience with this weapon during the pre-war years. As late as 1937, Pakenham-Walsh stated that it proved impossible for a CRE to obtain one mine, even unfilled, for demonstration purposes.

to rapid promotion. This was especially apparent in the Territorial divisions, with regular reservists finding themselves promoted to NCO status almost immediately. Training was also hampered by the severe winter weather, not least during periods of thaw when roads became impassable, meaning troops could not travel to firing ranges or exercises; this was the fate of the 1st Division's Exercise 'S' – to practice a movement of troops back to a defensive position on the Somme – which had to be cancelled.

A need to bring reality into collective training was also clearly recognised but difficult to implement. Peace time training often took place with reduced establishments and with equipment and fire often represented by a 'token'. In the absence of actual hostilities during the Sitzkrieg, training conditions were to some extent unreal and close to those during peace time. There was a need to accustom junior officers to handling units of a proper size and in replacing the 'token mentality'. This could only be addressed by the initiative of those with war time experience. Those with war experience were also relied upon to describe the experience of battle – for example being under fire and when to take cover from shell fire and when to continue advancing – to the large body of men with no such experience. Some field firing exercises did, however, add to reality in training. Second-Lieutenant Medley recalls one such exercise just before the cataclysm of 10 May when troops practised an advance supported by overhead fire from Bren guns firing off tripods and 3 inch mortars firing smoke.

As already stated, training became a high priority from December onwards, with no enemy attack expected until the spring. The period devoted to training was substantially increased and the period devoted to defence construction proportionately reduced from January onwards. This allowed larger scale exercises to be organised. The 5th Division, for example, held a full-scale exercise along the River Authie between 24 to 28 March to practice a night move, taking up a defensive position, a night attack and infantry co-operation with a tank attack. The 5th Division's exercise showed some serious deficiencies. In some cases, junior leaders had made no effort to interest their men in what was going on – in one instance, men were seen playing football in the FDL position! The night attack generally lost control after the troops passed through the initial crust of the defences. The process of issuing orders for a tank attack obviously needed improvement – the Brigadier and the battalion commander who were to co-operate with the tanks spent seven and a half hours preparing plans leaving company commanders only half an hour to return to their companies, collect their platoon commanders and issue orders. The result was that the infantry had no idea what they were supposed to be doing. The tanks showed too much crowding in the villages near the start line and would have been an easy target for enemy artillery. The carriers also acted like tanks, freely moving about with the first wave of tanks instead of rushing to one fire position to another, covering the flanks of the attack. The Divisional Commander concluded that far more practice was required in all these aspects and in particular that 'Junior Leaders require more training. Now is the time to get rid of the bad ones.'[40]

Montgomery ensured his 3rd Division practised operations they would likely be required to undertake: during 6 to 8 March, the Division practiced a night march to a river line, and a retirement to a second river line followed by a withdrawal to a prepared position. The distances covered by the 3rd Division's exercises were planned to be similar to the distance that would have to be covered in a move forward to the Dyle. One conclusion of the exercise was that having spent so much time on pillbox construction, there was a serious lack of training in ordinary field works. Many ordinary soldiers also could not understand the reason for such training; after having spent months on building a defensive position it was assumed that they would be occupied for a hard-fought engagement with the enemy. However, as events were to prove, this training was of immense value.

Time was also devoted to collective training in minor infantry tactics. Training guidance issued by the 2nd Division emphasised the need for company schemes involving the co-operation of arms and use of ground, and in particular an attack behind a barrage (represented by men with flags). The 17 Brigade encouraged battalion commanders to practice company schemes such as bombing attacks against trenches, training in assault bridging and use of assault boats, crossing obstacles, laying minefields and the tactical training of the carrier platoons in their defence role. The training of fighting patrols and snipers, both regarded as a lost art since the Great War, were also given high priority. This training took place in areas occupied by the infantry brigades, without the need to resort to hiring training areas, as long as damage was minimised and repaired as far as possible after. Such training could be very uncomfortable for the troops as noted by Second-Lieutenant Medley, who thought that practicing patrolling and 'crawling around with snow on the ground and an icy wind sweeping over the flat farmlands was not fun.'[41]

The 1 Guards Brigade took the opportunity of using the last ten days of January to 'restore the power to manoeuvre', which had been somewhat lost during the months of October to December when the priority was constructing defences. Company attacks on strongpoints were practised and the training of battalion fighting patrols co-ordinated. The existing defences provided a valuable resource for such training. They were used to study the attack on fortified positions or active defence. For training in defence, pillboxes could be manned and used to practice men in fire orders, observation and patrolling at night in the vicinity of the pillbox. In the attack, techniques to reduce a pillbox could be practised and also the art using ground for infiltration. Trenches could be used to practice bombing attacks. Smoke was allowed

40 TNA: WO167/21, 'Report on talk by Commander of 5 Div. on the Divisional exercises carried out from 24 – 28 March. 40.', SD & T Branch GHQ 1st Echelon War Diary.

41 R.H Medley, *Five Days to Live: France 1939-40* (Abergavenny: Dover & Company, 1992), p. 16.

to be used in training exercises provided they were not in the vicinity of the Belgian border. The 2nd Battalion Grenadier Guards improvised a gas chamber in a pillbox to test respirators!

The method for training in positional warfare and mobile warfare proposed by the 51st Division seemed sensible. The two brigades up in the line undertook training in positional warfare during breaks in working on the defences. This included maintaining a garrison in a proportion of pillboxes and carrying out reliefs as would be the case if in contact with the enemy. Existing pillboxes and trenches were also used for training in the offensive during positional warfare. The brigade in the rear was to concentrate on training in mobile warfare while not engaged in constructing the Divisional Reserve Line.

The training in the maintenance and operation of mechanical transport required new methods to be developed by workshops and Regimental Transport Officers as there was no previous experience in wartime with the scale of transport that the BEF was equipped with. The ability of the BEF to carry out Plan D would depend upon both the ability and morale of drivers and the condition of vehicles. As a general rule, well maintained wheeled vehicles could travel 150 miles a day and light tracked vehicles 100 miles a day. Subjects such as good driving, skilled maintenance, correct density of traffic, traffic discipline and correct loading of vehicles all required training and practice in order to attain these daily distances. It became apparent that civilian divers, whose numbers had swelled post-mobilisation, tended to close up to the vehicle in front in order to maintain touch, which had to be discouraged to avoid the severest form of aerial retribution. However, specialist drivers were in short supply, which made training learner drivers and civilian drivers on the crowded French roads difficult.

There were also difficulties in training the divisional cavalry and the 4th Battalion Royal Tank Regiment due to a lack of spares, such as tracks and sprockets. This placed a limitation on the use of vehicles for training. For example, I Corps ordered training to be stopped as vehicles had exceeded their track training mileage although individual vehicles which had not succeeded their track mileage could still be used to train drivers. A temporary halt to training in the Royal Armoured Corps was ordered in January due to the acute shortage of spare parts, especially tracks. Private George Andow, 4th Battalion Royal Tank Regiment, recalled he spent very little time training during the Sitzkrieg, instead whiling away many idle days in estaminets.

Prior to embarkation, the artillery had largely practiced for defence and attack in open warfare. The static defences planned by the Allies now required training in conditions of stabilised warfare. Instructions issued by GHQ emphasised the necessity of drills for the preparation of barrages, counter-battery fire and checking predicted fire. In addition, all ranks required practical training on the ground in survey work, laying out lines of fire and fire control and the maintenance of long cable communications. Officers had to learn the art of air-burst ranging. The artillery, just as the infantry, had to practice manning the defences. The I Corps manning exercise held in November stated that one position per troop was to be occupied during the manning exercise although no guns were to be brought into position if damage to cover was likely. If possible, regiments were to arrange for the occupation of one roving position after dark, the gun being withdraw before dawn. Regiments were to bring up such tractors and dragons as required, following laid down routes from the wagon line to the gun positions. Umpires would inform the batteries of the amount of ammunition expanded and the full procedure for replenishing ammunition from the wagon line was to be practiced although no ammunition was actually to be unloaded at the gun position. The medium and heavy artillery were to man all guns that were in action, although no guns were to be put into position especially for the exercise.

Collective exercises were not ignored for the field artillery. A typical example was an exercise carried out by 2nd Field Regiment with the 3rd Battalion Grenadier Guards and the 4th Battalion Royal Tank Regiment at Achiet Le Grand. A barrage plan was worked out and represented on the ground by a line of men with flags from the Regiment. The artillery also obtained permission to break wireless silence for training purposes. An exercise was held in early November with the RAF to practice RAF operators with battery ground sets.

The danger of gunners from the field artillery losing their sense of mobility in static conditions was just as valid a concern as that for the infantry. Field artillery could practice mobile warfare out of the line. Catling witnessed the training of a battery coming into action to support an imaginary infantry attack:

> Up the road the first troop was approaching. A 25-pounder on the move looks like a little train of three separate vehicles: the heavy tractor in front, the ammunition trailer with the detachable circular gun platform flat on top of it, and then the gun itself ... Through the flooded section of the road they came with sheets of water spurting from under them, up the hill, past the battery commander, almost to the top of the ridge. Then they turned off the road to the right and slid rapidly across a distant field to their positions.[42]

In all, Catling watched three troops rush into position and get their guns into action to support the imaginary infantry driving an imaginary enemy from a wood out of sight over the ridge.

For firing practice, guns had to be withdrawn from the front line. For instance, the 5th Heavy Regiment withdrew one 8-inch howitzer gun at a time, which proceeded with its sub-section to Calais for firing practice out to sea at full charge. Field guns could often make use of ranges provided by the French.

Field engineers struggled most to get away for a period of training, due to the demand on their time and the general shortage of engineers. Training was certainly needed – the 23rd Field Company noted that a newly arrived draft could barely slope arms. This Company had a spell out of the line for training in late March at Querrieu,

42 Catling, *Vanguard to Victory*, p. 15.

and the syllabus was probably typical for most engineer units. On route to the training area, the Company motor transport column was practised in air attack and had to take an alternative route to avoid an imaginary blockage on the main road. Once at Querrieu, it practised in physical training, bayonet fighting, and an infantry attack. The Company also practised with bridging and pontoon equipment at Daours on the River Somme. The change of scenery and a break in the daily monotony of defence works certainly did the field companies good as noted by the 11th Field Company: 'These stationary conditions and peaceful life have had a bad effect on the company and a change will certainly do everyone good.'[43]

One justified criticism levelled against the BEF – and GHQ in particular – was the lack of training in signals and communication. The French insistence in wireless silence was the reason given for this but I Corps managed to hold an exercise between HQ I Corps and 1st Division to practice the probable lack of telephonic communications which might arise during active operations. The failure of GHQ to organise similar exercises resulted in no common policy on the matter, so when differences arose these differences remained, and, according to Montgomery there was 'no firm grip from the top.'[44]

The time available for training of pilots was limited due to the need to be ready for immediate operations, but the operations, mostly reconnaissance or driving off enemy reconnaissance, did provide useful experience. The severe weather also limited air training just as it limited the training of the Army. With the unification of command of the AASF and the Air Component under Air Marshal Barratt, some useful training was carried out in the spring of 1940, including a number of tactical exercises in co-operation of the Army, such as flying over troops and helping pilots recognise suitable targets. At home, for those divisions in training for embarkation to France, some co-operation in training was also organised with the RAF. For instance, on 11 January 1940, the 50th Division held an exercise involving the move of the whole division. It moved north along the Cirencester – Northleach road and then occupied a defensive position; the RAF 'attacked' the column and the dispersal area.

However, other aspects of training for the pilots of the AASF were more problematic. Air Marshall Barrett was certainly aware of the risks to the Battle and Blenheim squadrons if they should be asked to carry out daylight bombing – the situation during the Battle of France and Flanders did call for this, with the predictable casualties. The need to avoid daylight bombing if possible required practice in night flying; however, the French forbade all night flying in the 'Zone of the Armies'. As for bombing ranges, the nearest was 400 miles away, near Perpignan on the Spanish frontier, requiring the wholesale evacuation of the squadron and its transport for something like a month.

Life was little better for the divisions mobilising back at home. Although the overriding principle was that all training should be concentrated on training for war,

43 TNA: WO167/908, 11th Field Company War Diary, 2 February 1940.
44 Montgomery of Alamein, KG, *The Memoirs of Field-Marshal Montgomery*, p. 56.

there were many difficulties and shortages to overcome to achieve this. Small arms ammunition was in short supply for practice and there were equipment shortages of all kinds. The situation with the 7th Battalion Worcestershire Regiment's transport, which consisted of just three carriers, five 15-cwt trucks and an Albion lorry, was typical. There was also a lack of ranges and areas in which to train. In many instances parks in towns which were close to billeting areas had to be utilised for training. *ATM No. 28,* which stressed that equipment shortages should be 'accepted cheerfully as all part of the day's work' and that much training could be accomplished '*without any equipment at all*' by determination, energy and imagination cannot have given commanders much comfort![45] As large numbers of men had to be trained intensively, training by demonstration and simple drills – which could include tactical demonstrations and simpler demonstrations such as the occupation of a defensive position, fighting patrols, wiring and reliefs – was highlighted as being particularly suitable. However, it was emphasised that tactical problems could not be solved by 'simple school solutions or by the use of a drill' – this was still a long way off from Battle Drill and Battle Schools adopted by the Army from 1942 onwards. The defensive role that the BEF was undertaking meant a high degree of training in digging field defences was required for units mobilising at home. It was emphasised that troops in contact with the enemy had to be able to dig themselves in as soon as the situation permitted: no matter how exhausted they were it was their duty to provide themselves with cover – 'sweat saves blood'. Just as the infantry had to be 'marching-fit', they also had to be 'digging-fit'. It was recommended that troops in training should carry out tactical digging training, for example digging a company sector.[46]

A typical battalion's experience – 3rd Battalion Grenadier Guards

The 3rd Battalion Grenadier Guards formed part of the 1 Guards Brigade, which was one of the brigades of the 1st Division. The other two battalions of the Brigade were the 2nd Battalion Coldstream Guards and the 2nd Battalion Hampshire Regiment. The Battalion served on the Gort Line throughout the Sitzkrieg, apart from a short spell on the Saar front, and their experience was probably typical of most battalions in the BEF.

The Battalion arrived at Templeuve by rail along with the 2nd Battalion Coldstream Guards on 3 October, having the honour of being some of the first troops to deploy

45 *ATM No.28: January 1940* (London: The War Office), p. 12.

46 *ATM No.24: September 1939* (London: The War Office), p. 10. This was further elaborated in *ATM No. 29*, which stated that every unit or formation should develop a defensive system in the vicinity of their quarters as part of individual and collective training, which could also be used to practice manning the trenches. An example of a company locality dug as part of training during the Sitz can still be found extant at the RSPB reserve North Warren in Suffolk. Subsequently, it was incorporated into the anti-invasion defences with the addition of three pillboxes.

to the BEF sector. They were met on the platform by the BEF Commander-in-Chief, Lord Gort, and HRH the Duke of Gloucester. After detraining, the Battalion marched to Genech, where 1, 2 and 3 Companies went into billets north of Genech while 4 Company was billeted in Genech. The Battalion HQ was established in the Château de Genech, a large unfurnished house built around the start of the 20th Century and left by its owner the previous year. The Château had been occupied by German HQ staff during the Great War.

On 4 October, the 1 Guards Brigade took over part of the frontier defences from the French, just east of Genech and three miles from the Belgian border, holding the entire 1st Division front with three battalions up (Figure 7.1). The Battalion held the centre (Figure 7.2), with the 2nd Battalion Coldstream Guards on the right and the 2nd Battalion Hampshire Regiment on the left. The Battalion position included six blockhouses and an anti-tank obstacle constructed in 1937, and according to the Battalion War Diary, 'very well done.' Approach roads had been mined while those crossing the anti-tank obstacle had concrete and steel road blocks. There was no communication to the posts except DSLR's; the civil telephone was taken over, with a woman at the exchange and signallers on duty to take any messages in English.

A report by the OC 1 Guards Brigade on the defensive line taken over by the Brigade noted that the six blockhouses taken over were 'All clean and the stores, to be handed over with each block house, were complete. Four Block Houses have been equipped with periscopes, but these are placed in such a position that they can be used only on an arc of 180 degrees.'[47] In the main, communication trenches and fire posts had been commenced but not completed. It was further noted that there was no depth to the position, although *points d'appui* had been sited to cover all the ground between but not covered by the blockhouses. According to the French plans, the *points d'appui*, were held by a machine gun supported in turn by light machine gun posts. Most had been dug, although would need to be altered to take a Bren but had not been wired. The OC 1 Guards Brigade considered that the siting of the *points d'appui* was excellent, the whole length of the wire obstacle taken in enfilade and approaches to the blockhouses well covered by cross fire. However, in some areas due to the nature of the ground, it was impossible to bring fire to bear in front of the blockhouses from these posts, and alternative posts were suggested. In the main, the nature of the ground also made bringing fire to bear in front of the anti-tank obstacle very difficult.

On relief, the French evacuated the area, leaving behind a working party which was working on a new front line (the Bachy Switch). Following a re-organisation which took effect on 9 October, the Brigade area became the area originally occupied by the Battalion's 1 and 2 Companies. The area occupied by 3 Company was handed over to the 3 Brigade and 1 Company area was handed over to the 2nd Battalion Coldstream Guards. The Battalion area (Figure 7.3) became the area occupied by

47 TNA: WO167/346, 'Report on the defensive line taken by this Battalion from 2nd Battalion 201st Regiment FRENCH INFANTRY on 4.10.39', 1Guards Brigade War Diary.

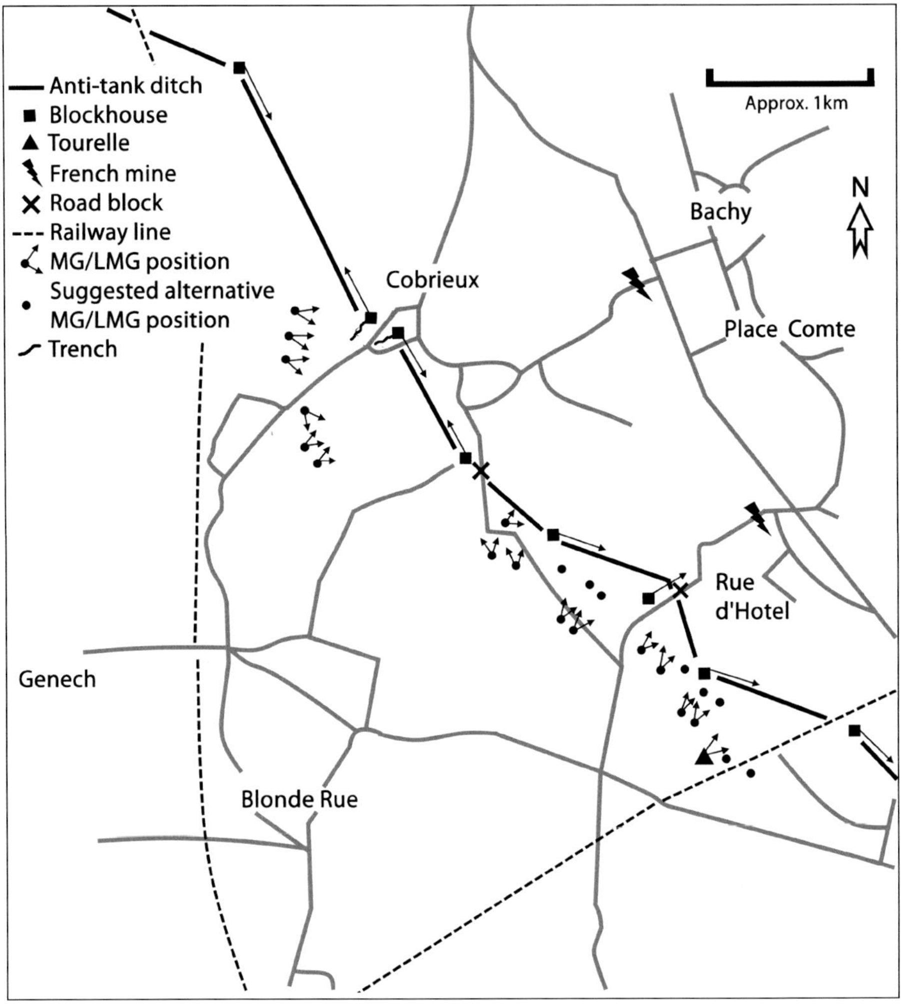

Figure 7.1: Map showing 1 Guards Brigade sector, 4 October 1939.

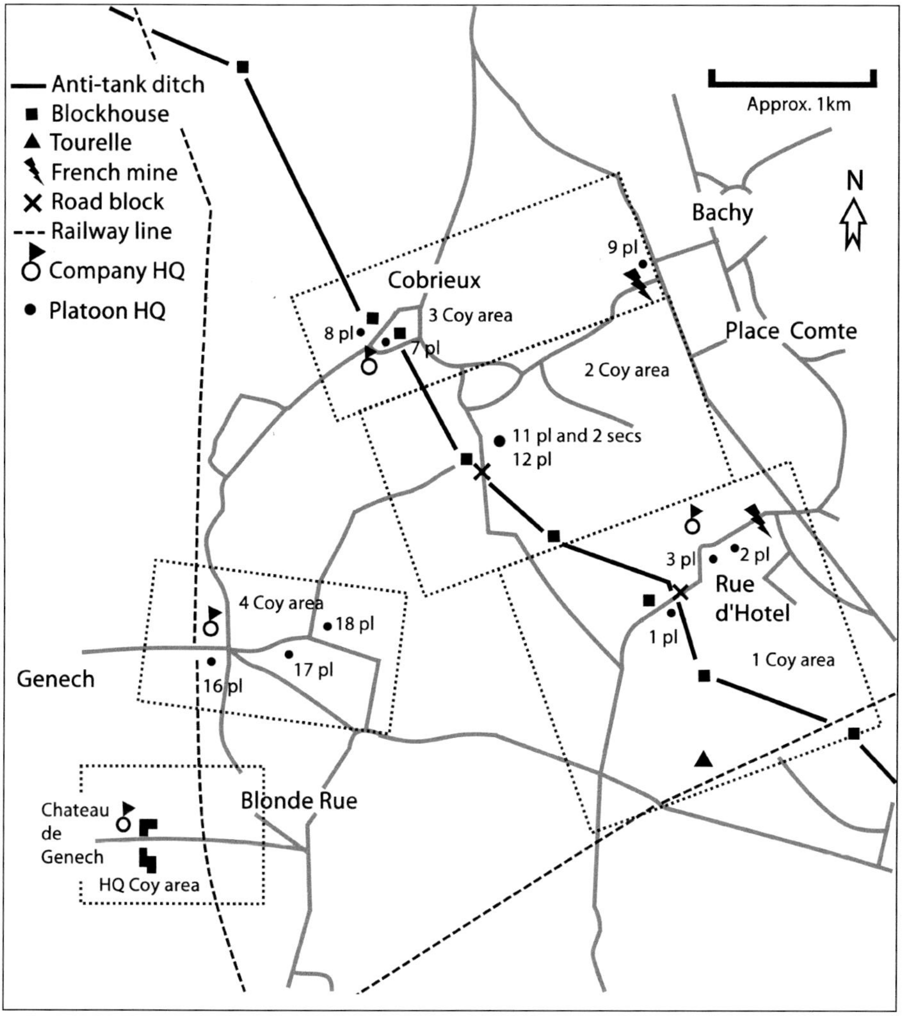

Figure 7.2: Map showing 3rd Battalion Grenadier Guards company localities, 4 October 1939.

its 2 Company, which included two blockhouses (no's 64 and 65). The 2nd Battalion Hampshire Regiment occupied the Brigade Reserve Line. Battalion HQ moved from the Château de Genech to Château du Fay.

At first the Battalion concentrated on improving its billets. Until it had been settled if the new line – the Bachy Switch – being dug by the French was to be garrisoned by the battalions of the Brigade, and until full details of the expected number of anti-tank guns, machine guns and artillery that would be made available, and the amount of engineer assistance that could be expected, it was only possible to make general recommendations on how to improve the position. Priority was to clear fields of fire, wire around the *points d'appui* and dig communication trenches from posts to the blockhouses.

The Battalion received instruction from the 23rd Field Company in the making of wattle fences for revetting. On 12 October, the troops commenced work on the platoon areas and cutting brushwood to make the wattle hurdles. The Battalion also had to find three double sentries to assist the French Customs on the Belgian frontier. To help foster good relations with the local community, time was found to help the local farmer pick his sugar beet crop on 13 October. The first of the 'sight-seers' visited on 18 October, when HRH the Duke of Windsor, accompanied by Lord Gort and the Corps and Divisional Commanders inspected the Battalion front. On 27 October, HRH the Duke of Gloucester also visited the Battalion's trenches.

Digging continued throughout the rest of October. Periods of heavy rain caused delays and problems, with constant drainage and repairs required to the trenches. In some cases, the trenches had to be abandoned and breastworks substituted. Shortages in boots, clothing and fuel for heating resulted in very unpleasant working conditions, as noted by the Battalion War Diary:

> [T]he men, with little or no experience of this type of work have got into it extremely quickly and work extraordinarily hard and well in spite of the fact that they work chiefly in pouring rain and thick mud. At the end of a day's work the men are soaking wet and covered in mud and the problem is how to avoid this, as they have nothing to change into. 1 lb per man per day for fuel is the present scale for cooking and heating and it chiefly goes in the former. The boots are becoming worn out and at present there is no new issue. The Battalion are buying French workmens' blue canvas trousers and they are invaluable. A small issue of gum boots and thigh boots has been made. At present only 150 second blankets are on charge to the Bn.[48]

The opportunity to visit the baths at the pit heads at Ostricourt must have been welcome. Some of the Battalion were lucky enough to attend a concert given by Miss Gracie Fields at Douai on 16 November. Sunday's also provided relief from the

48 TNA: WO167/702, 3rd Grenadier Guards War Diary 27 October 1939.

continuous digging with Church Parades and only maintenance work on trenches carried out for the rest of the day.

The Battalion also had to be prepared to garrison the line in the event of an attack. Blockhouse 65 was armed with two 25mm anti-tank guns while blockhouse 64 had one along with an anti-tank rifle. The anti-tank guns were manned by an anti-tank section while an infantry section was to fight with the Bren, anti-tank rifle, rifles and grenades. As the anti-tank gun was the most important weapon, the anti-tank section commander would assume command of the blockhouse in active operations. The anti-tank guns remained in the blockhouses at all times under the normal blockhouse guards. The guards had to wear battle order, less gas capes which were to be hung up in the blockhouse. On 25 October, loading trials were undertaken on the blockhouses to test their capacity for men, ammunition and stores.

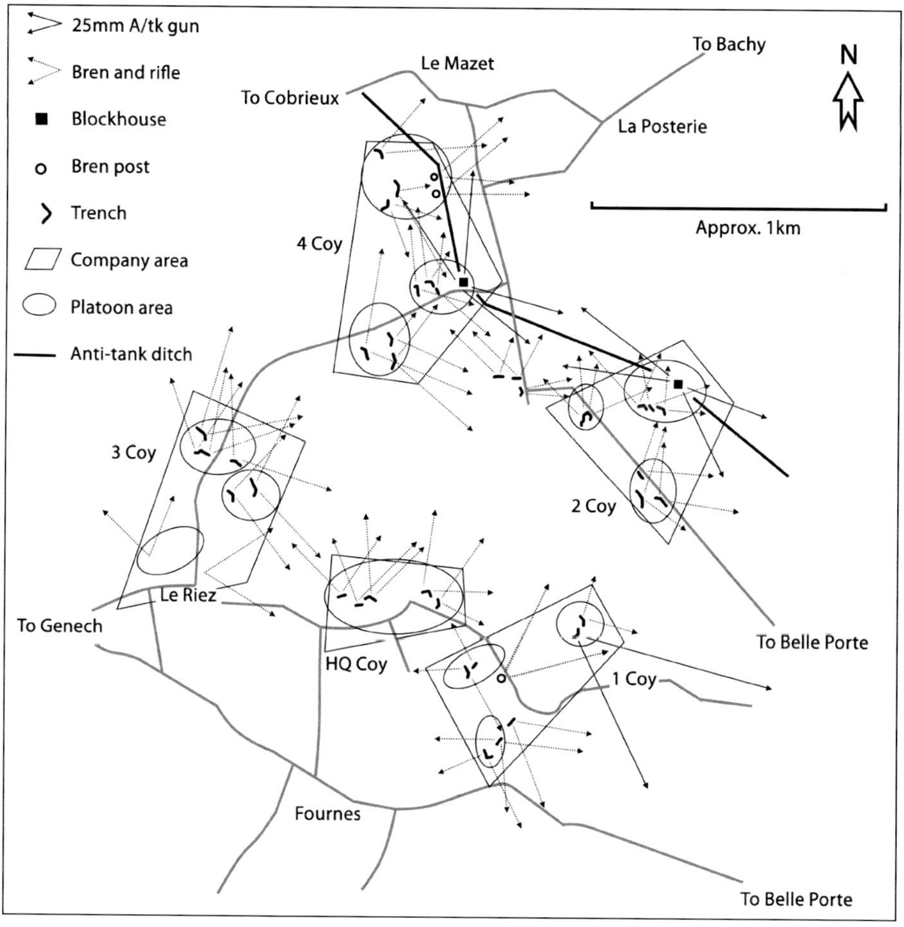

Figure 7.3: Map depicting 3rd Battalion Grenadier Guards positions, November 1939.

The only indication of the enemy was the 'usual air raid warning' at around 11:30 a.m. on most days. On one occasion, gunfire and aeroplane engines were heard, but nothing seen due to overcast conditions. The air raid warnings did not disrupt the work going on.

Work continued on the defences during November, and in addition the Battalion had to provide work parties for road repairs and Divisional fatigues. In addition, 1 and 3 Companies supplied working parties to work on the Brigade Reserve Line, leaving only maintenance parties in their own trenches. On 18 November, The Secretary of State for War, accompanied by Lord Gort, visited the Brigade front and saw the defences of 1 Company.

With the threat of a German attack receding during the winter months, more time could be given to training, including collective training in the rear area. On 22 December, instructions were received that blockhouse guards were to be discontinued. Instead they were replaced by a caretaker during the day and two at night, who were to lock themselves in the blockhouse and sleep inside.

On 1 February, the 1 Guards Brigade received notice that it was to move to the Saar Front. On 3 February blockhouses 64 and 65 were handed over to the 3 Brigade. In accordance with orders, on the following day, the Battalion entrained for Metz, the drums playing HQ and 2 and 3 Companies to the station. The Battalion War Diary states that the duty of the Battalion, while holding the *Ligne de Contact*, was to 'give warning of any attack. We hold the line until ordered to withdraw...Also we have to locate, report and confirm any enemy movement or dispositions or lack of.'[49]

On arrival on the Saar front, the first job of the Battalion was to help clear snow and ice from the streets, which was causing flooding in the billets. On 9 February, company officers went forward to recce their positions in the *Ligne de Contact*. The Battalion relieved the 1st Battalion Kings Own Yorkshire Light Infantry on 11 February – with the Battalion War Diary noting 'For the first time in this war the Battalion finds itself facing the enemy.'[50] The weather was cold, with 10 degrees of frost recorded that morning. In support of the Battalion were two platoons of the Cheshire Regiment (MG battalion), one anti-tank platoon and French artillery with eight 75mm and four 155mm guns. Up to six French officers from the 48th French Division were attached to the Battalion.

The *Ligne de Contact* was held with all four companies up. The duty of the forward posts was to keep the enemy under constant observation, reporting the least movement, however small. Fire could be opened up on small enemy parties up to 800 yards with rifles and Brens firing single shots during the day; for parties over 12 men and ranges greater than 800 yards, fire was to be with machine guns, Brens and mortars. During the night, fire could only be opened if the enemy could be clearly seen. Morning 'Stand To' was at 5:30 a.m. until the company commander was satisfied visibility was

49 Ibid., 'General Instruction No. 2', 7 February 1940.
50 Ibid., 11 February 1940

good enough. Evening 'Stand To' was at 4:30 p.m. until dark. Before 'Stand Down' in the morning, each company was to patrol its own wire and search dead ground, woods and villages as ordered.

Odd reports from the forward posts were received at Brigade HQ of individuals and small enemy patrols, but were never confirmed, and in the Brigadier's opinion, with perhaps one exception, no enemy patrol approached the forward posts of the Brigade sector during their stay. During the tour in the *Ligne de Contact*, fighting patrols consisting of an officer and 16 other ranks went out nightly, often crossing the River Hermsbach and penetrating 1,000 yards east but all were uneventful.

The Battalion was not impressed with the position it took over. The posts were ill sighted and badly constructed, not even being bullet proof with many falling in. The Battalion immediately set to work in improving the defences as much as the frozen ground conditions would allow – in reality just restricted to thickening up existing wire and laying out concertina wire as the ground was too frozen for digging or the planting of screw pickets for new wire obstacles. Obtaining the necessary stores was not an easy matter as according to the Battalion War Diary, 'wire, duck boards, and R.E. material...was scattered in every direction.'[51] This work continued daily during the Battalion's tour – during the day on positions out of sight from the enemy and during the night on posts under observation.

On the first day in the line, 20 mortar shells fell in the right platoon area of 4 Company. French posts immediately to the left of the Battalion were also shelled. On 13 February, 15 small shells fell in front of 1 Company. The following day, movement was heard in the direction of Waldwisse and Le Blauenberg, with the French artillery shelling the roads in this area intermittently. On 16 February, during the early morning, 10 shells fell in the right hand platoon area of 4 Company again, slightly wounding two men. At around 10:00 a.m., 22 shells fell in the area of 2 Company's right forward platoon, the War Diary noting it was 'excellent shooting' by the enemy. HRH The Duke of Gloucester, who was visiting the Battalion witnessed this shelling. Wire was cut and also the signal line to the Advance Company HQ. The shooting was thought to come from the area of Le Blauenberg Wood and the French 155mm battery in support of the Battalion fired 50 shells counter-battery into this area. Furthermore, during the day, the two French 75mm batteries fired 150 rounds at a suspected German working party in the wood. During the evening, the Battalion was relieved by the 2nd Battalion Coldstream Guards and moved back to the *Ligne de Recueil,* with 1 Company billeted at Rodlach while the other companies were billeted at St. Annes farm.

The Battalion spent 17 February resting and cleaning up. It snowed hard during the night and by early morning the snow was six inches deep. The *Ligne de Recueil* consisted of infantry posts with an anti-tank ditch in front, and for the duration of its stay in this position, the Battalion worked on improving the defences as much as

51 Ibid., 12 February 1940.

the ground conditions and supplies of materials would allow. Work on the posts was impossible as the ground was too hard to dig, so work on wiring to the general French plan was undertaken, although a shortage of French angle iron pickets limited the amount that could actually be undertaken. The Battalion also supplied a working party to carry out wiring in the *Ligne de Contact* on 19 February. The Duke of Windsor visited the Battalion on 22 February and saw the HQ and 4 Companies wiring at St. Francois La Croix.

The only excitement during this period in the *Ligne de Recueil* occurred during early morning on 18 February. Two sentries at the west end of St. Francois La Croix village challenged a shadowy figure that did not halt. Three shots were fired, the alarm sounded, and the guard turned out. The house in which the man had disappeared was surrounded and searched but no sign of him found. The village was carefully searched the following day, but again nothing found.

In his report on the 1 Guards Brigade tour of duty on the Saar Front, the Brigadier was surprised at the extent of the 'live and let live' culture that seemed to exist. In his opinion, there was too much movement during the day, including too many 'sight-seers', and not enough movement at night. Indeed, on arrival, he found that there seemed to be an idea that no movement should take place outside any post by night, or that the idea of shooting on sight was too prevalent. Although the use of fighting patrols was strongly encouraged, he felt that in general, given the very poor state of the defences, there was little alternative to continuing with such a 'live and let live' policy. He also noted a failure in company commanders to fully get a grasp on the defensive layout, and that many platoon and section commanders had never been shown a map of the line. Although the Battalion is not referred to directly in these criticisms, presumably they were implicated just as much as the other battalions of the Brigade.

On 22 February, the warning order for the return to *SD* Lille was received. The Battalion had two days relaxing in Metz, spent bathing and holding a swimming gala. The Battalion arrived back at Nomain on 29 February. The Battalion then moved to the rear area for training etc., moving back to Nomain on 1 April. Life was uneventful during April, with constant working parties on the forward defences, burying signal cable and concreting. On 11 April, Brigade Orders for Plan D were seen and work on orders and preparations were begun to implement the plan.

8

The Defences: Part I – Pillboxes

The BEF moved into the *SD* Lille in October 1939 and took over the line of blockhouses along the Franco-Belgian border from the French 51st Division. It was immediately evident that there was a need to construct additional field works and pillboxes to add depth the defence. Yet positional warfare characterised by these types of defensive works was something the British Army had largely forgotten about since the end of the Great War. Consequently, there was much debate and disagreement as to the role of pillboxes and their design which initially caused delay to the construction programme. Even when standard designs were issued, some units continued to make their own designs and modifications. Shortages of materials of all kinds and a harsh winter added further delay to the construction programme. Although the pillboxes may have had to been manned by either British or French troops, there was at times surprisingly little co-operation with the French in designing pillboxes that could house both French and British weapons.

French blockhouses on the FDL Line

The blockhouses in the *SD* Lille, *1ére Région Militaire*, were some of the last constructed as part of the 'New Fronts', and were rudimentary compared to the more substantial blockhouses in the Maginot Line or *SF* Maubeuge and *SF* Escaut. Typically, as we have already seen, the blockhouses were spaced at about 1,000 yards apart so that the ground between them could be covered by the fire of a 25mm anti-tank gun housed in each blockhouse (these guns had an effective range of up to 650 yards). However, in close country they were only a few hundred yards apart. The blockhouses could not bring fire to their immediate front, and in this regards, their layout was similar to the interval casements between the forts of the Maginot Line proper which were designed solely to fire along the anti-tank obstacle and had no forward firing artillery (Figure 8.1). The blockhouses usually had two loopholes, one for the anti-tank gun and one for the Hotchkiss light machine gun. As both guns only fired down the anti-tank ditch, loophole sizes could be kept to a minimum; the anti-tank gun loophole, for example, only allowed for a traverse of 30°. The smaller loopholes could be closed by means of slides, while the entrance to each blockhouse was fitted with thick steel doors. Instructions were issued to keep the hinges of the steel doors and the loophole slides well oiled.

Figure 8.1: Sketch of the French blockhouse *Bloc de Cysoing*, listed as No. 60 by the British. This was located on the original French *Ligne Principale* before the construction of the Bachy Switch. (TNA: WO 167/350)

The role of each blockhouse was solely to knock out enemy tanks and infantry that tried to cross the anti-tank ditch. In many cases a double blockhouse enfiladed two sections of anti-tank ditch. *Général* Condè, commanding French Third Army, who had formerly commanded in Lille, considered the double blockhouse enfilading two sections of anti-tank ditch as unsatisfactory but enforced on them by peace time economy. The anti-tank ditch stopped about 20 to 50 yards short of the blockhouse so that enemy infantry could not approach nearer to the blockhouse without being exposed to fire – i.e. the ditch did not encircle the blockhouse so as to avoid giving cover to the enemy infantry. To prevent tanks approaching the blockhouse, rails and anti-tank mines closed the gap between it and the anti-tank ditch.

The French realised that the most effective fire against a blockhouse would be direct fire against the loophole in support of advancing tanks and infantry. Siting pillboxes to fire in enfilade helped limit against this and the addition of an 'oreillion' (i.e. a wing wall) and steel shutters added further protection to the loophole.

In exposed areas likely to be subject to enemy artillery fire, blockhouses were constructed to be proof against 210mm (8 inch) shells, and in other areas proof against 150mm (5.9 inch) shells. Observation was either by periscope or a *cloche d'observation.* The exposed face of the blockhouse was protected by earth and rocks banked up against it, so that it was blind to the front. Although this concealed them fairly well from the front, they did show up as a rather visible grass mound. On taking over these blockhouses, British troops had to be reminded not to dig posts into this earth bank as it reduced the protection given by the bank to the blockhouse. A wire obstacle surrounded each blockhouse; in some cases the 2m high security fence, erected while construction of the blockhouse was being undertaken, was also retained.

These defences were for all practical purposes a single line of blockhouses defending a continuous anti-tank obstacle. In some cases these blockhouses were not even covered by flanking fire from adjoining posts and could be assaulted by infantry without the latter being subject to any fire whatever. The British also found that their 2 pdr anti-tank guns would not fit into the French blockhouses. To allow Bren guns or anti-tank rifles to be fired from the blockhouses, an addition of sandbags to the concrete platforms was required or simple timber rests fitted beneath the small sliding loopholes. Sandbags could also be used to make the main loophole smaller if using Bren guns or anti-tank rifles from it. The War Diary of the 23rd Field Company notes that minor alterations in two French blockhouses on the FDL Line were made to enable French 1 pdr guns – a number of which had been obtained by the BEF – to fit the blockhouse mountings. Trees and scrub also had to be cleared to create clear fields of fire; this also provided a small, but nevertheless, valuable supply of timber.

The intervening ground between blockhouses was typically covered by smaller posts, either *tourelles* (Figure 8.2) or *postes de tir*. The idea of the *tourelle* came from one of the lessons of the Great War: the devastating effect on attacking troops by a cleverly concealed machine gun. This led Gamelin to launch a study for a transportable turret for a machine gun, and the solution decided upon was to mount a *Mle* 1914 Hotchkiss 8mm in an armoured turret set into a concrete emplacement. There was also a suggestion to mount a 25mm anti-tank gun in a *tourelle*, but this proved to be too complicated. The function of the *tourelle* was to supplement the fire of the permanent fortifications and also to consolidate field defences following a campaign. They were effectively sunk into the ground for protection and concealment and would be hard to hit by larger calibre projectiles and would be proof against small arms fire or splinters from shells exploding nearby. Some of *tourelles* were modified by the BEF to take the Bren gun and in order not to disclose their positions – and as they could not hold more than two men – instructions suggested they were not to form part of a section post but instead be treated as a detached post. One *tourelle*, at Bachy Station, was later replaced with a pillbox. The *poste de tir* (*1ére Région Militaire* design) was a simple construction, being an irregular hexagon with loopholes only in the forward-facing sides, an entrance in the rear side and with 1m thick walls.

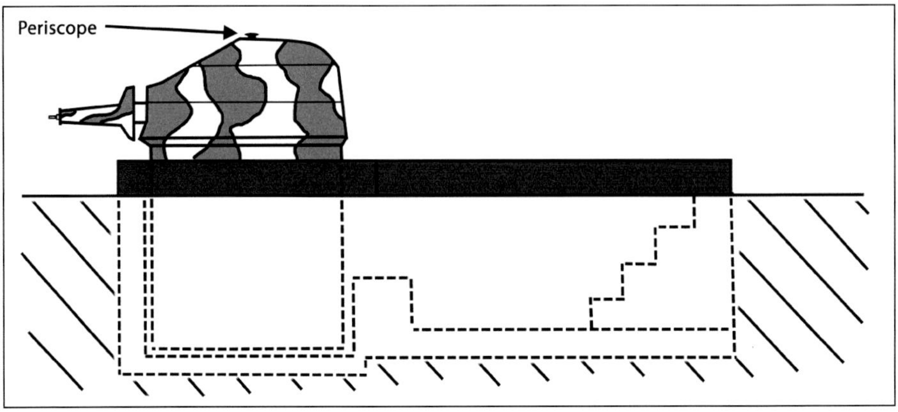

Figure 8.2: A sketch of a French *tourelle* of the type found in *SD* Lille

On the points dominating the high ground in the rear of the *Ligne Principale* in the non-urbanised sectors of Mont d'Halluin, Cysoing, Bachy and Mouchin the French had constructed a number of observation posts utilising the shell of a Renault *Mle* 1917 FT-TFS tank.

The French had made no use of the series of forts constructed in the 1880's which surrounded Lille and occupied dominant positions, considering it better and cheaper to start afresh. However, the British did make use of Fort Sainghin, which was incorporated into the Brigade Reserve Position, although they had to wait until the French had cleared away a dump of their aircraft bombs! In November, the garrison of the Fort consisted of one infantry company, one troop from the 20 Anti-tank Regiment and one platoon of the 2nd Middlesex (MG battalion).

When the 51st Division took over the front from the French in the area of Bailleul – Armentières, they inherited some exceptionally strong French blockhouses, much larger and stronger than on any other part of the BEF sector. Some contained an emplacement for a 75mm field gun as well as a 25mm anti-tank gun and machine guns. A projected blockhouse was to have room for two 75mm field guns in addition to a 25mm anti-tank gun and machine guns. But some pillboxes in this sector were also rather small. One such example had a single loophole for a light machine gun or machine gun, and it was apparently possible to build it in seven days. Another type had an inner shell of brick covered with concrete. The idea was to save on concrete, but it also gave the possibility to enable pillboxes to be built rather more quickly where a weaker structure could be accepted.

BEF pillbox design

The need for pillbox construction in the British sector was discussed as early as mid-September. It was recognised that as a minimum, standard designs in Army manuals (Figure 8.3) would have to be adapted to allow both French and British weapons to be mounted in them. Although from one point of view each pillbox should be designed for its special purpose, in practice considerable standardisation was required for large scale construction and to ensure economy in labour and material. The question of pillbox design in the BEF proved to be a 'much vexed question'.[1]

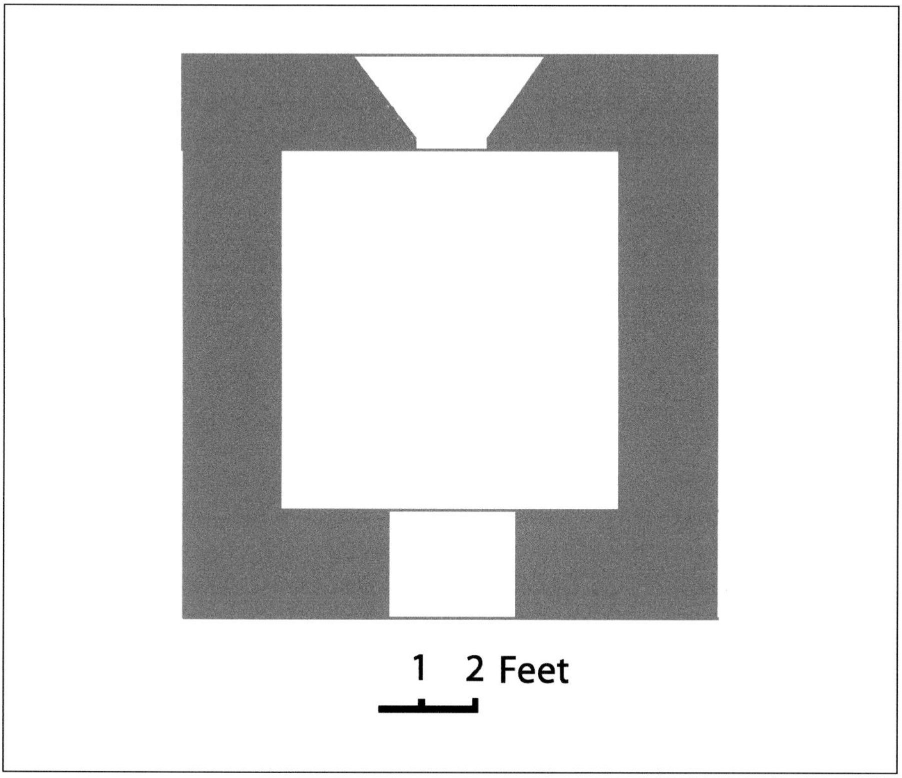

Figure 8.3: Pillbox for a single machine gun as illustrated in Plate 58, *Manual of Field Engineering Vol. II (R.E.), 1936*. The manual notes this was a pillbox for enfilade fire where concealment was necessary and only medium protection was possible. It is illustrated as partially sunken into the side of a bank. At least one example based on Figure 8.3 was constructed by the 11th Field Company. Work started on 14 October on a concrete machine gun emplacement (VIEUX CONDE), described as being of the type shown in the *MFE Vol. II* Plate V (although this is obviously a typing error). This was before any of the standard designs had been issued. It was completed on 10 November. However, the 11th Field Company's example is built on a concrete raft and not partially sunken.

1 TNA: WO167/43, GHQ Chief Engineer War Diary, 8 October 1939.

Opinion as to what form these designs should take and what exactly was the tactical role of a pillbox was very divergent and resulted in 'deplorable' delays in construction. At the time, very few RE officers had experience in the design of reinforced concrete to withstand shell fire. During their preliminary visit to France between 2 to 8 October, Brigadier Minnis and Colonel French, with the assistance of the Engineer-in-Chief, drew on the experience of French military engineers and collected plans of two pillboxes from *Colonel* Bertschi which were considered suitable for the BEF. From the start, 'X' Force intended to use prefabrication methods developed in the Great War such as the Rhys plate, bolted together in part hexagon shape. 'X' Force planned to use prefabricated steel or timber formwork and reinforcing bars bent and bundled into 'pillbox packs' which could be delivered to site for large scale production of pillboxes.[2]

On their return to London, arrangements were made with Messrs Blaw Knox Ltd for the immediate construction of steel shuttering for use with the two designs. However, on 13 October a message was received from France to delay production of the shuttering pending the arrival of the Deputy Engineer-in-Chief, Brigadier King, with further special designs. Brigadier King spent a week in London adapting and altering the designs to meet the British Army's requirements. In order to speed up the design of suitable prefabricated steel shuttering for the new pillbox designs, Messrs Blaw Knox Ltd was again asked to produce the shuttering. But once again, designs were altered, and Colonel French noted with obvious frustration: 'All this work was wasted as only one of these designs still holds good and that with some modifications.'[3]

On 15 October, the Chief Engineer noted that the matter of pillboxes needing to be capable of housing both British and French guns was still causing delays – 'This matter might have been thought out before' is the rather caustic comment in the Chief Engineer's War Diary.[4] In early November, this matter still appeared not to have been entirely resolved: one of the 3rd Division's Field Companies – 253rd Field Company – had started to build two pillboxes for a 25mm anti-tank gun, one at Lesquin and the other at Lezennes. During an inspection on 6 November, Brigadier King ordered that the designs should be modified so the pillboxes could take both the 25mm and 2 pdr guns. Work was halted on the Lesquin pillbox pending a modified design but work had progressed too far on the Lezennes pillbox to alter it.

According to Hore-Belisha, GHQ had 17 different designs of pillboxes at one point but could not make a decision as to which should be adopted. This was, he noted, the story of tank design over again when the British Army could not decide upon the role it wanted for tanks during the inter-war years. The Chief Engineer echoed

2 R.J.M. Sutherland, Dawn Iumn & Mike Chrimes, *Historic Concrete: Background to Appraisal* (London: Thomas Telford Publishing, 2001), p. 375.
3 TNA: WO167/1429, HQ, 'Appendix N. 34 – Report on "X" Force', "X" Force War Diary.
4 TNA: WO167/43, GHQ Chief Engineer War Diary, 15 October 1939.

these frustrations, expressing his opinion that the number of designs be reduced to a minimum to allow for rapid and efficient construction to take place. Once the designs had been settled, he considered it essential that lower formations should not be allowed to suggest alterations. He pointed out that 'brain waves' produced after work had started could slow the rate of construction by up to 80 percent. Some pillboxes were constructed before the official designs were finally decided upon. This could be a cumbersome affair, with a mock-up of the design being erected before any final decision was taken. A pillbox built by the 1st Division – when time included for pillbox and shuttering design was taken into account – took over a month to complete. In such circumstances, one can perhaps sympathise with Hore-Belisha.

As mentioned above, the tactical role of the pillbox caused much discussion and disagreement between the various formation commanders. The main questions regarding their role and aspects of design are summarised in the Chief Engineer's War Diary:

> i. Is the pillbox a self-contained fort with just sufficient men to man the weapons in the embrasures, or is it also a shelter for other men and weapons which take up position outside when the barrage lifts? Should we also have separate shelters for the latter?
> ii. Should frontal fire be provided at the expense of protection?
> iii. Is a large arc of fire and considerable change in elevation necessary for A/T guns, as large embrasures make pillboxes very vulnerable?
> iv. Should the close protection of the pillbox be by fire from inside, or purely passive by steel doors and shutters?[5]

As of 23 October, six designs had been approved as standard: five pillboxes and a simple shelter with no embrasures. However, because of the divergence in opinion as to the role of pillboxes, it was not until 16 November that GHQ issued the final designs for the five pillboxes. GHQ noted the standard designs would allow for minor modifications to suit various sites but stipulated that no other types were to be constructed. The standard of protection decided upon was that pillboxes should be proof against 5.9 inch shells, i.e. with a wall and roof thickness of 3ft 6in. Experiments were held back in England to see if a thickness of 4ft 6in was actually required, but no conclusions were reached. For key pillboxes in exposed areas and likely to be subject to heavy shell fire, one modification allowed was to build pillboxes proof against 8 inch shells, with a wall and roof thickness of 5ft 9in. Trials were also under way at home to test the thickness required to withstand close hits from the high velocity 6 pdr anti-tank gun under development.[6]

5 TNA: WO167/43, 'Policy regarding design of pillboxes', GHQ Chief Engineer War Diary.

6 Intelligence also suggested that the Germans were investigating attacking pillboxes using their 88mm anti-aircraft gun. The gun targeted the same spot, which was not possible with

The five pillbox designs finally settled upon were:

No 1 – a combined anti-tank and Bren pillbox, to fire solely along an anti-tank ditch (Figure 8.4 and 8.5). This was the largest pillbox constructed by the BEF. It basically consisted of two rectangular chambers, one for the anti-tank gun and one for the Bren gun. The chamber for the anti-tank gun projected beyond the Bren chamber. The two chambers were separated by an anti-ricochet wall. An 'oreillion' could be added to protect the loopholes from enfilade fire. It was almost certainly based on a prototype *1ére Région Militaire* design and one of the two designs supplied by *Colonel* Bertschi.

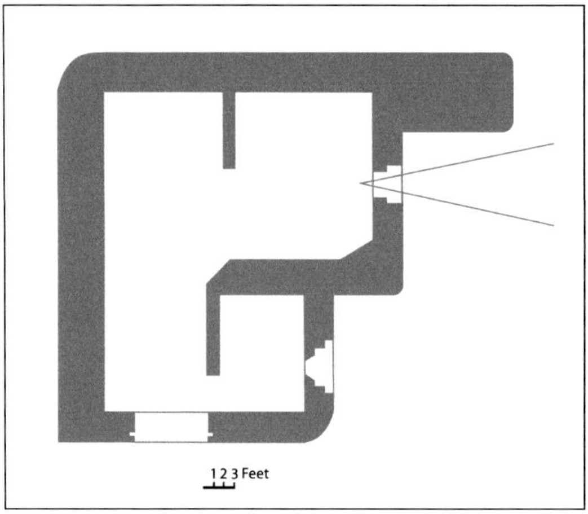

Figure 8.4: Plan of the combined anti-tank and Bren pillbox, allowing a 20° arc of fire.

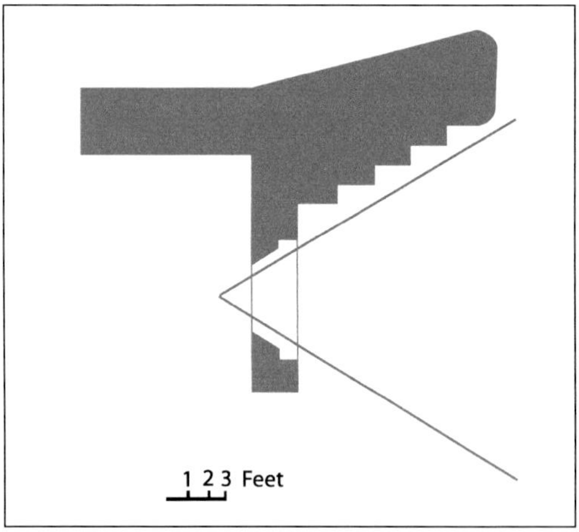

Figure 8.5: Embrasure and wing wall for a combined anti-tank gun and Bren pillbox, allowing a 60° arc of fire.

heavy artillery, and effectively drilled through the pillbox walls. Apparently, the Germans found that the occupants of a pillbox could not withstand such repeated shocks. This would force them to vacate the pillbox, which could them be stormed.

No 2 - Single MG emplacement (Figure 8.6). A rectangular shaped pillbox; an 'oreillion' could be added to protect the loophole from enfilade fire.

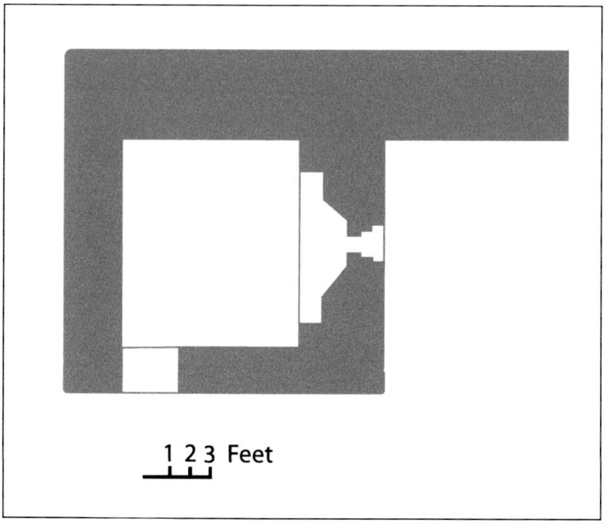

Figure 8.6: Plan of the single MG pillbox.

No 3 – Double MG emplacement (Figure 8.7). A rectangular pillbox with two forward facing embrasures; an 'oreillion' could be added to protect the loopholes from enfilade fire.

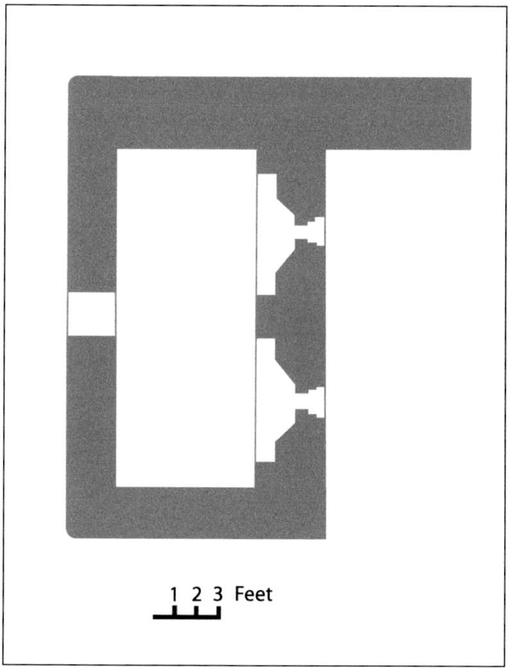

Figure 8.7: Plan of the double MG pillbox.

No 4 – Hexagonal Bren gun emplacement (Figure 8.8 and 8.9). A hexagonal pillbox for an infantry section, and the one design that had not changed much from the beginning. It was decided that no alteration would be required to take the larger sized infantry section. The garrison was usually not to exceed one Bren gun and a crew of three men, with the rest of the section fighting from field works to cover the flanks or rear of the pillbox. Arcs of fire overlapped at 80 yards. Often grouped in fours for all-round defence and the most numerous type of pillbox constructed by the BEF.

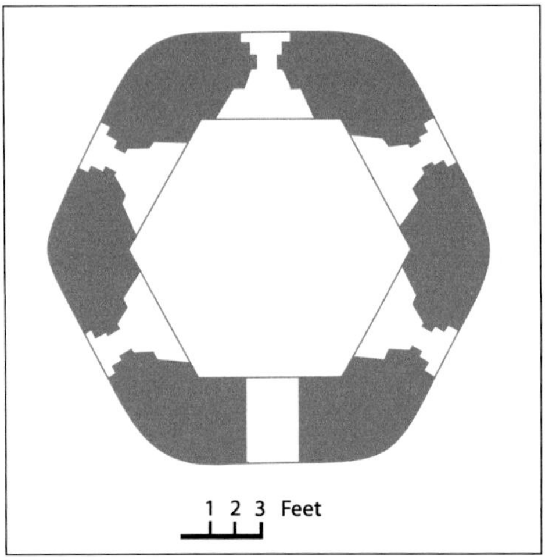

Figure 8.8: Hexagonal pillbox plan.

Figure 8.9: A hexagonal Bren gun pillbox. No camouflage has been added at this stage. (TNA: WO287/136)

No 5 – Single anti-tank gun emplacement (Figure 8.10). A rectangular shaped pillbox, to be sited in the rear of the forward defended localities to cover probable lines of advance by enemy tanks. An 'oreillion' could be added to protect the loophole from enfilade fire. Loophole shown is one of the 'X' Force drawings, giving a total arc of 68°.

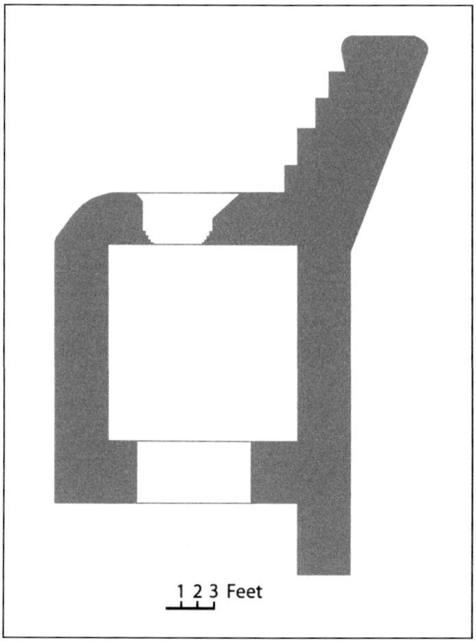

Figure 8.10: Single anti-tank gun pillbox plan.

Due to the sheer volume of concrete needed for pillbox construction, GHQ dropped the provision of simple concrete shelters; corrugated iron shelters were to be used instead. The concrete shelter had been intended for use by an infantry section, which would emerge from it after the passage of the enemy's barrage and AFVs. It could also be used as a company HQ, or a group of shelters could form a battalion HQ. Nevertheless, in February 1940, I Corps again raised the question of concrete protection for company and battalion HQs where it was not possible to construct mined dugouts. I Corps thought that such a pillbox should have two loopholes facing the flanks although a loophole for forward observation was not practicable; instead a periscope was required.

Other BEF concrete constructions included artillery observation posts and *postes de tir*. The *postes de tir* (Figure 8.11 and 8.12) were clearly based on the French *1ére Région Militaire* design and were intended for the close support of the FDL Line. They were designed to house either a 25mm anti-tank gun or a Bren gun. Some constructed by the BEF incorporated blocks on which to rest the gun, as typically found in the French blockhouses, and they were often sunk into the ground as deep as possible. Their simple design makes it difficult to distinguish between those constructed by the French and those by the British. Ironside raised doubts about the value of these small pillboxes:

> Small pillboxes as made in many cases by the French are unsuitable. They are uncomfortable to be in for more than a few hours and it would be impossible for a garrison to man them for three days or so as might be necessary in the event of hostile attack.[7]

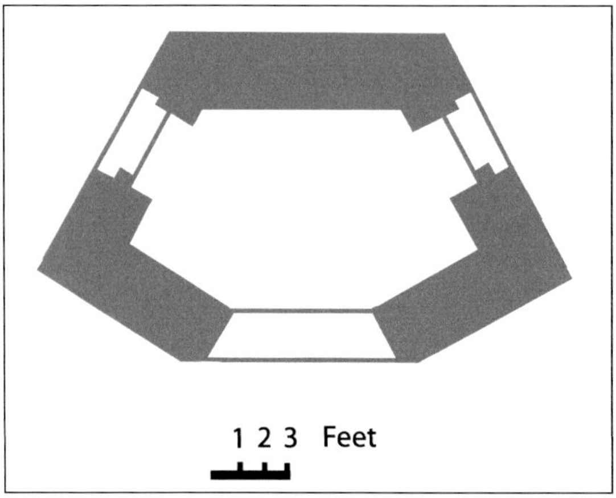

Figure 8.11: *Poste de tir* plan.

Figure 8.12: *Poste de tir* – French design and British built. Large loopholes enabled a wide field of fire. Note the open back and low roof. (TNA: WO287/136)

7 TNA: WO106/1777, 'Notes of C.I.G.S's visit to B.E.F. – 29th Nov. – 2nd Dec. 1939', 2 December 1939.

Perhaps in recognition of this, the CRE 1st Division issued orders that all *postes de tir* were to be constructed with 6 feet of head room. It is worth noting that some commanders found the smaller size more convenient for their requirements: for example, the engineers of the 4th Division prepared timber shuttering for the standard anti-tank gun and Bren pillbox, only for Division and Corps to decide that it was too big for what they required and so instead, a modified French *poste de tir* was constructed! Mention is also made in the CRE 1st Division War Diary of a 'Woollett' type pillbox for the 25mm anti-tank gun, but no further details are given; presumably a Divisional design based on the French *poste de tir* named after Lieutenant Woollett, 23rd Field Company.

Concrete observation posts were in the main simple rectangles with a narrow observation slit on the forward and side faces. On one brigade front, two observation posts were actually built into the French anti-tank ditch, with one in concrete, the roof parallel to the parados of the ditch. I Corps considered that French *tourelles* would make ideal observation posts and the matter of supply was taken up by GHQ. These *tourelles* would be best used where the concrete chamber could be dug deep into the ground. This was only possible to do on the higher ground during the summer months, so it can be inferred that few, if any, were actually constructed by the BEF as observation posts.

Not all new pillboxes in *SD* Lille were built to British standard designs after the arrival of the BEF. Until the relief of the French 51st Division by the 4th and 5th Divisions in December, *Colonel* Bertschi was responsible for the construction of pillboxes along this part of the front, using French concrete companies and civilian contractors. Following the relief, he was still responsible for completing pillboxes along the River Lys from Halluin to Deûlemont. He was allowed to build three types of pillbox along the river line: a large pillbox for an anti-tank gun and light machine gun, a pillbox for a single machine gun and a pillbox for a light machine gun. The French continued to build these pillboxes to French designs, and it was uncertain whether they would also take British weapons – on 8 December, a GHQ memo observed:

> It is hoped that Col. BERTSCHI will be able to obtain French designs of pill-boxes into which the British weapons will fit.[8]

The BEF pillboxes later provided some interest to the German General Staff, with it being reported that both Von Rundstedt and Göering had inspected an anti-tank gun and Bren pillbox built inside a barn near Neuville by the 7th Field Company.

8 TNA: WO167/2, 'Defence Sector LILLE', 8 December 1939, GHQ General Operations War Diary.

Anti-tank gun pillbox loophole

The design of the loophole for the anti-tank gun pillbox had not been finalised at the time the standard designs were issued. The variety of anti-tank guns available and the role of the gun was the complicating factor in loophole design.[9] The British were armed with French 25mm anti-tank guns, British 2 pdr anti-tank guns of two marks and some old 6 pdr tank guns that could be mounted on pedestals. A new mounting with a spilt trail had also been designed for the 2 pdr or a new 6 pdr gun currently under trial; the split trail was described as 'very unsatisfactory for pillbox work' but was not expected to be available for 12 months. In addition, if relieved by the French, they may have wished to use their 47mm anti-tank gun. If that was not enough, there were also reports of the possible acquisition of an Italian gun! A loophole had to be designed to take all these guns; a large loophole could accomplish this. It would, however, be very vulnerable.

Loophole size would also vary because of the role of the gun. Two roles were envisaged – those solely for the defence of an anti-tank ditch and those sited in the rear to cover the probable lines of advance of enemy tanks. To fire along a fixed line with, say, a traverse of 45° and limited elevation, a loophole of 5 feet by 2 feet would suffice. For an arc of fire of 90° with 30° variation in elevation, the loophole would have to be 10 feet by 4 feet. This was the loophole demanded by the anti-tank gunners, so full use could be made of their weapons.

Discussions on the loophole for anti-tank guns continued into the New Year. The 3rd Division, for example, simply specified that the size of each loophole was to be made to suit the conditions of the site. The War Diary of the 2nd Battalion 'X' Force notes that during a conference held on 14 January, the subject of the loophole for the anti-tank gun pillbox had not been finalised and all work on anti-tank gun emplacements was to stop at foundation level. The final solution decided upon was a five inch thick loophole plate carried in a frame which was set into the concrete, the idea originating from an offer by the French to manufacture steel loopholes for the BEF. Such plates were deemed necessary given the attention being paid by all armies to the methods of attacking pillboxes. The frame was a standard size and could take alternative removable loophole plates, suitable for any weapon or required traverse. The use of this type of loophole required a traversing sub carriage for the gun and gave a minimum traverse of 60°. To incorporate the loophole during construction, an opening in the front wall was to be left to take the loophole frame (5ft 6in by 4ft 6in) with a sill 1ft 6in above floor level and 3 inch pipes inserted in the roof for pouring

9 Pillboxes built to house a variety of anti-tank guns also caused GHQ problems with calculating the designated number of different weapons. In February I and II Corps were instructed to forward a list of all pillboxes in their area, giving particulars on whether they would take all types of anti-tank weapons or certain types only. The same information was also requested for all incomplete pillboxes.

concrete above the loophole frame. The War Diary of the 23rd Field Company notes the delivery of a loophole and frame to BACHY STATION anti-tank pillbox on 13 March, weighing two tons and requiring a crane lorry to unload.

Two trials were held in France to test the effectiveness of the new loophole plate and frame against the fire from various calibre guns. The first, held on 12 February, tested the method of attachment and protective qualities of loophole plates of French manufacture, held in a frame of steel and supported in a reinforced concrete wall, the whole representing the front of a pillbox of British design. The trial was carried out at a quarry 1,000 yards south of Vitry en Artois. A QF 2 pdr, firing practice Mk. VIII and Mk. I armour piercing projectiles, and a French QF 47mm gun, firing armour piercing rounds fitted with a ballistic cap and having two driving bands, were used to carry out the trials. The 2 pdr gun had a striking velocity of approximately 2,513 feet per second while the 47mm gun's striking velocity was approximately 2,721 feet per second. The concrete wall was not entirely representative of a pillbox for a number of reasons. First, the concrete was constructed using Cement Fondu to save time but full reinforcement was given. The concrete was 'green' in that it had only had four days to set. It was also constructed in frosty conditions and had no roof, so no support. However, the trial was not intended as a test of concrete penetration and these limitations were felt to be acceptable.

The conclusion of the trial was that the design gave a high level of protection, although a number of minor defects were noted. Firstly, it was found that the four bolts of the frame sheared by 'jump', but in spite of this the frame remained in position, most likely due to the 'riveting' action of the plate spreading in the frame. It was decided to use eight bolts instead, with a continuous strip separated from the frame by a small wooden fillet to absorb the 'jump'. Secondly, although a crack appeared in the frame, no extension of it was noted with subsequent hits; it was thought that the crack may have been caused by tension set up during casting. No change to the design was considered necessary. Finally, one shot struck the edge of the frame and glanced to the right, perforating the concrete wall. The shot did not hit any reinforcing bars in perforating the concrete. The easiest way to correct this was by adding more reinforcement bars.

On 4 March, a second trial was held, this time to assess the effect of a 25 pdr gun firing AP shot at a range of 60 yards. Again, the plate stood up well (Figure 8.13). Although one round did break off a piece of the plate on the right-hand side, the conclusion was that the loophole was still useable. The overall conclusion from these trials was that the frame and plate gave a high degree of protection.

Another solution to minimising the size of the loophole was to make the gun rotate at a point vertically under the centre of it. There were three possible ways of achieving this in principle:

1. A muzzle pivot mount which would achieve the ideal result. An undercarriage for both the 2 pdr and 25mm guns was developed that revolved on a pivot under the loophole.

Figure 8.13: The loophole plate and frame at the end of the trials held on 4 March 1940. (TNA: WO167/43)

2. A pedestal mounting which would permit the pivot to be close to the loophole.
3. A revolving shield on the gun.

The adopted solution was the pivot mounting and instructions were issued on 11 December that these mountings should be standard for all new anti-tank pillboxes and could also be fitted to existing pillboxes. By February they were being produced at the rate of about one per day, although it seems that they were not actually issued for installing in pillboxes until April. As a case in point, two were available to the 1st Division at the beginning of April and the 23rd Field Company was instructed to carry out experiments to convert the anti-tank gun and Bren pillbox and the 'Woollett' pillbox to accept these mountings. These pivot mounts could also be used with the new loophole frames and plates.

Medium machine gun pillbox loopholes

Machine gun pillboxes had to be situated, so their loopholes were aligned on to their predetermined task. This allowed a very small loophole, and it was also stated that small loopholes would counteract the temptation to disperse fire at the expense of the gun's allotted role. The Vickers guns were mounted in the pillbox using muzzle pivot mountings, of which 500 were initially sent over in October.[10] No such mount existed for the Bren gun and the War Office informed GHQ that if they were required, they would not be ready for some time.

Modifications to standard designs

It is perhaps no surprise, given the wide divergence of opinion with regards to the role of pillboxes, that several alterations to standard designs occurred. Some of these alterations were officially approved improvements and simplifications to designs and also recognition that a standard pillbox design would not fit every site. On the other hand, both corps and divisions also constructed their own designs – for example the War Diary of the 2nd Division notes with frustration that the standard designs were not suitable, in particular the anti-tank pillbox, and noted 'we shall have to improvise locally as best we can.'[11]

The II Corps design for a pillbox to house a 25mm anti-tank gun is a good example of the conflict between GHQ and unit formations in pillbox design that diverged from the standard designs. During a conference held by II Corps on 18 November, Brooke had specified that all anti-tank gun pillboxes in the forward areas should be constructed to take the 25mm anti-tank gun only. He even designed the pillbox mounting for this gun. Furthermore, he specified that for pillboxes not likely to be subject to plunging fire, a lesser degree of roof protection was acceptable, with a thickness of only 2 feet, while the walls had to be able to withstand German armour piercing shells fired from tanks. Concealment was all important for these pillboxes and the saving in the height of the roof would make this easier. GHQ had a number of objections to this design. Firstly, it was pointed out that the 25mm anti-tank gun may not be available in the future, so all anti-tank gun pillboxes should be able to take either the 25mm gun or the 2 pdr gun. Secondly, in cases where II Corps were proposing just 2 feet of reinforced concrete to aid concealment, GHQ pointed out that if concrete was to be used at all the roof should be at least proof against 5.9 inch shells – i.e. 3ft 6in thick .Thirdly, GHQ reminded II Corps of the advantages of using standardised designs: 'for the reason that supply of materials can be standardized [sic], and that all troops and formations in the B.E.F. may be fully cognizant of the type of pill-box to be occupied in any sector when relief of Corps or Divisions occur.'[12] A final point made to II Corps was that the GHQ anti-tank pillbox design made allowance for the incorporation of steel loophole plates.

10 Astonishingly, a new mount was designed later on that did not fit the BEF pillboxes!
11 TNA: WO167/203, 2nd Division General Staff War Diary, 22 November 1939.
12 TNA: WO167/2, 'Pillboxes', 11 December 1939, GHQ General Operations War Diary.

An observation loophole for the section commander in the double MG pillbox was a common modification – CRE 1st Division specified such observation loopholes in all double MG pillboxes in instructions issued on 3 January 1940 – but these observation loopholes were eventually prohibited from being incorporated by GHQ, presumably because they would weaken the front wall.

CRE 3rd Division intended to site its MG sections in an emplacement in which the single gun type of emplacement formed the basis of the design. As the guns had to be sited so their arcs overlapped slightly, the faces of the emplacements inclined slightly towards one another and it was noted that a separate design may be necessary for each location. Generally speaking, the two emplacements were to share a continuous roof; the inner walls only needing to be 1ft 6in thick and the space between the emplacements being the command post and provided with a loophole. It is probable that this design was never actually constructed, as no examples have been reported as extant.

In January 1940, the following approved alterations to anti-tank emplacements were notified in orders:

1. Loophole plate as described above, to replace loophole shown in standard drawing.
2. Periscope hole of 5 inches diameter to be left in roof.
3. Third row of vertical reinforcing bars.
4. Wing wall to be sloped off at 45°.
5. Two ventilators in side wall opposite wing wall.
6. Burster apron to be added.
7. Wing wall to be squared off in emplacements not yet excavated to simplify shuttering. This involved increasing the thickness of the front wall to 3ft 6in (Figure 8.14).
8. Wing wall to be omitted when emplacement faced the direction of enemy fire and the front and side walls to be increased to 3ft 6in thick.
9. A side entrance instead of rear entrance and no wing wall when the emplacement's back faced the enemy.

The same orders notified the following approved alterations to the double machine gun pillbox:

1. Cavity of 10 inches high by 6 inches deep and 26 inches long over loophole. This was to allow the rear cover of the Vickers gun to be opened in any position on the arc of traverse.
2. Loophole for an anti-tank rifle to be added into side wall when required. Loophole to be the same pattern as a Bren loophole.
3. Periscope hole of 5 inches diameter to be left in roof.
4. Right hand face of loopholes to be set back 3 inches.

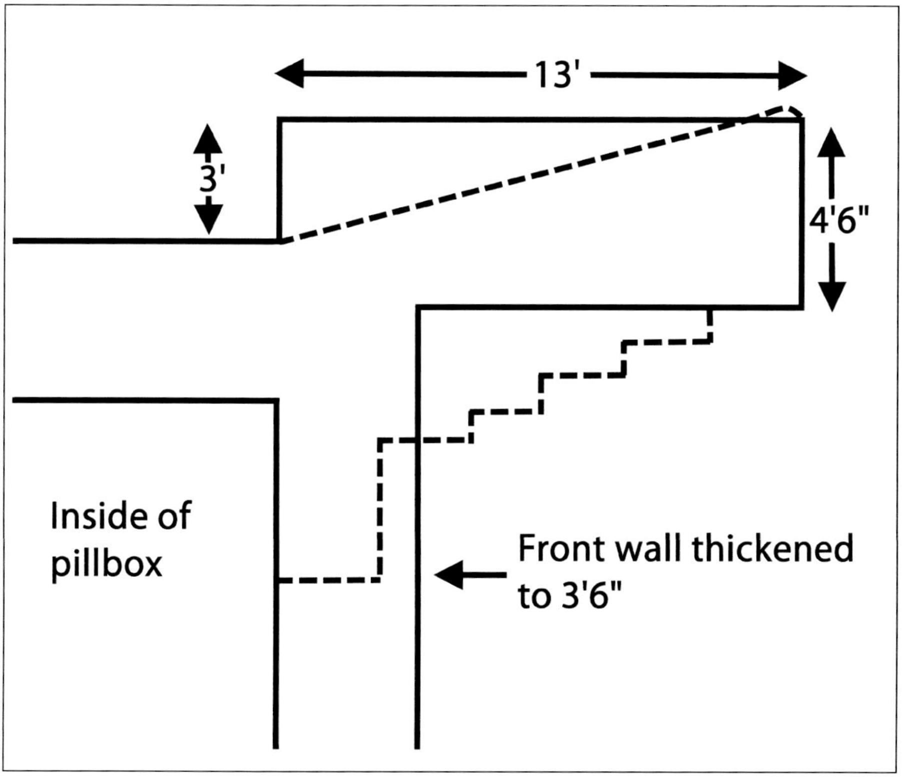

Figure 8.14: Modified wing wall squared off as notified in orders, January 1940.

5. Two ventilators in side wall opposite wing wall.
6. Burster apron to be added.
7. Wing wall to be omitted, front and side walls to be increased to 3ft 6in thick and side entrance changed if probable direction of enemy fire made such alterations advisable.

Alterations such as increasing wall thickness or variations in loopholes and entrances required modifications to standard shuttering and steelwork quantities. These alterations were to be made locally by the field park companies. Other alterations to standard shuttering could arise if a pillbox was constructed to blend in with its immediate surroundings. For example, if constructed to appear as an extension to a building, the wall of the building could be used as the outer shuttering for one of the pillbox walls.

Surplus loopholes

By January 1940 it had become apparent that some of the loopholes in the hexagonal Bren gun pillboxes were surplus to what was actually needed. On 21 January, Brooke, along with various Staff Officers, visited *Colonel* Bertchi's HQ for a machine gun demonstration against 'Bertchi Bricks' – a steel brick for altering the size of loopholes. Field park companies designed something similar with precast blocks for the inner and outer portion of the loophole. It had always been the intention of the Engineer-in-Chief to make available steel plates for this purpose, in particular due to the attention being paid in all armies to methods of attacking pillboxes, but there was a delay in their issue. However, some did question the use of such blocks or plates, with the pillbox garrison 'shut up like an oyster with the enemy ready to attack any chink which tries to open.'[13] The 2nd Division produced its own design, which was intended to guard against lamination of the concrete around the loophole plate, but the design was considered too complicated.

Either due to a shortage of anti-tank guns or a change in its role, at least one extant anti-tank gun pillbox has had its embrasure partly bricked up to form a loophole for a machine gun. It is interesting to note that similar situations arose in pillboxes constructed as part of Britain's anti-invasion defences, with many surplus loopholes blocked up with brickwork or concrete in 1941 and some anti-tank gun pillboxes converted to take light machine guns instead.

Periscope in anti-tank gun pillboxes

Serious doubts were raised in the spring of 1940 if the No. 1 of the gun team could identify the most dangerous tank from the periscope because of its limited field of view. If this was the case, it was recommended that the No.1 should use an observation slit and another member of the crew the periscope for general observations. If the No. 1 was to use the periscope, it was decided that some form of pointer was necessary inside the pillbox so that the gun could follow the direction of the periscope without the No. 1 having to direct it. Such a pointer of this nature was in development prior to the German invasion.

Mounting British guns in French pillboxes

As we have seen, one problem the British encountered when taking over French pillboxes was that the British 2 pdr anti-tank gun would not fit in them. There were similar problems in mounting the Vickers machine gun in loopholes designed for the Hotchkiss. Although early on *Général du Génie, Général* Philippe had undertaken that, in future, works constructed by the French would be designed to take weapons

13 TNA: WO167/43, 'Policy regarding design of pillboxes' GHQ Chief Engineer War Diary.

of both armies, the matter does not seem to have been adequately resolved. In January, the British lent the French a 2 pdr anti-tank gun and a Vickers machine gun so they could design mounts that would enable both guns to be used from French pillboxes; the *Service Klectro-Mecanique de Génie* was responsible for producing the designs. Their design for the 2 pdr gun mounting comprised of three pedestals made of small welded steel units with a heavy steel pin which had to rotate to absorb the shock of firing. They also designed a loophole from which the Hotchkiss and the Vickers machine guns could fire from, with a mounting with a simple adapter which would suit both guns. The French also requested the loan of a Bren gun so they could design an adapter to suit their mounting.[14] It also transpired that as late as March 1940, the French had little information on what the British were doing with regards to the design of loopholes or special gun mountings. It seems quite astonishing that this matter was still rumbling on after being noted as needing urgent attention back in October 1939.

Weapon Fumes

The potential poisoning of a garrison in a pillbox from fumes generated by weapon firing was an early concern in the BEF, especially if steel doors and loophole shutters were closed. On 4 November a weapon firing trial in a closed-up pillbox was held in the 3rd Division's area. Brooke records the event in his diary: 'Eighteen of us got into a pillbox, closed down all openings and then fired an anti-tank gun and a Bren through the apertures for five minutes to make certain that the fumes and gasses from the firing would not be such as to affect the garrison of the pillbox.' The experiment showed that fumes were not excessive, but Brooke remarked with humour that chances for promotion would have been helped if this was not the case, as the party present for the trial included one Lieutenant-General, one Major-General, two Brigadiers, one Colonel and three Lieutenant-Colonels – 'expensive 'white mice' for such a trial!'[15]

On a visit to the Maginot Line on 18 and 19 December, the Engineer-in-Chief noted that General Condè, commanding the French Third Army, did not place much store in wall ventilation. He considered that carbon monoxide from machine guns should be carried away by nozzle attachments. As anti-tank guns were unlikely to be used for continuous fire, he considered that a small hand operated fan fitted in each pillbox would cope with any carbon monoxide generated. GHQ decided to adopt a similar policy.[16]

14 The British went on to design something similar in late 1940 for use with pillboxes: The Turnbull mount, which comprised of a standard frame that could accept cradles for a Vickers, Lewis and Bren gun.

15 Alex Danchev & Daniel Todman (eds.), *War Diaries 1939-1945: Field Marshall Lord Alan Brooke* (Berkeley and Los Angeles: University of California Press, 2001), p. 13.

16 An interesting footnote to the ventilation issue is the results of trials held at Porton, published in a report dated 2 August 1940. It is of interest as it probably represents the

Loading trials

An interesting note in the 1st Division War Diary suggests that perhaps not enough thought had been given to manning the standard designed pillboxes for long periods. Instructions stated that when a pillbox of each design had been completed, the 21st Anti-Tank Regiment and the 2nd Battalion Cheshire Regiment were to carry out tests to see whether crews, food, water and ammunition could all be fitted into the pillbox or whether a proportion of the ammunition would have to be stored outside the pillbox in a shelter off the communication trench and provided with a concrete roof.

Pillbox for the Bofors A.A. gun

A Bofors gun could only be given limited protection as any parapet was restricted by the conditions of the site, the elevation required for the gun and the speed in which it had to come into action. The suggested protection was an emplacement of 20 feet square with revetted walls from four to six feet high and ammunition recesses. However, another suggestion was for a concrete shelter for the gun and crew, with two or three alternative positions in which the gun would be moved to for action. These positions would be about 200 yards from the pillbox, as this was the distance in which a gun could be got out of action and moved to the pillbox within eight minutes,

only example of a BEF designed pillbox built in Britain. The pillbox used for the trials was the BEF double machine gun emplacement with an interior of 700 cu.ft. and two embrasures each of 9 inch by 6 inch for Vickers machine guns. A hand operated blower was fitted to the pillbox which could deliver 150 cu.ft./min. of air with ease or 300 cu.ft./min. for about half an hour. Dissipation of smoke from the firing of two Vickers machine guns was measured photoelectrically. The results showed that in winds of 10 to 15 mph natural ventilation was almost as effective as forced ventilation, but forced ventilation was ten times as effective in cases of light winds. Forced ventilation was also four or five times more effective than using eight 4½ inch diameter ventilation ducts in the walls. Forced ventilation was twice as effective as an open door. Tests were also carried out with blast deflectors fitted to the guns. This showed that at half to one hour of steady firing (150 rpm or 75 rpm for each gun) the risk of dangerous levels of carbon monoxide could be virtually eliminated using blast deflectors and forced ventilation (forced ventilation produced a draft of about 7 mph so with blast deflectors the only carbon monoxide likely to enter the pillbox was from ejected cartridges). The trial also concluded that to be effective, ventilation ducts needed to be numerous and large, eight 4½ inch ducts being the minimum; 6 inch ducts with blast deflectors could almost eliminate the risk of carbon monoxide poisoning. To be of much use ventilation ducts had to be in walls facing the wind. As calm winds are most likely during early morning or late evening, in two cases advantage could be made of meteorological phenomena. Pillboxes sited on slopes could make use of the katabatic wind flowing downhill with ventilation ducts in the wall facing uphill or pillboxes sited on the coast could make use of onshore breezes with ducts in the rear wall. Perhaps one of the less practical suggestions was to use a canvas sail fitted to a duct leading into the pillbox, a few minutes warning of action only needed to trim the sail to receive the wind!

the reported time that a hostile battery took to open fire on a new target. The pillbox would be of a comparable size to an anti-tank gun pillbox, with internal dimensions of 16 feet by 10 feet and a door 6 feet wide and 6ft 6in high. As it would take six to eight weeks to construct the pillbox, it was considered that the possibilities of using this suggestion would be limited and none were built.

Pillbox Siting

Each division decided upon the sites and the types of each pillbox required. In order to construct a pillbox for its allocated role, arcs of fire and height of the muzzle had to be fixed at each site. Right from the start there were countless different opinions on the site and arcs of fire of pillboxes. Many pillboxes it seems were sited without any official order, presumably the result of 'getting on' and 'being seen to be doing something'. Even once the location and arcs of fire had been decided upon, these were frequently altered later. All of this added to the delay in pillbox construction, especially for the work that 'X' Force was brought over for. Colonel French noted that even if all the required personnel and plant of 'X' Force had been available at the start, no large-scale work could have commenced pending the settling of designs and site. Some pillboxes had to be sited in the vicinity of houses, which in a few cases necessitated requisition. Lieutenant D'Arcy remembered such an incident: 'there was a great deal of upset on the part of the family when they heard their garden was going to get a pillbox – but I was kept away from the recriminations and arguments'.[17]

Once the site had been decided upon, it was marked by pegging out or reference to existing features. The CRE 3rd Division specified that for anti-tank and machine gun pillboxes, the relevant officers of the anti-tank regiment and machine gun battalion had to be consulted and a full-scale canvas representation of the front of the emplacement erected on the site. As well as a grid reference, each site was given a name for easy reference, usually related to a location or nearby feature combined with the type of weapon the pillbox was to house (e.g. GENECH NORTH ANTI-TANK, GENECH NORTH MACHINE GUN).[18]. Progress on the building of

17 Joshua Levine, *Forgotten Voices: Dunkirk* (London: Ebury Press, 2011), P. 16.

18 In February 1940 GHQ instructed that a four-number system would be used to identify pillboxes. The first number referred to its position from front to rear. Thus '1' was in front of the anti-tank obstacle on the FDL Line, '2' was between the anti-tank obstacles of the FDL Line and the Brigade Reserve Position, '3' was between the anti-tank obstacles of the Brigade Reserve Position and the Divisional Reserve Position, '4' was between the anti-tank obstacles of the Divisional Reserve Position and the Corps Position, '5' was between the anti-tank obstacles of the Corps Reserve Position and the Second Position and '6' was in the rear of the Second Position. The second number indicated the divisional sector the pillbox was constructed in, the divisional sectors being numbered from right to left. The last two numbers indicated the number of the pillbox in the divisional sector, generally numbered from right to left. Thus, for example, a pillbox seventh from right in 4th Division's sector between the Brigade Reserve Position and Divisional Reserve Position anti-tank obstacles

pillboxes was tracked by the division or RE battalion building them and monthly progress reports submitted to corps, as described by Lieutenant Clarke:

> Our office is a first floor flat a few yards down the Comines road. Round the walls I have stuck charts with coloured pins showing the progress of pillbox construction, Bren, Machine-gun or Anti-tank gun. I have given them names beginning with B, M or T respectively. The map references never seems to be quite right. My draughtsman has just finished a tracing showing them all as yellow spots ringed with black so there will be no more arguments. Devote the day to checking my monthly report to my namesake at II Corps HQ hoping that it will not come back this time corrected in red ink.[19]

As the defences developed, each corps kept a complete record of them in the form of overlays on the standard 1:25,000 maps and the larger scale 1:10,000 maps. Some of these defences were plotted by aerial photos but most were plotted from general survey by the field survey companies.[20] It was intended these maps would be a complete record and thus facilitate reliefs.

Materials

To construct a reinforced concrete pillbox, the materials required are cement, sand, aggregate, reinforcing rods and shuttering. The rate of progress for the construction of the BEF's pillboxes was governed by the supply of these materials. On arrival in France, the Chief Engineer was informed by *Général* Phillippe that cement was in short supply and aggregate would have to be 'drawn from far away.' Large cement works did exist at Les Loisne, southeast of Barlin, but the French Government had requisitioned all the cement, and none could be bought without the sanction of the French Government. Steel bars were also in short supply. Supplies of steel bars and

would be numbered 3407. However, if War Diaries are anything to go on, it does not seem to have been used by units and formations.

19 Ralph Lionel Clarke, *Three Weeks to La Panne: A Diary of Dunkirk* <http://www.foxearth.org.uk/ThreeWeeksToLaPanne> (Accessed 25 August 2017).

20 When consideration was seriously being given to sending an Expeditionary Force to France, the decision was taken to mobilise a Survey Directorate and field survey units, which was implemented in August 1939. Each corps had a field survey company RE attached to corps HQ, made up of an HQ and two topographical sections. These field survey companies worked with the 'rearmament' map series, produced in the inter-war years in response to an increase in German hostility. This series of maps covered north-west Europe, and included the whole of Belgium, Holland and the part of north-east France bounded in the north-east by Belgium from the sea to Luxembourg and in the west by the sea coast on a line from Pas de Calais and in the south by a line running approximately from Paris to the Luxembourg frontier. This task was made difficult by the lack of co-operation of Belgium and Holland because of their neutrality.

cement do seem to have improved after these initial shortages, but the supply of sand and aggregate was always problematic for the BEF, and a couple of examples amply illustrate this point. On arrival at their allocated area of the front during October, the 1st Division discovered there were no local quarries and that the French had requisitioned all the local dumps of sand and aggregate. Arrangements had to be made to bring in supplies by barge from Soissons or Belgium. The CRE 2nd Battalion 'X' Force noted on 21 November that 100 tons of sand and aggregate was to be delivered every four days when 100 tons every two days was required for the works schedule.

At first, the BEF was allocated a number of gravel pits by *GQG* but in some cases, it was found that the allocated pits were already carrying out contracts for aggregates and the terms issued by *GQG* stated that these must be completed. In order to try and ensure smooth delivery of sand and aggregate, it was decided that all orders would be placed with *GQG* who would then place the order with owners of pits and make all the arrangements for delivering to the agreed supply regulating stations. This did not necessarily mean an instant improvement in matters; the 4th Division noted that the immediate consequence of these new arrangements was a glut in large aggregate and a shortage in small aggregate and sand, followed by a glut in sand! The Division also noted that the barges and trains were so unreliable that it was not worth making arrangements to unload them until they had actually arrived in their sidings otherwise working parties, grabs and transport were kept waiting or had to be cancelled at the last moment.

The demands on transport and labour to move sand and aggregate to the various pillbox construction sites resulted in some strange arrangements. To unload two barges of sand and aggregate on 8 December, the 2nd Division hired a crane which was operated by a French soldier on loan from the French Army. The grab was filled by men from the Field Ambulance, hoisted by the crane and emptied into lorries of the Divisional Ammunition Column who then delivered it to the various points at which it was needed.

The scale of the construction programme was always going to put pressure on the ability to maintain supplies of sand and aggregate. This was exasperated by the weather, first heavy rain then freezing conditions. During a period of heavy rain in early December, it was impossible to use barges due to the rising water levels and fast flows. Tugs could not pull full barges against the flow while empty barges could not get under bridges on their return journey. The rain was followed by freezing winter conditions from late December onwards, resulting in a deterioration in the condition of the roads. The winter was characterised by periods of snow, freezing temperatures and rapid thaws. It proved impossible to deliver sand and aggregate by road to many sites and supplies left over at completed sites could not be moved around. The freezing temperatures also caused problems with what little supplies that could be moved, for example frozen sand had to be cut out of rail trucks using compressor trucks. Sometimes, even compressor trucks could not break up the sand, as noted by the 5th Field Company on 25 January. This caused congestion at rail yards and other supplies could not be unloaded.

On the roads it was snow followed by thaw that caused problems, with some road closures and an increasing number of road accidents. Improvisation was required to keep the roads open, for instance the 23rd Field Company improvised four snow ploughs, dragged behind 30cwt trucks and a larger 10 feet plough, and spent two days in February clearing snow from roads. A rapid thaw in late February caused the roads to deteriorate rapidly. All roads except main roads had to be closed in 2nd Battalion 'X' Force's area on 27 February although special permission was given to deliver materials to some sites. Speed and weight restrictions had to be put in place as the thaw continued, which were as low as limiting lorries to 15cwt and a speed limit of 12 mph. Many third class roads remained closed as the pavé surface laid on earth had completely broken up. The War Diary of the 23rd Field Company notes the whole Company with the help of infantry working parties of up to 400 men were involved on road repairs from 1 March to 8 March. Pillbox construction almost ground to a halt as although sand and aggregate supplies continued to arrive at the railheads, it was impossible to deliver them to most of the construction sites.

The decision to deploy a third Corps of the BEF to hold part of the frontier defences placed even more pressure on supplies of sand and aggregate and pillbox construction was further delayed as a result during April.

Shuttering

As has already been noted, to achieve large scale production of pillboxes it was intended to use standard designs and prefabricated steel shuttering. Due to the changes in pillbox design early on, much work on designing prefabricated shuttering went to waste. The anti-tank gun and Bren pillbox was the largest of the BEF designs and was the least suitable for timber shuttering so 'X' Force decided to prioritise steel shuttering for this pillbox type at the expense of the smaller designs. The design of this pillbox was altered four times and by the time the first steel shuttering was expected in France, it had altered again! However, by January, external and internal steel shuttering sets were in use for all pillbox designs, although there were never enough available to meet the demands of the construction programme.

Steel shuttering was manufactured in lifts (2ft 6in, 2ft 0in and 2ft 0in for walls and 3ft 6in for the roof, to be erected in that order).[21] The internal and external corners were set to the full height of the pillbox and connected by horizontal ribs. The

21 Pillboxes were constructed in 'lifts'. Typical lifts for walls were 2ft 6in, 2ft 0in and 2ft 0in and 3ft 6in for the roof. Shuttering was supplied readymade for these lifts. This was because the shutters normally used would not withstand pressures exerted by more than 2ft 6in to 3ft 6in height of unset concrete, and this therefore was the maximum 'lift' which it was usual to pour in any one operation. Furthermore, if deeper layers were placed, a gradual increase in the water content of the upper layers would result on account of the increased pressure on the lower portions. Each 'lift' was built up in 6 inch to 12 inch layers, each layer being separately and simultaneously rammed.

shuttering was held in place by bolting to the horizontal ribs. Long bolts were used that were passed through the external and internal ribs, the shutters and one-inch pipe distance pieces. To dismantle the shuttering, the bolts were simply removed, and the distance pieces filled with fine concrete.

As well as steel shuttering, timber shuttering was widely used. Timber also had to be used for any non-standard design. Designs of timber shuttering were produced for the standard pillboxes, although the work of constructing it was delayed at first due to a lack of skilled carpenters capable of reading drawings. Timber shuttering was assembled at the engineer workshops and then delivered to site. For instance, the 7th Field Company set up a work shop to mass produce shuttering in a wool factory at Tourcoing: the mass production of beds and wool mattresses for the Company's billets was also carried out at the factory! Timber shuttering could be reused if treated with an application of form oil prior to use and thoroughly cleaned after use.[22]

Timber was naturally in much demand for all types of field engineering and supplies soon began to run short. The problem was compounded by new purchasing regulations which put a stop to units obtaining materials locally. At the end of November, instructions were issued to use sandbags as a substitute for external shuttering if timber was unavailable. It appears that there was no set procedure specified for the use sandbags as external shuttering and field companies were advised to determine the best method by trial and error. Two methods are described, both quite different as one incorporated the sandbags in the finished pillbox wall, while the other made no attempt to incorporate them.

The first suggested method was as follows:

1. Space outside vertical rods at 10-inch intervals instead of the normal 8 inches.[23]
2. Fill sandbags with a dry enough mix to prevent undue 'spreading' of the bag.
3. Start with a row of 'headers' laid between the rods, the rods forming the centre line of the row.
4. Rows of 'stretchers' were laid inside and outside the stretchers, taking care to 'break joint', using partly filled sandbags as 'closures'.[24]

22 The purpose of form oil was to prevent the shuttering from absorbing water from the concrete and to facilitate striking. Typical oils included waste engine oil, creosote, grease, limewash, soap solution and even clay slurry.

23 The military standard service sandbag measured 33 inch by 14 inch when empty. They were normally three-quarters filled and when laid should measure 20 inch by 10 inch, hence spacing the vertical reinforcing rods at 10 inch intervals.

24 Sandbags are normally laid in the same way as bricks and built on the 'English Bond' system. A 'header' is laid at right angles to the wall, a 'stretcher' with its longest side parallel to the wall.

5. Horizontal reinforcing rods were laid between the courses, irrespective of the intervals shown on plans.
6. Mortar or grout was laid over each course, paying particular attention to the vertical rods.
7. Build up to the 'lifts' of the internal shuttering before pouring.

The second method specified adding an additional apron, 2 feet wide and 1 foot thick, around the floor slab to take a concrete sandbag wall one 'header' thick. The sandbag wall was to be built outside the designed wall on the shuttering line as an extra, no attempt being made to retain it in the finished structure. If aggregate was not available for concrete sandbags, earth could be used but the base of the sandbag wall would need to be thickened, battering to a 'header' thick at the top of the wall.

Shuttering reports in War Diaries do show both earth and concrete filled sandbag shuttering being used for external shuttering, but no mention is made of the method used. Corrugated steel sheets seem to be the only other material used for shuttering as a substitute for prefabricated steel or timber; records show it was used for internal shuttering on a handful of BEF pillboxes while some extant pillboxes clearly show it was also used for external shuttering.

Construction methods

Before any construction could begin, the priority of the pillboxes needed to be determined: those that played a key role in the fire plan, particularly anti-tank gun pillboxes, had the highest priority. Plant and equipment, such as cement mixers and Decauville track, were in short supply so economy in moving these items around also had to be taken into account when deciding the programme of pillbox construction. Once the priority, site and arcs of fire of a pillbox had been decided upon, construction could begin.

The first task was to prepare the site and take delivery of materials and plant and equipment. The layout of the site needed to be planned to ensure good ingress and egress as inefficient approaches, especially during bad weather, would cause delay. Approach roads had to be improved or constructed in many cases to allow materials and plant to be delivered. On site, temporary roads and lorry turning circles were constructed if required; corduroy track or 2 inch to 3 inch slag were both used for this purpose. If no roads were nearby, Decauville track had to be laid to transport materials to site; for example at the site of NORTH SARTINE 25mm anti-tank gun pillbox it was necessary to lay 400 yards of Decauville track and use a 3½ ton Decauville locomotive for hauling 200 tons of sand and aggregate uphill.[25] Typically,

25 André Maurois recalls an amusing tale, where at one pillbox site a narrow-gauge railway had been hired from a local French contractor. The contractor said that his father had hired out the same rails and trucks to the BEF 25 years ago and that he would leave it to his son, as

a drawing was prepared for each site showing the arrangements for unloading points and storage of materials etc.

Careful thought had to be given to the location of plant and material dumps. Cement readily absorbs moisture from the atmosphere and rapidly deteriorates if exposed to damp. It had to be protected from the weather by placing on boards or on a platform raised above the ground and covered with tarpaulin sheets. Sand and aggregate had to be kept clean, especially from mud splashed by passing lorries. The same requirement applied to the storage of reinforcement rods. Any contamination of sand, aggregate or reinforcement would reduce its bond with the concrete. Corrugated steel sheets were provided for stacking sand and aggregates on while the best method of storing reinforcement was in racks. Some attempt was made on some sites to camouflage the dumps of sand and aggregate by covering with brushwood. The siting of the mixer was important; it should allow for the equal distribution of concrete. Materials had to be arranged suitably in relation to the mixer as it was easier to transport mixed concrete than the four separate materials (water, sand, aggregate and cement). Advantage could be taken of any differences in level in the site which permitted material to be moved downhill. Colonel French noted that if sites had been settled earlier, all this preparatory work could have been undertaken and construction started immediately once final designs had been issued.

In order to ensure accurate siting of loopholes and the subsequent accuracy of the pillbox, correct setting out was of the upmost importance. Templates were set up using timber (4 inch by 1 inch was recommended) cut to appropriate lengths and fixed to wooden pegs, shaped to the angles of the pillbox. The template had to be constructed at a sufficient distance to prevent damage during the course of the work. Nails were driven into the timber from which lines could be strung to define the inside and outside of the walls. The template remained in place during the course of the work and was set to one level so that the NCO in charge of the work could check his levels with boning rods.

Once the setting out was completed, the first stage in the construction of a pillbox was to excavate either for normal foundations or a pit for a concrete raft (also referred to as a plinth). For a pillbox to withstand being overturned or displaced by heavy shells a foundation depth carried 4 feet to 5 feet underground or a raft extending 5 feet to 6 feet beyond the pillbox walls was recommended. Given the nature of the terrain, if a raft was required, it also needed to be of quite a substantial depth; the 200th Field Company noted constructing a 4 feet thick raft for the BELISHA pillbox, a hexagonal Bren gun pillbox. The limits of the excavation were set by the template as described above. Additionally, it was recommended to extend the top 9 inches to form a 2 feet berm all-round the work. Given the low-lying nature of the land and its predominately agricultural use, water running into the excavation from spring water

'one never knows ...' (André Maurois, *The Battle of France* (London: John Lane the Bodley Head, 1940), p. 137).

or field drains broken during excavation was a problem at some sites. Cleaning out nearby ditches could aid drainage and pumps were available as a last resort.

Once the excavation was complete, foundations of brick or 2 inch clinker were laid to serve as the lower course of the pillbox raft in order to prevent churning up the soil while constructing the reinforcing mat. If the ground was very wet, it was also necessary to revet the sides of the excavation using rough wooden boards. When the lower course had been laid, the reinforcing mat was constructed, and the concrete poured. The vertical rods for the first lift of the pillbox were set into the raft, accurate spacing being obtained by either stringing lines from the template or using specially erected timber for setting out the reinforcement. The rods were set to a height so that 20 diameters would project above the first lift.

The next stage was to fix the horizontal reinforcing rods and erect the shuttering to the height of the first lift. The horizontal rods were wired to the vertical rods using No.10 SWG iron wire. The vertical rods were temporarily supported during pouring by wiring on a fastener. Pouring of the first lift could now take place.[26]

The concrete mix was expressed in nominal volumetric proportions, the usual mix for reinforced concrete being 1:2:3 i.e. one of cement to two sand to three aggregates, the ingredients of the mix being measured proportionally to one bag of cement. The records indicate a mix of 1:2:4 was also employed, which conveniently equated to one bag of cement, two cubic feet of sand (one barrow load) and four cubic feet of aggregates (two barrow loads). To ensure accuracy of the mix, barrows were occasionally tested with a gauge box. One man was told off at the mixing site to remove excess material from barrows or to top up barrows that appeared short. The mix was kept as dry as possible.[27]

Each lift had to be built up in 6 inch to 12 inch layers. Continuous ramming during pouring was essential. This was usually done by hand, using either a blunt piece of

26 An example of a reinforcing specification can be found in the CRE 3rd Division War Diary:
Floor – two mats, 6 inch square of ½ inch steel, the lower mat 3 inch above the bottom and the upper 3 inch below the surface of the floor.
Roof and walls – one mat, 6 inch square of ¾ inch steel, placed 3 inches from the inside surface of the wall or roof. One mat, 6 inch square of ½ inch steel, 6 inches above or outside the inner mat. Two mats 6 inch square of ½ inch steel 6 inches apart, the outer mat 3 inches from the outside surface of the wall or roof.
In the walls and roof, stirrups of ¼ inch steel placed horizontally and vertically respectively at 9 inch spacing to bind the mats together. Thomas Riordan, in *A History of the 7th Field Company RE*, notes that this differed from French methods where the walls and roof were built in one continuous operation, with horizontal reinforcement laid as the concrete reached the right level, ties not being used.

27 A certain minimum quantity of water is necessary to hydrate the cement completely. More water than this is necessary to make concrete sufficiently workable. Any excess of water over this amount will weaken the concrete because it will weaken the concrete paste. Density, permeability and shrinkage are also adversely affected by excess water. Its quantity should, therefore, be the minimum required to obtain the desired degree of workability.

timber or tampers made from ¾ inch or ½ inch diameter rods with 3 inch flat ends. Occasionally mechanical vibrators powered by compressor trucks were used.[28] Once poured and rammed into place, the concrete was not to be disturbed until the final set had taken place.

When the final set of the first lift had taken place, the next set of vertical rods were wired to the first set of rods, which as noted had been set to project 20 diameters above the first lift. The second set of vertical rods projected to roof level and required supporting during pouring. Horizontal rods were fixed, and shuttering built up to the level of the second lift and the second lift poured. This process was repeated for the third lift. The final stage was to prepare the shuttering and reinforcement for the roof before pouring the roof.

It was important to get the concreting around the loopholes right. Instances occurred where loophole shuttering had been fixed and attempts to pour the concrete under the loophole shutter. This never succeeded, especially in the case of the double machine gun pillbox, as the concrete would shrink away from the shuttering and leave a cavity. The correct method was to pour concrete up to the loophole height and then ensure it was screeded to a fair face before the loophole shutters were fixed.

The method of transporting concrete to the shuttering was by steel barrows or skips. For transporting at ground level, skips running on Decauville track provided with turntables were useful. As the height of the work increased, some method of lifting the concrete from ground level was required – either some form of hoist or ramps (either barrow ramps or Decauville track ramps – Figure 8.15). Decauville ramps were not to exceed a 1:10 gradient. Specifications for barrow ramps also stated that a gradient of 1:10 was not to be exceeded and that the ramps were to be 18 inches wide. Elevated barrow ways around the pillbox were specified at 2ft 3in wide. At first, materials to construct these ramps were in short supply; the 5th Field Company had to resort to obtaining tubular scaffolding from Paris. At times there was insufficient scaffolding or timber to construct these ramps. In such cases, the only option was to construct platforms. If a hoist was unavailable the only method of lifting the concrete from platform to platform was by shovelling. To do this successfully both the mixer and platforms had to be moved round the pillbox; a rough concrete floor or slag laid around the site greatly facilitated the process.

28 Ramming is necessary to ensure concrete is worked thoroughly into place, especially around reinforcing rods and shuttering. It should be rammed into place until it forms a quaking jelly-like mass with all trapped air expelled. Mechanical vibrators have the advantage that a drier mix unworkable by hand can be used, thus giving a concrete of greater strength with the same cement content. Shuttering can also be struck sooner with mechanically rammed concrete. Spading tools or straightened hoes were useful for 'slicing' the concrete against shutters or previously completed work, ensuring a close-knit surface free from voids.

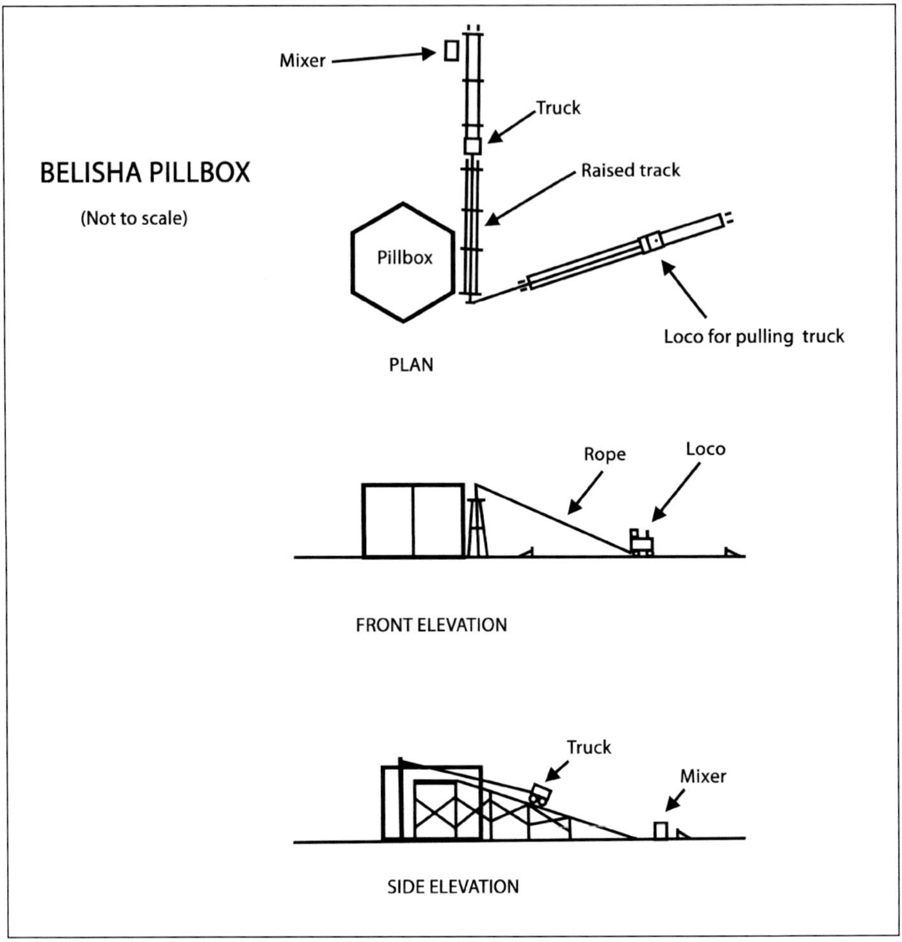

Figure 8.15: A method of lifting concrete from ground level by Decauville track ramps and a locomotive, used by the 200th Field Company to construct BELISHA pillbox.

Concrete hardens because of a chemical reaction between the cement and water. Once the pillbox was complete, measures had to be taken to ensure the retention of moisture in the concrete – this is known as curing. A variety of methods of curing could be used, such as continuous spraying with water, covering with hessian, sacking or similar materials saturated with water or leaving the shuttering in position for as long as possible and keeping it wet.

Table 8.1: Typical schedule of operations, labour and time for a 100 cubic yard pillbox built in good weather.

Operation No.	Operation	Labour	Time (hrs)	Tools and plant	Materials
1	Fixing steel reinforcement to floor level	2 steel fixers 4 unskilled	15	Wire nippers Two steel rules Three 1½ 1b hammers	Reinforcement binding wire 16 S.W.G. Chalk for marking steel Timber for templates and spacers
2	Concreting to floor level	1 mixer driver 2 concreters 14 unskilled	12	Mixer Wheelbarrows Shovels R.E measuring boxes 6'x6' timber platform Spading and ramming tools Screen board	Coarse and fine aggregates Cement Water Rough timber for shutters Nails, wire for ties
3	Fixing first lift steel, erecting entire internal shuttering and external shuttering for first lift	6 carpenters 4 steel fixers 12 unskilled	15	Carpenter tools Levels Wire nippers Steel rules	Timber for shuttering Nails -3",4" and 5" 6"x2" timber for templates and spacers Binding wire 9 S.W.G. Wire for shutter ties
4	Concreting first lift	As operation 2	8	Scaffolding and planks Watering cans Wire brushes Remainder as operation 2	As operation 2
5	Fixing steel and erecting shuttering for second lift	As operation 3	24	As operations 1 and 3	As operation 3
6	Concreting second lift	As operation 2	8	As operation 4	As operation 2
7	Fixing roof shutters and reinforcement	As operation 3	24	As operations 1 and 3	5 inch pipe for periscope Remainder as operation 2
8	Concreting roof	As operation 2	20	As operation 2 and 4	As operation 2
9	Curing	Unskilled	24	Hoses Watering can Sacking, hessian etc	Earth, sand and clay
10	Striking and cleaning shutters	Five skilled 25 unskilled	24		

To ensure work could take place in rainy conditions, a roof of corrugated iron sheets could be constructed over the pillbox. It was, however, the severe cold that caused serious delay to the pillbox construction programme, due to the difficulty of getting supplies of sand and aggregate to sites as already described and the difficulty of concreting in freezing temperatures. The period of disruption lasted from the end of December to 19 February when a rapid thaw set in. Although special measures could be taken to protect against frost (described below), for much of this period it was impossible to carry out any concreting at all.

Concrete which freezes before setting is complete and before it has become reasonably hard may disintegrate.[29] Generally, no concreting should take place when the atmospheric temperature is below 40 degrees F on a falling thermometer or below 36 degrees F on a rising thermometer unless special measures are undertaken: firstly, the temperature of the concrete has to be raised before pouring and secondly, while it sets a temperature maintained between 50 to 60 degrees F for four or five days if possible, and in no circumstances for less than 72 hours.

Concrete temperature could be raised by either heating the mixing water[30] or heating the aggregate with a brazier.[31] War Diaries of the field companies involved in pillbox construction show that both these methods were used. For example, on 20 December the 23rd Field Company noted that it was possible to pour the raft of a Bren gun pillbox and on 28 December pour the wall of a pillbox by heating water and aggregates. Instructions attached to the 200th Field Company's War Diary state that braziers for heating water and aggregates were to be left ready filled overnight and instructions given to light them at around 6:30 a.m. Working in these conditions was certainly unpleasant, especially the handling of the iron reinforcing bars; there was a danger of frost bite in men's fingers if they were not adequately protected.

Although heat is generated by the process of setting, further protection is necessary in very low temperatures (especially during the first hour after pouring when heat loss is at its greatest) to retain heat at 50 to 60 degrees F for at least 72 hours. Heat could be

29 Good quality concrete would not be permanently damaged after a certain amount of hardening had taken place; further hardening was merely delayed for the duration which it remained frozen.

30 A rise in 5 degrees F in the temperature of the mixing water produces a rise of approximately 1-degree F in the temperature of the concrete; thus, if the temperature is to be raised 20 degrees F, the water temperature should be raised to 100 degrees F. The maximum temperature to which water should be raised was about 180 degrees F. If water was heated above 50 degrees F the water and aggregate should be put in the mixer first, then after the drum has made a few revolutions the cement added. The object was to ensure the water was not too hot when it comes into contact with the cement otherwise a 'flash' set may take place.

31 When using braziers to heat aggregate, care had to be taken to ensure that heat was uniformly distributed and not localised, because otherwise the quality of aggregate may be become impaired from overheating. Furthermore, overheating may accelerate too greatly the setting time of the cement, or may evaporate the mixing water, resulting in the aggregate becoming covered with a thin film of dry cement.

retained in freshly poured concrete by covering with tarpaulins, thick sacking, straw or earth mattresses (sandbags or cement bags partially filled with straw or earth) and the use of braziers.[32] Various field company War Diaries show that all these methods were used to protect poured concrete. For instance, on 1 January the 23rd Field Company noted in their War Diary that braziers were left around poured concrete while it set. On 3 January, 15 degrees F of frost was recorded but the thermometer placed on the setting concrete at BACHY STATION pillbox did not fall below 36 degrees F. The War Diary again notes the use of braziers during and after pouring on 11 January and the use of corrugated iron sheets for windbreaks. However, on 9 February work was underway on pouring concrete for RUE D'HOTEL 2 pdr anti-tank gun pillbox and CARTER Bren gun pillbox when an intense cold set in during the afternoon and temperatures plummeted overnight resulting in the top layers of concrete freezing, which could not be protected due to a lack of coal for the braziers. It was noted that these layers would have to be removed the following day. While constructing a concrete plinth, the 11th Field Company erected a corrugated iron platform over braziers to bake aggregate and boil water before mixing. At the end of the day, a tent was made of lorry covers over the plinth and braziers lit to keep the frost out of the concrete. The War Diary recorded 'This was a great success but naturally the job took longer than usual and the plinth was not finished.'[33]

Earthing up and Burster courses

Pillboxes in the open could be given additional protection by placing a burster course and earth banks on the side likely to be exposed to enemy fire. As we have seen, adding a burster course was an approved alteration to the standard pillbox designs for ant-tank gun and machine gun pillboxes. For pillboxes sited close to an anti-tank ditch, the earth was easily won during the excavation of the ditch and transported to the pillbox site with dumpers. Concealment could be aided by either sowing grass seed or turfing. Any camouflage work, such as painting, had to be undertaken before earthing up. Burster courses were added to the exposed face of a pillbox before earthing up was carried out. If they were not added, the earth merely acted as a tamp for the exploding shell. Terre rouge or pavé stones were the most common materials used. By December, the question of providing reinforced concrete burster aprons on the enemy side of the pillbox was under consideration. This was apparently carried out on some pillboxes, for instance on MANSION HOUSE anti-tank gun pillbox by the 9th Field Company, although in March the 1st General Construction Battalion

32 If using braziers, the pillbox was enclosed in screens and the braziers lighted, low to the ground, inside the screens. Care had to be taken to ensure that the heat did not evaporate any water from the concrete. This was particularly important with steel shuttering, as steel shuttering has little insulation value compared to timber.

33 TNA: WO167/908, 11th Field Company War Diary, 4 January 1940.

RE noted that burster aprons would have to be omitted from new pillboxes due to a shortage of aggregate.

Concealment

Today, many of the pillboxes constructed by the BEF look very exposed. However, at least a good proportion of them would have been concealed. It was recognised that with the exception of painting, methods of concealing pillboxes would not survive battle. The object of concealment was therefore to deceive reconnaissance parties before battle and enable the pillbox garrison to achieve initial surprise. In general terms, the Engineer-in-Chief stated that concealment should deceive:

i. Aerial observation from a height of over 3,000 ft.
ii. The observer from a tank at a range of 300 yds.
iii. The artillery observer with glasses at a range of 1,000 yds.[34]

Little attempt seems to have been made to conceal pillboxes during construction in the open, unlike the French who were stated to attempt to conceal all theirs during construction. In practical terms, the British were probably right in the view that it was impossible to deceive the air camera from the fact that a pillbox was being built. Also, a pillbox certainly relied upon positive protection rather than on concealment compared to other forms of defence works. But it was subsequently possible to conceal the nature and size of the pillbox by camouflage. By February 1940, pillbox construction had reached a state where it was considered that much more attention should be given to camouflage on completion.

The first stage in concealing a pillbox was to remove all signs of construction in the neighbourhood and ensure that good track discipline was practised thereafter. Thus, each pillbox required an individual concealment scheme in relation to its surroundings. Concealment schemes for pillboxes could either be by artificial means (camouflage) or deception. The purpose of camouflage was to make the pillbox as inconspicuous as possible in relation to its surroundings – it was often its squat shape that gave it away. Deception attempted to alter the squat shape of the pillbox by a successful impression of another object or the use of dummy works.

The CRE 1st Division issued instructions that pillboxes, when completed, were to have a shed, barn or outhouse built over them to fit in with their surroundings. However, it was useless to attempt to disguise certain pillboxes, such as those near anti-tank ditches or in the open in the vicinity of trench systems. Such pillboxes had to be made as inconspicuous as possible by merging with the background. Those near anti-tank ditches could make use of the spoil from the ditch, with earth heaped

34 TNA: WO167/43, 'Camouflage of Pill Boxes', April 1940, GHQ Chief Engineer War Diary.

around the pillbox and sown with grass seed or laying turf. Exposed faces could be merged with disruptive painting which attempted to break up the outline of the pillbox (Figure 8.16). Steel wool was useful for loopholes and especially for those pillboxes which had an earth mound on the exposed side.[35]

The I Corps War Diary observed that 2nd Division painted all its finished pillboxes during January. Painting took practice to get right. The 11th Field Company noted that 'Our efforts in this direction have been somewhat armature.' The key faults were that faces were treated separately and not merged into one another, sharp edges to colours at the edges of the faces stood out and that the 'Whole treatment in some cases [was] rather futuristic and does not tone with the background.' However, with practice a good finish could be obtained. The Company completed a Bren gun post, and after three trials, 'perfect toning... [was] achieved with its surroundings. It is tacked on to a brick outhouse and fine old mottled brickwork effect has been produced. A corrugated roof has been put on.'[36] The frost held up painting as paint did not stick well to frozen concrete and the frost came out behind it. Batches of paint were also ruined by the frost and had to be sent back to a research laboratory for analysis.

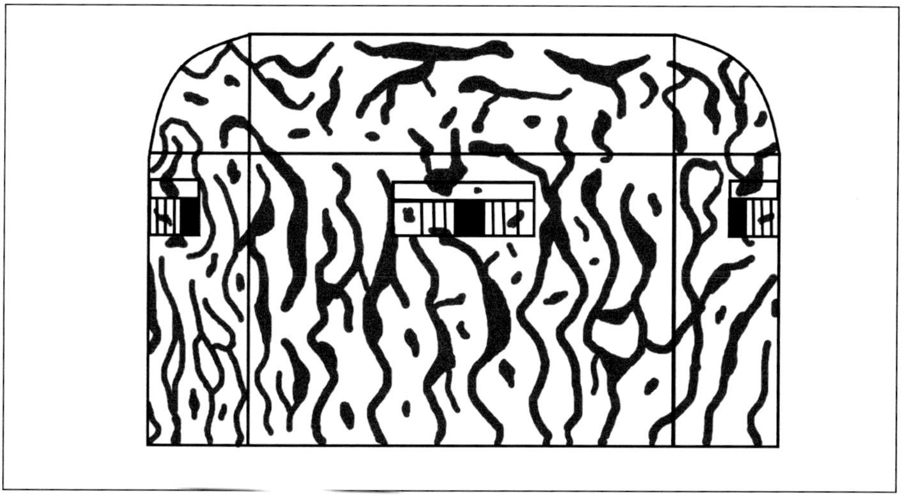

Figure 8.16: Sketch illustrating a disruptive painting scheme for a Bren pillbox, based on an original German photograph. It is broken up into small patches of dark and light to mimic similar ground patterns such as in orchards from the air. If the ground pattern was a plain surface, then a simpler treatment would be necessary.

35 Steel wool referred to rabbit wire netting 25 yards by 2 yards garnished with steel wool. Coarse and fine wool were applied to each roll in the proportion two thirds coarse and one third fine. The wool was rust proofed by Parkerising. A pure fine steel wool was also used for hand garnishing. Small arms ammunition and anti-tank gun rounds could be fired through it. The first order of 10,000 yds was shipped out in dark green and light earth. A bulk order for 600,000 square yards was placed in March.

36 TNA: WO 167/908, 11th Field Company War Diary, 26 January 1940.

The built-up landscape in much of the British zone, with the French architecture offering a variety of shapes and colours, meant that elaborate schemes of imitation were seldom required for disguise. The addition of a false tile roof and extensions in the form of a penthouse or lean-to shed could give the appearance of a barn, shed or outhouse. The camouflage could be enhanced by painting loopholes or constructing sandbag walls in neighbouring buildings. While working on the Corps Position, instructions issued by the 15 Brigade stipulated that camouflage on concrete works would take the form of tiles and a brick wall, one brick thick, on the outside of the concrete work. Similarly, a pillbox could also easily be made to appear as an extension to an existing building by constructing a brick wall one brick thick outside it. The choice of materials for constructing the disguise was important. It was clearly stated that corrugated iron should not be used because if it became dislodged it could block loopholes. Fibrous plaster, as used in cinema sets, was ideal as it was easily moulded to represent tiles, walls, doors, windows and so forth. It was also inexpensive and inflammable and stood up to the weather. If hit by shell fire it would disintegrate and not obscure the fire of the defence. However there was a trade off in its use as it diverted labour and transport, so was used only were it was considered essential to produce a convincing disguise.

Deception relied upon the free use of dummy pillboxes. On 22 February, the I Corps Camouflage Officer visited the 1st Division front when the question of dummy pillboxes was raised; the War Diary of CRE 1st Division noted that 'These are to be provided ready made from Corps as soon as possible. Considerable care will be needed in siting these from a tactical point of view.'[37] Dummy pillboxes could be constructed from scrim rabbit-wire and plaster on a frame. It was important that they should not be more obvious than the genuine pillboxes in the area and should therefore be camouflaged in a similar manor. It was also recommended that they should not appear suddenly but be constructed in a similar time span as real pillboxes. The War Diary of CRE I Corps records that the 105th Field Pack Company set up a workshop to manufacture dummy pillboxes. I Corps War Diary for March notes that during the month a total of nine dummy pillboxes were completed (three anti-tank, five machine gun and one Bren) and one dummy pillbox erected.

These techniques of concealment were to be widely used again on pillboxes constructed as part of Britain's anti-invasion defences.

Utilising First World War German pillboxes

When the 5th Division took over the part of the front held by the French 51st Division, Operating Instructions were issued stating that 'maximum use should be made of existing German pillboxes' in the Divisional Reserve Position. These

37 TNA: WO167/194, 1st Division Commander Royal Engineers War Diary, 22 February 1940.

German pillboxes were sited to oppose a breakthrough in a south-west direction from the Messines Ridge and the Ypres salient and were constructed in 1916 and 1917. In the most they consisted of three types – a twin machine gun emplacement, a single machine gun emplacement and shelters. Although over 100 still existed, with many in a good state of repair, not all were suited to the 5th Division Reserve Position Fire Plan so only a comparatively few could be utilised.

A good description of the solid construction of German pillboxes is given in Colonel E.G.L. Thurlow's booklet *The Pillboxes of Flanders*:

> The construction of the German concrete shelters and emplacements (Mannschafts –Eisenbeton – Unterstände or "Mebu" for short) was commenced in the Ypres area early in 1915 and was continued without interruption up to the commencement of the Battles of Ypres, 1917. The original idea of these concrete shelters was to provide protection for supports and reserves against the continuous fire of field guns and against individual shells from 15 c.m. field howitzers. These were followed by the solidly constructed blockhouses and machine-gun emplacements which provided such effective centres of resistance. The building of these structures was carried out by Fortress Engineers and Pioneers and also by Civil Engineers with previous peace-time experience in the construction of concrete work.
>
> Ferro-concrete was used from the very first in preference to plain concrete, but to begin with the reinforcement was not entirely satisfactory, as steel joists, screw pickets and any kind of scrap-iron were thrown in and buried in the concrete. Later, this form of construction gave place to ⅝ -inch round iron rods uniformly distributed over the whole structure, as it was found that the vibrations in girders, rails, screw pickets, etc., had a more disturbing effect on the mass concrete than the vibrations in the rods. The front walls and roofs of the shelters were from 2½ to 3 feet thick, and the surrounding earth was heaped up to a thickness of from 7 to 15 feet.
>
> At the start, sand and road material for the manufacture of the concrete was requisitioned locally, but later the gravel for the best quality concrete was brought from the Rhine through Holland *via* the Meuse and Scheldt in barges and by rail. It consisted of water-worn gravel, of flintstone and quartz broken to about ½-inch gauge. The sand was mostly coarse, sharp and clean. The best concrete shelters were quite capable of resisting direct hits by six-inch howitzers, heavy trench mortars and artillery of even greater calibre. In fact, in many cases the effect of shellfire on these structures was practically nil.[38]

38 Colonel E.G.L. Thurlow, DSO, psc, *The Pill-Boxes of Flanders* (London: Ivor Nicolson & Watson Ltd., 1933), p. 11.

A consequence of a pillbox's original purpose, some loopholes faced the wrong direction but others, although not perfect, were sufficient to almost give the required field of fire. Cutting new loopholes in existing concrete structures was a difficult task and required engineer assistance. Instructions specified that a careful reconnaissance was required before demands were made for new loopholes except for pillboxes that faced the wrong way. Most of the German pillboxes only had one or two loopholes. Thus, it would only be possible to fire the Bren gun and possibly the anti-tank rifle from cover; breastworks were required for the remainder of the section. Some German pillboxes were for shelter only, i.e. they had no loopholes. If these were used, breastworks were also required. At least one pillbox was used to give defilade cover to a 2 pdr anti-tank gun, the pillbox providing cover for the gun crew.

The OC 506th Field Company carried out a preliminary reconnaissance of pillboxes selected for occupation (table 8.2). In most cases, dirt had to be cleared out and in some cases, water pumped out. It was emphasised not to dump any dirt or material cleared out in the vicinity of the pillbox, otherwise this would betray its position. The infantry, as usual, supplied working parties to assist the engineers in the non-technical elements of work.

Fortified buildings

In urban areas such as in villages or towns, it made sense to site section posts in existing buildings. In most cases, the work required to bring them into a state of defence was fully reconnoitred but not commenced in order not to inconvenient the occupants. In the first instance, work would have included the strengthening of walls with sandbags and loop-holing – such a task was stated to take about two hours from the time of arrival at the house. The 15 Brigade, for example, when working on the Corps Position specified that a reserve totalling 40,000 sandbags was to be held which could be used for no other purpose than the interior defence of buildings. If time allowed, further strengthening could include shoring up of roofs with timber and strengthening with concrete and even adding a false roof with a burster and air layer. In order to reduce the number of buildings taken over for defence works, the 6 Infantry Brigade specified that pillboxes could be built under the cover of existing civilian buildings such as unoccupied buildings and barns, or if these were not available then constructing one before work on the pillbox was begun. A small number of buildings were actually prepared for defence, especially in situations when trench digging was impossible; for example, by the 3 Brigade in Mouchin and Bercu.

Some buildings were also to be demolished to clear lines of fire. Instructions in the 1st Grenadier Guards War Diary noted that such houses were to be prepared, even if occupied; liaison officers were to explain to the inhabitants that charges would only be blown in the event of an enemy advance and would be removed only when it was apparent that the sector was not to be a theatre of operations!

Given the lack of concrete available for unit HQs, cellars were an obvious alternative, and most brigade operating instructions specified that reconnaissances

Table 8.2: Schedule of German pillboxes earmarked for occupation in 5th Division Divisional Reserve Position and remarks of work required.

Location	Unit	Immediate work required	Remarks
709481	206 A.Tk Battery	Old German pump repaired.	A pump supplied by Brigade. Pillbox used as defilade cover for a 2 pdr gun. Gun detachment cover in pillbox.
709479	K.O.Y.L.I.	Diversion of existing field drain or spring that was flooding pillbox. Supply force pump until thus repaired. Recce air shaft with a view to conversion to a loophole. If feasible, cutting airshaft to loophole size.	Section post for K.O.Y.L.I.
707474	K.O.Y.L.I.	Nil.	Garrison for one section of K.O.Y.L.I.
696459	Y. & L.	Recce for level inside ceiling and ground outside with view to a loophole firing N.E.	Recce to be reported back to Brigade commander who would decide if it was to be carried out. Garrison for one section of Y. and L.
694460	Y. & L.	Chamber edge of existing loophole. Recce possibility of enlarging opening for steel observation shutter to take a Bren gun.	Chambering edge to be carried out forthwith. Enlarging opening to be carried out if feasible. Garrison for a platoon less one section of Y. & L.
689458	Y. & L.	Nil.	Garrison for one section of Y. & L.
687461	Y. & L.	Cut loophole facing N.E.	To be put in hand forthwith. Garrison for one section of Y. & L.
686458	Y. & L.	Nil.	Garrison for one section of Y. & L.
688456	Y. & L.	Nil.	Garrison for H.Q. Coy. Y. & L.

should be carried out for suitable HQs and Battle HQs. Work on shoring up cellars on buildings selected as HQs could be carried out straight away.

On the Saar Front, the 59th Field Company undertook what was described as a 'rather urgent' fortification of Grindorff village. This work was designed to be proof against grenades and bullets rather than shelling. Three houses were interconnected and windows and walls loopholed, and doors barricaded and made bullet proof.

9

The Defences: Part II - Field Works and Obstacles

Today, the only remnants of the BEF's defences are the concrete pillboxes, and it could be easy to forget that pillboxes formed only part of the defences. Pillboxes were not built in isolation but would have been supported by fire trenches and breastworks – actually, to be correct, pillboxes supported the field works by adding strength, and not the other way around. The defences were further enhanced by employment of obstacles, carefully sited to stop and canalise enemy tanks and infantry, so they could be destroyed by the fire of the defence. As with pillboxes, the task of constructing field works and obstacles was hampered by a shortage of materials and the harsh winter weather, with digging either washed away with heavy rain or all but impossible in frozen ground. The fact that the French *Ligne Princiaple* was sited on low-lying ground in the southern portion of the BEF sector because of its close proximity to the border with Belgium rather than on tactical grounds exasperated the problems caused by the wet weather. On the Saar Front, defences were rudimentary compared to the Gort Line. They consisted of isolated section posts with log cabins used for shelters, HQs and to house machine guns.

Infantry field works

The organisation of *SD* Lille for protracted defence has been described in Chapter 3. The initial intention of GHQ was to develop a full trench system along the FDL Line and the Brigade Reserve Position in accordance with *FSR Vol. II 1935*. The defence was then to be developed in depth further behind. The supporting weapons – machine guns and anti-tank guns – were to be sited in the general trace of the trench system. Only a limited amount of field defences had been completed by the French since mobilisation, consisting of communication trenches and a few fire positions. If possible, these were to be incorporated into the defences; if this was not possible, they could act as alternative positions or dummy positions.

Trenches

GHQ notified formations that trench systems should be developed in line with the sequence laid out in the relevant Field Engineering manuals.[1] At first, an extensive skeleton trench system was to be prepared with shallow crawl trenches dug to a depth of 3 feet. Then, platoon posts, machine gun positions, anti-tank gun positions and HQs were to be completed. Finally, the whole system of trenches between the posts and communication trenches were to be fully dug and completed. The intention of carrying out work in this order was to confront the enemy with an extensive trench system, forcing him to disperse his fire as well as providing alternative positions for the defenders. If work was concentrated on the main fire positions first, then the enemy would be able to deduce not only the location but also the strength of the garrison. However, the digging of full trench systems was to prove not viable due to the long fronts that had to be held and adverse weather conditions.

The platoon locality was to form the framework of the defence, but each locality was to be planned on a much larger scale than considered the norm or for the garrison available; i.e. it was a framework to build upon as time went on (Figure 9.1). Under these circumstances, a frontage of 100 yards was considered suitable for a platoon (the normal frontage being 60 – 70 yards). The section posts within a platoon locality were to be carefully sited and not just be the haphazard joining up of rifle pits: they had to be sited to fulfil the role allotted to the platoon, i.e. resistance to the front and mutual support to other localities to the flanks. Small trees (except fruit trees) and scrub could be cleared without further reference, and in consideration for local farmers, approaches to fields were not to be entrenched. Although each platoon only had three rifle sections plus an HQ section, the number of section posts was not to be limited to this number. Allowance also had to be made for emplacing Bren guns, anti-tank rifles and 2 inch mortars and in some cases 25mm anti-tank guns. The wider than normal fronts would facilitate offering a greater number of alternative positions and help to conceal the actual occupied positions from the enemy. At least one brigade recognised that the considerable lengths of unoccupied trenches could be of use to the enemy and instructed that plans should be prepared to render these trenches uninhabitable or at least uncomfortable for the enemy by wiring up or booby traps if time allowed and also the exact registering by trench mortars.

Section post fire trenches were to be dug to the specifications given in *Manual of Field Engineering (All Arms) 1933*, i.e. the standard three task trench.[2] Layouts

1 *Manual of Field Engineering Vol. I (All Arms) – 1933* and *Manual of Field Engineering Vol. II (RE) – 1936.*

2 In the first instance – Task I – a trench 3ft 6in wide and 3 feet deep was excavated, the spoil used to build up a parapet. This trench was then widened – Task II – and the spoil used to further build up the parapet until it was bullet proof, the rest being thrown on the parados. Finally, it was to be further deepened to allow a passage way – Task III – the spoil thrown onto the parados.

Figure 9.1: A text book trench platoon post. It has been revetted with XPM and corrugated iron. The rubble on the fire step gave a good grip. The parados is higher than the parapet and the wide berm prevents it from crumbling into the trench. The turf has been replaced on the parapet. (TNA: WO287/136)

were either to be zigzag, bastion or a modification of either depending on ground conditions. Instructions issued by the 9 Brigade specified that spoil from the traverses was to be placed in mounds, so that every third or fourth mound could hide a pillbox. Communication trenches linking up platoon localities had to allow men to walk upright without exposure, and the standard dimensions were 6 feet wide at the top, 6 feet deep and 2 feet wide at the bottom with parapets on both sides. As practiced in the Great War, GHQ required trenches to be named for easy reference. Soldiers often came up with their own names: for example, one trench was named 'Gort Blimey'!

The width and length of a standard fire trench did not give adequate protection against air attack or prolonged bombardment. In consequence, it was stated that shelter trenches not exceeding three feet in width should be dug close to each fire position, for example cut out the back of a traverse, in which the garrison other than sentries could remain in such periods. Corrugated iron was used to give some protection against the weather. Simple trench shelters with 12 inch to 2ft 6in roofs along the principal of 'cut and cover' provided protection against shrapnel and shell splinters. Contemporary photographs show many improvised designs for shelters and troops had to be reminded to stick to the official specifications for shelters as such 'amateur designs' were often not safe.

The GOC 1st Division was ahead of the game as he emphasised the value of deep narrow slit-trenches against tanks, as they could not crush down the trench if it was in good firm ground, and they could also not depress their guns low enough to fire into such trenches. However, ground conditions were against him, as they tended to collapse in the poor soil unless well revetted.

It proved to be one of the wettest autumns since the end of the Great War. The monthly rainfall recorded in Lille for October and November 1939 was 144mm and 156mm respectively, which was over double the average for the preceding decade (70mm and 63mm respectively).[3] Such volumes of rainfall soon resulted in water-logged ground and this largely determined the feasibility of developing trench systems. On the higher ground occupied by the 3rd Division, this was achievable in places, and for instance the 7 Guards Brigade did manage to dig considerable lengths of trenches (Figure 9.2). In the low-lying ground occupied by I Corps, where water was met just below the surface, many partially dug trenches had to be abandoned and breastworks constructed instead. As a result, in I Corps area no continuous trench system was dug, with digging confined to section posts.

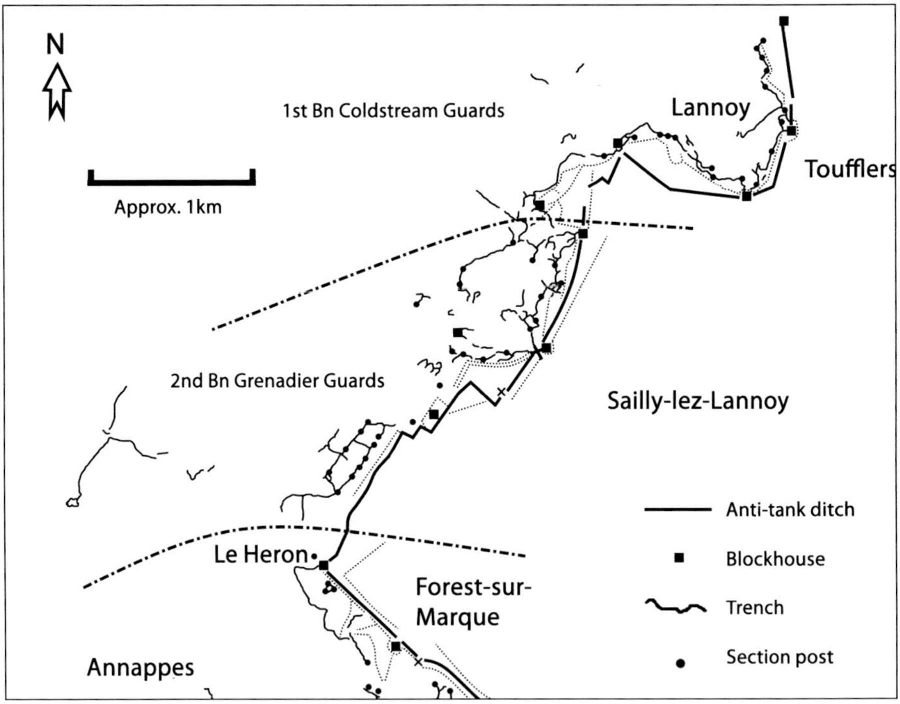

Figure 9.2: Map to illustrate trench system dug by 7th Guards Brigade.

3 Source: https://climexp.knmi.nl/data/pa7015_1929: 1939. dat.

Digging trenches in the pouring rain was difficult and miserable work as recorded by Catling: 'there is plenty of water in the trenches now. The men are digging them quickly and deeply, but the water streams in with the rain and oozes in from the sides as they dig.'[4] On the 7 Guards Brigade's front the trenches were described as 'small mill streams' in many places following heavy rain over the night of 25/26 October. Working on the Corps Reserve Position, the 2nd Battalion Bedfordshire Regiment was tasked with holding the Bois De Phalempin near a village called Petit Attiches. In his book, *Five Days to Live*, Second-Lieutenant R.H. Medley gives a vivid description of the havoc caused by the rain on entrenching in this wood:

> Our daily task was to develop fire bays and connecting trenches for the whole company position. At the end of the first week all sections had completed their fire bays and a good start had been made on connecting trenches – then the rain came...It rained and rained, and we carried on digging, but work was now delayed whilst water was pumped out of the trenches. Eventually, the water level in the ground rose and our digging was awash.[5]

From bitter experience, it soon became apparent that it was essential to dig drainage ditches before digging trenches and to keep them in good repair. The 1st Battalion Royal Berkshire Regiment recorded that each trench required at least one drain, and every drain in the village of Bercu was opened up, the whole eventually draining into the anti-tank obstacle. Such drains had to be revetted with wire netting or brushwood hurdles and could be as long as 200 yards (Figure 9.3). Agricultural drains did not help matters, causing flooding and damage to many trenches. In many instances, as already noted, the rain led to commanding officers deciding to abandon trench digging and build up breastworks instead; for example, on 20 October, the OC 3rd Battalion Grenadier Guards decided to abandon 25 percent of trenches worked upon and construct breastworks instead. Even if trenches were currently in a serviceable condition, it was recognised many would be flooded by winter and as a result reconnaissance's for alternative positions for breastworks were carried out. This was especially the case where troops had utilised existing ditches which were dry at the time to enable rapid construction of trenches.

It was not only the weather which delayed trench digging. There was a general shortage of entrenching tools, with for instance the 3rd Division's War Diary noting 'all units ask for more.'[6] Wood required for revetting was always in short supply. Initially, the BEF estimated that 1,000,000 pickets and 10,000m^3 of squared timber

4 Skene Catling, *Vanguard to Victory: An Account of the first months of the British Expeditionary Force in France* (London: Methuen & Co. Ltd., 1940), p. 10.
5 R.H. Medley, *Five Days to Live: France 1939–40* (Abergavenny: Dover & Company, 1992), p.11.
6 TNA: WO167/218, 3rd Division General Staff War Diary, 17 October.

Figure 9.3: A drain 200 yards long from a trench leading into the anti-tank obstacle. Before digging this drain, the water in the trench was up to the fire step. (TNA: WO287/136)

of various sizes were urgently required at the front to satisfy the countless competing demands for timber. Many troops were tempted to cut surrounding brushwood for revetting material, often removing valuable cover for the defences and without the permission of landowners. Such cutting caused serious damage to woodland and disputes with landowners were frequent. For instance, the 2nd Battalion Dorsetshire Regiment had cut revetting material from the Forest of Marchiennes during most of October, but was stopped from doing so because of damage to the wood, and instead they had to resort to angle iron and rabbit netting. Forestry experts were brought over to investigate how best to clear up the damage caused to woodlands; for example Major Gordon was tasked with cleaning up the woods in the 1st Division's area. The shortage of timber meant only fire positions and essential communication trenches to them or to pillboxes could be revetted and provided with duckboards. This lack of revetting resulted in collapse and slips in places. From November onwards, it was the supply of brushwood that largely governed the progress of work on the trenches because in the conditions it was useless to dig trenches if they could not be revetted immediately. Many units resorted to acquiring materials lying about, 'apparently serving no useful purpose'. For instance, during November the *Société nouvelle des briqueteries du Nord* complained to the *1ére Région Militaire* about the 'requisition' of 300 corrugated iron sheets. Instructions were soon issued to bring these practices to a halt, following numerous complaints from French citizens.

Another factor that hindered the work was a lack of experience in trench digging – in the main, peace time training was limited to digging weapon-pits only – which resulted in numerous mistakes being made in the construction of trenches with immunity from enemy action. Poor revetting was perhaps the most common mistake; it was noted that when the soil froze then thawed, poorly revetted trenches collapsed and the demand on labour for repairs was far greater than that required for digging them in the first instance! Other common faults were smoothing off the parapet and parados to make the trench look neat – this was wrong and potentially dangerous, as a man firing over a parapet was very obvious compared to the smooth line of the parapet or the background of a straight parados – and unnecessarily long fire bays and traverses too short. As men were not actually occupying the trenches, they were also liable to forget the need for the provision of latrines.

Nevertheless, despite these difficulties, by the end of October, most rifle and machine gun battalions had completed section posts and prepared alternative positions. In most cases these had not been linked by a trench system except on the 3rd Division's front as noted above. On 3 November, the 1st Division issued orders stating that no communication trenches were to be dug, but the trace of all communication trenches worked out should still be marked on maps so they could be completed at a later date if required. Progress continued throughout November and by the end of the month I Corps reported that all section posts had been completed on the FDL Line, Brigade Reserve and Divisional Reserve Positions. Progress slowed later in the year due to the freezing conditions, making digging impossible. After the thaw set in towards the end of February, many of the trenches required draining with the use of pumps and repairing as they had suffered collapse in places.

For the most part, no attempt was made to camouflage trenches from aerial observation; instead reliance was placed upon the extent of the trench network to make it difficult for the enemy to locate the actual fire positions. Crawl trenches were the prime means of achieving this. *MTP No. 26 – Notes on Concealment and Camouflage* elaborates further:

> Trench systems cannot be directly concealed, and deception must be resorted to instead. The most satisfactory method is by presenting the enemy with a continuous system alike in all parts so that he cannot pinpoint centres of resistance or discover the organization [sic] of the defence. Such a system is likely to take time to complete and, if it has been developed regularly, as for instance by expansion from section posts, the enemy will have opportunity for discovering the organization [sic] during the early stages of the work. It is most important, therefore, that from the very start there should be digging at places other than those to actually occupied. The crawl trench method of rapidly connecting up

> the occupied and dummy weapon-pits throughout the system, has for its chief objective the defeating of the enemy air or ground observer in this way.[7]

However, in cases where a full trench system was not developed some brigades did issue instructions for camouflaging section posts; for example, the 1 Guards Brigade issued instructions that when dug, section posts were to be covered with branches and bushes etc. to give some attempt to hide them from aerial observation. Section posts in woods could also be easily concealed with the use of natural materials and nets (Figure 9.4).

Figure 9.4: A well concealed section post sited under trees. The use of natural materials, no fresh spoil showing, and the use of nets all help to conceal the post.

Infantry breastworks

It has already been described how heavy rain led to some completed trenches being abandoned and breastworks constructed instead. On some parts of the front, particularly in the 2nd Division's area, when digging was commenced water was a met just below or in some cases immediately below the surface. In such circumstances,

7 *Notes on Concealment and Camouflage – M.T.P. No. 26* (London: The War Office, 1939), pp. 15–16.

there was no alternative but to construct breastworks, as described by Signaller R Brown, HQ Coy 2nd Norfolk Regiment:

> It was a water-logged area and in some places we couldn't dig deep enough. We tried to go down about six feet but could only manage four then we had to build revetments above and make our own wattle hurdles out of wood and fill them with soil and stones to build it above ground. We had pumps going if the trench was any depth to take water out all the while.[8]

One advantage of breastworks over trenches was that they could be sited on lower ground or reverse slope positions so to avoid observation but still allow for a reasonable field of fire. GHQ specified that if it was necessary to construct breastworks, they must be constructed in accordance with the *Manual of Field Engineering (All Arms) Vol. I,* with care taken to make the parapet bullet proof and the parados splinter proof (although later it had to be admitted that the illustrations in this manual showed the parapet and parados the same height which was wrong; the parados should be higher than the parapet).

At first, a shortage of sandbags hampered the construction of breastworks. Second-Lieutenant R.H. Medley, having had to abandon trench digging continued his narrative:

> The decision was now made to build up a lengthy and time-consuming task as earth had to be dug and moved to provide earthworks in front and behind the selected position. The soldiers worked with a will, but progress seemed very slow...The completion of No 2 Section position above ground took some eight weeks...We had a problem in obtaining sandbags – as only one hundred were available for the battalion – the situation eased later. Rumour had it that all initial supplies of sandbags had been used for key buildings in England![9]

Brooke, writing in his diary on 22 October, was scathing about a vital supply shortfall:

> Still very short of sandbags, when one remembers the lavish use made of sandbags at home in localities that will never see a bomb, it makes one's blood boil to be so short out here.[10]

Incredibly, the French had also asked the BEF during October if they could supply them with 20,000,000 sandbags urgently!

8 Peter Hart, *The 2nd Norfolk Regiment: From Le Pardis to Kohima* (Barrnsley: Pen & Sword Books Ltd., 2011), p. 28.
9 Medley, *Five Days to Live*, p. 11.
10 Alex Danchev, & Daniel Todman (eds.), *War Diaries 1939–1945: Field Marshall Lord Alan Brooke* (Berkeley and Los Angeles: University of California Press, 2001), p. 9.

The lack of peace time training in breastwork construction showed when an officer from GHQ, Lieutenant-Colonel Godfrey-Faussett, made visits to field defences and was requested to report back his findings to the Chief Engineer. He was amazed to find that on not one occasion that he visited troops working did he see a RE officer or NCO advising the infantry. He concluded that the infantry was working hard and enthusiastically on unfamiliar work in bad soil, but making a lot of mistakes that could have been put right by engineer advice. Common mistakes he found included the proper bond of sandbags not being used, badly made brushwood hurdles which in some cases were falling apart before they had even been put in place, and wire anchorages for hurdles not far back enough. He believed that this would lead to breastworks caving in when thaw followed frost. He also discovered that the 'trench' between breastworks was often too wide giving little protection. In one case, he found a fire step on either side of the breastwork. The officer stated that he had been ordered to do this to provide all round fire. However, it just made the trench unnecessarily wide; for all round fire alternative positions should be provided. In one or two cases, borrow pits for breastworks were right up against the outer edge of the breastwork, with a risk that the breastwork would slide into the borrow pit!

At least some of those constructing breastworks had little faith in them, and probably with good reason. Captain Henry Faure Walker, HQ 7 Guards Brigade recollected:

> We made the best of a bad job by erecting breastworks. These consisted of peat and were revetted by the kind of basketwork fascines of which one saw drawings from the Crimean War. They would not have stopped a bullet, or a shell, and would probably have been washed away by heavy rain.[11]

Breastworks were difficult to camouflage. If they could be sited on the edge of woodland, this would help conceal them. For those sited in the open, for example to command an anti-tank obstacle, they could be camouflaged to represent dumps of sugar beet, haystacks, piles of brushwood or whatever else harmonised with the ground on which the breastworks were constructed.

The necessity to cover blockhouses and anti-tank obstacles in the flat countryside led to the construction of some extraordinary breastworks because fire positions needed to be built upwards to achieve this. For instance, the 2nd Battalion Grenadier Guards had to build some breastworks 8 feet high as defenders had to see over the anti-tank obstacle, which was a revetted bank on the near side of a river, 6 feet high. Perhaps the most extraordinary breastworks constructed by the BEF were some of those of A Company, 2nd Battalion Norfolk Regiment constructed in the Rumegies area as recalled by Captain Barclay:

11 Joshua Levine, *Forgotten Voices: Dunkirk* (London: Ebury Press, 2011), p. 17.

> Many of my platoon section positions were breastworks and some even were built in trees to raise them off the ground sufficiently to give a field of fire – with of course an enormous 'build up' or foundation underneath. We had to make hurdles, stiffened up by either lopped off trees or great thick stakes and filled with earth. They were quite extraordinary and really, seemingly ridiculous. Enormously high breastworks in front and a splinter proof back drop behind, otherwise they resembled trenches in trees.[12]

These breastworks were built to cover the stream L'Elnon, the FDL Line anti-tank obstacle in this area. It had been chosen as an anti-tank obstacle by the French because of its close proximity to the border, not because of its tactical value. Captain Barclay remembers that these breastworks were always popular with the 'VIP' sightseers because nobody had ever seen anything like them before (or would ever likely see anything like them again).

Machine gun posts

As we have already seen, the key machine guns of the defence were to be emplaced in concrete pillboxes. For other guns, or until the pillboxes had been constructed, some type of field work was required. If possible, these field works were to be situated in areas not likely to be subject to enemy artillery concentrations. The machine gun posts that would do the greatest damage to the enemy, and escape damage themselves, would be those completely concealed and camouflaged, and great care was required to ensure that posts remained concealed. Use of the environment was made to conceal guns, for example in hen houses, outhouses, edges of woods and orchards etc. In open country conditions, posts probably consisted of simple field works such as those described in the 2nd Battalion Cheshire Regiment's War Diary. Given the task of preparing positions for penetration fire tasks on the 1st Division's front, the Battalion prepared two-gun positions comprising of two standard 6 feet square gun platforms connected by a communication trench with an observation post between the two guns. The standard camouflage equipment for machine guns in the field consisted of a spider frame, complete with a telescopic support which supported a 14 feet by 14 feet garnished net. However, more elaborate use of netting and natural foliage was used to cover the prepared field works. A few machine guns were placed in the FDL Line to cover the intervening ground between blockhouses. In such cases concealment was paramount and cut and cover dugouts with a 12 inch thick concrete roof were considered enough. These could be incorporated into a trench system to appear as a traverse.

12 Francis Peter Barclay, IWM interview <http://www.iwm.org.uk/collections/item/objects/8000793> (Accessed 24 August 2017).

When constructing a machine gun post in the field, trucks were instructed not to leave the road and thus prevent a track identifying its location. Instead, tools and materials were to be offloaded on the road and carried to the post. All work was to be carried out under camouflaged nets and other suitable camouflage material such as brushwood and scrub, unless the site was already under cover from aerial observation. Once completed, they were not to be occupied until attack was imminent so as to avoid making tracks.

AA Bren guns

For infantry Bren guns sited in an AA role, square emplacements and not circular ones were specified, as from the air they would resemble other works such as latrines, refuse pits etc. Instructions stated they should be about 5 feet deep with some sort of simple shelter for the sentry. When not occupied, they could be covered with wire netting garnished with scrim or hessian.

Infantry field works on the Saar Front

The BEF also experienced great difficulty digging in along the Saar Front because of the frozen ground. The 1 Guards Brigade, which toured the Saar Front in February, reported that all they could achieve was the building a few log cabins well back in the woods, to which at least men from the forward posts could be withdrawn for rest and to cook meals. On their tour, the 15 Brigade noted that not a single post they took over was bullet proof and as the earth was so frozen it was impossible to fill sandbags. An attempt was made to get down to soft earth by blowing small charges, but it was found the holes created froze solid in a short time. Other factors that limited what could be achieved were the difficulty of finding working parties with battalions having all four companies in the line and the fact that materials had to be brought up to the front using mules and infantry work parties.

It was not until the freeze ended that work on improving the defences could begin in earnest. During April, the 59th Field Company dug a number of new section posts along the lines of those already dug in *SD* Lille. Each section post, typically for 10 men, consisted of fire bays linked up with short communication trenches and a 'cut and cover' dugout that could hold six men. Digging was described as hard work, the ground being impermeable clay and water in the surface had to be drained away first. With the use of catchment drains and digging the drain before any other digging was carried out, the clay remained dry and workable. Revetment was of brushwood or XPM. The parapet was constructed of at least two layers of sandbags filled with earth. The parados was constructed higher than the parapet to break up the outline of the post. As the posts were isolated, latrines had to be provided for each post. No attempt was made to link up the section posts with communication trenches.

Log cabins provided shelter and some protection for machine guns on the Saar Front. During February, D Company, 2nd Battalion Cheshire Regiment, was detached from the Battalion and placed under the command of the 1 Guards Brigade on the Saar front and its war diary provides a good description of the type of machine gun post taken over from the French. The Company took over two-gun positions in Bizing Wood and two in Winkelmerter Wood. The gun positions in Bizing Wood consisted of log shelters reinforced with earth and sandbags and set back about 20 yards into the wood. There was sufficient room inside for four men to sit. The guns pointed though apertures which could be closed by boards placed outside. Directions for fixed lines were obtained by using aiming posts during the day and aiming lamps by night. The gun positions were wired all-round, with a mass of trip wires inside the perimeter which it was decided to remove to allow the section to move freely about while inside the perimeter. The position overlooked the valley of Heltenbach, an anti-tank obstacle at the time, and the gun arcs were entirely frontal and plunging fire. The gun positions at Winkelmerter Wood were similar, except smaller and appeared lower as they were dug down a little and again located just inside the wood. The gun arcs were also frontal, covering the Hermes Bach and Hermes Wald. An observation post for one of the guns was in the top of a tree adjacent to the gun position. In neither case were the positions or fire tasks considered entirely suitable; it being preferable to locate the guns closer to the line of FDLs and firing in enfilade. The weather conditions prevented the construction of new positions and the only work that could be carried out was strengthening the current positions to withstand the thaw when it arrived.

Log cabins were also used as HQs. The 59th Field Company describes the construction of a number of partially sunk log cabins for use as a battalion HQ in L'Oberterwald, making use of a large amount of fallen fir trees. First an excavation and drain were dug. A raised floor, about 9 inches off ground level, was laid in three strips to facilitate removal if the cabin started to flood and the drain became choked. Heavy steel troughing was used for the roof. The whole cabin was then earthed up. The road up to the HQ was under enemy observation, and before work could begin a screen had to be built to conceal movement.

Artillery field works

Artillery was not given concrete protection, but instead emplaced in field works (Figure 9.5). These field works generally consisted of gun pits with sandbag screens. At first, as we have already seen, there was an acute shortage of sandbags which made fortifying the gun positions difficult. In some instances, use had to be made of four-gallon empty petrol tins filled with earth to supplement sandbags as a temporary measure. Gun platforms could be improved with the construction of wheel beds and tail supports. These were improvised with materials at hand, acquired honestly or otherwise, and one troop for instance incurred the displeasure of a local farmer by removing bricks for use in the gun position which 'were not for sale'. Dugouts and PAD slit trenches were prepared for the protection of the gunners. As with infantry trenches, the heavy rain flooded many gun pits and the only option was to build up.

Figure 9.5: A gun pit for a 25 pdr field gun. The caption on the photograph notes bad sandbagging as all the sandbags on the left are headers. (TNA: WO287/136)

Although the decision was taken early on not to provide field artillery with concrete protection, the commander of I Corps was still concerned about the provision of overhead cover for guns in modern warfare. He noted that standard elephant iron shelters were not large enough for the 25 pdr. In response, the CE I Corps did design a portable corrugated iron shelter. The War Diary of the 23rd Field Company mentions an 'experimental' gun pit for a 25 pdr with the provision of overhead cover using elephant iron.

A good quality platform was vital for the medium and heavy guns. To get the guns into position for action when the BEF first arrived in *SD* Lille, temporary standings were constructed with any material at hand as engineering material was in short supply. The 5th Heavy Regiment's War Diary notes that 'home made' standings using hurdles and ash were only moderately successful. Bricks were also frequently used for standings. Throughout October and November work was carried out to provide proper platforms for the guns. Platforms were usually of a continuous heavy timber decking laid on top of a mattress of rubble and expanded metal. In some cases concrete was used. It was not always easy moving the guns from the temporary standings to the newly constructed platforms. On 6 November, the 5th Heavy Regiment attempted to move a gun from a standing to a platform. During the move, an air raid alarm was sounded, and the Scammell gun tractor moved into cover. The weight of the gun broke into a hidden sewer. It took a day to rescue the gun. Another of its guns could not be moved onto a new platform by a Scammell gun tractor due to the bogey nature of the ground; the War Diary records that manpower – 115 men – was required to complete the task!

In order to prevent enemy aerial reconnaissance from discovering the position of gun pits, camouflage netting had to be erected before work started on digging the gun pit and digging carried out underneath it. Furthermore, it was recommended practice that dummy positions should be dug first for deception purposes. For artillery weapons, camouflage equipment was standardised in two sizes: a 30 feet by 30 feet frame with 29 feet by 29 feet net for field artillery and 36 feet by 36 feet frame with a 35 feet by 35 feet net for medium artillery. The centre of the net was garnished thickly with strip canvas or opaque patches, thinned out towards the edges to prevent pronounced shadow. Due to the shortage of camouflage material, vehicle nets were used to supplement gun nets. The shortage of camouflage material remained into December, I Corps War Diary noting that 'improvised materials' were used where possible. With the likely move forward into Belgium, there was a general policy to replace twine camouflage nets with wire nets, the camouflage twine nets being retained for any forward movements. In villages, buildings, such as open barns, could also be used to conceal guns.

For anti-tank guns sited in the field and not in concrete pillboxes or under cover, simple gun pits were prepared. It was necessary that these remained hidden until it was necessary to open fire. The standard camouflage equipment consisted of a 24 feet by 24 feet garnished net supported by a large spider clamped to the gun shield, but this was found to be not entirely satisfactory as it limited the traverse of the gun and if a wide field of fire was required it would have to be thrown off. Thus other means were necessary to camouflage guns such as the use of painted scrim canvas, coir mats, natural foliage and every other means of concealment available.

Bofors AA guns at the front were emplaced in sandbagged gun pits, with a short communication trench linking the gun pit to a shelter dugout for the crew. Catling describes one dugout as 'constructed of corrugated iron, lengths of railway line, sandbags and all sorts of odds and ends, including the excavated remains of what were dug-outs occupied by Germans in the last war'.[13] These dugouts were often named by the troops: 'Dirty Dick's' and 'Café Anglais', being two examples, the latter visited by the King when touring the front. The space inside the dugouts was often reminiscent of the Great War:

> The furnishing and décor is of the 1914-18 style: rather severe, everything of unvarnished wood – floor boards, seats, panelling. To the left are box seats, a table. To the right is a brightly burning stove, whose chimney goes up through the roof. On each side of the stove are heavy, wood-framed, wire-netting-seated divans, each six feet long and one of them with a frame above it in the manner of a ship's bunk.[14]

13 Catling, *Vanguard to Victory*, p. 7.
14 Ibid, pp.19–20.

Camouflaging such gun positions was difficult, particularly the disposal of spoil. If the layout of the position could be made to conform to the general rectangular pattern of the countryside, this could go a long way to concealing a position. It was suggested that if the movement of guns and the construction of the posts damaged this pattern, it would be necessary to remove all crops and plough the ground in a rectangular shape. A firm track discipline, if combined with planned and firm tracks laid down early on, could also substantially reduce damage to the surrounding area.

Obstacles

The purpose of obstacles, both natural and artificial, according to the military manuals of the time was twofold:

> i. To hold attacking troops under the close fire of the defence, so that they may be destroyed by that fire.
> ii. To restrict the freedom of manoeuvre of an attack, and to herd it into pockets where it can be effectively dealt with by the fire of the defence.[15]

Obstacles of the first category are known as protective obstacles while those of the second category are known as tactical obstacles. Some obstacles, if they acted as a deterrent to attack, were in effect both tactical and protective. As with other aspects of the defence, they had to be sited in depth and to a definite tactical plan. They had to be covered by the fire of the defence otherwise their value was limited to the time required for its unopposed passage. However, the effect of strong natural obstacles, such as rivers, could have an appreciable effect in limiting the probable lines of attack by AFVs. The British also recognised that in modern mechanised warfare, attacks tended to gravitate towards roads, so obstacles should commence from roads.

Anti-tank obstacles

The principal consideration for the BEF defences was the need to defeat a mass tank attack. Although both the flanks of the BEF were secured with good natural anti-tank obstacles (River Lys on the north flank and the inundated Scarpe on the south flank), there was little in the way of natural anti-tank obstacles on the rest of the front. Artificial obstacles such as anti-tank ditches and minefields were necessary to both economise on the use of anti-tank guns and to cover the gaps between natural obstacles. The need to update pre-war ideas on anti-tank obstacles to meet the threat of modern tanks meant that many anti-tank obstacle trails were started in France, and were continued back home at Farnborough.

15 *Engineer Training – 1937* (London: HMSO, 1937), p. 127.

Anti-tank Ditches

During the inter-war years, the British had little faith in long stretches of continuous artificial obstacles in the open such as anti-tank ditches as they required an immense amount of labour to construct and would be well known to the enemy, and would, therefore, be of little value. However, ditches could be prepared in the artificial peace of the Sitzkrieg, unlike mines which could only be laid when imminent contact with the enemy was likely. The extreme shortage of anti-tank mines also necessitated the need for ditches.

Anti-tank ditches, described by one writer as 'a kind of elongated hencoop for steel hens',[16] were sited on the same principal as other obstacles i.e. protectively along the front and tactically to canalise the attack into areas from which they could be best dealt with by the weapons of the defence. Ditches had to be enfiladed by fire from anti-tank guns and machine guns since the enemy would easily succeed in crossing them if left unmolested (Figure 9.6). When the BEF took over the *SD* Lille, only a single anti-tank ditch existed, which had been sited so as not to yield any French territory rather than on tactical grounds. The French tended to build their anti-tank ditches in straight lengths. In some cases, there was a kink at each blockhouse to prevent the anti-tank guns from being able to fire directly at the neighbouring blockhouse, but on occasions the ditch was straight between two blockhouses which would have allowed this to happen. Gaps in the anti-tank ditches, for example at blockhouse sites, were closed with Champs de Rails (Figure 9.7).

Figure 9.6: French built anti-tank ditch, with blockhouse sited in line with the obstacle for enfilade fire. (TNA: WO287/136)

16 Colin Coote, (introduction), *War Pictures by British Artists,* (London: OUP, 1942), introduction.

Figure 9.7: French Champs de Rails consisting of four rows of rails of unequal height and wired as an obstacle to infantry as well. The obstacle is continued in the background by a ditch. (TNA: WO287/136)

Typically, the French ditches were about 5 feet deep and, in many places, had no revetting (Figure 9.8). The slope down from the enemy side was about 45°. GHQ considered these ditches would become passable if subjected to a bombardment. In places where the ground was too marshy to allow the trench to be dug to its full depth the obstacle was completed by means of a breastwork, which, as we have seen, made them difficult to cover with weapon fire. With the harsh winter weather, many of the French dug ditches fell into a state of bad repair in many places.

Not all French anti-tank ditches were as well prepared. In the Bailleul – Armentières area taken over by the 51st Division, it was discovered that a considerable part of the French anti-tank ditch was too narrow and had not been revetted, so that it was not an effective obstacle. In places, it was also found the French had used the road side ditch and bank as a tank obstacle, with rails placed on the top of the bank.

Although the French generally relied upon single or double pillboxes firing along straight stretches of ditch in both directions, this was not the case everywhere. On the 6 Brigade's front the anti-tank ditch was formed from the stream L'Elnon. The blockhouses were sited in the rear of the ditch, so could not command it but could oppose attempts to cross it. The Brigade started work on a second ditch, so aligned that the existing blockhouses could enfilade it, but had to abandon the attempt as the winter weather closed in.

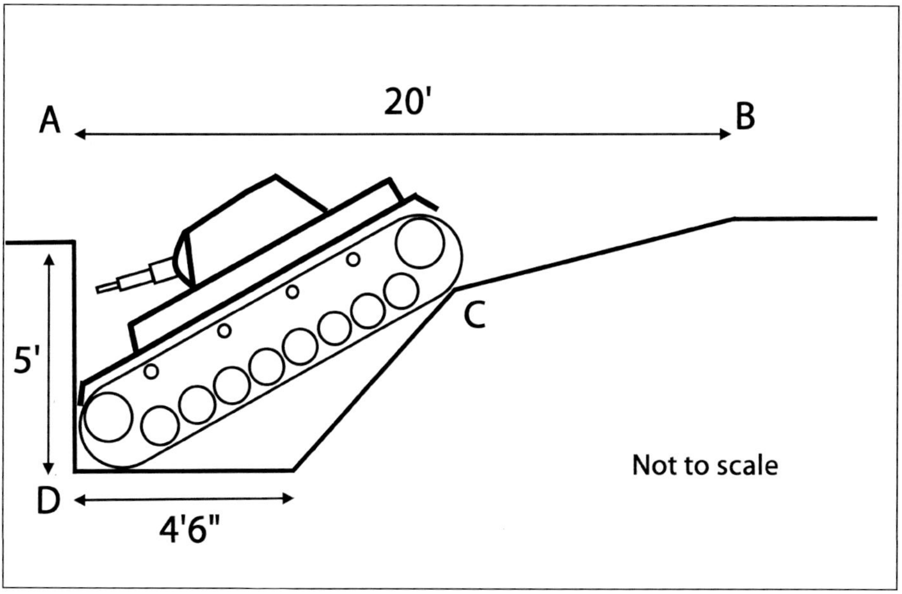

Figure 9.8: Sketch to illustrate a French anti-tank ditch. The French constructed the ditch so that it was too wide to be crossed by any known tank (A to B). As the tank passes point B, it starts to go downhill, and if it passed point C its falls with its nose at point D. It now rests with its nose at point D and tail at point C with the remainder of the tracks off the ground, giving the minimal amount of purchase from the tracks. From A to B it is in full view of the anti-tank gun in one of the blockhouses. If enemy infantry tried to get into the ditch to bridge it, they would likewise be in full view of the light machine gun in the blockhouse.

The BEF immediately planned and began work on a series of positions in depth each covered by a continuous anti-tank obstacle, consisting in the main of anti-tank ditches. Defended localities were not, however, to be provided with an all-round artificial anti-tank ditch because of the labour involved and the fact it would give the position of the locality away. Instead, use was to be made of tank proof obstacles such as woods and villages in which to site localities, with an artificial anti-tank ditch linking up these natural obstacles. Where canals, rivers and streams did exist, these were incorporated into switch lines. Rivers and streams could easily be improved by deepening and widening with a dragline and building up and revetting the rear bank (Figure 9.9). For example, the 3rd Division made use of the River Marcq from where it bends just south of Bouvines to Pont-à-Marcq. However, this could cause problems with covering the obstacle by weapon fire, as already noted above. The second position was to make full use of the canal lines: Canal de la Sensée – Canal de la Haute Deûle – La Bassée Canal.

Figure 9.9: A small stream improved as an anti-tank obstacle by revetting the rear bank with brushwood and raising the height of the bank with earth. Such raised banks could cause difficulties in covering the obstacle with weapon fire. (TNA: WO287/136)

In principal, the BEF decided to complete anti-tank ditches in the forward areas with short angled sections rather than long straight sections as was the French practice, with each section running slightly to the front from each pillbox to avoid them shooting at each other. The anti-tank weapons would now fire at a slight angle into the ditch and not straight down it; this had the advantage that no one tank could mask the fire of the anti-tank gun. As we have already seen (Chapter 6) existing straight ditches were converted to angled sections along parts of the 4th and 5th Divisions front by digging stretches of new ditches in a bastion trace in front of the existing ditch. The specification for the layout of the anti-tank ditch along the Corps Reserve Position is described in Chapter 5.

GHQ issued a standard design for an anti-tank ditch (Figure 9.10). This design specified that the ditch should be dug to a minimum depth of 5 feet below ground, but the deeper the better. A minimum width of 18 feet from the point from which an attacking tank would start overbalancing to the top of the opposite face of the ditch was specified. The width of the bottom of the ditch should be a maximum of 6ft 6in; the tank must be made to tip downwards into the ditch. In practice, the actual dimensions would be limited or adapted by the type of machinery in use, the length of available revetting posts or if utilising an existing ditch. Mechanical excavators could only achieve a depth of around 5 feet at first but with larger dragshovels that became available from late November a depth of 7 feet to 7ft 6in could be achieved. In most cases, a ditch was dug by a drag shovel and dragline working together. The drag shovel took the lead, taking out the vertical wall and flat bottom of the ditch while the dragline followed, taking out the battered slope (Figure 9.11). In the flat parts of country, especially in I Corps sector, it was essential that the excavated spoil did not provide cover to attacking infantry or obscure the fire of the defence. To discourage tanks from attempting to jump the ditch (apparently, it had been ascertained that the light German tanks going at full speed could jump as much as 30 feet if provided with a take-off hump), the excavated spoil on the side nearest the enemy was sloped as steeply as possible.

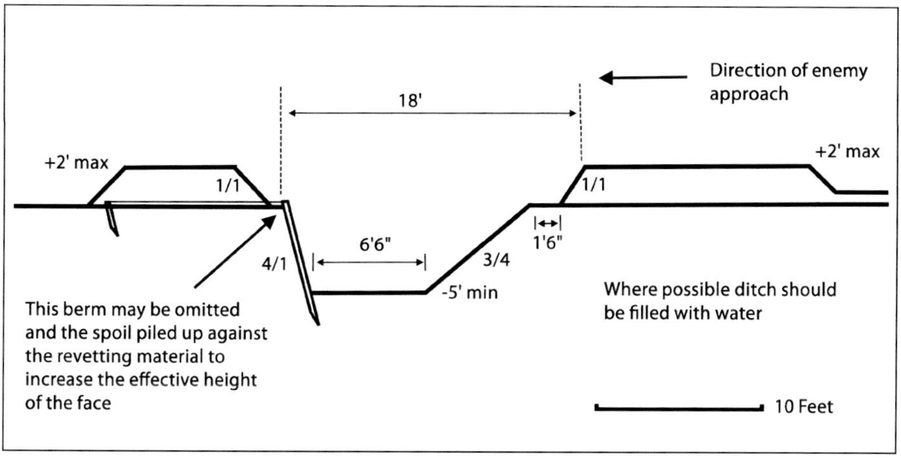

Figure 9.10: GHQ standard design for an anti-tank ditch.

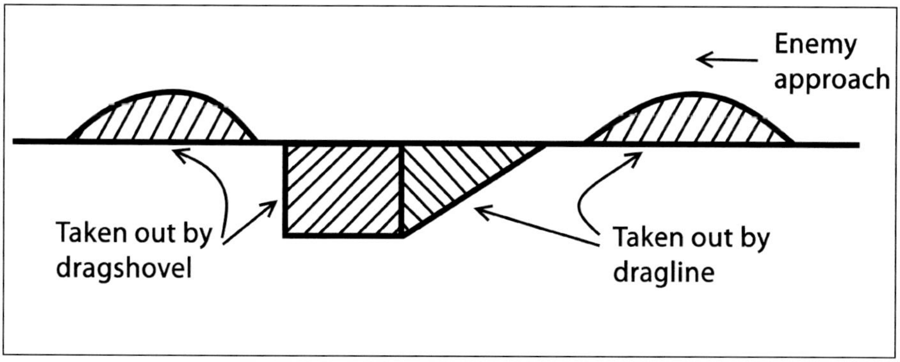

Figure 9.11: Method of working a dragline and drag shovel together in digging an anti-tank ditch.

However, in some cases the anti-tank ditches were dug by hand, either before excavators became available or because of the shortage of excavators when available (Figure 9.12). In October, the 7th Field Company started digging an anti-tank obstacle by hand along the 11 Brigade's front, digging a 30-yard stretch to full depth by hand in five hours. However, work soon became impossible due to heavy rain. The 1st Battalion East Surry Regiment, working with the Company, reported that it took two men to lift one shovel of mud! When the 5th Division took over part of the front from the 51st French Division, digging the anti-tank ditches had to be by hand until mechanical excavators became available. Likewise, the 1 Guards Brigade was instructed to dig an anti-tank ditch in the Genech area, using entirely labour, both from the Brigade and the 1st Division. The daily work party was 30 men, the men working in pairs and each pair expected to complete 6 feet of ditch per day. Each man was provided with a barrow, so one man would be filling a barrow while his mate would be emptying the other barrow. The men were expected to change tasks every hour or so. The 234th Army Field Company, preparing defences in the Seclin area, reported that a company of 66 men, with 33 armed with shovels and 10 with picks, completed digging 23 yards in a six-hour day. While employed on digging a ditch by hand Lance Corporal Hector Morgan, 1st Battalion Loyal Regiment, was able to use his mining skills, demonstrating to others how to undercut an embankment with a pick so that the weight of the soil did most of the work.

All ditches had to be revetted to prevent them collapsing.[17] The 135th Excavating Company had its own factory at Douai where revetting materials were received, then dressed and distributed to sites. Revetting consisted of hurdles supported by uprights. Uprights had to be close together so if one was destroyed by shellfire, the revetment would not fail. They also had to be anchored well back. Hurdled brushwood or XPM were the most satisfactory materials as they would not give purchase to a tank if destroyed unlike the concrete revetment slabs in use by the French. Corrugated iron sheets and timber could also be used, but their use was discouraged due to the shortage of these materials.

It was soon discovered that in wet ground conditions revetment had to be carried out on the steep wall immediately behind the excavators otherwise it simply fell in within minutes of being dug (Figure 9.13). Excavators could easily push in revetting posts but when the ditch was dug by hand, augers had to be used to dig holes for the posts. During the first half of December, a period of almost continuous rain meant that pumping and dams had to be resorted to hold back water and so permit the revetting party to work. However, the 101st Army Field Company did devise a system for revetting flooded ditches although unfortunately no further details are given in the War Diary.

17 The OC 234th Army Field Company, working in the Seclin area, concluded by questioning local inhabitants that a well and closely revetted anti-tank obstacle would last the winter.

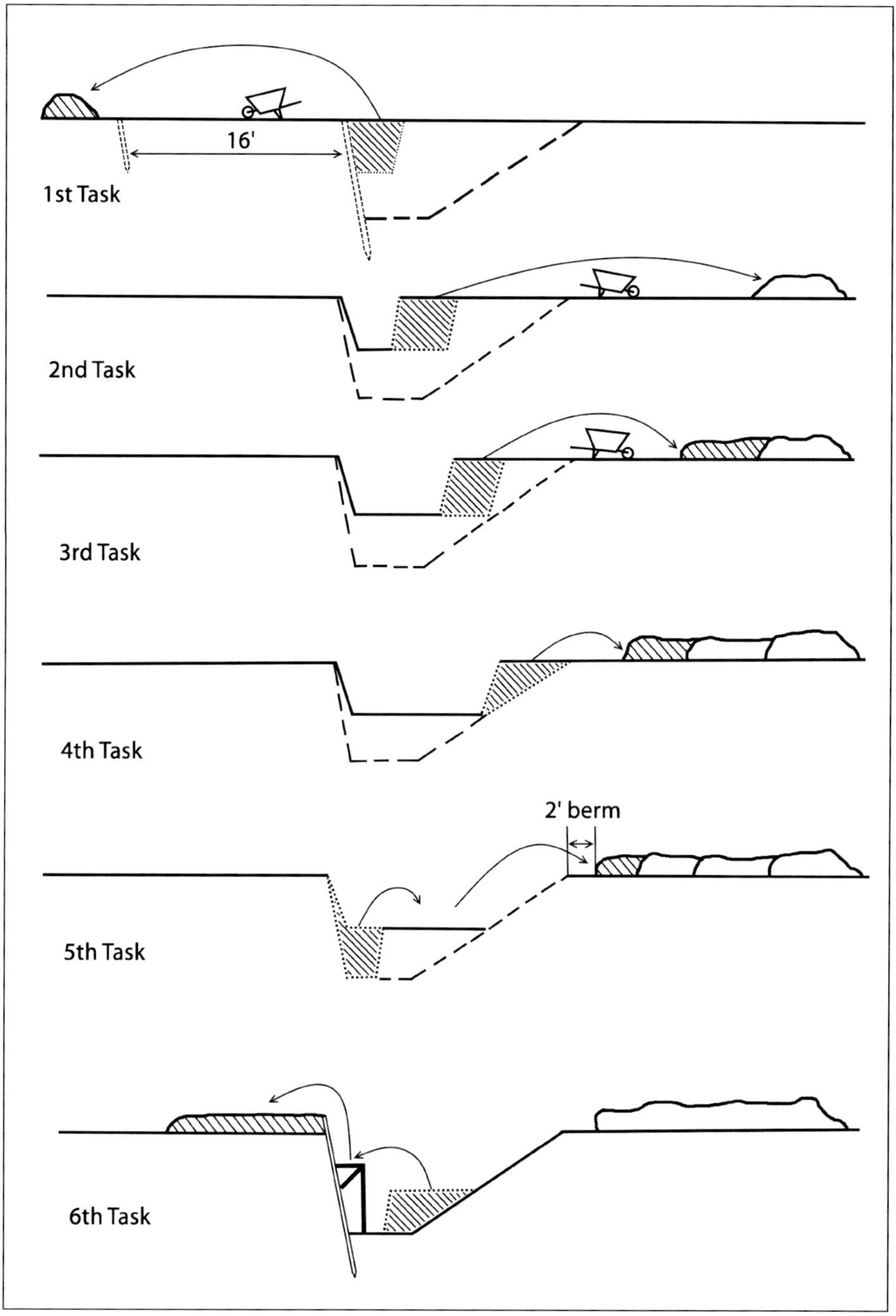

Figure 9.12: Diagram to illustrate the method of digging an anti-tank ditch by hand.

Figure 9.13: An anti-tank ditch dug to the full depth possible by an excavator, then immediately revetted. Long stakes are closely spaced and pushed in with the excavator. In this image the revetting material is corrugated iron sheets, which was unusual. (TNA: WO287/136)

The amount of materials required for revetting ditches was substantial. For a day's work for a Labour Company of about 250 men divided into four platoons, the following material was required:

600 x 9 ft by 4 inch to 6 inch butt poles
600 sq yards of hurdles
600 sq yards of XPM or 1 inch rough boards
600 x 4 ft by 3 inch to 4 inch pickets
25,000 ft of 10 or 11 gauge wire
6,000 ft of 14 to 15 gauge wire

It was always a struggle to provide sufficient supplies to ensure revetting work was not held up. The severe frosts during January and February 1940, when no digging was possible, at least allowed a supply of materials to be built up.

In certain circumstances it proved impossible to revet the ditches. The solution was to dig a 'V' shaped ditch with a dragline, about 20 feet to 30 feet wide and 8 feet to 9 feet deep. In the spring, when ground conditions improved it was anticipated the ditch could be converted to the standard pattern by driving poles half way down one bank, putting in place revetment material and wiring back the poles, then filling in behind with a bulldozer or drag shovel the original spoil.

The French considered that anti-tank ditches were more effective if wet rather than dry and the Chief Engineer repeated this advice. It was recommended that every effort be made to fill ditches with water that were not naturally full, either by damming or diverting streams. If a ditch could not be kept wet, instructions stated it had to be filled with wire to prevent them from being used as trenches by enemy infantry, and to impede men attempting to make crossings for tanks. However, given the shortage of wire, it is unlikely that any ditches were actually filled as such; this was a task in all likelihood that would have only been carried out if contact with the enemy was imminent.

Some improvements to the standard ditch were later notified in orders. Instructions issued in December 1939 required the elimination of the long slope down into the ditch as it exposed the revetment unduly to fire from tank guns. On 19 March, orders were issued to strengthen the revetment of all existing anti-tank ditches by planting willow-tree cuttings. Cuttings of 18 inches to 24 inches in length were to be planted 36 inches apart up against the revetment, at the bottom of the ditches. It was intended that the trees would grow to form a willow tree fence, supporting the existing revetment.

In order to allow troops to move throughout brigade sectors once the ditches had been dug, and to allow farmers to reach their fields, temporary bridges were erected over the anti-tank ditches. Thought also had to be given to concealed crossings to allow counter-attacks to be carried out. One interesting observation from Gort on the anti-tank ditches was they were not being prepared with reference to the counter-attack. He considered that units should have room to form up for a counter-attack, the frontage of the counter-attack being the proportion of an equilateral triangle to the distance of the objective. It is difficult to see how the conflicting requirements for continuous anti-tank obstacles, designed to disrupt tank manoeuvre, and room for forming up and manoeuvre in a counter-attack could be both met.

Despite the vast resource put into digging the ditches, trials showed they were not as effective as thought. The OC 9 Brigade attended a set of trials held by the 4th Battalion Royal Tank Regiment on 2nd December and one conclusion was 'that tanks can cross our present type of A.Tk. obstacle in four different ways'.[18] Unfortunately there is no description given in the Brigade's War Diary of the methods of crossing the ditch.[19] The trials concluded that soft ground was actually the greatest handicap to tanks rather than the ditches.

18 TNA: WO167/364, 9 Infantry Brigade War Diary, 2 December 1939.

19 The German Panzer Mk. II could cross a 6 feet trench and climbing a 3 feet vertical face, the Mk. III performance figures were 7 feet and 3 feet and the Mk. IV 8 feet and 3 feet. For

Anti-tank Minefields

Anti-tank mines provided the best means of forming a rapid anti-tank obstacle where no efficient obstacle existed. If an anti-tank obstacle was not continuous, one of the most important uses of mines was to close gaps in that obstacle. They also had the advantage that the obstacle could be constructed in much greater depth than a single stretch of anti-tank ditch.

At first, there was an acute shortage of anti-tank mines available to the BEF with only enough to close gaps in the anti-tank obstacles such as at roads, and to cover concealed gaps left in the obstacle until they were required for counter-attack by the 4th Battalion Royal Tank Regiment. *Général* Georges considered that a figure of 3,000 mines per km was required to create effective anti-tank obstacle; given the shortage of mines this emphasised the need to use artificial anti-tank obstacles such as ditches. In cases where it was not desired to construct a permanent artificial anti-tank obstacle, such as on roads, instructions stated that minefields were to be laid at close spacing (i.e. one yard apart) in one to three rows to allow quick lifting.

To make up the shortfall in mines, an issue of the French type was made, with 4,000 supplied to I Corps and 6,000 to II Corps of which 2,000 were to be allocated to the French 51st Division. GHQ hoped that there would be sufficient anti-tank mines issued before the end of winter to allow mines to be stored near where they were required, but a reserve also had to be held back for a possible move to the River Escaut. By the end of February, I Corps was able to notify the 1st and 2nd Divisions that 10,000 mines would be allotted to each division for use in the frontier position. With a more plentiful supply, minefields could be planned along the whole front of the FDL Line in conjunction with the anti-tank obstacle. At the end of December, I Corps suggested to GHQ that minefields should also be laid in a 'box' around areas in which enemy tanks might penetrate on likely tank 'runs'. The suggested layout for these minefields was 10 rows with mines 10 yards apart. In all cases, detailed plans were to be drawn up for minefields, but mines were not to be laid until authority had been given by GHQ.

On 21 April, CE I Corps inspected damage caused by a dump of 1,000 Mk. III anti-tank mines blowing up. A crater in a roadway of approximately 70 feet diameter and 22 feet deep was left. In St. Leger, a quarter of mile away, tiles were ripped off roofs, plaster fell from ceilings, and many windows were broken. The crater was filled in by a bulldozer from the 135th Excavator Company.

comparison, a British Cruiser's performance was 7 feet and 3 feet. It was impossible for any of these tanks to cross a ditch dug to GHQ specifications unaided.

Converting a Railway Line into an anti-tank obstacle

The Chief Engineer issued instructions that plans were to be drawn up to prepare the railway line running across the Divisional Reserve Line as an anti-tank obstacle by tilting up the rails. Alternative sleepers could be used as supports. Railway banks were also enhanced as an anti-tank obstacle (Figure 9.14).

Figure 9.14: A railway bank made into an anti-tank obstacle by cutting a vertical face and revetting with closely spaced stakes and brushwood. (TNA: WO287/136)

Road Blocks

Roads, where they passed through an obstacle zone, needed carefully prepared blocks as they were the weakest points in the obstacle zone. The French used concrete blocks and removable steel anti-tank rails to close roads along the line of the forward blockhouses. No details in War Diaries are given on the concrete block element of a road block, but what looks like a so-called concrete 'dragons tooth' can still been seen by the side of a pillbox at Cysoing. This type of road block was to be frequently used in Britain's anti-invasion defences. On taking over these blockhouses, garrisons carried out frequent practice in placing these obstacles in place. The British also used rails to close gaps in the anti-tank ditches they dug, particularly at pillbox sites and roads. Not less than five rows of 90lb rails were specified. Rail road blocks were also constructed along the Second Position. During the 4th Battalion Royal Tank Regiment trials already referred to above, it was concluded that rails were largely ineffective in stopping tanks as they simply bent. This conclusion was supported by the results of experiments held in England.

BEF Operational Instructions clearly indicate that concrete was also to be used for road blocks on the principal approach roads; for example, 3rd Division's Operational Instruction No. 1 specified a block designed so that traffic could only pass through it at a slow pace allowing effective fire to be brought against enemy armoured vehicles as they negotiated the obstacle. Large concrete slabs supporting immovable rails are noted in the 234th Army Field Company's War Diary. Again, similar blocks were to appear in Britain's anti-invasion defences.[20]

Wire could also be used to stop tanks on roads and tracks. Trials were undertaken to assess the performance of various tanks against Dannert wire obstacles.[21] Trials at Farnborough on 7 March tested three types of obstacle – a picketed triple coil fence of the infantry type obstacle, five loose single coils at 10 yards spacing and two concertinas arranged in a U shape – against an Infantry A.11 tank. The triple coil fence performed badly as the pickets prevented sufficient wire being fed into the tracks. The obstacle consisting of five loose coils was also insufficient to stop a tank; apparently the Germans recommended 10 coils. A single U-shaped block also could not be relied upon to stop a tank, and if such a block was to be used it was recommended that a minimum of three sets of U type blocks should be erected. Further trials were held at Farnborough on 20 April using Infantry tanks A.11 and A.12. An A.11 tank passed through an obstacle at 10 mph consisting of seven rows of unpicketted wire 10 yards apart but stopped after 200 yards, the wire having been dragged under the skirting plate and wrapping around the sprockets and idlers. The light tank Mk. VIB coped much better, not only in crossing but also in clearing away the obstacle. Earlier trials had stopped the light tank, perhaps indicating that the Dannert wire being supplied to the BEF was of inferior quality to wire imported from Germany before the war. The recommendation from the trial was to use Dannert wire in triple rows as in the infantry obstacle, but not picketted.

20 Brooke, when he became Commander-in-Chief Home Forces, was not impressed with this type of defence: 'Another form of defence which I found throughout the country and with which I was in total disagreement consisted of massive concrete road-blocks at the entry and exit of most towns and villages. I had suffered too much from these blocks in France not to realise their crippling effect on mobility ... I stopped any further constructions and instructed existing ones to be removed where possible'. See Arthur Bryant, *The Turn of the Tide: Based on the War Diaries of Field Marshal Viscount Alanbrooke* (London: Collins, 1957), p. 198.

21 Concertina wire – oil tempered barbed spring-steel coil wire – which as its name suggests, could be pulled out to form a long, round fence. It was invented during WW1 by Herr Dannert, and the name 'Dannert' wire was retained by the British.

Main roads entering the Corps Reserve Position, such as the Seclin – Lille road, were not to be blocked permanently, although permission was given to block some minor roads. Instead temporary blocks consisting of farm vehicles and carts, Dannert wire and anti-tank mines were to be established close to section posts. As an alternative to constructing permanent blocks, the OC 234th Army Field Company suggested carrying the anti-tank ditch through the road and bridging the gap with a small 5-ton bridge which could be erected and dismantled by unskilled labour as circumstances demanded. He was given permission to try this method on a minor road at Martinstart. The bridge was constructed by embedding bank seats for RSJ road bearers the day before cutting the ditch through the road. The bridge could then be assembled within half an hour of completing the ditch. Trials showed that six men could dismantle the bridge in four and a half minutes after the passing of the last vehicle. This was done by throwing the decking into the obstacle, lifting the RSJ road bearers out of their sockets on the enemy side and drawing them forward until the opposite end drops into the ditch, and left to embarrass.

A mine crater made a formidable anti-tank obstacle in a road, track or railway, especially if deviation was difficult. They were planned extensively on the *SD* Lille Front and to a degree on the Saar Front (for example, see Figure 5.4 for mine craters planned on the 1st Division's front). The French had already prepared and charged (with melanite) mine chambers in the *SD* Lille before the BEF took over. The mined points were organised into *groupements*, commanded by a French Engineer officer, having under him about a dozen NCOs and men. They were billeted in the immediate neighbourhood of the points. The French also prepared mine chambers along the Bachy Switch, which became part of the FDL Line in February 1940. French mine chambers were marked either by pavé laid in the opposite direction or a small stone at the side of the road bearing the letters 'G.M'. The BEF prepared mine chambers usually consisted of concrete pipes or steel tubes sunk about seven feet into the ground, with two in echelon (Figure 9.15). These would have been charged with 50lb to 80lb ammonal. These mine chambers were an entirely British responsibility, although their position was reported to the French. Shelters were constructed behind the blockhouses to store the ammonal.

On 14 March, the 1st Division carried out a demonstration, attended by *Colonel* Bertschi, blowing two road craters in prepared concrete 6ft 6in mine chambers. Charges used were 100lb and 150lb ammonal, which formed craters 36 feet wide by 11feet deep and 39 feet wide by 12 feet deep respectively. Experiments were also carried out on destroying a pavé road using a drag shovel fitted with a three-tine ripper. It was found that about a third of a mile of pavé road could be destroyed in an hour.

The BEF constructed a variety of road blocks on the Saar Front. In the village of Halstroff, three road blocks were constructed consisting of timber breast walls, the gaps between them filled with rubble. The blocks were staggered so that traffic could still pass between them but had to negotiate an 'S' bend and slow down to 5 mph. Two examples of road blocks were constructed at Grossenwald. The first took the form of

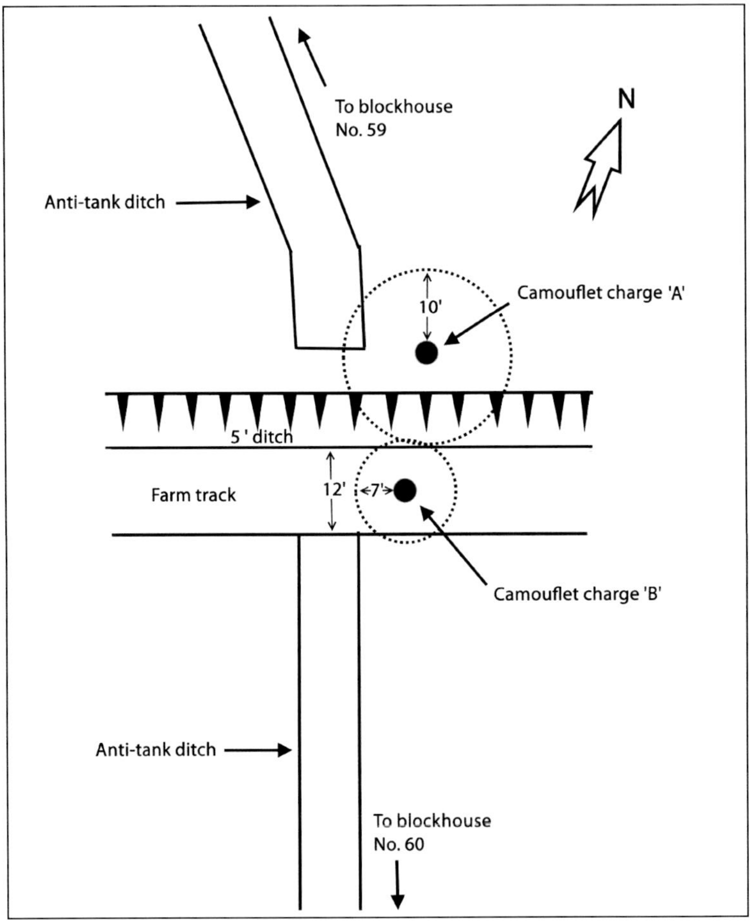

Figure 9.15: Plan showing British prepared mine chambers to block the junction of a farm track with the anti-tank ditch between blockhouses No. 59 and 60 on the original French *Ligne Principale* in the 1st Division's sector. Two camouflet charges were to be made using 6-inch diameter steel tubes sunk 7 feet into the ground. Each was to be charged with 50lb of ammonal in waterproof tins and tamped. The charges would make two linked craters, one 7 feet in diameter and the other 10 feet in diameter.

a triple concertina wire fence and four rows of holes in the road in which mines could be placed. The second type consisted of a number of logs sunk 3 feet to 4 feet into the ground in pairs. Between them were laid rails, with an 8 feet gap in the centre of the road with a removable rail. A moveable road block, to specifications provided by the French, was constructed on the road between Monerea and Halstroff. The block closed the gap caused by the road in the *Ligne de Receuil* anti-tank ditch. The block was supposed to consist of rails of varying lengths, but the French were only able to supply two lengths, 2.9m and 4m.

A number of blocks were constructed around Bizing village. These were designed to be proof against lighter armoured vehicles only, as in the event of a large scale attack the village was to be evacuated. Figure 9.16 shows the road blocks in the village. Block 'A' consisted of baulks held in place by angle iron pickets and filled with stones. Block 'B' consisted of a wire entanglement and shallow trenches in which anti-tank mines could be placed. Block 'C' was a staggered breast wall, made of 12 feet posts sunk 3 feet into the ground, sawn logs for revetment and the space filled with large stones. The gap between the breast walls was closed with knife rests fitted with boards to take anti-tank mines. A series of demolitions were also carried out. At 'D', on either side of a culvert, two 37lb ammonal charges at a depth of 6 feet were fired, resulting in a crater of 35 feet long, 27 feet wide and 9 feet deep. In order to connect blocks 'B' and 'C', a block of craters was made at 'E'. The largest charges were two of 50lb, three of 80lb and one of 75lb, with a number of smaller charges made to link up the obstacle. Finally, to join obstacles 'C' and 'D', a stream was improved to give a ditch with a 3ft 6in bank and 10 feet wide, revetted with wire netting and angle iron.

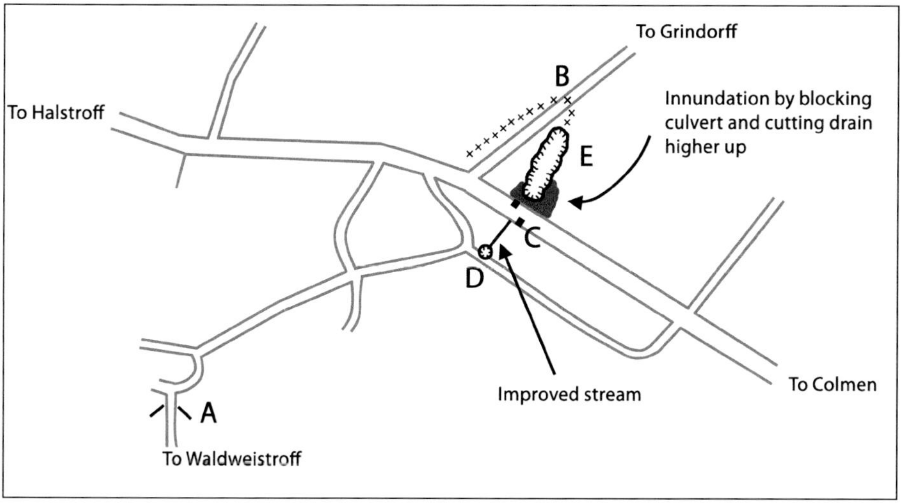

Figure 9.16: Sketch showing road blocks constructed at Bizing village.

Demolitions

The French had also prepared bridges along the frontier and certain important railway bridges for demolition. A further series of demolitions along the canal lines in the rear were also projected by the French, which were in the process of being charged as the BEF moved into the line. GHQ discovered that not all the canal demolitions were within *Colonel* Bertschi's responsibility and the authority of two French commanders was required to fire the charges. Responsibility for the canal line demolitions within the BEF sector was eventually transferred to GHQ, which issued instructions that all road and rail bridges over the line not already prepared for demolition were to be prepared for demolition immediately. This also included alterations to demolition chambers prepared by the French to take melanite, which the BEF did not have. Small chambers were driven behind retaining walls of bridge abutments and boxes for explosives made to fit and fix to girders with ring mains and methods of firing planned. GHQ also raised the matter of barges apparently not in use along the canals of Sensée, Haute-Deûle and La Bassée as they could be utilised by the enemy as bridges to cross the waterways, negating the effect of any demolitions, and asked the French for their removal. The French pointed out that the vast proportion of barges could not be removed as they were required for the transportation of coal to Paris. A certain number were also required for the evacuation of the Northern region should it become necessary. Nevertheless, the French did agree to remove barges not currently in use or required, which satisfied GHQ as in the event of hostile activities in *SD* Lille there would be few abandoned barges left. Ultimately though, GHQ concerns were found to be valid, as when the BEF fell back onto the Gort Line in May 1940, many barges had to be destroyed to prevent them being used by the enemy to cross the River Lys (see Chapter 10).

Similar demolitions were also to be prepared on the line Marchiennes – Montreuil and the Seclin Canal on the Corps Reserve Position. Bridges on the Haute Deûle Canal along the western outskirts of Lille were not to be prepared for demolition, although plans were drawn up, including calculations of charges required, to carry out this work if it ever became necessary.

The normal channel of orders for firing demolition charges was via the *Commandant SD* Lille. In an emergency, formation commanders (not below commanders of infantry brigades) or the French personnel could fire the charges on their own responsibility. In an extreme emergency, British as well as the French firing detachments could fire the charges. Railway bridges of first priority could only be demolished on the orders of the *Commandant SD* Lille.

Infantry Obstacles

Wire and anti-personnel minefields were the chief obstacles to infantry. When the BEF took over the *SD* Lille from the French, the only infantry obstacles that had been completed were wiring immediately to the rear of the anti-tank ditch and around the blockhouses.

Wire obstacles

GHQ described the French wire obstacle along the length of the anti-tank ditch and around the blockhouses as being 2ft 6in high and about 9 feet wide, supported on wooden posts. It was considered weak by British standards. On 13 October, GHQ notified I and II Corps that an allocation of 40 tons of wire was now available in order to complete the wire obstacle immediately behind the FDL Line anti-tank ditch and to surround all completed pillboxes with a wire obstacle. However, Dannert wire was unavailable as all stocks were being held back for a possible advance into Belgium.

By December, sufficient wire was available for obstacles in front of the FDL Line consisting of two double apron fences with two lines of Dannert concertina wire between them (Figure 9.17) and one double apron fence in front of the Brigade and Division Reserve Positions.[22] In some places, a pyramid of Dannert wire was constructed between the double apron fences, such as along the Bachy Switch – 'A most effective looking obstacle' according to the War Diarist of the 23rd Field Company.[23] About every 300 yards, staggered gaps were left for infantry patrols. Instructions specified that the wire should not be sited too close to the anti-tank ditch, as it would then be destroyed by artillery fire directed on the ditch. In CRE 1st Division War Diary, instructions specified that the wire obstacle had to be close enough to the ditch to allow the infantry to lob grenades into the ditch from behind it, but far enough away to allow patrols to pass between it and the ditch. On the Second Position, following the release of the mobile reserve of barbed wire held by I and II Corps for a possible move forward to the Escaut, there was sufficient wire to erect one double apron fence covering crossing points only. There was still insufficient wire for the Corps Position and Switch Lines. By February, sufficient wire was available to allow for a further belt of double apron fence and one or two coils of Dannert wire along the whole front exclusive of the River Lys. If not already carried out, this additional wire was to be used to create a belt of wire in front of the foremost anti-tank obstacle in the first instance. In all cases of constructing wire obstacles, farming interests had to be taken into account; if it would cause great inconvenience, the wire was not to be erected but held on the spot so it could be erected when required.

22 A double apron fence consists of three horizontal wires fixed to pickets, sloping wires (called diagonals) leading from the top of the pickets to anchorage pickets, and three horizontal wires fixed on each side to the diagonals. These horizontal wires, together with the diagonals, are called the 'front and rear aprons'. It was a difficult obstacle to cut or climb over, and two or three apron fences were difficult to destroy by artillery fire. The gap between apron fences could be filled with loose wire or concertinas. The concertina wire was secured by pickets, either screw pickets or angle iron pickets if no screw pickets were available or the ground was unsuitable for their use. When extended to 50 feet, a Dannert concertina has a diameter of approximately 3 feet. Further extension would result in a reduction of this diameter, which was not desirable. Thus, 50 feet was adopted as the standard length for extending Dannert concertinas. Barbs were longer and more unevenly spaced than on normal barbed wire.

23 TNA: WO167/916, 23rd Field Company War Diary, 28 November 1939.

Figure 9.17: A British built wire obstacle consisting of two rows of double apron fence with two lines of concertina wire between. (TNA: WO287/136)

Away from the anti-tank ditches, tactical and defence wire was to be sited but not laid. Instructions specified that it was to be sited carefully and not in rings around localities as this would give the position away. Rather it was to be laid out in intersecting belts of wire that could be covered by the fire of automatic weapons and which would shepherd the attackers into the fire of these weapons.

The bitter winter weather made work on infantry obstacles in the Saar sector all but impossible. Although the French promised as much barbed and concertina wire as the British could use, the ground was too hard to plant screw pickets or hammer in angle iron pickets. To overcome this, a form of concertina wire was improvised using normal barbed wire and tied to existing wire to make a reasonable obstacle. In Peter Hart's book on the 2nd Battalion Norfolk Regiment, an account is given by Private Ernie Farrow, Pioneer Section, HQ Company, of the struggle to put up wire in these conditions:

> We had this Dannert wire, round rings of wire. This came up, lorry loads of it. We had to get this out at night in the dark in certain positions. We took an iron stake out with us and tried to drive it into the ground. The ground was frozen stiff. Because we couldn't get it in very far, we had a rope and two of us would stand back with this rope on the top of the post to hold it back. Then they'd pull

> this Dannert wire out, hundreds of yards of it and make it fast at the other end. Then we'd find a small stake to drive into the ground again to hold the dammed thing up straight which was a heck of a job.[24]

Anti-personnel Minefields

Anti-personnel mines were only to be used in front of the FDLs, in areas where enemy patrolling and concentrations were likely to form up or pass. They were also to be laid in the FDL anti-tank ditch when dry. As was the case with anti-tank mines, they were only to be laid when contact with the enemy was imminent.

Booby Traps

Booby traps were only an option when in close contact with the enemy, i.e. on the Saar Front. For instance, because of active enemy patrolling, a simple controlled booby trap was constructed at Hartbuch: electric leads from a front line post ran out into no-man's land to six charges, each charge consisting of two slabs of gun-cotton placed with a quantity of broken glass. However, it was found that the charges did not scatter the glass far enough so 5lb ammonal charges were used instead. At first, the charges were fired using a car battery, then later with a small torch battery. On 21 April, all the charges were fired but no enemy casualties were found, although the ammonal charges made considerable craters!

Inundations

Inundations provided an effective obstacle against both infantry and tank attacks. They could only be used in conditions when purely static defence was required, as once formed, they rendered the area impassable to all but the lightest traffic for long periods. The French had prepared plans to inundate the area around Marchiennes by blocking the canal and closing sluices along the Scarpe waterway. These inundations were under the control of the French First Army, although they could not be put into effect until ordered by *GQG* – as the 2nd Division put it: 'we gather that these plans are very hush-hush and that only General Gamelin himself can order them.'[25] However, this scheme affected the 2nd Division unfavourably because it would inundate roads near Marchiennes in a position of their area which was already insufficiently roaded. The French later agreed to bank two roads that the 2nd Division required to be kept open. It was also noted that some of the proposed schemes along the Marcq could also affect BEF defensive positions.

24 Hart, *The 2nd Norfolk Regiment,* p.34.
25 TNA: WO167/203, 2nd Division General Staff War Diary, 12 October 1939.

The BEF also drew up a list of possible inundations. The intelligence for some of these schemes dated back to the Great War; for instance, schemes for inundations by closing sluices along the Lys and Deûle waterways were drawn up by the Second Army BEF in 1917.

Woodland Obstacles

Woods provided good anti-tank obstacles as well as providing cover in which to hide defensive posts. In some woodlands selected for defence, arrangements were made for blocking rides by felling trees across them. These were to be felled on brigade orders only, and should the frontier position be occupied, pioneers were to be stationed by the trees in question ready to fell them should this be ordered. Infantry obstacles were also to be constructed to block rides in the form of an abatis.

10

The Battle Of France and Flanders and Aftermath

A German offensive in the spring of 1940 was widely anticipated, and Gamelin expected it would come through the Low Countries. However, what the Germans achieved came as a complete surprise: the *Schwerpunkt* was through the supposedly impassable Ardennes. Once the infantry and engineers had established crossings over the Meuse, the shock action of tanks shattered the weak French front in this area, and the panzers did not then try to roll up the French front but instead raced straight to the Channel, cutting off the LoC to the Allied armies in the north. The BEF, which had raced forward into Belgium in accord with Plan D was forced to retreat. After only 12 days it found itself back on the Gort Line. After only three weeks it had been evacuated from the beaches of Dunkirk. Following the evacuation, the British Army began to hurriedly prepare defences at home in anticipation of Hitler's next move: the invasion of Britain. The layout of the anti-invasion defences had clear parallels to the defences constructed by the BEF in *SD* Lille and were widely criticised as being 'Maginot minded' by some senior commanders who had been through the retreat.

Case Yellow

Following the collapse of Poland, Hitler ordered his generals to prepare for the invasion of the Low Countries and France. The generals had little confidence in defeating France and the plan they produced reflected this and was not that ambitious. Basically, it was a repeat of the Schlieffen plan: the German Army would wheel through the Low Countries with the aim of capturing forward air bases to carry out attacks on Britain and France, and perhaps destroy a portion of the Allied forces in the north. One German officer, *Generalleutnant* Erich von Manstein, had little confidence in this plan. The Belgian plain was not good country for tank operations, and he believed the plan would inevitably result in a long war of attrition which Germany could not hope to win. Instead, Manstein proposed an armoured thrust through the Ardennes and over the Meuse to good tank country that continued all the way to the Channel. Manstein's plan was true Blitzkrieg: he did not envisage traditional battles of encirclement or rolling up the enemy front once the tanks had broken through enemy lines. Instead, he planned an armoured thrust straight to the Channel, cutting off the LoC to the Allied forces concentrated in the north and the areas of country in which Allied forces would have to redeploy for counter-attacks. German forces would still advance through the Low Countries to divert attention from the main attack and pin down the Allies in the north. The further the Allied armies advanced into Belgium as a result of Plan E or D, the better this suited Manstein's plan (Figure 10.1). If successful, the plan would result in the destruction of a major part of the Allied armies and the collapse of France. The plan impressed Hitler, who himself had considered the idea of cutting of the Allied armies south of Namur. It also promised him the quick victory he needed. The final version of the German plan, based on Manstein's ideas, allocated two army groups to the invasion: Army Group A (*Generaloberst* von Rundstedt) which was to attack through the Ardennes and was assigned most of the panzer divisions and Army Group B (*Generaloberst* von Bock) which would advance through the Low Countries, with the aim of distracting the Allied armies in the north. Army Group C (*Generaloberst* von Leeb) would keep up pressure on the Maginot Line to prevent the French moving the interval troops to the threatened area.

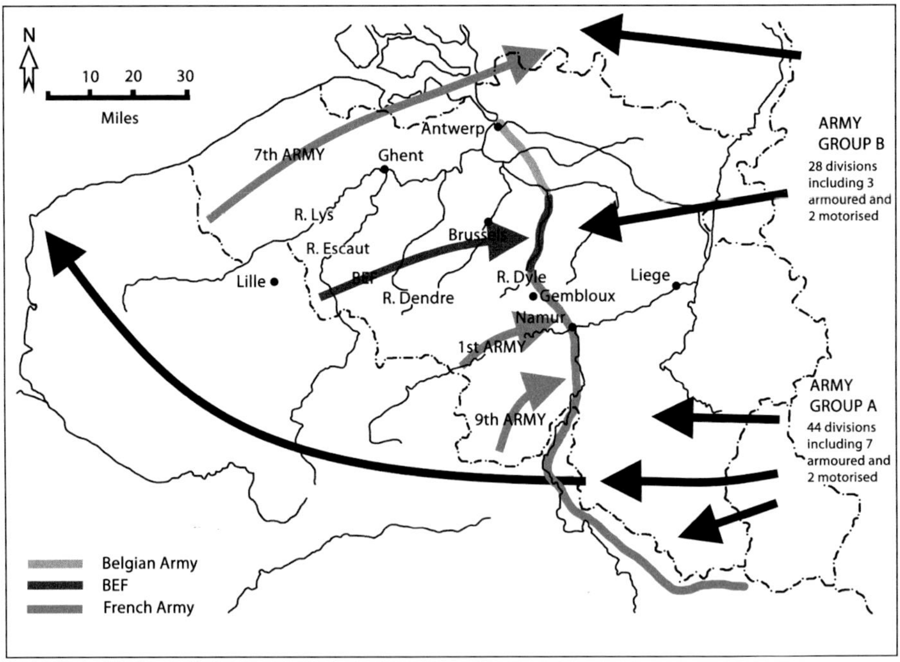

Figure 10.1: Opposing Plans: Plan D and Plan Yellow.

Opening Moves

In the early morning of 10 May, the long-awaited German attack commenced. The first reports indicated that the German attack was unfolding as Gamelin had expected. Plan D was put into effect and the French First Army Group, which included the BEF, moved into Belgium and dashed forward to reach the Dyle Line before the Germans. The BEF spearhead comprised of I and II Corps; III Corps remained in reserve. The British had anticipated that the Germans would do everything possible to interfere with the move forward by bombing and the use of parachute troops. The advancing columns of the BEF were provided with strong fighter support for protection against German bombers. The brigades of III Corps picketed areas for the BEF spearhead to pass though, and despite many reports of German parachute troops landing, not a single person could be found who had actually seen any descending to earth. Neither did the German bombers interfere with the BEF move into Belgium as most were needed to support the thrust through the Ardennes and the attack on Holland. By 13 May, the BEF was safely deployed on the Dyle. I Corps had the 1st and 2nd Divisions in the line with the 48th Division in support while II Corps had the 3rd Division in the line, supported by the 4th Division. The 5th and 50th divisions were in reserve. III Corps was now ordered forward to hold a layback position on the River Escaut. The French First Army discovered, as had been feared, that there was no effective anti-tank obstacle covering the Gembloux Gap. As a consequence, Georges decided to push out advanced troops to the Perwez Line (the anti-tank obstacle on this line was not only unfinished but was also badly sited) to cover the Gembloux Gap.

The divisions tasked with forming a layback position on the Escaut also wasted no time in digging in. For instance, Brigadier Smyth's 127 Brigade dug in along the Escaut on 15 and 16 May; the battalions of his Brigade contained a number of miners, and 'they got down to their job with a will'.[1] He also managed to obtain a mechanical excavator for the 5th Battalion Manchester Regiment to dig an anti-tank ditch on Mont St. Aubert. They were destined never to hold this position, as the 127 Brigade was selected to be the basis of one of Gort's 'stop-gap' forces – Macforce (described in further detail below). Moreover, on 15 May, the 135th Excavator Company moved an elevating grader and two excavators to dig an all-round anti-tank obstacle round a village northwest of Oudenaarde (northeast of Tournai), blocking the exit from a crossing over the River Escaut,

At first, it did not go well for the Allies in the north. The Germans seized a bridgehead at Maastricht, turning the main Belgian defence lines along the line of the Meuse and the Albert Canal. German glider troops landed on Fort Eben Emael, compelling the Fort to surrender when the 4th Panzer Division reached the Albert Canal. With the fall of the Fort, the main line of Belgian resistance was broken, and

1 Brigadier Sir John Smyth, VC, MC, MP, *Before the Dawn: Two Historic Retreats Dunkirk 1940. Burma 1942*(London: Cassell & Co. Ltd., 1957), p. 42.

the other forts on the line soon fell. The French Seventh Army outran its supports and supplies in the dash to Breda, and was severely battered and compelled to fall back to Antwerp with much of its armour lost. Holland surrendered on 14 May. But, despite these events, the Allied position in northern Belgium was not a total disaster. The BEF had safely arrived on the Dyle, while the Belgian Army securely held the left flank after withdrawing from the Albert Canal. The French First Army held the southern flank and was effectively holding German attacks. Still convinced this was the German *Schwerpunkt*, the French ordered the strategic reserve to move forward in support of the First Army.

Battle of the Bulge

The Allies were entirely focused on the actions in northern Belgium and failed to realise the importance of reports of German forces moving through the Ardennes, largely dismissing them as 'Fifth Column' or a secondary attack. Gamelin's plan required the French Second and Ninth Armies to move a short distance into Belgium. The Second Army's role was to anchor the French Army's flank from Sedan to the Maginot Line while the Ninth Army was to hold the Meuse south of Namur and link up with the First Army. Both Armies sent their armour and cavalry into Belgium not realising that 44 German divisions which included seven Panzer divisions – having easily dealt with Belgian resistance – were rapidly approaching them. As the German armour moved through the 'impassable' Ardennes, they met and overwhelmed the cavalry of the Ninth and Second Armies. By 12 May the German panzers had reached the Meuse and the French realised that this was the German *Schwerpunkt*. As the French began to prepare the move of reserves to the area, there was no panic as they expected the Germans to pause and prepare a deliberate attack to cross the Meuse.

The Germans did not wait. Using 77mm anti-aircraft guns, dive-bombers and tank guns as a substitute for artillery, which had not yet reached the leading panzer divisions, the German infantry and assault engineers had established three bridgeheads over the Meuse by the end of 13 May: *Panzerkorps* Hoth at Dinant, *Panzerkorps* Reinhardt at Monthermé and *Panzerkorps* Guderian at Sedan. The Germans quickly exploited the bridgeheads in what was known at the time as 'The Battle of the Bulge'.

Georges cancelled the movement of the strategic reserve north and issued orders for it to move in support of the Ninth Army. The French Seventh Army was also now moving down from the north to reinforce the Ninth Army, but it had no hope of arriving in time. Georges assembled the last reserves of armour, the 1st *DCR*, 2nd *DCR* and 3rd *DCR* into position for a counter attack. The 2nd *DCR*, moving up behind the Ninth Army, attempted to assemble right in the path of the advancing panzers. The 3rd *DCR* failed to counter-attack and was instead used to form part of a last-ditch defensive line. The 1st *DCR's* counter-attack ended in disaster. With the failure of these counter-attacks the Ninth Army collapsed. The Ninth Army consisted mainly of older reservists, many who had not completed their training, and was poorly equipped. Nevertheless, it had made the Germans fight for their bridgeheads and had there been properly co-ordinated counter-attacks on 13 and 14 May the Germans may well have been pushed out of them.

Crisis

By 15May, it was no longer a 'bulge' in the French line. The panzers had ripped through the French positions into open country and moving in a westerly direction they threatened to cut off the First Army Group to the north. On this day, the French Prime Minister Reynaud phoned Churchill and told him the war was lost. Churchill flew to France and met Gamelin the following day. Churchill asked him where the strategic reserve was, to which the latter is said to have replied 'there are none'. Gamelin later claimed he had not answered 'there are none' but 'there are no longer any'. But in terms of the unfolding campaign, it amounted to the same thing.

Moreover, on 15 May, an Allied conference held at the Château Casteau decided to ensure closer integration of the Allied armies in the north; the King of the Belgians and Gort accepted co-ordination by General Billotte as Georges' representative. It was now obvious that a prolonged stand on the Dyle was out of the question. Although the BEF and the Belgian's on their left had not been seriously tested, the French First Army had given ground under German pressure. This, along with the German victory in Holland and the rapidly disintegrating French Ninth Army, meant new measures were required and a withdrawal to the Escaut was decided upon. On 16 May the order for this was given to the First Army Group. This was to be done in bounds, firstly to the Senne Canal which lay between the Dyle and the Dendre. British troops could not understand the order, as they were holding firm against German attacks.

The BEF and the Belgians successfully carried out the withdrawal from the Dyle to the Senne Line, running from Charleroi to Brussels and on to the Willebroeck Canal. However, the news of the breach in the French line directly on the right threatened the BEF: if the panzers turned north in the direction of Lille, they would cut clean behind I and II Corps. Gort ordered General Roderick Petre to form a layback position pivoting on Arras, using the 23rd Division and a brigade from the 12th Division. To counter the immediate threat of the panzers swinging north, he ordered Major-General Mason-Macfarlane to form a 'stop-gap' force – a mixed force of armour and infantry known as Macforce – and to move at once to the River Scarpe. Further back, towards the Somme, other units in the rear such as general construction companies, Royal Army Service Corps units and even a mobile bath unit placed their own localities into as state of defence.

On the night of 17 May, the Allied armies fell back again to the line of the Dendre. The following night they withdrew safely to the Escaut. The French First Army's line did not continue south towards Cambrai but instead bent westward along the River Sensée compelling Gort to immediately dispatch the 50th Division to take up positions along the line of the canal running northwest from Douai to La Bassée to further strengthen the BEF's southern flank. Georges attempted to block the path of the advancing panzers by ordering the 23rd Division to occupy 16 miles of the Canal du

Nord – the last good tank obstacle in the path of the panzers – while the French were to hold the southern 14 miles, but they never arrived. This is perhaps not surprising as from 16 May the German advance had cut communications between *GQG* (Gamelin) and HQ North-East Front (Georges). Also, on that date, communications between Georges and the HQ French First Army Group (Billotte) ceased. From 17 May, Gort had no direct land telephone lines to the Belgium HQ on his left, the French First Army on his right and HQ North-East Front behind. Co-ordination between the BEF, the French and Belgians had practically ceased.

By 17 May the panzers had reached St Quentin and by 18 May they had captured Péronne. All that stood in their way to the coast was the 23rd and 12th Divisions. It will be recalled these were Territorial divisions which had been sent out to France for labour duties and to continue their training. They had spent most of their time working on the LoC and aerodrome construction in the rearward areas; their training was far from complete and they were certainly not equipped as fighting divisions. On 19 May the German armour was across the Canal du Nord and racing towards the sea. The 23rd and 12th Divisions had practically ceased to exist and had only delayed the panzers for a few hours.

The 19 May was to prove a critical day. Gamelin had recovered some of his nerve and was forming a new army along the line of the Somme using divisions withdrawn from other parts of the line and felt that action was needed to maintain the link between the eastern armies and the armies in the north. It was the last chance to cut off the German spearhead. Gamelin's Directive No.12 issued on 19 May stated:

> Rather than allow the First Army Group to be encircled the boldest action should be taken, on the one hand by opening up if necessary, the way to the Somme and on the other by launching specially mobile forces against the rear of the German armoured divisions followed by divisions of motorised infantry. It seems that at present there is a gap behind their first wave.[2]

But the French Prime Minister Paul Reynaud decided on this date to suspend Gamelin and recalled Weygand from Syria to replace him. Decisive action was required: Weygand did not provide this. Instead, he cancelled Gamelin's counter-attack and decided to go on what he later called his 'odyssey' to find out the situation for himself. Two days later, he decided Gamelin's plan was the best option but by now it was far too late.

On this grave day, Gort considered his options. He believed nothing could stop the panzers reaching the sea. Already his LoC were cut and he was fighting on the forward echelons of ammunition. There was no possibility of the 1st Armoured Division – his one hope of reinforcement – could reach him. The German advance had forced the Air Component to abandon its French airfields and return to England, so

2 Major L. F., Ellis, *The War in France and Flanders 1939–1940* (London: HMSO, 1953), p. 114.

air support for the BEF would become unreliable in the near future.[3] Gort had three options. In the event of a successful counter-attack from the south he could stay on the line of the Escaut or at least the frontier defences. He could order a further fighting withdrawal to the line of the Somme, but this would mean abandoning the Belgians to their fate. However, by this time the enemy were already in Amiens and this option was not practical or even seriously considered. His last option was to withdraw to the coast and use the port facilities at Dunkirk to evacuate the men of the BEF, although it would mean abandoning all the heavy guns, vehicles and equipment. At 1:30 p.m., Pownall telephoned the Director of Military Operations and Plans at the War Office and presented these alternatives to him.

Gort also realised he would now be fighting two distinct battles, with little prospect of a co-ordinated Allied effort in the north as Billotte seemed incapable of providing this. The front in the east, currently on the Escaut became known as the Eastern battle and the battle that was to develop in the rear of the BEF the Western battle. Gort continued to establish 'stop-gap' forces to secure the position of the BEF. Polforce, under Major-General H.O. Curtis, was set up to safeguard the Canal Line in the area of St. Pol – Carvin and Usherforce, under Colonel C.M. Usher, to secure Dunkirk.

The War Cabinet did not accept Gort's third option of a withdrawal to Dunkirk and Ironside was dispatched to France to assess the situation. Ironside arrived early morning on 20 May at Gort's HQ with instructions from the War Office that 'the B.E.F. was to move southwards upon Amiens, attacking all enemy forces encountered and to take station on the left of the French army.'[4] This was the new army that Gamelin was forming along the line of the Somme. Gort knew this was impossible as the main body of the BEF was fully engaged along the whole of the Escaut Line.

Yet, Gort still thought a combined attack from the north and south might work. He had ordered the 5th Division to join the 50th Division in the area of Vimy for an attack south towards Cambrai, scheduled to take place on 21 May. This would at least narrow the gap between the eastern and northern armies, and perhaps Weygand could attack from the south. However, arrangements with the French were far from satisfactory. Ironside went to meet Billotte to arrange co-operation with the French First Army but found him in a state of complete depression. Ironside lost his temper and shook Billotte by the buttons of his tunic. This seemed to work and Billotte 'drew himself up to attention' and agreed to make an immediate plan to attack. Weygand agreed to attack from the south with the French Seventh Army. At this stage, the gap from Arras to the Somme was only 25 miles and if the attack was successful it would cut off the German armoured columns from the slower moving supporting infantry coming up behind.

3 The AASF was also forced to abandon its airfields following the German breakthrough, and work started on four new airfields further back in the neighbourhood of Orleans. Although forced to abandon these new sites after only four days' work, progress had reached a state were fighters could land at all four.

4 David Divine, *The Nine Days of Dunkirk*, (London: Faber & Faber, 1959), p. 42

On 21 May, Gort learned from the French that their First Army could not attack until 22 May or even 23 May. Gort felt he could not delay the preliminary move in the attack, so Frankforce – the name given to force comprising of the 5th and 50th Divisions under the command of Major-General H.E. Franklyn – was ordered to move forward and clear the area south-west of Arras. Frankforce's immediate objective was to secure the line of the rivers Scarpe and Cojeul. This was to be followed up by securing the Sensée the following day, and thence towards Bapaume and Cambrai. The French provided part of a mechanised cavalry division (*Général* Prioux) to operate on the flank of Frankforce. Frankforce ran straight into Rommel's armour. The Germans had been expecting counter-attacks from the north and south, and so at last it seemed they had materialised. The vigour in which Frankforce pushed its attack unsettled the Germans.

Rommel described the attack 'as a very heavy battle against hundreds of enemy tanks and following infantry' and reported back the situation to Rundstedt.[5] Rundstedt wrote in 1945:

> A critical moment in the drive came just as my forces had reached the Channel. It was caused by a British counter-stroke southward from Arras on May 21. For a short time it was feared that our armoured divisions would be cut off before the infantry divisions could come up to support them.[6]

Frankforce attacked with strength of only two battalions and 58 Mark I and 16 Mark II tanks. The main conclusion that can be drawn from the Arras action is that the German armoured spearhead was in a vulnerable position, and the German High Command was concerned that it could be cut off before the infantry came up in support. Weygand had had four days in which he could have acted, but he failed to do so.

Meanwhile on the same day Weygand, along with Billotte, met the King of the Belgians at Ypres to try and persuade him to withdraw his armies to the Yser to cover the combined attack by the BEF and the French First Army to the south. As Weygand's plans involved the BEF, Gort was sent for but Weygand had left before he arrived. Weygand's plan involved an attack from the north by eight divisions. The BEF would provide two of these divisions, the French First Army the rest. Weygand issued his Operation Order No 1, which put forward the decisions at the Ypres conference, and it included the following paragraphs:

> II. The only way to hold, and beat, the Germans is by counter-attack.
> III. The forces necessary for such a counter-attack are already in being within the group, which is moreover much too thick on the ground.[7]

5 Ibid., p.44.
6 Ibid.
7 Ellis, *The War in France and Flanders,* p. 112.

The Belgians had the impression that Weygand was not aware of the true situation and they were quite right in their assessment. Weygand apparently thought the forces in the north were much stronger than the armies assembling on the Somme and should carry the main weight of the counter-attack. This was not the reality. Gort was fully engaged on his Eastern front and was attempting to build his Western front to guard against the left hook of the German armour. The Belgian Army was fighting on a 60-mile front and was also running out of ammunition and had declared it could retire no further than the Lys as it was tired and disintegrating. The French First Army was also in no state to comply with Weygand's Operation Order. A report sent to Weygand on 25 May by a senior staff officer, *Commandant* Fauvelle, outlined the real state of French First Army:

> The First Army had, in actual fact, only three divisions left which were in a fit state to fight. These only had a day's artillery ammunition in addition to that in the boxes of the batteries, and a day's provisions.[8]

Withdrawal to the Gort Line

As already noted, Gort arrived at the Ypres conference after Weygand had left. During subsequent conversations with Billotte and the King of the Belgians, Billotte stated the French First Army was 'too tired' to take place in any offensive operations. Gort had already decided that the Escaut Line could not be held for more than 24 hours and had examined the possibility of withdrawing to the old frontier positions to take advantage of the pillboxes, trenches and anti-tank ditches. This retirement was agreed upon at the conference, with the Belgians agreeing to pull back to the River Lys. On the right, French formations would hold the frontier positions through which the British troops would withdraw and come into reserve. Further north, British forces withdrawing from the Escaut would fall in line with the French forces already mentioned and hold the frontier defences as far as Halluin. It was further hoped that Belgian forces could relieve the British in the sector Halluin – Courtrai on the night 23/24 May, the British forces relieved also passing into reserve. The British formations remaining on the frontier position would come under the command of the French First Army. The British forces in reserve would be available for the planned counter-attack to link up with the French forces on the Somme line.

The Anglo-French front now ran along the frontier defences from Halluin to Maulde, where it then pivoted onto the Canal Line, which extended from the Escaut to La Bassée and thence to St Omer and the sea while the Belgians held the River Lys from Halluin to Ghent (Figure 10.2). At this moment in time, the British held the Canal Line, a length of some 85 miles, with no more than 20,000 men and all

8 Divine, *The Nine Days of Dunkirk*, p. 248.

that could be organised were a series of 'stops' and demolitions. Anti-tank guns in particular were in short supply and there was barley sufficient to cover all the crossings. The shortening of the line by the withdrawal from the Escaut allowed the 2nd and 48th Divisions to assemble southwest of Lille for deployment in defence of the Canal Line. Macforce was no longer needed in the south following the concentration of the French First Army and was ordered to move to a more northerly sector of the Canal Line in the Nieppe Forest area. The 44th Division was held in GHQ reserve. Sadly, Billotte was fatally injured in a car crash on the way back from the conference to his HQ. There was now nobody in place aware of what had been discussed at the Ypres conference to co-ordinate the action of the northern armies.

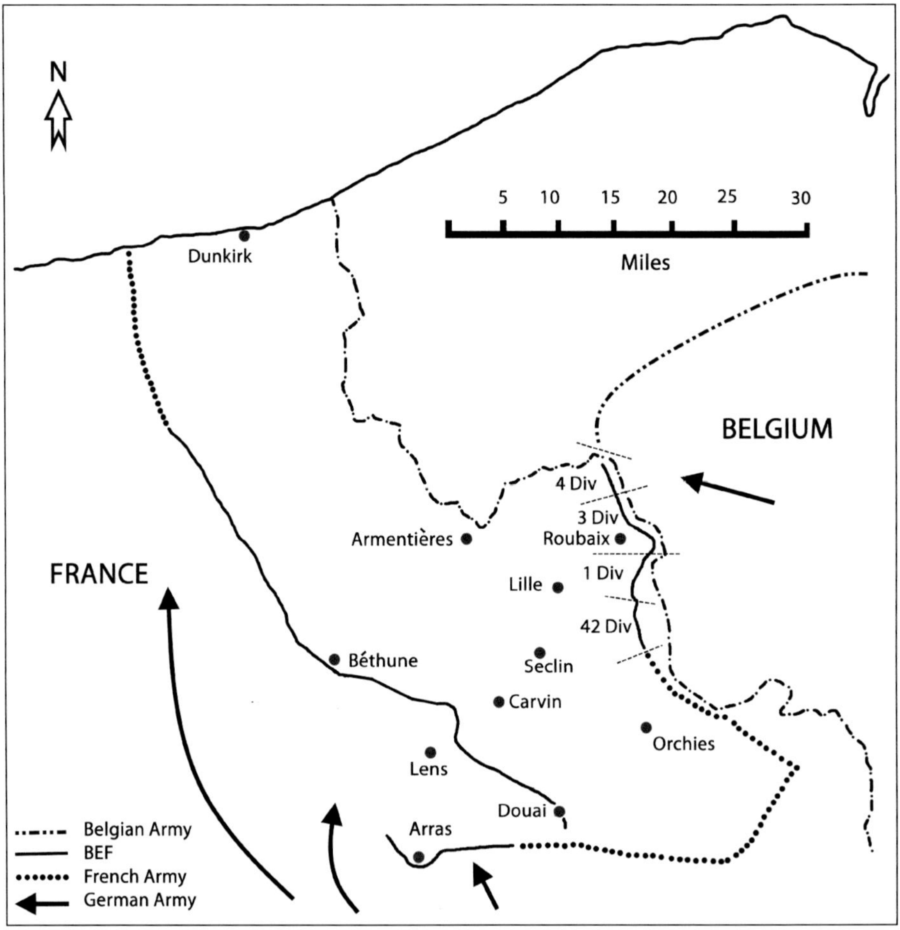

Figure 10.2: Withdrawal to the Gort Line: situation on 23 May.

Pownall well described the desperate situation the BEF was in on the Escaut and the need for the withdrawal and the establishment of a reserve:

> It should give us three divisions in reserve which is vital – at present G.H.Q. reserve consists *of one cavalry regiment* – a most dangerous situation but brought about by the need to hold two fronts, one of which *should* have been done by First French Army … We hold a front on the Escaut of seven divisions, each about 10,000 yards, with no corps reserves at all. Two divisions are on the Arras-Scarpe front, a necessary defence and an attempt to get the French to do something themselves there. And we have defensive posts manned by any old people, the 'labour' Territorial divisions, R.E. construction companies, anyone we can lay hold on thrown together, dished out with a few anti-tank rifles, some field guns and anti-tank mines. These line the Canal from Douai to Aire (and are to be extended to the sea at Calais) together with such centres of communication as Albert, Doullens, St Pol, etc. The B.E.F. is fighting hard on two fronts and defending itself in posts all the way back to the sea. How long can this continue?[9]

The withdrawal to the old frontier positions had been exhausting for the troops and at times confusion prevailed. The story of the 1st Battalion Royal Berkshire Regiment is no doubt typical. After successfully disengaging from the Dyle, the Battalion withdrew from the Senne Line to the Dendre on 18th May, arriving at Gamarages [sic] at 3:00 a.m. 'in a state of exhaustion and it was obviously impossible to march any further.'[10] The battalion had marched 40 miles in just over 28 hours. The CO decided to halt and billet the troops, which was not difficult as Gamarages was being rapidly evacuated and there was plenty of vacant accommodation. The Battalion did not rest for long as Gamarages was in no man's land; at 9:30 a.m. troop carriers arrived and most of the Battalion embussed and moved back to Wodecq. Some had to start on foot, marching to Grammont and acting as rear guard but further transport arrived and the whole Battalion was eventually able to travel by motorised transport.

The Battalion was looking forward to a rest and re-organisation, but this was not to be as at 3:00 p.m. the warning of the move back to Tournai was received. The move to Tournai was chaotic, and is best described in the words of the Battalion War Diary:

> At about 2300 hrs, however, the Bn was embussed and the column moved off. Just before RENAIX we ran off all our existing maps and felt reasonably confident that there would be some form of traffic control there. Our confidence was misplaced and the main square of RENAIX was full of a motley collection of tpt [transport] feverishly driving round and round looking for an outlet. The

9 Brian Bond (ed.), *Chief of Staff: The Diaries of Lieutenant-General Sir Henry Pownall* (London: Leo Cooper, 1972), p. 332.

10 TNA: WO167/706, 1st Royal Berkshire Regiment War Diary, 18 May 1940.

> C.O. made a recce before allowing the Bde column to go on and probably lose its way, and we moved on through traffic blocks which even London couldn't rival. It was the worst M.T. move the Bn had yet experienced, constant stopping and starting and drivers continually falling asleep. [11]

The Battalion arrived in Tournai at about 6:00 a.m. on 19 May amongst much confusion as the town was in the process of being evacuated. The town was bombed as the Battalion waited to be guided into its defensive position. The position was situated in the suburbs south of Tournai, behind the River Escaut. It was a strong position, mostly in buildings and on a forward slope. Tournai was repeatedly shelled and bombed, and refugees and stray Belgian soldiers were reported as giving 'considerable trouble'. In the evening, several men from the Kings Shropshire Light Infantry and 4/7th Dragoon Guards, who had been cut off, swam the river to the British lines.

On 20 May, enemy recce parties had reached the area and were successfully sniped at. Tournai continued to be shelled by mortars and artillery, causing some casualties while several alarmist rumours circulated, a practice which was strongly discouraged afterwards.

On 21 May, the Battalion moved into reserve, allotted a position in a wood south of St. Maur. It was another strong position, with excellent fields of fire and observation, but was also an obvious position so was heavily shelled on a frequent basis. The Battalion War Diary records that the troops worked hard on digging and wiring, heartened by the news that they were at last going to stand and fight. It seems that the troops on the ground did indeed think they were going to stand on the Escaut as Lille was canvassed for 5,000 men to dig the Divisional Reserve Line; guides, tools and lorries were laid on but only five Frenchmen turned up.

However, at 10:00 p.m. on 22 May the Battalion began to withdraw to the Gort Line in the vicinity of Bercu because of the decision reached at the Ypres Conference of 21 May. The Battalion arrived at 4:00 a.m. on 23 May and moved into the line at the main Tournai – Orchies road to Blockhouse 70, mostly occupying trenches it had dug before the move into Belgium.[12] The position still required a lot of work, which was begun immediately. French troops began to arrive during the day, as agreed at the Ypres Conference and by midnight the relief was complete, and the Battalion prepared to move into GHQ reserve. Some comfort must have been awarded to the troops on the discovery of a train at Bachy station by the arriving French troops which was full of ordnance stores of clothing; the Battalion War Diary notes that this 'was immediately looted and soon both French and British were completely re-equipped.'[13]

11 Ibid, 18 May 1940.
12 Most battalions that retired to the Gort Line were not lucky enough to end up back were they started from, which resulted in lost time as necessary recognisances were undertaken.
13 TNA: WO167/706, 1st Royal Berkshire Regiment War Diary, 23 May 1940.

Although the withdrawal to the Gort Line had been carried out successfully by the morning of 23 May, the situation of the Allies seemed hopeless. The German panzers had reached the coast; Boulogne was under heavy attack and Calais would also be by the end of the day. The panzers had also reached the Canal Line at St. Omer and Arras was hopelessly outflanked. Troops in the rear area of the LoC, which included the long-awaited Armoured Division, were finally removed from Gort's command and placed under the command of General Sir Henry Karslake. The BEF and the French First Army were in a precarious position, effectively trapped in a pocket stretching southwards from the coast for some 70 miles, only 25 miles wide at its widest point and 13 miles wide at its narrowest. Ammunition and supplies were desperately short and, on this day, the BEF was put on half rations.[14] All hope of the attack with eight divisions had gone, although the French First Army had actually recovered enough to launch an attack with the strength of about two divisions. The attack met little resistance until Cambrai, but the advance was then broken up by dive-bombers, the force withdrawing to its original line.

At 6:00 p.m. the situation suddenly changed. Rundstedt decided to halt the German armour on the line of the Aa Canal. He had lost 50 percent of his AFVs to enemy action and wear and tear. The countryside, now broken by dykes and flooded areas, was much less favourable to armour. He was convinced by Frankforce's counter-attack and the stubborn defence of Arras that he would face heavy losses if he advanced further. He was also convinced that the French Army still intact in the south was of considerable strength and that he had to conserve his own strength to prepare for *Fall Rot* – Operation Red – the attack south across the Somme. On the following day Hitler confirmed Rundstedt's order. Hitler still felt victory against the Allied northern Armies was certain as they would be destroyed by Bock's armies attacking down from Belgium and trapping them against the halted armour. Bock had other ideas though. He felt the key place to strike was at the junction of the Belgian and British Armies, aiming at a breakthrough towards the sea. This would also avoid having to come up against the Lille defences.

Meanwhile, in the east the enemy pressure on Arras continued and Gort realised that the town and the high ground to the north could not be held as a springboard for an attack to the south and ordered Major-General Franklyn to withdraw behind the Canal Line in the area around Seclin. This would still mean they would be ideally placed for any further counter-attack to the south. The lull in the fighting due to the enemy pause on the Canal Line made it possible for Gort to complete the reorganising

14 Montgomery believed that placing the BEF on half-rations made little difference. He was probably right as most divisional RASCs managed to round up abandoned cattle and were able to keep up a fair supply of fresh meat. Other sources of food included abandoned warehouses and deserted shops in Lille. The 42nd Division RASC, for instance, managed to serve up tinned asparagus and lobster to supplement rations. One of the abandoned shops they came across belonged to the upmarket firm Messrs. Felix Potin and the requisitioned stock was nicknamed the 'Felix' ration.

of his forces after the withdrawal from the Escaut and Arras. The 'stop-gap' forces – Frankforce, Petreforce, Polforce and Macforce – could be abolished and replaced by divisions freed because of the new shorter front in the east. I and II Corps would hold the British sector of the frontier line and III Corps the Canal Line. A change before this plan was implemented resulted in the withdrawal of III Corps (consisting of the 5th and 50th Divisions and First Army Tank Brigade) from the Canal Line, so it could prepare for a combined counter-attack with the French to begin on 26 May. The counter-attack, put forward by the British, envisaged an attack southward between the Escaut Canal and the Canal du Nord with the objective Havrincourt – Marcoing. It was hoped that *GQG* could co-ordinate this with the operations allegedly taking place to the south. The Canal Line was to be held with the 44th and 46th Divisions.

By 24 May Weygand had given up hope of the joint counter-attack. He was now aware of the true state of the French First Army and that the attack from the south could not now materialise. He blamed the situation on the British Army having decided to 'withdraw forty kilometres in the direction of the ports at a moment when our forces from the south were gaining ground towards the north to join up with the Allied Armies of the North.'[15] There was no truth in this – only Frankforce had withdrawn and only to the Canal Line, and was now making arrangements with General Blanchard (who had replaced Billotte) to attack south with two or three French divisions supported by 200 tanks. In addition, Weygand's claim that the French Seventh Army was advancing from the south showed just how out of touch he was with the situation on the ground – no progress had been made and the enemy held the line of the Somme in strength.

Moreover, on this day, a new threat arose in the Eastern battle as Bock opened his attack on the junction between the Belgian and British armies. By 7:00 a.m. on 25 May, the enemy penetration of the Belgian front was reported to be a depth of a mile and a half for 13 miles between Menin and Desselghem. Gort also expected the German attack to resume in the west, exploiting the bridgehead at St. Omer but the Eastern battle was his most imminent danger and he sent the last of the GHQ reserve, consisting of a brigade of infantry and two machine gun battalions, to General Brooke on the left flank of the BEF.

At around 7:00 a.m. in the morning, Sir John Dill arrived to discuss the situation with Gort. Dill became convinced of the seriousness of the situation and reported back to the Prime Minister:

> There is NO blinking the seriousness of the situation in the northern area. B.E.F. is now holding front of eighty-seven (87) miles with seven divs. in line exclusive of remnants of three T.A. labour divs. which are being used as stops on bridges... two B.E.F. divs. in reserve preparing attack in conjunction French for evening 26. Germans in contact along whole front and are reported to have penetrated

15 Ellis, *The War in France and Flanders*, p. 142.

> Belgian line north-east Courtrai yesterday evening. In above circumstances attack referred to above cannot be important affair.[16]

Gort's position was an unenviable one. He had been ordered by Weygand, Georges, Blanchard and the British Government to attack south, but he had also been tasked with the safety of the BEF by London. Just before 6:00 p.m., he walked into Pownall's office and said: 'Henry, I've had a hunch. We've got to call off the 5th and 50th Divisions from the attack to the south and send them over to Brookie on the left'.[17] This was only possible because in the east the BEF was entrenched in the old frontier positions. David Divine has likened the situation to a child extending a brick wall by taking a brick from one end and placing it at the other end. Gort's decision saved the BEF. Just after he had made his decision, news came in that a gap had been forced between Gheluwe and the River Lys and that the Belgians had no reserves left and had no way of closing it.

In the intervening time, British forces in the old frontier positions were largely unmolested from 23 to 26 May except for bombing and shelling by artillery and mortars. Troops and engineers were able to concentrate on improving the defences, carrying out demolitions of canal and river bridges, road cratering, laying anti-tank mines to cover gaps in the anti-tank ditches and carrying out contamination of petrol installations in Lille. The only British division to undertake any offensive action of note while on the Gort Line was the 3rd Division when its 8 Brigade carried out a reconnaissance in strength on 23 May. It was ordered to start at 7:00 p.m. and be completed by 9:30 p.m. All three battalions took part and were ordered to advance north-east of Wattrelos to a railway line about 1,000 yards in front of the forward positions to clean up any enemy in the intervening area. Machine guns of the 2nd Battalion Middlesex Regiment provided flank protection. The action indentified one enemy unit in the area but suffered losses of nine officers wounded (of whom three were missing), four other ranks killed, four missing and 97 wounded and five carriers lost. The Official history records that little purpose was severed for such high casualties.

The 4th Division had withdrawn back to the line Halluin – Tourcoing and was on the left of the British Front, taking over the old 5th Division front. Immediately after they arrived, field companies were ordered to undertake preparations for cratering all roads entering the position where they crossed the anti-tank ditch which had been constructed during the winter. The Divisional commander decided that Halluin should form part of the position, so section posts had to be dug and wired in front of Halluin, connecting the existing defences with the River Lys, which formed the boundary with the Belgian Army. The laying of anti-tank mines, loopholing walls, preparing buildings for defence, constructing road blocks and demolishing buildings

16 Ibid., p. 147.
17 Divine, *The Nine Days of Dunkirk*, p. 54.

to clear lines of fire were all undertaken. [18] A water tower overlooking the position was demolished on the second attempt. Lieutenant Clarke thought that this time the BEF really was going to stand and fight it out and that it had 'plenty to fight with': he notes that on 24 May he had 'never seen such a concentration of formations...the white triangles of 1 Div and the crossed keys of 2 Div. as well as the TA divisions'.[19]

On 24 May, orders were given for blowing all craters entering Halluin and to prepare all bridges over the Lys for demolition. In addition, all barges on the Lys were to be destroyed. Lieutenant Clarke describes this unpleasant business of making the bargees homeless:

> I walk across the field towards it, [the barge] and up the gang plank. There are lace curtains and china ornaments and an elderly couple very frightened. I give them ten minutes to pack their belongings and get out. They ask me where they are to go, and I cannot help them. ..Behind me black smoke curls up from the burning houseboat.[20]

Clarke also rushed down to the Halluin bridge to see it was destroyed as the Belgians appeared to have withdrawn and the enemy was seen on the far river bank. Enemy columns could also be observed on the Menin – Ypres road. This compelled the 4th Division to extend its left front along the River Lys, forming a defensive flank. Preparations for the demolition of crossings over the Ypres – Comines canal, which was found to be dry and only an anti-tank ditch in places, were undertaken.

When the 3rd Division fell back to the Gort Line – the troops driving back quantities of cattle with them – it took over the original 4th Division front along the line of Roubaix – Tourcoing. Clarke was ordered to leave immediately for HQ 3rd Division on 21 May to show them where all the engineer work was, especially the pillboxes. HQRE 3rd Division was apparently not impressed:

> They do not think that 4 Div. has done very much work at all. They wish they were in their old sector where they have dug a continuous fire trench from end to end as well as building twice our number of pillboxes.[21]

He went on to observe:

18 Whilst organising the defences, in at least one instance British troops attempting to occupy a French blockhouse found themselves locked out of it, the previous occupants having left and taken the keys with them!

19 Ralph Lionel Clarke, *Three Weeks to La Panne: A Diary of Dunkirk* <http://www.foxearth.org.uk/ThreeWeeksToLaPanne> (accessed 25 August 2017).

20 Ibid.

21 Clarke, *Three Weeks to La Panne.*

> In general, they have had no difficulty in finding our pillboxes [i.e. those built by 4th Division] but do not think much of their siting. But our efforts will be useful in diverting enemy attention away from the fieldworks they are building for themselves.[22]

The 2nd Battalion Bedfordshire Regiment, 10 Infantry Brigade, formed part of the 4th Division. Second-Lieutenant R.H. Medley, whom we have already met and now Acting Second in Command C Company, gives his experience of the retreat to the Gort Line during those hectic days:

> Captain Johnson went off to an Orders Group and on his return gave us new orders to withdraw to Mouscron on the French frontier. The battalion was to begin its move at 2200 hrs and 'C' Company was to cover its withdrawal. We lay up covering two roads leading into the main withdrawal route and saw 'A', 'B' and 'D' Companies pass through. Once they were passed, we followed along behind. Pte Rayner our cook, had acquired a goat which supplemented the milk ration and started off leading his newly acquired milk supply. Captain Johnson ordered it to be let loose when we arrived at a final check point. The Brigadier retrieved the situation by lifting the goat in the back of his vehicle.
>
> The long march back became more exhausting as the East Surrey territorial battalion ahead of us were dead beat and the pace became slower and slower. One of their soldiers shot himself in sheer desperation at about 0200 hrs. Eventually our route left the cross-country tracks for a metalled road and the pace improved. We crossed the frontier at Mouscron at about 0900 hrs and found Captain Johnson and the CQMS waiting for us at the National Range de Tir with a hot breakfast. My batman on his own initiative brought me a mess tin of food and quite rightly I received a just rocket for accepting it before all the soldiers had been fed.
>
> The march back that night had covered some eighteen miles and the march discipline was something to be proud. No one fell out. We were now in an excellent position in depth with two anti-tank ditches each covered by pillboxes and some wire. The Company took up positions in the National Range de Tir which had walls at right angles to the front. Trench positions were sited, and holes knocked in the walls to provide fields of fire. We spent the night in the firing bay. It at least provided some cover. The next day, the 24th May, a Tiger Moth with Belgian Air Force colours flew around about one hundred feet above our positions. Probably manned by a German aircrew! I had been told to liaise with the KOSB on our right flank. I met Lt Anderson and CSM Smith...I also met McEachran whom I was next to meet up with again at Shrewsbury after our return to England when we caught up on what had passed in the intervening

22 Ibid.

> days. His soldiers were digging in in a cemetery and sappers were planting charges to blow craters on all routes to our front. There was little ground activity and on 25th May the battalion frontage was contracted, and "C" Company abandoned positions in the Range de Tir and provided a third line in depth some four hundred yards further back.[23]

Medley recorded that things warmed up on the 26 May, with frequent bouts of shelling forcing the troops to stay in their trenches. That night, he could here gunfire behind him on the right and the situation on the left was not good as the Belgian Army was being driven back towards Menin. The following day, Medley experienced more pronounced shellfire, with the positions he was occupying now being overlooked by the enemy from high ground on the left. At 2:00 p.m. orders were received for a move to protect the left flank and C Company embussed at 2:30 p.m. to deploy along the Ypres – Warnetan road, leaving A and B Companies to hold the frontier positions. This remaining force was caught up in the fighting along the Ypres – Comines Canal and suffered many casualties. The 4th Division Engineers (7th, 59th and 225th Field Companies) were also caught up in this battle and used as a whole to carry out a counter-attack. Pakenham-Walsh states this was probably an example of the whole of a division's engineers used in an infantry role unique to the Corps of the RE.

The 2nd Battalion Cheshire Regiment (MG battalion) also fell back to the vicinity of Roubaix, just south of Mouscron, with its HQ at Marcq-en-Baroeuil. Its A Company was situated forward at Bailleul, just west of the Escaut. The Germans succeeded in crossing the Escaut in this sector at first light on 23 May and several counter-attacks failed to dislodge them. The Germans were, however, stopped from any further progress by the joint efforts of A Company and the 3rd Battalion Grenadier Guards. It was a carrier of the Grenadiers which moved the Cheshire's Vickers machine guns and ammunition to a position in which they could engage the enemy at 800 to 1,100 yards that made this possible; all the Cheshire's trucks were in the wagon line, five miles to the rear. At 4:00 p.m., A Company received orders to withdraw behind the defences of Roubaix. One section of No. 6 Platoon, under the command of Lance-Corporal Renshaw received the order to prepare to withdraw but not the subsequent order to withdraw. He discovered they were surrounded and decided to stay put until first light and then make an attempt to get away. After many detours due to enemy parties, they eventually reached the British FDLs and Lance-Corporal Renshaw was subsequently awarded the MM for his bravery and leadership in getting his platoon away. On 24 May, it was announced by wireless that the Germans were in Arras and Amiens, giving the Battalion its first indication of the extent to which the BEF was encircled in the south. Supplies were running short and everyone was on half rations. On 25 May, A Company's No. 4 Platoon shot two Germans out of a tree (believed

23 R.H. Medley, *Five Days to Live: France 1939–40* (Abergavenny: Dover & Company, 1972), pp. 34–35.

to be observers) with a burst from a Vickers at 800 yards. Three other ranks of this platoon joined a patrol of the 1st Battalion The Loyal Regiment which captured a patrol of eight Germans, all drunk in an estaminet only 300 yards beyond the anti-tank ditch!

The southern sector of the old frontier positions was held by the 42nd Division. Its 127 Brigade was holding the line from Gruson to Ascq, and its OC, Brigadier Sir John Smyth, VC, MC, gives a good description of the Brigade's time in the frontier position:

> My brigade started moving slowly back as soon as it was dark, and just before midnight the other two brigades began their long trek back from the Escaut. Not a shot was fired, and, as day broke, we peered through the wire at a completely blank and peaceful countryside. It was only then that the Germans realised what had happened and it was not until the afternoon that we saw their first patrols advancing. This was Wednesday, 22nd May, but we had lost all count of time and the men were literally asleep on their feet. So, I took advantage of a peaceful afternoon to give as many men as possible a few hours' sleep. By that evening the brigades had been sorted out and we were holding a 4,000-yard front from Gruson to Ascq, with our brigade H.Q. at Sainguin [sic]. During the late afternoon of 23rd May, German patrols made contact all along the front and that night they made a somewhat tentative attack, covered by a concentration of heavy mortars which we had not experienced before, and which made a rather terrifying din. However, the men soon found that few casualties were caused and that the noise was the worst thing about them. In fact, the men were rather enjoying themselves now that they had had a good sleep. They had most of them never fed so well in their lives, for the deserted farms were simply crawling with chickens, ducks and pigs and it seemed a pity to leave them to the coarse palates of the Germans troops ... The 24th and 25th May found us still holding the Lille defences with brigade H.Q. at Sainguin [sic]. The Germans had been probing our front but had made no serious attempt to dislodge us. Our real trouble was, as always, the extent of the front we had to hold, which meant that there always had to be a very large proportion of men in action and too few getting any rest. German aircraft were constantly overhead, and their artillery was ranging on roads and bridges behind our front. All mails from England had ceased and we were put on half rations. The latter did not worry us much to begin with because we were living on the country, but a complete stoppage of letters and newspapers has always depressed the British soldier. We did have our wireless sets, however, and it was obvious from the news that the position of the B.E.F. was becoming very grim...All civil control seemed to have broken down entirely and we had to find military police all over our area to regulate the difficult but important civilian traffic. On Sunday, 26th May, the situation on our front was quite serene, but the Highland Light Infantry battalion H.Q. narrowly escaped a direct hit from a bomb and suffered a very severe shaking. Our complete air

> inferiority was both irksome and demoralising. Even the ordinary functions of nature had to be performed with one eye on the skies, and by day, movement was only possible in small parties.[24]

The 5th Battalion Manchester Regiment were one of the battalions in 127 Brigade, commanded by Ronald France, a Territorial officer whom Brigadier Smyth had successfully kept in post despite Gort's suggestion that Territorial officers commanding battalions be replaced with regular officers. The Battalion was bussed to the Gort Line on 22 May after Macforce was dissolved. Its task was to hold part of the line around the Gruson area as the BEF withdrew from the Escaut. The War Diary describes its position as consisting of a 'fully prepared A/Tk ditch, with 6 pillboxes and [a]small secondary ditch'.[25]

A gap was discovered in the anti-tank ditch, which was blocked by anti-tank mines (5 yard spacing in 10 rows) by the Royal Engineers. On 23 May, several enemy reconnaissance aircraft were seen overhead, and one plane bombed a road one mile east of the Battalion position. During 24 May, the Battalion was occupied in digging weapon-pits and clearing civilians and cattle from the front line. Many of these civilians were returning from Douai, which was now in German hands, or had been turned back from St Pol by enemy troops. The first enemy troops were also seen; one party of eight men and one of 30 men. B Company opened fire on a party of 30 men at 1,000 yards range while C Company shot up a motor cycle combination. An enemy machine gun was reported in woods 1,400 yards in front of the position and five rounds of 3 inch mortar were fired into the wood. The enemy began shelling the frontline pillboxes and also fired intermittent heavy mortar rounds in to the area. That night, the Battalion received one fatality and one seriously wounded when the leader of a patrol stepped on an anti-tank mine.

The 25 May was a relatively quiet day, with some intermittent shelling by mortars. An enemy observation balloon was seen, presumed to be spotting for heavy mortars which were shelling the railway line. Engineers and the Battalion pioneers were preparing all bridges in the area for demolition, replacing them with planks ready for a rapid withdrawal. On 26 May, news was received that the French had given way at St Amand and that the Battalion was to be prepared to move to Armentières. The Battalion arrived at Armentières on 28 May and took up positions on the River Lys at Le Bizet. On the move back, one of the Battalion's lorries was caught by an enemy armoured fighting vehicle, the driver being killed.

When the BEF advanced into Belgium, the field companies stopped working on the defences, immobilising their plant and collecting starting keys and handles to pass onto the general construction companies which continued to work on the Gort Line defences as planned. For instance, the 667th General Construction Company

24 Smyth, *Before the Dawn*, pp. 64–66.
25 TNA: WO167/789, 5th Manchester Regiment War Diary, 22 May 1940.

continued work on pillboxes up to 17 May, when the first signs that things had not gone well were evident when orders were received to 'stand to' and sections ordered to guard bridges at St. Amand and to put Rumegies into a 'state of defence' and block roads. On 18 May, the OC reported to 2nd General Construction Battalion at Orchies asking for further instructions about blocking roads at Rumegies as the roads were filling up with refugees. He was taken to GSO 1 MacForce and ordered to proceed to Carvin forthwith and place this town in a state of defence, including blocking roads from the southeast and east.

The journey to Carvin was difficult owing to road congestion but by 5:00 a.m. on 19 May sections were at work assembling farm carts, implements etc. for road blocks. The War Diary noted the following:

> During the period at CARVIN, the Refugee-traffic ie – on foot, bicycles, carts, motors – was very great. At times it would go South, then West to La Bassee [sic], & then almost reverse its direction. On 3 occasions the OC felt justified in sending into hospital at LENS obviously ill children with their parents. Only 1 baker (out of 3) remained at his post, a farmer at the southern entrance to the town. The bakery worked like niggers. Many refugees were half-starving.[26]

The Company continued to guard all road blocks (five in total) until 3:00 p.m. on 21 May when an officer of the 6th Battalion York & Lancaster Regiment arrived with instructions for the Company to move to Oiginies and work under them. The Company established itself in Chateau Wood and started digging weapon pits for the Yorks & Lancs. Work continued on these positions the following day and the Company lived 'on the country.' Pigs, potatoes etc. were requisitioned or taken. No bread was brought, unless there was a surplus after the needs of refugees had been met.

On 23 May the OC Yorks & Lancs arrived and with instructions that he was to move off with his Battalion, taking the transport of 667th General Construction Company with him; the Company wisely held onto four trucks to transport its tools etc. On 25 May the OC 2/5th Battalion Sherwood Foresters appeared, and the Company began digging weapon pits around Chateau Wood for their C Company. On 26 May, the Company was ordered to move to Steenvoorde and begin its move to Dunkirk. The whole Company had been safely embarked by 6:30 a.m. on 28 May.

Dunkirk

By 26 May, three German divisions were approaching the position taken up by the 5th Division while two were now in close contact with the old frontier positions. One more was in close support. As we have seen, British divisions in the Gort Line were

26 TNA: WO167/1034, 667th General Construction Company War Diary, 19 May 1940.

not heavily attacked during the day, although they were subject to heavy shelling and some bombing, with enemy artillery ranging in on the blockhouse line. British observers in the forward positions noted large formations of enemy units moving north but owing to the shortage of ammunition and the need to husband the remaining stocks, the artillery could not engage them. The German plan was to provide for a holding attack on the frontier positions to pin down the BEF while the main thrust struck towards the general area of Ypres at the hinge of the BEF and Belgian forces. The British had managed to obtain a copy of these plans when a British patrol had shot up a German Staff car and Brooke's placing of the 5th Division was made in light of these plans.

The situation in the west was also becoming more desperate. The German halt order did not prevent attempts to widen the bridge heads across the Canal Line. A particularly strong attack developed against the 2nd Division's front and in the general area of St. Venant. This was a preliminary move which was to develop into a pincer movement on Kemmel with the object of linking up with Bock's Sixth Army. The halt order also did not apply to German units in the south, and a heavy enemy attack developed against the French First Army, with the aim of trying to link up with units of Army Group B attacking towards Seclin.

On this day, key decisions were taken both by the German High Command and the British Government. In light of the slow progress of Bock's armies, Hitler's HQ issued an order for an attack from the west by armoured groups and infantry divisions in the direction of Tournai – Cassel – Dunkirk. Meanwhile in the morning, the Secretary of State for War had sent a telegram to Gort informing him that the Government had received information that the planned French offensive from the south could not be launched in sufficient strength to link up with the Northern Armies. Later, Gort received a second telegram:

> [N]o course open to you but to fall back upon coast...M. Reynaud communicating General Weygand and latter will no doubt issue orders in this sense forthwith. You are now authorised to operate towards coast forthwith in conjunction with French and Belgian Armies.[27]

Operation 'Dynamo', the code name for the evacuation of the BEF, was ordered to commence. Late on this day, Gort appointed Sir Ronald Adam to organise the defence of Dunkirk.

On 27 May the German drive resumed, with an attack east on a 35 mile front between Gravelines and Robecq and another towards Armentières and Kemmel, to cut off the BEF and the French First Army and link up with Bock's Sixth Army. Holding its position in the face of the strongest German action against British troops in the entire campaign, the 2nd Division practically ceased to exist on this day.

27 Divine, *The Nine Days of Dunkirk*, p. 86.

Along the Canal Line, the 'stops' at Lestrem, Hazebrouck, Cassel, Arneke, Ledringhem and Wormhoudt continued to be a thorn in the side of the Germans, causing them some delay. In the east, Bock's 6th Army attacked the 5th and 50th Divisions, but failed to exploit the gap that had opened up between the remnants of the Belgian Army and the BEF.

During an Anglo-French conference held on this day, a message was received from the Belgian King, who stated he feared that 'a moment is rapidly approaching when he can no longer rely upon his troops to fight or to be of any further use to the B.E.F.', and that he would be 'obliged to surrender before a debacle.'[28] But at least the conference did decide on a perimeter for Dunkirk, with the British responsible from Nieuport along the canals through Furnes to the old town of Bergues and the French from the limits of Bergues to Gravelines.

Almost immediately following the message from the Belgian King, Gort received a telegram from Weygand: 'General Weygand makes a personnel appeal to General Gort. The British Army must participate strongly in the necessary joint counter-attacks. Situation demands hard hitting.'[29] Weygand failed to mention with what these hard-hitting attacks were to be made with, as the BEF and French First Army had two pincers closing in on them and were short of ammunition and petrol.

The 2nd Division's stand and sacrifice and the other holding actions allowed the BEF to slip away. The 3rd Division disengaged from the frontier defences and moved north behind the front of the 50th division to extend the flank towards the new Dunkirk perimeter.[30] Behind them the 4th and 42nd Divisions fell back onto the line of the River Lys and formed a defensive flank from Comines to Armentières. The French III Corps held the river line from Armentières to Estaires.

On 28 May, Bock took advantage of the Belgian surrender and launched an attack on the coast, pivoted on Ypres. They were met in the coastal area around Nieuport by the 12th Lancers, which Gort had kept in GHQ reserve, and the Germans were delayed just long enough for Adam's measures to organise the defence to take effect. Brigadier Lawson managed to move up a mixed force of gunners, engineers and anti-aircraft gunners fighting as infantry and with elements of the French 60th Division the Germans were held.

In the west, the 'stops' fell one by one, but new ones were established behind them – Quaëdypre, Wylder, Bambecque, Vyfweg and Bergues. The 'stops', along with the difficult terrain for AFVs, led to a drastic change in opinion by Guderian, who came to the conclusion that 'Further tank attacks would involve useless sacrifice of our best

28 Ibid., pp. 95–96.
29 Ibid., p. 96.
30 Montgomery describes this manoeuvre as the most difficult he had to perform in the campaign, involving a night move of the whole Division within a couple of thousand yards of the 5th Division front, where a fierce battle had raged all day and was still going on. The following day, Montgomery learned of the Belgian surrender, leaving his left flank completely uncovered.

troops.'[31] The Germans hesitated on this day. Although it is hard not to believe that if they had pushed home the attack, they would have carried Dunkirk, the decision was made to withdraw the armour from the battle for overhaul and repair in preparedness for Case Red. *Reichsmarschall* Göering promised Hitler that the *Luftwaffe* would destroy the Allied armies in the north.

One tragedy of this day was the loss of the French First Army, which became cut off in the quadrilateral of canals south-west of Lille. Blanchard had decided to stand on the Lys in the absence of any orders to the contrary from Weygand or Georges. He sent a telegram to Weygand that Gort was withdrawing on his own initiative. Weygand asked the President of the Council to lodge a protest about 'Gort's too selfish attitude'.[32] This was despite being informed by the British Government that its policy was still to stand by their Ally – the evacuation was seen as a way of reuniting the severed forces in the north and south by transfer by sea via England. It is clear, even at this stage in the campaign, that neither Weygand nor Blanchard understood the perilous situation of the Allied forces in the north. With the exception of the French III Corps and the Cavalry Corps, which were bought out by *Général* de la Laurencie, the French First Army fought on bravely, but uselessly, until 1 June when they surrendered with the honours of war.

By 29 May, Brooke had established a rearguard line from Noordschote through Proven to Poperinghe. That morning, the Germans had come up to this line and from thereafter it was under heavy shellfire. At dusk, the general withdrawal to the Dunkirk perimeter began, which was completed by 30 May. The perimeter held until 2 June when Captain Tennant, Senior Naval Officer at Dunkirk was able to signal: 'B.E.F. evacuated.' However, the Battle of France was not yet over – it continued for another three weeks as the Germans launched Case Red: the destruction of the Allied armies in the south and the occupation of France.

The success of Operation Dynamo was in part due to Germans errors: mention has already been made of the halt orders while the *Luftwaffe* wasted much time in attacking troops on the beaches – it should have gone all out for the ships at the first moment. In periods when it did this, shipping losses were high, forcing the Admiralty to momentarily withdraw all modern destroyers from the evacuation on 29 May and limiting evacuation to the hours of darkness from dusk on 1 June. Had the *Luftwaffe* focused entirely on attacking the ships from the start of the evacuation, Göering's promise to his *Führer* may well have been realised. Nevertheless, the Allied strategy lay in ruins and Germany had won a great victory. But the BEF was safely back home and now as part of Home Forces was assisting with the nationwide endeavour to build defences to resist an invasion of Britain. Its experience in preparing defences and maintaining aerodromes was to be put to good use.

31 Divine, *The Nine Days of Dunkirk*, p. 107.
32 Ibid., p. 108.

Aftermath: Britain's anti-invasion defences

Gordon Barclay, in *If Hitler Comes: Preparing for Invasion Scotland 1940,* has demonstrated that Britain's anti-invasion planning was not a homogeneous entity that appeared suddenly to a coherent plan. It was the result of a complex relationship between shifting defence policy and shortcomings in British military and naval thinking, especially in misunderstandings of German intentions, preparedness and capability for mounting an invasion. This subject is outside the scope of this book, and the following discussions will focus on the summer of 1940, where clear parallels can be drawn with the BEF defences in France and the subsequent rejection of static defence, and concrete defences in particular.

As we have already seen in Chapter 2, the main perceived threat against Britain in the lead up to war was from the air; there was little fear of invasion. This changed from October 1939 onwards, largely it is thought because of German propaganda which worked hard to suggest a combined attack from seaborne troops and parachutists in order to tie up British troops in the defence of the Britain. The Commander-in-Chief Home Forces – General Kirke – was required to prepare plans to deal with this threat and in November 1939 he produced the 'JC Plan'. Its name was derived from two code words: 'JULIUS' indicating a likely invasion and 'CAESAR' that invasion was imminent.

The JC Plan worked from the premise that an invasion could not be successful unless the Germans seized a port or ports by the use of airborne troops. The JC plan intended to defeat an attack by inflicting maximum damage on airborne troops as they landed and collected. If airborne forces became established, a cordon was to drawn around them in order to immobilise them until counter-attack troops could move up to eliminate them. It was an eminently sensible plan, although there was a lack of trained and equipped troops to properly carry it out – a recurrent theme! The invasion scare went up a notch in April 1940 with the German invasion of Norway; now the control of the seas by the Royal Navy seemed less certain. Troops prepared for active service were to be stationed along the Scottish and English East Coasts to meet an invasion. Portions of these troops were to be made mobile by the provision of transport. Those in an advance state of training in Aldershot and Southern Command would be in GHQ reserve. Yet still, on the ground, little was accomplished except for the digging of a few weapon pits and providing 18 pdr guns for the protection of the Scottish ports of Aberdeen and Dundee and in Eastern Command the ports Lowestoft and Ramsgate.

On 27 May Ironside replaced Kirke as Commander-in-Chief of Home Forces. By 2 June, the evacuation from Dunkirk was complete and Britain now became a theatre of war, with Home Forces operating under conditions much the same as the BEF had in France during the Sitzkrieg. It must have felt like déjà vu to Ironside. In fact, he faced a much more perilous situation with regards to equipment shortages than the BEF did when it sailed over to France in 1939. The formations in the United Kingdom at the time were still undergoing training and few had reached a sufficient standard or possessed the necessary equipment to take on enemy troops in mobile warfare. Although the troops evacuated from Dunkirk were experienced in battle, they were disorganised and had lost all their heavy equipment and transport. In total, Ironside had at his disposal 15 infantry divisions, one armoured division and 57 Home Defence battalions and the Local Defence Volunteers (LDV) formed in mid-May.[33] Only limited numbers of 25 pdr field guns and 2 pdr anti-tank guns remained in Britain and only a handful of obsolete light tanks were available to the armoured division.

In Ironside's opinion, a large part of the Army was fit only for static defence – exactly the same point he and Lieutenant-General Dill had made with regards to the BEF back in the autumn of 1939. In this sense, the Sitzkrieg and Britain's anti-invasion planning in the summer of 1940 shared the characteristic of a static defence imposed on the Army. Nevertheless, despite being forced to instigate a static defence scheme to defeat an invasion, Ironside emphasised 'All our energies must be put into stopping this [the establishment of a German bridgehead in England]. No waiting for more troops to come up. Our mobile forces must attack at once regardless of losses and nip the landing in the bud. We cannot inculcate that idea too much into everybody concerned.'[34] A strong mobile reserve was crucial to Ironside as this was the only way of influencing the battle. However, such a reserve simply did not exist in June 1940. Ironside envisaged more men being withdrawn from static defence into mobile counter-attack formations as the training and equipment situation improved, but this would take time.

GHQ Operating Instruction No. 1, issued on 5 June while the French were still fighting, envisaged a German seaborne and airborne invasion of Britain, using the shortest crossing routes available in order to achieve surprise and concentration of forces, including air cover for the invasion. The possibility of subsidiary operations in the Shetlands, Ireland or the north of Scotland had also to be taken into account. An invasion was expected to open with simultaneous attacks by parachute troops to capture landing grounds for the use of troop-carrying aircraft and attacks on communications and other vital points. This would be combined with a seaborne invasion, with numerous AFVs landed in the first flight. The most likely point of attack was speculated to be between the Wash and Newhaven, with areas with good beaches being selected to land transports carrying AFVs or the seizing of port facilities to unload AFVs. It was recognised that as the Germans continued their advance in France, this 'danger area' would increase.

33 The use of parachute troops during the first days of the attack on Holland produced a sense of hysteria in Britain, with visions of parachutists and fifth columnists popping up all over the place. The War Office hastily put in place a scheme for 'Local Defence Volunteers' to watch out for these parachutists and fifth columnists and hopefully alleviate public fears and prevent outbreaks of vigilantism. The scheme was largely based on General Kirke's idea for the formation of a Defence Force on a town and village basis, giving the utmost latitude to local knowledge and enterprise. Churchill renamed the LDV as the Home Guard in July 1940.

34 Colonel R. Macleod, DSO, MC & Denis Kelly (eds.), *Time Unguarded: The Ironside Diaries 1937-1940* (New York: David McKay & Company Inc., 1963), p. 346.

The general policy for defence laid out in Operation Instruction No. 1 was 'that there would be no withdrawal', and if the enemy gained a foothold, he was to be driven out as soon as possible.[35] This was to be achieved by demolitions and blocks on communications designed to prevent or delay the expansion of any enemy foothold. Defences were to be of 'concrete construction and provided with overhead cover' where possible.[36] Beaches selected for defence would be protected by wire, concrete blocks and minefields, all protected by light machine guns in pillboxes. Commands were also to obstruct all possible landing grounds within a five mile radius of certain specified ports, within the Metropolitan Area of London and within a five mile radius of all beaches practicable for a seaborne landing. The Air Ministry was responsible for the obstruction of all possible spaces were landings could take place within a five mile radius of RAF landing grounds.

After the events in France, Ironside's greatest fear was the prospect of enemy armoured formations running riot if they penetrated the defences. However, the English countryside was different from the wide rolling open areas of Poland and France and thus much less suitable for the employment of AFVs, which would be largely restricted to roads. Ironside had great faith in the LDV and saw their role as a vital one in forming the basis of a road defence in great depth and avoiding the tragedy that unfolded in France:

> I shall get a great deal out of these L.D.V.s. It will differ according to the man who is in charge. I put down the following:
> 1. Static defence of village by blocks to prevent armoured columns moving.
> 2. Information from bicycle patrols issuing from the village.
> 3. Moltoff [sic] cocktails to deal with tanks from the windows of houses.
>
> If we can get this going, we ought to make easy movements through the country impossible and to avoid [repeating] the spectacle of France having her guts torn out without any effort being made to deal with the aggressor. All the troops cowering behind a water obstacle [i.e. the French Armies assembling along the Somme] and facing nothing. Not fighting but waiting while their very entrails were being torn out. A pitiable sight.[37]

Ironside elaborated on the role of the LDV in a speech he made to the leaders of the LDV. In this speech, he stated that in France wherever there was a block, the Germans columns turned off. However, there were precious few blocks in France restricting their movement. In the rural areas of Britain, Ironside wanted every village or group of houses to be blocked to prevent the enemy from 'just rushing about where he likes'

35 TNA: WO166/1,' Operating Instruction No. 1', 5 June 1940, GHQ Home Forces General Operations War Diary.
36 Ibid.
37 Macleod, DSO, MC &Kelly (eds.), *Time Unguarded*, pp. 345–346.

which 'was the great failure in France.'[38] For towns, Ironside told the LDV leaders he wanted 'blocks on the roads leading in so as to stop the man [i.e. the enemy] coming in into your centre and clawing your guts out'.[39] Ironside also saw the provision of information to enable GHQ to best deploy its mobile columns to deal with the enemy as a vital role for the LDV. For mobile forces, Ironside had to improvise. He created troops of three motor cars with Brens commanded by a Tank Corps officer, christened 'Ironsides'. These were to form motor columns with infantry in lorries. To tackle tanks, he hoped to have a number of 6 pdr and 12 pdr guns mounted on lorries. Ironside was under no illusion that these were adequate substitutes for tanks, but they might get lucky with a shot and knock out a German tank. Ironside was also temporarily handicapped by the decision to prioritise the re-equipping of the BEF to return to France – although until dispatched they would be available for home defence – as it meant no more equipment for home defence troops.[40]

With the final defeat of the French, Germany was now truly at the gates of England and everyone expected Hitler's next move would be the invasion of Britain (Figure 10.2 and 10.3).[41] Ironside reasoned that the British 'coastline is terrific in length and we may be attacked at any point of it, owing to the fact that the Germans may start from Norway, the Baltic, Holland or France. They may even take Ireland first and so extend the possibility of landing still further to the west.'[42] There was a real fear at the time that the Navy could not guarantee to foil a seaborne invasion because of the narrow waters and German aircraft operating from coastal airfields. German airborne forces could land anyway where in Britain or Ireland. The lack of anti-tank guns, artillery and AFVs necessitated another static defence scheme, with the principles of FSR somewhat modified to take into account these shortages and the long fronts that would have to be held to guard against any invasion.[43] The general policy for this new defence scheme was set out in GHQ Operating Instruction No. 3.

38 Charles Grave, *The Home Guard of Britain*, p. 71.
39 Ibid., p. 72.
40 Montgomery says in his memoirs that there was in England only sufficient transport and armament to equip one division. It was decided to give this to his 3rd Division and to get that Division ready to go back across the Channel and join up with the British forces still fighting with the French Army. Brooke was to be Commander-in-Chief of this second Expeditionary Force. Montgomery's 3rd Division was equipped and ready to be sent back across the Channel by the middle of June but the French capitulated on 17 June.
41 With hindsight, we now know that Hitler's real intentions were to the East and not Britain. However, to keep up the pressure on Britain he issued his famous *Führer* Directive No. 16, which ordered the preparations for the invasion. Although the German Navy viewed the prospects of undertaking an invasion of Britain with dismay, they still achieved a great feat in assembling the necessary barges required to transport the invasion force. The Army greeted the Directive with enthusiasm and made tremendous efforts to be ready to carry out the invasion. Hence at the time, the fear of invasion was entirely reasonable, and the anti-invasion defences a sensible precaution.
42 Macleod, DSO, MC & Kelly (eds.), *Time Unguarded*, p 374.
43 The issue of long fronts and equipment shortages was recalled somewhat humorously by General Hollis in *War at the Top*. When visiting the beaches of St. Margaret's Bay near

Figure 10.3: 'Storm before England's gates' (Authors collection).

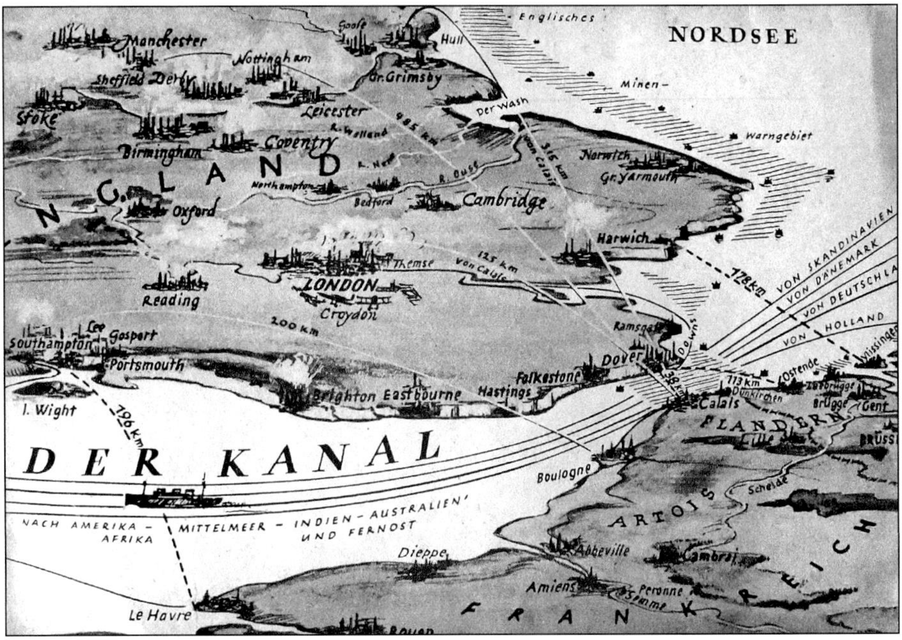

Figure 10.4: England's gates (Authors collection).

Ironside planned to hold the coast as a 'crust', with beaches suitable for landing AFVs selected for defence. The defence of such beaches was based on strongpoints consisting of emergency coastal batteries (old naval 6-inch guns mounted on holdfasts and given splinter-proof concrete protection) and other strongpoints at various points along the beach, especially at sections suitable for tank exits. These strongpoints were to consist of pillboxes and anti-tank obstacles such as concrete blocks, minefields and underwater metal spikes. In terms of FSR, this 'crust' was to be the outpost zone, designed to give warning of any landings, prevent raids and delay a full-scale invasion for as long as possible to allow mobile reserves to move forward and drive the enemy back into the sea. As virtually nothing had been done with respect to constructing beach defences prior to Ironside's tenure as Commander-in-Chief Home Forces, troops had to quickly dig in to face the imminently expected invasion. This naturally resulted in the defences taking on a linear form at first and the long fronts held also necessitated sacrificing depth so that the beaches could be adequately covered.

Dover with Churchill, the officer in charge of the anti-invasion defences explained that he only had three anti-tank guns in the whole of the brigade, which was to cover five miles of this stretch of coast, with just six rounds for each gun. He wondered whether he was justified in firing one of these to show the men how the gun worked!

Behind the beach defences, Ironside planned for a series of occupied 'stops' consisting of defended continuous anti-tank obstacles designed to hold up and delay enemy mechanised forces that had penetrated the beach defences until what mobile forces existed could deploy for the counter-attack. These 'stops' – cumulating in the 'GHQ zone of 'Stops'', also referred to as the GHQ reserve positions or the GHQ anti-tank stop-line, which was sited to cover London and the important industrial areas – comprised the main position (Figure 10.4). 'Stops' were of the same two types prepared by the BEF: natural obstacles such as water ways or artificial such as anti-tank ditches. Both types were to be protected by pillboxes, field works, wire, demolitions, road blocks, and where appropriate minefields. The artificial anti-tank ditches were dug to the standard BEF specifications while the style of road block consisting of a permanent concrete element and removable rail element were also largely based on those built by the BEF and the French. The main aim of Ironside's plan was to achieve great depth in the anti-tank defence. The limited numbers of anti-tank guns available were primarily to be employed along these 'stops', the rest used for beach defence. The most mobile guns were to be retained in the mobile columns.

There can be little doubt that Ironside's scheme was influenced by the experience gained in constructing the defences of the Gort Line and the Battle of France and Flanders – in which some success was achieved in delaying the enemy by holding a series of water obstacles and 'stops' – which allowed the Army to conclude that its 'tactical conceptions of the defence have on the whole stood the test.'[44] Although Ironside was aware it would be impossible to garrison all of these 'stops', he insisted that work begin immediately in preparing the necessary anti-tank obstacles and pillboxes. Ironside never intended the 'stops' to function as a succession of defensive lines in the first instance. Rather, they were a response to the recognition that Britain lacked sufficient mobile forces to operate over the whole area in which the Germans may attempt an invasion. In the first instance, they were to form 'bounds' for mobile counter-attacking forces moving forward by forming a stabilised position from which to launch a counter-attack. Second, they were to act as 'stops' to delay enemy armour if it was successful in pushing inland from beachheads, gaining time for the counter-attack forces to deploy. Only as a last resort were they to act as defensive lines.

Typically, each command establishment commenced work on preparing a 'Command Line', designed to be a complete anti-tank obstacle to block any further progress of enemy AFVs that had successfully penetrated the beach defences.[45] Such command 'stop' lines were provided with a high density of shell proof pillboxes. Numerous

44 *ATM No. 33*, (London: The War Office, July 1940), p.14. *ATM No. 34* went on to note that reports from the BEF showed that the field engineering designs of the time were generally sound.

45 Home Forces was split into administrative areas referred to as 'Commands'. In 1940 there were six commands: Scottish, Northern, Eastern, Aldershot, Southern and Western Command, although Aldershot Command had no defence forces under its command unlike the other Home Commands.

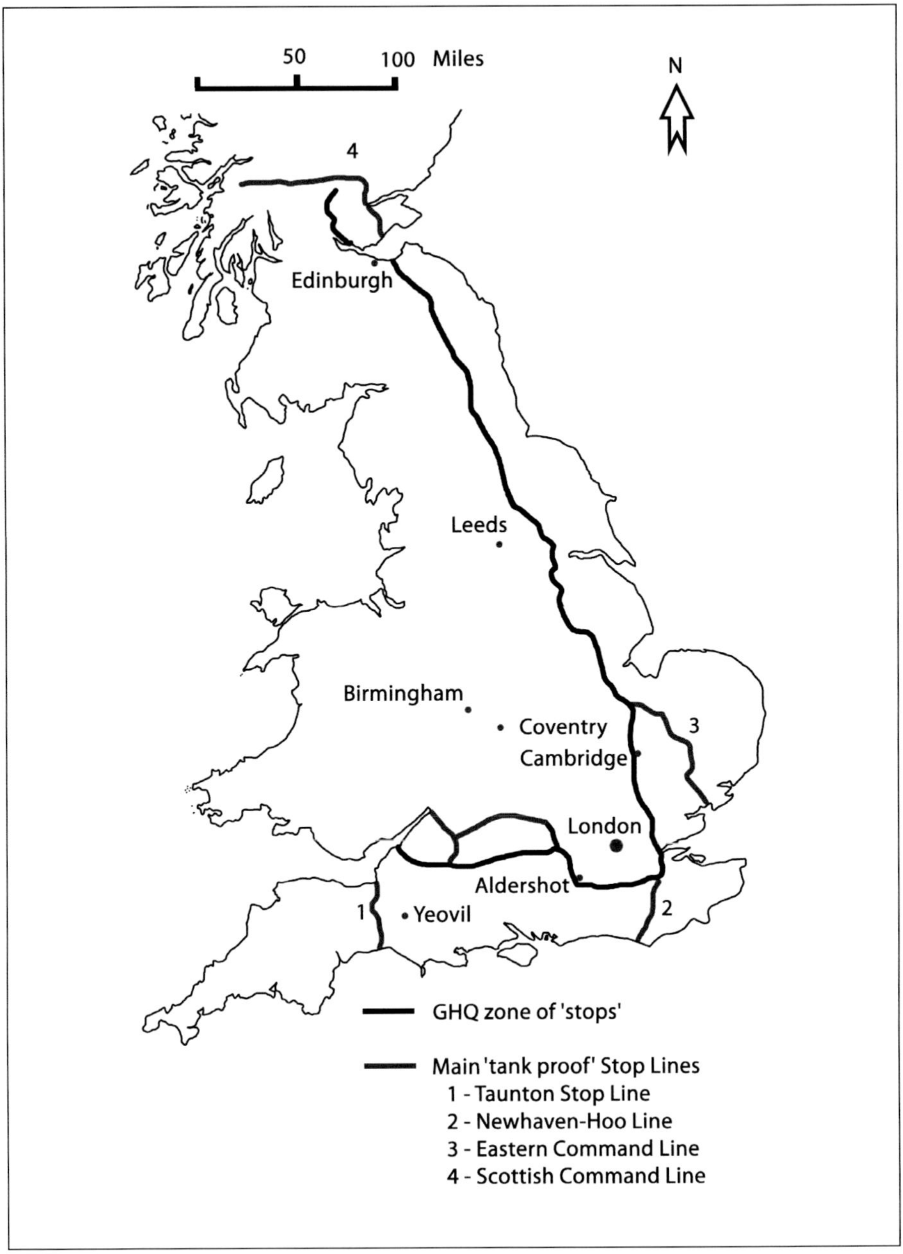

Figure 10.5: The planned GHQ zone of 'stops' and other major tank-proof 'stops', July – August 1940.

divisional 'stops', or switch lines, mainly utilising water ways, railway cuttings and embankments were sited to link up the main command lines and to disrupt or canalise the enemy advance into pockets where they could be ultimately destroyed. The divisional 'stops' were not intended to be a formidable anti-tank obstacle such as the command lines, but mostly relied upon the demolitions of crossings as a delaying effect or acting as a deterrent. The density of pillboxes along these switch lines was substantially lower than the stronger command lines, with most pillboxes only being proof against bullets.

The GHQ zone of 'stops' was to be sited in depth, with a zone of demolitions in front of it. As Colin Alexander notes in his book *Ironside's Line*, it was planned to be a chain of anti-tank obstacles and defended localities in effect forming a single static position running across the whole length of Britain, parallel to the Channel and North Sea and extending over 800 miles. Ironside's insistence on constructing the GHQ zone of 'stops' simultaneously with the beach defences and other 'stop' lines was a departure from the BEF policy of working on the defences from the front to the rear. The reason for this was twofold. Firstly, the resource of civil labour for concrete work was considerable. Secondly, Ironside emphasised the necessity for the provision of 'an occupied stop somewhere in [the] rear'[46] to prevent enemy armour roaming freely as it had done in France and, as well, on 7 June the Chiefs-of-Staff had instructed him to prepare inland defences to protect London and the main industrial and urban centres of Birmingham, Sheffield and Leeds from direct attack following a successful enemy landing. Seen in the context of June 1940, the importance assigned to the GHQ zone of 'stops' can be understood, given there was serious doubt about the Royal Navy or the virtually non-existent beach defences being able to prevent a full scale invasion. However, the policy had the effect of limiting the amount of work that could be done elsewhere because of the sheer volume of resources that the GHQ zone of 'stops' consumed. The GHQ zone of 'stops' rarely attained the level of depth planned for due to shortages in construction materials, especially cement. Indeed, in July Ironside had to restrict the construction of concrete defences along the GHQ zone of 'stops' to the south of the Wash.

The LDV were to add depth to the 'stops', as outlined above, by denying the road network to enemy AFVs and making the Germans having to fight their way through every village and town. They also had a key role in providing the necessary information to ensure the most mechanised and well equipped troops Ironside had could be deployed to where they were needed. These were organised into a separate Corps (IV Corps) independent from the commands. IV Corps was split into a southern and northern group, located north and south of London to be able to strike at any landings along the south-east and east coasts of England.

Just as the BEF had had to undertake survey work from scratch in France with regards to siting the defences, so did Home Forces, as it transpired that no complete

46 *ATM No. 33*, p. 17.

investigation of beaches suitable for enemy landings or suitable landing grounds for enemy airborne forces had been carried out. Details on roads, railways and rivers existed but had to be compiled. Even then, it was found that some proposed 'stops' would easily be breached because of low water levels during the summer months. Given the seriousness of the situation, the commands could not wait until this information was collected and were forced to use any means at their disposal. This forced extemporisation resulted in many mistakes – as was the case in France – which could have been avoided if previous planning had been possible, and it is also fair to say that some of the defences were sited with rather more enthusiasm than tactical knowledge. It also resulted in a lot less homogeneous approach to defences than taken by the BEF as each command and even division pursued its own ideas.

However. a change in emphasis on the defences was soon to come. The German methods of attack employed during the Battle of France and Flanders and the perceived failure of static defence had a lasting influence on senior soldiers such as Brooke and Montgomery. Both, along with many other senior officers openly criticised GHQ Operating Instruction No. 3 and its emphasis on static defence. For instance, Montgomery wrote in his memoirs:

> I found myself in disagreement with the general approach to the problem of the defence of Britain and refused to apply it in my corps area, and later in the South-Eastern Army. The accepted doctrine was that every inch of the coast line must be defended strongly, the defence being based on concrete pill-boxes and entrenchments on a linear basis along the coastline.
>
> There was no depth in the defensive layout and few troops available for counter-attack. Inland, "stop lines" were being dug all over England; when I asked what troops were available to man the stop lines, I could get no clear answer. There were no troops.
>
> My approach was different. I pulled the troops back from the beaches and held them ready in compact bodies in rear, poised for counter-attack and for offensive action against the invaders ... On the beaches themselves all I would allow was a screen of lightly equipped troops, with good communications and sufficient firepower to upset any landing and cause it to pause.
>
> My whole soul revolted against allowing troops to get into trenches and become "Maginot-mined"; any offensive action would then be out of the question, and once the linear defensive system was pierced it would disintegrate. My idea of the defence was that it must be like a spider's web; wherever the Germans went they must encounter fresh troops who would first subject them to heavy fire and would then attack them.[47]

47 Bernard Law, Viscount Montgomery of Alamein, *The Memoirs of Field-Marshal Montgomery* (London: Collins, 1958), pp. 74–75.

The Prime Minister also viewed the 'stop' lines and their pillboxes as another doomed Maginot Line. He decided to replace Iornside with the younger Brooke, who shared his views and had also seen action in the Battle of France and Flanders. Although within days of taking over command Brooke had condemned static defence lines in favour of a more aggressive defence based on mobile counter-attack, he was no more able to deliver this at first than Ironside was, as he still faced the same problems: namely the poor state of training of most troops in this type of warfare and the continuing equipment shortages.

Nevertheless, Brooke did make two immediate changes. Firstly, he stopped all further work on the GHQ zone of 'stops'. The defences of the nodal points[48] along the GHQ zone of 'stops' were to be retained but organised into 'anti-tank islands' and given all round defence. Secondly, as observations of the German preparations for Operation Sealion – the invasion of Britain – indicated the south-east coast of England was the point where landings would be made, Brooke was able to prioritise these beaches, along with those of East Anglia, for defence. They were now to be held as FDLs of the main zone of defence, rather than the outpost zone as planned by Ironside. But, despite these changes, it would be quite wrong to think that static defence disappeared with the appointment of Brooke. New 'stop' lines, anti-tank ditches and linear beach obstacles were still being laid out in 1941. Also, although divisions responsible for the defence of the coastline gradually re-organised the linear network of posts hastily constructed in July to September 1940 to FDLs, this did not necessarily mean defence in depth was always achieved. Many commanders well understood that stretches of anti-tank ditches or other obstacles were not under observation or fire and platoon posts could be 1,000 yards apart, meaning they could not effectively mutually co-operate in defence.

Even so, the work put in hand by Ironside and Brooke in the nine months following Dunkirk did eventually result in an integrated and complex defence of prepared battlefields, running from the coastline to the heart of the country and the engineering achievement was phenomenal. For the beaches selected for defence, field works were dug and strengthened by the provision of pillboxes, wiring schemes completed, minefields laid, and other obstacles put in place against landing barges and tanks that made it ashore. Many miles of anti-tank ditches were dug along the various 'stop' lines and in the rear of the beaches, and water courses enhanced as anti-tank obstacles. Schemes were drawn up for belts of demolitions in depth, from the beaches up to the command lines and along the GHQ zone of 'stops'. Towns and villages had been fortified for all-round defence. The total number of pillboxes built in Britain for the defence of beaches, 'stops', aerodromes and other vulnerable points is estimated to be around 28,000. Home Forces certainly benefited from the experience of the BEF in the rapid construction of defences. Pakenham-Walsh noted that the RE

48 The term nodal point was used to describe towns and villages which the main road network ran through.

units were better placed than most as they not only possessed the knowledge gained in France, but also most of the equipment they required was in common use in civil engineering practices in the country. At this critical time, the RAF also benefited from the experience gained in France, as by the end of June 1940 no less than 134 airfields had RE maintenance parties assigned to them, the majority from reassigned general construction companies raised for this type of work.

By 1942, the improvement in the training and equipping of the Army had allowed Brooke's change in emphasis to be achieved. 'Stop' lines had been abandoned, replaced instead by a network of strongpoints designed to delay or deny German armour progress through towns and villages. He had also been able to increase the mobile forces, leaving the defence of much of the coastline to lower establishment beach defence divisions, and inland to the Home Guard. But all of this had much in common with Ironside's thinking and it is interesting to speculate if he had remained in post as the equipment shortages eased and progress was made in training the Army for mobile operations, would he have moved away from static defence based on the 'stop' lines to a defence based on a network of strongpoints and aggressive counter-attack? Most likely he would have done.

Changing attitudes to pillboxes

The lack of any prepared plans by Germany for an invasion of Britain following the fall of France also gave Home Forces an 'unexpected opportunity' to construct concrete defences, and today, the pillbox is the iconic object that characterises both the Gort Line and Britain's anti-invasion defences. The intended purpose of pillboxes in Britain's anti-invasion defences was much the same as the BEF's pillboxes: to house the principal weapons of the defence. It should be noted that the majority of the infantry would have fought from field works: the role of the pillbox was again – or at least it should have been – to strengthen the field works rather than the other way round. The pillbox was considered of value only in positions which had to be held indefinitely and at all costs, such as beaches suitable for landings and nodal points.

GHQ Home Forces was more relaxed about pillbox design than the BEF. Although the War Office Department of Fortifications and Works (DFW) did issue a series of standard designs in May 1940 which could be issued to building contractors, these were intended as suggestions rather than fixed designs. The DFW deigns were also intended to aid mass production in much the same way as in the BEF, allowing contractors to assemble 'pillbox packs' of standardised quantities of reinforcement rods, shuttering and pre-cast loopholes.[49] The remarkable diversity of pillbox designs

49 Pakenham-Walsh, in his *The History of the Corps of Royal Engineers Vol. VIII,* describes an example were one Chief Engineer rang up a building contractor and asked him to build 200 pillboxes on a 50 mile stretch of coast line and to complete the job in three weeks. This

constructed throughout Britain testifies to the fact that each command, corps and even division had their own ideas on pillbox designs.

None of the standard BEF designs were built as part of Britain's anti-invasion defences. However, they undoubtedly influenced design. The hexagonal Type 22 pillbox is the most common example built as part of the anti-invasion defences, and it is very similar to the BEF hexagonal Bren pillbox (especially the expanded shell proof versions built by V Corps in Southern Command along the GHQ Red and Blue Lines and those built by Eastern Command (to CRE Colchester drawing 1113) along the Eastern Command Line), which itself may owe its origins to the hexagonal pillboxes built along the East Coast during the latter part of the Great War when a German invasion was also feared. The standard Bren embrasure found in all shell proof pillboxes in Britain's anti-invasion defences is clearly based on the BEF Bren embrasure. The Type 28 anti-tank gun pillbox and the Type28a anti-tank gun and Bren pillbox are simplified versions of the BEF designs, but the anti-tank gunners seemed to have won the argument about a wide loophole to allow a wide field of fire, as the loopholes in anti-tank pillboxes in Britain are generally much wider than those found in the BEF's pillboxes. This characteristic was also shared with pillboxes built for the medium machine gun and was no doubt due to the much larger fronts that had to be covered. A number of pillboxes built by Scottish Command incorporating loopholes protected by wing-walls and a small number of rectangular double Vickers machine gun pillboxes built with the two embrasures facing in the same direction on the Scottish Command Line shared characteristics with those built by the BEF. The Northern Command lozenge pillbox is remarkably similar to the variant BEF Bren lozenge pillbox.

The defences built to resist invasion were designed to 'meet the weapons which the enemy is most likely to bring.'[50] GHQ considered it unlikely that defences in Britain would have to be able to withstand the deployment of heavy guns as was the case on the Continent. Such equipment would unlikely be available to parachute troops or airborne troops. Neither would they be likely mounted in light or medium tanks, which would probably be the first to be landed by sea. Consequently, the majority of beach pillboxes and those defending the divisional and corps 'stop-lines' were only bullet proof (i.e. walls and roof 12 to 15 inches thick). Shell proof pillboxes (3ft 6in thick) were largely reserved for the main command lines and the GHQ zone of 'stops', because if the enemy got this far, he would likely have the time to bring up the necessary heavy artillery required to destroy pillboxes.

Yet, the weapons of 1939–40 were capable of inflicting serious damage to pillboxes built to these standards, as British experiments with the 2 pdr gun and German experiments with the 88mm gun had clearly demonstrated. As early as August 1940

was achieved. In Chapter 5, we saw how it was suggested that a large building contractor be hired to build pillboxes along the line of the River Lys so the job could be got on with!

50 TNA: WO199/2527, Pillboxes, MO3 memo.

the question of pillbox reinforcement was raised and by 1941 it was widely accepted that if concrete defences were to be used, they should be effective against the best weapon the enemy could produce, but not against the exceptional weapon. The German equivalent of the British high velocity 6 pdr anti-tank gun was taken as a criterion. Continuing on from tests started during the Sitzkrieg, a Research Board carried out trials on the thickness of reinforced concrete that would be required to stop a shot from the 6 pdr anti-tank gun. The Board also felt confident in calculating the requirements needed to stop the German 88mm gun.

A pillbox capable of stopping such weapons would need to be likely 6 feet thick. It was recognised that such work would require a huge amount of labour and materials, both in short supply. It would not be possible to carry out such work in all commands simultaneously, so it was recommended that priority be given to Southern and Eastern Commands on vulnerable areas. The Chief Engineer recommended that the following level of protection should be provided:

a. Protection in the walls to meet an attack by an 88mm gun at 500 yards allowing for the impact of six shots in a 6-foot square.
b. Protection in the roof to withstand a 250-kilo bomb.

The Board's research never reached the stage of a practical pillbox design. Two designs were, however, produced by DFW and issued by the War Office. It was noted that these designs were not the special case on which the Research Board had been working on – a pillbox proof against any type of gun. These drawings were for anti-tank gun pillboxes to be used on the coast. One was to have a 6 feet thick wall on the exposed flank, with 3ft 6in thickness on the other walls and a 1ft 6in inch thick roof. None were ever built.

Existing pillboxes could also be strengthened. Bullet proof pillboxes could be increased to 3ft 6in thick. Designs for this work were to be prepared locally. The main principle to be followed was to add a reinforced concrete wall on the 'vulnerable side'. If existing loopholes were no longer required, a key for the new wall could be obtained by filling them up. The wall could either be bought up to the height of the roof, but this would then require cutting out new loopholes or a compromise could be adopted and just bring the reinforcement up to the level of the existing loopholes. Some pillboxes were upgraded in such a manor, mostly those built for airfield defence. Another way of 'strengthening' a pillbox was the blocking up of surplus loopholes. GHQ noted that many a pillbox was 'riddled' with loopholes, rendering it a 'death trap'. Numerous pillboxes had some of their loopholes blocked by brickwork or concrete. A similar situation had occurred in France, where the BEF used pre-cast blocks or steel plates for the same purpose.

The tactical use of pillboxes was always in question, as it had been in France. The DFW designs had been produced before the fall of France: although the infantry type pillboxes had been designed to hold Bren guns, the losses of equipment following the evacuation of was enormous meaning in many cases rifles would have to replace Brens, going against the general thinking that concrete protection would not be provided for riflemen. To clarify the situation, the War Office issued guidance for the defence of pillboxes in Infantry *Training 1937, Supplement No 1 – Tactical Notes for Platoon Commanders 1941*:

1. The concrete pill box is a great aid to defence if intelligently used; if not, it may become a death-trap.
2. Concrete is a protection against bullets, shell splinters, and weather. Sometimes it affords protection against shell fire. If properly camouflaged, it is also a protection from ground and air observation.
3. Many concrete posts are not complete protection against a direct hit from as shell or from an aerial bomb. They all have the disadvantage of limiting the field of view and the field of fire. The garrison will be unable to use all their rifles at one and the same time because of the fewness of the loop-holes. Finally, the garrison is hindered in the employment of the hand grenade and bayonet.
4. Therefore, the garrison of a pill box locality will act as follows:

a. The sentry or sentries on duty will be stationed outside the pill box, where they can see and hear all round them.
b. Temporary cover from view, shell fire, and aerial bombing may be sought inside the pill box; but beware that the enemy are not creeping towards you under this covering fire, whilst you are hiding inside.
c. When the attack comes, the light machine gun or machine gun will fire from the pill box, if it can carry out its task, if not, it must come out to a prepared position.
d. Those men who cannot use their weapons inside must man the trenches outside–where they can do their duty.
e. (e) If the pill box is surrounded–except for those who can fire from the loopholes, the garrison will fight outside, where they can employ all their weapons to the best advantage.[51]

Throughout 1941 pillboxes were still an important part of defence schemes although to be used tactically as outlined in the 1941 Supplement to Infantry Training. This did not, however, stop some doubting the value of concrete in defences:

51 *Infantry Training, 1937: Supplement, No. 1 – Tactical Notes for Platoon Commanders* (London: The War Office, 1941), p. 16.

> The injurious effects of static defence and excessive reliance on elaborate concrete defences on morale and initiative are well known and are often described as fostering a "Maginot Complex".[52]

Yet, the fear of a 'Maginot Complex' had been raised as early as July 1940 in *ATM No.33* which made the point that the 'occupation of defensive positions and the construction of concrete emplacements' for any period of time was 'dangerous to both morale and discipline.'[53] And, in August 1940, *ATM No. 35* was much more forthright on the evils of static defence and concrete:

> Troops must not be led into battle in the belief that the "prepared positions" to the rear exist primarily to offer them refuge in the face of a determined enemy. Over-reliance on static defensive measures and concrete fortifications will kill the fighting spirit of any army.[54]

Pillboxes were finally condemned firstly because they imposed a rigid static layout on the defence, with flexibility only obtained by abandoning them, and secondly because to resist modern weapons they would have to be built to an incredible thickness as already noted. Earth works providing all round defence were the better option and by 1942 the pillbox was seen redundant as a defence work. A GHQ memo, *Construction of Field Defences,* dated 23 February 1942 notes:

> All experience of modern warfare ... points most strongly to the fact that the pillbox is not a suitable type of fortification for either coastal or nodal point defences.[55]

52 TNA: WO199/44, 'Copy of paper submitted to M.O.3. The War Office on the choice of concrete or earthworks for deliberate field defences', 13 April 1941.

53 *ATM No. 33,* p. 15.

54 *ATM No. 35* (London: The War Office, August 1940), p. 6. This was repeated in the pamphlet *The Officer and Fighting Efficiency* published in February 1941. Further evidence for this point of view on static defences came from operations in the Western Desert between December 1940 and January 1941 when the British attacked the Italian defences at Bardia. These defences consisted of a continuous anti-tank ditch defended by a series of mutually supporting redoubts with concrete communication trenches and dugouts with concrete roofs and garrisoned by 30 to 50 men armed with anti-tank weapons and light and heavy machine guns. There was little depth to the defence, with the majority of Italian troops committed to a static role in the front line. The British concluded that the Italian concept of the defence was based on a series of 'little circular "Maginots"'. The garrisons showed little fight once the British armour had penetrated behind their positions – 'if only because a *trapped garrison cannot fight* whatever the state of its morale. The garrison of a pillbox, if it begins to fight at all, must feel that it is trapped even before it starts to hit back, and commanders should take heed of the psychological implications of the use of pillbox systems of defence'. (*ATM No.39* (London: The War Office, April 1941), p.12).

55 TNA: WO 199/2527, 'Construction of Field Defences', 23 February 1942.

The British had to change their view on concrete defences following the disastrous 1942 Dieppe raid – Operation JUBILEE. This raid demonstrated the need to rethink methods of assaulting German fixed defences if any future Allied landings in Europe were to succeed. One of the first full-scale trials for the preparation of D-Day was Exercise Kruschen, ordered in December 1942 and held in Suffolk during the first half of 1943. The object of the exercise was to investigate methods of land assault against strongly defended positions. It is illuminating that one of the first full-scale trials for D-Day was not concerned with the actual landings but investigated the problem of overcoming the pillboxes, minefields and anti-tank ditches that would be encountered inland of the Atlantic Wall and along the Siegfried Line. The subsequent development of specialised assault tactics on a fortified position built upon much of the research put in hand by the British Army during the Sitzkrieg. This work was continued post Dunkirk and following Exercise Kruschen Home Forces produced a provisional pamphlet, *A Drill for The Assault on a Highly Defended Locality,* which as its title suggested, was a drill to overcome the fire of the defence, the breaching of the obstacle (i.e. an elaborate obstacle consisting of mines, wire and an anti-tank ditch or wall) and the destruction of the garrison.

The concept of an 'engineer' tank was also adopted following the debacle of Operation JUBILLEE. This was to eventually lead to the formation of the 79th Armoured Division and its specialised armour – Assault Vehicle Royal Engineer (AVRE). Major-General Hobart was given command of the Division, and was tasked with developing the technique of assault in Western Europe with specialised forms of armoured vehicle such as amphibious tanks, searchlight tanks, mine destroying tanks, flame throwers etc., bringing together assault tanks and engineers under one senior officer. This specialised armour is most widely known as 'Hobart's funnies'. In particular, Hobart was instructed to continue the work begun in Exercise Kruschen, i.e. developing methods to overcome strongly defended positions:

> A technique for the assault on prepared defences was evolved in Exercise "KRUSCHEN" and is to be issued as a pamphlet by this Headquarters to form the basis for training by all formations. This technique is, however, not complete. With the resources with which your units are gradually becoming equipped, you will further develop the technique.[56]

The attack on pillboxes was best undertaken with a combined assault and the role of the infantry was not ignored. Following on from experience in Italy, where pillboxes had to 'be reduced one by one' and with D-Day looming, *ATM No. 48* emphasised 'A point of training that requires constant practice is the platoon or section attack

56 TNA: WO205/64, 'Training Directive to Maj-Gen P.C.S. Hobart, CB, DSO, OBE, MC', 18 May 1943, 79th Armoured Division, Organisation, Equipment, Training, Part I.

on pillboxes.'[57] Britain was unique in developing specialised armour to work with the infantry in a combined arms assault on a strongly fortified position and this undoubtedly saved lives.

Changes in thinking about the operation of the defence

The principal of defence in depth remained unchanged following the events of May 1940, although the organisation and operation of a position in defence did gradually change following the experiences in modern armoured warfare and can be traced through *MTP No.23 Part II – The Infantry Division in the Defence* issued in 1942 and *MTP No. 3 – The Defence* issued in 1943. Any thought of defending continuous anti-tank obstacles, such as characterised by the Gort Line and Britain's anti-invasion defences built in the summer of 1940, was thoroughly discarded by 1943.

MTP No.23 still described a main position consisting of a system of anti-tank localities organised in depth covered by at least one anti-tank obstacle covering the entire width of the position. Rivers and railway lines if passing through a series of cuttings and over steep embankments were considered suitable obstacles. If these did not exist, then artificial obstacles such as ditches and minefields would need to be created. In this sense, it was very similar to *Operations - MTP No. 23 Part II: Defence – 1939.* Yet, gone now was the confidence of a strong anti-tank defence proving an insurmountable obstacle for armoured units as it was accepted that 'Anti-tank weapons have not the same ascendancy over the armoured fighting vehicle as has the machine gun over troops unprotected by armour.'[58] It was expected that the enemy would often make deep penetrations into the defensive position with armour, but it was now emphasised that the defender would have to rapidly convert a defensive battle into a battle of encounter using armoured formations on ground which was known and in circumstances beneficial to the defender.

The layout of the defence was still largely the same as described in the 1939 pamphlet. In prolonged defence, localities were to be developed rapidly to form an extensive trench system so as to conceal the actual positions of the garrison. The importance of roads to enemy armoured formations was emphasised, and localities were to be sited so as to deny the use of roads to the enemy. Localities were to be formed by linking up natural obstacles such as woods, villages or groups of houses or artificial obstacles if no natural obstacles existed. The role of artillery, anti-tank guns and medium machine guns remained largely unchanged from the 1939 concept of the operation of the defence.

57 *ATM No. 48* (London: The War Office, May 1944), p.20.
58 *Operations – MTP No. 23: Part II – The infantry Division in the Defence* (London: The War Office, 1942), p.1.

But, by 1943 the operation of the defence had completely changed although the underlying principles remained the same. According to *MTP No. 3*, static defence no longer had any role:

> Although the recognized [sic] principles of war have lost none of their relevance under modern conditions, the techniques of defence, owing to the power of modern weapons, including aircraft, has changed and has become more offensive instead of purely static ... A major lesson of this war is that purely static defence can no longer succeed.[59]

The idea of a continuous defensive front covered by an anti-tank obstacle had also gone:

> Our pre-war ideas of the power of natural or artificial obstacles to stop, or at least delay, the advance of both mechanized [sic] and dismounted troops have been considerably changed by events. The campaigns in EUROPE, EAST AFFRICA and MALAYA have shown that, when the attacker is properly equipped and trained, and resolutely led, few obstacles will prevent movement unless covered by adequate and sustained fire.
>
> Rivers, marsh, or jungle will not prevent determined men from advancing on broad fronts and infiltrating through, or round defended areas. River lines or mountain ranges cannot stop airborne, or on occasion waterborne, troops from landing on the defenders' side of the obstacles and disorganizing [sic] the defence. Mines of all types, wire or ditches will not stop penetration on narrow fronts, provided the attacker concentrates adequate fire power to support well organized [sic] assault troops.[60]

In many other respects the layout of the defence remained similar, although as alluded to above, it was no longer formed by linking up a continuous anti-tank obstacle. Having stated that, full advantage of obstacles was still to be taken for the protection of defended localities, but they were now regarded mainly as a means of disorganising and canalising an enemy attack into areas where it could either be dealt with the fire power of the defence or by counter-attack; they could not be relied upon to halt an attack. The river line was still regarded as having great value for delay but could not be fully covered without a great expenditure of troops and weapons, probably to the detriment of counter-attack forces.[61] Mines and booby traps combined with wire

59 *MTP No.3 – The Defence* (London: The War Office, 1943), pp.2–3
60 Ibid.
61 Many in the BEF had been surprised with the success the Germans had in crossing water obstacles using rubber boats and doubts about the effectiveness of water obstacles had been raised as early as July 1940 in *ATM No. 33*, which also raised the issue of the long frontage to be held. Additionally, it noted that water obstacles also confined the defender and limited

were regarded as the most inconvenient and deadly obstacle to an attacker. There is no mention of anti-tank ditches in *MTP No. 3*.[62]

The style of defence outlined in *MTP No. 3* is the so-called 'island defence system', where the defensive zone was organised as chain of self-contained localities in great depth. Each locality was to act as a 'fortress' from which to bring fire against an attacker who had penetrated between the localities and to act as pivots for counter-attacking forces. If the enemy used tanks, the defence still aimed 'to isolate the tanks from their unarmoured support in the form of engineers, infantry, machine guns and anti-tank guns.'[63] Battalion localities had to be within small arms and anti-tank gun support of one another although brigade localities were sited so that the gaps between them could be covered by supporting artillery. The gaps between corps would depend upon the type of ground, the counter-attack forces available and the size of the defended zone. These gaps could be large. Aggressive defence was essential 'with a powerful highly mobile counter-attack force in hand to destroy the enemy' should he penetrate between or outflank the defended localities.[64] As one book written during the war put it, in order to avoid the defence being smashed by shock action, 'a moving shield, rather than a fixed one, is the true answer to the moving sword, for it can thrust in all directions.'[65]

Field defences now consisted of narrow slit trenches with fire bays notched into the sides because 'the old pattern fire trench is valueless against air attack.'[66] The use of artillery, medium machine guns and anti-tank guns in the defence remained largely unchanged. Interestingly, *MTP No. 3* still emphasised a good line system as the principle means of inter-communication, with wireless only becoming the principle means in the later phases of the defensive battle. This was largely because of the greater carrying capacity of line communications and the need to preserve wireless security – much the same reasons as given in Signal *Training (All Arms) 1938*.

the ability of carrying out an aggressive defence. However, it did acknowledge that provided 'bridges are blown, and the obstacle covered by fire and under observation, a water line is probably a more difficult obstacle for the A.F.Vs. to cross than any other.' (*ATM No. 33*, p. 17).

62 Although the use of ditches as anti-tank obstacles are not mentioned in *MTP No.3*, the style of anti-tank ditch dug by the BEF and the 'V' style anti-tank ditch are still illustrated in *MTP No. 30 Part III: Obstacles – 1943* and *Royal Engineers Reconnaissance Pocket Book – 1944*.

63 *MTP No. 3 – The Defence, p.30*

64 Ibid., p. 4.

65 Admiral Sir Reginald Bacon, KCB, KCVO, DSO, Major-General J.F.C. Fuller, CB, CBE, DSO, Air Marshall Sir Patrick Playfair, KBE, CB, CVO, MC, (eds.) *Warfare Today* (London: Odhams Press Ltd., no date), pp. 93–94.

66 *MTP No.3 – The Defence*, p. 15. In August 1941 *ATM No. 40* stated that 'Slit trenches should be dug rather than the elaborate field defences described in pre-war manuals. The slogan should be, "The narrower the better."' (*ATM No. 40* (London: The War Office, August 1941).

The importance of air power was now clearly stressed, both as a powerful harassing and counter-attack weapon:

> By intense and sustained air action against the attackers L of C and his dumps and forward concentrations, his preparations can be greatly delayed and disorganized [sic]. During the counter-attack battle considerable effect can be achieved by direct air support.[67]

Montgomery's conduct of the Battle of Alam Halfa (31 August – 6 September 1942) was the first example of the British Army employing a modern defence, when at last, it could rely upon fully co-ordinated air support and a strong tank force for the mobile counter-move.

67 Ibid., p. 3. It is interesting to note that air power was not mentioned until page 37 in *MTP No. 23*.

11

The Gort Line Today

Although the urban area centred on Lille has expanded much since the end of the Second War, much of the BEF sector along the Franco-Belgian frontier south of Gruson is still open countryside. In the extreme north-east of the BEF sector, open countryside can also be found around Halluin. The trenches, breastworks and anti-tank ditches have long been levelled, and the barbed wire entanglements cleared, but many BEF pillboxes and French blockhouses still survive. This book is not intended to be a guide book to the extant archaeological remains of the Gort Line: however, the following is a simple itinerary, based on visits the author made while travelling south from Ypres to visit the Somme battlefields. This itinerary will allow the visitor to view all the standard BEF pillbox designs plus a series of French constructed blockhouses. For those wishing to study the area in more depth, Appendix IV will hopefully be of use.

Please note no right of access is implied in this itinerary. However, if you park sensibly and do not obstruct tracks or entrances into fields, and do not walk across any fields in crop, I have personally never encountered any problems in walking a short distance into a bare field to get a closer look at a pillbox.

Itinerary

Leave the A17 / E42 at junction 3 and take the D93 to Baisieux. At the T junction with the D941 turn left. After a short distance, turn left for Cysoing at the cross roads with the D90. After passing under the motorway, several British and French pillboxes soon come into view. This area was on the boundary between 1st (I Corps) and 3rd Division (II Corps). The French blockhouses were constructed in 1939 as part of the new FDL Line – the Bachy Switch. The Royal Engineers began work on pillboxes in this area from November onwards to add the required depth to the line. It is possible to park safely on several farm tracks off the D90 to explore the pillboxes.

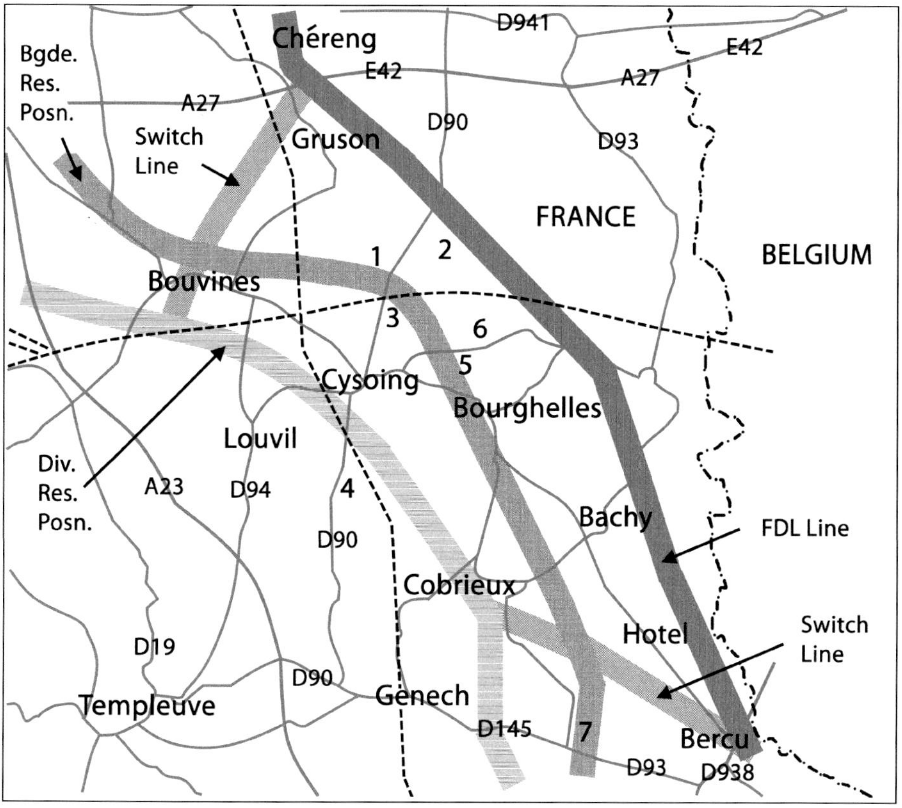

Figure 11.1: Map showing suggested tour in the Cysoing area. See Figures 11.6 to 11.30.

West of the D90 can be seen a number of hexagonal Bren pillboxes arranged in groups of four for mutual support, a partially complete double MG pillbox and a couple of single anti-tank gun pillboxes, built on the revised trace of the Brigade Reserve Position just into the 3rd Division's sector (No. 1 on Figure 11.1; Figure 11.2). These Bren pillboxes all have an almost domed roof, created by rounded corners. There is nothing in the records to explain this variation officially. It could be just the result of different shuttering design, or perhaps as Mike Osborne has suggested, a modification to aid the deflection of direct hits by shells. One of the Bren pillboxes has been demolished, probably a post-war attempt to remove it, but also possibly by German engineers testing the strength of the pillbox. The two anti-tank gun pillboxes differ slightly in design. One is the standard design, with a stepped orellion, or wing wall, and has the steel frame for the loophole plate. The other has a simpler rectangular wing wall and time has been taken to add a rendered finish, perhaps as part of its camouflage scheme. It does not have the loophole frame added. There is also a single

French blockhouse, built in 1939 as part of the Bachy Switch; the track leading up to it is still made of the traditional pavé surface. On the east side, additional Bren pillboxes can be seen as well as another French blockhouse (listed as Bloc de Campin, *1ére Région Militaire* pattern 'B' by Dépret) with the large earth bank to the front still in place (No. 2 on Figure 11.1). This is blockhouse No.6 in Captain K.G. Exham's and Captain Smith-Dorrien's report on the Bachy Switch dated 10 October 1939, when it was then at foundation level (see Table 5.5, Chapter 5). One of the Bren pillboxes was still only half complete when the BEF dashed into Belgium on 10 May 1940. A small *poste de tir* for a light machine gun can also be seen; corrugated steel sheets have clearly been used for the shuttering and line of five air vents have been added in the front wall. This was no doubt sited on the FDL Line to cover the gap between the two French blockhouses, but would have been a very isolated post.

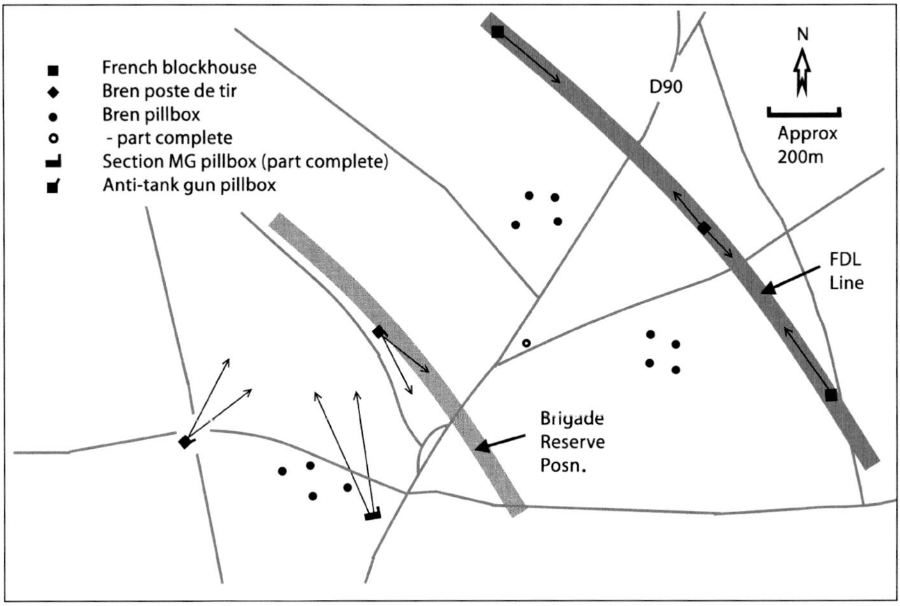

Figure 11.2: Map showing the cluster of pillboxes to the east and west of the D90, north of Cysoing.

Following the visit to these pillboxes, continue along the D90 towards Cysoing. As you pass over the railway line, go straight over the roundabout and park by the communal cemetery (No. 3 on Figure 11.1). Walk back north and in the first field after the cemetery there is another double MG pillbox, this one being complete. This example is of interest as it still has the two mounts for the Vickers machine gun. These are of the pattern used in the Great War, and an extant example of one dating from 1918 can be seen in a pillbox at Hénencourt, a village fortified as a strong point after the German advances. This pillbox also has the cavity above the loophole, to allow the rear cover of the Vickers to be opened on the arc of traverse, and the observation slit between the two loopholes. Air vents for fumes generated from weapon firing can be seen in either side of the pillbox.

After visiting this pillbox, the cemetery is also worth a visit to see the village war memorial and six British graves dating from May 1940. Four belong to men of the 4th Royal Tank Regiment. They formed part of the 1st Army Tank Brigade along with the 7th Royal Tank Regiment, which was ordered forward to harbour at the Forêt de Soignes at the southeast edge of Brussels when the German invasion of the Low Countries began. Following the German advance, they were ordered to move back southwest by train from nearby Enghien. Unfortunately, no flatbed trailers could be found so the Brigade had to drive southwest towards Tournai by road. It was a difficult journey with the roads congested by refugees and constant attention by Stukas, and it was a Stuka attack that killed these four men, the first war dead of the Royal Tank Regiment. One of the other graves belongs to Flight Sergeant G Mackenzie, a pilot of the ill-fated 253 Squadron. This Squadron was formed at Manston, originally for shipping protection with Blenheims. However, it was subsequently decided to equip the Squadron with Hurricanes, and it became operational on 3 April 1940. Following the German invasion, the Squadron was formed into two flights, each amalgamated with a flight from 111 Squadron to form composite a squadron. The idea was to have half of each Squadron remaining at home and the other half in France. 'A' Flight 253 Squadron flew across the Channel daily, operating from French airfields and returning to Manston while 'B' Flight was sent to Lille. On 'B' Flights first combat, it lost three pilots, including Sergeant Mackenzie, all to ME109's of *Jagdgeschwader* 3. Shortly after, 'B' Flight was withdrawn back to England. In all, 253 Squadron lost half its pilots, including the Squadron leader and both Flight commanders. The final grave is to an unknown.

From the cemetery continue south along the D90. After crossing the railway line on the southern edge of Cysoing, look out for a hard standing on the edge of Cysoing Wood (also known as Bois de Taissonniere) which will be on your left-hand side (No. 4 on Figure 11.1). From here, walk a short distance south along the road and you will come across an anti-tank pillbox just inside the wood. This pillbox –named BOIS DE TAISSONNIERE – was started by the 1st Division (which explains its non-standard design) but was taken over by the 228th Field Company 'X' Force. The 228th Field Company was taken from the 49th (West Riding) Division. This Division's sign during the Great War and the inter-war years was the white rose of Yorkshire, which can be seen on the pillbox (the Divisional sign of the polar bear on a black background was not adopted until the Division served in Iceland). The pillbox was located in the rear of the original *Ligne Principale*, which became the Divisional Reserve Position following the siting of the Bachy Switch. At the time of writing it was also possible to walk along the central east-west ride of the wood towards the railway line to see two *Tourelles*.

Retrace your route back to Cysoing and turn right at the cross roads with the D955 (Rue Roger Salengro) then pick up the Rue de Tournai. You are again back in the area of the Bachy Switch. Along the Rue de Tournai another pillbox for a machine gun section can be seen (No. 5 on Figure 11.1). In front of it, what appears to be an anti-tank 'dragons tooth' can be seen. On the left hand side, an artillery observation post (THE TRENCH) and *a poste de tir* for a 25mm anti-tank gun (SPINDLEY WOOD) can be seen (No. 6 on 11.1). Both of these are on the revised trace of the 1st Division's Brigade Reserve Position following the incorporation of the Bachy Switch into the FDL Line. As you continue along the Rue de Tournai, which becomes the Chaussée Brunehaut a number of Bren pillboxes and French blockhouses are also viewable. Pick up the D93 to Wannehain. In Wannehain, take the Route de Bachy to Bachy, passing a couple of French blockhouses.

From Bachy, pick up the Rue de Saint-Amand / Route Nationale (D955) and head south to Mouchin. At Bercu, you could take a small diversion along the D93 towards Genech to see a variant machine gun section pillbox (BELLE PORTE) which has a loophole in each side protected by a wing wall instead of both guns firing frontally (No. 7 on Figure 11.1). This pillbox was on the revised trace of 1st Divisions Brigade Reserve Position. As you leave Mouchin, roughly following the line of the *Ligne Principale* in the 2nd Division's sector, two sets of two pillboxes for a single machine gun can be seen (No. 8 on Figure 11.3). Some units favoured placing the two guns of a machine gun section in single-gun pillboxes rather than the double-gun pillbox. These are probably pillboxes M.G.F (c) and (d). You can park by the side of a memorial to five American airmen from the 327th Bomber Squadron, 92nd Group, who died on a mission on 9 October 1942. From the memorial you can then walk to the pillboxes for a closer view. Continue along the D955 to the next house on the right-hand side. An artillery observation post – VEHICLE SHED – can be seen by the side of the house (No. 9 on Figure 11.3). Soon after, at the next cluster of buildings on the left-hand side another machine gun pillbox can be seen built onto the side of a farmhouse to obtain concealment by making it appear as an outbuilding (No. 10 on Figure 11.3).

Keep on the D955 until Rumegies then take the D327 towards the Belgium border. Here you can see the old border post with an interesting display and also the stream L'Elnon which formed the anti-tank obstacle for the *Ligne principale* in this area (No. 11 on Figure 11.3). A track leading southeast from the border post takes you to two variant Bren pillboxes. These are lozenge in shape, with three forward facing Bren loopholes. They were no doubt built to cover the stream L'Elnon, filling in the gaps between the French blockhouses. In the rear can be seen massive poste *de tir* for a 25mm anti-tank gun, presumably constructed by the French.

From here, return back to Rumegies and follow the signs for Orchies, picking up the Rue de la Caisse / Rue de Tournai. This takes you past VIEUX CONDE pillbox, constructed by the 11th Field Company and one of the first constructed by the BEF to a pre-war design (No. 12 on Figure 11.3). Continue towards Le Masures and the take the D127 towards Aix. In Aix, take the D126 towards Haut Hameau to view several

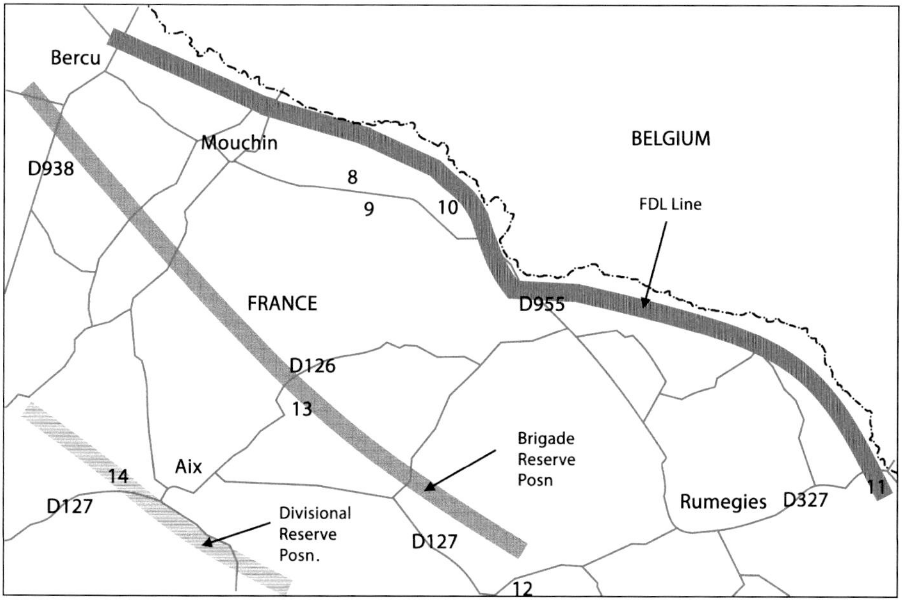

Figure 11.3: Map showing suggested tour in the area around Mouchin and Aix. See Figures 11.31 to 11.41.

pillboxes sited on the 2nd Division's Brigade Reserve Position, including an anti-tank gun pillbox – probably PRUNELLE POST – and a double MG pillbox (No. 13 on Figure 11.3). Retrace your route to Aix and continue on the D127 towards Nomain. This road takes you along the Aix – Nomain ridge – a section of the 2nd Division's Divisional Reserve Position – where a number of Bren and machine gun pillboxes can be seen (No. 14 on Figure 11.3). It can also be appreciated how the ridge dominated the ground to the east.

At the cross roads with the D938, turn left towards Orchies. From Orchies take the D954 to Mons-en-Pévèle. As you approach Mons-en-Pévèle it is easy to see how it dominates the area and why it was the corner stone of the Corps Position. It is worth parking near the church and enjoying the views. A short detour north from Mons-en-Pévèle along the D120 takes you to two 2 pdr anti-tank gun and Bren pillboxes, arranged at angles to each other so they could enfilade the anti-tank ditch without danger to each other (No. 15 on Figure 11.4). Both have stepped oreillions and steel loophole frames. From Mons-en-Pévèle you can follow the D954 to pick up the A1/E17 Autoroute du Nord.

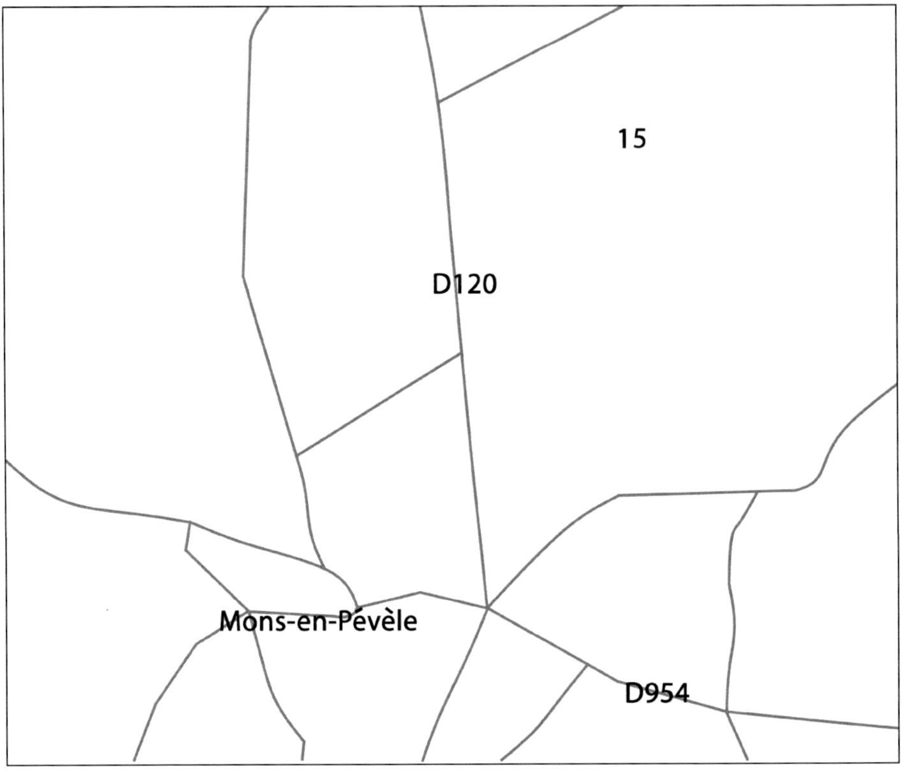

Figure 11.4: Map showing the two anti-tank and Bren blockhouses at Mons-en-Pévèle. See Figures 11.42 to 11.44.

To see the German pillboxes dating from the Great War as utilised by 5th Division in its Divisional Reserve Position, one needs to travel up to the area north of Lille between Quesnoy and Linselles. There are numerous pillboxes of this type in the area, but two that were to be prepared by the 506th Field Company for the 6th Battalion York and Lancaster Regiment are easily located (Nos. 16 & 17 on Figure 11.5).

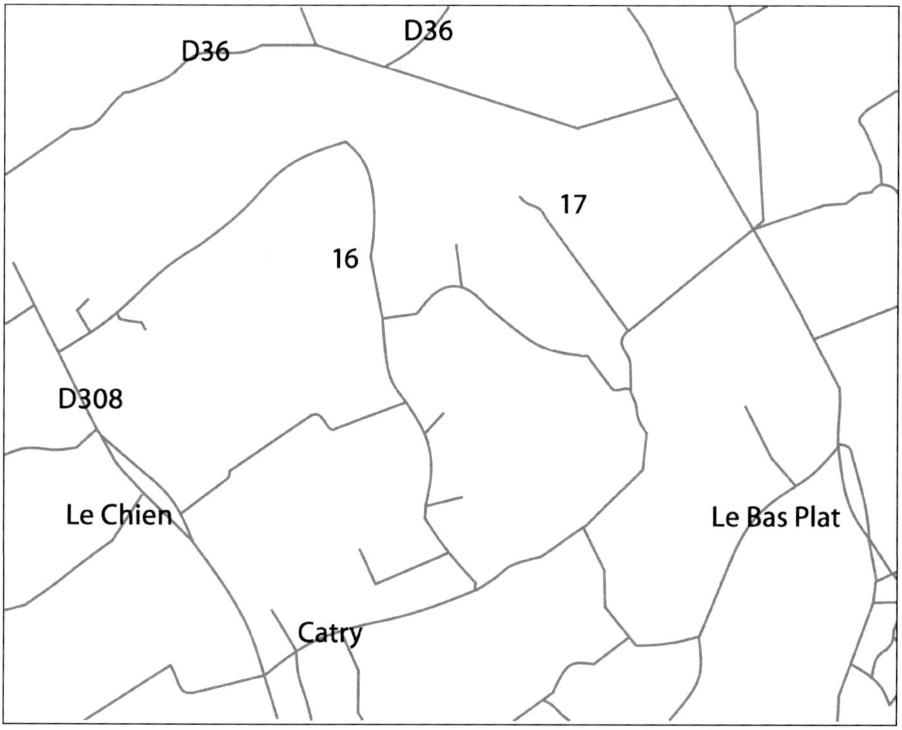

Figure 11.5: Map showing the location of two German WW1 pillboxes used by the BEF. See Figures 11.45 to 11.47.

Figure 11.6: French blockhouse, Cysoing, constructed in 1939.

Figure 11.7: Interior of Fig. 11.5 showing the block on which the French 25mm anti-tank gun was mounted.

Figure 11.8: Surviving French pavé road in the Cysoing area.

Figure 11.9: Hexagonal Bren gun emplacement, Cysoing.

Figure 11.10: Pillbox landscape, Cysoing, showing the typical placing of hexagonal Bren gun pillboxes in groups of four for mutual support.

Figure 11.11: Single anti-tank gun emplacement with a simple wing wall, Cysoing.

Figure 11.12: Single anti-tank gun emplacement with a stepped wing wall, Cysoing.

Figure 11.13: Part completed hexagonal Bren gun emplacement, Cysoing.

Figure 11.14: *Poste de tir* for a light machine gun, Cysoing.

Figure 11.15: French blockhouse, listed as Bloc de Campin, *1ére Région Militaire* pattern 'B' by Dépret.

Figure 11.16. Double machine gun emplacement, Cysoing.

Figure 11.17: Interior of double machine gun emplacement showing one of the gun mounts. Note the observation slit, an unofficial modification later prohibited by GHQ, and the cavity over loophole to allow the rear cover of the Vickers gun to be opened in any position on the arc of traverse, which was an approved GHQ alteration.

Figure 11.18: British graves in Cysoing communal cemetery.

Figure 11.19: Interior of the anti-tank gun pillbox BOIS DE TAISSONNIERE.

Figure 11.20: The emblem of the white rose of Yorkshire embossed on BOIS DE TAISSONNIERE pillbox (Tim Thurlow).

Figure 11.21: French *Tourelle* on the west side of the railway, Cysoing Wood.

Figure 11.22: French *Tourelle* on the east side of the railway, Cysoing Wood.

Figure 11.23: Double machine gun emplacement, Rue de Tournai.

Figure 11.24: What appears to be an anti-tank 'dragons tooth'.

Figure 11.25: Artillery observation post, named THE TRENCH.

Figure 11.26: *Psote de tir* for a 25mm anti-tank gun, named SPINDLEY WOOD.

Figure 11.27: French blockhouse (listed as Bloc du Moulin Mathon, *1ére Région Militaire* pattern G3 by Dépret) on the Route de Bachy.

Figure 11.28: BEF hexagonal Bren gun emplacement covering the rear of a French blockhouse (listed as Bloc de Bercu Pont d'Or, *1ére Région Militaire* pattern G by Depret) alongside the D955. Note the turf on the roof to aid concealment from the air.

Figure 11.29: Variant double machine gun emplacement alongside the D93.

Figure 11.30: One of the loopholes in the double machine gun emplacement alongside the D93.

Figure 11.31: Memorial to airmen from the 327th Bomber Squadron, 92nd Group.

Figure 11.32: Pair of single machine gun emplacements, just south of Mouchin on the D955.

Figure 11.33: Artillery observation post by the side of a house, south of Mouchin on the D955.

Figure 11.34: MG emplacement built onto the side of a farmhouse, south of Mouchin on the D955.

Figure 11.35: The stream L'Elnon, which formed part of the anti-tank obstacle in the French *Ligne principale*.

Figure 11.36: BEF lozenge shaped pillbox for Bren guns / riflemen.

Figure 11.37: Interior of lozenge pillbox showing the three forward facing Bren loopholes.

Figure 11.38: *Poste de tir* for a 25mm anti-tank gun.

Figure 11.39: VIEUX CONDE pillbox for a machine gun, one of the first pillboxes built by the BEF. Again, note the turf on the roof to aid concealment from the air.

Figure 11.40: Single anti-tank gun emplacement, lacking a wing wall, on the Aix – Nomain ridge.

Figure 11.41: Double machine gun emplacement, Aix – Nomain ridge.

Figure 11.42: Two 2 pdr anti-tank gun and Bren Gun emplacements, Mons-en-Pévèle.

Figure 11.43: One of the two 2 pdr anti-tank gun and Bren Gun emplacements, Mons-en-Pévèle.

Figure 11.44: Loophole for a 2 pdr anti-tank gun in one of the emplacements at Mons-en-Pévèle. Note the loophole frame.

Figure 11.45: German 1914-18 pillbox used as a post for a garrison of one section of York & Lancs.

Figure 11.46: Another German 1914-18 period pillbox also used as a post for a garrison of one section of York & Lancs. This pillbox required cutting a new loophole firing NE

Figure 11.47: The new loophole cut by of 506th Field Company firing NE.

12

Final Thoughts

Reflecting on the events of May 1940, RSM Cyril Freebrey observed:

> We were put to work to continue the defences through France to the coast by building the Gort Line, and this was straight out of the First World War textbook. Trench lines were paced out by the officers on reverse slopes, marked with white tape then dug out with pick and shovel. We dug strong points and pillboxes, dressing stations and rallying points. We felled trees to clear lines of fire and used the timber to reinforce steep-sided ditches to trap tanks. Looking back on it you can see we were thoroughly trained and superbly equipped to win the First World War. If we had fought the Battle of the Somme trained and equipped as we were in 1939 it really would have been all over by Christmas, no sweat. But the Germans, unsporting as ever, had changed the rules without telling us. We were twenty years behind the times and didn't know it yet.[1]

For someone who went through the traumatic three weeks of May 1940 after spending the previous winter digging, such a view is understandable. Today, the BEF's commanders are still widely perceived as having a 'Maginot mentality', obsessed with a Great War linear style of static defence from concrete works. But is this fair?

1 David Freebrey (ed.), Guardsman *and Commando: The War Memoirs of SM Cyril Freebrey, DCM* (Barnsley: Pen & Sword Books Ltd., 2008), pp. 9-10. Cyril Freebrey was not the only veteran to state he was taken by surprise with the German methods in attack. Clearly, the lessons from Poland were not fully disseminated during training, either because of the freedom given to senior commanders to set training programmes meant they did not ensure such information was passed down, or the lack of opportunity to experience tanks in training or because the message simply got lost amongst all the mud, digging and concreting. Montgomery expressed an opinion similar to Cyril Freebrey: 'the Army entered the Second World War in 1939 admirably organised and equipped to fight the 1914 war, and with the wrong officers at the top' See Bernard Law, Viscount Montgomery of Alamein, *The Memoirs of Field-Marshal Montgomery* (London: Collins, 1958), p. 39.

To try and answer this question, and the others posed in the Introduction, it is worth remembering how the years following the end of the Great War shaped the BEF of September 1939. During the 1920s, the fact that Britain had achieved most of her war aims was soon forgotten by the public, and the Great War was increasingly seen as one of futile sacrifice. The politicians reflected this view of the wider public and were determined that Britain would never again be dragged into a Continental war. To deal with a resurgent Germany, a policy of appeasement was adopted. British politicians believed Hitler did not want to drag Germany into another large-scale Continental war and that if a political settlement could be reached with German grievances over the Versailles Treaty, war could be avoided.

As tensions in Europe increased, the over-riding fear of British politicians was that Nazi Germany might attempt a knockout blow with a huge bomber offensive. Britain responded with a series of schemes to expand the RAF, largely focusing on building bombers to act as a deterrent to any threat by Germany to lay waste to British cities. If war should break out again on the Continent, British politicians were determined to fight a war of limited liability. British naval power would keep the sea lanes open while a powerful bomber force would act as a deterrent to any German aggression. In such a scenario, no need was seen to maintain a large army. Out of the three armed services, it was the Army that suffered the most during the period of the ten-year rule. It was only following the Munich Crises that politicians began to realise that war was inevitable, and that France may not be able to withstand a German attack alone. Arrangements were put in hand to expand the Army by doubling the size of the Territorial Force and introducing conscription, and to send an Expeditionary Force to the Continent.

Britain's military leaders had not forgotten the combined arms tactics that Britain excelled in during the last year of the Great War. British military doctrine was based on mechanised combined arms tactics, fully recognising the role of air support. This applied equally to the defence as well as the attack. However, the Army lacked any defined role other than that of a colonial police force and was starved of the equipment necessary for such a doctrine and had been unable to effectively train in it due to these matters. The RAF also thought that co-operation with the Army was a wasteful use of valuable bombers which would be much better employed hitting the enemy's war industry.

The consequence of the ten year rule and the rapid expansion of the Army from early 1939 onwards was that the British Army of 1939 did indeed more closely resembled the 'army of civilian volunteers that had fought on the Somme in 1916 than to the high-tech, well-co-ordinated behemoth that had advanced to victory in 1918.'[2] Initially, Britain could only send over to France an Expeditionary Force of four divisions, of which just two were fully trained, with a promise of 32 divisions within two years' time. Britain was the junior partner in the coalition with France

2 Daniel Todman, *Britain's war: Into Battle 1937-1941* (London: Allen Lane, 2016), p. 220.

and had to go along with French ideas on the way the war was to be fought. In such circumstances, senior British commanders realised that the Expeditionary Force could do little more than dig in and hope to hold on.

The BEF sailed to France with no clearly defined operational role other than to hold the frontier defences alongside the French. The defences that the BEF took over consisted of just a single anti-tank ditch covered by blockhouses at about 1,000 yards apart which were not necessarily built on a natural defensive position. The first priority had to be to prepare field defences centred on the French frontier defences to meet the expected imminent German attack. Once the initial danger of attack had passed, the BEF turned its attention to developing a defensive system in depth.

The layout of the Gort Line was very much in keeping with the tactical teaching of the day, with full provision for FDLs and depth in the rear. The country of the *SD* Lille was ideally suited to defence, and the BEF commanders were right to emphasise this. There were plenty of natural anti-tank obstacles, such as streams, woods, ribbon style villages and the large urban areas of Lille, Tourcoing and Roubaix. Full use of the natural strength of the position was made and enhanced by anti-tank ditches linking up the natural obstacles. The fire plans of all weapons were co-ordinated with the obstacles to create inter-locking fields of fire, with full provision made for alternative fire positions and, with the use of switch lines, minefields and a programme of demolitions, tank killing areas were created. The landscape in places provided excellent opportunities to conceal machine guns and anti-tank guns, but if this was not possible concrete cover was provided. All field, medium and heavy artillery were on mobile mountings and not fixed permanently in one position. This allowed the guns to make full use of alternative fire positions, providing a degree of mobility within the defensive position. The BEF's pillboxes fitted in with the defence doctrine as they were small works designed to strengthen field works and located in a chain of defended localities laid out in depth. In this sense, the Gort Line was not a defensive system based on a linear line of large fixed permanent concrete forts and was tactically superior to the Maginot Line.[3] To counter the paralysis of transport and communications inflicted by the *Luftwaffe* that characterised the Polish Campaign, alternative command centres and means of opening up new transport switches were provided for. The BEF also planned for an integrated air defence, which would ultimately form an extension of ADGB.

However, positional warfare was a role that the British Army had largely forgotten about during the inter-war years when it focused on its role as a colonial police force. This resulted in both improvisation and delay in the construction of the defences. It is a fair criticism that this should have been appreciated when the decision was made

3 The French tried to solve the problem of the immobility of the Maginot Line defences by garrisoning tank units and interval troops equipped with normal field weapons and artillery in the rear, but this had the effect of tying up tanks and troops which would have been of better use elsewhere.

to send over an Expeditionary Force to the Continent, which would have a defensive role. Further confusion arose as a result of Hore-Belisha deciding the Army should build for the 'new concept of fortress warfare' and with good intentions sending over 'X' Force to achieve this. This 'interference' in military matters by a politician enraged both Gort and Pownall and cumulated in the 'Pillbox Affair'. There were also many disagreements within the BEF as to the role required of pillboxes and it took some time to finalise designs. There were numerous problems and delays in sourcing enough materials and equipment for concrete construction. The position with field works was little better. At first, a continuous trench system was to be built. Then, it was decided no attempt would be made to dig a continuous trench system. Much effort was wasted digging in water-logged ground. The lack of pre-war training in field engineering showed, with many trenches and breastworks badly constructed. Little progress could be made in AA defence due to the acute shortages of AA guns in the BEF and the shortages of fighter aircraft, the majority which were retained at home for ADGB.

Despite all these issues, by May 1940 it is fair to say the Gort Line was beginning to resemble the carefully prepared battlefield in zones of depth that had been planned. Churchill noted that the construction of the Gort Line appeared to be keeping pace with the rate the Germans were extending their Siegfried Line, despite the German advantages of home resources and forced labour. Along much of the British zone, some defence in depth had been achieved by holding vital localities in considerable strength. The Gort Line was not seriously tested in battle so only tentative comments can be made with regards to whether it would have held up or seriously disrupted a major German attack. Brigadier Sir John Smyth certainly thought that the defences built by the BEF would at least cause havoc amongst the attacking German infantry following a tank breakthrough:

> I looked at the defences long and critically, trying to visualise how an approaching German force would tackle them. At first sight they appeared very strong and the dug ditch was certainly – as it stood and *if* it stood – a complete tank obstacle. But it was very conspicuous and could soon have been flattened by artillery bombardment. In fact, the whole defence system was rather too obvious and, as a lot of it had been built by civilian labour, it was probable that the Germans knew a great deal about it. Moreover, each battalion had to hold far too long a front. The greatest strength of this particular brigade sector lay in the very cleverly concealed machine-gun posts in the reserve areas. They had been situated not in concrete emplacements, but in hen-houses and other unlikely places. I came to the conclusion that the main obstacles would not hold up a strong force with air superiority for long, but that determined troops holding these rearward concealed positions might inflict enormous causalities on attacking infantry.[4]

4 Brigadier Sir John Smyth, VC, MC, MP *Before the Dawn: Two Historic Retreats Dunkirk*

An integrated defence consisting of trenches, wire, minefields, demolitions, pillboxes and anti-tank ditches sited in depth on ground well known to the defender could require a 'bloody slogging match' to overcome them if defended by resolute troops.[5] The British put a large resource into investigating methods to overcome such defences from the start of the Sitzkrieg right up to D Day, including the development of specialised armour. Although there is little value in dwelling too much on speculative history, if the Allies had decided to stand on the frontier defences, the Gort Line would likely have required just such a 'bloody slogging match' to overcome if seriously attacked – especially if we remember many of the German tanks in use in 1940 were the obsolete PzKw I and II. The French and British frontier defences would probably have halted the German offensive, resulting in a period of stagnated trench warfare on Allied terms as both sides fought to a standstill.[6]

1940. Burma 1942 (London: Cassell & Company Ltd., 1958), p. 26. To be fair, not all British officers agreed with Smyth's conclusion. Colonel William Morgan, GSO 1st Division, arrived in France in January 1940 and as he recalled, 'I don't remember having any confidence in the strength of the [Gort] line. It might have been a useful stopgap – but no more'(Joshua Levine, Forgotten *Voices: Dunkirk* (London: Ebury Press, 2011), p. 16).

5 The Siegfried Line is an example in case. Following the success of the Battle of Normandy in 1944, Montgomery had frequent disputes with Eisenhower – the Supreme Allied Commander-in-Chief – over strategy, largely based around Montgomery's belief that the Germans had to be prevented from being able to fight a static battle in the Siegfried Line by a concentrated thrust in the north which would outflank the defences: a kind of Schlieffen plan in reverse. Montgomery believed that overcoming such defences would severely slow down the Allies and drag out the war. However, Eisenhower preferred a broad front advance, partly for political reasons and also to be able to take advantage of any weak points in the German defence, but this strategy committed the American forces to a frontal attack on the Siegfried Line. Even though largely neglected for four years and hopelessly out of date, Neil Short concludes that the Siegfried Line, hastily garrisoned by new raw recruits and the shattered remnants of the German Army that had escaped the debacle in France, delayed the Americans with remarkable success, inflicting casualties of 7,024 killed, 35,155 wounded and 4,860 missing and captured on the American First Army alone in the period of fighting for the Line up to the German Ardennes offensive. Had Hitler decided to fully man the Siegfried Line instead of launching his ill-fated Ardennes offensive, the American casualties would likely have been much greater.

6 This is not hard to imagine as most fighting during the Second World War actually did involve periods of stagnated trench warfare; there were only a few periods of highly mobile warfare such as the Battle of France and Flanders, North Africa and the period immediately following the Allied breakout of the *bocage*. However, the nature of trench warfare was different to that in the Great War, where the front effectively became petrified, and many in the BEF certainly recognised this. Most of the trench warfare during 1939–45 was from hastily dug slit trenches which could be quickly occupied or abandoned. We have seen in Chapter 9 how the 1st Division commander emphasised the value of slit trenches against tanks. During the fighting in France and Flanders, the 1st Liverpool Scottish also noted the value of this style of trench: 'we found that small slit trenches were a complete answer to dive bombing' and that not 'a single man in the Division was killed by a dive bomber if he was in a slit trench' (TNA: WO166/4433, 1st Liverpool Scottish War Diary, Operational

The BEF's commanders are often criticised for continuing to build the Gort Line after Gamelin had decided in November that the only options to meet a German invasion of Belgium would be an advance to the Dyle or the Escaut. Gort's critics state he should have prioritised the training of his Army rather than continue to build useless fortifications. This argument ignores two points: firstly, continuing to develop the Gort Line was entirely in keeping with the principle of defence in depth and constructing a rear position in case of the failure of the Belgian manoeuvre and secondly, Gamelin was still stating that the move into Belgium would only be carried out if it was certain the Belgians could delay the Germans long enough for the Allies to establish a defensive line. It should be remembered that by November, the BEF had only dug itself in along the FDL Line, with little added depth. The British were far less certain than the French that any move into Belgium would be a success because of the Belgian refusal to enter staff talks, meaning all planning had to be done largely with second hand maps and with what intelligence could be gleaned, and because of the weak state of the Belgian defences along the Dyle Line (see Appendix II). Another critical point to make is that the BEF was still getting mixed messages of its operational role from the War Office with forces diverted from it for operations in Scandinavia. Also, successive discrepancies between British and French strategy against Germany directly, or indirectly in the Balkans, also caused uncertainty. The result was that the French succeeded in blocking British plans of action and the British the French plans: there was no unified strategy to fighting the war, but instead only improvised solutions. Under these circumstances, continuing to work on the defences was an entirely sensible precaution.

The British accepted Gamelin's Plan D as it fitted in with their long held fear of the Low Countries falling into the hands of a strong power hostile to Britain. However, many thought the dash into Belgium meant abandoning the Gort Line and 'ensuring that willy-nilly the work of a whole winter should be rendered useless.'[7] Not quite, but it is easy to understand the frustration of those who held this view at the time. By 22 May the BEF was back on the Gort Line and very glad of its strong defences. The Gort Line now fulfilled its role as a fallback position. It allowed Gort to economise his forces in the east and build up a reserve, at first intended for a counter-attack to the south to link up with the French Army assembling on the Somme, but ultimately sent to Brooke to plug the hole in the Allied line created by the German breakthrough on the Belgian Army's front.

The BEF was not sufficiently equipped to train and prepare for first class modern mechanised warfare, but it did train for the two roles it was expected to carry out: a

Instruction No. 27). With regards to the value of slit trenches in defensive lines, it was found they gave good cover against artillery and mortar fire until the enemy had got the positions pinpointed. As many alternative positions as possible were the answer to this.

7 Lt. Colonel Ewan Butler & Major J. Selby Bradford, *Keep the Memory Green: The First of the Many France 1939-40* (London: Hutchinson & Co. Ltd., no date), p. 73.

rapid dash to a river line (the possibility of a withdrawal was not ignored in training) and holding a stabilised front. Additionally, experience of being in close contact with the enemy was gained with tours to the Saar Front. Although standards in training were undeniably inconsistent throughout the BEF, it had certainly reached a sufficient level of training to carry out its part in Gamelin's plan for the advance into Belgium and to dig in along the Dyle. Subsequently, during the Battle of France and Flanders, the BEF was also able to inflict heavy casualties on the German Army – then arguably the best in the world – and fight a successful retreat in close contact with the enemy by hastily organising a series of defensive positions.[8] Commanders and troops were able to put into practice the training and experience of preparing field defences gained during the Sitz.[9] This was despite the many obstacles to training: the continuous working parties on the defences, the harsh winter weather and restrictions due to crops in the field. Opinion amongst many of those who successfully made it back from Dunkirk was adamant that the British soldier man for man could beat the Germans.[10]

Following Dunkirk, Britain faced imminent invasion, with a largely untrained Army and precious little equipment to meet it with. Again, static defence was all the Army was capable of. Ironside was unfortunate in the timing of his appointment as Commander-in-Chief Home Forces: it came at a time when practically nothing had been done to prepare Britain for invasion and this again resulted in an extemporised approach to the defences at first. But at least Home Forces was operating under much

8 Although the BEF successfully fought its way back to Dunkirk, it has to be admitted that the retreat was chaotic at times; exposing shortcomings in command and control and communications. The German error in not pressing the attack at the critical stage also played a large part in the BEF getting away.

9 Presumably it was this type of scenario of active campaigning that Pownall had in mind when he stated in his diary on 25 October 1939 'what better practical training than the preparation of a defensive position?' (Brian Bond (ed.), *Chief of Staff: The Diaries of Lieutenant-General Sir Henry Pownall* (London: Leo Cooper, 1972), p. 249).

10 *ATM No.*33 also stated that the 'British soldier is man for man at least the equal if not better than the German' *ATM No. 33*, p. 14). Captain John Horsfall certainly thought that the German Army was not as good as it was often portrayed: '[T]he 7th Panzers suffered a large number of quite unnecessary casualties through incompetence, arrogant bullheadedness and lack of individual training. Their field craft was non-existent and the tactical handling at regimental level was bad – scarcely attempted in fact. The standard of weapon training was poor save with their machine gunners, and their ability as marksman was negligible' (John Horsfall, Say *Not the Struggle...* (Kineton: Roundwood Press, 1977), p. 166). He also thought that the Germans relied on 'bludgeon' tactics with the Panzers, treating the infantry as 'cannon fodder'. The Germans were also impressed with the qualities of the British, as illustrated by a report prepared in August 1940 by the German IV Corps which had fought against the BEF. It noted 'The English soldier has always shown himself to be a *fighter of high value.* Certainly, the Territorial divisions are inferior to the Regular troops in training, but where morale is concerned, they are their equal' (Major L. F. Ellis, *The War in France and Flanders 1939–1940* (London: HMSO, 1953), p. 326). None of this detracts from the stunning German victory, but it does illustrate that the BEF did perform creditably in the Battle of France and Flanders, although it was way too small to make a difference.

the same conditions as the BEF had during the Sitzkrieg, allowing time to begin to put things right. Ironside's scheme was a reaction to the lack of hard-hitting mobile forces and preparedness in the Army, and he undoubtedly relied upon the experience that officers and men had gained along the Franco-Belgian border. However, his policy of static defence was widely criticised, and he was soon replaced by Brooke who favoured a mobile aggressive defence. Concrete defences were finally declared redundant in 1942 and any thought of defending a continuous anti-tank obstacle had been rejected by 1943. Nevertheless, back in June 1940, Ironside faced the same problems as the BEF had in September 1939: just as the BEF had been fit only for preparing a static defence in September 1939, it is difficult to see how Ironside could have planned anything else than a similar style of static defence. Certainly, in the summer of 1940 none of Ironside's critics ever explained where the trained men and AFVs necessary for a more aggressive mobile defence were to come from and following his removal work on static defences did not cease.

In writing this book, I have come to believe that the Sitzkrieg was not a period wasted by the BEF or even one marked by stupidity, opinions still widely held today. The BEF was largely a product of Britain's grand strategy during the inter-war years and it was ill-prepared and ill- equipped to meet the expected German Blitzkrieg. The Gort Line defences were a necessity of the time, rather than the deliberate choice of a generation of 'Colonel Blimp' officers determined to refight the Great War. Given the circumstances, and the knowledge possessed at the time by those who had to make the decisions, it is difficult to see how the BEF could have done anything different. Dunkirk was ultimately a result three factors. Firstly, the failure of the Allies to form a fully functioning alliance and the absence of any combined staff or organisation to formulate and execute a strategic direction of the war should not be underestimated as a cause of the Allied failure. Secondly, the ill-fated Breda Variant to Plan D deprived the French of the best elements of their mobile reserve, essential for a successful defence in depth.[11] Thirdly, the breakdown of French command and control resulted in giving up the Meuse bridgeheads too easily and then not being able deliver the right type of counter-attack at the right place at the right time. These were the main reasons for the Allied debacle, not the reliance on static defences – the so called 'Maginot mentality'. The BEF, caught up in the French collapse, found itself back on the Gort Line during the Battle of France and Flanders and its defences gave Lord Gort a brief but desperately needed respite in the eastern battle.

11 In Chapter 4, it was noted that back in September 1939 some did not believe Germany could win success in the West unless the Allies were forced to disperse their effort. In effect, this is exactly what the Breda variant to Plan D achieved, by ensuring the best elements of the French strategic reserve had no hope of influencing the main battle. Even Montgomery recognised that events might not have been as bad as they were if Georges had got his way and the French Seventh Army had been kept in reserve instead of being pushed forward.

Appendix I

BEF Officer reports on French Pillboxes

Engineer-in-Chief's visit to the Maginot Line

On 18 and 19 December, the Engineer in Chief and Deputy Engineer in Chief visited the French Third Army on the Maginot Line in the area Soutrich, north of Thionville and close to the Luxembourg border. This area was selected by the French for the visit, as it demonstrated most of the principles and details of the Maginot Line, and also because in this neighbourhood a considerable number of pillboxes and anti-tank obstacles had been, or were in the process of being, constructed. The report of the visit gives some further interesting insights to the defence of the Maginot Line and French pillboxes.

The new pillboxes were all built in the neighbourhood of the Maginot forts and were designed to strengthen the Line. None had been built, or were in the process of being built, in the more forward lines. The French considered the provision of fortifications in peace time and war time as entirely different. In peace, they considered it advisable to construct numerous works, provided with the maximum protection and housing the maximum number of weapons. In wartime however, such works took too long to construct. Instead it was better to concentrate on constructing a larger number of small pillboxes, to take one or two weapons at the most. They considered that each pillbox should be able to withstand one hit of the heaviest artillery (9 inch calibre). Given ample reinforcement, 1m or 1.2m thick walls was sufficient for this.

The pillboxes seen by the Engineer in Chief were all quite small, designed either to hold a 25mm anti-tank gun or a machine gun. Most of the anti-tank gun pillboxes faced the front, or at least obliquely to the front, with a wide traverse and consequently large loopholes. The French stated that about 50 percent were sited for frontal fire and 50 percent for enfilade fire. Walls and roof were stated to be 1m thick and the foundations sunk 1.5m or 2m into the ground. Most of the machine gun pillboxes were sited to fire in enfilade. However, in the case of reverse slopes, with a short field of fire, they were sited for frontal fire with a wide traverse. These machine gun pillboxes were also 1m thick except on the loophole face where thickness was reduced to limit the size of the loophole. To make up for this, a burster course of steel rails was provided in front up to the level of the bottom of the loophole. It has to be noted that the hilly countryside of Lorraine differed from that of Lille; in Lille the terrain was much flatter and there was little to defilade from the front, so fire would be from enfilade in the vast majority of cases.

Tactically, the French considered every pillbox should be capable of holding out even if the enemy had surrounded it. For this it was necessary to give some protection to the entrance, either with sandbags or concrete, and that fire from within the pillbox should be able to cover the entrance. If possible, holes from which bombs could be rolled should be provided on every face that the enemy might approach. It was also considered necessary to provide the loopholes with tank proof shutters and that theses should be put in place if a tank was advancing on a pillbox using its gun directly towards the loophole, until the tank had turned to a more vulnerable angle.

All pillboxes were built by engineer labour. All materials such as reinforcing bars and shuttering were prepared in a central workshop at Thionville and delivered to site. The approximate time for construction of a pillbox after delivery of materials was three weeks.

The main anti-tank obstacle consisted of five rows of champs de rails with a thick wire entanglement in front and behind. It was covered by the fire of all arms from the cupolas of the forts. Along certain parts of the obstacle, special mines formed of shells activated by steel rods were placed at the last row of rails.

In considerable depth behind the main obstacle, were two rows of excavated and revetted anti-tank ditch. They were enfiladed by machine guns only but were covered by fire from anti-tank guns in pillboxes behind the ditches firing to the front with a wide traverse and by the fire of the main guns in the forts. In contrast, the anti-tank ditches and wire obstacles that were being constructed several miles in front of the main forts were not covered by close fire and there was no intention to do so.

Report by Lieutenant J.A. Warre, 12th Lancers, on the French defences north of Bavai

This reconnaissance was carried out ostensibly as a road reconnaissance and not a detailed reconnaissance of the defences of the area. The defences that Warre recorded were all from a motor vehicle and so no details of the defences were obtained from French troops. His report, dated 14 December, does still have some interesting observations and contrasts with the apparent lack of action of the French 51st Division on the left of the BEF.

Warre notes that the defences in the Bavai area were in an advanced stage although not yet completed. He observed a considerable number of French troops working hard, in some places under very bad weather conditions, to complete them. It was believed the troops in the area were from the 1st Regiment Zouaves and the 1st Regiment

Mitrailleuse. Bavai is just west of Maubeuge, so would have been the part of the French defences that secured the BEF's right flank.

He noted that the pillbox designs were the same French types as found on the BEF front. In several places they were situated in the middle of the anti-tank ditch, in which case there was another ditch in front of the pillbox (in contrast to the Lille defences, where anti-tank rails were used). In most cases the pillboxes were exceedingly well camouflaged with trees and brushwood. He was unable to tell if the pillboxes housed anti-tank guns or machine guns, but noted they were well sited on forward slopes of a rise over looking a valley giving excellent fields of fire. There were nearly always fire trenches besides them and communication trenches running to the rear from the pillboxes. He also observed communication trenches running forward of the anti-tank ditch to what he presumed were observation posts.

The main tank obstacle was an anti-tank ditch, faced with wattle. In very damp areas, the wattle facing had been replaced with concrete. He noted three separate wire obstacles. The only tank obstacle along the river line running through Longueville was a double line of steel rails which he did not consider very formidable.

Warre observed two strongly fortified areas – the Bois de la Leniere and the Malplaquet crossroads. He noted many pillboxes in the Bois de la Leniere and that sections of the wood had been cleared to give a wide field of fire.

MO4 Observations on French First Army and 16 Corps, 5 November 1939

MO4 noted that the French First Army and 16 Corps were working on rear positions as well as the forward positions. The French were working on the principle of not so much as to make a continuous line but to select desirable areas of defence and make centres of resistance capable of all round defence. Two centres of resistance were the Forest of Mormal and the Forest of Nouvion. Tank obstacles and pillboxes were included in the defence. Similar defences were being constructed between Vervins and Montigny-en-Ostrivent, also using woods and forests, 'which the French seem to like as bases for the centres of resistance.'[1]

Dépret notes that between September 1939 and May 1940, the French First Army had completed 295 blockhouses with 39 in hand. This was against a target of 242 set by *Groupe d'armées no.1* (396 required for a front of 66km, with 154 blockhouses existing as at September 1939, requiring an additional 242 blockhouses). On the other hand, the French Seventh Army on the BEF's left had only completed 62 with four in hand between September 1939 and May 1940 against a target of 260.

1 TNA: WO106/1638.

Appendix II

Belgian Defences

There were divergent views in Belgium on how the country should be defended against a German invasion. One opinion was that the German's should be met in fortified defences along the border, while others held that the main battle positions should not be along the border, but in the heart of the country, allowing time for mobilisation and allies to come to Belgium's help. The result was a dispersion of effort, with a border position based on the Albert Canal and the Liége defences, and inland, a battle position based around Brussels.

The Belgian forces mobilised amounted to 16 divisions, of which six were active, six were 1st reserve and four were 2nd reserve. Of that number, 13 divisions lay between Antwerp and Liége, of which five were in the area of Liége and Maastricht. One division was at Namur. The Albert Canal was 60 to 100 metres wide with 6 feet of water and constituted an excellent anti-tank obstacle. The Belgians had constructed machine gun emplacements every 500 metres or so designed to give enfilade fire along the obstacle. The old forts of Liége had been modernised in the sense that new forts had been built underneath the old ones, the old construction being used as a burster overhead. These forts had no artillery heavier than field artillery. Behind the forts lay the anti-tank obstacle of the River Meuse. In front of the Liége forts there were other considerable forts to the east and south; these were however isolated and did not form a continuous line. Further south lay the Belgian Ardennes where a great deal of demolition had been prepared although it was not a defensive area. Further west lay Antwerp, which had old forts which had not been modernised although would still provide useful infantry shelters.

The Belgians had also started constructing an intermediate defensive system round Brussels, linking the Namur defences to the Antwerp defences, utilising the River Dyle as an anti-tank obstacle. The Allies understood the Belgians were constructing an artificial anti-tank obstacle running south across the Wavre plateau, covering an area vulnerable to tank attack known as the Gembloux Gap where no natural anti-tank obstacle existed. Plan D was to see the BEF advance into Belgium to take up a sector on this inland battle position – the Dyle Position – to meet the German invasion. Last minute information revealed that the Belgian artificial anti-tank obstacle did not cover the dangerous Gembloux Gap as had been understood, but was sited further east, along the line Namur – Perwez – Louvain, and was by no means complete. This did not directly affect the BEF as they had an excellent natural anti-tank obstacle formed by the Dyle; however, the situation was different for the French First Army, which had no natural obstacle and was much more dependent upon the artificial obstacle the Belgians were constructing.

The DYLE river intermediate position

British intelligence on the Dyle Position was hardly encouraging:

> the attached notes on the DYLE River position show that it is far from being fully developed. It has a more or less continuous anti-tank obstacle. The northern part of the position has a wire obstacle throughout most of its length, with some field works and some concrete pill boxes: but these works, so far as we know, are confined to forward defences. In the southern sector even the forward defences are only "in progress".[1]

In detail, the notes summarised the progress of work along the various sections of the Dyle Position:

> SECTOR NAMAUR [sic]
> Nine old forts exist. Whilst the remaining 7 of them have been modernized [sic], the two on the north west of the town linking up with the new line have not been modernized [sic].
> South of the MEUSE the three modernized [sic] forts have had some 33 Pill Boxes built in the intervals.
> North of the Meuse a line of de Cointet obstacle with behind it three lines of barbed wire each 15 feet wide and 80 yards apart has been built between MARCHES LES DAMES (on r. MEUSE) – inclusive RHISNES. (About 8 miles).
>
> SECTOR RHISNES – WAVRE (About 20 miles).
> Work on defences in progress with object of making a continuous trench system, wired and protected by a de Cointet type obstacle. Preparations for building concrete emplacements are reported and the M.A. Brussels estimates that the A.Tk. obstacle should be complete by now.
>
> SECTOR WAVRE – LOUVAIN (About 15 miles).

1 TNA: WO106/1777, memo by DCIGS on visit to France, 1 February 1940.

Main defensive position is west of the DYLE, the level of which between WAVRE and LOUVAIN has been raised by the construction of a dam at LOUVAIN.
The existing defences consist of a continuous belt of wire east of the river with field works and a certain number of concrete pill boxes west of the river. It is believed that the Belgians intend to construct another belt of wire and a second A.Tk. obstacle west of the river. The railway embankment east of LOUVAIN is being improved to make an A.Tk. obstacle and a covering position is being prepared on the high ground east of LOUVAIN.

SECTOR LOUVAIN – LIERRE (About 18 miles).
Main position consists of a number of pill boxes. Between LOUVAIN and THILDONCK the A.Tk. obstacle is the Canal and west of the Canal positions have been dug and heavily wired.
Between THILDONCK and the river DYLE north of HAECHT an A.Tk. ditch has been dug. Between here and the ANTWERP defences, the A.Tk. obstacle is provided by the inundations on the GRAND and PETIT NETHE rivers. The intervals between the floods being filled with a de Cointet obstacle.[2]

2 Ibid, 'The DYLE river intermediate position (NAMUR – WAVRE – LOUVAIN – ANTWERP)', 1 February 1940.

Appendix III

Attack on a Fortified Position

The special characteristics of an attack against a fortified enemy position – as articulated in *FSR Vol. II 1935* – are that the enemy defences would be elaborate and extend to a great depth and covered by obstacles that would need to be pierced or broken before the infantry could advance. For tanks, the attacker would have to devise some means of enabling them to cross the obstacles or must make the first attack with infantry to clear the obstacles. Great resources of material would be required to deal with enemy defences in position warfare – especially artillery – and preparations would take considerable time. Operations may have to be carried out in distinct phases over several days before finally breaking through the organised defences. The French were broadly in agreement with these characteristics.

For an attack against Germany, the Allies considered that the most favourable situation would be if the Germans had invaded Belgium and been halted on the line Namur – Louvain – Antwerp – Breda as they would then be exposed to an Allied counter-attack in open country and would have lost the support of the Siegfried Line. If the Belgium theatre was not available, a direct attack on the Siegfried Line would be required which would be a battle of brute force – a 'modernized [sic] Verdun or Somme' – with no exploitation possible until having emerged from the fortified system.[1] The excellence of German equipment and the organisation of Germany's internal railways would always allow Germany to bring up forces necessary to check any Allied attack. To have any chance of success, the Allies reasoned that incontestable superiority of resources compared to Germany would be necessary. This need not be absolute, as long as local superiority could be obtained. The Allies estimated that 130 to 140 divisions would be required for the offensive and to guard the Franco-Belgium border against German counter-attacks, against 150 to 160 German divisions. This would require a contribution of 40 British divisions. Thus, the spring of 1941 was the earliest that the Allies would be in a position to begin such an offensive. Nevertheless,

1 WO193/157, 'Conditions for the resumption of the offensive on the Western Front', Siegfried Line and Note on Attack on Fortified Towns.

preparations were undertaken to ensure that the offensive could be undertaken with prospects of success.

The French produced several detailed memorandums on the attack against fortified positions and the following details are from the assessments of July and September 1939. French ideas were largely in accord with British thinking on an attack in position warfare.

Any attack debauching from the frontier would meet an outpost zone and the main battle zone of the Siegfried Line. The outpost zone would consist of an echelon of strong points consisting of small concrete posts and a belt of demolitions, designed to slow up the enemy's advance to the main zone. The outpost zone was expected to be as wide as 12km in places. The main zone consisted of a complete infantry obstacle, anti-tank obstacles, numerous small concrete works of between 1m and 1.5m thick echeloned on a variable depth, each position giving flank protection to its neighbour.

The French considered that the fortification of frontiers, such as the Maginot Line and the Siegfried Line, gave the infantry a 'new' problem. Because of the solidity of forts, the infantry was prevented from taking action against them except against their embrasures. The British were inclined to agree and considered that new tactics and the development of existing weapons would be needed to overcome such fortifications. This development of weapons would take time to bring to the stage of practical use, and then there would be the need to train troops in their use. Even if the number of divisions required could be concentrated by the spring of 1941, there would likely be further delays in accumulation the specialised material for such an operation.

In its strongest parts, the main position of the Siegfried Line was as deep as 2km or 3km. The rear edge of this zone often consisted of a chain of strong concrete works, often on a reverse slope, forming the framework of a final 'stopping line'. To overcome such concrete works, trials held by the French at their experimental centre at Bourges convinced them calibres of 220mm (8.8 inch), 280mm (11.2 inch), 370mm (14.8 inch) and even 400mm (16 inch) would have to be employed. The breaching of the infantry obstacle by artillery was regarded as particularly problematical due to the obstacle often being on reverse slopes; it would always require a very heavy expenditure of ammunition.

The French believed that an attack on a fortified front could only succeed if the attack was on a wide front; otherwise only a narrow deep pocket would be gained, making it difficult to pass through reinforcements and supplies and making it easy for an enemy counter-attacks. A breakthrough operation would be divided into a succession of phases. Firstly, preliminary operations would be required, with the aim of gaining contact with the enemy and preventing him from carrying out his demolition programme. The second phase would be the penetration and capture of the main position on a front which would be limited in size by the amount of heavy artillery available. The third phase would be overcoming any hastily prepared defences the enemy had constructed in order to seal the breach in his line. The final phase would be the exploitation of the breakthrough. There would be delays between each phase due to the need to plan methodically and bring up the necessary means for each phase.

In order to carry out such an operation, a considerable material resource was required. Firstly, a powerful force of artillery with a plentiful supply of ammunition would be required for the preparation of the attack, the destruction of concrete defence works and obstacles and the neutralisation of the enemy defensive fire. Secondly, a strong force of tanks would be required for infantry support, and to act in independently during the exploitation phase. If available, specialised armour, capable of passing over obstacles and provided with armament capable neutralising concrete emplacements not destroyed by the artillery would be very beneficial. Thirdly, a strong air force would be required to provide air cover for all stages of the operation and prevent enemy bombing operations from paralysing the movement forward of reserves. Lastly, a whole host of specialised equipment would be necessary such as smoke to blind the enemy defences, chemical weapons to reduce the enemy's morale, means of crossing obstacles, especially water ways, and re-establishing communications.

In detail, the taking of the outpost zone would be a rapid operation; utilizing the fact that organisation of an outpost position was not continuous. The concrete posts would be assaulted by specialist teams, having been paralysed by employment of smoke and placing other screens, such as fascines and sandbags, in front of the weapons of the defence. Once the outpost line had been breached and contact made with the main defensive position, methodical preparations could be made for the actual rupture of the main fortified position. This would always take a considerable amount of time. Continuous artillery fire, day and night, would be required to demolish obstacles and concrete works as well as lessening the powers of resistance by shaking the morale of the defenders. The artillery would also be required to undertake counter-battery fire to neutralise enemy artillery. The time required for this artillery preparation would depend upon the number of concrete works that would need to be destroyed.

The main attack would be supported by strong artillery support and specialised heavy tanks (smaller tanks would run the risk of becoming held up by obstacles or the ground cut up by the artillery fire). Concrete forts which had not been neutralised by the artillery would be dealt with by special detachments of infantry consisting of engineers and rifle companies reinforced with flat trajectory weapons (e.g. the 75mm field gun or the 47mm and 25mm anti-tank guns) which could destroy the embrasures of the fort and the specialised tanks. The main attacking infantry would continue their advance once any remaining forts had been neutralised, leaving mopping-up parties to deals with the remaining defenders. These mopping-up parties would be also be armed with specialist weapons such as flame throwers and incendiary grenades. Thus the advance would take the form of the infantry carrying out a succession of small assaults carefully boxed in by artillery fire, and in particular the use of smoke shells. If numerous concrete works had escaped destruction by the artillery fire, the advance may be as little as 1km a day. Once the initial breach had been made, attempts would be made to widen it on the flanks and in the rear. As the time taken to carry out these operations would always be lengthy, the enemy would have plenty of time to make the disposition of his reserves. A new attack would be required to completely break through the fortified front. The enemy would probably not have had time to complete anti-tank obstacles in the rear were his reserves were deployed, allowing the use of cruiser tanks (*chars de manoeuvre d'ensemble*) in this phase. Once this had been achieved, the breakthrough would be exploited by the mass deployment of tanks (*DCRs*, *DCMs* and tank battalions). The French considered that to ensure command and control of such attacking units, a divisional frontage should be limited to 1,200m or 1,500m.

The British had also started to study the problem of attacking the Siegfried Line. Work had begun on constructing a typical section of the Siegfried Line on Salisbury Plain – consisting of about half a mile of metre-thick concrete wall and a dozen pillboxes – for large scale exercises and experimenting with a number of devices for overcoming German permanent fortifications. A model of a portion of the Siegfried Line, together with an air photograph, map and annotated tracing, was issued to certain divisions at home. Officers were encouraged to come up with novel and innovative methods for overcoming the defences, the best suggestions forwarded to the War Office. Experiments included various bridging devices (including one a self-propelled mounting and one that could be pushed ahead of a tank), a bulldozer mounted on a Mk I tank for fast infilling of trenches, a roller fascine that could be pushed ahead of a tank to fill wide ditches and trenches, a coconut fibre matting for unrolling over barbed wire, explosive charges that could be fired from inside a tank to destroy concrete teeth and similar obstacles, anti-mine devices (such as rollers or skids pushed in front of thanks to explode mines and ploughs to turn mines to onside), a Bangalore torpedo that could be laid in front of a tank and a tank mounted flamethrower. Special tanks designed for static warfare against fortifications were also under development such as the Mk IV 'Shelled Area Tank' – the Stern 50 ton tank – and a tank carrying a De Thoren searchlight for use at night and for dazzle purposes.

The type of artillery required was also being studied. The British did not think that conventional howitzers, even if firing delayed action fuses, would be effective against concrete. Experiments were being undertaken with a heavy 9.2 inch gun firing heavy piercing shells with base fuses such as used at sea and mounting heavier high velocity guns firing solid shot rounds on tanks, given the success of trials using the 2 pdr gun on concrete. The new general-purpose French 75mm gun was considered a superb gun but was too big to fit into the Stern tank.

Mine warfare was not neglected. Mechanical means had also been developed for soil removal: either by conveyor belt or hydraulic ejection. Two machines had also been developed that could tunnel by compressing the soil, removing the problem of soil disposal altogether.

A. 20 Stern Tank: First attempt at specialised armour

As noted above, early consideration was given to the need for a specialised tank capable for breaking through the defences of the Siegfried Line. The specifications for an Infantry Tank suitable for supporting an offensive on the Western Front stipulated that it had to be capable of crossing shelled ground, have a speed of not less than 10 mph, have good trench crossing capacity, and have armour that could resist anti-tank fire and armament for dealing with anti-tank defences. The French technique (Char B tank) was to employ a low velocity, high calibre gun mounted in the hull firing a HE shell (75mm gun) for dealing with earthworks and a high velocity, smaller calibre gun (47mm gun) firing solid shot mounted in a turret for breaking up dragon's teeth, steel rails and concrete pillboxes. In addition to these, it was considered desirable to have a machine gun either side of the tank capable of firing to a flank and means of putting down smoke, as defences would have to be destroyed while the tank was stationary.

The British experimental tank for this role was the Infantry Tank Mk. IV, known as A.20. It weighed nearly 40 tons and carried a crew of seven (commander, gunner and loader in the turret, driver, forward gunner and two machine gunners). It had a 24 inch broad track, with a ground pressure expected to be less than 10lbs per square inch. The suspension consisted of a set of independent mounted track rollers with double concentric coils springs. Ground clearance was about 2 feet. The engine fitted to the pilot model was a 300bhp 12-cylinder Meadows engine. The length of the tank was around 27 feet and it was expected that it could cross trenches 12 feet wide.

The armour was composite. The hull armour was a novel design, consisting of two continuous plates of D.1 machineable steel, with an air space in between. These plates were 19mm thick and bolted to a plate of 25mm C.T.A., giving a thickness of only 63mm but firing trials suggested it was equivalent to a 90mm casting and could keep out a 2 pdr round shot at 35 yards range. Frontal plates and the turret were also composite.

The tank was armed with a 2 pdr gun and 7.92mm Besa in the turret coaxially mounted, and also a 2 inch smoke mortar. In the centre of the front plate of the hull was a second 2 pdr gun on a gimbal mounting giving 7.5° traverse to either side. On either side of the hull was a 7.92mm Besa in a ball mounting giving a 90° traverse.

The tank did have a number of problems, mostly centred on its armament, and doubts about this had been raised in various quarters. Major W. M. Blagden RE, a technical officer, was sent over from France during 12 April to 1 May to view a series of tank trials, including the pilot model of the new Infantry Tank A.20. Although impressed with some of the novel design features, he largely confirmed the doubts about its armament. Firstly, the 2 pdr gun could not be used to destroy earthworks and showed the need to develop a gun specifically for the task they were intended for and not merely an adapted field gun. The turret was mounted too far back so the gun could not be sufficiently depressed. This would make it difficult to deal with concrete dragon's teeth, the intended purpose of the gun. The cramped space in the fighting compartment made it impossible to use the side mounted Besa's with parallel mounted telescopic sights. A special periscopic telescopic sight was devised but the view from it was too restrictive. Tests had also shown that the Meadows engine only produced 240bhp which was considered inadequate. An alternative engine – a 350bhp engine manufactured by Vauxhall Motors – was in the process of being sourced.

Although work on the design of the A.20 was continued following Dunkirk, the design was ultimately abandoned because of the excessive weight, which reached 80 tons for the final version. However, the British did not give up with the development of specialised armour: several attachments were designed for the Churchill tank and operated by the 79th Armoured Division.

Appendix IV

Pillboxes Constructed / Planned by the BEF – Extracted from War Diaries

---

The table below lists the pillboxes and other concrete structures constructed or at least sited by the BEF compiled from X' Force, RE field companies and GHQ down to division level war diaries. It should not be regarded as a complete record, as details recorded in the relevant war diaries vary considerably.

The Military Grid references were converted to decimal points by utilisation of the web programme *Coordinates Translator* <http://www.echodelta.net>. Note such conversations only have an accuracy of +/- 200 metres.

Useful electronic sources that detail many of the Gort Line's remaining pillboxes are as follows:

<www.wikimaginot.eu>
<www.attila-77250.fr>

Structure	Name	Military Grid Ref	Con. Grid Ref	Comments
?		621483	50.73741, 2.94463	
?		622479	50.73387, 2.9491	
?	Warneton West	627498	50.75121,2.95177	
?	Warneton East	628499	50.75217, 2.9531	
?		641495	50.74932, 2.97185	
?		677515	50.7693, 3.02101	
German pillbox		686458	50.71865, 3.03879	WW1 pillbox.
German pillbox		687461	50.72139, 3.03994	WW1 pillbox.
German pillbox		688456	50.71696, 3.0418	WW1 pillbox.

German pillbox		689458	50.71881, 3.04303	WW1 pillbox.
?		692510	50.76566, 3.04269	
German pillbox		694460	50.72089, 3.04993	WW1 pillbox.
German pillbox		696459	50.7201, 3.05285	WW1 pillbox.
?		699509	50.76515, 3.05269	
?		699511	50.76695, 3.05251	
German pillbox		707474	50.73418, 3.06708	WW1 pillbox.
German pillbox		709479	50.73878, 3.06948	WW1 pillbox.
German pillbox		709481	50.74058, 3.0693	WW1 pillbox.
?		710521	50.77654, 3.0672	
?		711521	50.77659, 3.06862	
A/tk gun pillbox	G'DS Obeaux	713426	50.69143, 3.07977	Recced April. Wing wall on right. Type B foundation raft. Weapon 3ft above ground level. C/L of arc 290 deg.
Sec MG pillbox	Le Lazard	715414	50.68077, 3.08365	Wing wall on right. Floor to be 3ft below ground level if possible. C/L of arc 327 deg.
A/tk gun pillbox	White Horse Two	717422	50.68806, 3.08578	Wing wall on right. C/L of arc 287 deg.
A/tk gun pillbox	Fort Bondues One	717427	50.69255, 3.08534	Recced in April. 8in proof. Bren loophole at back of entrance. Right wing wall. Right of arc on fence.
Sec MG pillbox	Fort Bondues West Two	717428	50.69344, 3.08525	No wing wall. C/L of arc 319 deg.
A/tk gun pillbox	Fort Bondues West Three	717428	50.69344, 3.08525	Ramp required for gun. No wing wall. C/L of arc 276 deg.
Sec MG pillbox	Fort Bondues Two	717429	50.69434, 3.08517	Recced in April. 8in proof. Raft. Entrance on left hand side. Right wing wall. C/L of arc 315 deg.
A/tk gun pillbox	Fort Bondues West One	718429	50.6944, 3.08658	Ramp required for gun. No wing wall. C/L of arc 329 deg.

A/tk gun pillbox	Fort Bondues Three	718429	50.6944, 3.08658	Recced in April. 8in proof. Raft. Entrance on left hand side. Right wing wall. C/L of arc 328 deg.
A/tk gun pillbox	Fort Bondues Four	718429	50.6944, 3.08658	Recced in April. 8in proof. No wing wall. C/L of arc 75 deg.
?		719517	50.77345, 3.0803	
A/tk gun pillbox	Detombe Farm	720425	50.69092, 3.08976	Left or no wing wall; if no wing wall, front wall to be 3ft 6in thick. C/L of arc 92 deg.
A/tk gun pillbox	Fort Bondues East One	720428	50.69361, 3.08949	Ramp required for gun. No wing wall. C/L of arc 102 deg.
Sec MG pillbox	Fort Bondues East Two	720428	50.69361, 3.08949	No wing wall. C/L of arc 89 deg.
Sec MG pillbox	Fort Bondues Five	721427	50.69277, 3.09099	Recced in April. Normal foundations (not raft). Bren loophole on right for a/tk rifle. No wing wall. C/L of arc 67 deg.
?		721517	50.77356, 3.08313	
A/tk gun pillbox	Marcq North	722419	50.68564, 3.09311	Wing wall on left. C/L of arc 114 deg.
Fortified house		723140	50.43522, 3.11872	A/tk gun in house if Corps position occupied.
A/tk gun pillbox		723140	50.43522, 3.11872	Side walls and roof bullet & splinter proof. For a 25mm gun by house.
Fortified house		723146	50.44061, 3.1182	A/tk gun in house if Corps position occupied.
?		723517	50.77367, 3.08596	
?	Knightsbridge	724164	50.45683, 3.11805	
?	Sloane Square	725164	50.45688, 3.11946	
A/tk gun pillbox	Wambrechies Road South Two	725417	50.68401, 3.09752	Wing wall on right. C/L of arc 350 deg.
Sec MG pillbox	Wambrechies Road South One	727419	50.68592, 3.10017	Wing wall on right. C/L of arc 332 deg.
Bren pillbox	Gueldre Road One	727424	50.69041, 3.09974	Three loopholes called for but instructions to put in five. C/L of arc 139 deg.

Bren pillbox	La Chantrelle	727428	50.694, 3.09939	Three loopholes called for but instructions to put in five. C/L of arc 59 deg.
A/tk gun pillbox	Gueldre Road Two	728425	50.69136, 3.10106	Wing wall on right. C/L of arc 348 deg.
Bren pillbox	La Chantrelle Two	728426	50.69226, 3.10097	Recced April. Door facing cottages. Raft required.
A/tk gun pillbox		729158	50.45261, 3.12551	Concrete flooring, side walls, back wall and roof. Bullet and splinter proof. For a 2 pdr gun.
Sec MG pillbox		729159	50.45261, 3.12551	In orchard, Rue du Debort.
?	St. James Park	729159	50.45261, 3.12551	
A/tk/MG pillboxes		729161	50.45441, 3.12534	Three concrete emplacements for two MG and one A/tk gun.
?	Victoria	729161	50.45441, 3.12534	
A/tk gun pillbox	White Horse	729421	50.68783, 3.10282	Left or no wing wall; if no wing wall, front wall to be 3ft 6in thick. C/L of arc 99 deg.
A/tk gun pillbox	Wambrechies Road North One	730422	50.68878, 3.10415	Wing wall on right. C/L of arc 359 deg.
A/tk gun pillbox		731139	50.43477, 3.13005	In orchard. Back wall bullet and splinter proof. For a 2 pdr gun.
Platform		731153	50.44734, 3.12884	Concrete platform for A/tk gun.
Bren pillbox	Wambrechies Road North Four	731422	50.68883, 3.10556	Recced April. Door facing cross roads. Raft.
Bren pillbox	Wambrechies Road North Two	731423	50.68973, 3.10548	Three loopholes called for but instructions to put in four. C/L of arc 354 deg.
Bren pillbox	Wambrechies Road North Three	732424	50.69068, 3.1068	Four loopholes called for but instructions to put in five. C/L of arc 94 deg.
Sec MG pillbox	Entrepot One	733418	50.68535, 3.10874	Wing wall on right. C/L of arc 326 deg.
Fortified house		734142	50.43763, 3.13401	A/tk gun in house if Corps position occupied.
Fortified house		734153	50.4475, 3.13306	A/tk gun in house if Corps position occupied.

?	Westminster	734153	50.4475, 3.13306	
A/tk gun pillbox	Entrepot Two	734419	50.68631, 3.11006	Wing wall on right. C/L of arc 336 deg.
?		734524	50.78056, 3.10092	
?	Charring Cross	735153	50.44756, 3.13447	
A/tk gun pillbox	Lesquin North	735322	50.59928, 3.11989	No wing wall. Front wall to be 3ft 6in thick. On right of existing gun pit. C/L of arc 70 deg.
Bren pillbox	Entrepot Four	735421	50.68816, 3.1113	Recced April. Raft. C/L of arc 293 deg.
Bren pillbox	Canal Three	736414	50.68193, 3.11332	Recced April. C/L of arc 73 deg.
Bren pillbox	Gamand Crossing	737304	50.58323, 3.12427	Raft required. C/L of arc 75 deg. Recced 16 April.
Bren pillbox	Ulster Six	737333	50.60927, 3.12176	Normal foundations. Entrance into trench. C/L of arc Brewery chimney. Recced 16 April.
Bren pillbox	Lezennes East Four	737342	50.61735, 3.12098	Recced in April. Normal foundations. Entrance into trench. C/L of arc brewery fence.
Bren pillbox	Canal One	737414	50.68198, 3.11474	Recced April. Door facing back. Raft. C/L of arc factory stack.
Bren pillbox	Entrepot Three	737419	50.68647, 3.1143	Recced April. Door towards fort. Raft. C/L of arc on factory stack.
Bren pillbox	Lezennes East Three	738341	50.6165, 3.12248	Recced in April. Normal foundations. Entrance into trench. C/L of arc brewery fence.
Sec MG pillbox	Gamand Factory	739309	50.58783, 3.12665	Recced in April. Left wing wall. 1 ft of wing wall for observation. C/L of arc 75 deg.
Sec MG pillbox	Lezennes Road Three	739327	50.60399, 3.1251	Wing wall on left.
Bren pillbox	Ulster 5	739331	50.60758. 3.12475	Normal foundations. Entrance into trench. C/L of arc 51 deg. Recced 16 April.
Bren pillbox	Lezennes East One	739339	50.61476, 3.12406	Recced in April. Normal foundations. Entrance into trench. C/L of arc water tower.
A/tk gun pillbox	Lezennes East Two	739340	50.61566, 3.12397	Recced in April. No wing wall. C/L of arc centre of ditch.

Sec MG pillbox	Gamand Railway	740303	50.5825, 3.12858	No wing wall. In front of trenches. Normal foundations. C/L of arc 58 deg. Recced 16 April.
Bren pillbox	Gamand Orchard	740305	50.5843, 3.12841	Normal foundations. C/L of arc A/tk ditch running east. Recced 16 April.
Bren pillbox	Gamand North	740306	50.58519, 3.12832	Raft required. C/L of arc Sainghin Church. Recced 16 April.
Sec MG pillbox	Merchin Garden	740315	50.59327, 3.12755	Sec MG pillbox modified as a Pl HQ with two Bren loopholes in garden wall. Recced 16 April.
Bren pillbox	Ulster Four	740333	50.60943, 3.12599	Normal foundations. Entrance at back. C/L of arc 26 deg. Recced 16 April.
Bren pillbox	Lezennes Brickery Two	740345	50.62021, 3.12495	Recced in April. C/L of arc 135 deg. Door to trench. Raft required.
Bren pillbox	Gamand Bridge	741308	50.58704, 3.12956	Normal foundations. C/L of arc water tower. Recced 16 April.
Bren pillbox	Merchin South	741314	50.59243, 3.12904	Raft required. C/L of arc Sainghin Church. Recced 16 April.
Bren pillbox	Merchin North	741315	50.59337, 3.12896	Normal foundations. Omit left hand firing towards farm. C/L of arc 67 deg. Recced 16 April.
Sec MG pillbox	Merchin	741316	50.59423, 3.12887	Wing wall on right. Pegged out in barn. Leave roof support. C/L of arc 5 deg.
Bren pillbox	Merchin Plot	741316	50.59423, 3.12887	Normal foundations. C/L of arc cross roads blockhouse. Recced 16 April.
A/tk gun pillbox	Lesquin Road One	741320	50.59782, 3.12852	Modified A/tk and Bren firing both ways down ditch. Sited in ditch.
Bren pillbox	Lezennes Road Four	741326	50.6032, 3.12801	Normal foundations. Entrance into trench. C/L of arc 152 deg. Recced 16 April.
Sec MG pillbox	Lezennes Road Two	741331	50.60769, 3.12757	Wing wall on left.

A/tk gun pillbox	Ulster One	741332	50.60859, 3.12749	Wing wall on right. Hedge marks front. C/L of arc 11 deg.
Bren pillbox	Lezennes Brickery One	741343	50.61846, 3.12654	Recced in April. C/L of arc on first pylon to right of church spire. Door facing Briqueterie. Raft.
Bren pillbox	Lezennes Brickery Three	741347	50.62206, 3.12619	Recced in April. C/L of arc on right corner of Lezennes East.
?		741531	50.78723, 3.11022	
A/tk gun pillbox	Merchin Hut	742316	50.59428, 3.13028	Wing wall on left. Modified A/tk (Type B foundations). C/L of arc 137 deg. Recced 16 April.
A/tk gun pillbox	Lesquin Road Two	742321	50.59877, 3.12985	No wing wall. Left of arc takes in ditch. Behind existing gun pit. C/L of arc 44 deg.
Bren pillbox	Lezennes Road Five	742326	50.60326, 3.12942	Normal foundations. Entrance into trench. C/L of arc cross roads blockhouse. Recced 16 April.
Bren pillbox	Lezennes Road Six	742327	50.60416, 3.12933	Normal foundations. Entrance into trench. C/L of arc 101 deg. Recced 16 April.
Sec MG pillbox	Observatory	742372	50.64455, 3.12544	
A/Tk gun pillbox	Briqueterie One	742378	50.64994, 3.12492	
Bren pillbox	Merchin Willow	743317	50.59523, 3.1316	Normal foundations. C/L of arc water tower. Recced 16 April.
A/tk gun pillbox	Lezennes Road One	743329	50.60601, 3.13057	Wing wall on left. Behind existing gun pit with same arc.
A/tk gun pillbox	Ulster Two	743332	50.6087, 3.13031	Wing wall on left. Centre of loophole on line of ditch. Side entrance on right. C/L of arc 125 deg.
Bren pillbox	Ulster Three	743333	50.6096, 3.13022	C/L of arc chimney right of water tower. Recced 16 April.
Sec MG pillbox	Galilee Four	743350	50.62486, 3.12875	Recced in April. C/L of arc at right angles to track. Loophole facing rail track also on left facing down rail track.
Bren pillbox	La Semeuse One	743357	50.63114, 3.12815	Recced 25.3.40.

Platoon HQ	Arab House Three	743358	50.63204, 3.12806	Recced 25.3.40.
Sec MG pillbox	Briqueterie Two	743379	50.65089, 3.12625	
Sec MG pillbox	Lezennes East	744345	50.62043, 3.1306	Wing wall on left. Retain existing breastworks. A/tnk rifle loophole on right. C/L of arc 125 deg.
Bren pillbox	Phoenix Park Two	744347	50.62222, 3.13042	Recced in April. C/L of arc on second pylon to right of church spire.
Bren pillbox	Galilee One	744349	50.62402, 3.13025	Recced in April. Raft. C/L of arc down road.
Bren pillbox	Arab House Two	744359	50.63299, 3.12939	Recced 25.3.40.
A/tk gun pillbox	Briqueterie Three	744378	50.65005, 3.12774	
?	Temple	745152	50.44721, 3.14862	
A/tk gun pillbox	Gamand East	745304	50.58367, 3.13555	Wing wall not required; front wall 3ft 6in thick. C/L of arc 99 deg.
Bren pillbox	Galilee Two	745349	50.62407, 3.13166	Recced in April. C/L of arc on Annappe Church. Raft required.
Sec MG pillbox	Les Touquets	745350	50.62497, 3.13158	No wing wall; retain existing wall as a feint. C/L of arc 30 deg.
Bren pillbox	La Semeuse Two	745357	50.63125, 3.13097	Recced 25.3.40.
Sec MG pillbox	Flers North One	745371	50.64382, 3.12476	
A/tk gun pillbox	Flers North Two	745372	50.64472, 3.12968	
A/tk gun pillbox		746151	50.44636, 3.15011	In enclosure, Le Bourgage. Standard pattern for a 25mm A/tk gun.
?	Blackfriars	746151	50.44636, 3.15011	
Bren pillbox	Galilee Three	746349	50.62413, 3.13307	Recced in April. C/L of arc on ditch. Door facing house on road.
A/tk gun pillbox	Arab House One	746359	50.6331, 3.13221	Recced in April. Left wing wall. Special loophole on back side for Bren or A/tk rifle. C/L of arc on back side of right hand ditch.

A/tk gun pillbox	Arab House One	746360	50.634, 3.13212	Recced 25.3.40.
Sec MG pillbox	Meadow Farm One	746380	50.65196, 3.1304	
Bren pillbox	Flers South	747365	50.63855, 3.1331	Recced 25.3.40.
A/tk gun pillbox	Meadow Farm Two	747379	50.65111, 3.13189	
A/tk gun pillbox	Golf Club One	747385	50.6565, 3.13138	
Sec MG pillbox	Golf Club Two	747385	50.6565, 3.13138	
A/tk gun pillbox		748152	50.44737, 3.15284	
Bren pillbox	Phoenix Park One	748347	50.62244, 3.13607	Recced in April. C/L of arc where road disappears. Raft required.
Platoon HQ	Flers Shelter	748366	50.6395, 3.13443	Recced 25.3.40.
Bren pillbox	Cemetery Three	748367	50.6404, 3.13434	Recced 25.3.40.
Sec MG pillbox	Cemetery One	748369	50.64219, 3.13471	
A/tk gun pillbox	Cemetery Two	748369	50.64219, 3.13471	
A/tk gun pillbox	Flers East Two	750366	50.63961, 3.13725	Recced 25.3.40.
Fortified house		751144	50.44035, 3.15774	A/tk gun in house if Corps position occupied.
A/tk gun pillbox		751144	50.44035, 3.15774	Wood stack by house. Standard pattern for a 25mm gun.
?	Mansion House	751144	50.44035, 3.15774	
Bren pillbox	Flers East One	751367	50.64056, 3.13858	Recced 25.3.40.
Fortified house		752145	50.4413, 3.15906	MG in house if Corps position occupied.
?	Monument	753141	50.43777, 3.16081	
?	Cannon Street	753143	50.43956, 3.16064	
?	Liverpool Street	754134	50.43154, 3.16281	

A/tk gun pillbox	Fretin Brewery	754279	50.56172, 3.15039	
Bren pillbox	Sainghin West Six	754304	50.58417, 3.14824	
A/tk gun pillbox		755132	50.4298, 3.16439	End of garden. Side walls, back wall and roof bullet & splinter proof. For a 2 pdr gun.
A/tk gun pillbox	Moorgate	755132	50.4298, 3.16439	
A/tk gun pillbox	Du Bonnet House	755133	50.43069, 3.1643	
?	Mark Lane	755135	50.43249, 3.16413	
A/tk gun pillbox	Sainghin West Three	755302	50.58242, 3.14982	Entrance in left side, facing direction of fire; wing wall to be on right, facing direction of fire; bearing 266 deg.
Bren pillbox	Sainghin West Five	755305	50.58512, 3.14956	
Bren pillbox	Sainghin West Seven	755305	50.58512, 3.14956	
A/tk gun pillbox	Sainghin West Two	755307	50.58691, 3.14939	Wing wall on right facing direction of fire; bearing 339.
?	Kings Cross	756121	50.41997, 3.16673	
?	Farringdon	756122	50.42087, 3.16665	
Bren pillbox	Sainghin West Four	756305	50.58517, 3.15097	
A/tk gun pillbox		757125	50.42362, 3.1678	Side walls and roof bullet & splinter proof. For a 2 pdr gun by house.
?	Aldersgate	757125	50.42362, 3.1678	
A/tk gun pillbox	Sainghin West One	757305	50.58523, 3.15238	Wing wall on right facing direction of fire; bearing 43 deg.
Fortified house		758124	50.42278, 3.16929	MG in house if Corps position occupied.
A/tk gun pillbox	Peronne Blue	758290	50.57182, 3.15508	Wing wall on right. C/L of arc 10 deg.
?	Port des Vaches	759115	50.41475, 3.17146	Three concrete emplacements each for eight men.
Bren pillboxes		759116	50.41565, 3.17138	Two pillboxes, Pont du Vaches.

A/tk gun pillbox.		759314	50.59342, 3.15443	
Sec MG pillbox	Fort Sainghin Five	761300	50.58096, 3.15845	Wing wall on left. Recced 1-4 April.
Sec MG pillbox	Fort Sainghin Five	761300	50.58096, 3.15845	Recced in April. Left wing wall. 8in proof. C/L of arc 140 deg.
A/tk gun pillbox	XS10	761528	50.78564, 3.13811	Two anti-tank rifles. Firing SE and NW respectively along tank obstacle.
Sec MG pillbox	Fort Sainghin Four	762302	50.58281, 3.15969	Recced in April. Right wing wall. 8in proof. C/L of arc 336 deg.
Sec MG pillbox	XS8	762506	50.76595, 3.14213	Firing NW and SE respectively along tank obstacle.
A/tk gun pillbox		762526	50.7839, 3.1404	Constructed by Com. *SD* Lille. Pillbox for a 25mm gun and A/tk rifle. Firing SE
A/tk gun pillbox		763294	50.57568, 3.16179	For a 2 pdr gun.
A/tk gun pillbox		763294	50.57568, 3.16179	
Bren pillbox	Fort Sainghin East Two	763300	50.58107, 3.16127	C/L of arc 155 deg. Recced 1-4 April.
Bren pillbox	Fort Sainghin North	763303	50.58376, 3.16102	C/L of arc 6 deg. Recced 1-4 April.
?	C16	763484	50.74625, 3.14544	French, completed
A/tk gun pillbox		763506	50.766, 3.14354	Constructed by Com. *SD* Lille. Pillbox for a 25mm A/tk gun and light MG.
Sec MG pillbox	Peronne Palace	764287	50.56945, 3.1638	C/L of arc 17 deg.
Bren pillbox	Fort Sainghin East One	764302	50.58292, 3.16251	C/L of arc 60 deg. Recced 1-4 April.
Sec MG pillbox		765288	50.5704, 3.16512	MG emplacements for four guns.
A/tk gun pillbox		765292	50.57399, 3.16478	For a 2 pdr gun.
A/tk gun pillbox		766292	50.57405, 3.16619	Fort Sainghin emplacement.
?	C15	766479	50.74193, 3.15012	French, completed

A/tk gun pillbox		766494	50.75539, 3.14882	Constructed by Com. *SD* Lille. Pillbox for 25mm A/tk gun and light MG. Firing east to cover inter-Brigade boundary
A/tk gun pillbox	XS5	766494	50.75539, 3.14882	25mm and light MG. Firing E to cover inter-Brigade boundary.
A/tk gun pillbox		766522	50.78053, 3.14641	Constructed by Com. *SD* Lille. Pillbox for 25mm A/tk gun and A/tk rifle. Gun firing SE down obstacle, rifle NW down obstacle.
Sec MG pillbox	XM5	766522	50.78053, 3.14641	Firing NW and SE respectively along tank obstacle.
Sec MG pillbox	Peronne North	767288	50.57051, 3.16794	Wing wall to be on right facing direction of fire; bearing 347 deg. Front face to be in brick.
Bren pillbox	Peronne East One	767288	50.57051, 3.16794	C/L of arc 40 deg. Recced 1-4 April.
Bren pillbox	Fort Sainghin South	768299	50.58044, 3.16841	C/L of arc 179 deg . Recced 1-4 April.
Sec MG pillbox	Fort Sainghin Four	768302	50.58313, 3.16815	Wing wall on right. Recced 1-4 April.
A/tk gun pillbox		768506	50.76627, 3.15062	Constructed by Com. *SD* Lille. Firing NE beyond foremost obstacle
A/tk gun pillbox		769314	50.59396, 3.16854	
Sec MG pillbox	XMC1	769506	50.76633, 3.15204	Firing NE.
A/tk gun pillbox		770322	50.6012, 3.16926	For a 2 pdr gun.
A/tk gun pillbox		770324	50.603, 3.16909	For a 2 pdr gun.
A/tk gun pillbox	Euston Square	771111	50.41181, 3.18866	
A/tk gun pillbox.		772111	50.41187, 3.19007	Pont du Croquet, Standard pattern for a 25mm gun.
Bren pillbox		772111	50.41187, 3.19007	Three pillboxes.
?	Pont du Croquet	773112	50.41282, 3.19139	Four concrete emplacements each for eight men.

A/tk gun pillbox		773498	50.75937, 3.15839	Constructed by Com. *SD* Lille. Pillbox for a 25mm A/tk gun and light MG.
A/tk gun pillbox	XA13	774498	50.75942, 3.1598	For a 2 pdr and light MG. Firing East to cover Brigade boundary.
A/tk gun pillbox		774508	50.7684, 3.15894	Constructed by Com. *SD* Lille. Pillbox for 25mm A/tk gun and light MG. Firing NE along obstacle.
A/tk gun pillbox	XS2,North Dronkat	774508	50.7684, 3.15894	For a 25mm and light MG. Firing NW along obstacle.
A/tk gun pillbox		775286	50.56915, 3.17939	For a 25mm gun.
A/tk gun pillbox		775286	50.56915, 3.17939	Fort Sainghin emplacement.
Sec MG pillbox	La Trie One	775386	50.65893, 3.17084	Wing wall on left. C/L of arc 203 deg. Recced April.
A/tk gun pillbox		775507	50.76755, 3.16044	Constructed by Com. *SD* Lille. Pillbox for 25mm A/tk gun and light MG. Firing SE along obstacle.
A/tk gun pillbox	XS1, South Dronkart	775507	50.76755, 3.16044	For a 25mmr and light MG. Firing SE along obstacle.
Bren pillbox	Rooky Lane Four	776283	50.56651, 3.18106	C/L of arc 185 deg. Recced 1-4 April.
Bren pillbox	Rooky Lane Two	776285	50.56831, 3.18089	C/L of arc 35 deg. Recced 1-4 April.
Bren pillbox	Bouvines West	776297	50.57908, 3.17986	C/L of arc 153 deg. Recced 1-4 April.
Sec MG pillbox	Alsatian Lodge Eight	776392	50.66437, 3.17174	Wing wall on right. Opposite side of road behind cottages. C/L of arc 331 deg. Recced in April.
Bren pillbox	Alsatian Lodge Ten	776392	50.66437, 3.17174	Opposite side of road end of cottages. C/L of arc 51 deg. Recced in April.
Bren pillbox	Alsatian Lodge Eleven	776392	50.66437, 3.17174	Opposite front of cottages. C/L of arc 167 deg. Recced in April.
Bren pillbox	Rooky Lane Three	777285	50.56836, 3.1823	C/L of arc up ride. Recced 1-4 April.
Bren pillbox	Bouvines South	777290	50.57285, 3.18187	C/L of arc 30 deg. Recced 1-4 April.

Bren pillbox	Bouvines Marcq	777301	50.58273, 3.18093	C/L of arc 32 deg. Recced 1-4 April.
A/tk gun pillbox		777317	50.59709, 3.17956	For a 25mm gun.
Bren pillbox	Alsatian Lodge Six	777390	50.66263, 3.17332	In field in front of white cottage. C/L of arc 233 deg. Recced in April.
Bren pillbox	Alsatian Lodge Five	777391	50.66353, 3.17323	Corner or orchard. C/L of arc 148 deg. Recced in April.
BH, sec MG	Alsatian Lodge One	777392	50.66442, 3.17315	No wing wall. C/L of arc 118 deg.
A/tk gun pillbox	Alsatian Lodge Three	777393	50.66532, 3.17306	Wing wall on right. In garden near present dump. C/L of arc 73 deg. Recced in April.
A/tk gun pillbox	Alsatian Lodge Seven	777393	50.66532, 3.17306	Wing wall on right. In coppice near present dump. C/L of arc 50 deg. Recced in April.
Bren pillbox	Alsatian Lodge Nine	777393	50.66532, 3.17306	In coppice near present dump. C/L of arc 21 deg. Recced in April.
?	C14	777497	50.75869, 3.16414	
MG pillbox		778332	50.61061, 3.17969	MG emplacements for two guns.
Bren pillbox	Alsatian Lodge Four	778392	50.66448, 3.17456	On end of row of cottages. C/L of arc 118 deg. Recced in April.
Sec MG pillbox	Alsatian Lodge Two	778393	50.66538, 3.17448	Wing wall on left.
?	C11	778493	50.75515, 3.16589	
?	C13	778497	50.75874, 3.16555	
A/tk gun pillbox		779309	50.59002, 3.18307	For a 25mm gun.
?	C10	779487	50.74982, 3.16783	
?	C12	779495	50.757, 3.16714	French, completed.
A/tk gun pillbox		780338	50.61611, 3.182	For a 25mm gun.
Bren pillbox	Twin Farm Seven	780388	50.661, 3.17773	Recced in April.
A/tk gun pillbox	Twin Farm Six	780389	50.66189, 3.17764	Wing wall on right. At back of wood. C/L of arc 347 deg. Recced in April.

A/tk gun pillbox	XFC1	780501	50.46244, 3.16804	For a25mm gun and light MG. Firing SE into 4th Div area.
?	C9	780502	50.76334, 3.16795	
?		781108	50.40966, 3.20297	Four concrete emplacements each for eight men.
A/tk gun pillbox		781108	50.40966, 3.20297	Area Pont du Cattelet. Standard pattern for a 25mm gun.
Bren pillbox		781108	50.40966, 3.20297	Three pillboxes.
Bren pillbox	Twin Farm Two	781387	50.66015, 3.17923	Door towards wagon shed. Side parallel to shed.
Sec MG pillbox	Twin Farm Three	781387	50.66015, 3.17923	Wing wall on left. Loophole enlarged to give 4½ deg depression and 7½ deg elevation. C/L of arc 200 deg.
Sec MG pillbox	Twin Farm Four	781388	50.66105, 3.17914	Wing wall on right. C/L of arc 56 deg.
?	C7	781497	50.7589, 3.1698	
Bren pillbox	Twin Farm One	782387	50.66021, 3.18064	Door 60 deg to wall. Side parallel to wall.
A/tk gun pillbox	Twin Farm Five	782388	50.66111, 3.18055	Wing wall on right. C/L of arc 43 deg.
?	C6	782496	50.75806, 3.1713	
?	C8	782499	50.76075, 3.17104	
A/tk gun pillbox	La Frete S	783262	50.54804, 3.19271	
?		783263	50.54894, 3.19263	
A/tk gun pillbox		783294	50.57677, 3.18999	Fort Sainghin Emplacement.
Sec MG pillbox	Bouvines East	783295	50.57767, 3.1899	Wing wall on left. To be built to appear as an extension to existing building.
Sec MG pillbox	Green Shutters One	783391	50.66385, 3.18171	Wing wall on right. Doorway on left. C/L of arc 348 deg.
A/tk gun pillbox	Green Shutters Two	783392	50.66475, 3.18162	Wing wall on right. C/L of arc 333 deg.
?	B6	783485	50.74824, 3.17366	French, completed.
A/tk pillbox	Louvil	784269	50.55438, 3.19353	For a 25mm gun and Bren gun.

Bren pillbox	Red Lodge One	784391	50.66391, 3.18312	Recced in April.
?	C2	784494	50.75637, 3.1743	
Bren pillbox	Red Lodge Two	785391	50.66396, 3.18453	Recced in April.
?	C5	785493	50.75553, 3.1758	
?	C3	785494	50.75643, 3.17572	
?	B5	786482	50.74571, 3.17816	French, completed.
?	B3	786485	50.784, 3.1779	
?	B4	786489	50.75199, 3.17756	
?	C4	786495	50.75738, 3.17705	
Bren pillbox	Hem Fork	787379	50.6533, 3.18838	Door towards house. C/L of arc 129 deg.
?	C1	788490	50.753, 3.1803	
Bren pillbox	Goodge Street	789195	50.48821, 3.20685	
A/tk gun pillbox	Les Patures	789256	50.54298, 3.20168	
Bren pillbox	Peronne E Two	789287	50.57081, 3.19904	C/L of arc 45 deg. Recced 1-4 April.
Sec MG pillbox	Bouvines Station	789294	50.57709, 3.19845	No wing wall. Existing wall to be left as shuttering for front face.
?	B2	789485	50.74857, 3.18215	
A/tk gun pillbox	Great Portland Street	790105	50.40745, 3.21587	
Bren pillbox	Hem Plaform	790370	50.64538, 3.19339	C/L of arc 190 deg. Recced in April.
?	Pont du Cattelet	791105	50.40751, 3.21728	Four concrete emplacements each for eight men.
Bren pillbox		791105	50.40751, 3.21728	Two pillboxes, Pont du Cattelet.
A/tk gun pillbox		791106	50.4084, 3.21719	Pont du Cattelet. Standard pattern for a 25mm gun.
Bren pillbox		791106	50.4084, 3.21719	Pont du Cattelet.
Bren pillbox	Hem Halt	791372	50.64723, 3.19463	C/L of arc 118 deg.

Bren pillbox	Cinder Lane	791375	50.64992, 3.19438	C/L of arc 105 deg.
Bren pillbox	Brickery Vale	792375	50.64998, 3.19579	Recced in April.
?	A3	792457	50.72359, 3.18879	French, completed.
?	B1	792473	50.73796, 3.18742	French, completed.
Sec MG pillbox		793247	50.53511, 3.20808	
Sec MG pillbox	Bouvines North	793303	50.58539, 3.20333	Wing wall on left. C/L of arc 121 deg.
?	A1	793452	50.71916, 3.19063	French, completed.
?	A2	794454	50.72101, 3.19187	
?	A5	794468	50.73358, 3.19068	French, completed.
Artillery OP		795223	50.51367, 3.21293	
Bren pillbox	La Vallee Orchard	795378	50.65283, 3.19977	C/L of arc 120 deg.
?	A4	795463	50.72914, 3.19252	French, completed.
A/tk gun pillbox	Bois de Taissonniere	796267	50.55323, 3.21061	
A/tk gun pillbox	Hedge End	796308	50.59004, 3.20713	
Bren pillbox	La Vallee Cutting	796380	50.65468, 3.20101	Arcs down cutting both ways.
A/tk gun pillbox	Cysoing	797272	50.55777, 3.2116	
Bren pillbox	Trambridge One	797387	50.66102, 3.20183	Recced in April.
Bren pillbox	Trambridge Two	797388	50.66192, 3.20174	Recced in April.
A/tk gun pillbox	Trambridge Three	797388	50.66192, 3.20174	No wing wall. C/L of arc 155 deg. Recced in April.
A/tk gun pillbox		798278	50.56321, 3.2125	
Sec MG pillbox		800438	50.70697, 3.20172	
A/tk gun pillbox.		801244	50.53285, 3.2196	

Artillery OP	61	801271	50.55709, 3.21732	R bearing 336 deg, L bearing 103 deg; arc 127 deg.
Sec MG pillbox	Genech North MG	802245	50.53201, 3.2211	
Fortified house		802265	50.55197, 3.22487	
A/tk gun pillbox	Bowler Hat	802310	50.59216, 3.21543	
MG pillbox		803244	50.53296, 3.22242	Two small pillboxes for a MG section.
A/tk gun pillbox	Genech North A.T	803246	50.53475, 3.22225	For a 2 pdr gun.
Artillery OP		803271	50.5572, 3.22014	
A/tk gun pillbox		803391	50.66494, 3.20996	For a 2 pdr gun.
Sec MG pillbox	La Riez M.G	804243	50.53211, 3.22391	
Sec MG pillbox		804292	50.57611, 3.21977	
Sec MG pillbox	Cemetery M.G	804294	50.5779, 3.2196	Observation slit bearing 253½ deg. Arc 45 deg.
A/tk gun pillbox	Cemetery A.Tk	804295	50.5788, 3.21952	For a 25mm gun. R bearing 144 deg, L bearing 84 deg; arc 60 deg. Subsidiary loophole for a Bren on fixed line (R bearing 9 deg, L bearing 309 deg; arc 60 deg).
Sec MG pillbox	Shrine	804297	50.5806, 3.21935	Wing wall on right. Entrance on left hand side and ventilators in back wall. C/L of arc 330 deg.
Sec MG pillbox		806224	50.51516, 3.22834	
Sec MG pillbox	La Belle Vue	806244	50.53312, 3.22665	
BH, A/tk	Cobrieux C.	806255	50.543, 3.22572	

Bren pillbox	Cemetery	806290	50.57442, 3.22276	R bearing 124 deg, L bearing 64 deg. Two subsidiary loopholes for Bren on fixed line (R bearing 184 deg, L bearing 124 deg; arc 60 deg and R bearing 64 deg, L bearing 4 deg; arc 60 deg).
Artillery OP		806293	50.57711, 3.22251	
A/tk gun pillbox	Roller	806302	50.58519, 3.22174	
A/tk gun pillbox	La Belle Vue A.T	808227	50.51796, 3.2309	
Sec MG pillbox		808231	50.52155, 3.23056	Firing NE towards Belle Porte.
Sec MG pillbox	Blonde Rue South M.G	808232	50.52245, 3.23048	Guns firing NE to Belle Porte.
Sec MG pillbox		808418	50.68945, 3.21473	
Bren pillbox	Fence	809286	50.57099, 3.22733	R bearing 121 deg, L bearing 61 deg; arc 60 deg. Two subsidiary loopholes for rifles (R bearing 61 deg, L bearing 1 deg; arc 60 deg and R bearing 181 deg, L bearing 126 deg; arc 60 deg).
Sec MG pillbox	Shrine East	809295	50.57907, 3.22657	Wing wall on right. Entrance on left hand side and ventilators in back wall. C/L of arc 7 deg.
A/tk gun pillbox	La Riez A.T	810246	50.53513, 3.23211	
Bren pillbox	Rosery	810284	50.56925, 3.22891	R bearing 99 deg, L bearing 39 deg; arc 60 deg. Two subsidiary loopholes for rifles (R bearing 39 deg, L bearing 339 deg; arc 60 deg and R bearing 339 deg, L bearing 279 deg; arc 60 deg).
Sec MG pillbox		810402	50.67519, 3.21892	
Bren pillbox		811397	50.67076, 3.22076	
A/tk gun pillbox	Blonde Rue South A.T	812232	50.52267, 3.23611	

Sec MG pillbox		812234	50.52446, 3.23594	
A/tk gun pillbox		812392	50.66632, 3.22259	For a 2 pdr gun.
A/tk gun pillbox		813235	50.52541, 3.23727	
BH. A/tk	Cobrieux South East	813250	50.53888, 3.236	
Sec MG pillbox		813276	50.56223, 3.23381	
A/tk gun pillbox	Chalk Pit	813283	50.56851, 3.23322	For a 25mm. R bearing 2 deg, L bearing 302 deg; arc 60 deg. Subsidiary loophole for Bren on fixed line (R bearing 92 deg, L bearing 32 deg; arc 60 deg).
Bren pillbox		813399	50.67266, 3.22341	
Sec MG pillbox		813418	50.68972, 3.2218	
A/tk gun pillbox	Blonde Rue East A.T	814234	50.52457, 3.23876	For a 2 pdr gun.
Sec MG pillbox	Fourness	814237	50.52726, 3.23851	
Battalion Battle HQ		814282	50.56767, 3.23472	
Artillery OP	Hounds ditch	814297	50.58114, 3.23345	R bearing 313, L bearing 133; arc 180 deg.
Bren pillbox		814300	50.58383, 3.2332	
Sec MG pillbox	Tonkin	815286	50.57131, 3.23579	
Bren pillbox	Box & Cox	815299	50.58298, 3.23496	
Sec MG pillbox	Cobrieux North	816263	50.55072, 3.23914	Grid bearing of centre of arc 97 deg; no a/tk rifle loophole; observation slit; walls 3ft 6in thick.

Bren pillbox	Cottage	816284	50.56937, 3.23737	R bearing 74 deg, L bearing 17 deg; arc 60 deg. Two subsidiary loopholes for rifles (R bearing 134 deg, L bearing 74 deg; arc 60 deg and R bearing 194 deg , L bearing 134 deg; arc 60 deg).
Artillery OP	Trench	816287	50.57266, 3.23711	R bearing 306, L bearing 136; arc 190 deg.
Bren pillbox	North ditch	816295	50.57945, 3.23644	For a 25mm gun.
Artillery OP		816298	50.58214, 3.23619	
A/tk gun pillbox	La Posterie North West	817258	50.54628, 3.24097	
Poste de Tir	Spindley Wood	817288	50.57322, 3.23844	
Signal Test Point		818289	50.57417, 3.23976	
A/tk gun pillbox	Bourghelles West	819281	50.56704, 3.24185	For a 25mm. R bearing 3½ deg, L bearing 303½ deg; arc 60 deg. Subsidiary loophole for a Bren on fixed line (R bearing 273½, L bearing 213½ deg; arc 60 deg).
Sec MG pillbox	Hau Du Bois	820228	50.51951, 3.24772	
Bren pillbox	Chateau du Fay	820246	50.53567, 3.2462	
A/tk gun pillbox	La Posterie North	820261	50.54913, 3.24494	
A/tk gun pillbox	Le Carnoy	821218	50.51058, 3.24996	
Bren pillbox	Moulin	821292	50.57702, 3.24374	
A/tk gun pillbox	Les Patures East	822171	50.46843, 3.25531	
A/tk gun pillbox		822219	50.51153, 3.25129	For a 2 pdr gun.
Sec MG pillbox		822219	50.51153, 3.25129	
Sec MG pillbox	La Posterie	822258	50.54655, 3.24801	

A/tk gun pillbox	Les Patures	822279	50.5654, 3.24625	For a 2 pdr gun. R bearing 109 deg, L bearing 39 deg; arc 70deg.
Sec MG pillbox	La Rotoir M.G	823213	50.5062, 3.2532	
A/tk gun pillbox	Bois de Berou South	823227	50.51877, 3.25203	For a 2 pdr gun and Bren gun.
Bren pillbox		823258	50.5466, 3.24942	
Bren pillbox		823259	50.5475, 3.24934	
Sec MG pillbox	Bourghelles South	823272	50.55917, 3.24824	Walls 3ft 6in thick; a/tk rifle loophole on right; observation slit.
Artillery OP		823282	50.56815, 3.2474	
A/tk gun pillbox	Bourgelles North	823283	50.56905, 3.24732	For a 25mm. R bearing 111 deg, L bearing 51 deg; arc 60 deg. Subsidiary loophole for a Bren on fixed line (R bearing 21 deg, L bearing 321 deg; arc 60 deg).
Bren pillbox	Corner House	823285	50.57084, 3.24715	
Bren pillbox	Windmill	823289	50.57444, 3.24681	
Sec MG pillbox		824229	50.52062, 3.25327	
A/tk gun pillbox		824233	50.52421, 3.25293	For a 25mm gun and Bren gun.
A/tk gun pillbox	Belle Porte	824233	50.52421, 3.25293	For a 2 pdr gun and Bren gun.
Sec MG pillbox		824236	50.5269, 3.25268	
A/tk gun pillbox	Cense de Cobrieux West A.T	824243	50.53319, 3.25209	
A/tk gun pillbox	La Posterie South East	825252	50.54132, 3.25274	
Bren pillbox	Road House	825284	50.57005, 3.25006	
Sec MG pillbox		826206	50.50007, 3.25801	

MG pillbox	M.G.R.3 (a)	826216	50.50905, 3.25717	Two pillboxes, one MG each.
MG pillbox	M.G.R.3 (b)	826218	50.51085, 3.257	Two pillboxes, one MG each.
A/tk gun pillbox	Cense de Cobrieux South A.T	826239	50.5297, 3.25524	
Bren pillbox		826240	50.5306, 3.25516	
Bren pillbox	Belisha	826240	50.5306, 3.25516	
Bren pillbox	Butcher's	826266	50.55395, 3.25298	
Bren pillbox	Bachy West	826266	50.55395, 3.25298	
Artillery OP	Avenue	826268	50.55574, 3.25281	R bearing 338, L bearing 76; arc 98 deg.
Bren pillbox	Marsh	826278	50.56472, 3.25197	
Bren pillbox	Calvaire	826285	50.571, 3.25138	R bearing 137 deg, L bearing 77 deg; arc 60 deg. Two subsidiary loopholes for rifles (R bearing 197 deg, L bearing 137 deg; arc 60 deg and R bearing 77 deg, L bearing 17 deg; arc 60 deg).
Bren pillbox	Mathon	826286	50.5719, 3.2513	R bearing 96 deg. L bearing 36 deg; arc 60 deg. Two subsidiary loopholes for rifles (R bearing 36 deg, L bearing 336 deg; arc 60 deg and R bearing 336 deg, L bearing 276 deg; arc 60 deg).
A/tk gun pillbox	La Commune	827218	50.5109, 3.25841	
Sec MG pillbox		827236	50.52706, 3.2569	
Bren pillbox		828193	50.48851, 3.26191	
Bren pillbox	V.R.S (a), (b), (c)	828216	50.50916, 3.25999	Three pillboxes.
A/tk gun pillbox	Boucherie	828259	50.54777, 3.25638	For a 2 pdr gun. R bearing 286 deg, L bearing 196 deg; arc 90 deg.

?		828260	50.54867, 3.2563	To drawing E.C.6.
A/tk gun pillbox	V.R.2 (y)	829225	50.51729, 3.26064	For a 2pr gun.
Sec MG pillbox		829247	50.53705, 3.2588	
Bren pillbox	Orchies Road Post	830201	50.4958, 3.26406	
Signal Test Point		830267	50.55506, 3.25853	
sec MG pillbox		831201	50.49585, 3.26547	
Bren pillbox		831252	50.54164, 3.2612	
Sec MG pillbox		831255	50.54434, 3.26095	
Bren pillbox	Wilsons	831268	50.55601, 3.25986	
Bren pillbox	Worthing	831279	50.56588, 3.25893	
Bren pillbox	Brighton	831282	50.56858, 3.25868	
Bren pillbox		832108	50.4124, 3.27464	
Bren pillbox		832190	50.48603, 3.2678	
A/tk gun pillbox	L.W.4 (x)	832214	50.50758, 3.26579	For a 2pr gun.
A/tk gun pillbox		832215	50.50847, 3.26571	For a 2pr gun.
A/tk gun pillbox	V.R.2 (t)	832222	50.51476, 3.26512	For a 25mm gun.
Bren pillbox	V.R.2 (a), (b), (c)	832223	50.51566, 3.26504	Three pillboxes.
A/tk gun pillbox		832224	50.51656, 3.26495	Double fronted pillbox with 25mm anti-tank gun; built within barn.
A/tk gun pillbox		832224	50.51656, 3.26495	
Signal Test Point		832236	50.52733, 3.26395	

A/tk gun pillbox	Rue D'Hotel	832249	50.539, 3.26286	For a 2 pdr gun.
Sec MG pillbox	Orchard	832255	50.54439, 3.26236	R bearing 155 deg, L bearing 110 deg.
A/tk gun pillbox	Farmyard	832257	50.54619, 3.26219	For a 2 pdr gun. R bearing 165 deg, L bearing 95 deg; arc 70 deg.
?		832257	50.54619, 3.26219	To drawing E.C.6.
Bren pillbox	Green Mound	832263	50.55157, 3.26169	
Bren pillbox	Citadel	832264	50.55247, 3.2616	
Bren pillbox	Chambers Post	833200	50.49506, 3.26837	
Bren pillbox	Bachy Cemetery	833263	50.53647, 3.2631	
Bren pillbox	Place Comte North	833263	50.55163, 3.2631	
Bren pillbox	Orchard OP	833266	50.55432, 3.26284	
Bren pillbox	Kings	833267	50.55522, 3.26276	
Bren pillbox	Orchard	833267	50.55522, 3.26275	
Artillery OP		833267	50.55522, 3.26276	
BH, Bren	Bachy North	833268	50.55612, 3.26268	
Bren pillbox	Carters	833269	50.55701, 3.26259	
Bren pillbox		834208	50.5023, 3.26911	Three pillboxes.
A/tk gun pillbox		834211	50.50499, 3.26886	For a 2 pdr gun.
Bren pillbox	Place Comte	834259	50.54809, 3.26484	
A/tk gun pillbox	L.W.4 (y)	835215	50.50863, 3.26993	For a 2 pdr gun.
Bren pillbox	V.R.1 (a), (b), (c)	835218	50.51133, 3.26968	Three pillboxes.

Bren pillbox	Cense Montifaux South	835245	50.53557, 3.26742	
Bren pillbox	Adams	835246	50.53647, 3.26734	
Bren pillbox	Cense Montifaux North	835247	50.53737, 3.26725	
Bren pillbox		836218	50.51138, 3.27109	For two Brens.
A/tk gun Emplace-ment		836230	50.52216, 3.27008	For a 2 pdr gun - concrete walls and platform.
Bren pillbox	Barn	836246	50.53652, 3.26875	
Bren pillbox	Webbs	836257	50.5464, 3.26783	
Bren pillbox	Place Comte South	836257	50.5464, 3.26783	
Bren pillbox	L.W.3 (a), (b), (c)	837213	50.50694, 3.27291	Three pillboxes.
A/tk gun pillbox	L.S.3 (T)	837230	50.52221, 3.27149	For a 25mm gun.
A/tk gun Emplace-ment		837231	50.52311, 3.27141	For a 2 pdr gun - concrete walls and platform.
A/tk gun pillbox	Rue D'Hotel (Pigstye)	837252	50.54196, 3.26965	For a 2 pdr gun.
Bren pillbox	Gebbels	837254	50.54376, 3.26949	
Bren pillbox	Garden	837254	50.54376, 3.26949	
A/tk gun pillbox	North Sartine	837261	50.55004, 3.2689	25mm and Bren.
Bren pillbox		838189	50.48545, 3.27632	
Bren pillbox	Le Dernier Sou	838201	50.49622, 3.27532	
MG pillbox	M.G.R.2 (b)	838207	50.50161, 3.27482	Two pillboxes, one MG each.

A/tk gun pillbox	L.W.3 (x)	838211	50.5052, 3.27449	For a 2 pdr gun.
Special pillbox in building	L.S.3 (a), (b)	838230	50.52226, 3.2729	Two pillboxes.
Bren pillbox	Cathedral	838243	50.53393, 3.27181	
Bren pillbox	Hau D'Hotel	838248	50.53842, 3.2714	
A/tk gun pillbox	South Sartine	838256	50.54561, 3.27073	'Wollett' pillbox for a 25mm gun.
A/tk gun pillbox	Bois Jacocb Group	839188	50.4846, 3.27782	Bois Jacob Group (Ruth, Rachael, Rebecca). A/tk gun and Bren gun.
A/tk gun pillbox	Bois Jacocb Group	839198	50.49358, 3.27698	Bois Jacob Group (Ruth, Rachael, Rebecca).
Bren pillbox	Bois Jacob Forward	839199	50.49448, 3.2769	
Bren pillbox	Bois Jacocb Group	839199	50.49448, 3.2769	Bois Jacob Group (Ruth, Rachael, Rebecca).
MG pillbox	M.G.S.2	839227	50.51962, 3.27456	Two pillboxes.
Bren pillbox	L.L.3 (a), (b), (c)	839235	50.52681, 3.27389	Three pillboxes.
A/tk gun pillbox	Bachy Station	839243	50.53399, 3.27322	For a 2 pdr gun
A/tk Emplace-ment		840225	50.51788, 3.27614	For a 2 pdr gun - concrete walls and platform.
Bren pillbox	L.L.4 (a), (b), (c)	840233	50.52506, 3.27547	Three pillboxes.
Bren pillbox		840240	50.53135, 3.27488	
?		840242	50.53314, 3.27472	To drawing E.C.6.
Bren pillbox		840251	50.54122, 3.273986	
Bren pillbox		841193	50.4892, 3.28021	
Bren pillbox		841200	50.49404, 3.24162	

A/tk gun pillbox	L.W.2 (x)	841208	50.50267, 3.27896	For a 2 pdr gun.
MG pillbox		841209	50.50357, 3.27888	Two pillboxes.
MG pillbox	M.G.R.2 (a)	841209	50.50357, 3.27888	Two pillboxes, one MG each.
Bren pillbox	L.S.4 (a), (b), (c)	841226	50.51883, 3.27746	Three pillboxes.
Fortified house		841233	50.52512, 3.27688	For one section and two Brens.
Bren pillbox	L.W.2 (a), (b)	842208	50.50272, 3.28037	Two pillboxes.
Fortified house	L.W.2 (c)	842208	50.50272, 3.28037	For one section and two Brens.
Bren pillbox	L.S.2 (a), (b), (c)	842229	50.52158, 3.27862	Three pillboxes.
A/tk gun pillbox	L.S.2 (t)	842230	50.52248, 3.27854	For a 25mm gun.
A/tk Emplace-ment		842230	50.52248, 3.27854	For a 2 pdr gun - concrete walls and platform.
Bren pillbox		842233	50.52517, 3.27829	Two pillboxes.
Bren Pillbox	Bachy Station North	842249	50.53954, 3.27695	Bren on fixed line, R bearing 154 deg, L bearing 54 deg; arc 60 deg. Two subsidiary loopholes for Bren or rifle (R bearing 34 deg, L bearing 334 deg; arc 60 deg and R bearing 334 deg, L bearing 274 deg; arc 60deg).
Sec MG pillbox		843197	50.4929, 3.2827	
Bren pillbox	L.S.1 (a), (b), (c)	843225	50.51804, 3.28036	Three pillboxes.
A/tk gun pillbox		843231	50.52343, 3.27986	
A/tk gun pillbox	L.C.4 (t)	843233	50.52522, 3.27969	
Bren pillbox	L.C.4 (c)	843233	50.52522, 3.27969	

Bren pillbox	L.L.1 (a)	843237	50.52881, 3.27936	
Bren Pillbox	Bachy Station South	843241	50.53241, 3.27903	Bren on fixed line, R bearing 34 deg, L bearing 334 deg; arc 60 deg. Two subsidiary loopholes for Bren or rifle (R bearing 154 deg, L bearing 94 deg; arc 60 deg and R bearing 214 deg, L bearing 154 deg; arc 60deg).
?	Willow Hedge	844198	50.49385, 3.28402	
Bren pillbox	Willow Corner	844198	50.49385, 3.28402	
Bren pillbox	L.S.G. (a), (b), (c)	844203	50.49834, 3.2836	Three pillboxes.
Bren pillbox	L.W.1 (a), (b), (c)	844206	50.50103, 3.28335	Three pillboxes.
Bren pillbox	L.L.1 (b), (c)	844233	50.52528, 3.2811	Two pillboxes.
Artillery OP	Tower	845224	50.51725, 3.28326	
Special pillbox in building		845233	50.52533, 3.28251	For one section. Double fronted pillbox built within barn.
Special pillbox in building	L.C.4 (a)	845233	50.52533, 3.28251	For one section and two Brens.
Bren pillbox	L.C. 3 (a), (b), (c)	845235	50.52712, 3.28234	Two pillboxes.
Bren pillbox		845235	50.52712, 3.28234	Two pillboxes.
Bren pillbox	R.A. Standing	846197	50.49306, 3.28692	
Bren pillbox		846201	50.49665, 3.28659	
Bren pillbox		846232	50.52448, 3.284	Two pillboxes.
Bren pillbox		846233	50.52538, 3.28392	Built into corner wall.
A/tk gun pillbox		847197	50.49311, 3.28833	

A/tk gun pillbox	L.C.1 (c)	847232	50.52454, 3.28541	Built into corner wall.
A/tk gun pillbox		847232	50.52454, 3.28541	
Bren pillbox	L.C. 1 (a), (b)	847234	50.52633, 3.28525	Two pillboxes.
Bren pillbox	Lannay Road Post	848200	50.49586, 3.28948	
Bren pillbox	L.E.3 (a), (b), (c)	848205	50.50035, 3.28907	Three pillboxes.
Bren pillbox	R.S.4 (a), (b), (c)	848221	50.51471, 3.28774	Three pillboxes.
Sec MG pillbox	M.G.S. 1	848221	50.51471, 3.28774	Two pillboxes.
A/tk gun pillbox	L.E.3 (x)	849204	50.4995, 3.29056	For a 2 pdr gun.
A/tk gun pillbox	L.W.1 (x)	849206	50.5013, 3.29039	For a 2 pdr gun.
A/tk gun pillbox		849221	50.51477, 3.28914	A/tk gun and one section.
Artillery OP	Cowshed	849228	50.52105, 3.28856	
Bren pillbox	L.R.4. (a), (b), (c)	849230	50.52285, 3.2884	Three pillboxes.
Bren pillbox	L.R.3. (a), (b), (c)	849233	50.52554, 3.28815	Three pillboxes.
Bren pillbox	R.S.3 (a), (b), (c)	850220	50.51392, 3.29064	Three pillboxes.
Sec MG pillbox		851199	50.49512, 3.29379	
MG pillbox	M.G.R.1 (b)	851200	50.49602, 3.29371	Two pillboxes, one MG each.
A/tk gun pillbox		851218	50.51218, 3.29221	A/tk gun and one section.
Bren pillbox	R.S.2 (a), (b), (c)	851218	50.51218, 3.29221	Three pillboxes.
Bren pillbox	Cameron Mess	852200	50.49607, 3.29512	
Bren pillbox	R.S.1 (a), (b), (c)	852217	50.51133, 3.2937	Three pillboxes.

Bren pillbox	R.L.4. (a), (b), (c)	852226	50.51941, 3.29295	Three pillboxes.
Bren pillbox	L.R.1 (a), (b)	852232	50.5248, 3.29246	Two pillboxes.
?		852271	50.55982, 3.28921	
Bren pillbox		852288	50.52121, 3.29279	Two pillboxes.
MG pillbox	M.G.R.1 (a)	853200	50.49612, 3.29652	Two pillboxes, one MG each.
A/tk gun pillbox	L.E.2 (x)	853204	50.49971, 3.29619	For a 2 pdr gun.
Bren pillbox		853226	50.51947, 3.29436	Behind dividing wall of butcher's shop property and abattoir.
Bren pillbox		853226	50.51947, 3.29436	For one section and two Brens.
Special pillbox in building	R.C.4 (a)	853226	50.51947, 3.29436	Two loopholes.
Bren pillbox	R.L.3. (a), (b), (c)	853229	50.52216, 3.29411	Three pillboxes.
Sec MG pillbox		854199	50.49528, 3.29801	
Bren pillbox	L.E.2 (a), (b), (c)	854207	50.50246, 3.29735	Three pillboxes.
Bren pillbox	Iron Gates	855201	50.49713, 3.29926	
Bren pillbox	R.L.1 (a), (b), (c)	855227	50.52047, 3.2971	Three pillboxes.
Bren pillbox	L.E.S (a), (b), (c)	856205	50.50077, 3.30033	Three pillboxes.
A/tk Emplace-ment		857222	50.51609, 3.30033	For a 2 pdr gun - concrete walls and platform.
A/tk gun pillbox	R.C.4 (t)	857223	50.51699, 3030025	For a 25mm gun.
A/tk Emplace-ment		857223	50.51699, 3.30025	For a 2 pdr gun - concrete walls and platform.
Bren pillbox	R.C.4. (a), (b), (c)	857224	50.51788, 3.30016	Three pillboxes.

Fortified house		857224	50.51788, 3.30016	For one section and two Brens.
Sec MG pillbox	Helon Prone	858200	50.49639, 3.30356	
Bren pillbox		858202	50.49818, 3.3034	
Bren pillbox	L.E.1 (a), (b), (c)	858209	50.50447, 3.30282	Three pillboxes.
A/tk gun pillbox	L.E.1(x)	858209	50.50447, 3.30282	For a 2 pdr gun.
A/tk gun pillbox	L.E.1 (y)	858209	50.50447, 3.30282	For a 2 pdr gun.
Bren pillbox		858225	50.51883, 3.30149	Two pillboxes.
Bren pillbox	R.C.3. (a), (b)	858227	50.52063, 3.30132	Two pillboxes.
A/tk gun pillbox	Prunelle Post	860203	50.49919, 3.30613	
Sec MG pillbox	Haut Hameau	860204	50.50008, 3.30605	
Sec MG pillbox	M.G.F. (c), (d)	860221	50.51535, 3.30464	Two pillboxes.
Bren pillbox	R.C.1. (a), (b), (c)	862225	50.51905, 3.30712	Three pillboxes.
Bren pillbox		863200	50.49665, 3.3106	
MG pillbox	M.G.F.(a), (b)	863221	50.51551, 3.30886	Two pillboxes.
Bren pillbox	R.R.3. (a), (b), (c)	863223	50.5173, 3.3087	Three pillboxes.
Bren pillbox		864202	50.4985, 3.31184	
Bren pillbox	Pigmy Post	865202	50.49855, 3.31325	At stage of plinth dug and lined on 3 May.
Artillery OP	Vehicle Shed	865220	50.51472, 3.31176	
Bren pillbox		866201	50.49771, 3.31474	
A/tk gun pillbox		866201	50.49771, 3.31474	

Bren pillbox	R.R.2. (a), (b), (c)	866225	50.51926, 3.31276	Three pillboxes.
A/tk gun pillbox		867200	50.49686, 3.31623	
MG pillbox		868195	50.49243,3.31805	For one MG.
MG pillbox.		868195	50.49243, 3.31805	For one MG.
A/tk gun pillbox		868198	50.49512, 3.31781	
Bren pillbox		869199	50.49607, 3.31913	
Fortified house	School	870207	50.50331, 3.31988	
Section post		870219	50.51408, 3131889	To be built into a lean-to brick and tile building in unoccupied farm. Two loopholes N & S. Also reinforced and loopholed wall on W side of farm building abutting road.
Fortified house		870219	50.51408, 3.31889	For one section and two Brens.
Bren Pillbox	R.R.1. (a), (b), (c)	870220	50.51498, 3.3188	Three pillboxes.
A/tk gun pillbox		871196	50.49348, 3.3222	
Bren pillbox		871216		
Special pillbox	R.R.1 (d)	871219	50.51413, 3.32029	Special pillbox with five loopholes.
Special pillbox	R.R.1. (e)	871219	50.51413, 3.32029	Special pillbox with three loopholes.
Artillery OP	Hell Fire Corner	871219	50.51413, 3.32029	
Bren pillbox	Bois Aix Pigsty	872210	50.50611, 3.32245	
Two man Bren Post	Orchard Post	872211	50.507, 3.32236	
Fortified house	Chicory Factory	873211	50.50706, 3.32377	Not yet designed.

Two man Bren Post	Brearley's Post	873216	50.51155, 3.32336	
Bren pillbox	Suicide Copse Left	874193	50.49095, 3.32667	
Bren pillbox	Dornoch Left	874205	50.50172, 3.32568	
Sec MG pillbox	Vieux Conde North	875187	50.48561, 3.32857	
MG pillbox	Vieux Conde	875187	50.48561, 3.32857	Type is listed as M.F.E. Vol. II, Plate V but this is a mistake, presumably should be Plate 58. The only pre war design used by the BEF.
Bren pillbox		875193	50.491, 3.32807	
A/tk gun pillbox	Dornock Right	875205	50.50177, 3.32708	For one a/tk gun and one Bren gun.
Bren pillbox	Dornock Centre	875206	50.50267, 3.327	
Artillery OP		876194	50.49195, 3.3294	
Two man Bren Post	Planard Left	876216	50.5117, 3.32758	
Fortified house	Kent Cottage	876216	50.5117, 3.32758	
Fortified house	Stone Henge	876216	50.5117, 3.32758	
Two man Bren Post	Planard Right	877216	50.51176, 3.32899	
Bren pillbox		879193	50.49121, 3.3337	
Two man Bren Post	Belzanois	879204	50.50109, 3.3328	
A/tk gun pillbox	Belzanois	879204	50.50109, 3.3328	For one a/tk gun and one Bren gun.
Bren pillbox	Broadway Left	881209	50.50568, 3.3352	
Fortified house	Broadway Rear	882208	50.50483, 3.33669	
Bren pillbox	Breadway Centre	882209	50.50573, 3.33661	

Bren pillbox	Broadway Right	883208	50.50489, 3.3381	At stage of plinth dug and lined on 3 May.
Bren pillbox	Corfe Left	884208	50.50494, 3.33951	At stage of plinth cast.
?	La Bougrie	884210	50.50674, 3.33934	Sited only.
Fortified house	La Bougrie	884211	50.50763, 3.33926	
Two man Bren Post	77 Block House	884213	50.50943, 3.3391	
Bren pillbox		885188	50.48703, 3.34256	
Bren pillbox	Corfe Rear	885207	50.50409, 3.341	At stage of plinth dug and lined on 3 May.
Bren pillbox	Corfe Right	885208	50.50499, 3.34092	At stage of plinth cast.
Bren pillbox	Provost Left	888205	50.50246, 3.34539	
Bren pillbox	Lone Post	888209	50.50605, 3.34506	Not yet sited.
?	Provost Centre	889205	50.50251, 3.3468	At stage of plinth dug and lined on 3 May.
?	Provost Right	890204	50.50166, 3.34829	Sited only.
A/tk gun pillbox	Rumegies East	891200	50.49812, 3.35002	Special design required.
Two man Bren Post	78 Block House	891210	50.50742, 3.35765	
Bren pillbox	New Street B	892200	50.49819, 3.35143	
Bren pillbox	Villa Left	893197	50.49553, 3.35308	
Bren pillbox	New Street A	893200	50.49823, 3.35284	
Bren pillbox	New Street C	893201	50.49913, 3.35276	Sited only.
Bren pillbox	Villa Right	895198	50.49654, 3.35582	Sited only.
Two man Bren Post	Lozelles	895207	50.50462, 3.35508	
Fortified house		897207	50.50472, 3.3579	Three houses, Cul du Four, Four Oaks and Coleman Row.

Two man Bren Post	Old Square	898201	50.49939, 3.3598	
Fortified house	Bull Ring	900194	50.49321, 3.36319	Not yet designed.
Two man Bren Post	Witton	901197	50.49595, 3.36435	
Fortified house		901202	50.50044, 3.36394	
Bren pillbox	La Triee Two	Exact location not settled		Recced April.
Bren pillbox	La Triee Three	Exact location not settled		Recced April.
Bren pillbox	La Triee Four	Exact location not settled		Recced April.
Bren pillbox	International One	Exact location not settled		On same side of factory. Recced April.
Bren pillbox	International Two	Exact location not settled		Recced April.
Bren pillbox	La Vallee Factory	Exact location not settled		Recced April.
Sec MG pillbox	Pommiers Grange One	Exact location not settled		
Bren pillbox	Pommiers Grange Two	Exact location not settled		
Sec MG pillbox	North Road House One	Exact location not settled		Wing wall on left.
A/tk gun pillbox	North Road House Two	Exact location not settled		
Bren pillbox	Canal Two	Exact location not settled		Recced April. Raft required.
Bren pillbox				Total of 12 pillboxes 853217 - 848222 (50.51139, 3.29511 - 50.51561, 3.28765).
Bren pillbox				Total of 12 pillboxes 845225 - 835225 (50.51815, 3.28318 - 50.51761, 3.26909.

Bibliography

Primary Sources

The National Archives (TNA), Kew, London

CAB/65/3/9, Confidential Annex to W.M. (39), 19th, Conclusions, Minute 3.
CAB/67/5/28, Supply of Labour for the British Expeditionary Force.
WO32/4612, Future Reorganisation of the British Army.
WO106/1605, Anti-tank, Issue of Weapons to Regiments.
WO106/1626, Use of Gas on the Western Front.
WO106/1638, French Intelligence and plans; defences.
WO106/1640, German Intelligence, Plans 1939/40.
WO106/1664, Possible Future Operations: Western Front.
WO166/1685, General Strategy.
WO106/1686, British Defences and Tactics.
WO106/1777, The British Front.
WO106/1720, Appreciations.
WO166/1, GHQ Home Forces, General Operations War Diary.
WO166/796, 1st Armoured Division, General Staff War Diary.
WO167/2, GHQ, General Operations War Diary.
WO167/13, GHQ, Major General Royal Artillery War Diary.
WO167/14, GHQ, Anti-Aircraft Branch, 1st Echelon War Diary.
WO167/21, GHQ, SD & T Branch War Diary.
WO167/43, GHQ, Chief Engineer War Diary.
WO167/48, Camouflage Factory War Diary.
WO167/124, I Corps, General Staff War Diary.
WO167/129, I Corps, Chief Engineer War Diary.
WO167/127, I Corps, Commander Corps Royal Artillery War Diary.
WO167/148, II Corps, General Staff War Diary.
WO167/155, II Corps, Chief Engineer War Diary.
WO167/169, III Corps, General Staff War Diary.

WO167/175, III Corps, Chief Engineer War Diary.
WO167/190, 1st Division, General Staff War Diary.
WO167/193, 1st Division, Commander Royal Artillery War Diary.
WO167/194, 1st Division, Commander Royal Engineers War Diary.
WO167/203, 2nd Division, General Staff War Diary.
WO167/207, 2nd Division, Commander Royal Engineers War Diary.
WO167/218, 3rd Division, General Staff War Diary.
WO167/221, 3rd Division, Commander Royal Engineers War Diary.
WO167/230, 4th Division, General Staff War Diary.
WO167/233, 4th Division, Commander Royal Engineers War Diary.
WO167/244, 5th Division, General Staff War Diary.
WO167/247, 5th Division, Commander Royal Engineers War Diary.
WO167/258, 12th Division, General Staff War Diary.
WO167/262, 23rd Division, General Staff War Diary.
WO167/266, 42nd Division, General Staff War Diary.
WO167/275, 44th Division, General Staff War Diary.
WO167/286, 46th Division, General Staff War Diary.
WO167/289, 48th Division, General Staff War Diary.
WO167/300, 50th Division, General Staff War Diary.
WO167/314, 51st Division, General Staff War Diary.
WO167/346, 1 Guards Brigade War Diary.
WO167/348, 2 Infantry Brigade War Diary.
WO167/350, 3 Infantry Brigade War Diary.
WO167/352, 4 Infantry Brigade War Diary.
WO167/357, 6 Infantry Brigade War Diary.
WO167/359, 7 Guards Brigade War Diary.
WO167/362, 8 Infantry Brigade War Diary.
WO167/364, 9 Infantry Brigade War Diary.
WO167/366, 10 Infantry Brigade War Diary.
WO167/368, 11 Infantry Brigade War Diary.
WO167/370, 12 Infantry Brigade War Diary.
WO167/372, 13 Infantry Brigade War Diary.
WO167/376, 15 Infantry Brigade War Diary.
WO167/378, 17 Infantry Brigade War Diary.
WO167/459, 4th Battalion Royal Tank Regiment War Diary.
WO167/467, 2nd Field Regiment RA War Diary.
WO167/471, 10th Field Regiment RA War Diary.
WO167/537, 4th Medium Regiment War Diary.
WO167/536, 3rd Medium Regiment RA War Diary.
WO167/566, 5th Battery, 10 Heavy Regiment RA War Diary.
WO167/571, 1st Survey Regiment RA War Diary.
WO167/575, 13th Anti-tank Regiment RA War Diary.
WO167/578, 21st Anti-tank Regiment RA War Diary.

WO167/698, 1st Coldstream Guards War Diary.
WO167/700, 1st Grenadier Guards War Diary.
WO167/701, 2nd Grenadier Guards War Diary.
WO167/702, 3rd Grenadier Guards War Diary.
WO167/706, 1st Royal Berkshire Regiment War Diary.
WO167/713, 1st Border Regiment War Diary.
WO167/724, 1st Cheshire Regiment War Diary.
WO167/727, 2nd Dorset Regiment War Diary.
WO167/728, 2nd Durham Light Infantry War Diary.
WO167/789, 5th Manchester Regiment War Diary.
WO167/832, 2nd Lincolnshire Regiment War Diary.
WO167/850, 2nd East Yorkshire Regiment War Diary.
WO167/903, 5th Field Company RE War Diary.
WO167/905, 7th Field Company RE War Diary.
WO167/907, 9th Field Company RE War Diary.
WO167/908, 11th Field Company RE War Diary.
WO167/916, 23rd Field Company RE War Diary.
WO167/917, 26th Field Company RE War Diary.
WO167/919, 38th Field Company RE War Diary.
WO167/921, 59th Field Company RE War Diary.
WO167/925, 101st Army Field Company RE War Diary.
WO167/944, 135th Excavator Company RE War Diary.
WO167/957, 170th Tunnelling Company RE War Diary.
WO167/962, 200th Field Company RE War Diary.
WO167/972, 216th Field Company RE War Diary.
WO167/985, 234th Army Field Company RE War Diary.
WO167/1000, 253rd Field Company RE War Diary.
WO167/1001, 254th Field Park Company RE War Diary.
WO167/1022, 655th General Construction Company RE War Diary.
WO167/1034, 667th General Construction Company RE War Diary.
WO167/1234, Labour Personnel Centre War Diary.
WO167/1429, HQ, "X" Force War Diary.
WO167/1422, Commander Royal Engineers, Advanced Air Striking Force War Diary.
WO167/1430, 1st Battalion "X" Force War Diary.
WO167/1432, 2nd Battalion "X" Force War Diary.
WO190/867, Review of the Situation after first Month of War: Indication of a German Attack on the Western Front.
WO193/157, Siegfried Line (and Note on Attack on Fortified Towns).
WO197/6, Note on The Attack of Fortified Lines.
WO197/10, Defences of the Franco – Belgian Frontier.
WO197/11, Visits to War Office, GHQ and BEF: General Correspondence.
WO197/13, AFVs, Employment.

WO197/17, Conferences between C. in C. and French Comds.
WO197/26, Occupation and Defence Works of Lille Sector.
WO197/47, Report on Visit to Saar, 3 and 12 Infantry Brigades.
WO197/63, Establishment of an Air Fighting Zone.
WO197/66, GHQ BEF Pamphlets No's. 1-24 (incomplete).
WO197/73, Armament and Fighting Arrangements of Proposed New Infantry Tank Mk. IV.
WO199/44, Concrete defences – Policy.
WO 199/2527, Pillboxes.
WO205/264, 79th Armoured Division: Organisation, Equipment, Training, Part I.
WO277/36, Training in the British Army.
WO287/136, Initial Organization of the Field Defences in the B.E.F. 1940.
WO287/226, Tactical and Technical Notes on the German Army.

Official Manuals and other documents

Army Training Memorandum No. 24 - 27: War (London: War Office, September–December 1939).
Army Training Memorandum No. 28 - 33: War (London: War Office, January–July 1940).
Army Training Memorandum No. 39: War (London: War Office, April 1941).
Artillery Training Vol. II: Gunnery, 1934 Supplement No. 2 – 1940 (London: War Office 1940).

Divisional Standing Orders (London: War Office, 1939).

Engineer Training – 1937 (HMSO, 1937).

Field Service Regulations Vol. I: Organization and Administration – 1930 (London: War Office, 1939 edition).
Field Service Regulations Vol. II: Operations – General 1935 (London: War Office, 1935).
Field Service Regulations Vol. III: Operations – Higher Formations 1935 (London: War Office, 1935).
Field Engineering (All Arms) MTP No. 30 Part III: Obstacles – 1940 (London: War Office, 1940).

Guide to Mechanical Equipment (BNAF, 1944).

Infantry Training (4-Company Organization) 1914 (General Staff, 1914).
Infantry Training 1937: Training & War (London: War Office, 1937).
Infantry Training, 1937: Supplement, No. 1 – Tactical Notes for Platoon Commanders (London: War Office, 1941).
Infantry Section Leading 1938 (London: HMSO, 1938).

Manual of Field Engineering Vol. 1 (All Arms) – 1933 (London: War Office, 1933).
Manual of Field Engineering Vol. II (R.E.) – 1936 (London: War Office, 1936).
Military Engineering (Vol.II): Defences – 1925 (London: War Office, 1925).
Military Engineering Vol. XIX – Concrete: Part I Practical Work (London: War Office, 1944).

Notes on Concealment and Camouflage – MTP No. 26 (London: War Office, 1939).

Operations - MTP No. 23 Part II: Defence – 1939 (London: War Office, 1939).
Operations – MTP No.23 Part III: Appreciations, Orders, Intercommunications and Movements – 1939 (London: War Office, 1939).

Royal Engineers Reconnaissance Pocket Book – 1944 (London: War Office, 1944).
Royal Engineers Supplementary Pocket Book No. 5A – Roads (London: War Office, 1946).

Signal Training (All Arms): 1938 (London: War Office, 1938).
Small Arms Training, Volume I Pamphlet No.5: Anti-tank Rifle (London: War Office, 1942).
Small Arms Training, Volume I Pamphlet No. 19: Anti-tank Gun (25-mm. Hotchkiss, Mark I on 25-mm. Carriage, Mark I) (London: War Office, 1939).
S.S. 210: The Division in Defence (General Staff, 1918).
Statistics Relating to the War Effort of the United Kingdom (London: HMSO, 1944).

Tactical Handling of Anti-tank Regiments – MTP No. 19 (London: War Office, 1939).
The Defence – MTP No.3 (War Office, 1943).
The Infantry Division in the Defence – MTP No.23 Part II (London: War Office, 1942).
The Officer and Fighting Efficiency (War Office, 1941).

Secondary Sources, Memoirs and Personal Accounts

Paul Addison & Angus Calder (eds.), *Time to Kill: The Soldier's Experience of War in the West* (London: Pimlico, 1997).
Colin Alexander, *Ironside's Line* (Storrington: Historic Military Press, 1999).
Martin S. Alexander, *The Republic in Danger: General Maurice Gamelin and the Politics of French Defence, 1933–1940* (Cambridge: CUP, 1992).
Alan Allport, *Browned Off and Bloody-Minded: The British Soldier Goes to War 1939–1945* (New Haven and London: Yale University Press, 2015).
Christopher Andrew & Jeremy Noakes (eds.), *Intelligence and International Relations 1900 – 1945* (Exeter: Exeter University Publications, 1987).

Admiral Sir Reginald Bacon, KCB, KCVO, DSO, Major-General J.F.C. Fuller, CB, CBE, DSO & Air Marshall Sir Patrick Playfair, KBE, CB, CVO, MC, (eds.),

Warfare Today: How Modern Battles are Planned and Fought on Land, at Sea, and in the Air (London: Odhams Press Ltd., no date).

Gordon Barclay, *If Hitler Comes: Preparing for Invasion Scotland 1940* (Edinburgh: Birlinn Ltd., 2013).

D. A. Barlone, *French Officer's Diary: 23 August 1939 – 1 October 1940* (Cambridge: CUP, 1942).

Gordon Beckles, *Dunkirk and After: The Campaign and Evacuation of Flanders* (London: Hutchinson & Co. Ltd., n.d.).

Ian Frederick William Beckett & John Gooch, *Politicians and Defence: Studies in the Formulation of British Defence Policy* (Manchester: Manchester University Press, 1981).

Brian Bond, *Britain's Two World Wars against Germany: Myth, Memory and the Distortions of Hindsight* (Cambridge: CUP, 2014).

Brian Bond, (ed.) *Chief of Staff: The Diaries of Lieutenant-General Sir Henry Pownall* (London: Leo Cooper, 1972).

Robert Boyce (ed.), *French Foreign and Defence Policy 1918–1940: The Decline and Fall of a Great Power* (London and New York: Routledge, 1988).

Arthur Bryant, *The Turn of the Tide: Based on the War Diaries of Field Marshal Viscount Alanbrooke* (London: Collins, 1957).

Stephen Bull, *German Assault Troops of the First World War: Stosstrupptaktik The First Stormtroopers* (Stroud: Spellmount, 2007).

Lt. Colonel Ewan Butler & Major J. Selby Bradford, MBE, MC, *Keep the Memory Green: The First of the Many France 1939–40* (London: Hutchinson & Co. Ltd., n.d.).

Skene Catling, *Vanguard to Victory: An Account of the first months of the British Expeditionary Force in France* (London: Methuen & Co. Ltd., 1940).

Comité D'Histoire De La 2e Guerre Mondiale, *Francais et Britanniques dans la Drôle de Guerre* (Paris: Editions du Centre National de la Recherche Scientifique, 1979).

Winston Churchill, *The Second World War: Volume I – The Gathering Storm* (London: Cassell & Co. Ltd., 1948).

Winston Churchill, *The Second World War: Volume II – Their Finest Hour* (London: Cassell & Co. Ltd., 1949).

Lloyd Clark, *Blitzkrieg: Myth, Reality and Hitler's Lightning War – France, 1940* (London: Atlantic Books, 2016).

Anthony Clayton, *Paths of Glory: The French Army 1914–18* (London: Cassell, 2003).

Basil Collier, *The Defence of the United Kingdom* (London: HMSO, 1957).

J.R. Colville, *Man of Valour: Field-Marshall Lord Gort VC* (London: Collins, 1972).

Colin Coote (introduction), *War Pictures by British Artists* (London: OUP, 1942).

Alex Danchev & Daniel Todman (eds.), *War Diaries 1939–1945: Field Marshall Lord Alan Brooke* (Berkeley and Los Angeles: University of California Press, 2001).

General Charles De Gaulle, *The Army of the Future* (London: Hutchinson & Co. (Publishers) Ltd, c.1940)

Len Deighton, *Blitzkrieg: From the Rise of Hitler to the Fall of Dunkirk* (London: Jonathan Cape, 1979).

Julien Dépret, *Le Nord, Frontière Militaire, Tome 2: L'organisation defensive de Dunkerque à Mézières 1919–1940* (SPEI/Pulnoy, 2005).

David Divine, *The Nine Days of Dunkirk* (London: Faber & Faber, 1959).

Richard Dorney, *An Active Service: The Story of a Soldier's Life in the Grenadier Guards, SAS and SBS 1934–1958* (Solihull: Helion & Company., 2005).

Major L. F. Ellis, *The War in France and Flanders 1939–1940* (London: HMSO, 1953).

Harold Faber, *Luftwaffe: An analysis by former Luftwaffe Generals* (London: Sidgwick & Jackson, 1979).

Desmond FitzGerald, *Many Parts: The life and Travels of a Soldier, Engineer and Arbitrator in Africa and Beyond* (London: Radcliffe Press, 2007).

Robert T. Foley, *German Strategy and the Path to Verdun: Erich von Falkenhayn and the Development of Attrition 1870–1916* (Cambridge: CUP, 2005).

David Freebrey (ed.), Guardsman *and Commando: The War Memoirs of SM Cyril Freebrey, DCM* (Barnsley: Pen & Sword Books Ltd., 2008).

David French, *Raising Churchill's Army: The British Army and the War against Germany 1919–1945* (Oxford: OUP, 2000).

Charles Grave, *The Home Guard of Britain* (London: Hutchinson & Co. (Publishers) Ltd., n.d.).

Major-General Heinz Guderian, *Achtung – Panzer! The Development of Armoured Forces their Tacics and Operational Potential* (London: Brockhampton Press, 1999).

Gun Buster, *Battle Dress* (London: Hodder & Stoughton, 1941).

Liddell Hart, *The Defence of Britain* (London: Faber and Faber limited, 1939).

Guy Hartcup, *Camouflage – The History of Concealment & Deception in War* (Barnsley: Pen & Sword Books Ltd., 2008).

Peter Hart, *The 2nd Norfolk Regiment: From Le Pardis to Kohima* (Barnsley: Pen & Sword Books Ltd., 2011).

Ian Hay, *Arms and the Men* (London: HMSO, 1950).

Ian Hay, *The Battle of Flanders* (London: HMSO, 1941).

John Horsfall, *Say Not the Struggle ...* (Kineton: The Roundwood Press, 1977).

J.E. Kaufmann & H.W. Kaufmann, *Hitler's Blitzkrieg Campaigns: The Invasion and Defense of Western Europe, 1939-40* (Conshohocken: Combined Books, 1993).

J.E. Kaufmann & H.W. Kaufmann, *Fortress France: The Maginot Line and French Defenses in World War II* (Mechanicsburg: Stackpole Books, 2007).

J.E. Kaufmann & H.W. Kaufmann, Aleksander Potocnik, Lang Patrice, *The Maginot Line: History and Guide* (Barnsley: Pen & Sword Books Ltd., 2011).

Anthony Kemp, *The Maginot Line: Myth & Reality* (London: Frederick Warne (Publishers) Ltd., 1981).

John Kennedy, *The Business of War: The War Narrative of Major-General Sir John Kennedy GCMG, KCVO, KBE, CB, MC* (London: Hutchinson & Co. Publishers Ltd., 1957).

Jon Kimche, *The Unfought Battle* (London: Weidenfeld & Nicolson, 1968).

Bernard Law, Viscount Montgomery of Alamein, *The Memoirs of Field-Marshal Montgomery* (London: Collins, 1958).

James Leasor, *The Experiences of General Sir Leslie Hollis KCB, KBE: War at the Top*, (London: Michael Joseph Ltd., 1959).

Joshua Levine, *Forgotten Voices: Dunkirk* (London: Ebury Press, 2011).

Eric Linklater, *The Highland Division* (London: HMSO, 1942).

Bernard Lowry, *Pillboxes and Tank Traps*, (Oxford: Shire Publications, 2014).

Colonel R. Macleod DSO, MC & Denis Kelly (eds.), *Time Unguarded: The Ironside Diaries 1937–1940* (New York: David McKay Company Inc., 1963).

John Masefield, *The Twenty-five Days: The Flanders Campaign and the Rescue of the BEF from Dunkirk 10 May – 3 June 1940*. Introduction by Jon Cooksey (Barnsley: Pen & Sword Books Ltd., 2004).

André Maurois, *The Battle of France* (London: John Lane the Bodley Head, 1940).

R.H. Medley, *Five Days to Live: France 1939–40* (Abergavenny: Dover & Company, 1992).

Charles Messenger, *The Blitzkrieg Story* (New York: Charles Scribner's Sons, 1976).

Jerry Murland, *Retreat & Rearguard Dunkirk 1940: The Evacuation of the BEF to the Channel Ports* (Barnsley: Pen & Sword Books Ltd., 2016).

T.H. O'Brien, *Civil Defence* (London: HMSO, 1955).

Mike Osborne, *Pillboxes of Britain and Ireland* (Stroud: Tempus, 2008).

Major-General R. P. Pakenham-Walsh, CB, MC, *History of the Corps of Royal Engineers Vol. VIII 1938–1948: Campaigns in Franc and Belgium, 1939–40. Norway, Middle East, East Africa, Western Desert, North West Africa, and Activities in the U.K.* (Chatham: The Institute of Royal Engineers, 1958).

Timothy Harrison Place, *Military Training in the British Army, 1940–1944: From Dunkirk to D-Day* (Abingdon: Routledge, 2008).

Barry R. Posen, *The Sources of Military Doctrine: France, Britain, and Germany Between the World Wars* (Ithaca and London: Cornell University Press, 1984).

Thomas M. J. Riordan, *A History of the 7th Field Company RE 1939–1946*, (Published by the author, 1984).

Mike Rossiter, *I Fought at Dunkirk: Seven Veterans Remember the German Invasion of France* (London: Bantam Press, 2012).

Anthony Saunders, *Trench Warfare: 1850–1950* (Barnsley: Pen & Sword Books Ltd., 2010).

Hugh Sebag-Montefiore, *Dunkirk: Fight to the Last Man* (London: Penguin Books, 2015).

Neil Short, *Hitler's Siegfried Line* (Stroud: Sutton Publishing Limited, 2007).

Nick Smart, *British Strategy and Politics during the Phoney war: Before the Balloon Went Up* (Westport: Praeger Publishers, 2003).

Brigadier Sir John Smyth, VC, MC, MP, *Before the Dawn: Two Historic Retreats Dunkirk 1940, Burma 1942* (London: Cassell & Company Ltd., 1957).

Dawn Iumn Sutherland & Mike Chrimes (eds.) *Historic Concrete: Background to Appraisal* (London: Thomas Telford Publishing, 2001).

Major-General Julian Thompson, *Dunkirk: Retreat to Victory* (London: Sidgwick & Jackson, 2008).

Daniel Todman, *Britain's War: Into Battle 1937–1941* (London: Allen Lane, 2016).

Colonel E.G.L. Thurlow, DSO, psc, *The Pill-Boxes of Flanders* (Ivor Nicolson & Watson Ltd., 1933).

Robert Tombs & Emile Chabal (eds.), *Britain and France in Two World Wars: Truth, Myth & Memory* (London: Bloomsbury, 2013).

Neil J. Wells, *Verdun: An Integrated Defence* (Uckfield: Naval & Military Press Ltd., 2009).

Thomas Wictor, *German Assault Troops of World War I* (Atglen: Schiffer Military History, 2012).

Colonel G. Williams, OBE, *Citizen Soldiers of the Royal Engineers Transportation and Movements and the Royal Army Service Corps 1859 to 1965* (The Institute of the Royal Corps of Transport, n.d.).

Henry Wills, *Pillboxes: A Study of U.K. Defences 1940* (London: Leo Cooper, 1985).

Electronic Sources

Francis Peter Barclay, IWM interview, <http://www.iwm.org.uk/collections/item/object/80007933>

Ralph Lionel Clarke, *Three Weeks to La Panne: A Diary of Dunkirk* <http://www.foxearth.org.uk/ThreeWeeksToLaPanne>

Monty Groan, *Retreat to Dunkirk* <http://bbc.co.uk/history/ww2peopleswar/stories/12/92281312.5>

General the Viscount Gort VC, KCB, CBE, DSO, MVO, MC, *Official Despatches*, Supplement to the London Gazette <http://www.ibiblio.org/hyperwar/UN/UK/londongazette>

Elizabeth Kier, *Culture and Military Doctrine: France between the Wars* <web.stanford.edu/class/polisci243b/readings/kier.pdf>

Christopher B. Leach, *The Belgium Question in French Strategic Planning and Army Doctrine between the Wars* <http://summit.sfu.ca/item/3811>

General James Lois Moulton, IWM interview <http://www.iwm.org.uk/collections/item/object/80006634>

Robert Parker, *"Ouest la Masse de Manoeuvre?": Maurice Gamelin and the Lessons of Blitzkrieg in Poland* <spectrum.libary.concordia.ca/977623/1Parker_MA_F2013.pdf>

Brett Steel, *Military Reengineering between the World Wars* <http://www.rand.org/content/dam/rand/pubs/monographs/2005/RAND_MG253.pdf >

Captain Cyril Moseley Townsend, *Diary of 40725 Captain Cyril Moseley Townsend 2 DLI* <http://www.durhamlightinfantry.webs.com/2dlidyledunkirk1940>

Captain L. Twomey, *Notes on attachment to French Arty. Groupement supporting the British SAAR Force* <http://www.wargunner.co.uk/58th/58thtwomey>

Dunkirk – 7th Battalion Worcestershire Regiment (1939-40) <http://worcestershireregiment.com/h_dunkirk_7thBn.php>